The Philanthropy Reader

Philanthropy is both timeless and timely. Ancient Romans, Medieval aristocrats, and Victorian industrialists engaged in philanthropy, as do modern-day Chinese billionaires, South African activists, and Brazilian nuns. Today, philanthropic practice is evolving faster than ever before, with donors giving their time, talents, and social capital in creative new ways and in combination with their financial resources. These developments are generating complex new debates and adding new twists to enduring questions, from 'why be philanthropic?' to 'what does it mean to do philanthropy "better"?' Addressing such questions requires greater understanding of the contested purpose and diverse practice of philanthropy.

With an international and interdisciplinary focus, *The Philanthropy Reader* serves as a one-stop resource that brings together essential and engaging extracts from key texts and major thinkers, and frames these in a way that captures the historical development, core concepts, perennial debates, global reach, and recent trends of this field. The book includes almost 100 seminal and illuminating writings about philanthropy, equipping readers with the guiding material they need to better grasp such a crucial yet complex and evolving topic. Additional readings and discussion questions also accompany the text as online supplements.

This text will be essential reading for students on philanthropy courses worldwide, and will also be of interest to anyone active in the philanthropic and nonprofit sectors – from donors and grantmakers, to advisers and fundraisers.

Michael Moody is the Frey Foundation Chair for Family Philanthropy at the Johnson Center for Philanthropy at Grand Valley State University, USA.

Beth Breeze is Director of the Centre for Philanthropy at the University of Kent, UK.

'*The Philanthropy Reader* is a significant addition to the growing body of knowledge about the theory and practice of effective giving. In one volume, readers can now find the full range of ideas that have shaped the field in recent decades by some of the field's most interesting and provocative thought leaders. This book is at once a great place to start for newcomers to philanthropy, a compelling resource for scholars and teachers, and a place where practitioners can find the concepts and frameworks they need to raise the quality of their giving.' – *Professor Peter Frumkin, Center for Social Impact Strategy, University of Pennsylvania, USA*

'This reader is the number one destination for anyone who wants to get familiar with the study of philanthropy. The editors have compiled the most comprehensive and systematic collection of major contributions to date – highly recommended to practitioners, students and scholars.' – *Professor Helmut Anheier, President and Dean, Hertie School of Governance, Germany*

'As an accessible and concise collection of key texts on "elite philanthropy" offering global insights into monetary giving by donors and institutions, this reader is an invaluable and timely reference point for scholars on the African continent as "African philanthropy" and "philanthropy in Africa" is on the horizon as a multidisciplinary field of study at the university level.' – *Dr. Susan Wilkinson Maposa, author of 'The Poor Philanthropist: how and why the poor help each other', South Africa*

'Finally, the book long awaited by scholars, practitioners, and students of philanthropic activities all over the world has been published. This excellent collection of global perspectives on philanthropy opens a window through which both Western and non-Western readers can view the scale and significance of philanthropy'. – *Professor Toru Shinoda, Faculty of Social Sciences, Waseda University, Japan*

'A much-needed selection, this is a treasury of perspectives amidst the blur of daily declarations of disruption. Ably curated by two leaders in our field, this is bound to be a standard resource for students and practitioners.' – *Amir Pasic, Dean, Lilly Family School of Philanthropy, Indiana University, USA*

'An invaluable and comprehensive resource for every student and practitioner with an interest in philanthropy.' – *Johanna Mair, Visiting Scholar, Stanford Center on Philanthropy and Civil Society, USA and academic editor of Stanford Social Innovation Review*

'A treasure trove of ideas, debates, findings and recommendations for the study, practice and policy of philanthropy, this marvelous collection of essential essays will guide students of philanthropy for generations to come.' – *Professor René Bekkers, Center for Philanthropic Studies, Vrije Universiteit Amsterdam, The Netherlands*

The Philanthropy Reader

Edited by
Michael Moody and
Beth Breeze

LONDON AND NEW YORK

First published 2016
by Routledge
2 Park Square, Milton Park, Abingdon, Oxon OX14 4RN

and by Routledge
711 Third Avenue, New York, NY 10017

Routledge is an imprint of the Taylor & Francis Group, an informa business

© 2016 selection and editorial material, Michael Moody and Beth Breeze; individual articles, the contributors

The right of the editors to be identified as the authors of the editorial material, and of the authors for their individual chapters, has been asserted in accordance with sections 77 and 78 of the Copyright, Designs and Patents Act 1988.

All rights reserved. No part of this book may be reprinted or reproduced or utilised in any form or by any electronic, mechanical, or other means, now known or hereafter invented, including photocopying and recording, or in any information storage or retrieval system, without permission in writing from the publishers.

Every effort has been made to contact copyright holders for their permission to reprint material in this book. The publishers would be grateful to hear from any copyright holder who is not here acknowledged and will undertake to rectify any errors or omissions in future editions of this book.

Trademark notice: Product or corporate names may be trademarks or registered trademarks, and are used only for identification and explanation without intent to infringe.

British Library Cataloguing in Publication Data
A catalogue record for this book is available from the British Library

Library of Congress Cataloging in Publication Data
Names: Moody, Michael P., editor. | Breeze, Beth, editor.
Title: The philanthropy reader / edited by Beth Breeze and Michael Moody.
Description: Abingdon, Oxon ; New York, NY : Routledge, 2016.
Identifiers: LCCN 2015044175| ISBN 9781138903586 (hardback) |
ISBN 9781138903593 (pbk.) | ISBN 9781315696805 (ebook)
Subjects: LCSH: Charity. | Charities. | Humanitarianism.
Classification: LCC BJ1533.P5 P45 2016 | DDC 361.7/4--dc23
LC record available at http://lccn.loc.gov/2015044175

ISBN: 978-1-138-90358-6 (hbk)
ISBN: 978-1-138-90359-3 (pbk)
ISBN: 978-1-315-69680-5 (ebk)

Typeset in Bembo
by Florence Production Ltd, Stoodleigh, Devon, UK

Printed and bound in Great Britain by
TJ International Ltd, Padstow, Cornwall

Contents

Editors' introduction to The Philanthropy Reader xi

Section 1: WHAT IS PHILANTHROPY? 1

Editors' introduction 3

1.1 Why philanthropy matters 7

Robert Payton and Michael Moody, Taking philanthropy seriously 9
Beth Breeze, UK philanthropy's greatest achievements 17
Philanthropy New York, Key contributions to society by philanthropic foundations 23

1.2 Contested definitions of philanthropy 29

Marty Sulek, On the classical and modern meanings of philanthropy 31
Siobhan Daly, Philanthropy as an essentially contested concept 37
Anne O'Brien, Colonialism and the meaning of philanthropy 39

1.3 Different lenses for studying and explaining philanthropy 43

James Andreoni, The economic explanation of philanthropy 45
Rob Reich, A political theory of philanthropy 50
Robert Wuthnow, A cultural explanation of compassion 53
Christian Smith and Hilary Davidson, How generosity enhances well-being 60
Samir Okasha, Biological altruism 63
René Bekkers and Pamala Wiepking, Eight mechanisms that drive charitable giving 67

1.4 The balance of public and private in philanthropy 73

Dwight F. Burlingame, Philanthropy is not the same as altruism 75
Alexis de Tocqueville, Self-interest rightly understood 78
Peter Frumkin, Strategic giving for public and private value 81

Section 2: PHILANTHROPY ACROSS TIME AND PLACE 87

Editors' introduction 89

2.1 Complex history 95

Hugh Cunningham, A history of Western philanthropy 97
Kevin C. Robbins, The centrality of philanthropy over time 105

2.2 Contested history 109

Frank Prochaska, Great Britain has the greatest philanthropic tradition 111
Olivier Zunz, Philanthropy's place in American history 115
Thomas Adam, The European roots of North American philanthropy 119
Joanna Handlin Smith, Reflections on philanthropy in China 121
Karen Wright, Generosity versus altruism: US versus UK 125

2.3 Continuity and change across eras 129

Scott Davis, Lessons from antiquity and the Middle Ages 131
Gertrude Himmelfarb, Lessons from the nineteenth century 133
Hillel Schmid and Avishag Rudich-Cohn, Elite philanthropy in contemporary Israel 137
Pushpa Sundar, Philanthropy in the building of modern India 139
Cynthia A. Sanborn, Philanthropy in Latin America 144

2.4 The role of religion, race, gender and geography 149

Warren F. Ilchman, Stanley N. Katz and Edward L. Queen II, Philanthropy in the world's traditions 151
Sudhir Alladi Venkatesh, Race and philanthropy 156
Kathleen D. McCarthy, Women in philanthropy 159
John R. Bryson, Mark McGuinness and Robert J. Ford, Geography matters: the case of English almshouses 164

Section 3: BEING A PHILANTHROPIST: CALLINGS AND CRITIQUES 167

Editors' introduction 169

3.1 Why should people give?: religious and secular calls 175

John Wesley, Give all you can 177
Dalai Lama, The ethic of compassion 180

Peter Singer, The rich should give 183
Michael Ignatieff, The needs of strangers 189

3.2 Why do wealthy people give?: elite donor statements 193

Paul G. Schervish, Why the wealthy give 195
Andrew Carnegie, The gospel of wealth 201
Bill Gates, Caring and complexity 205
Xin Zhang, I never dreamed I'd be a philanthropist 208
Victor Pinchuk, Giving back for the next generation 211
Ilana F. Silber, Civic anger among major donors 213

3.3 Critiques of elite donors 215

Francie Ostrower, Philanthropy, prestige and status 217
Teresa Odendahl, Philanthropy serves the interests of the rich 220
Benjamin Soskis, The importance of criticizing philanthropy 223

3.4 Philanthropy versus the alternatives 227

Jim Lacey, Business is better than endowed foundations 229
Marvin Olasky, Charity is better than government 231
Polly Toynbee, Thank goodness the poor don't rely on philanthropy 233
Gara LaMarche, Democratic critiques of big foundations 235
J. Gregory Dees, An emerging alternative: social entrepreneurship 238

Section 4:
PHILANTHROPISTS AND BENEFICIARIES:
A COMPLEX RELATIONSHIP 243

Editors' introduction 245

4.1 Giving and receiving 251

Aristotle, On benefactors and beneficiaries 253
Seneca, On benefits 255
Moses Maimonides, Eight levels of giving 257

4.2 Philanthropy as a type of gift 259

David H. Smith, What is a gift? 261
James Allen Smith, In search of an ethic of giving 263

4.3 When philanthropic gifts go wrong 267

Mike W. Martin, The harms philanthropy can do 269
Michael Moody, Seek to do good, but do no harm 270
Jane Addams, The subtle problems of charity 276

4.4 Being a giver, being a recipient 279

Ellen Ross, The meaning of charity for donors and recipients 281
Susan A. Ostrander and Paul G. Schervish, Giving and getting 284
Julie Salamon, A human exchange of equals in New York 291

4.5 What is the right relationship between those who give and those who get? 297

Marco H. D. Van Leeuwen, Amsterdam in the Golden Age 299
Alan Fowler and Susan Wilkinson-Maposa, Horizontal philanthropy in southern Africa 304
Halima Mahomed and Bhekinkosi Moyo, Power and philanthropy in Africa 308

Section 5: PHILANTHROPIC PRACTICES AND INSTITUTIONS 313

Editors' introduction 315

5.1 The practice of asking, the practice of granting 321

Henry A. Rosso, A philosophy of fundraising 323
Booker T. Washington, I am not a beggar 327
Joel J. Orosz, Humane grantmaking 329

5.2 Foundations: roles and critiques 335

Joel L. Fleishman, What foundations do 337
Helmut K. Anheier and Diana Leat, The creative value of foundations in a democracy 342
Joan Roelofs, Foundations and hegemony 346
Filiz Bikmen, Foundations in Turkey 349

5.3 Should corporations give? 353

Milton Friedman, The social responsibility of business is to increase its profits 355
Thomas W. Dunfee, The legitimacy of corporate philanthropy 360
Felipe Aguero, Corporate social responsibility in Latin America 364

5.4 New methods and blurring boundaries 369

Mark R. Kramer, Catalytic philanthropy 371
Lester M. Salamon, The revolution on the frontiers of philanthropy 379
Antony Bugg-Levine and Jed Emerson, Impact investing and blended value 381

Weiyan Zhou *et al.*, Social enterprises and impact investing in China 387
Angela M. Eikenberry, Giving circles are changing philanthropy 391
Lucy Bernholz, Edward Skloot and Barry Varela, Technology and the future of philanthropy 394

Section 6: DEBATES ABOUT MAKING PHILANTHROPY BETTER 401

Editors' introduction 403

6.1 On philanthropic decision-making 409

John D. Rockefeller, The difficult art of giving 411
Charles Bronfman and Jeffrey Solomon, To give is to choose 415

6.2 How do we know if philanthropy does any good? 419

Paul Brest, A decade of outcome-oriented philanthropy 421
Michael Hobbes, The problem with big ideas 429
Dan Pallotta, What if everything we've been taught about charity is dead wrong? 437

6.3 New – or not so new – ways of improving philanthropy 439

Matthew Bishop and Michael Green, How the rich can save the world 441
Michael Edwards, The emperor's new clothes 448
Charles Handy, The New Philanthropists 453
Beth Breeze, How new is the 'new philanthropy'? 455
Olga Alexeeva, The Gucci bag of new philanthropy 460

6.4 Is 'being effective' the only worthwhile yardstick? 465

Peter Singer, What is effective altruism? 467
Eric Friedman, Philanthropy is broken – here's how to fix it 475
William Schambra, The emerging threat of effective altruism 483
Paul M. Connolly, Balancing the head and heart in philanthropy 488
Thomas J. Tierney and Joel L. Fleishman, From aspirations to impact 493

Sources and copyright information 500
Index 505

[illegible]
[illegible]
[illegible]
…ments of philanthropy

Section 6
DEBATES ABOUT [illegible] PHILANTHROPY [illegible]

6.1 [illegible] 409

John D. Rockefeller, The difficult art of giving 411
Charles Bronfman and Jeffrey Solomon, [illegible] 415

6.2 How do movements in philanthropy [illegible]

[illegible]

Editors' introduction to *The Philanthropy Reader*

I: The need for a philanthropy reader

Philanthropy is essential, and everywhere

Philanthropy is an ancient tradition and a hot trend spreading around the globe. It is both timeless and timely. It was debated by Aristotle, and is now promoted by Bill Gates. Ancient Romans, medieval aristocrats and Victorian industrialists engaged in philanthropy, as do modern-day Chinese billionaires and Brazilian nuns.

People freely giving what they have – time, talent, treasure – to make their society a better place has been practised in some form in every human civilisation we know of. Still, while some aspects of philanthropy transcend time and place, others vary dramatically across cultures and evolve significantly over time. And even within a particular culture in a particular time and place, philanthropy encompasses a remarkable diversity of activities, actors, motives, institutions and ideas. It includes massive international grantmaking foundations as well as modest giving circles among people living in the same neighbourhood. It includes gala dinners for high net worth donors in the big city and tiny charity food drives in the most remote rural communities.

Today, philanthropic practice is evolving faster than ever before, both in those places where it has a long, institutionalised history and those where it has remained mostly local and informal. Even people who feel they have a good understanding of this tremendously complicated and diverse phenomenon now regularly encounter new expressions of the philanthropic impulse, newly invented methods for giving (online or off), and new hybrid types of institutions that blur the lines between philanthropy and business. Reflective philanthropic practitioners are asking enduring questions in new ways with new tools and using criteria for measurement – questions such as 'What is effective philanthropy?' and 'How can philanthropy address the root causes of social problems?'

Whatever form it takes, philanthropy in the broad sense of 'voluntary action for the public good' is a social practice that almost everyone engages in at some point, and the consequences of voluntary action certainly touch everyone's lives in one way or another. It is a fundamental human activity in response to two crucial, timeless aspects of the human condition: that things often go wrong and things could always be better. In many places, societies rely on philanthropy to address some of their most vexing social problems, to do some of their most urgent public work, and to express some of their most heartfelt beliefs and values.

Understanding of philanthropy is often limited, and sometimes mistaken

Despite its ubiquity and importance, the understanding of philanthropy is, for the most part and among most people, either very partial and scant, or downright misconceived. This is not because of a lack of capacity to comprehend, so much as a lack of opportunity and resources to develop a better understanding, as well as the sheer complexity of the subject itself.

Most people never take a course in philanthropy at any level of schooling. They never get assigned a book such as this Reader. The systematic teaching of philanthropy is a fairly recent phenomenon, and while it is spreading rapidly in places such as the US and Europe – there are even some globally available online courses in philanthropy – it is still mostly limited to a handful of institutions, the occasional elective course within a different field of study or a few specialised (often highly priced) private training programmes.

Most people learn about philanthropy, then, in informal, self-directed, haphazard ways, and many times this learning is more observational and experiential than studious. We learn about philanthropy when our school collects toys to send to needy children on the other side of the globe, or when we see our parents dress up to attend some strange event called a 'fundraiser,' or when we hear in the news about some famous wealthy person making a donation to a worthy cause. And we might pay attention to all these things because of the praise that is often given to these 'philanthropists', or perhaps the vehement criticisms levelled against them.

This practical learning has the drawback of being necessarily shaped by where we live. Growing up in Cape Town will give someone a very different understanding of the role, motives and norms for giving than growing up in Copenhagen, Cairo or Caracas. The specific familial, religious, ethnic, professional and other paths we lead in life will bring us into contact with different mixes of philanthropic experiences that shape our understanding. And those who are primarily on the giving side often have a very different view of philanthropy than those primarily on the receiving side, including a lack of awareness that sometimes they are also, respectively, recipients and donors.

The same can be said for those who study philanthropy, as more and more scholars do these days. They, too, approach this subject with their particular disciplinary lenses on – lenses that will zoom in on certain aspects of the phenomenon while ignoring or discounting other aspects. Economists or biologists will focus on certain questions about, for example, what financial incentives or evolutionary imperatives might cause otherwise self-interested people to make voluntary sacrifices for the good of others. Meanwhile, political scientists and sociologists ask different questions, such as about the civic role or community embeddedness of philanthropy. Scholars interested in macro-level social dynamics will present one picture of philanthropy, while those interested in micro-level individual behaviour will present quite another. Historians and anthropologists might see philanthropy as a contextualised product of particular times and places, while psychologists might see it as a widespread human response to certain stimuli. Philosophers focus on the fundamental nature and morality of philanthropy, while public policy scholars focus on the intersection with state action and how to incentivise greater giving.

Both the limited practical learning about philanthropy by individuals and the partial disciplinary understandings of scholars are aggravated by the fact (noted earlier) that philanthropy is an exceedingly diverse and complicated social practice, and one that is evolving especially rapidly these days. It is not surprising that our understanding of philanthropy is at least limited, and often amiss.

The need to bring together writing about philanthropy

Despite its obvious importance and recent growth, philanthropy is only just becoming a serious subject of scholarly inquiry and instruction. However, this does not mean there has been a lack of writing about philanthropy over time or by scholars from various disciplines. Philanthropy has been a source of fascination, reflection and sometimes critique by many of the most respected thinkers throughout history. And today, philanthropy is an interdisciplinary topic attracting scholars working in many fields.

Yet as the study of philanthropy – by students of all ages, as well as by thoughtful practitioners and reflective donors – grows, the field still lacks many of the resources needed to help those students and eager readers. For one thing, it lacks a 'one-stop' reading resource, bringing together the most engaging extracts of key texts and major thinkers, and framing these in a way that captures the nature, development, importance and diversity of the field. This book fills that gap.

This volume includes many writings about philanthropy – from throughout history, around the globe and across scholarly disciplines – that might not be known or accessible to readers, especially given the limited prior understanding of philanthropy noted above. In doing so, it seeks to equip readers with the thoughtful guiding material they need to better grasp and practise such an essential yet complex and rapidly changing topic.

II: What this Reader covers

What we mean by philanthropy

The word 'philanthropy' means different things to different people; it is a complex and contested term that can be ideologically loaded. Etymologically, it means 'love of humankind,' but in practice it is often used to refer to significant donations of money to charitable causes. However, philanthropists often donate their time, talent, voice, influence and social capital alongside their financial resources, and they often come to believe that the transformational change they seek is best achieved through giving a combination of assets.

Our focus in this volume is primarily on what we can label 'elite giving' – especially monetary giving by donors and institutions considered wealthy by global standards – although a great many of the selections here explicitly apply to the broader meanings of philanthropy: to non-monetary gifts, to philanthropic acts by all sorts of people, and to informal giving and helping. We made this decision because, while we respect the impact and meaningfulness of these other forms of philanthropy, elite giving is a significant portion of this field in practice, is often of particular interest to students, as well as to donors, advisors and practitioners, and is the locus for much of the innovation in philanthropic discourse and practice that we want to include in this book. That said, and in keeping with our intention to showcase the complexity and cultural specificity of philanthropy in theory and in practice, we also include excerpts concerned with topics such as mutual aid, practical compassion, poor-to-poor giving, volunteering and voluntary associations, and other non-elite forms and concepts of philanthropy. We also include many readings that make fundamental critiques of elite giving.

Aims of this Reader

Audience

The book is primarily aimed at three audiences:

- students of philanthropy taking courses at universities across the world;
- the growing cohort of reflective practitioners working in the field of philanthropy and non-profits/NGOs, including charity managers, fundraisers, consultants and other professionals in this field; and
- individual donors looking for an authoritative resource and a source of diverse insights and inspiration to guide their philanthropic learning.

Given the reach of philanthropy into the daily lives of everyone around the globe, we also hope this selection of curated readings will appeal to a general audience, as well as to more niche groups, such as philanthropy advisors, who will find this book a useful and handy resource to give their clients, and those teaching courses on philanthropy who might find the structure helpful in organising, framing and introducing the subject.

Sources and further resources

The needs and interests of this diverse readership have guided our selection, which includes a mixture of academic and non-academic sources. We have chosen the most important scholarly writing found in academic monographs, edited collections and learned journals, as well as influential pieces originally published in journalistic and popular media – both print and online – and extracts from biographies and autobiographies. To keep a sharp focus on philanthropic attitudes and activity as they are expressed in practice and as they vary across real times and places, we have not included any extracts from fiction or poetry.

The reading selections have been carefully curated, excerpted and organised into six Reader sections. Section overviews add value to the selections by drawing out the key issues, concerns and debates within and across the extracts. In addition, the Reader's accompanying eResource provides various supplementary resources of interest to varied audiences, including discussion questions, instructional aids and links to further useful resources.

Scope of this Reader

As noted above, the selections contained within this Reader are focused on the concept, practice and theory of philanthropy, with a particular focus on elite giving. But that focus sits alongside an ambitious goal to provide an international, historically informed and multidisciplinary perspective – and to do so in a way that highlights contentious issues and provides alternative angles on key debates.

International

The selections in this Reader reflect philanthropy as practised internationally. We have chosen to bring a global perspective into the core content of all six sections, rather than having a separate section dedicated to this topic. Keeping an international frame of reference throughout the Reader demonstrates how philanthropic thinking and practices are always embedded in culture and context. Putting side-by-side contributions from often radically different geographical locations helps to highlight crucial questions about the universality of philanthropic approaches, the variations in cultural assumptions about the proper place of philanthropy in relation to the marketplace and government in achieving social ends, the connection of philanthropy to faith traditions, and many other issues that are deeply influenced by and embedded in context and culture. Presenting the international perspectives in this way also invites readers to see how their own cultural context influences how they think and act as students, philanthropists and practitioners.

Historical with a contemporary focus

One feature of contemporary society is a general lack of historical knowledge, despite awareness that taking the 'long view' is necessary to understand present-day phenomena. Philanthropy is one such aspect of social and economic life that benefits from being firmly located in its proper historical context. We know that philanthropy has existed in every historical era, and yet at best we often look back only a few decades to make sense of the present, disregarding the centuries of activity, experience and learning that came before. For this reason, we embed a historical perspective throughout the Reader, including readings from as far back as the fourth century BCE, and we also have a subsection of readings on 'philanthropy across time' within Section 2.

Yet as our readers are studying and practising philanthropy in the here and now, these historic sources are complemented with a plethora of timely and influential readings from the present and very recent past. These readings cover the most current challenges and trends in philanthropy today – from technological changes, to hot debates over effectiveness, to emerging innovations and the so-called 'new philanthropy'.

Multidisciplinary

Despite efforts to develop the field of philanthropic studies, most scholars still view philanthropy as a topic, not a discipline. This may impede its uptake within traditional higher education institutions that organise teaching along disciplinary lines, but the advantages of having no obvious academic home include the avoidance of silos that afflict most specialisms – leading to increasingly deep but narrow knowledge – and the opportunity for input from all relevant disciplines. In this Reader, we showcase important and influential writing by people wearing numerous academic labels – and some who wear none – including historians, economists, sociologists and philosophers. Mixing extracts from these various sources within the covers of this book enables the reader to see similarities and differences in disciplinary approach, and may encourage greater cross-disciplinary collaboration in future research.

Embracing debate and dissent

The philanthropic space is – and always has been – complex and contested. This is all the more true as the pace of growth and innovation in the field quickens. In keeping with our goal to fully represent the reality of the field, we weave contentious and controversial issues throughout the Reader, rather than constrain them within a single 'key debates' section. In the section overviews, we highlight where readings engage directly with arguments in other readings, with the intention of providing a balance of perspectives and raising important questions for dialogue and reader reflection.

As noted earlier, we also strive to shine a spotlight on dissent and critique concerning philanthropy itself. While we include extracts that highlight the unique role that philanthropy plays in society, it is not our intention to produce a polemic in defence of philanthropy, but rather to produce a tool to help readers think about philanthropy within their own contexts, and through engagement with a variety of arguments.

Section summaries

Section 1: What is philanthropy?

The subject of this Reader is complex and contested, so the volume starts by exploring this fundamental question. Readings here examine the definition of philanthropy, why it exists, what makes it distinctive, how it balances the public and the private, and how different scholars from different disciplinary perspectives go about studying it.

Section 2: Philanthropy across time and place

This section highlights the variety, complexity and contested nature of philanthropy that becomes evident when it is viewed in historical context and in different geographic regions. It also points to some degree of continuity across eras, and highlights the role of religion, race, gender and geography.

Section 3: Being a philanthropist: callings and critiques

People are called to become philanthropists for many reasons – some religious, some secular, some very philosophical, some very personal. After reviewing diverse statements of these reasons, including some written by wealthy donors, this section turns to critiques of philanthropists and of philanthropy itself, from arguments about elite giving perpetuating the status quo, to arguments against philanthropy from both the political Left and Right.

Section 4: Philanthropists and beneficiaries: a complex relationship

The relationship between those who give and those who receive raises many thorny issues and questions, which are explored in this section. Contributions from the Ancient Greeks to contemporary thinkers discuss the nature of philanthropic gifts and their potential harms, as well as the experience of being on either side of the exchange, and the 'right relationship' between philanthropists and beneficiaries.

Section 5: Philanthropic practices and institutions

This section examines the core practices and roles of institutionalised philanthropy, covering the practices of asking and of grantmaking, and the legitimised roles and critiques of foundations and of corporate giving. It also reflects on how creative innovations in the field are changing many of these practices and institutions, often in ways that blur the boundary between for-profit and non-profit.

Section 6: Debates about making philanthropy better

Philanthropists throughout history have noted the difficulties inherent in giving well, and have pioneered new approaches to achieve more effective outcomes. This section reviews the development of these ideas, and ends with a set of readings offering alternative perspectives on yardsticks for measuring philanthropic success.

III: Notes on creating the Reader

Choosing and editing the selections

The selections in this Reader are either partial or full reprints from previously published texts, rather than new pieces of writing or heavily revised extracts. The vast majority are excerpts, with only a few cases where the original was short enough to be reproduced in full.

In choosing the sources and selecting the pieces to use, we had to make many difficult decisions. Often, our choices were guided by the intentional scope and aims of the Reader described above – i.e., to make sure each section reflected the volume's international and interdisciplinary orientation, our sensitivity to variations across time and place, and our interest in exploring all sides of key debates in the field. Our toughest and most consequential editorial decision, however, was to include shorter selections from a bigger and more diverse list of original texts, rather than fewer but longer selections. Put another way, we decided to emphasise breadth, variety and comprehensiveness over depth.

Of course, these editorial decisions necessitated more careful editing of the full original texts than we would otherwise prefer. Often, this entailed including only a certain section of the original piece, but in other cases we made more precise edits. All edits were designed to keep the particular excerpt focused on the specific topic of the subsection within which it appears. Other minor editing involved taking out statements that are transient (such as links to then-current affairs), which only make sense in the original published context, or other such reasons. We indicate all places where edits were made using ellipses and brackets.

The selections in the Reader do not include bibliographic references, citations or footnotes/endnotes that were in the original published work. Again, this was to allow us to include more pieces of shorter length, as well as to provide a standard format. However, if a particular author or source is referred to by name in the text, that remains *in situ* but with the citation removed. We also gave each reading a title that reflects the specific topic of the excerpt and how it fits into the flow of topics of that section; in some cases, this title is the same as the original piece. The original format, as published, was retained for each reading whenever possible, including the use of British or American editorial style.

Full information on the original source for each excerpt in this Reader is available in the list provided at the end of the volume. We *strongly encourage* all readers to retrieve the original piece and read it in full. There are so many other interesting and helpful elements to all the edited readings than we are able to include here, and the full original texts provide greater context, more depth, additional illustrations, complete bibliographic details and other things that serious readers will find useful.

The accompanying eResource to this Reader has links to online versions of the full original texts – when available – as well as a list of other sources and readings related to each section of the Reader. Even with our decision to include a longer list of readings, there is a large body of further great writing on these topics that we could have included, and we list many of them on the website and encourage you to explore.

Acknowledgements

This Reader has been a labour of love for both editors, who hope this collection of readings will help to grow the field of philanthropic studies, to support reflective practice and to encourage thoughtful donors.

We could not have produced the Reader without the financial support, academic collegiality and practical assistance of a large number of people, all of whom we thank most sincerely, especially:

Our funders: Pears Foundation in the UK, especially Trevor Pears and Bridget McGing, and the Gandyr Foundation in Israel, especially Judith Yovel Recanati and Ronit Amit – for funding to enable the editing work to take place and to cover the cost of permissions.

Our International Advisory Committee: Michael Alberg-Seberich, Ronit Amit, René Bekkers, Dwight Burlingame, Shuki Erlich, Daniela Fainberg, Lijun He, Johanna Mair, Wendy Scaife, Toru Shinoda, Theo Sowa, Andrés Spokoiny and Susan Wilkinson-Maposa – for reviewing our draft selections, making additional suggestions and helping to fill gaps in our knowledge of philanthropy around the world.

For practical assistance: Katie Kirouac and Alicia Chiasson, whose hard work and good humour kept the project on track. Helen Wooldridge for careful inputting of texts, and Debs Sowrey for managing the project finances.

Finally, thanks to our ever-supportive other halves: Karen Zivi and Michael Breeze.

Section 1

WHAT IS PHILANTHROPY?

Editors' introduction

Overview

The subject of this Reader is complex and contested, so the volume starts by exploring the fundamental question: What is philanthropy? Readings here examine the definition of philanthropy, why it exists, what makes it distinctive, how it balances the public and the private, and how different scholars from different disciplinary perspectives go about studying it. It is a testament to both the complex and the mostly understudied nature of our subject that we need to start with an entire section devoted to these basic – yet revealing – questions.

While philanthropy is something that all of the readers of this volume will have some ideas about – and, as the readings in this section show, it is something that touches all of our lives in meaningful ways – there is by no means widespread agreement about the definition of philanthropy, why it exists, what makes it distinctive, or how we should think about and study it. Philanthropy as we present it in this volume is also exceedingly diverse in its expression and complicated in its practice.

When we combine this complexity of philanthropy with the fact that it is often connected to some of the most cherished values and strong passions in any culture, it is clear why we need to devote this first section to exploring what philanthropy means.

There is no single answer to the question, 'What is philanthropy?' This is because:

- Most people, even professionals working in philanthropy, have a fairly limited knowledge of the field in all its diversity. We usually don't study philanthropy in the same way we study government, business or other major spheres of social life.
- The nature of philanthropy varies in different national, cultural, historical and social contexts. It takes on a different complexion in different times and places – as illustrated throughout this Reader.
- Scholarly attempts to answer this question come from many perspectives and diverse disciplines, from economics, to sociology, to history, to political science, even to evolutionary biology.
- People experience philanthropy in distinctive ways depending on their identity in play at any given time – e.g. as wealthy donors, as recipients of charity, as professional fundraisers, as informal helpers.

The 'essentially contested' nature of the concept is noted by many of the readings in this section, but that does not mean philanthropy is essentially controversial – though it sometimes is. Rather, it means the definition and use of 'philanthropy' is often debated, and more, that these debates raise difficult yet essential questions, as is the case with other such contested concepts such as 'democracy' or 'art'.

The readings in this section explore many fundamental questions, and help bring to the surface a number of the core issues about philanthropy addressed throughout this Reader. Issues such as:

- Is philanthropy voluntary or obligatory? Is it private or public? Is it purely other-directed and altruistic, or is there an element of self-interest and egoism? How do people explain why they do it? Is philanthropy only something rich people do?
- Why is philanthropy important to individuals and to society? Why do we value it so much and expect so much from it? How do we explain the emergence of philanthropy in so many places?
- How can and should we study philanthropy? What aspects of the subject are revealed, and what is obscured, when we look through the lens of a particular scholarly discipline?

To address these questions, the readings here are grouped into four subsections.

Why philanthropy matters

The first three readings introduce a broad conception of philanthropy and discuss the often underappreciated importance and quite impressive scope of philanthropic activities – both the 'greatest achievements' of philanthropy in the past, and the enduring ways that it impacts our everyday lives.

The working definition of philanthropy informing this whole volume – 'voluntary action for the public good' – comes originally from Robert Payton. As noted in the Robert Payton and Michael Moody reading here, this is a deliberately broad and affirmative conception of the subject, encompassing not just voluntary giving, but also voluntary service and association. 'Philanthropy' defined in this way is meant to be an umbrella term – or as Payton and Moody say, a 'circus tent' term – to stand alongside 'government' and 'business'.

Philanthropy is a positive human response to the uncertainties of the human condition, and so deserves a positive definition that captures the range of ways humans try to make the world better through voluntary action. These diverse philanthropic responses are found in many corners of social life across the globe, manifested in voluntary action to educate children, help the poor, save the environment, preserve heritage, serve the sick, care for the elderly, and so on.

As noted in the introduction to this volume, we take a special focus here on elite giving, and the other two readings in this section – from Beth Breeze and from the organisation Philanthropy New York – examine some of the greatest achievements of institutional and major donor giving in the UK and US, respectively, as an illustration of just how pervasive philanthropy is and why it matters. As you look through those lists – from the abolition of slavery to the polio vaccine, from famine relief to Sesame Street – imagine a world in which donors and charitable foundations had not made these investments.

Contested definitions of philanthropy

Being careful at the start of this volume to explore the nuances of the definition of philanthropy is not a matter of scholarly positioning. Rather, this is a way of introducing the core questions and diverse manifestations of this contested yet powerful concept.

Readings in this section show how the meaning of philanthropy has developed over time, from Ancient Greece, to colonial Australia, to the contemporary Western academy. Anne O'Brien shows, for instance, how the concept of philanthropy that had developed in Britain up to the eighteenth century was imported to the Australian penal colonies and mingled there in close association with the welfare state paternalism of the governing authorities.

The debate over the meaning of philanthropy, then, is embedded in the specific circumstances of those historical places, but there are also some recurring issues inherent in the concept that these readings note. One of these is whether philanthropy is truly 'voluntary' or if the moral duty to give makes it somewhat 'obligatory'. Another is how to reconcile the *public* focus of philanthropic actions with the *private* nature of the actors choosing to give to public purposes. Marty Sulek also shows how philanthropy sometimes refers to the intent of the action, and sometimes to the consequence. As Siobhan Daly explains, it is in these essential contests over meaning that the complexity of philanthropy is revealed.

Different lenses for studying and explaining philanthropy

We also want to be clear at the start of this volume that there is not one way – let alone one 'best' way – to study this complex, contested subject. In fact, as the study of philanthropy expands, it is essential that we embrace multiple lenses of analysis lest we find ourselves lost in disciplinary *cul de sacs* or discouraging new scholars who might take insightful new approaches. A multidisciplinary approach is most suitable, because philanthropy touches on the core subject matter of so many disciplines – from the economy and the state, to culture and motivation, to human nature and evolution.

Different ways of seeing the world, from different scholarly disciplines, involve defining and explaining philanthropy somewhat differently, using their own disciplinary theories and concepts. This section samples many – though certainly not all – of those approaches, and reveals how each lens shines a unique light on the subject, highlighting certain features while minimising others.

Philanthropy in the various readings in this section is explained as: behaviour that exists because it provides a 'warm glow' for self-interested actors (James Andreoni) and behaviour that survives because it serves reproductive fitness for a species (Samir Okasha). Other readings look at how the state incentivises philanthropy (Rob Reich), and how culture provides multiple messages that we use to make sense of our giving in ambivalent ways (Robert Wuthnow). The readings here also identify what experimental evidence tells us about the mechanisms that drive charitable giving (René Bekkers and Pamala Wiepking), as well as what research tells us about the psychological and emotional consequences of giving (Christian Smith and Hilary Davidson). We can see disciplinary variation in the terms used in this set of readings as well, from 'altruism', to 'giving', to 'compassion', to 'generosity'.

The balance of private and public in philanthropy

One key conceptual duality runs through all sorts of different disciplinary understandings. This is the question of the balance of the private and the public, a balance that is the crux of both many scholarly debates and many practical concerns about philanthropy. Philanthropy is defined as private action pursuing a public goal, and is driven by both internal and external motives. It is about doing good for others and for society, but it also has clear and multiple benefits for the individual. Philanthropy creates both private and public value – one does not negate the other – and this makes it more complicated to assess.

Dwight F. Burlingame's essay addresses this duality by explaining the value of a conceptual distinction between philanthropy and altruism, arguing they are both important but not equivalent. This harks back to a classic point made by Alexis de Tocqueville, who marvelled at how Americans in the early nineteenth century were quite comfortable with the notion that something could be in the public interest *and* also beneficial to their own self-interest. In fact, this notion was helpful in motivating people to work towards that public interest. Peter Frumkin elaborates on this duality, arguing that effective strategic giving needs to balance both the public and private values that it creates.

Discussion questions

- What role does philanthropy, as described in these readings, play in your own life? How would your life be different if philanthropy didn't exist?
- What are the pros and cons of a broad definition of philanthropy? What might be better or worse if we define philanthropy more narrowly – e.g., as just giving by wealthy people or by big foundations? Do we really even need or want one definition in a complex global world?
- What do the different disciplinary approaches to explaining philanthropy – from economics, political science, psychology, evolutionary biology and others – have in common, if anything? Which approach is the most helpful for understanding philanthropy as you've experienced it?
- Does it diminish philanthropy to say that there is personal benefit from doing it? Why or why not? How can we know when the private and public benefits of philanthropy are in balance, and what does being out of balance look like?

1.1 Why philanthropy matters

Taking philanthropy seriously

Robert Payton and Michael Moody, 2008

What is philanthropy? An initial summary

[I]n our experiences thinking about and doing philanthropy in some professional capacity – over the course of about 50 years for one of us, a mere 20 years for the other – we have never stopped asking the question, "What is philanthropy?" Our simple answer has not changed. It is the same answer proposed by the senior one of us many years ago in a previous book: *philanthropy is "voluntary action for the public good."*

[. . .]

Our definition itself encompasses many things. Of course it includes voluntary *giving*, when we give our money, either in cash or in property, often on the spot but more often by check – or even by deferred bequests, so-called "planned giving," that will come out of our estates one day. But our definition also includes voluntary *service*, when we give our time and, sometimes, our talent; *and* our definition includes voluntary *association*, the organized activity without which most voluntary giving and service would be ineffective or even impossible.

[. . .]

Taking philanthropy seriously

Philanthropy, in the broad sense in which we define it, permeates our lives, whether we are conscious of it or not. There are few things that affect as many aspects of our lives as philanthropy, and yet there are few that are less well understood. Philanthropy is as important in our lives as are law and medicine, subjects about which we know tremendously more than we know about philanthropy. Philanthropy is an essential tool in our collective attempts to solve public problems, yet there is too little – or only ill-informed – consideration of philanthropy in our public conversation. Unlike business, philanthropy does not have its own regular section in the daily newspaper; unlike politics, philanthropy rarely makes the front page. Yet in the United States alone there are millions of volunteers at work as you read this, thousands of checks totaling millions of dollars are in the mail today to thousands of philanthropic organizations and institutions, some better known to you than rock groups, college football teams, or breakfast cereals.

[. . .]

Despite its prevalence in the culture, few Americans have thought very carefully about philanthropy – what it is, how it works, its motivations, its results, what part it plays in our society and in the world, the arguments for it and against it. Because philanthropy is commonplace, most people have opinions about it in this broad sense, but these opinions are often uninformed. For example, many Americans think that most philanthropic giving comes from large foundations like the Ford Foundation and from large corporations like Microsoft. In fact, a whopping 83 percent of all dollars given philanthropically in the US are given by *individuals*, *not* corporations or foundations. Similarly, many people assume that most if not all of the funds received and distributed by nonprofit organizations in the US come from philanthropic contributions. In fact, only a small percent of the revenues of the nonprofit sector – only one dollar out of every eight received, by one measurement – comes from private giving. As a whole, American nonprofit groups receive less from private giving than from government, and their largest source of revenue by far is neither private giving nor government grants but *fees* for the services and goods they sell.

Americans also do not have a widely shared understanding of why we do so much of our public work through philanthropy. Political and policy debates that reference philanthropy often reveal an alarming ignorance about the tradition and the sector. Relying on "charities" to deal with public problems becomes an election-year rhetorical prop or a way to shift responsibility; philanthropy is often spoken of as if it were infinitely expandable in scale and conveniently malleable in scope. The media has a hard time explaining the reason for tax exemption, or the crucial differences in types of tax-exempt organizations.

Our opinions about philanthropy are uninformed largely because philanthropy is something we have learned about only informally and often haphazardly from family, church, and following tradition. We have not studied it the way we have studied our economic life, our political life, or even our spiritual life. We give less attention to it than we do to golf and tennis, movies and television, clothes and cosmetics, diet and exercise.

[. . .]

[W]hen we say philanthropy permeates "our lives" and that "everyone" should understand it better, we mean to include people around the globe, in different cultures and nations each with their own distinctive philanthropic tradition . . . [W]e believe the understanding of philanthropy we present here will allow people immersed in other traditions, and people practicing philanthropy in other societies – especially in other democratic nations – to take philanthropy seriously in their own neck of the global woods. The activities that we call philanthropy look somewhat different in different societies: the relative size of this sector and its relationship with government and government funding vary, the cultural traditions of giving and service vary, the types of institutional structures and labels vary, and so on.

[. . .]

Philanthropy is important and interesting

Philanthropy deserves greater attention because it is important and interesting; more important and interesting than most people realize. Anything involving as many as half of all adult Americans, on a regular basis, voluntarily giving away their time and money would seem to be important. Anything that is at the center of current public debates about social welfare (e.g., what role should faith-based charities play in feeding the hungry?), human rights, the environment, and a hundred other issues, including our personal character and virtue and sense of social responsibility, would seem to be important. Philanthropy is a mode of action that shapes our individual lives and the world around us in ways that are far more extensive than most people realize. And philanthropy is important because we often measure others, and sometimes we measure ourselves, by the way we help others in need, by the way we help our neighborhoods and communities, by the money and time we donate to causes we believe in.

[. . .]

Philanthropy is an ancient, universal, and diverse tradition

Most of the activities we label "philanthropy" have been going on for a very long time. Organized charity is older than democracy and capitalism, older than Christianity and Buddhism, older than societies and many other traditions that no longer exist. Charity in its less organized, spontaneous form, as ad hoc individual expression, is as old as humanity itself; we can safely consider it universal.

Similarly, the practice of some form of organized philanthropy is common to all of the great religions and civilizations of the world. But this universality does not mean there is not great diversity in philanthropy across the world and over time. The tradition takes a distinctive form in each culture. The fact that organized philanthropy is so ancient and widespread means that cultures have many different philanthropic traditions, and philanthropy has taken many forms. People have tried many things in the name of philanthropy: from saving children to saving trees, from saving refugees to saving old buildings, from saving symphony orchestras to saving stray dogs. People have used many words and labels for the activities, the values, and the purposes of philanthropy: charity, reform, liberation, voluntary action, eleemosynary, altruism, nonprofit, benevolence, generosity, good works, and many more. People have also justified and practiced philanthropy in many different ways (not all admirable, we might point out): from giving alms because it is required by God to organizing a males-only benevolent society to preserve the status quo in a village, from annoying fundraising telephone calls during the dinner hour to more subtle appeals brought up offhandedly over drinks among friends.

[. . .]

Everyone has a connection to philanthropy

As we noted earlier, philanthropy deserves more attention because everyone has some experience with philanthropy. Not all the experience is positive, nor is everyone actively engaged in philanthropy, but the experience of giving and receiving assistance is, for all practical purposes, universal. This is true for Albanians and for Alabamans.

Despite our limited formal knowledge of philanthropy, most everyone can share some draft version of their "philanthropic autobiography" if the occasion arises. Our connection to philanthropy may go back to a childhood experience of donating money or food items at school or church, or of going door-to-door soliciting donations for UNICEF or the Red Cross. We have probably continued to give money – some of us sporadically, some regularly. We may have responded to letters requesting a donation. We may have given money to people who asked us for it on the street. We may have made similar token gifts to organizations simply because we were asked. We may have made regular contributions to our favorite charities. We may have attended social or cultural events where at least some of the proceeds from ticket sales went to a charity. Chances are good that we have also volunteered our services at some time, whether for our church, our children's school, or the local soup kitchen on Thanksgiving.

Many, if not most, of the readers of [this] have also been on the receiving end of philanthropy – not necessarily direct charity, but philanthropy. The good works of others, past and present, permeate our lives. One of the most troubling inadequacies of the definition of philanthropy as voluntary giving or helping is that it focuses too much attention on the giver. This belies the fact that philanthropy is about receiving as much as about giving. And for most of us, benefiting from philanthropy is not about our own hunger or homelessness, but is about benefiting from social change or stewardship. All Americans are recipients, in a way, of philanthropic acts such as Andrew Carnegie's gifts to start public libraries across the US. Even if you've never used a public library personally, you've benefited indirectly (if only through lower taxes) from the higher literacy rates and afterschool child care that public libraries provide.

[. . .]

More generally, there is no such thing as being wealthy beyond the need of the voluntary assistance of others. If helping others is universal, being helped is equally so. In such relations, we are close to an existential understanding of the human condition. We are all vulnerable. We have all benefited from philanthropy in some form. We were all infants once.

Most of us don't consider ourselves among "the vulnerable." Until, that is, we realize that someone close to us is but a wayward cell or two from a life-threatening disease. Or until we realize that some of those in dire need of charitable aid following a disaster like a tsunami are wealthy Western tourists. At that point the things we value most highly may rest on someone else's philanthropy, perhaps the forgotten donation of a total stranger of an earlier generation, perhaps the voluntary commitment of the stranger we meet in the emergency aid tent.

This is an important and interesting subject, one we must take seriously.

[. . .]

The scope of philanthropy

As we noted earlier, philanthropy deals with the most important social and moral issues affecting society, as well as our individual lives. In fact, these crucial issues confronting society – moral issues like social welfare, human rights, the environment – often arise as salient issues first in this "third sector," this public space where the voluntary work of society is carried out. Our moral and political agenda is often set by voluntary associations who advocate for something to be put on that agenda, like women's rights or laws against gay marriage.

Philanthropy has been a significant influence in social, political, religious, moral, economic, scientific, and technological affairs. The spectrum of causes advocated by philanthropic organizations extends from efforts to limit air pollution to efforts to define the rights of children, from providing exhibition opportunities for artists to providing hospice care for the terminally ill, from saving refugees to saving old buildings to saving stray dogs. Philanthropy has been influential in shaping the outcome of issues in religion, education, health, social welfare and human services (including family, children, and youth), the arts and humanities, cultural preservation, community service, sports and recreation, international relief and development, the environment, on and on.

The practices of philanthropy are as various as the needs they serve. The list of human needs in the New Testament that begins "I was hungry and you gave me food" is a part of the cultural and philanthropic literacy of the West. Food and drink, companionship and compassion, medicine, liberation, work, education, worship, music – all are needs to which philanthropy responds with voluntary gifts of money or service. The strategies that are available are dictated by the needs. In the case of refugees, for instance, those strategies would include relief and rescue, rehabilitation, return, and economic development.

However, when assessing the scope of philanthropy, we must again remind ourselves that there is a vast and largely uncharted ocean of informal, spontaneous, interpersonal philanthropy. We make a mistake in measuring the scale and scope of philanthropy if we neglect or forget about the pervasive, character-shaping good works that are immediate, direct, or personal – the domain of traditional benevolence, love of neighbor, civility, and tolerance, the "ordinary virtues" if you will. As we noted earlier, we do not have adequate ways to measure the impact of all this sort of work on people, on the communities in which they live and work, and on the nation and the world. But this informal philanthropy clearly matters, especially to those receiving the help, whether they are our closest friends or a stranger. We must think of philanthropy as encompassing both the spontaneous, individual acts of kindness and the planned, organized efforts that ensure acts of kindness are not ineffective or short-lived.

[. . .]

A broad, affirmative conception of philanthropy

"Voluntary action," as we define it, encompasses both voluntary giving *and* voluntary service, the former usually referring to gifts of money and the latter to gifts of time. But we also include voluntary association as a third form of voluntary action. Voluntary association is the vehicle or instrument for philanthropic giving and service; it organizes gifts of money and time to accomplish public purposes. Philanthropy's impact on society is only possible because of voluntary associations.

Our definition of philanthropy is broader than most, and this is by design. The single word *philanthropy* is used here to encompass many things, as the single word *business* does, and as *politics* does. Philanthropy and business and politics are "umbrella terms," even though "circus tent" might be a more useful metaphor. Under the circus tent called philanthropy, one would find a diverse array of topics and terms: gifts and grants, volunteers and trustees, foundations and endowments, special events and fundraising, advocacy and reform, Alternative Spring Breaks and service learning, scholarships and awards, and many more.

Defining philanthropy as voluntary action for the public good assumes that philanthropy is manifest in action, not simply in purpose or intention. However, the definition also specifies that action, to be classified as philanthropic action, must have a particular purpose, mission, or intention – the purpose to achieve some vision of the public good. While this public good purpose might be mixed in with other, even selfish reasons for action, the action should be considered philanthropic, in our view, if it is voluntary and if it is seen by the actor as action to achieve the public good – or at least *a* public good. The point is that, taking all the pieces of our definition together, we argue that *both* the intentions and the actions of philanthropy are important.

Another way to approach this issue is to try to identify the objectives of "voluntary action for the public good." A useful way to classify these objectives is to boil them down to two general types: 1) to relieve the suffering of others for whom one has no formal or legal responsibility, and 2) to improve the quality of life in the community, however one defines that idea. The first objective involves such things as meeting basic needs such as food, shelter, clothing, and medical attention; the second involves enhancing the life – cultural, educational, recreational, etc. – of a community, however big or small. The range of specific philanthropic activities designed to achieve one or the other of these objectives is diverse, from direct service to organizing to fundraising to advocacy. But both of these objectives have a prominent *moral* dimension; that is, they require intervening in other people's lives presumably for their benefit in some way. [I]n our conception of philanthropy, this moral dimension is the most important characteristic of the subject.

[. . .]

The story of philanthropy in any culture records a moral quest that has shaped the moral agenda of that culture across the generations . . . [T]he history of philanthropy is the "social history of the moral imagination." Philanthropy is a primary way that humans enact their moral visions of what is good, visions which always differ among people and groups within any single society. Humans use philanthropic action to relieve suffering or meet other pressing needs, to improve the quality of life or civic capacity in our communities, to advocate for or express ideas or values or identities, to experiment with new ideas for social change as well as to preserve traditions in the face of impending change. All of these and more are specific roles for philanthropy that can be encompassed by a broad, affirmative conception of philanthropy.

[. . .]

The context for philanthropy

Philanthropy appears, in some form, in all cultures and civilizations and through all recorded history. It seems there is something about the world, and about humans in this world, that calls philanthropy into being. Philanthropy is a response. But to what? What is it about the world that causes us to respond philanthropically, that makes philanthropy seem to be a reasonable response?

[. . .]

The human problematic

Like it or not, we humans face difficult problems in this world. This means there are questions that humans everywhere and always must attempt to answer. These fundamental problems and questions are the inevitable reality we call the *human problematic.* The human problematic is defined by two other basic realities: the first is the *human condition*; the second is *human nature.* It is this human problematic that sets the context for why philanthropy exists in the world.

Philanthropy exists because of two truths about the human condition:

1. things often go wrong, and
2. things could always be better.

First, *things often go wrong.* Systems fail. Natural and human, social and political, economic and biological systems fail, and as a consequence humans suffer. As we grow up, we all learn by experience as well as by observation that in many situations individuals and societies are overwhelmed by circumstances either natural or man-made, that we sometimes can't cope without help. It is through no lack of will or desire or moral fiber that brings starving Ethiopians to the brink of death by starvation. It is through no ethnic flaw or cultural decay that people find themselves swept away by a tsunami. We are all vulnerable to suffering, even if some of us are more vulnerable to certain types of suffering than others.

Philanthropy is an act of response to this inevitable suffering; we shouldn't forget there are other possible responses. Also, we shouldn't forget that sometimes what is going "wrong" is disputed or that the definition of wrong varies across cultures, groups, and times. Whether husbands routinely beating their wives is seen as an example of something going wrong or not depends on when and where and who you ask, and this will then influence whether philanthropy or any other intervention is called for. In fact, philanthropic action itself – the exercise of the moral imagination – is often part the process of declaring which "conditions" are defined as "problems." What we do to make things better reveals what we consider to be going wrong.

Second, *things could always be better.* That is, humans can imagine ways in which life could be more agreeable, comfortable, congenial, pleasant, fruitful, productive, profitable, etc. Philanthropy is an expression of this human moral imagination that seeks to improve the quality of life. [. . .] Of course, "could always be" does not necessarily imply "will always be." Philanthropy is about trying to make things better, sometimes in the face of dauntingly unfavorable odds.

These two features of the human condition set the stage for humans to respond to problems, and *the philanthropic tradition is the history of this response.* In the stream of this tradition usually called "charity," we respond to suffering and distress and acute need; in the stream of this tradition usually called "philanthropy," we respond to our awareness of ways we can improve the quality of life. Both streams mingle in a shifting current with the political forces of order and the economic forces of the market, all adapting to one another and to the natural course of the river of humanity.

What makes the philanthropic response to the human condition difficult is that the human condition is uncertain. Many of the most fundamental threats to human well-being are far beyond human control. The media make it possible for us to observe the incredible power and destructiveness of routine natural phenomena like earthquakes, floods, hurricanes, and volcanic eruptions. But humans themselves are capable of behavior that tests our most generous definition of the human; we often make the human condition worse. We delude ourselves if we forget that barbarism is usually rationalized as necessary and that this usually leads to acts of even worse barbarism. Most wars, civil and otherwise, contain evidence of this. And, of course, the media makes it possible for us to observe these acts of barbarism, regardless of where they occur.

Human nature – the other reality contributing to the human problematic – leads us not only to make things worse. However, it is also human nature, in part, that impels us to respond philanthropically. Yes, it is hard to deny what many people believe, that egoism and self-interest are "just human nature." But we need not deny this in order to accept that the opposite quality, altruism, is also "just human nature." Concern for others is a defining characteristic of humans. We see this illustrated time and again in the philanthropic response to the human condition.

One conclusion to draw from all of this is that life is problematic. Utopia is a useful way of thinking how things might be better; it is not useful to expect that things will ever be perfect or even settled. A problematic life in a problematic universe is, apparently, inevitable. That humans, both individually and in society, are also problematic seems to be another inevitable reality. The combination of those different kinds of problems often leaves us trying to make sense of evil and misfortune – and of goodness and joy. And we often make sense of these things through our philanthropic response.

UK philanthropy's greatest achievements

Beth Breeze, 2006

The secret of philanthropic success

Philanthropists use their private wealth to affect the public good. They do not need to persuade voters or shareholders of the merits of their schemes and can therefore deploy their money in ways that differ from both public and private sector spending: they can be more innovative, act faster and take greater risks.

Innovation

Philanthropists have a strong track record in being innovative, identifying new needs and proposing new solutions to old problems. For example, the hospice movement applied new thinking to help people die with dignity and 'green issues' were first brought to public attention by environmental campaign groups.

Speed

Unencumbered by the need to pass legislation or argue for pots of public spending, philanthropists can react more flexibly and quickly to meet new, urgent needs. For example, voluntary organisations were the first to provide services for people with HIV and AIDS.

Risk-taking

Freed from the need to be accountable to the electorate or to pacify the media, philanthropists can take greater risks and pursue the causes and concerns that motivate them, which may include providing support for asylum seekers, visitors for prisoners or services for other marginalised and unpopular groups.

[. . .]

Given the nature of the problem that this report seeks to address – that people are generally unaware of the successful outcomes of UK philanthropy – this research is based on the opinions of the small, though rapidly increasing, body of 'philanthropic experts' living and working in the UK.

[. . .]

Historic and modern philanthropy

The 'historic' and 'modern' categories used in this research were designed to counter the tendency to admire the philanthropy of the Victorians above the modern day and ensure we identified sufficient contemporary achievements. In previous ages, when the state's role was largely confined to defending borders and waging war and the public purse provided negligible welfare, the voluntary efforts of individuals in tackling social problems inevitably appear more significant. It is important to recall that, whilst charities are sometimes collectively described as the 'third sector,' they were in fact the first to provide basic services to those unable to pay for them, such as education, health and housing.

Modern philanthropy in the UK is rarely treated with the respect and appreciation shown to such acts in earlier times. This is partly due to the prevailing cynicism of our times, manifested in a suspicion that self-interest is the primary motivation behind philanthropic acts. It is also partly due to a lack of understanding of the role available for philanthropy in a welfare state society. A survey conducted in 1948 found that the vast majority of the population felt philanthropy had been made superfluous by the creation of the welfare state. Yet, as our findings show, there remain innumerable ways for private philanthropy to complement and co-operate with tax-funded provision.

[. . .]

Findings

The greatest achievements of historic (pre-1900) UK philanthropy are:

1 Provision of social services before the creation of the Welfare State.
2 Campaigning which led to the abolition of the slave trade.
3 Provision of education and leisure opportunities for all.

The largest area of pre-1900 philanthropic achievement identified by our experts is the provision of a wide range of social services, paid for and provided by philanthropists, long before the state took responsibility for the welfare of its citizens. In addition to the well known tradition of the rich giving alms or poor relief to the needy, multiple nominations were made for philanthropists' efforts in providing housing for the poor, almshouses for the old, care for orphaned and abandoned children, basic educational institutions as well as health care and hospital fees for those unable to afford to consult private medical practitioners. The philanthropic roots of a range of public services were also highlighted, including the ambulance service, probation service, social workers, universities and care for those injured fighting for their country.

> The probation service has its roots in the common law practice of releasing offenders on condition that they kept the peace and would come for judgement if called. During the late nineteenth century, voluntary societies, led by the Church of England Temperance Society, appointed missionaries to the London Police Courts. Their initial function, to reclaim drunkards, was later extended to other offenders who were released into the care of missionaries on the condition that they accepted their guidance. This philanthropically-organised system continued until 1907 when supervision was given a statutory basis, allowing courts to appoint and employ probation officers.

Whilst these are now viewed as essential governmental-funded responsibilities, and increasingly as public-private partnerships, they were all originally funded and provided by private individuals. The direction of travel does not always flow from philanthropy to the public sector as occasionally provision is taken over by the private sector. For example, mass access to clean water supplies was originally organised through the funding of public water fountains by town guilds and rich merchants and is now a commercialised business.

The final type of philanthropic effort identified in this area is the research effort, first funded and undertaken by the Rowntree family philanthropists, which captured and analysed the extent of poverty in the UK. This evidence helped to create the firm foundations on which the British welfare state was eventually built.

In 1899, Joseph Rowntree and his son, Seebohm, studied the extent and causes of poverty in the York slums. The work of these early social researchers, funded by philanthropy, demonstrated the extent of poverty in Britain, helped to undermine the myth that the poor were entirely responsible for their own situation and contributed to the reform of the Poor Laws and the introduction of state support for the poor. The Rowntree research helped to create an evidence base for those who argued the necessity of tax-funded, state-organised welfare and is said to have directly influenced the Beveridge Report which set out the blueprint for Britain's Welfare State. The three Rowntree funds (Joseph Rowntree Foundation, Joseph Rowntree Charitable Trust and the Joseph Rowntree Reform Trust) have continued to support research as a means of bringing about social justice.

The single most frequently named historic achievement was the philanthropic efforts of those involved in financing and running the campaign to end the slave trade. The Society for the Abolition of the Slave Trade was founded in 1787 by Granville Sharp and Thomas Clarkson, and the contribution of William Wilberforce is most widely remembered. But many thousands of individual philanthropic men and women joined the campaign, ran local groups, raised funds, distributed pamphlets and worked collectively for decades to secure the successful passage of the 1807 Abolition of the Slave Trade Act and the 1833 Slavery Abolition Act.

The third most popular type of historic philanthropic achievement is the widespread provision of education and leisure opportunities. Apprenticeships are identified as a charitable objective in the oldest known records of British philanthropy. A range of schools were founded to cater for the needs of poor children who had to work for most of the week, including Ragged schools, Charity schools and Sunday schools. The ongoing needs of the working adult population to learn and gain new skills has been consistently funded by voluntary contributions. One of the best known philanthropic efforts of this type is the mass provision of public libraries funded by Andrew Carnegie. The turn-of-the-century founding of the Carnegie UK Trust led to hundreds of libraries being built across the country, with an open access policy that brought educational opportunities and a love of literature to ordinary people.

[. . .]

Finally, in this category of achievements, are the philanthropic efforts that ensured the existence of sporting facilities, public parks and open access to the countryside and significant buildings. This latter is epitomised by the work of the National Trust, founded in 1895 by renowned Victorian philanthropists including Octavia Hill, who was also named by our experts for her work in social housing and is therefore a key figure in two of the three pre-1900 achievements.

> Octavia Hill (1838–1912) was a remarkable Victorian woman, involved with a variety of philanthropic achievements that continue to enhance the quality of life in the UK today. Multiple nominations were received for two of her projects: the provision of quality homes for the poor and the preservation of open spaces for all. Hill's pioneering work in improving housing standards with the aim of making, in her words, "*lives noble, homes happy, and family life good*" is described as laying the foundations of the modern profession of housing management. Her belief in the value of fresh air and the joy of plants and flowers lay behind her success in creating a number of London's public parks and her co-founding of the National Trust in 1895. The Trust now cares for over a quarter of a million hectares of countryside, 700 miles of coastline and hundreds of significant buildings. Its work depends on the gifts of the rich who donate property and land and on the smaller donations of over 3 million members whose subscriptions support the Trust's ongoing work.

The greatest achievements of modern (post-1900) philanthropy are:

1 Famine relief and long-term aid to developing countries.
2 Health research and pioneering health services.
3 Campaigning which led to major social change.

Despite our prediction that historic philanthropic successes would dominate nominations, the achievement most frequently cited overall was the philanthropic response to famine and poverty in developing countries. A fifth of nominations came in this category, with the three most frequent mentions being the establishment of the Oxford Committee for Famine Relief (now known as Oxfam), the response to the 1984 news coverage of the Ethiopian famine which led to Live Aid, and indirectly to Comic Relief, Live 8 and Make Poverty History, and the Jubilee Debt campaign which resulted in billions of pounds of unpayable debt being cancelled.

> Oxfam began life as the Oxford Committee for Famine Relief, which first met in 1942 with the aim of getting essential supplies to people affected by blockades during the Second World War and raising funds for war refugees. After 1945, the committee recognised the need to continue efforts to relieve world-wide suffering and Oxfam (as it has been known since 1965) went on to play a major role in disaster relief and tackling the root causes of poverty. In October 1984, TV footage of famine in Ethiopia (especially the BBC news report by Michael Buerk) prompted unprecedented public generosity. Initiatives like Band Aid and Comic Relief followed, raising funds for Oxfam's work, as well as for other international aid organisations. Oxfam was a key partner in the 2005 Make Poverty History campaign and continues to mobilise hundreds of thousands of volunteers, campaigners and donors.

[. . .]

The second theme that emerged in the nominations for modern philanthropic achievements is health research and pioneering health services. The three most cited nominations in this area are the establishment of hospices to provide dignified and pain-controlled environments for the dying, the philanthropic response to the AIDS epidemic which provided preventative education and support for sufferers before the state grasped the scale of the problem and the enormous scientific enterprise that resulted in the mapping of the human genome in which the Wellcome Trust was a major partner.

> The Wellcome Trust, which currently has assets of over £11 billion, was established in 1936 as a result of legacy left by Sir Henry Wellcome to fund research to improve human and animal health. A number of Wellcome Trust projects received nominations, including the development of antimalerial drugs and the establishment of the UK Biobank. But Wellcome's contribution to the international Human Genome Project received most nominations. Funding from the Trust not only paid for the sequencing of one-third of the human genome but also ensured that this information, on what is described as the 'recipe book' of life, was kept in the public domain. The Wellcome-funded UK work was led by Sir John Sulston who argued strongly that sequence data should be released freely and as rapidly as possible, enabling researchers all over the world to access this information free of charge. This tremendous boost for global biomedical research is therefore a direct result of a philanthropic act made seven decades ago.

[. . .]

The third main area of achievement continues the tradition of the slavery abolitionists in using campaigning as a technique to bring about significant social change. Nominations for successful philanthropically-funded campaigns cover an enormous area of social terrain including the right for women to vote, the banning of handguns after the Dunblane massacre and the ban on the production and use of landmines and other explosive remnants of war. An inter-related set of campaigns resulting in equalities legislation received multiple nominations, including the repeal of Section 28, equalisation of the age of consent and the Civil Partnership Act.

> The campaigning charity, Stonewall, receives no public funding and is entirely reliant on donations and sponsorship. Founded in 1989, it successfully co-ordinated a campaign to repeal Section 28 of the Local Government Act, which was designed to prevent the 'promotion' of homosexuality in schools. A recent achievement resulted in the Civil Partnerships Bill, enacted in December 2005, giving lesbian and gay couples the same rights as heterosexual couples in matters such as pensions, inheritance and recognition as next-of-kin. By September 2006 over 15,000 couples had registered their civil partnerships. One of our experts described this campaign as *"a major milestone in equality that was delivered by philanthropy as result of an intelligent, focussed and ambitious campaign."*

[. . .]

Conclusion

This report is a celebration of the achievements of philanthropy in the UK. It contains ample evidence that the decisions of individual women and men, rich and not-so rich, to give away some of their money can, and has, changed the world for the better.

It is undoubtedly true that philanthropy alone cannot claim credit for the entirety of every achievement described above, but it is equally true that the role played by philanthropic funding is frequently overlooked. Money is an essential ingredient in creating social change and bringing about social justice, yet those who willingly provide the funds are often at best ignored and at worst vilified. This report seeks to challenge the dominant cynicism and suspicion held by many people regarding the motives of philanthropists.

Key contributions to society by philanthropic foundations

Philanthropy New York, 2008

Foundations often serve as society's research and development arm by funding programs to explore new problem-solving approaches that the public and private sectors cannot or will not explore.

[. . .]

The following are a list of well-known innovations that can be traced to foundation funding over the past 100 years:

Public libraries

The US library system today is enormous; our 16,000 library outlets are visited nearly 1.5 billion times a year and house a variety of resources, from newspaper articles and research references to adult and children's fiction books, audio and video resources, and internet terminals, all free for public use. Yet less than a century ago, the idea of equal access to books and educational materials was revolutionary and controversial. The vision and action of one man, Andrew Carnegie, helped to create more than 2,500 libraries worldwide during the early 1900s. For Carnegie, the library was the manifestation of one central theme in his philanthropic philosophy – self-betterment – and nearly every community that requested support from Carnegie or the Carnegie Corporation of New York received it. By the 1920s, Carnegie's library gifts surpassed $39 million and had led to the construction of 1,679 public libraries in 1,406 communities in the United States alone. Today, these libraries are an integral part of the nation's public library network.

Yellow fever vaccine

By the beginning of the 20th century, Boston and Baltimore had experienced a total of 50 yellow fever epidemics. Communities such as Charleston, SC, Galveston, TX, and New Orleans, LA had lost tens of thousands to the illness, and victims were being buried day and night. To eradicate this disease, in 1915 the Rockefeller Foundation launched a 30-year, all-out effort to find a vaccine. Foundation physicians and scientists traveled to the cities and jungles of South America and West Africa, where they set up on-site laboratories and investigated causes of yellow fever. Although many Rockefeller researchers died of the disease during the course of their work, in 1936 their efforts paid off with the development of the first successful yellow fever vaccine. In 1938, more than 1 million people were vaccinated (with a 90 percent success rate) and during World War II, more than 34 million doses were manufactured and distributed free to health agencies and Allied governments. In 1951, foundation scientist Dr. Max Theiler received the Nobel Prize in Medicine for his work on the yellow fever vaccine.

[. . .]

Insulin to treat diabetes

Prior to the discovery of insulin, diabetic patients suffered under radical dietary restrictions and treatment plans with little hope for recovery. In 1916, the Carnegie Corporation of America, still in its infancy, received a project proposal from Dr. Nathaniel Carter for a study of treatment for the disease. It was accepted, and he started his research at Cottage Hospital in Santa Barbara, whose trustees, recognizing the importance of his work, funded the construction of a research laboratory adjoining the hospital. Although Dr. Potter died just three years later, his successor at the Potter Metabolic Clinic, Dr. William Sansum, later oversaw work to improve the insulin extraction process. This led to the administration of the first dose of insulin produced in the United States to an adult patient, in May of 1922. The patient, a fifty-one-year-old man terminally ill with diabetes, lived to age ninety with insulin treatments. Through collaboration with researchers at the University of Toronto who had successfully treated the first child patient, large-scale production of insulin commenced later that year, and by late 1923, insulin began to appear on drugstore shelves. Although diabetes is still a worldwide problem, it is estimated that insulin has saved and elongated the lives of millions of people living with the disease.

[. . .]

Rocket science

The development of rocket science was a necessary precursor to space exploration and technologies such as satellite communication, which touches our everyday lives in innumerable ways. Although the NASA program is now government-run, it was private foundation money that initially allowed a scientist to experiment and discover the technology that allowed rockets and humans to go into space. After having built a rocket that could travel in a vacuum, physics professor Robert H. Goddard received a small grant of $5,000 from the Hodgkins Fund of the Smithsonian Institution to build a high-altitude version of the rocket. He succeeded in 1926, when he launched a rocket that flew 41 feet in the air for 2.5 seconds. Subsequent launches caught the attention of neighbors and reporters, who considered his efforts a joke. One well-connected man, Harry Guggenheim, however, took Goddard's efforts seriously. Guggenheim consulted with Charles Lindbergh on the feasibility of Goddard's ideas, and ultimately, Lindbergh persuaded Guggenheim's father, whose wealth came from the family empire in mining, to provide support over a four-year period for Goddard's work. The Daniel and Florence Guggenheim Foundation subsequently funded Goddard's work for 11 years, leading the US to become the first nation to place a man on the moon.

The Pap smear

Today, cervical cancer is one of the easiest cancers to treat when caught early. Until the 1940s, however, it was the deadliest of all forms of cancer among women, owing in large part to the lack of a simple, inexpensive test for diagnosing the disease. In 1923,

Dr. George N. Papanicolaou discovered that cervical cancer could be diagnosed before a woman presented any symptoms. Although he reported his findings, pathologists dismissed them, unwilling to believe cancer could be detected in individual cells. In 1941, however, the Commonwealth Fund took a chance on Papanicolaou, offering him a $1,800 research grant that was considered "highly speculative." Papanicolaou later wrote, "At a moment when every hope had almost vanished, The Commonwealth Fund . . . stepped in." Through this support, Papanicolaou was able to prove that exfoliative cytology revealed cellular irregularities even before they had become cancerous, far earlier than biopsy could. The effect was quick and tremendous, and by 1960 the American Cancer Society estimated that not only had over 6 million American women received Pap tests (named for Dr. Papanicolaou), but that deaths from uterine cancer had been reduced to half of what they would have been otherwise. Pap smears, as they are called today, are now the basic and routine diagnostic technique for detecting cervical cancer.

The polio vaccine

In December 1994, the Pan American Health Organization announced that polio had finally been eradicated from the Western Hemisphere. Previously, however, the world lived in fear of the deadly, crippling effects of this disease, and outbreaks reached pandemic proportions in Europe, North America, Australia, and New Zealand during the first half of the 20th century. In 1948, however, Dr. Jonas Salk received a $35,000 grant from the Sarah Scaife Foundation (later known as the Sarah Mellon Scaife Foundation) to establish and equip a virus laboratory at the University of Pittsburgh. By 1952, the now-famous Salk vaccine was developed and on April 12, 1955, this life-saving discovery was announced to the world. Following the widespread use of the vaccine in the mid-1950s, the incidence of poliomyelitis declined dramatically in many industrialized countries. A global effort to eradicate polio began in 1988, led by the World Health Organization, UNICEF, and The Rotary Foundation. These efforts have reduced the number of annual diagnosed cases by 99 percent, from an estimated 350,000 cases in 1988 to 1,997 cases in 2006. Currently, polio remains endemic in only four countries: Nigeria, India, Pakistan, and Afghanistan.

White lines on highways

After working with Thomas Edison as a teenager, Dr. John V. N. Dorr eventually became internationally known for his innovations in the field of metallurgical engineering. In 1940, he established a foundation in his name with the initial purpose of supporting the fields of chemistry and metallurgy exclusively. By the early 1950s, however, his thoughts had started to shift to more simple solutions to everyday problems. Dr. Dorr postulated that at night, when rain, snow or fog impaired vision, drivers hugged the white lines painted in the middle of highways. Dorr believed this led to numerous accidents and that painting a white line along the outside shoulders of the highways would save lives. He eventually convinced highway engineers in Westchester County, New York and in Connecticut to test his theory along stretches of highway with curves and gradients. The initial results seemed promising, but highway officials were reluctant to pursue Dorr's suggested course of action due to the high cost of shoulder striping, at $150 per mile, as well as some skepticism regarding the true effectiveness of the initiative. The Dorr Foundation continued to advocate strongly for the cause, however, and after subsequent positive studies in Ohio, New Jersey and Rhode Island – including one which showed a 37 percent decrease in fatalities and injuries – the highway shoulder line gained universal application and acceptance. Although state funds are now used to paint white lines on the shoulders of the nation's highways, every person who travels in a motor vehicle is indebted to Dorr and his foundation for the implementation of this life-saving discovery.

Public broadcasting

In December of 1964, the First National Conference on Long-Range Financing of Educational Television Stations called for a study of the role of noncommercial education television in society. The Carnegie Corporation subsequently agreed to finance the work of a 15-member national commission, resulting in the publication of its landmark report, "Public Television: A Program for Action," on January 26, 1967. The report popularized the phrase "public television" and greatly assisted the legislative campaign for federal aid for such an initiative. The Public Broadcasting Act of 1967, enacted less than 10 months later, chartered the Corporation for Public Broadcasting (CPB) as a private, nonprofit corporation. The law initiated federal aid through the CPB for the operation, as opposed to the funding of capital facilities, of public broadcasting. The CPB initially collaborated with the pre-existing National Educational Television system, but in 1969, decided to start the Public Broadcasting Service (PBS). A public radio study commissioned by the CPB and the Ford Foundation conducted from 1968–1969 led to the establishment of National Public Radio, a public radio system under the terms of the amended Public Broadcasting Act. Today, nearly 89 million people are estimated to watch public television during any given week.

[. . .]

Sesame Street

In an average week, Sesame Street reaches 16 million viewers, and is the most widely viewed children's series in the world. Although the show is self-supporting today, this was not always the case. During the early 1960s, the National Education Association endorsed the idea of making preschool education available to all children, but funds available within school budgets were not sufficient for such programs. In 1966, the Carnegie Corporation of New York underwrote a feasibility study on the use of television for preschool education; the same grantmaker, along with the Ford Foundation, the Corporation for Public Broadcasting, and the US Office of Education then pledged over $6 million in funding to start Children's Television Workshop. On November 10, 1966, Sesame Street premiered on public television to an astonishing 1.5 million viewers during its first week. Today, Sesame Street is understood as one of the most successful television ventures ever, and is seen in more than 120 countries. An estimated 77 million Americans watched the show as children, and it has won more than 118 Emmy awards, the most for any television series.

Emergency 911

Efforts to create a national emergency medical response system began in 1966, when the National Safety Act authorized funds for ambulances, communications and training programs. These efforts were augmented in the early 1970s when the Robert Wood Johnson Foundation provided 44 grants in 32 states for regional emergency medical services – the largest sum of private funds ever allocated for this purpose. The Foundation program demonstrated the concept of a regionalized, systematic approach, and was highly successful at improving outcomes for patients. Following these grants, the federal government stepped in and made a series of grants that resulted in today's nationwide 911 system.

1.2 Contested definitions of philanthropy

On the classical and modern meanings of philanthropy

Marty Sulek, 2010

Widening usage in 4th century BCE Athens

[I]t is clear that the use and meaning of *philanthrôpía* evolved considerably between the mid-5th and late 4th centuries BCE. Many schools of thought in classical Athens – sophistic, poetic, philosophical, and oratorical – played pivotal roles in propelling this evolution: coining, refining, and redefining the meaning of *philanthrôpía* to suit their various rhetorical purposes. Given the extreme divergence in the outlooks of these various schools, as well as the interminable social and political conflicts in which their members were frequently enmeshed, it should come as little surprise to learn that their usage of the word also widely varied. Generally speaking, though, these various modes of usage may be arranged under six broad categories, according to the nature of the primary subject to which it refers:

- theological, in reference to divine beings;
- philosophical, in reference to the knower, knowledge, learning, culture, and other associated concepts;
- political, in reference to rulers, magistrates, civic leaders, laws, and other political entities;
- ontological, in reference to an innate affection for, or attraction to, human beings in the nature of a person or thing;
- social, in reference to the possession of certain social graces, such as courtesy, kindness, friendliness, or gregariousness; and
- fiduciary, in reference to financial generosity.

There is considerable room for overlap in such conceptions, of course; and, indeed, among the classical Greeks, a person would have been considered deficient in his *philanthrôpía* if he possessed only one aspect of it while fundamentally lacking in the others [. . .]

Although there is considerable variety in the usage of *philanthrôpía* among ancient authors, there is also a fairly consistent association of it with the highest ideals of civilized humanity; and because Athens was situated at the epicenter of Greek philosophical life, Athenian conceptions of *philanthrôpía* were frequently informed by philosophical ideals. Particularly in its philosophical mode of usage, *philanthrôpía* became practically synonymous with the concept of *paedeía*, or the conscious shaping of human intellect through education and acculturation, with the aim of attaining the virtues.

[. . .]

Modern definitions of philanthropy

Sir Francis Bacon (1561–1626) is the first English writer to employ philanthropy in a discernibly modern sense, and to imbue it with the full depth of meaning intended by the ancient philosophers. Bacon employs *philanthrôpía* only once as a word in his published works, in the 13th essay of a collection first published in 1612. Titled "On goodness and goodness of Nature," this essay is nothing less than an extended meditation on the very meaning of philanthropy, given the thrust of its opening sentence:

> I take goodness in this sense, the affecting of the weal of men, which is that the Grecians call *philanthrôpía*; and the word humanity (as it is used) is a little too light to express it.

Bacon thus considers *philanthrôpía* to be synonymous with "goodness" and "affecting the weal of men," which he then goes on to describe as the *habit* of doing good. Goodness of *nature*, by contrast, he describes as the *inclination* to do good. Bacon's conception of *philanthrôpía* and goodness thus correlates to the Aristotelian conception of virtue, as consciously instilled habits of good behavior. Bacon further declares goodness to be the greatest virtue of the mind, answering to the theological virtue of charity and admitting of no excess except error.

[. . .]

A series of authoritative dictionaries published over the course of the 18th, 19th, and 20th centuries provides an invaluable aid for tracing the historical evolution in the meaning of philanthropy subsequent to Bacon's seminal use of the term. Undoubtedly, the most influential of these early modern English dictionaries was compiled by the celebrated man of letters and lexicographer, Samuel Johnson (1709–1784). As Winchester notes, "Johnson's work set standards for all future English dictionaries." First published in London in 1755, Johnson's dictionary defines philanthropy as simply

> love of mankind; good nature.

It then goes on to reference a prominent instance of its use by Joseph Addison (1672–1719) in Addison's *Spectator*, a popular early-18th-century British literary magazine, where he writes,

> Such a transient temporary good nature is not that *philanthropy*, that love of mankind, which deserves the title of a moral virtue.

For Addison, then, as for Johnson, philanthropy must be a constant and consistent feature of a person's character to be deserving of "the title of a moral virtue." A temporary good humor would thus not qualify as philanthropy, even if it resulted in an ostensible act of charity and/or achieved a beneficial aim or outcome as a result.

[. . .]

The next great dictionary project in the English language was undertaken by Noah Webster (1758–1843), who has been described as a founding father of the American intellect [. . .] In this first edition, Webster defines philanthropy as

> the love of mankind; benevolence towards the whole human family; universal good will. It differs from friendship, as the latter is an affection for individuals.

Webster's conception of philanthropy as "benevolence toward the whole human family" may be seen to take an important cue from a close associate of his in the Federalist Party, Alexander Hamilton (1757–1804). In the first installment of the Federalist Papers, Hamilton published what is likely the single most prominent instance of the use of philanthropy as a word in American English.

[. . .]

As the 19th century progressed, philanthropy became increasingly employed in reference to the many new charitable societies dedicated to social and political reform that arose after the American Revolution in the early American republic, as described by de Tocqueville, and in England following the Industrial Revolution. At the same time, philanthropy also became increasingly employed in reference to the generous benefactions made to this new generation of charitable institution by the wealthy industrialists these revolutions helped produce. In the process (and much to the chagrin of some of the more preeminent, classically trained philosophers of the period, such as Emerson, Thoreau, and Nietzsche), the classically influenced meaning of philanthropy, as reflected in Webster's definition, became almost entirely eclipsed by popular usage: either to describe a sociopolitical movement, or to describe donating money to charitable institutions that embodied that movement.

[. . .]

In terms of the wider English-speaking world, the most authoritative reference is generally held to be the *Oxford English Dictionary (OED)* [. . .] The current online version of the *OED* defines philanthropy as

1a. Love of mankind; the disposition or active effort to promote the happiness and well-being of others; practical benevolence, now esp. as expressed by the generous donation of money to good causes.
1b. The love of God for humanity. Now *rare.*
2. A philanthropic action, movement, or agency; a charity. Chiefly in *pl.*

[. . .]

Contemporary academic definitions

The precise meaning of *philanthropy* is a matter of some contention within contemporary academic circles, its definition being largely dependent on the particular interests of the scholar employing the term. Nevertheless, there are some working definitions to which the scholarly community associated with the field of "philanthropic studies" most commonly subscribes. One of the more widely accepted of these is the one employed by Lester Salamon, who defines philanthropy as

> the private giving of time or valuables (money, security, property) for public purposes.

He then goes on to characterize philanthropy as

> one form of income of private non-profit organizations.

[. . .]

Salamon's definition of philanthropy, as essentially synonymous with charitable donations, is generally taken as a given by most scholars of philanthropy today, though with some notable exceptions. Some historians, for example, point to a distinction that arose in the late 19th century between "Christian charity," which primarily sought to alleviate the sufferings of the poor, and "scientific philanthropy," which sought, instead, to address the root causes of poverty to bring about permanent solutions to it and other social ills. Those drawing this distinction often point to the seminal influence of the Rockefeller philanthropies under the direction of Frederick Gates, with their novel emphasis on applying the findings of scientific research, particularly within the field of medicine, to solve previously intractable social problems. Others point to Andrew Carnegie, who attempted to encourage self-reliance among his beneficiaries in a conscious effort to avoid the "pauperism" he thought dependence on charity tended to foster. Still others point to the rise of associational life in early-19th-century America as marking the decisive transition from charity, understood as giving between individuals, to philanthropy, understood as an institutionally channeled humanitarian response to conditions of the poor.

[. . .]

Scholars within the field of philanthropic studies from more varied backgrounds define philanthropy both more broadly and more precisely. Robert Payton's definition, as "voluntary action for the public good," offers one of the primary alternatives to Salamon's definition within the field of philanthropic studies. A blend of "Paytonian" and "Salamonion" shades of meaning may also be discerned in the definition of philanthropy proffered by Jon Van Til as

> the voluntary giving and receiving of time and money aimed (however imperfectly) toward the needs of charity and the interests of all in a better quality of life.

A particularly interesting aspect of Van Til's definition is the crucial importance he places on intent. He considers philanthropy to encompass all acts of voluntary giving to meet charitable needs, even if that aim is never attained, just so long as the donor aimed to achieve "a better quality of life for all." The underlying assumptions of this definition have often been questioned; by Carnegie, for example, in his famous critique of charity's unintended consequences, where he writes: "Of every thousand dollars spent in so-called charity to-day, it is probable that nine hundred and fifty dollars is unwisely spent – so spent, indeed as to produce the very evils which it hopes to mitigate or cure." Serious challenges have also been mounted, though, to the more robust assumptions behind Payton's definition of philanthropy as voluntary service to a public good. As Paul Schervish points out, for example, many things not philanthropic (e.g., government and the market) also serve the public good; furthermore, philanthropic behavior is frequently defined more in terms of its "obligatory" rather than its "voluntary" nature. Given this state of affairs, Schervish chooses, instead, to define philanthropy as:

> a social relation governed by a moral obligation that matches a supply of private resources to a demand of unfulfilled needs and desires that are communicated by entreaty.

Like Van Til, then, Schervish also understands philanthropy as acting to meet unfulfilled human needs or wants. By contrast, though, he sees this process as governed by a moral obligation to meet expressed needs rather than stemming primarily from the good will, intent, or volition of the donor.

From this brief survey of contemporary academic definitions of philanthropy, a number of disagreements may be discerned as to its precise meaning, even among the leading scholars in the field of philanthropic studies. In particular, there is fundamental disagreement over:

- Whether philanthropy is voluntary, or whether it is compelled by factors such as moral restraints, social obligations, and the like.
- Whether philanthropy serves a public purpose, a public good, a charitable need, or simply a communicated want or desire.
- Whether philanthropy is an intent to achieve a particular aim, is the actual attainment of that aim, or is just simply a private act of giving.

A synthesis of modern definitions

As varied and even contradictory as early modern, contemporary, and academic definitions and usage of philanthropy can sometimes be, they nevertheless share a sufficient degree of commonality to synthesize them into an overall framework of meaning. One way to do this would be to arrange them according to the nature of the phenomenon to which they refer, as follows:

- *Literal*: Encompassing references to the literal meaning of philanthropy in ancient Greek as the love of mankind.
- *Archaic*: For usages now considered largely obsolete, such as those referring to philanthropy as the "love of god for humankind" or as being synonymous with "humanity."
- *Ideal*: To describe the attainment of ideal aims, goals, outcomes, or objectives in terms of meeting a need, attaining a good, and/or advancing human happiness and well-being.
- *Ontological*: To describe an innate desire, moral sentiment, psychological predisposition, or other such aspect of human nature that impels people to want to help others.
- *Volitional*: To describe the good will, intent, or readiness to voluntarily help others.
- *Actual*: To describe an objective act, such as giving of money, time, or effort, to a charitable cause or public purpose.
- *Social*: To describe a relation, movement, organization, or other such social entity larger than the individual that embodies an explicitly defined charitable cause or good.

[. . .]

Conclusion

In conclusion, the findings of this article's research on the historical evolution of the meaning of philanthropy may be summarized as follows:

1. Philanthropy has (had) a variety of differing, albeit closely interrelated, shades of meaning in its historical, contemporary, common, and academic usage.

2 The meaning of philanthropy has evolved along a discernible historical trajectory, the analysis of which yields insight into its full nature.
3 There are significant parallels in the evolution of the use and meaning of philanthropy between the classical and the modern eras: in both, philanthropy is initially employed as a specialized theological and philosophical term by an educated elite to describe a catalyst of human progress; later, it is adopted by ever-wider circles in civil society to describe a range of more conventional and ostensible public virtues.
4 The meaning of philanthropy considerably narrowed during the 20th century, both in its common and academic usages, to refer almost exclusively to charitable giving.

Philanthropy as an essentially contested concept

Siobhan Daly, 2012

Different scholars approach the definition of philanthropy in different ways and disagree about the significant defining features of philanthropy. The meaning of philanthropy has also evolved and altered in different ways over time, within and across different contexts. These features of the concept of philanthropy enhance the risk of it being rendered confused and ambiguous. 'Philanthropy' is a term that is used interchangeably with other terms such as 'charity', 'benevolence', 'giving', 'donating', 'voluntary sector', 'non-profit organisation' and 'NGO' often without adequate regard to the need to be clear about what is meant by each of these terms. The implications of how we approach conceptualisation and, indeed, the importance of clarity and conscious thinking in relation to concepts, have received some attention from scholars. For instance, Muukkonen considers how our understanding of concepts such as 'philanthropy' and 'third or voluntary sector' and how we articulate the nature of the relationships between them affects the 'framing' of the study of these phenomena. Srivastava and Oh underline the epistemological dilemma encountered in the study of philanthropy in the Global South, specifically: 'does the definition and practice of philanthropy in a northern context hold in a developing one?' Scholars engaged in the study of philanthropy in Asia and Latin America have posed similar questions.

Payton and Van Til assert that philanthropy is an essentially contested concept. Gallie defines essentially contested concepts as those which 'inevitably involve endless disputes about their proper uses on the part of their users'. He also proffered seven defining criteria of essentially contested concepts and discussed examples including democracy, social justice and art. Although Payton does not discuss these criteria specifically, he argues that philanthropy is 'an idea that is bent and distorted by attempts to contain within it a diversity of human phenomena that resist generalisation and categorisation'. He also suggests that the essential contestability of the concept of philanthropy is reflected in normative debate about the purpose(s) of philanthropy; the nature of the motivations encapsulated by the concept of philanthropy and fundamental (ideological) disagreement about how 'philanthropy' should be manifested. Similarly, Van Til argues that the variety of ways in which the concept of philanthropy is articulated and employed leads scholars 'in profoundly different directions' not only regarding the meaning, but also the value and purposes attributed to philanthropy. As an essentially contested concept, Payton argues that philanthropy is 'a slippery idea which none of us can seize firmly and claim exclusive rights to'.

[. . .]

A number of scholars underline the voluntary character of philanthropy that is central to Robert Payton's definition of philanthropy. However, it is contested by Schervish who posits that the moral sense of virtue which is, in his view, inherent to philanthropy may be compelling rather than voluntary, that is, shaped by an array of factors from religious beliefs to peer pressure. [. . .] [S]cholars differ as to whether 'charitable need' or charity should be articulated as a separate concept. From some perspectives, there is a case to be made for what is effectively the disaggregation of philanthropy. For example, Gross argues that whilst 'charity' implies compassionate, person to person giving, 'philanthropy' connotes rational and institutionalised giving, which seeks to achieve grand objectives in society. Whilst not disputing this particular interpretation of charity, Ostrower argues that philanthropy is a broad concept, which 'includes charity, but also encompasses the wider range of private giving for public purposes'.

[. . .]

Sulek suggests that the synonymy of philanthropy with 'charitable donations' is 'generally taken as a given' by the majority of those engaged in the study of philanthropy. However, the concept of philanthropy has also been defined with reference to the foundation form alone. To the lament of some commentators, philanthropy is also associated with wealthy individuals. Indeed, in the United Kingdom, particularly in the twentieth century, 'philanthropy' has become 'more synonymous with charitable foundations and trusts and being a philanthropist synonymous with the largesse of rich individual donors'. The extent to which philanthropy should be associated with a 'sector' is also the subject of debate. In fact, Peter Frumkin argues that there is substantial 'diversity and confusion' regarding the range of philanthropic actors which make up the field. He suggests that the list of actors who engage in philanthropy ranges from individuals who make donations to charities in their local area; to wealthy donors who seek to make a long-lasting impact on society, to big foundations, corporate foundations, community foundations and the range of vehicles that have become prominent in recent years to facilitate philanthropy from informal giving circles to donor-advised funds. These recent developments, part of what is often referred to as the 'new philanthropy', have added a further dimension to the debate about the form of philanthropy. The 'new philanthropy' has, in part, been characterised by the development of new vehicles for, and approaches to, philanthropy. In this sense, the internal complexity of the concept of philanthropy is interlinked with the evolution of the concept, which, in turn, leads to further interpretations of the form private giving takes.

[. . .]

The concept of philanthropy has been modified in accordance with the evolution of societies, economies and politics (particularly, the role of the state). There is a rich historical literature which documents and critically analyses the development of philanthropy over time in different countries, complemented by the chronological mapping of the evolution of the concept of philanthropy. Whilst much of this work is focused on the United States, our understanding of the evolution of philanthropy in other countries worldwide has been enhanced in recent years. Historians are leading the way in considering how the open character of the concept of philanthropy poses particular challenges in relation to the establishment of 'analytic equivalence' in efforts to compare across time and space. At the heart of debates relating to openness, there are also concerns about the resonance of the concept of philanthropy, within and, indeed, outside the academy.

Colonialism and the meaning of philanthropy

Anne O'Brien, 2014

In the last couple of decades, philanthropy has taken off. Offering tax concessions, exposure to markets and scads of social capital, donation has been built into the business models of most large corporations. 'Ordinary people' also give – their most likely 'profile' is that of a middle-aged woman with higher than average income and education. But the use of 'philanthropy' to refer primarily to corporate or individual benefaction is a relatively recent revival, despite the long history of giving in Australia. Indeed, the word had largely fallen out of use by the mid-20th century: 'Like courtly manners', it was 'suspect', according to the Principal of Women's College in Brisbane in 1951. And it would seem to have stayed that way until the mid-1990s. When Elizabeth Cham, Director of the newly enlarged umbrella organisation Philanthropy Australia, started in 1996 to contact the press to raise the profile of giving, she was advised to choose a different word. Over the next decade 'philanthropy', both the term and the activity, became fashionable – an 'innovative, growing, influential and high performing sector' as Philanthropy Australia's website now describes it. Its rise was an international phenomenon, both product and pillar of the revival of the market economy. Given the fulsome tradition of American giving it is not surprising that Bill and Melinda Gates are among its highest-profile global ambassadors, but Australia seeks to foster its own tradition: it seemed only natural when a Macquarie banker and philanthropist, for example, was named 'Australian of the Year' in 2011.

If philanthropy today is mostly associated with giving away money, its meanings at the moment of Australia's colonisation in the late 18th century were broader and richer [. . .] But what *did* it mean then? Literally, of course, it has always referred to a 'love of humanity' – like today's benefactors, it sought to promote the welfare of others. But how can we trace the history of an idea at once so noble, so elusive but so inviting of scepticism? These questions are particularly pertinent for countries of the British world like Australia, for British claims on benevolence were deeply felt. Long before the First Fleet sailed benevolence had been integral to the identity of the English elite – the 16th-century Poor Laws were its statutory proof – and in the 18th century a new transatlantic sensibility that saw 'irresistible compassion' as natural to all humanity kindled even greater self-consciousness among the British of their own 'humanity'. One of its manifestations was the voluntary organisation: philanthropy had long been enmeshed in the paternalist structures of manor and village with landowners responsible for those they knew, but in the 18th century it became the work of committees of volunteers coming together in the public sphere to assist strangers.

[. . .]

A study of voluntary welfare is particularly important in Australia because the relationship between the state and voluntarism was unusually close. Government played a central role in the foundation and development of the Australian colonies but rather than weakening philanthropy I argue that this intimacy strengthened it. Indeed paternalism, with its obligations and responsibilities, was an important component in the governance of the early penal colonies. From the time of Macquarie (1810–22), most of the governors subsidised philanthropy, and it remained the main provider of assistance in the nineteenth century. Even after the introduction of pensions and benefits at the turn of the 20th century philanthropy was an important buffer against primary poverty. In the small communities that developed across the continent in the 19th century leading citizens operated on both sides of the 'moving frontier' between the state and voluntary sector and at certain pivotal moments key individuals could exercise considerable power. In Victoria, for example, the Moravian missionary, Frederick Hagenauer, became Secretary of the Aborigines Protection Board in the 1880s, where he was instrumental in passing a law whose draconian consequences were suffered by generations of Aborigines; in NSW during the next decade a ginger group of clergy, MPs and charity workers were influential advocates of the old age pension, which provided a degree of autonomy for aged settlers but excluded 'Asiatics' and 'aboriginal natives of Australia'.

Philanthropy's discursive powers were strong in this colonial context. Settlers' rejection of a poor law attested to their preference for voluntarism and, as expressions of faith and civic duty, their organisations fashioned ideas about deservedness that flowed back into state action. But the absence of a poor law confronted philanthropists with an anomalous task: they had to be seen to be weeding out the undeserving and ensuring the 'genuinely' needy were being treated humanely, but they could not entirely abandon the desperate. Their published reports, at once seeking to prevail upon the public and demonstrate efficiency, fluctuated between displays of compassion and assertions of rigor and were often shaped by the political preoccupations of the day. It is telling, but perhaps not surprising then, that different cultures of blame developed in different colonies: in former convict colonies, such as Tasmania, philanthropists were rarely troubled by doubts as to the depravity of their clients, whereas in gold-rich Victoria, the legacy of 'the pioneer' led to philanthropists emphasizing misfortune rather than culpability in the lives of the poor. While such discursive differences did not always flow into the experience of those in their way, they sometimes did – and not just in treatment by charities but cemented in policy.

[. . .]

A long history of philanthropy sheds new light on social policy as it developed in this settler society. There is now a well-established international literature arguing that Australia has been distinctive in constructing a welfare state focused on the white male wage-earner: the corollary of privileging his efforts to support a family was a system of welfare supported by general revenue that was means-tested, targeted and residual. But despite the clearly gendered and raced nature of this welfare state there has been little sustained, integrated historical analysis of how race and gender ideologies specifically shaped and maintained it. Philanthropy offers the opportunity for these connections to be made. It not only provided care for those overlooked by the state; it was also central in maintaining the structures of thought and practice that perpetuated the system. In the 19th century, colonisation itself – even as it was known to dispossess the original owners – was envisaged as a philanthropic solution for Britain's grinding poverty; and in immigrants' flight from the Poor Law, the dependent wife became a sign of colonial success. By the late 19th century, when the alliance between labour and new liberalism was forging the mechanisms of the wage-earners' state, the combination of reinvigorated evangelical Christianity and progressivism in old and new voluntary organisations reflected and reinforced white women's dependence and Aboriginal people's marginalisation. Philanthropy worked in myriad ways, mostly reinforcing these patterns but sometimes challenging them.

1.3 Different lenses for studying and explaining philanthropy

The economic explanation of philanthropy

James Andreoni, 2006

Introduction

Philanthropy is one of the greatest puzzles for economics. A science based on precepts of self-interested behavior does not easily accommodate behavior that is so clearly unselfish. How can unselfish behavior be reconciled with self-interest?

One explanation is that charitable giving is not unselfish at all. One who gives to medical research may hope one day to benefit from its findings. A person who gives to public broadcasting may expect to enjoy improved programming. A benefactor of the opera may seek to hire more talented performers. A second justification, sometimes called "enlightened self-interest," is a step removed from pure selfishness. A comfortably employed person may give to poverty relief in order to keep the institution in place, banking on the rare event that he may himself be impoverished someday. But these clearly cannot be full explanations. What about the person who gives to famine relief on another continent? Or the environmentalist who contributes to saving a rare species that she never expects to see? And what about charitable bequests – such gifts have no chance of affecting consumption of a person while alive. These examples raise a third explanation: Altruism toward others or toward future generations may be a motivator in giving, and gifts are made to maximize a utility function that includes the benefits to others or to society in general. While these three explanations are distinct, an economic theorist would model them all the same. Since each implies a concern about the total supply of the charitable good or service, albeit for different reasons, each could be modeled identically as private gifts to a pure public good.

Notice that all three of these explanations are best suited to situations in which one's own contribution has a measurable impact on the charitable good. When the good is large in scale and when donors are many, it becomes difficult to accept that people can actually experience the impact of their gifts. As a result, free riding may predominate.

In these cases, a fourth explanation for giving may be more attractive: People may get utility – a "warm-glow" – from the act of giving.

A fifth possibility is that our economic discipline of self-interested behavior is simply not well suited to explain philanthropy. Humans are, after all, moral beings. Perhaps our behavior is constrained by moral codes of conduct that make our choices unexplainable by neo classical models of well-behaved preferences and quasi-concave utility functions. While this argument undoubtedly has merit, it represents the last refuge for the economic theorist.

[. . .]

Regardless of the reasons for its existence, there is clearly a strong public policy interest in philanthropy. First, private philanthropy can substitute for public sector provision of goods and services. With individuals to provide poverty relief or support for the arts, there is less need for the government to do so. As such, it becomes essential to understand how private charity is provided and how it interacts with public provision. Second, governments have historically treated charitable donations with tax-favored policies, such as the charitable deduction in the US. What are the effects of these policies on giving and on tax collections? Third, there are obviously enormous efficiency concerns. How is this set of public and private institutions co-existing to provide public charitable services, and is there a more efficient configuration of these institutions? What is the best policy for providing public goods?

[. . .]

Theoretical foundation

Hochman and Rodgers and Kolm were the first to recognize that charitable giving, motivated out of altruism, creates a public good out of charity. Even if, for instance, the recipients of the charitable services are individuals and are given private goods, such as income transfers, day care, or housing, the fact that others feel altruistically toward these individuals means that the private consumption of these charity recipients becomes a public good.

Similar arguments hold for other charities that provide private goods. Education dollars benefit the students and faculty of the institution, but because the donors also take pride in the quality of the institution, the donations act as public goods. Gifts to health care will benefit the patients of hospitals, and medical research will help those with particular maladies, but the fact that givers value these outcomes, in general, again makes them into public goods. Similarly with the arts. The patrons of the museum or opera will get the direct benefits of any gifts, but the fact that the giver values these benefits received by others makes the donations public goods to the donors.

[. . .]

Neutrality: crowding out

In 1984 Russell Roberts made a bold assertion in the *Journal of Political Economy*: The great expansion of government services for the poor since the Great Depression was accompanied by an equal decline in charitable giving for the poor, with the result that the government dollars had no net effect on alleviating poverty. The same was true, he claimed, for all public-private partnerships in providing public goods. His empirical evidence was all impressionistic, and his main basis for his assertion was theoretical.

Roberts' claims were built upon a model of Warr. Warr showed that any "small" lump sum tax on donors that is contributed to the public good will completely crowd out private donations. The substitution will be dollar-for-dollar.

[. . .]

Few people, I expect, are willing to adopt the full slate of predictions from a model of pure public goods – a classic *reductio ad absurdum*. How, then, can we modify the model of charitable giving to get a more realistic picture of giving to public goods?

Warm-glow giving

The model of pure public goods is an extremely natural model to turn to, so what made it such a poor predictor? Certainly the goods people are giving to are pure public goods, and certainly people have feelings of altruism that make them demand these goods. So what needs to change to make the model more realistic and more predictive?

[Empirical studies of crowding out] rely on one feature of the pure public goods model: all else equal, individuals are assumed to be indifferent between all the *sources* of the contributions to the charity, are indifferent to the *means* by which the good is provided, and only care for the total supply of the public good. Simple introspection (an often dangerous avenue to take) reveals that there are many other considerations to giving that may make people *not* indifferent to the means of providing the good. As stated in the introduction, humans are moral – they enjoy doing what is right. They are also emotional, empathic and sympathetic – they enjoy gratitude and recognition, they enjoy making someone else happy, and they feel relieved from guilt when they become a giver. Put more simply and more generally, people may experience a "warm-glow" from giving. All of these moral compunctions and emotional exchanges mean that people are not indifferent to their own voluntary gift and the gifts of others. They strictly prefer, all else equal, that the gifts come from themselves.

[. . .]

The dominance of warm-glow

[A]s the size of the charity grows, all giving due to altruism will be crowded out, leaving only giving due to warm-glow. This accords naturally with the observation that giving $100 to an organization that collects millions is motivated more by an admiration for the organization than for any measurable effect of the marginal donation. That does not, however, imply that altruism is not important – the two are surely tied together. Just like hunger tells a person it is *time* to eat but taste buds tells the person what they *want* to eat, it is altruism that should tell you what to give to, but warm-glow tells you how much to give.

Should warm-glow count in social welfare?

Now that we have explored the implications of the warm-glow assumption, demonstrated its importance, and verified the assumption on empirical grounds, we are faced with a deep and significant question: How should warm-glow giving factor into calculations of social welfare?

This is as much a philosophical question as it is an economic one. Reasonable people will likely differ on the answer. On one hand, we should not question preferences. On the other hand, however, we can easily imagine cases where a (paternalistic) government would improve well-being by ignoring those preferences. Perhaps the best way to understand this question is through a series of examples and analogies.

[. . .]

[C]onsider a laboratory experiment to provide public goods. In this experiment, the exact same game is presented in two frames, one positive and one negative. In the positive frame subjects are given 100 units of money to keep, but are told they can contribute any share of it to a public good, thus creating a positive externality for other subjects. In the negative frame they are told that all the money is already given to the public good, but that they can withdraw up to 100 units to keep, thus creating a negative externality. What happens? People don't seem to be bothered that much by creating a negative externality, although they don't like the "cold-prickle" they feel, but really enjoy the warm-glow of creating positive externalities. Does this mean it is socially preferred to provide more of the public good when giving donations creates a warm-glow than in the world where withdrawing donations creates a cold-prickle? What is happening in this game is that there is utility from the act of making the choice, and this "choice utility" is again biasing choices. Since the only difference in these worlds is the frame which prejudices the decisions – whether the economy is endowed with money in the public good (like a commons) or in the private good (as with charitable giving) – it seems that we would want a social criterion that would give us the same directive in both cases.

What about this hypothetical situation: Imagine two pairs of friends. Each pair meets every week for lunch at the same restaurant and always orders the same thing. Al and Andy each pay for their own meals, while Bob and Brad take turns picking up the tab. The B friends get a warm-glow from giving a gift to each other each week. Can we say they are better off than the A friends? Maybe, but maybe not. Bob and Brad are constantly in a state of having to retire a debt. So, while buying lunch for the friend is improving utility, it may be the debt they are paying off has lowered their utility in the first place. Hence, it is just as likely that the mutual gift-giving friends are actually worse off than the self-sufficient friends. As economists, we have no way of knowing.

Next, a related point on the "power of the ask." Fundraisers know that to get money donated, you have to ask for it. And, most often you either get nothing or you get the amount you asked for. Think of how you feel when colleagues ask you to give to a cause, buy Girl Scout cookies, or sponsor their kids' sports teams. Although you cringe when they approach, you give because saying no would be even more painful than saying yes. Hence, giving has a marginally positive effect on your utility – but it was "the ask" that lowered it in the first place. By providing public goods through charities, we are creating obligations, guilt, and social pressure among people that they relieve by giving to charity. The giving creates warm feelings, provides social praise, and may actually build valuable relationships. But even with successful charitable fundraising, do the positive feelings of giving outweigh the negative feelings of the burdens of obligation and guilt? Again, we have no way of knowing.

Finally, consider this experimental data collected by Kahneman and Knetsch. They ask people a series of questions about how much they are willing to contribute to a public good. Each successive question they ask involves an environmental public good that embeds the public good in the prior question – environmental cleanup on a local level versus regional level versus national level. Thus, stating a smaller number when moving to a larger scale would be logically inconsistent. What they find is that the answer to the first question they ask is, on average, about $25, and the answer to the second is about $50. But this is true whether the first question is about the local, regional or national good. Hence, the good itself seems not to matter for the willingness to pay. Kahneman and Knetsch instead argue that the answers to these questions are simply maintaining a self-image of being an environmentalist. What if the warm-glow of giving to a public good is exactly the same as this? When a fundraiser calls and asks for a donation, the gift is simply buying a self-image that says "I am a decent and generous person," or perhaps less positively, "I am not cold-hearted and selfish." This is a demand that, as in Say's law, would not have been generated had the supply of fundraisers for charitable causes not emerged in the first place. So, whether and how this "spin-off" good should be counted in social welfare will depend on whether the social planner has any direct interest in creating this market in the first place. That is, does society have a direct interest in creating a market for maintaining self-images? Lacking any argument that it does, then the creation of this market should not in itself affect the social welfare goals of proving the efficient level of charity.

These examples have illustrated four principles that militate against counting warm-glow in welfare:

1. Choices in the real world are distorted by the institutions within which they are made. These biases prey on decision frames, incomplete information, and naive decision makers. Optimal social policy should have as a goal decisions that would be made in an idealized world where there are no decision frames, no missing information or knowledge, and no social distortions.
2. Different institutions for providing public goods bring up different emotions or sentiments simply by creating different environmental cues. Even small or seemingly innocuous changes may have big effects on behavior. This "decision utility" does not itself represent any new consumption, but only utility gained by the process of generating consumption. While such decision utility may affect society's choice of institution to reach social goals, the determination of these social goals, that is the social welfare calculations, should be independent of such decision utility.
3. Even if we were to include warm-glow, we are not sure whether it should increase or decrease welfare. If giving to charity is relieving a guilty feeling, then although it certainly increases utility to give, it does not necessarily mean utility is higher than it would be if the government had forced the contribution through taxation.
4. What if warm-glow giving is purchasing some other good that, while related, is totally separate from the charity itself, such as maintaining a self-image? What is society's interest in creating this spin-off good? If there is no compelling social interest in creating this good, it seems like its existence should have no effect on the calculation of the socially optimal level of the public good itself.

These four points present a (partial) list of the reasons why counting warm-glow in social welfare calculations is either problematic or potentially misleading. In my own view, it is most prudent and most informative to first recognize that behavior is chosen by people seeking warm-glows, but then to set the social welfare maximizing goals that makes no adjustment for warm-glow in aggregating welfare. That is, all social welfare prescriptions should be made without counting warm-glow, but should be constrained by behavior that is dictated by seeking warm-glow.

A political theory of philanthropy

Rob Reich, 2011

The practice of philanthropy is as old as humanity. People have been giving away their money, property, and time to others for millennia. What's novel about the contemporary practice of philanthropy is the availability of tax incentives to give money away. The charitable contributions deduction in the United States is less than 100 years old, created by the US Congress in 1917 shortly after the institution of a system of federal income taxation in 1913. Similar incentives built into tax systems exist in most developed and many developing democracies.

More generally, laws govern the creation of foundations and nonprofit organizations, and they spell out the rules under which these organizations may operate. Laws set up special tax exemptions for philanthropic and nonprofit organizations, and they frequently permit tax concessions for individual and corporate donations of money and property to qualifying nongovernmental organizations. In this sense, philanthropy is not an invention of the state, but ought to be viewed today as an artifact of the state; we can be certain that philanthropy would not have the form it currently does in the absence of the various laws that structure it and tax incentives that encourage it.

Contemporary practice, in which philanthropy is structured by a regulatory framework of incentives, is not the norm, but the historical anomaly. Previously, the state protected the liberty of people to make donations of money and property, but did not provide incentives for doing so. Two natural questions arise: Why have such incentives and what is their justification in a liberal democracy?

[. . .]

What rules should govern private charity in a liberal democracy? Consider this simple framework to motivate the question. Assume, first, that there is a private property regime of some type. Assume, second, that there is some kind of income tax. Individuals have private property, in particular some income or wealth, and then they have been duly taxed on it. After being taxed, they have money or property they wish to give away for charitable purposes. What now?

The default position of a liberal democratic state regarding charitable giving, it seems to me, ought to be strict nonintervention: Individuals should possess the liberty to give their money or property away to whomever they please. Restrictions on that liberty, such as with estate taxation or campaign finance restrictions, stand in need of justification; the state bears the burden of showing why such restrictions are necessary or permissible, consistent with justice. In parallel form, I suggest that incentives for people to exercise their liberty to give their money away also stand in need of justification; the state bears the burden of showing why such incentives are desirable and consistent with justice.

This returns us to my original question: What is the justification for the current practice in the United States and elsewhere of providing tax incentives for citizens to make charitable contributions? Because the tax incentive constitutes a subsidy – the loss of federal tax revenue – it is no exaggeration to say that the United States and other countries currently subsidize the liberty of people to give money away, foregoing tax revenue for an activity that for millennia has gone unsubsidized by the state. The United States has the most generous subsidy structure. Charitable giving in 2008 exceeded $300 billion, costing the US Treasury more than $50 billion in lost tax revenue. Why does the United States do this?

The remainder of this essay lays out and assesses three possible justifications for the existence of tax incentives for charitable giving. I focus special attention on the incentive mechanism currently used in the United Sates and in many other countries: the charitable contributions deduction, a deduction of charitable gifts from a citizen's taxable income.

[. . .]

Tax base rationale

The justification rejects entirely the claim that the deduction is a subsidy. The deduction constitutes, instead, the fair or appropriate way to treat the donor; deductibility is *intrinsic* to the tax system. First promulgated by William Andrews, the basic argument is that deducting charitable contributions is necessary to properly define an individual's taxable income. If taxable income is construed, as according to the standard Haig – Simons definition, as personal consumption and wealth accumulations, then charitable donations ought not be included in a person's tax base. The reason is that charity cannot be equated with personal consumption, because charitable gifts redirect resources from private and preclusive consumption to public and nonpreclusive consumption. Andrews concludes that "a deduction should be allowed whenever money is expended for anything other than personal consumption or accumulation." Tax scholar Boris Bittker offers a similar argument, concluding that charitable donations ought not count as consumption because, in making a voluntary donation, the donor is made worse off (with respect to others at the same income who do not make a donation), relinquishing use of resources that could have been directed to personal benefit.

Unlike subsidy justifications, the tax base justification focuses on the fair treatment of the donor; it does not inquire into the goods produced with the donation or the efficiency with which these goods are produced.

[. . .]

Subsidy rationale

The more typical defense of the charitable contributions deduction – and one that does, even if sometimes only implicitly, take into account a broader theory of social and economic justice – is that the state accomplishes something of important social value by providing subsidies for people to be charitable. The state provides incentives for charity because it is believed that the incentives stimulate the production of something of greater social value than what the state could have produced on its own, had it not offered the incentives.

The subsidy therefore counts as a tax expenditure, the fiscal equivalent of a direct spending program. When the state allows citizens to deduct their charitable contributions from their taxable income, the state foregoes tax revenue, which is to say that all taxpayers are affected. They are affected in (at least) two important ways. First, they stand to lose some portion of the benefit they receive from direct governmental expenditures. If every citizen gains some fraction of the total revenue of the federal budget, the loss of billions of dollars in tax revenue through the deduction lowers every citizen's fractional benefit. Second, citizens lose in democratic accountability, for the foregone funds are not accountable, or even traceable, in the way that direct government expenditures are. To give an obvious example, citizens can unelect their representatives if they are dissatisfied with the spending programs of the state; the Gates Foundation also has a domestic and global spending program, in part supported through tax subsidies, but its directors and trustees cannot be unelected.

Thus, the success of the subsidy rationale depends on whether the benefits brought about by the subsidy exceed the costs of the lost tax revenue.

[. . .]

Pluralism rationale

The pluralism rationale comes in several stripes and cannot be called a unified theory. The basic idea is that the tax incentive to make charitable donations should not be justified on the basis of assessing the discrete social goods, or outputs, of the various nonprofit organizations funded through these donations. Instead, the tax incentive is justified for its role in stimulating or enhancing the voice of citizens in the production of a diverse, decentralized, and pluralistic associational sector, which is in turn thought to be a bedrock of flourishing liberal democracy. If nonprofit organizations are the institutional face of associational life, then stimulating charitable donations to a wide array of nonprofits might amplify the voice of citizens and enhance civil society to the overall benefit of liberal democracy. Rather than focus on the matrix of goods produced by charitable organizations, the focus here is on the creation and sustenance of a diverse slate of organizations themselves. The public good or social benefit being produced is civil society itself, not the catalogue of public goods or benefits produced by the roster of organizations that constitute civil society.

Note that this is still a subsidy theory, but there is no necessary demand that the subsidy be treasury efficient. Even if there is a net loss to the treasury in the production of the social goods generated by nonprofit organizations – if the state could more efficiently deliver these goods itself – the pluralism rationale holds that the subsidy is nevertheless worthwhile. Of course, there is no bias against the efficient production of goods, but the pluralism rationale does not demand efficiency for the success of the argument. The state might justifiably forego tax revenue for the sake of fostering citizens' voices and the sustenance of a pluralistic associational sector.

[. . .]

I believe this pluralism rationale has merit, and that it may indeed supply reason to subsidize the liberty of people to give their money away for charitable or philanthropic purposes. But however compelling the pluralism rationale may be, it cannot be said to sit behind the current design of tax-supported giving in most countries. Providing tax deductions for individuals who make charitable gifts does not honor the pluralism rationale but rather, I think, undermines and makes a mockery of it.

A cultural explanation of compassion

Robert Wuthnow, 1991

An American paradox

Several miles from where I live stands a large manor house that bears the name of Tolstoy's beloved estate. I invent nothing in reporting this. The name is emblazoned in large white letters, twice – once on either side of the iron gates that stand guard in front of the villa. It was put there by the third wife of the owner in memory of the great writer from her homeland. A visit to this estate was also about to reveal something of the character of compassion in America.

At exactly 10:13 p.m. on a cold evening in late November the iron gates swung open, letting an orange and white emergency vehicle speed through. At the bottom of the hill that sloped gradually away from the highway, nearly shielded from view stood the manor house. Those lucky enough to have been inside said it was one of the finest mansions in all the world. There were ninety-six rooms spread out symmetrically across three floors, and in back was a large doghouse with its own air-conditioning system and a brass staircase. The owner, everyone knew, was the founder of one of the largest companies in the world. His profits were said to be among the highest in the world. He had had the good sense to find a way to make money by marketing comfort to the suffering. Cynics said he made a nickel every time a schoolboy scraped his knee, a quarter every time a woman had her period. But now, as the emergency vehicle wound its way down the long driveway, the owner lay bent in agony, clutching his chest with the desperate intensity of a man near death.

The driver of the emergency vehicle brought it to a screeching halt under the large portico at the front of the house. From the passenger side a lanky young paramedic jumped out, barked an order to the driver, and bounded up the steps toward the door. On the way, he muttered another quick command to his companion, who caught his eye and grinned widely; then both disappeared inside.

In less than a minute and a half Jack Casey and his assistant had sized up the situation, loaded the ailing gentleman into the emergency vehicle, taken vital signs, radioed the local hospital, and begun their ascent back up the driveway to the main road. The mission had been accomplished with the smooth efficiency of trained professionals.

For Jack Casey, tonight's call was simply part of a familiar routine. Within the past twenty-four months he had responded to more than five hundred such calls. He had also dragged people from burning buildings, helped his teammates cut through the twisted wreckage of automobiles to reach trapped drivers, and risked his personal safety responding to cases where victims were stabbed by their own family members. Once, not long before this, he had swum through icy water fully clothed without a life jacket, dragged an unconscious woman back through the water to shore, and administered cardiopulmonary resuscitation just in time to save her life.

But Jack had done none of these things as a paid professional. Like millions of Americans, he was an unpaid helper who gave his time freely because he cared for others.

[. . .]

Volunteering is one of the ways Americans show care and compassion. Not many have the opportunity or the training to show it as dramatically as does Jack Casey: of all the volunteer jobs people listed in the Independent Sector survey, less than 1 percent were related to fire or rescue-squad work. But volunteering is a way to reach out, to do what one can, to use one's skills, often in quiet ways, to make the community a better place. In fact, many of our community organizations depend largely on volunteers for their very existence. Approximately 31 million people do volunteer work each year for their churches or synagogues. Twenty million provide free services to schools, tutoring programs, and other educational organizations. Sixteen million donate time to some kind of hospital, nursing home, clinic, or health agency.

Formal volunteering is only one of the ways in which Americans show care and compassion. In small ways, millions of Americans also extend a helping hand informally to their neighbors, relatives, and friends. They visit them in the hospital, help them through personal crises, lend money, provide a sympathetic ear when one is needed, and encourage those they care about to give up addictive behaviors. According to a national survey I conducted for this volume, six people in ten visited someone in the hospital during the past year. Three in four had at one time or another helped a relative or friend through a personal crisis, and half of these had helped someone through a crisis during the past year. Six persons in ten had lent more than one hundred dollars to a relative or friend – half within the past year. Slightly more than half the population had tried to get someone to stop using alcohol or drugs – 29 percent in the past year.

[. . .]

If this were the whole story we might well raise our collective chins, stick out our chests, and tell our detractors that the picture of America is brighter than they had supposed. The level of volunteering and caring in our society suggests an image of wholesomeness, health, nurturing, and goodness. But this Wonder Bread image of American society is only half the loaf, still preposterously different from Tolstoy's bread labor. There is another side to our character.

Although millions of hours are donated to volunteer activates each year, this effort falls far short of what is needed. I mentioned earlier that two-thirds of the American people have visited someone in the hospital in the past year and a quarter have taken care of someone seriously ill in their homes. But thousands of people have no one to care for them. Substantial numbers in our society fear they could not count on anyone for help if they or a member of their family became seriously ill. Nearly four in ten (37 percent) feel they could not count on their immediate neighbors. Almost as many (36 percent) think they could not depend on church or synagogue members for help. One person in three doubts it would be possible to count on relatives outside the immediate family. And when it comes to volunteer and government agencies, the proportions who express doubt are even higher. Half the population think volunteers in their communities could not be counted on for help; two people in three think this about social welfare agencies.

As a society we pay lip service to altruistic values, but these values must be seen in the context of our other pursuits, the majority of which focus on ourselves rather than others. From the variety of breakfast cereals in our supermarkets to the vast efforts we make to spend quiet evenings and weekends alone, our behavior demonstrates that we cherish individual freedom almost as deeply as life itself. If we talk incessantly about "community," we live our lives in a way that says individual freedom is better. Ours is a society that places equally high value on the dogged determination and long hours of hard work it takes to achieve individual success. We are also a society in which self-interest, whether in money, physical health, self-expression, or matters of the heart, assumes a dominant role in our thinking.

[. . .]

Collectively, these values make up what is popularly referred to as American individualism. They are among our most widely shared values. They are deeply embedded in the mythic legacy we have all inherited. The American frontier, with its cowboys and pioneers, symbolizes freedom and the rewards of hard work. Heroes like Abraham Lincoln and Davy Crockett conjure up images of nonconformity, being true to one's own convictions, and the ability to succeed. In the twentieth century, these heroes of the past live on while a new generation of rugged individualists takes its place alongside them: the astronaut who finds glory in hard work and freedom in the vast frontiers of outer space, the movieland adventurer (Indiana Jones, Han Solo, Rambo) who strikes out on his own and defies everyone's expectations, the figure of a Jonathan Livingston Seagull who finds strength deep within and rises to miraculous heights, and the real estate magnate who plays his or her hand more skillfully than everyone else and trumps them all in the deal's cleverness.

We saw earlier that three-quarters of the American people say helping people in need is very important to them and nearly two-thirds say giving time to help others is very important. These figures represent a high level of agreement about the importance of being concerned for others. But an equally large share of the population, according to my survey, attaches high value to the various aspects of individualism we have just considered. The extent to which personal freedom is valued is evident in the fact that seven persons in ten (71 percent) say it is either absolutely essential or very important to them to "be able to do what you want." Our collective love affair with the success ethic is revealed by the vast majority of the public (78 percent and 77 percent, respectively) who say it is very important to them to be successful in their work and to live comfortable lives. An even higher proportion – 88 percent – say taking care of themselves (one way of expressing our attachment to self-interest) is very important.

[. . .]

What strikes me most about Jack Casey, in addition to the volunteer activities he describes, is the fact that even his choice of language consistently puts others first. He gives much of the credit for his own interest in first aid to the scout leader he had been "lucky" enough to have in the fifth grade. He describes his involvement with water safety in high school as merely a "rare opportunity." He says he could not take credit for the outdoor-action program because "the kids do all the work."

Nor are his efforts to help others limited to these volunteer activities. In daily life he finds himself trying to be helpful just by meeting the little needs of those around him, such as providing transportation. "Somebody'll call me up at midnight and ask me to drive them to the airport, so I will; or somebody'll call me at three in the morning and ask me to pick up their friend at the train station. So I'll say, sure I'll pick them up." Pausing to reflect for a moment, he adds, "I'm inclined whenever someone asks for help to try and help them. That's just the way I am. I guess it's part of my self-image to picture myself as someone who other people can rely on."

In all these ways Jack Casey epitomizes caring and compassion. His desire to help others has taken him well beyond the bounds of most people's commitments to their communities. If the typical volunteer donates five hours a week, Jack donates at least fifteen. If the average American has visited someone in the hospital, Jack has made sure the sick and injured have got there in the first place. But there is another side to Jack Casey.

He also prides himself on being a rugged individualist: someone who not only thinks for himself and does what he wants to but also refuses to burden his friend or let himself be dependent on anyone. "I'm the kind of person who likes to be relatively independent of other people," he says. That means not having – and not needing – a "specific reference point," such as a group of friends who support one another or a stable community with which to identify.

Jack's individualism also involves taking care of himself emotionally, even if this means denying some of his feelings. His brand of individualism shows little patience for the touchy feely kind of person who focuses on his or her emotions. He speaks disparagingly of his sister ("a person with a huge heart who can't take care of herself") and his friends who are constantly "stressed out" about little things. Jack's brand of individualism is more that of the rugged stoic. "I always have too much to do to get stressed out about it all the time." He says he has discovered that "after a while you just have to develop an iceman personality."

[. . .]

How is it that Jack Casey is able to be such a rugged individualist and so deeply compassionate at the same time? How is it that he manages to risk his life in the service of others and yet hold firmly the conviction that he is Number One? How does he manage to devote himself so selflessly to the community and still claim to be the iceman who depends on no one?

How is it that we as a people are able to devote billions of hours to volunteer activities, to show care and compassion in so many ways to those around us, and still be a nation of individualists who pride ourselves on personal freedom, individual success, and the pursuit of self-interest? How do we reconcile these paradoxical elements in our tradition?

[. . .]

Caring and/for our selves

Making sense of why we do things is never easy. When it involves complex motives and several alternative languages for describing these motives, it becomes even more difficult. The various stories Jack Casey tells about his behavior illustrate these difficulties. He is an exceptionally thoughtful, caring, and articulate young man, and yet he develops several narratives about himself that are neither internally consistent nor entirely compatible with one another. He can talk fluently about some of the self-interested reasons why he gives of himself to help others; at the same time, he recognizes the limitation of these reasons. He recognizes that he continues to show care and compassion even when such gratifications cannot account for his actions, but he admits that his behavior remains puzzling to him. His story about the terror of seeing someone die and not being able to help provides an explanation for his entry into rescue-squad work. But his inability to articulate a meaningful story of his present activities, including his apparent lack of language to explain his sense of altruism and to express the emotional qualities of compassion, raises serious doubts about the durability of his commitments.

[. . .]

For me the essential question in all this is: "Is compassion really possible in our society?" I do not mean voluntarism, care giving, helping behavior, prosocial activity, or similar words that have been invented to give compassion a more contemporary ring. I mean compassion in the old-fashioned sense (for it is an old-fashioned word) – what in most languages means "to suffer with" and in other languages means simply "to feel with," what the Good Samaritan was moved with when he came across the injured man on the Jericho road.

Is compassion possible? Of course, one might say. Look at the statistics on giving time to charitable and social-service organizations. Of course it is possible. And there would be even more of it if people had more free time and were encouraged to give. What we need are more effective appeals, better advertising, more attention to the incentives that make people willing to give, more consideration of the situations in which it becomes possible to give. Or, one might say, look at the feelings of which compassion consists. Of course compassion is possible, at least for most people. A mother catches her hand in the bathroom door; on seeing her grasp it, wincing with pain, her infant daughter does the same. Compassion is natural unless some abnormal experiences cause it to be lost.

None of this is what I have in mind. When I ask whether compassion is possible, I mean, is it culturally possible? Are we able to interpret our behavior – to ourselves and to others – in a way that makes sense, in a way that makes sense of it as compassion? Is it possible for us to think of ourselves as persons who have shown compassion, as persons who are capable of showing compassion, as persons who are (at some level) compassionate? Moreover, is it possible for us to think of ourselves collectively in this way? Are we a compassionate people? Or, perhaps more realistically, does compassion play an important role in our society? And, if so, what is that role?

[. . .]

When I talk about "acts of compassion," then, I do not mean a particular set of behaviors, taken simply at face value, such as a visit to the hospital or an afternoon of volunteering at a center for abused women. I mean the cultural framework as well: the languages we use to make sense of such behaviors, the cultural understandings that transform them from physical motions onto human action. The discourse in which such behavior is inscribed is no less a part of the act than is the behavior itself. The possibility of compassion depends as much on having an appropriate discourse to interpret it as it does on having a free afternoon to do it. To ask whether compassion is possible, therefore, is to ask about the languages on which its very conceivability depends.

But to ask about language inevitably moves us from the level of the individual to the level of society. Each of us must use language to make sense of our individual experiences [. . .] We all use the words our language gives us. But they are not the words of our own invention. They are the languages we find available in our culture. They reflect broader themes about what it means to be an American.

[. . .]

[W]e all must struggle to find out what it means to be compassionate in the unique context of American society. I believe deeply that we all struggle with that issue, whether we are volunteers or people who help our neighbors informally or just individuals who find ourselves needing community. We have to discover how to reconcile our caring for others with the pervasive individualism that so often fragments our society and our lives. I believe we succeed for the most part in doing this – better, at least, than many of our society's critics suggest.

But we also pay a price. We begin with ourselves. We worry a lot about our motives. We pay great heed to the language of good feelings. We struggle even to adapt our religious values and our sense of ethical responsibility to the fragmented society in which we live. These pursuits are all issues that deserve our attention, for they structure much of our thinking about the possibility of being compassionate in a self-interested world. But in the end, we must return to the question of society itself. We must ask, does caring for others primarily help "our selves," as individuals, or can it also help "ourselves," as a society?

[. . .]

Talking about motives

Our culture supplies a number of repertoires to draw from whenever we want to construct an account of our motives for caring. These repertoires are reproduced in sermons and speeches. They can be found in books and articles discussing the motives of public figures. In more ordinary contexts they are simply evident in the conversation we hold with our acquaintances and with ourselves.

The biblical tradition has been a rich source of arguments about the importance of caring. I have mentioned the role played historically by sermons about love of neighbor such as those of John Winthrop and John Witherspoon. Through the many denominations and faiths that make up the mosaic of American religion these admonitions have continued to play a prominent role in our culture. Variously interpreted, the biblical tradition teaches compassion as a duty to divine law, as a response to divine love, and as a sign of commitment to the Judeo-Christian ethic.

[. . .]

The idea that compassion may in some way be a natural impulse continues to have resonance in our society. Researchers are now studying small children to see if some primary disposition toward empathizing with others' pain may lie at the root of compassion. In the philosophical and ethical literature one finds similar ideas. One author who has carefully examined the ethical basis of compassion argues, for example, that "the impulse to act in behalf of the present other is itself innate." She goes on to explain that "it lies latent in each of us, awaiting gradual development in a succession of caring relations."

[. . .]

Another, perhaps more pervasive, tradition in which we understand compassion also hails from the Enlightenment. Although utilitarianism has been popularized in ways that neither its originators would recognize nor its contemporary advocates concur with, its main arguments can be traced to the writings of David Hume, Jeremy Bentham, and John Stuart Mill in the eighteenth and nineteenth centuries. Utilitarianism is an ethical system and a political theory that stresses the consequences of actions for people in general; that is, an action's utility for the common good. Among its more debated tenets is the view that people can and should pursue their own interests, even their own pleasures, as a way of maximizing the good of all.

[. . .]

One other tradition supplies an important repertoire with which to interpret our motives for compassion. It often mixes with the other traditions we have just considered. But it is also important in its own right (as we shall see). It is a secular version of the religious teaching that loving one's neighbor is of value. It emphasizes the role of desire or will: what motivates one to care is simply the desire, the wish, the decision to show compassion. It gains reinforcement from the fact that so much of our charitable behavior is institutionalized in the so-called voluntary sector – the sector where people presumably care simply because they want to. It is part of the logic that grows from our society's emphasis on freedom, individual autonomy, and willpower.

[. . .]

This, it seems to me, is the cultural significance of accounts. Motive-talk provides connections with our cultural heritage. It associates us with the various values we have been taught to accord prominence. It tells others that we cherish these values. Our ability to care may not depend on giving one account rather than another. But being able to give some account makes it possible to conceive of our behavior as caring. By linking it with broader values we place it in a context. Our accounts define the cultural meaning of our caring; our caring in turn becomes a reflection of our broader values.

How generosity enhances well-being

Christian Smith and Hilary Davidson, 2014

[We have] established a clear association between the practice of generosity and Americans' greater well-being in life. The central question of this chapter concerns how the causal forces that produce that association actually work. Does generosity causally produce greater well-being? Or is it actually greater well-being that causes more generosity?

[. . .]

Well-being causally influencing generosity

Let us consider first the ways that greater well-being in people's lives likely causally influences more generous practices. This is the response of the causal skeptics. They are not hard to think of. Some of them very likely include the following causal mechanisms:

1 *Positive mental outlook*. People who are happier, healthier, and more purposeful in life will, all other things being equal, tend to have a more positive, hopeful outlook on life and the possibilities for doing good in the world than those who are less happy, healthy, and purposeful, and so will be more generous in various ways.
2 *More energy*. People who are happier, healthier, and more purposeful in life will, all other things being equal, tend to have more energy to spend on matters beyond their own personal concerns than those who are less happy, healthy, and purposeful, and so will be more generous in various ways.
3 *More money*. People who are healthier (though not necessarily more happy or purposeful) will, all other things being equal, tend to have more money to spend on matters beyond their own personal concerns than those who are less healthy, insofar as health problems tend to consume money and may curtail people's ability to work in the paid labor force, and so will be more generous in various ways.
4 *Social network connections*. People who are happier, healthier, and more purposeful in life will, all other things being equal, tend to be better connected to and more engaged in a wider range of social relationships in a broader variety of institutional settings than those who are less happy, healthy, and purposeful – and those social ties will provide more opportunities to engage through invitations and requests in generous practices, and so they will be more generous in various ways.

These kinds of explanations for how greater well-being in life may facilitate higher levels of generosity make great sense. We have good reasons to think that they help to explain the difference the significant association between generous practices and life well-being that we observed . . . Our account . . . does nothing to deny them. We accept these explanations as part of a larger picture of complex causal dynamics. But, we also suggest, they are only *part* of the picture, only one side of a complicated, two-sided dynamic that we need to better understand.

[. . .]

[W]e proceed with the belief that generosity and well-being are mutually influencing. Greater well-being can casually encourage more generosity. But practices of generosity can also casually enhance people's well-being. Part of making the case for this bidirectional model of causation involves spelling out specific causal mechanisms by which generosity can increase human well-being. It is to this task that we turn next.

Nine interrelated causal mechanisms

[. . .]

1. Generosity often fosters and reinforces positive emotions and reduces negative emotions in givers, which tends to lead to greater happiness and health.

[. . .]

2. Generosity often triggers chemical systems in the brain and body that increase pleasure and experiences of reward, reduce stress, and suppress pain, which tend to lead to greater happiness and health.

[. . .]

3. Generosity increases personal agency and self-efficacy, which tends to enhance happiness and health.

[. . .]

4. Generosity often creates positive, meaningful social roles and personal self-identities for generous givers to live out, which tends to lead to greater happiness and health.

[. . .]

5. Generosity tends to reduce maladaptive self-absorption, which tends to produce greater happiness and health.

[. . .]

6. Practicing generosity requires and reinforces the perception of living in a world of abundance and blessing, which itself also increases happiness and health.

[. . .]

7. Generosity expands the number and density of social-network relational ties, which tends strongly to lead to greater happiness and health.

[. . .]

8. Generosity tends to promote increased learning about the world, which often leads to greater happiness and health.

[. . .]

9. Generosity tends to increase givers' physical activity, which usually leads to greater happiness and health.

[. . .]

Caveats

We want to be clear: not every act or practice of generosity necessarily improves happiness, health, and purpose in every participant's life. Many generous practices do, it seems . . . However, general causal mechanisms can affect individual people differently. Some people may be more susceptible to generosity's well-being enhancing effects than others. All of the mechanisms examined above also interact differently in specific cases with particular people's health conditions, family settings, geographical and neighborhood contexts, socioeconomic status, general outlook on life, lifestyle practices, risk behaviors, and more. Human bodies and social life are complicated. Nothing is necessarily predictable or guaranteed in any given instance, even if the overall pattern of associations and causes is pretty clear for the population. We are dealing here, in other words, with probabilities, likelihoods, and tendencies that apply to most people, not with universal laws or formulas that work for everyone.

[. . .]

Summary and conclusion

These nine causal mechanisms, and perhaps others, help to explain why it is that more generous people tend to be significantly more happy, healthy, and purposive people. It is not just that generosity is caused by some greater original well-being. The well-being itself is also caused in part by practices of greater generosity. In multiple, complex, and interacting ways, bodies, brains, spirits, minds, and social relationships are stimulated, connected, and energized by generous practices in ways that are good for people. Thus, as a result of the generous practices themselves, those who live more generous lives also tend to enjoy greater well-being in life.

Biological altruism

Samir Okasha, 2013

In evolutionary biology, an organism is said to behave altruistically when its behavior benefits other organisms, at a cost to itself. The costs and benefits are measured in terms of *reproductive fitness*, or expected number of offspring. So by behaving altruistically, an organism reduces the number of offspring it is likely to produce itself, but boosts the number that other organisms are likely to produce. This biological notion of altruism is not identical to the everyday concept. In everyday parlance, an action would only be called "altruistic" if it was done with the conscious intention of helping another. But in the biological sense there is no such requirement. Indeed, some of the most interesting examples of biological altruism are found among creatures that are (presumably) not capable of conscious thought at all, e.g. insects. For the biologist, it is the consequences of an action for reproductive fitness that determine whether the action counts as altruistic, not the intentions, if any, with which the action is performed.

Altruistic behavior is common throughout the animal kingdom, particularly in species with complex social structures. For example, vampire bats regularly regurgitate blood and donate it to other members of their group who have failed to feed that night, ensuring they do not starve. In numerous bird species, a breeding pair receives help in raising its young from other "helper" birds, who protect the nest from predators and help to feed the fledglings. Vervet monkeys give alarm calls to warn fellow monkeys of the presence of predators, even though in doing so they attract attention to themselves, increasing their personal chance of being attacked. In social insect colonies (ants, wasps, bees and termites), sterile workers devote their whole lives to caring for the queen, constructing and protecting the nest, foraging for food, and tending the larvae. Such behavior is maximally altruistic: sterile workers, obviously, do not leave any offspring of their own – so have a personal fitness of zero – but their actions greatly assist the reproductive efforts of the queen.

From a Darwinian viewpoint, the existence of altruism in nature is, at first sight, puzzling, as Darwin himself realized. Natural selection leads us to expect animals to behave in ways that increase their own chances of survival and reproduction, not those of others. But by behaving altruistically an animal reduces its own fitness, and so should be at a selective disadvantage vis-à-vis one which behaves selfishly. To see this, imagine that some members of a group of Vervet monkeys give alarm calls when they see predators, but others do not. Other things being equal, the latter will have an advantage. By selfishly refusing to give an alarm call, a monkey can reduce the chance that it will itself be attacked, while at the same time benefiting from the alarm calls of others. So we should expect natural selection to favor those monkeys that do not give alarm calls over those that do. But this raises an immediate puzzle. How did the alarm-calling behavior evolve in the first place, and why has it not been eliminated by natural selection? How can the existence of altruism be reconciled with basic Darwinian principles?

Altruism and the levels of selection

The problem of altruism is intimately connected with questions about the level at which natural selection acts. If selection acts exclusively at the individual level, favoring some individual organisms over others, then it seems that altruism cannot evolve, for behaving altruistically is disadvantageous for the individual organism itself, by definition. However, it is possible that altruism may be advantageous at the *group* level. A group containing lots of altruists, each ready to subordinate their own selfish interests for the greater good of the group, may well have a survival advantage over a group composed mainly or exclusively of selfish organisms. A process of between-group selection may thus allow the altruistic behavior to evolve. *Within* each group, altruists will be at a selective disadvantage relative to their selfish colleagues, but the fitness of the group as a whole will be enhanced by the presence of altruists. Groups composed only or mainly of selfish organisms go extinct, leaving behind groups containing altruists. In the example of the Vervet monkeys, a group containing a high proportion of alarm-calling monkeys will have a survival advantage over a group containing a lower proportion. So conceivably, the alarm-calling behavior may evolve by between-group selection, even though within each group, selection favors monkeys that do not give alarm calls.

[. . .]

The major weakness of group selection as an explanation of altruism, according to the consensus that emerged in the 1960s, was a problem that Dawkins called "subversion from within." Even if altruism is advantageous at the group level, within any group altruists are liable to be exploited by selfish "free-riders" who refrain from behaving altruistically. These free-riders will have an obvious fitness advantage: they benefit from the altruism of others, but do not incur any of the costs. So even if a group is composed exclusively of altruists, all behaving nicely towards each other, it only takes a single selfish mutant to bring an end to this happy idyll. By virtue of its relative fitness advantage within the group, the selfish mutant will out-reproduce the altruists, hence selfishness will eventually swamp altruism. Since the generation time of individual organisms is likely to be much shorter than that of groups, the probability that a selfish mutant will arise and spread is very high, according to this line of argument. "Subversion from within" is generally regarded as a major stumbling block for group-selectionist theories of the evolution of altruism.

If group selection is not the correct explanation for how the altruistic behaviors found in nature evolved, then what is? In the 1960s and 1970s a rival theory emerged: kin selection or "inclusive fitness" theory, due originally to Hamilton.

[. . .]

Kin selection and inclusive fitness

The basic idea of kin selection is simple. Imagine a gene which causes its bearer to behave altruistically towards other organisms, e.g. by sharing food with them. Organisms without the gene are selfish – they keep all their food for themselves, and sometimes get handouts from the altruists. Clearly the altruists will be at a fitness disadvantage, so we should expect the altruistic gene to be eliminated from the population. However, suppose that altruists are discriminating in who they share food with. They do not share with just anybody, but only with their relatives. This immediately changes things. For relatives are genetically similar – they share genes with one another. So when an organism carrying the altruistic gene shares his food, there is a certain probability that the recipients of the food will also carry copies of that gene. (How probable depends on how closely related they are.) This means that the altruistic gene can in principle spread by natural selection. The gene causes an organism to behave in a way which reduces its own fitness but boosts the fitness of its relatives – who have a greater than average chance of carrying the gene themselves. So the overall effect of the behavior may be to increase the number of copies of the altruistic gene found in the next generation, and thus the incidence of the altruistic behavior itself.

[. . .]

Reciprocal altruism

The theory of reciprocal altruism was originally developed by Trivers as an attempt to explain cases of (apparent) altruism among unrelated organisms, including members of different species. (Clearly, kin selection cannot help explain altruism among non-relatives.) Trivers' basic idea was straightforward: it may pay an organism to help another, if there is an expectation of the favor being returned in the future. ("If you scratch my back, I'll scratch yours".) The cost of helping is offset by the likelihood of the return benefit, permitting the behavior to evolve by natural selection. Trivers termed this evolutionary mechanism "reciprocal altruism."

For reciprocal altruism to work, there is no need for the two individuals to be relatives, nor even to be members of the same species. However, it is necessary that individuals should interact with each other more than once, and have the ability to recognize other individuals with whom they have interacted in the past. If individuals interact only once in their lifetimes and never meet again, there is obviously no possibility of return benefit, so there is nothing to be gained by helping another. However, if individuals encounter each other frequently, and are capable of identifying and punishing "cheaters" who have refused to help in the past, then the helping behavior can evolve. A "cheat" who refuses to help will ultimately sabotage his own interests, for although he does not incur the cost of helping others, he forfeits the return benefits too – others will not help him in the future. This evolutionary mechanism is most likely to work where animals live in relatively small groups, increasing the likelihood of multiple encounters.

[. . .]

But is it "real" altruism?

The evolutionary theories described above, in particular kin selection, go a long way towards reconciling the existence of altruism in nature with Darwinian principles. However, some people have felt these theories in a way devalue altruism, and that the behaviors they explain are not "really" altruistic.

[. . .]

The key point to remember is that biological altruism cannot be equated with altruism in the everyday vernacular sense. Biological altruism is defined in terms of fitness consequences, not motivating intentions. If by "real" altruism we mean altruism done with the conscious intention to help, then the vast majority of living creatures are not capable of "real" altruism nor therefore of "real" selfishness either [. . .] The contrast between "real" altruism and merely apparent altruism simply does not apply to most animal species.

[. . .]

Where human behavior is concerned, the distinction between biological altruism, defined in terms of fitness consequences, and "real" altruism, defined in terms of the agent's conscious intentions to help others, does make sense [. . .] What is the relationship between these two concepts? They appear to be independent in both directions, as Elliott Sober has argued. An action performed with the conscious intention of helping another human being may not affect their biological fitness at all, so would not count as altruistic in the biological sense. Conversely, an action undertaken for purely self-interested reasons, i.e., without the conscious intention of helping another, may boost their biological fitness tremendously.

[. . .]

Contrary to what is often thought, an evolutionary approach to human behavior does *not* imply that humans are likely to be motivated by self-interest alone. One strategy by which "selfish genes" may increase their future representation is by causing humans to be *non*-selfish, in the psychological sense.

Eight mechanisms that drive charitable giving

René Bekkers and Pamala Wiepking, 2011

[Note from the editors: There are no brackets and ellipses in this extract because the authors themselves made the selections from the original.]

An overwhelming body of knowledge is available on philanthropy in the social sciences. Research on philanthropy appears in journals from very different disciplines. We present an overview of research on determinants of charitable giving from all disciplines.

Why do people give?

Experiments in economics, sociology, social psychology, biology, and marketing have shown how situations can be created that encourage giving. The situations in these experiments are created by researchers, which allows for causal inferences about determinants of giving. From these experiments, conclusions can be drawn about why people give. We reviewed this literature and identify eight mechanisms as the key mechanisms that have been studied as determinants of philanthropy. They are (a) awareness of need; (b) solicitation; (c) costs and benefits; (d) altruism; (e) reputation; (f) psychological benefits; (g) values; (h) efficacy.

Below we present the eight mechanisms that drive giving. The order in which the eight mechanisms are presented does not reflect the importance or causal strength of the mechanisms. Rather, the order corresponds to the chronological order in which they affect giving in the typical act of donation. For each mechanism, we present the main effect. In many cases, these main effects can be moderated (or sometimes mediated) by other factors. Moderating factors are factors that weaken or strengthen the effect of the mechanism: conditions or personal characteristics that interact with the main effect.

Mechanism 1: awareness of need

Awareness of need is a first prerequisite for philanthropy. People have to become aware of a need for support. Awareness of need is a mechanism that is largely beyond the control of donors, preceding the conscious deliberation of costs and benefits of donating. It is the result of actions of beneficiaries (who seek help) and charitable organizations (who communicate needs to potential donors).

The effects of need have been documented mostly in social psychology, beginning with a series of field experiments from the mid 1960s onwards. In these experiments, a variety of helping behaviors were studied. Generally speaking, the degree of need for help is positively related to the likelihood that help will be given.

Experiments usually manipulate need by exposing participants to needy victims. In focus groups, donors cite knowing a (potential) beneficiary as a motive for charitable contributions. Survey studies also suggest that awareness of need is increased when people know potential beneficiaries of a charitable organization. Awareness of need is facilitated by the (mass) media. More extended media coverage of an earthquake, for example, has a strong positive relationship with private contributions supporting those affected. In turn, the amount of attention the media pays attention to beneficiaries' needs depends on, among others, the number of beneficiaries (or those affected in the case of disasters), and the demographic and psychological distance between potential donors and beneficiaries.

Mechanism 2: solicitation

A second mechanism that precedes the conscious deliberation of various types of costs and benefits of donating is solicitation. Solicitation refers to the mere act of being solicited to donate. The way potential donors are solicited determines the effectiveness of solicitations. The effects of different methods are captured by the other mechanisms. Studies on solicitation have appeared in journals from a variety of disciplines, including marketing, psychology, and economics.

A large majority of all donation acts occurs in response to a solicitation. According to survey studies, in 1996 in the US, 85 percent of donation acts are preceded by a solicitation for a contribution. In the Netherlands, 86 percent of the donation acts are preceded by a solicitation. The evidence from these cross-sectional studies is complemented by the earlier experimental finding showing that actively soliciting contributions rather than passively presenting an opportunity to give, increases the likelihood that people donate. The implication is that the more solicitations for donations people encounter, the more likely they are to give. Survey studies in marketing and sociology usually find that receiving a higher number of solicitations for charitable contributions is associated with increased philanthropic activity. This does not imply that fundraising organizations should mindlessly increase the number of individuals receiving their appeals, as receiving too many requests for donations results in irritation and consequently lower compliance rates.

Mechanism 3: costs and benefits

The third mechanism covers the material costs and benefits associated with donating, defined here as "tangible monetary consequences of making a donation." Effects of costs and benefits are most often documented in studies in economics and marketing.

It is clear that giving money costs money. When the costs of a donation are lowered, giving increases. This is not only true for the absolute costs, which can be lowered through fiscal incentives, but also for the perception of the costs of a donation. This is not to say that philanthropy is motivated by material self-gain because a donation by definition costs money. Economists have studied the empirical effects of the price of giving on philanthropy using survey data and tax files in many papers since the 1970s. A meta-analysis shows that estimates of the price effect are generally negative, but vary widely between studies, depending on the scope of the sample and the statistical methods used. More recent estimates of price effects, based on econometric models developed for the analysis of panel data, tend to be lower than estimates from earlier studies.

Occasionally, donations to charitable organizations buy benefits: e.g., services or other "selective incentives." For instance, when donors to universities, museums, or symphony orchestras get access to exclusive dinners, meetings, or special concerts. Offering access to exclusive services in exchange for contributions brings giving closer to buying. There is a danger in offering material benefits for charitable contributions. When people receive material benefits for helpfulness, they tend to undermine self-attributions of helpfulness, which reduces the effect of prosocial self-attributions on future helpfulness.

Mechanism 4: altruism

An obvious reason why individuals may contribute money to charities is because they care about the organization's output, or the consequences of donations for beneficiaries. Economists, who dominate the study of this mechanism, have labeled this motive "altruism." Purely altruistic motivation (in the economic sense) would lead individuals who learn about an increase in contributions by others with US$1 to reduce their own contribution with US$1. This is called a "crowding out" effect. Numerous studies in economics have sought to estimate the magnitude of crowding out. Results of empirical studies testing for crowding out effects show that crowding out may exist, but is often less than perfect: A US$1 dollar increase in governmental spending decreases private giving with less than US$1. Some studies find no crowding out effect at all, and some studies even find crowding in effects. One study found that increased government support was correlated with a higher number of donors, but with lower average private contributions.

Theoretically, the often less than perfect crowding out implies that other and perhaps more powerful things besides altruism motivate donations. From the behavior of donors we can infer that they do not care so much about the public benefits generated by their contributions. The private benefits or selective incentives for contributions dominate altruistic motives. Hence donors may be called "impure altruists." In practice, the findings imply that charitable donations are unlikely to make up for severe government cuts in nonprofit funding.

Mechanism 5: reputation

The mechanism of reputation refers to the social consequences of donations for the donor. Reputation is studied most often in psychology and economics, together accounting for about two thirds of the studies on this mechanism.

Giving is usually viewed as a positive thing to do, especially when giving reduces inequality, and when giving is less costly, beneficiaries are not to blame and is more effective. Thus people who give to charitable causes are held in high regard by their peers. They receive recognition and approval from others. Laboratory experiments with abstract public goods games by economists and social-psychologists reveal that individuals are willing to incur costs to recognize generous contributions. Conversely, not giving damages one's reputation. This is especially true when donations are announced in public or when they are directly observable. Opportunities to gain or maintain a positive reputation (naming) or avoid a bad one (shaming) in social situations promote giving.

Mechanism 6: psychological benefits

Giving not only yields social benefits but also psychological benefits for the donor. A large majority of all studies on this mechanism is conducted by (social) psychologists who have shown that giving may contribute to one's self-image as an altruistic, empathic, socially responsible, agreeable, or influential person. In addition, giving is in many cases an almost automatic emotional response, producing a positive mood, alleviating feelings of guilt, reducing aversive arousal, satisfying a desire to show gratitude, or to be a morally just person.

There is ample evidence from studies on helping behavior that helping others produces positive psychological consequences for the helper, sometimes labeled "empathic joy," "warm glow" or "joy of giving." Recent evidence from neuropsychological studies suggests that donations to charity result in activity in brain regions that are known to activate our reward system. There are several reasons why humans may have pleasurable psychological experiences on giving: people may alleviate feelings of guilt (avoid punishment), feel good for acting in line with a social norm, or feel good for acting in line with a specific (prosocial, altruistic) self-image.

Positive moods in general may motivate giving. A positive mood may also be induced by the question "How do you feel today?" Most people answer positively to this question ("I'm fine, thank you") and are subsequently more likely to comply with a request for a donation. This is called the "foot-in-the-mouth effect." Simply telling prospective donors that donating will put them in a good mood increases giving, especially when victims are depicted as innocent. Donors also self-report "feeling good" as a motive for donating to charitable causes. Survey studies have also provided evidence of a link between an altruistic self-image and charitable giving.

Mechanism 7: values

In the eyes of donors, the works of nonprofit organizations may make the world a better place. Attitudes and values endorsed by donors make charitable giving more or less attractive to donors. Donations can also be instrumental to exemplifying one's endorsement of specific values to others, but this is captured by the mechanism of reputation. Studies on the effects of values are most often published by journals in sociology, psychology, and philanthropic studies.

Endorsement of prosocial values generally has a positive association with charitable giving. Because values are difficult if not impossible to manipulate, experimental studies on the effects of social values on philanthropy are virtually nonexistent. Survey studies, mostly conducted by sociologists and marketing scientists, show that people who have more prosocial values are more likely to give because they are motivated to make the world a better place. Typically, religious values are related to prosocial values.

Through giving, donors may wish to make the distribution of wealth and health more equal; they may wish to reduce poverty, empower women, safeguard human rights, to protect animals, wildlife, or the ozone layer. Supporting a cause that changes the world in a desired direction is a key motive for giving that has received very little attention in the literature. The desire for social justice is most often studied in relation to philanthropy. A stronger similarity between personal values and organizational values increases the probability that a donation to that particular organization is made.

Mechanism 8: efficacy

Efficacy refers to the perception of donors that their contribution makes a difference to the cause they are supporting. Efficacy is most often studied in philanthropic studies, economics, and psychology, respectively. Survey studies reveal that when people perceive that their contribution will not make a difference, they are less likely to give or leave a charitable bequest. These findings may be the result of reverse causality and/or justification. Although efficacy has been studied extensively in the helping behavior literature, we have been unable to locate any experimental studies on philanthropy that manipulated efficacy. Providing donors with information about the effectiveness of contributions has positive effects on philanthropy. It appears that financial information is especially influential among committed donors.

Perceived efficacy is a likely explanation for the effects of leadership donations and seed money that have been studied extensively by economists. When people see that others give to a charity, they can take this as a signal that others have confidence in the organization. The leadership effect was described earlier by social psychologists as a "modeling effect." A matching offer by a third party (e.g., one's employer or the government) can also have a legitimizing effect: People will think that the third party had enough confidence in the organization to offer the matching contribution. Endorsement of a charity by a high status person is also likely to generate higher donations through a legitimization effect.

Surveys reveal that donors have an aversion against expensive fundraising methods, although donors often overestimate fundraising costs of charitable organizations. Perceptions of efficacy are related to charitable confidence and perceptions of overhead and fundraising costs. Donors who have more confidence in charitable organizations think their contributions are less likely to be spent on fundraising costs and overhead. Such beliefs about the efficacy of charitable organizations are likely to promote giving.

How do the mechanisms relate to each other?

The relative influence of each of the eight mechanisms – whether donations are primarily made in response to awareness of need, solicitation, costs and benefits, altruism, reputation concerns, psychological rewards, or efficacy – is unclear. Multiple motives are likely to operate simultaneously and the mix of these motives differs over time, place, organizations, and donors. It is also likely that the eight mechanisms have interactive effects (e.g., that awareness of need may promote giving more strongly when efficacy is high). We think that identifying systematic patterns in the mix of the mechanisms and interactions among them is an important task for future research.

Throughout our review, we have distinguished experimental from survey studies. Each of these methods has its own advantages and disadvantages. Experiments typically test for short-term effects of manipulations, create artificial conditions, and rely on small groups of participants (university students). Strictly speaking, results cannot be generalized to the general population. The advantage of experimental control is the potential to draw causal inferences. Survey studies typically investigate donations over a longer period to real organizations among population samples but cannot be used to infer causation. Much would be gained by combining the strengths of the two methods. We hope that with this review, researchers using either method will become more aware of the insights gained in studies using the other method.

1.4 The balance of public and private in philanthropy

Philanthropy is not the same as altruism

Dwight F. Burlingame, 1993

Does the motivational theory of altruism commonly used today serve as an effective foundational base for a definition of philanthropy as we know it? I argue that it does not because of its limiting nature. Altruism is one end of a continuum which is anchored by egoism on the other. Both motives come together in the human condition to form a cooperative venture to achieve nearly all ends in society.

[. . .]

Altruism can be defined as unselfish action for the welfare of others or, as the *Oxford English Dictionary* states it, "devotion to others" or "regard for others as a principle of action." This is contrasted with the definition of "egoism" as "regard for one's own interest." The term "altruism" was coined by Auguste Comte and his followers in the 19th century.

[. . .]

Altruism is not the single motive for defining philanthropy, nor is it necessarily the desired operational motive. It is further not very fruitful to attempt to explain philanthropic action by emphasizing either one motive (altruism) to the exclusion of the other (egoism) when the prevailing evidence clearly indicates that both motives are jointly at work causing the philanthropic action to occur. This premise is based, in part, upon the argument put forth by my colleague William Dean that "altruism elevates the moral agent and diminishes the moral object (the one to whom the altruistic act is aimed). Therefore, even on its own terms, the use of altruism can be morally counterproductive." Dean argues that altruistic acts glorify the moral agents, because they can give without any thought of return, and reduce the moral objects, because they can receive without a need to differentiate.

It seems that, at least in part, when philanthropy adopts altruism as its motive, critics of philanthropy are led to argue that the philanthropic tradition perpetuates an elitist view which puts the receiver in an inferior position. In contrast, my definition utilizes our understanding of prosocial behavior, which allows one to avoid at least one of the contested issues identified by Robert Payton in his definition of philanthropy as "voluntary action for the public good." "Philanthropy as voluntary giving and receiving (of money and/or effort) intended for public purposes" creates a value-neutral definition to, as Mike Martin has argued, leave room for moral assessment to be done based on individual cases. It is important for me to emphasize that I am not suggesting that philanthropy has not, on the whole, "been efforts to make things better, or to make them less bad," as Payton has said. Rather, I am saying that oftentimes many people do not know that this is the case, particularly as philanthropy is viewed from a particular cultural or economic position, and in fact what has been claimed as philanthropic may not have been. Therefore, by not including the moral judgment in the definition as it relates to the aims of philanthropy, we still allow for the moral discourse to be applied to individual cases, and at the same time, include the moral "sentiment and imagination" as it is applied to communities.

The definition of altruism is not the appropriate avenue to seek a foundational basis for a definition of philanthropy because one does not need to make a choice between acting altruistically and egoistically in order to act in the interest of the common or public good. This does not imply, however, that a choice is never warranted. Nor does it argue that conflict doesn't exist between egoism and altruism. Rather, it argues that a moral problem surfaces only when the interest of self and the interests of others conflict.

Let me further clarify the elements of my definition of philanthropy as a way to eliminate some, but not all, vagueness as to the territory that is included in this encompassing notion of philanthropy.

First a word about the term voluntary: Voluntary, for our purposes, seems to be most closely tied to the notion that the act is not politically coerced or financially remunerated (in contrast to the power of government to tax); it is intended as giving and, in a legal sense, it is done without profit or payment. In contrast to the dictionary's definition, I do not think of behavior done willingly as always voluntary. For example, I may pay my taxes or a fine willingly in my role as a good citizen, but this is not voluntary.

Second, giving and receiving implies a relationship; you cannot have a philanthropic act without a minimum of two parties. These parties can be individuals or institutions. The exchange can be money or time. As has been pointed out by Ostrander and Schervish, in the relationship between donor and recipient, "The general tendency is for donors to occupy positions that give them substantially more active choice than recipients about how to define the philanthropic transaction and how to take part in it." They further develop a model of donor-led and recipient-side strategies which conceptualizes philanthropy as a social relation. It is important to add that I see the roles in this relationship as very fluid. One moment one may be a receiver and the next moment one may be a donor. The social relationship perspective allows for transferability of the definition across cultures and over time. It also recognizes that intermediary institutions and groups play an important role in connecting donors and recipients and in influencing and advising both donors and recipients.

"Public purposes" consist of virtually all social aims which fall outside the sphere of immediate family and friends; these acts are not done to make a profit or in response to government regulation. This definition includes more than the IRS's limited definition as contained within Section 501(c)3 of the Internal Revenue Code. Political campaign volunteers, mutual-aid groups, professional groups advancing the public good – all count as philanthropy in this sense. The fact that there are economic rewards for certain acts of philanthropy does not prevent the act from being philanthropic; it may in fact encourage more philanthropy.

This definition also allows for the recognition that philanthropy can be ineffective and even wasteful: it can be ridiculous to some and saving grace to others; it can invade and blur the borders of the other sectors; and it allows for much of philanthropy, in fact, to be made up of "the social history of the moral imagination" – that is, both moral choice and moral obligation.

Reviewing the definitional question allows me to clarify further the often blurred concepts in so much of the discourse about the voluntary, philanthropic, nonprofit or third sector. Philanthropy, it seems, is best thought of in terms of a type of action which is prevalent in all sectors. As Ostrander and Schervish pointed out, "The nonprofit sector is no more exclusively the realm of philanthropic relations than the for-profit sector is exclusively the realm of commercial relations." Van Til, after reviewing many approaches to defining philanthropy, also argues for an understanding that philanthropy "pervades all other sectors and institutions."

In summary, it clearly does not follow that acting in one's self-interest will automatically produce bad or misanthropic consequences. Likewise, acting altruistically does not always guarantee positive or philanthropic consequences. Philanthropy is best described and understood when its definition takes into consideration concepts that include both the interest of self and the interest of others. Or, as Tocqueville so elegantly defined it, "Self-interest rightly understood."

Self-interest rightly understood

Alexis de Tocqueville, 1840
(translated by Henry Reeve, 1899)

How the Americans combat individualism by the principle of self-interest rightly understood

When the world was managed by a few rich and powerful individuals, these persons loved to entertain a lofty idea of the duties of man. They were fond of professing that it is praiseworthy to forget oneself and that good should be done without hope of reward, as it is by the Deity himself. Such were the standard opinions of that time in morals.

I doubt whether men were more virtuous in aristocratic ages than in others, but they were incessantly talking of the beauties of virtue, and its utility was only studied in secret. But since the imagination takes less lofty flights, and every man's thoughts are centered in himself, moralists are alarmed by this idea of self-sacrifice and they no longer venture to present it to the human mind.

They therefore content themselves with inquiring whether the personal advantage of each member of the community does not consist in working for the good of all; and when they have hit upon some point on which private interest and public interest meet and amalgamate, they are eager to bring it into notice. Observations of this kind are gradually multiplied; what was only a single remark becomes a general principle, and it is held as a truth that man serves himself in serving his fellow creatures and that his private interest is to do good.

I have already shown, in several parts of this work, by what means the inhabitants of the United States almost always manage to combine their own advantage with that of their fellow citizens; my present purpose is to point out the general rule that enables them to do so. In the United States hardly anybody talks of the beauty of virtue, but they maintain that virtue is useful and prove it every day. The American moralists do not profess that men ought to sacrifice themselves for their fellow creatures because it is noble to make such sacrifices, but they boldly aver that such sacrifices are as necessary to him who imposes them upon himself as to him for whose sake they are made.

They have found out that, in their country and their age, man is brought home to himself by an irresistible force; and, losing all hope of stopping that force, they turn all their thoughts to the direction of it. They therefore do not deny that every man may follow his own interest, but they endeavor to prove that it is the interest of every man to be virtuous. I shall not here enter into the reasons they allege, which would divert me from my subject; suffice it to say that they have convinced their fellow countrymen.

Montaigne said long ago: "Were I not to follow the straight road for its straightness, I should follow it for having found by experience that in the end it is commonly the happiest and most useful track." The doctrine of interest rightly understood is not then new, but among the Americans of our time it finds universal acceptance; it has become popular there; you may trace it at the bottom of all their actions, you will remark it in all they say. It is as often asserted by the poor man as by the rich. In Europe the principle of interest is much grosser than it is in America, but it is also less common and especially it is less avowed; among us, men still constantly feign great abnegation which they no longer feel.

The Americans, on the other hand, are fond of explaining almost all the actions of their lives by the principle of self-interest rightly understood; they show with complacency how an enlightened regard for themselves constantly prompts them to assist one another and inclines them willingly to sacrifice a portion of their time and property to the welfare of the state. In this respect I think they frequently fail to do themselves justice, for in the United States as well as elsewhere, people are sometimes seen to give way to those disinterested and spontaneous impulses that are natural to man; but the Americans seldom admit that they yield to emotions of this kind; they are more anxious to do honor to their philosophy than to themselves.

I might here pause without attempting to pass a judgment on what I have described. The extreme difficulty of the subject would be my excuse, but I shall not avail myself of it; and I had rather that my readers, clearly perceiving my object, would refuse to follow me than that I should leave them in suspense.

The principle of self-interest rightly understood is not a lofty one, but it is clear and sure. It does not aim at mighty objects, but it attains without excessive exertion all those at which it aims. As it lies within the reach of all capacities, everyone can without difficulty learn and retain it. By its admirable conformity to human weaknesses it easily obtains great dominion; nor is that dominion precarious, since the principle checks one personal interest by another, and uses, to direct the passions, the very same instrument that excites them.

The principle of self-interest rightly understood produces no great acts of self-sacrifice, but it suggests daily small acts of self-denial. By itself it cannot suffice to make a man virtuous; but it disciplines a number of persons in habits of regularity, temperance, moderation, foresight, self-command; and if it does not lead men straight to virtue by the will, it gradually draws them in that direction by their habits. If the principle of interest rightly understood were to sway the whole moral world, extraordinary virtues would doubtless be more rare; but I think that gross depravity would then also be less common. The principle of interest rightly understood perhaps prevents men from rising far above the level of mankind, but a great number of other men, who were falling far below it, are caught and restrained by it. Observe some few individuals, they are lowered by it; survey mankind, they are raised.

I am not afraid to say that the principle of self-interest rightly understood appears to me the best suited of all philosophical theories to the wants of the men of our time, and that I regard it as their chief remaining security against themselves. Towards it, therefore, the minds of the moralists of our age should turn; even should they judge it to be incomplete, it must nevertheless be adopted as necessary.

I do not think, on the whole, that there is more selfishness among us than in America; the only difference is that there it is enlightened, here it is not. Each American knows when to sacrifice some of his private interests to save the rest; we want to save everything, and often we lose it all. Everybody I see about me seems bent on teaching his contemporaries, by precept and example, that what is useful is never wrong. Will nobody undertake to make them understand how what is right may be useful?

No power on earth can prevent the increasing equality of conditions from inclining the human mind to seek out what is useful or from leading every member of the community to be wrapped up in himself. It must therefore be expected that personal interest will become more than ever the principal if not the sole spring of men's actions; but it remains to be seen how each man will understand his personal interest. If the members of a community, as they become more equal, become more ignorant and coarse, it is difficult to foresee to what pitch of stupid excesses their selfishness may lead them; and no one can foretell into what disgrace and wretchedness they would plunge themselves lest they should have to sacrifice something of their own well-being to the prosperity of their fellow creatures.

I do not think that the system of self-interest as it is professed in America is in all its parts self-evident, but it contains a great number of truths so evident that men, if they are only educated, cannot fail to see them. Educate, then, at any rate, for the age of implicit self-sacrifice and instinctive virtues is already flitting far away from us, and the time is fast approaching when freedom, public peace, and social order itself will not be able to exist without education.

Strategic giving for public and private value

Peter Frumkin, 2006

Public needs and private values

All philanthropic activity involves a choice about how to join public needs with private commitments in a way that is both beneficial for others and satisfying for the giver. Without both dimensions working closely together, philanthropy can degenerate either into a bland and disconnected exercise in administering transfer payments or into a selfish and shallow indulgence of the leisure class. While it is tempting to view the value proposition in philanthropy – the choice of what goal or mission to pursue – as involving a zero-sum trade-off between public benefits and private satisfaction in which more of one implies less of the other, this would be grossly misleading. The most strategic forms of philanthropy are those that start with a tight and energizing link between the donor's passions and the community's needs that leads to high levels of both public impact and private satisfaction.

Unfortunately, too many donors conceive the public and private dimensions of philanthropy as constituting distinct and irreconcilable starting points that frame a fateful choice. From one extreme perspective, the call of philanthropy demands the conscious abrogation of the self and the pursuit of the most urgent community needs. From this vantage point, philanthropy produces tangible results that meet critical needs left unmet by the market and that government has failed to fulfill adequately. This conception of giving is understandable, given the range of human problems that present themselves to all donors. Faced with issues such as youth violence, drug abuse, failing public schools, and a lack of affordable housing, donors can be led to sublimate their own interests and values and focus instead on the world. Almost all donors begin their search for a cause without an awareness of the massive scope of problems that could legitimately benefit from their attention. With pressure coming from many directions, it is tempting for donors to think of their giving as an agnostic and selfless response mechanism that should be driven by public needs. This perspective is actually rendered far more nuanced by the nature of the concept of public needs.

There are two fundamental dimensions to the concept of public needs. The first relates to who is doing the defining. Here there is an important distinction between definitions of public needs that are arrived at through collective deliberation and those that are set in place by individuals. The struggle to define public needs can often take place in the sphere of politics, although many times in philanthropy the definition of a public need is simply whatever the donor or a foundation's trustees declare is a need. While there is no simple answer to how many people are needed to agree before a problem becomes a legitimate human need, one thing is clear. There is pressure from the many stakeholders in philanthropy to spread responsibility beyond the donor to include others. One challenge in this move is maintaining a semblance of coherence and specificity, because there is an inverse correlation between the number of people engaged in decision making and the ability of parties to reach narrow and precise agreement on terms. Individual donors may be able to set down clear statements about what they believe are public needs, but large groups, even entire communities, may find it considerably more difficult to agree on the precise nature of public needs and their relative priority.

The second dimension is more complex and relates to the character of the definition that is advanced, which can be positive or normative in nature. Some believe that needs are nothing other than facts subject to measurement and specification through research. The social sciences have long aspired to render objective, positivistic assessments of public needs through surveys and field research. Against this perspective, there will always be those who assert that a concept as contested as "public needs" must be defined in normative terms, owing to the subjective nature of the concept. Those engaged in political advocacy make compelling moral arguments about the significance of certain public needs and why they should not be overlooked. This process leads to the construction of normative arguments that are designed to guide decision making. Often donors are hesitant to proceed on anything less than solid positivistic definitions of needs for fear that they lack the facts necessary to sensibly discharge their responsibilities. Ironically, many donors also have serious doubts about the capacity of researchers to provide much guidance in terms of the objective conditions and needs of communities. Thus, donors can and do find themselves caught between the desire for grounding and the sense that such grounding is hard to ever carry out systematically. It is in this context that more overtly normative arguments about public needs often surface and win the day. Without good data, claims from stakeholders about the "right thing to do" take on greater weight and more persuasive power.

[. . .]

One good indication that no clear, compelling hierarchy of charitable causes can be defined, based on either of these two central dimensions to public needs, lies in the enduring reticence of the tax code about treating any particular type of nonprofit differently from all the rest. Soup kitchens receive the same tax treatments as avant-garde theaters. Community health clinics working in desperate urban settings have no advantage over suburban historical societies. All public-serving nonprofit organizations are treated the same because the alternative, a differentiated treatment of charities based on their social contribution, is simply unworkable.

If the nature of public needs defines one side of the conceptual playing field of philanthropy, the other side is marked by the character of the private values and commitments enacted through giving. Philanthropy allows donors to speak to the world about what they believe is valuable. Starting with the heartfelt beliefs of the donors, it is possible to construe philanthropy as an expressive activity that allows individuals to project their values into public space. Having earned or acquired money legitimately and not having to give any of it away, some wealthy individuals simply conclude that the primary factor driving their giving should be their own personal satisfaction. Seen from this perspective, giving is a way for donors to feel better about themselves. This may lead donors to support organizations that have been personally significant – a college that the donor attended or a hospital that prolonged the donor's life. When the private values of the donor are a starting point, charitable giving takes on an expressive character that is quite distinct from the espoused needs and desires of the broad public. Reciprocity and the sense of giving something back does not necessarily lead to the most pressing public needs being selected for funding. Rather, it often leads straight into the personal life experiences and values of the donor.

For every donor, there are some causes that pull on the heartstrings and then tug on the purse strings. The transition from appeal to action is often based on the strength of the donor's private values, commitments, and beliefs and how they relate or do not relate to the appeal being made. Rather than seek to sublimate the personal connection and passion of donors, it may be best to simply acknowledge it and seek to capture its capacity to mobilize giving. After all, on almost every major issue or topic, there are usually forces arrayed on both sides, each supported by their own group of dedicated donors. For philanthropy to work, donors need to be matched to the issues that speak to them so they can see their giving as a form of expression and action on behalf of causes or missions that matter.

[. . .]

Not everyone is willing to embrace the private nature of the philanthropic impulse so quickly. Rather than accept the passions and commitments of givers as a source of strength and vitality for the field, some attempt to construe the private values as a threat to a rational and effective philanthropy. The sometimes bizarre and extreme ideas of donors must be held to some kind of account so that publicly subsidized giving can meet its full potential. Interestingly, those who tend to have reservations about the role of private values in philanthropy tend to overlap fairly consistently with those who believe that philanthropy should be directed at the most pressing human needs or who want to see communities have a greater say in the allocation of philanthropic funds. Only when one is willing to take a more nuanced point of view on the nature of public needs does the potential value added of a donor-driven, personalistic philanthropy come into full focus. Not only is it impossible to take private values out of individual philanthropy, but to do so would surely weaken the performance of philanthropy and undermine its ability to mobilize large amounts of money.

The private values of donors interact with public needs, and philanthropy is enriched when the two find some overlap. It is an elusive and complex intersection in which private values need to find resonance with community desires. Dueling perceptions of public needs can collide and make the location of this intersection elusive. What is striking about philanthropy is that in the cases where this confluence of forces has occurred, impressive results have been achieved for all parties. Nevertheless, in the many cases where this intersection is not achieved, philanthropy can and does take alternative or mixed forms that are greater or lesser approximations of strategic giving.

Four forms of value creation

Although the concepts of public needs and private values are highly contested and problematic, it is still possible to sketch out a framework that allows one to understand the main forms of philanthropic value creation. To do so, it is necessary to introduce a somewhat different, though related, distinction. Giving can be understood to possess two very different dimensions, one of them instrumental and the other expressive. First, philanthropy is an important instrument for the accomplishment of public purposes, no matter how or by whom they are defined. Donors play an important role in supporting nonprofit organizations in a broad array of fields. Gifts and grants can be a central support mechanism that allows nonprofits to offer the services on which their clients depend. When they succeed in achieving public purposes, defined in any of the many possible ways, donors deliver something of instrumental value. As such, giving has an instrumental dimension that is measured in terms of the concrete outcomes it produces. In a search for validation and learning, the programmatic outcomes are increasingly being measured and evaluated using metrics borrowed from business. That philanthropy is valuable because it is a useful tool for the accomplishment of public purposes is the core of what I call the instrumental dimension of giving.

Second, giving can be seen as valuable because it allows donors to express their values and commitment through gifts to others. The very attempt to act publicly can be a satisfying end unto itself. The value that is created may be entirely psychic, arising simply from expressing commitment, caring, and belief. The expressive quality of giving suggests that a narrow focus on programmatic outcomes distracts from what may be the deeper meaning of philanthropic action, which springs from the self-actualization experienced by those who give or volunteer. This is what I call the expressive dimension of giving.

The expressive and instrumental dimensions of giving can complement one another or they can create tensions. Under the right circumstances, the values that drive donors can be harnessed to produce better and more effective grantmaking. In some ways, this connection seems obvious. Committed donors are more likely to work hard to create value through their giving than donors who feel detached and removed from their philanthropy. When the values, commitments, and beliefs of the donor find expression in philanthropy, they can become at odds with the instrumental purposes that the donor is seeking to achieve.

As donors deliberate over how to balance these two critical dimensions, four main options emerge. First, giving can be purged of private values and be aimed at very narrow and specific public needs; what will result, however, is a form of giving that resembles old-fashioned charity, in which money simply passes quietly and uncreatively from one person to another through an intermediary organization. Second, giving can be infused with donor values and passions and be directed at a purpose that neither the community nor the donor can reasonably argue is urgent or important. This will generate a form of expressive giving that privileges the donor's needs, but that does not meet the test of effectiveness. Third, giving can be directed at the public needs of affected communities in ways that are potentially far reaching, with the donor's values and input screened out of the equation. In such cases, a kind of instrumental giving will emerge directed at delivering results, even if innovation and passion are missing. Finally, there is a kind of giving in which public needs are successfully married to deeply held beliefs and commitments of donors. It is this strange and elusive combination that I seek to illuminate here.

To better understand the interaction of these two dimensions, one can construct a map that tracks along two axes the critical difference between the instrumental and expressive dimensions of giving. The four forms of value creation presented here (see Figure 1.1) are ideal types, in that they represent pure concepts. In practice, the boundaries around these types are almost always loose and shifting. More often than not, giving combines two or more of these types, either because the donor's approach to giving has multiple dimensions within a single chosen field of activity or – when the donor's substantive interests are diffuse – the donor's approach is different across the multiple fields of activity in which giving takes place. In the first instance, where giving is focused, for example, on education, donors may experiment with highly

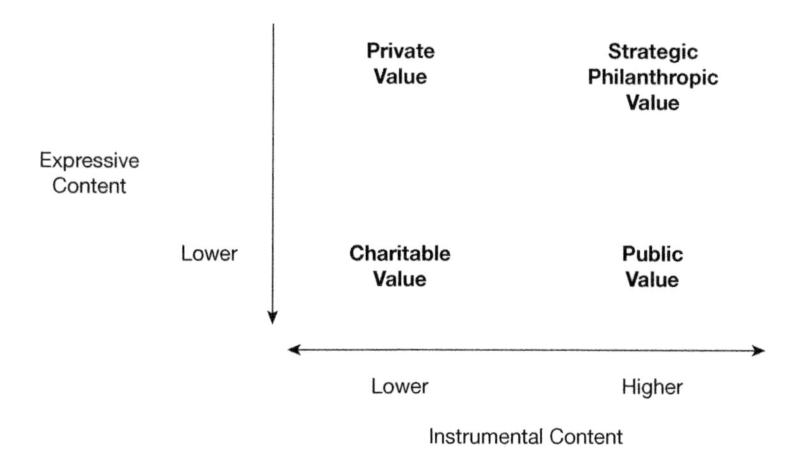

Figure 1.1 Four forms of value creation

expressive forms of giving when supporting a class gift to the undergraduate institution they attended, while at the same time wanting to make a more instrumental gift that will create institutional change at a leading teaching hospital with which the donor has no affiliation. In the second instance, where philanthropic interests are broad, giving may combine, for example, charitable support for disaster relief in the developing world with expressive giving for an advocacy organization working on an issue close to the donor's heart. Even with these caveats, it is still possible to begin to sketch the landscape of value creation in philanthropy by distinguishing the kinds of private commitment and public purpose that is pursued.

Section 2

PHILANTHROPY ACROSS TIME AND PLACE

Editors' introduction

Overview

Philanthropic activity is evident in every historical era and in every society that has been studied across the globe. It is also promoted by every major religion and is a core component of secular humanitarianism. Its omnipresence often goes unremarked, reflecting what we might call (adapting Hannah Arendt's famous phrase), the "banality of benevolence."

This second section contains key readings providing diverse explanations of the presence and persistence of philanthropy across time and place. The 16 selected extracts give a flavour of the deep roots of both the practice of philanthropy and the enduring interest in understanding the structures, motivations and implications of this aspect of social life.

It is important to recognise that philanthropy is not just something that is "done" everywhere and at all times; it is also something that people have thought about extensively and debated heatedly, just as we continue to do today. Examining the existence and right role of philanthropy – and how that might differ according to the historical and cultural context, as well as the socio-demographic characteristics of givers and receivers – raises profound questions that touch on some of the most difficult issues we face as humans, including changing understandings of the nature of our responsibility to others, what it means to live a "good life" in different times and places, and how philanthropy fits into ideas about this good life.

The variety and reach of these questions – which have troubled donors and commentators for centuries – reminds us that philanthropy is, in a sense, both a noun and a verb: it is a thing as well as an activity, attitude and outlook. Philanthropy creates tangible outputs that leave a physical trace, and it also inspires actions that propel human behaviour in a wide variety of ways that are less easy to capture and record. Philanthropy as a noun is simpler to note and discuss for it shows up, to use Pushpa Sundar's arresting phrase, in the "institutional efflorescence" funded by private donors, such as buildings and monuments. But philanthropy as a verb is trickier to quantify. Frank Prochaska's conception of philanthropy as "the history of kindness" is a start, yet as many authors throughout this Reader note, there is also a 'dark side' of philanthropy to be taken into account.

Collectively, the readings in this section demonstrate that philanthropy is a social act involving social institutions, rather than simply a financial transaction, so it is always a product of its time and place. Yet the readings also demonstrate many common concerns that transcend historic eras and geographic boundaries.

While remaining cognisant of cross-cutting themes, the readings in this section are organised into four subsections.

Complex history

The history of philanthropy is complex and to some extent contested, just as the present-day concept is. It is also partial – there is far more written about the Western experience. Some histories tell a relatively simple tale of rise and decline (and rise again); others are inherently Whiggish (especially in Europe), tracking the progress of philanthropy only insofar as it relates to the growth of tax-funded provision; others chart trajectories within one nation or town, one particular religion, or within one cause area such as hospitals. The two readings included in this subsection demonstrate that understanding the history of philanthropy involves being willing to resist a search for simplistic roots and linear narratives of progress, and to look beyond the tangible contributions of past donors to fully understand their impact.

The complexity of the topic requires historians of philanthropy to think like geologists, according to Hugh Cunningham, who describes nine strata or layers of philanthropic giving accumulated over time that continue to influence the present. This non-linear approach emphasises the need for an "outward-looking" analysis that includes the ever-changing context for philanthropy. As well as influencing the physical world, such as the building of cities, Kevin Robbins notes that philanthropists have influenced the articulation of civic values over time, and been instrumental in shaping the moral imagination of their contemporaries.

Contested history

Different nations and eras lay claim to "owning" or "perfecting" philanthropy, notably Victorian England and the contemporary US, but intercultural transfers mean other older nations can also make the case that they influenced these more well-known centres of philanthropic practice. The readings in this section illustrate the grounds for making such claims, and demonstrate different perspectives on both founding myths and examples of excellence.

We begin with Prochaska's argument that "No country on earth can lay claim to a greater philanthropic tradition than Great Britain," followed by Olivier Zunz's historical review of how and why philanthropy has been central in the American century, as a result of the convergence of big money philanthropy and the emergence of mass giving. Thomas Adam points to the European roots of elite philanthropy, arguing that transatlantic visitors on the "Grand Tour" returned to North America with new notions about the role of philanthropy in upper-class life and its contribution to shaping social distinctions. The explosion of new institutions, such as art galleries, as a result of this intercultural transfer leads Adam to describe philanthropy as "the most bourgeois behavior." By contrast, Joanna Handlin Smith finds that in another place and another era – eleventh-century China – philanthropy was peripheral to elite identity. Her description of the emergence of benevolent societies in the late sixteenth century, and accounts of the good deeds of the illiterate in the late Ming era, illustrate that philanthropy in China has not traditionally been monopolised by any one class.

Tying several of these threads together, we end this subsection on contested histories with Karen Wright, whose comparison of philanthropy in the UK and the US emphasises the complexity of differences between the political structures, social attitudes and roles of charitable giving on either side of the Atlantic. Wright also notes that other countries and cultures may suffer similar simplistic assessments in an era when the export of American civic concepts and strategies has become increasingly popular.

Continuity and change across eras

Philanthropy has taken distinctive forms in different eras as a result of being embedded in the dominant ideas and beliefs of the time, and being influenced by contemporary forms of social organisation. This section explores different views on how philanthropy was perceived and practised across the globe in Antiquity, the Middle Ages, the Victorian period and the contemporary era.

The selections highlight much continuity. For example, the role of religion, reputational benefits and the pervasive philanthropy of the poor are seen to be commonplace whether the focus is on ancient times, nineteenth-century Britain or contemporary Latin America. But we can also identify differences over time in relation to how philanthropy is practised and viewed, as well as the enthusiasm with which it is undertaken.

G. Scott Davis' recognition of the plurality of forms and understandings that underlie the concept of philanthropy over time leads him to argue for the discontinuity of the classical with the late antique and medieval meanings of philanthropy. He also warns against trying to understand philanthropy and related concepts using modern interpretations of these activities, their motives and their goals.

That the goals of philanthropic activity are inconsistent across time and place is demonstrated by the next two extracts. Gertrude Himmelfarb paints a picture of Victorian philanthropists as "incorrigible moralists" pursuing the moral, spiritual, cultural and intellectual elevation of the poor, whereas Hillel Schmid and Avishag Rudich-Cohn find contemporary elite philanthropists in Israel concerned with pursuing both a radical liberal ideology and a desire to play an important role in the national effort to create a new society. Yet consistency is also evident, most obviously here in the role of religious faiths – respectively, Christianity and Judaism.

Sundar's description of the role philanthropy played in founding modern India draws attention to the shift from building physical institutions to using private resources to attempt to change mindsets, such as views about *sati* and the caste system. This reading also casts interesting light on the widely assumed notion that twentieth-century Americans were the first to found charitable foundations with generalist goals "for the good of all mankind." Sundar describes an Indian philanthropist, N. M. Wadia, who set up his eponymous foundation in 1909 for the benefit of all, irrespective of creed or community – predating both Rockefeller and Carnegie. These sorts of claims and counterclaims over philanthropic innovation deserve further scholarship.

Finally in this subsection, Cynthia A. Sanborn reports that Latin American philanthropy has recently increased in scope, scale and ambition, with patterns of giving similar to those in developed countries, including substantial support for elite activities despite the persistence of extreme poverty. However, local traditions of solidarity among the marginalised, including immigrant groups, the role of the Catholic Church and the impact of liberation theology all shape the specific response of philanthropy over time in this region.

The role of religion, race, gender and geography

The final subsection explores the impact of four key variables: religion, race, gender and geography. These socio-demographic factors are widely discussed in the literature, but the ways in which they have shaped philanthropy remain open to debate. The extracts raise issues such as the close connection between all major religions and philanthropy, the impact of race relations and normative views on gender, and the problems of philanthropic particularism.

All religions exhort followers to share their assets, but they differ in the amounts suggested and the timing of gifts across the annual calendar, as well as their edicts and advice on the manner in which gifts should be made. Warren F. Ilchman, Stanley N. Katz and Edward L. Queen II's study was one of the first comparative studies of the social and historical conditioning of philanthropy, making the important point that "philanthropic acts become the preeminent means by which people attempt to realize their understanding of cultural values, to practice what their culture preaches."

Sudhir Alladi Venkatesh notes that philanthropy can be "a conflictual or troubled field" with practices of helping and giving money being shaped by, and in turn shaping, our understandings of race and ethnicity. Similarly, Kathleen D. McCarthy explores questions of explicit and implicit power in relation to gender, noting the extent to which government, the market and religion have shaped the role of female philanthropy and philanthropists in different national settings.

The final selection in this section argues that geography matters because much philanthropy is locally embedded. The geographical-legal articulation of donor intent – in the case of this study, with regards to setting up almshouses – creates "sentimental spaces" that restrict the distribution of charitable benefit and, as John R. Bryson, Mark McGuinness and Robert J. Ford note: "The geography of need and the geography of charity established to meet that particular need do not necessarily coincide. They may even run counter to each other."

This – and other – critiques of philanthropists are taken up further in Section 3, and implications for the relationship between donors and beneficiaries are expanded upon in Section 4.

Discussion questions

- Why might philanthropy be overlooked, despite existing in every historic era and in every geographic region? Why is it important for us to look at philanthropy's variation across time and place? How might this help us improve our own philanthropy?
- List some examples of philanthropy as a thing you can see and touch (e.g. a grantmaking foundation, an international "NGO"), and philanthropy as an intangible action or attitude (e.g., a kind gesture, charitable impulses). How are these two connected, and what happens if they are disconnected? Does this dual existence of philanthropy as a noun and a verb make it more complicated to grasp?
- Choose any country or region, and name some factors (such as social, political and economic developments) that have shaped the nature of philanthropic responses in that part of the world. How might this history of philanthropy in that region be "contested" by others? How should we handle claims that certain societies have been especially influential in shaping philanthropy elsewhere?
- Do you agree that philanthropy is always a product of its time? Why or why not? Think of some examples that show how the meaning and focus of philanthropy has changed over the centuries, and some examples of how it has stayed the same.
- How do normative views about gender and race shape practices associated with giving money, and how has philanthropy, in turn, shaped views about gender and race?

- Is the development of philanthropy over time more accurately characterised by the concept of "continuity" or "change?" Focusing on the role that religion plays in philanthropic ideas and practices, how is this continuity or change manifested?

2.1 Complex history

A history of Western philanthropy

Hugh Cunningham, 2016

Historians of philanthropy need to think like geologists. Stop the clock at any time, say 1850 in Europe, and you will find strata or layers of philanthropic giving accumulated on top of each other. The philanthropy of the past leaves its material record, its buildings, its legal documents, its charitable gifts, its assumptions and practices, in layer after layer. The present adds a topsoil of the latest projects, but the lower layers continue to exercise their influence, sometimes in the form of outcrops from earlier ages of giving.

Excavators of the first stratum seize on Aristotle (384–322 BCE) who wrote that to give money 'to the right person, in the right amount, at the right time, with the right aim in view, and in the right way – that is not something anyone can do, nor is it easy'. Twenty-first-century philanthropists love to quote this: philanthropy, it seems to say, is not easy, but to engage in it has the sanction of ancient wisdom. In fact Aristotle was exploring how to achieve a mean between wastefulness and stinginess; for him the truly virtuous person, in the words of Roger Crisp, 'is unlikely to stir himself to help the vulnerable'.

The Greek word *philanthrôpía* originally referred to the relationship of the gods to humans; it came to be applied to rulers who were generous to their subjects, and then to the wealthy more generally. It incorporated the notion of a return *philanthropon* from the recipients in the form of honours heaped on the donor – it was a form of gift exchange, a quid-pro-quo. Often it referred to a relationship between wealthy individuals, indicative of a cast of mind as much as the conferring of a gift. [. . .] Philanthropy was given a new twist by early Christians, but as a term it soon disappeared from view before re-emerging in the late eighteenth century.

The second stratum is made up of the teachings of the Bible and of the early Christian Fathers, of their interpretation from the twelfth century onwards, and of the medieval world of giving. At their root was a sense of justice, that the poor should be relieved by the rich. The Christian Fathers argued that all property belonged to all men.

[. . .]

If there was an obligation to give, it was also increasingly argued that it should be done with discrimination. The *Summa elegantius* (c.1169) asserted that 'In almsgiving there should be distinction between people. You had better give to your own than to strangers, to the sick rather than to the healthy, to ashamed rather than aggressive beggars, to the have-not rather than to him that has, and amongst the needy, first to the just and then to the unjust. That is ordered charity'. The distinction between the deserving and the undeserving poor, with a long and unfinished history ahead of it, was in place.

[. . .]

The experience of Italian cities helps to capture the scale and reach of late medieval charity. It was 'chiefly intended for the respectable, the innocent, and the holy'. Hospital building had taken off in the twelfth and thirteenth centuries – by 1383 there were twenty-one in Genoa alone, some housing and caring for the elderly, others foundling hospitals for abandoned babies. Confraternities, perhaps best seen as mutual aid self-help organisations, began to proliferate in the fourteenth and fifteenth centuries. By 1521 Venice had at least 120 small confraternities and five large ones. In the middle years of the fifteenth century cities began to build great hospitals, partly to bring some coherence and order to a charitable world where there were too many institutions with overlapping missions. They also began to develop the micro-credit schemes known as Monti di Pietà, making small loans to the worthy poor.

The third stratum originated in the later Middle Ages and was dominant until the late nineteenth century. The socio-economic fact underlying it was the existence of poverty among a substantial proportion of the population. Finding that about one-third of the population of mid-eighteenth-century Florence applied for public poor relief, a percentage similar to that in England, Peter Laslett concluded that 'Everything points to the existence within European traditional societies of a sizeable block of the population looking to the collectivity to get by'. In famines or epidemics, one-third of the population might rise to half. Some of this poverty was of a kind known to the Middle Ages, the poverty of the elderly, of widows, of the sick, of children. But on top of this there was poverty among men of working age. In face of the endemic problem of poverty, the belief that the poor were closer to Christ than the rich was less frequently voiced. On the contrary it was their idleness, their fecklessness, their immorality which impressed itself. Extensive poor relief strategies were adopted, and charity became inextricably bound up with them.

In the administration of poor relief the distinction, so fundamental to modern thinking, between private donations and state funding made little sense. [. . .] The innovation in England at the beginning of the seventeenth century of taxing people to pay for poor relief was sometimes described as charity; the Poor Law and the Charitable Uses Act both, and not coincidentally, date from 1601. In Italy the words for poor relief and charity were used interchangeably. The Société Philanthropique de Bruxelles (1828) was founded by private initiative, subsidised by local government and had the mayor of Brussels as its president. No one could say where the private ended and the public began.

[. . .]

Beginning in the late fifteenth century, and of fundamental importance, there was a decisive shift from charitable action initiated and controlled by the Church to one where laymen were the dominant force. This did not mean that Christianity ceased to be a vital force in the world of charity, rather that charity shifted its focus from giving to religious causes to attending to 'the secular needs of humanity', and that laymen were conspicuous in its funding and organisation. As Cissie Fairchilds has expressed it, 'the merchants of almost every major town in Western Europe began in the late fifteenth and early sixteenth centuries to establish new charities, which they, and not the Church, would control'. [. . .] The central text of this new approach was *De Subventione Pauperum* written by the Spanish humanist, Juan Luis Vives, in 1526, addressed to the Consuls and Senate of Bruges, and soon enjoying Europe-wide renown. Vives noted how 'The young children of the poor are villainously brought up, they [mothers] and their sons lying outside the churches or wandering round begging'. The solution to the problem was to place these children in institutions. Sometimes existing hospitals for poor or abandoned children were taken over and measures to improve discipline enacted, usually with the provision of education for the brighter ones. In due course the boys might be apprenticed, and dowries paid for the girls. This was Christian humanism in action, instilling discipline, offering the possibility of advancement, lay-controlled, but suffused with a religious ethos, whether Protestant or Catholic.

[. . .]

Early modern charity was proud to be in the public eye. It was urban and promoted as an adornment of any town or city. It was an inducement to the poor to migrate from the countryside – only England, with its parish-based poor law from the beginning of the seventeenth century, offered much help to the rural poor. Once the poor, and particularly their children, became inmates of institutions, they became enmeshed in a philanthropic world which was dependent for funds and reputation on public display.

[. . .]

Over the course of the roughly 350 years (1520–1870) during which charity and poor relief were virtually coterminous, there emerged three distinctive new strata with a long life ahead of them. The first (our fourth stratum) originated in England in the late seventeenth and eighteenth centuries. Historians in the early twentieth century described what happened as 'associated philanthropy'. Instead of there being a multiplicity of individual one-off acts of giving, people came together to promote a cause they believed in; they formed societies; they funded themselves through annual subscriptions from members, the latter having the right to elect the governors of the charity; they published annual reports. These initiatives in organisational form bore a similarity to the contemporaneous development of financial institutions in the City of London, especially joint-stock companies. The causes they were drawn to in the late seventeenth century were the establishment of charity schools, the provision of employment in part through the building of workhouses, and the formation of Societies for the Reformation of Manners. If from one angle they look like an outpouring of organised Christian zeal, from another they seem primarily concerned with social control. The same could be said for a key development of the eighteenth century, the establishment of hospitals. A concern for health had to fight for prominence against a range of other purposes that it was thought a hospital could serve, these neatly encapsulated in the title of a sermon delivered in 1746: 'Hospitals and Infirmaries Considered as Schools of Christian Education for the Adult Poor: and as a Means Conducive Towards a National Reformation in the Common Peoples'.

[. . .]

The new hospitals described themselves as 'voluntary'. They were carving out a role for themselves which was independent of both state and church. They were run by unpaid volunteers; even doctors who worked in them did so without receiving any fee, though the prestige and networking that accrued to them was often more than adequate compensation. More important, the hospitals received no money directly from the state, though some from Poor Law Guardians who sent patients to them. They were, it can be argued, laying the foundations of 'civil society'.

Civil society was also evident in Hamburg where the establishment in 1788 of the General Poor Relief was the outcome of over twenty years of reforming effort. It reinvigorated the campaign against begging, it looked for ways to get paupers back into work, but above all it was marked by a recognition that, as Johann Georg Büsch put it, 'the common man earns too little to live on'. A growing city like Hamburg, its population swollen by migrants whose livelihoods were dependent on the ups and downs of global trade, required 'a restructuring of charity', 'a new type of philanthropy', one that was responsive to the need to get workers who fell ill back into work. Poor relief began to extend beyond paupers. The emphasis was on providing medical relief in the home with domiciliary visits to the poor by doctors and other volunteers, themselves inspired by humanitarianism and a service ethic. The ideas and practices generated in Hamburg spread to other German towns, and although the escalating expense led to much debate on the merits of the system, domiciliary visiting of the poor remained a crucial element of philanthropic action through the nineteenth century.

[. . .]

The fifth stratum becomes identifiable towards the end of the eighteenth century: it ceases to be anachronistic to write about 'philanthropy'. Francis Bacon in the early seventeenth century had equated what "the Grecians call *philanthrôpía* with goodness [. . .] affecting of the weal of men," but the word only became widely used with the Enlightenment. Like the revolution to come, it was French, and it reflected a powerful strand of anti-clericalism in French society, a strong critique of existing charities and an optimistic belief that in a well-ordered society human beings would throw off the chains, both physical and psychical, that restricted them. The background to it was a collapse in donations through wills to existing charities, and increasing socio-economic pressures. The foundation of the Société Philanthropique de Paris in 1780, though it had little impact in its first five years, was a landmark. In a 1787 manifesto it declared that philanthropic activity was the main duty of a citizen. Hitherto charitable giving had been incited by the belief that it was a duty incumbent on Christians. Now it became, as it remains, the mark of true citizenship. The Société Philanthropique was not a total break with the past, far from it. It became in the nineteenth century the repository of conservative attitudes. Nevertheless this late eighteenth-century moment effectively marks the beginning of 'philanthropy' as something which might be distinguished from 'charity'.

Philanthropy crossed the Channel from France to England in the 1780s. The first person in England to be described as a philanthropist was John Howard who toured and reported on prisons and similar institutions in Britain and Europe, urging reform. In 1786 he became 'John Howard, the philanthropist', seen as a lover of humankind, more famous for the 42,033 miles that he calculated he had travelled than for any money he might have given. It was in the 1780s, too, that Robert Young, long-resident in France, returned to his native England, and was there instrumental in founding the Philanthropic Society to reform young criminals or those in danger of becoming so. For many years it looked as if philanthropy would be located on the left of the political spectrum. Right-wing newspapers jeered at 'Tom Paine the Philanthropist'. 'Every philanthropist should be a reformer', wrote the Unitarian George Dyer, echoed by the historian G. J. Barker-Benfield for whom 'from the latter eighteenth century, reform and philanthropy were nearly interchangeable'.

[. . .]

But this radicalism of philanthropy died away. Philanthropy began to align itself with the dominant social and economic ideology of the time, political economy. Political economists preached market solutions to social problems. They were above all concerned that wages should be determined by the market. Earning a living through wages was fundamental both to a successful economy and to personal morality. Charity in its old forms, political economists argued, undermined that [. . .] Nothing did more harm, it was said in 1815, than 'the misplaced benevolence of the charitable and humane'.

This was an attack on charity and on that much-heralded eighteenth-century virtue, 'benevolence'. In the 1820s claims were made for 'philanthropy' as the means by which political economy could set bounds to unlimited charity. Teaching the poor 'the knowledge of the laws which regulate wages', it was said, '[. . .] depends in a great measure upon the exertions of enlightened philanthropists'.

[. . .]

Philanthropy and political economy, it seemed, were to be allies against 'the lazy shape of charity'. By the 1860s, however, there were mutterings about 'a misguided and sanguine philanthropy', about 'Misdirected Philanthropy'. Philanthropy seemed to be no better than the charity or benevolence from which it was trying to emancipate itself.

If nagging doubts had entered some parts of the philanthropic world by mid-century, other parts of it proclaimed confidence in what they were doing. Inheriting from the Enlightenment a belief in the transformative power of well-run institutions, they focused their attention on the young, and in particular on young males who seemed likely to go astray. Criminality and its prevention lay at the heart of much early philanthropy [. . .] and was international in nature. [. . .] The Philadelphia Society for Alleviating the Miseries of Public Prisons, formed in 1786, was closely linked through Benjamin Rush with people with similar concerns in England, notably the Quaker doctor, J. C. Lettsom, and John Howard. By personal correspondence which then found its way into friendly newspapers, reformers on one side of the Atlantic kept themselves informed of initiatives on the other. The London Society for the Improvement of Prison Discipline, formed in 1816, was open about its indebtedness to Philadelphia. The men involved in these exchanges had wide interests, extending, for example, to opposition to slavery, and they were filled with enthusiasm for what Rush called 'the extension of the empire of humanity'.

[. . .]

This tradition of sharing experience and good practice was given a Continental European dimension with the foundation of the Rauhes Haus near Hamburg by Johann Hinrich Wichern in 1833. The Rauhes Haus in its turn inspired the foundation in France in 1840 of the agrarian colony of Mettray, near Tours. Dutch, English and Belgian philanthropists flocked to Mettray and copied it. The Englishman, Matthew Davenport Hill, was so impressed that he wrote that 'No Mahommedan [. . .] believes more devoutly in the efficacy of a pilgrimage to Mecca, than I do in one to Mettray'. This 'philanthropic tourism', as Jeroen Dekker has called it, was a notable feature of philanthropy in the first half of the nineteenth century. Across Europe, though in different forms in different countries, there was 'a firm conviction that *their* nation could be transformed by means of philanthropy'.

The degree of faith in the reforming potential of institutions is best exemplified in the building of asylums in the United States after 1830. By 1850 in New York State there were twenty-seven public and private institutions caring for children. In the country as a whole the seventy-seven private orphanages of 1851 had increased to 613 by 1880, with a further 474 founded over the ensuing twenty years. By then there was a counter-blast to placing children in particular in what came to be described as 'barracks'. Americans coined the word 'institutionalised' to describe a child who was 'mechanical and helpless from the effect of asylum life'. What followed in response were in part attempts to improve domestic institutions, to organise them on a smaller scale, but also in part a new major experiment in social engineering, the emigration of children from the environment of the city to the countryside, that countryside often on the other side of the world. American East coast children were taken to the Mid-West, British children shipped to Canada and later to Australia.

This belief that children thrived only in the countryside reflected another aspect of philanthropic change in the nineteenth century. Until then it had been reasonably assumed that the prime purpose and function of philanthropy was to shift resources from the rich to the poor. By the middle of the nineteenth century the target of philanthropy shifted from the poor to the town or city. Of course the poor constituted a large part of the urban problem, but they were not the whole of it. Philanthropists began to think that they could best improve their societies by providing their cities with a civic infrastructure of public parks, art galleries, museums, concert halls and libraries. It was one of the attractions of this form of philanthropy that it escaped the censure of political economists, another that the benefactor's name often became attached to the donation. It was linked, too, to another novelty of nineteenth-century philanthropy, an early example of what we now call 'social enterprise', the attempt to relieve housing problems by 5 per cent philanthropy – an investment in building new apartment blocks for the respectable working class that would have the distinct attraction of bringing the donor a 5 per cent return. This belief in the civilizing impact of cultural institutions, in his case libraries, reached its height in the work of the Scot who emigrated and made a fortune in the United States, Andrew Carnegie.

In 1869 the English feminist, Josephine Butler, distinguished between feminine and masculine forms of philanthropy, the latter marked by 'large and comprehensive measures, organizations and systems planned by men and sanctioned by Parliament'. If these masculine forms dominated publicity as they do much history, it was nevertheless the case that the distinctive feminine forms of philanthropy had profound social and political consequences. It was not simply that women vastly outnumbered men in charitable activity, important though that was – in 1893 it was estimated that half a million women in England worked 'continuously and semi-professionally' in philanthropy. Perhaps more significant in the long term, middle-class women found in philanthropy a space where they had a degree of autonomy and an ability to influence outcomes, creating what Kathleen McCarthy has described as 'parallel power structures' to those of men. In the United States the outcome was that welfare measures focused on the needs of women and children rather than, as in Europe, of men.

If philanthropy at its outset was secular in outlook, this was not to last. Christians were soon attracted to the ambition and optimism that inspired philanthropy, and brought their own distinctive approach to the aim of regenerating society. And whereas secular philanthropists focused their attention, for the most part, on home soil, evangelical Christians had the world in their sights – and this forms the sixth stratum. There were earlier forerunners, not least in Latin America, but it was from the late eighteenth century onwards that what Alison Twells has termed 'global missionary philanthropy' came close to being a reality. The long-standing sense that relief to the poor should be prioritised on those born and bred in the locality gave way, not without controversy, to a belief that there was both an opportunity and a duty to bring the benefits of Christianity and civilisation to the 'heathen' overseas. Which should come first, Christianity or civilisation, was much debated, but that the two were intimately connected was not in doubt. Missions gained a legitimacy previously lacking by adopting some of the optimistic language of the Enlightenment and of philanthropy: the Bible, according to a Dutch pamphlet of 1801, contained 'the true grounds and rules of civilisation' and knowledge of it had to be spread by Protestant Europeans, 'the principal members of the great household of humanity'. In Britain, simultaneously forging an empire, the 1790s was an important decade: the Baptist Missionary Society sent a mission to India in 1792, the London Missionary Society set itself up in Tahiti, Tongatapu and Marquesas in 1796 and by the end of the decade the Methodists and the Church Missionary Society were in West Africa. The British initiative was soon taken up by Protestants in other countries, Americans, Germans, Danes, Swedes and Norwegians. The Roman Catholic Church, battered by the assaults on it in the French Revolution, was slower in the field, but by the 1830s was making its mark. It is arguable that Christian missions form no part of philanthropy, but the counter-argument, that out of funds that came primarily from the West, they were expanding education and health as well as proselytising, is a powerful one. Missions were 'diverting much of [Britain's] charity to religious causes overseas'. In the twentieth century, particularly after the Second World War, secular versions of global philanthropy set themselves up alongside the missionary ones.

A seventh stratum in the history of philanthropy surfaced in the later nineteenth century, eventually disconnecting the intimacy of the link between philanthropy and poor relief. The state, it began to be argued with increasing force, was better placed than philanthropy to resolve the social and cultural problems that beset so many lives. If philanthropy in the nineteenth century had to pitch itself in relation to political economy, by the twentieth century it was doing so also in relation to the state. In the nineteenth century the mixed economy of welfare had allowed a growth of both state and philanthropic initiatives. Neither was without criticism, what the British called 'grand-motherly legislation' as much as philanthropy. What was new by the end of the century was that the state was poised to intrude into areas that had hitherto been the preserve of philanthropy. Philanthropy, it was argued, was patchy in its coverage, condescending in its attitudes and with insufficient resources for the scale of the problems thrown up by urban and industrial society. Many rejected it on democratic and socialist grounds. If the political economists who had so scared philanthropists can be seen as on the right of the political spectrum, those who championed the role of the state were on the left. A pincer movement was strangling philanthropy, or at least many forms of it.

[. . .]

The outcome was that philanthropy as the solution to poverty was seen as playing a role secondary to and separate from the state. The public/private divide which is impossible to disentangle for most of philanthropy's centuries now came to be thought of central importance. Philanthropy might pioneer new approaches for the state later to adopt, it might try to fill the gaps which the state did not cover, it might, and increasingly did, run services on behalf of and financed by the state, but it was not and no longer aspired to be the lead actor. Some people began to ask whether it had any future role. Others, like Elizabeth Macadam in Britain (1934) talked up a 'new philanthropy' consisting of a partnership between statutory and voluntary services. The history of philanthropy was written as a prelude to the history of the welfare state, a perhaps well-meaning but insufficient attempt to cope with social problems that were beyond its capacity.

This was largely a European discussion and diagnosis. Across the Atlantic, fuelled by vast fortunes, a new kind of philanthropy was born, an eighth stratum. It was the age of foundations, established, in the words of one of them, 'for the improvement of mankind'. The Carnegie, John D. Rockefeller Sr., the John D. Rockefeller Jr., the Edward Harkness, the Russell Sage were all founded in the early twentieth century, all aiming, as Frederick Gates, Rockefeller Sr.'s advisor put it, on giving wholesale, not retail. Emancipated by their wholesale approach from having to grapple with individual poverty, or indeed with poverty at all, they were free to aim at the eradication of disease or the improvement of agricultural yields. There were 27 foundations in the United States by 1915, over 200 by 1930. Linking up with progressive reformers, they believed that the solution to deep-rooted problems lay in science and research, not in giving directly to the poor. The beneficiaries of their largesse were likely to be universities and research institutes, especially in the social sciences.

The ninth and final stratum in the history of philanthropy emerged with the criticism of welfare states that started in the 1970s and grew with exponential speed from the 1980s onwards. It coincided with a marked increase in inequality and in the relative wealth of the very rich. High taxation levels disappeared as entrepreneurs argued that they were a disincentive to investment, risk-taking and hard work. The resulting superfluity of ready money in the pockets of high net worth individuals gave a new confidence to philanthropists that they had a role to play and the money with which to play it. Another 'new philanthropy' was born. Some of its propagandists, lauding 'philanthrocapitalism', saw it as capable of solving the world's most deep-rooted problems, a happy marriage of capitalism's efficiency and entrepreneurship applied to disease and poverty, to higher education and the arts.

The history of philanthropy has too often been written in an either/or way. Either as something to celebrate and take inspiration from, or as a cautionary tale of man's (and it is almost entirely a male story) over-optimistic hopes of what could be achieved, not unmixed with a degree of vanity and self-promotion. A geological approach helps to free us from the either/or approach. It suggests that strata laid down centuries ago still work their influence, and it draws attention to the ways in which philanthropy is constantly claiming novelty while often only reverting to old models and ways of thinking. Its history is as much circular and repetitive as progressive and linear, not least because there is only a limited number of ways of trying to resolve poverty and the problems associated with it, and they are likely to recur, or run alongside each other.

The centrality of philanthropy over time

Kevin C. Robbins, 2006

Even a brief survey of philanthropy's history in the West shows the densely interconnected social, economic, legal, political, religious, artistic, and psychological dimensions of the subject. Over time, philanthropists and the institutions they created to perpetuate their generosity have played central roles in the building of cities and the articulation of civic values. Charitable actors and organizations have long been essential in the formation, communication, and teaching of religious principles. Donors did not merely build churches. Their generous, at times selfless behavior also catalyzed doctrinal disputes and generated sectarian movements that led to entirely new religions. Rituals of giving worked in part to differentiate castes and reinforce social hierarchies, especially in cities. Givers' ambitions and anxieties contributed to the development and revision of Western law codes. Ceremonies of just donation also moderated class tensions and became an important theater for symbolizing social norms and contracts. Using charity as conspicuous compassion, contenders for supreme governing power sought to demonstrate their moral aptitude for rulership.

More broadly, entire systems or regimes of philanthropy have clashed and modified continuously in Western history. Particular eras, such as the fifth century BCE, the first century CE, late antiquity, the fourteenth century CE, the Reformations, and the nineteenth century, stand out as periods of great human experimentation to redefine and better administer philanthropy. Vital contemporary trend lines that emerge from these experiments can be summarized as the rationalization, secularization, capitalization, nationalization, and professionalization of philanthropy and its agents. Within this dynamic, the scrutiny of donor behavior and potential recipients of aid increases dramatically. Endorsements of spontaneous, indiscriminate largesse drop off and the paradigm of socially responsible generosity moves toward stringent premeditation and selectivity in giving. Self-assertion increasingly supplants self-denial as a spring for benevolence with a greater attendant risk that philanthropists may be denounced as vain, self-serving egoists. The economic and political obsolescence of aristocrats, hastened by enterprising and rebellious merchants, renders noblesse oblige impractical as an ideology of modern giving. The status of donor, even patron, is democratized to admit a far wider array of competitors for social distinction via thoughtful giving and rigorous selection of worthy beneficiaries. Existing charities bureaucratize and new cadres of expert philanthropists form to counsel wise giving and steward the liquid capital amassed by "nonprofit" organizations. A more diverse body of donors is recruited in a culture of perpetual fundraising and more frenetic gift solicitation enabled by the evolving mass media of print and communication.

Attentiveness to the long history of individual and collective charitable action in the West enables better understanding of how the nonprofit sector and its supporters behave today. Such knowledge leads to many new topics of research. Heavily reliant on the benevolence of private givers and volunteers, many modern charitable nonprofits survive in large part because of the compulsions toward external or communal service experienced by private donors. Historical analysis suggests that donor motives are usually, if not always, plural in nature and do not derive solely from benefactors' most religious or ethical precepts. However, knowledge of charity's essential place but varying strength or intensity in different codes of Western religious practice over time can help in comprehending the deeper springs and directions of gift flows, most of which have gone and still go to religious organizations. Just as likely, tacit self-interest, fear of humiliation, rampant patriotism, and a poignant quest for psychic or worldly comfort may combine to produce the human actions and emotions of confraternity and compassion. What is the mix of emotions and motives that drive donor behavior now? How charitable institutions incorporate and modify the ideals that supporters bring to them also requires more careful attention and historical insight because these processes are potentially crucial to the maintenance – and the disturbance – of social order.

Prior civilizations, such as the Greeks, had no qualms whatsoever about identifying as "philanthropic" donor behaviors that were both overtly and tacitly coerced by the communities in which benefactors lived. The Greeks' own elaborate lexicon of *philanthropy*, in which the word took on multiple new meanings over time, should prompt us to wonder about the accuracy, scope, and limitations of the term as used in our modern tongues today. Where did all the ancient meanings of philanthropy go? And what do current definitions of the term tell us about the historic philanthropies we have accepted and those we have rejected in shaping the operations of the nonprofit sector?

As both beneficiary and target of accumulated legal privileges and judicial investigations over time, the current nonprofit sector exists in dynamic symbiosis with the forces of justice and state government. European and American archives document a long quest for a law of charity in the West. That jurisprudence, now luxuriant, is the net result of cross-fertilizations between positive and customary law occurring in the legal histories of several ancient and modern cultures, including Greece, Rome, Byzantium, medieval Christian Europe, and England. Examples from these civilizations show philanthropy's historic power to integrate human communities and to moderate their socioeconomic tensions. These phenomena suggest that charities have contributed their own informal laws or implied contracts, creating commonwealths by articulating the needs of minorities and smoothing relations between different social strata. Do modern philanthropies, often bureaucratically organized and expertly managed, continue to exert these pacific powers?

Has the more recent advent of scientific philanthropy, with its rational and professional pretensions, enhanced or diminished philanthropy's capacity for popular and consensual peacemaking? As epitomes of Renaissance philanthropy, civic confraternities are celebrated for offering alternatives to the existing social order. Can the same be said for these modern nonprofits that, under a regime of rationalized and nationalized philanthropy, only manage to survive through the sale of services and direct grants or contracts from governments? From a historic perspective, does the sector now subvert or sustain the status quo?

Finally, philanthropists have been instrumental in expanding (and occasionally contracting) the moral imagination of their contemporaries. Can the professionalized and bureaucratized agents of an expanding and increasingly competitive modern nonprofit sector, now far more vulnerable to harsh media scrutiny, achieve similar public trust and influence? Historic charitable organizations contended to set and reset the bounds of civilization, often by striving to exemplify civilized behavior in their own operations and assistance. Retracing the steps by which they did so primes us to recognize whether and how they may do so now.

2.2 Contested history

Great Britain has the greatest philanthropic tradition

Frank Prochaska, 1990

No country on earth can lay claim to a greater philanthropic tradition than Great Britain. Until the twentieth century philanthropy was widely believed to be the most wholesome and reliable remedy for the nation's ills, a view that is not without adherents today. For every affliction, individual or social, physical or spiritual, the charitable pharmacopoeia has a prescription or at least a palliative. Disease, old age and immorality are perennial problems. Others come and go with the elements or the trade cycle.

[. . .]

As befits a nation in which philanthropists are ubiquitous, enormous sums have been contributed, representing a massive redistribution of wealth. But while financial records exist for many charities, it is impossible to measure the overall sums contributed to philanthropy in a single year or to compare the percentage of national income redistributed at different periods. Some individuals have given away millions of pounds. Eighteenth- and nineteenth-century families at almost every level of the social scale commonly tithed their incomes to charitable causes. A study of middle-class households in the 1890s established that on average they spent a larger share of their income on charity than on any item in their budget except food. A survey of working-class and artisan families in the same decade showed that half of them subscribed weekly to charity and about a quarter of them also made donations to church or chapel. Even after the beginning of this century the sums contributed each year, not including church and chapel collections and unremembered alms, far exceeded government expenditure on poor relief. Philanthropic receipts for London alone, observed *The Times* in 1885, were greater than the budgets of many European states.

[. . .]

It is suggestive to think of the history of philanthropy broadly as the history of kindness. This conveys the importance of philanthropy at all social levels and reveals its implications for individuals, families and communities. The standard definition of philanthropy, or charity, is love of one's fellow man, an inclination or action which promotes the well-being of others. It thus includes benevolence within classes as well as between them; it encompasses a neighbourly visit or a widow's mite as well as the momentous decisions of great charities with international connections and legislative programmes. Cast widely to include informal, domestic expressions of kindness, the philanthropic net catches virtually everyone at one time or another.

[. . .]

The familial and immediate character of so much charitable work is never more striking than in the case of working-class philanthropy, the charity of the poor to the poor. The survey of working-class and artisan families already mentioned reveals that philanthropic subscriptions were not limited to the rich. To ignore this fact is to miss an important feature of working-class life and to encourage a narrow understanding of philanthropy which can reduce it simply to a reflection of class conflict. Historians, perhaps unconsciously, tend to perpetuate the view of many middle-class Victorians, who, according to the Chartist John Collins, had little idea 'that working men possessed any feeling or humanity'. As he was aware, the sympathies of the poor were often expressed privately, and the relative dearth of written evidence of their kindness to one another helped to make its extent underestimated. But those with a first-hand knowledge of working-class life were well aware that egalitarian beneficence came naturally to the poor. Fellow feeling, remarked W. R. Greg in reviewing *Mary Barton*,

> can only exist in its fullest extent among persons of the same condition, surrounded by the same circumstances, inured to the same privations – who know what the distress they are called upon to mitigate was their own yesterday, and may be their own again to-morrow.

[. . .]

The need in poor neighbourhoods was often such that it could not be satisfied by spontaneous, informal acts of kindness; thus the poor organised. Many of their societies came and went with the seasons, for example soup kitchens in which the labouring classes handled the operations entirely. Servants set up their own charities to look after servants in distress. Navvies, who had a marked sense of self-help, established sick clubs and visiting societies, complete with navvy officials. Formal subscriptions were taken up, sometimes by trade unions, friendly societies or benefit clubs, often simply by neighbours with common needs and worries. Such donations served a great variety of purposes, from support for infant schools to assisting transported prisoners. At their best, working-class charities were preventive. In Seven Dials in the early nineteenth century a group of workingmen formed the West Street Chapel Benevolent Society in which a committee of twelve met weekly to inspect the books and plan the campaign of relief and religious conversion. The well-run West Birmingham Relief Fund, established in 1892 by workingmen, gave advances to the disabled and paid rent for deserving cases. Working-class philanthropy and self-help commonly merged in medical causes. Well over half of the income of several general hospitals outside London came from humble subscribers.

[. . .]

The degree to which charity saturated people's lives, both givers and recipients, is difficult to imagine for anyone who has grown up in the shadow of the welfare state. A glimpse of the Rothschild Buildings in the East End, themselves a part of late Victorian 'philanthropy at 4 per cent', is as telling as the life at Carrow Works. Apart from the extensive network of casual benevolence performed daily by the residents, organised societies luxuriated. Run mostly by women, often with the assistance of the poor of the tenements, they included: Sick Room Helps' Society, Jews' Lying-in Charity, Israelite Widows' Society, Jewish Soup Kitchen, Whitechapel Children's Care Committee, Boot Club, Clothing Club, Children's Penny Dinner Society, Ragged Schools' Union, Bare Foot Mission, Children's Country Holiday Fund, Jewish Ladies' Clothing Association and a Savings Bank run by St Jude's School.

[. . .]

Charity within the privileged classes represented one of the fastest growing forms of philanthropic endeavour from the late eighteenth century onwards. Many institutions made annual grants to applicants, focussing on particular professions and localities. Typical of these were the Society for Relief of Widows and Orphans of Medical Men in London and its Vicinity, the London Clergy Orphan Fund and the Royal Navy Benevolent Society. Some charities, like the National Benevolent Institution, founded in 1812, provided pensions to a wider range of applicant, including indigent gentry, decayed merchants and former tutors and governesses. The growth of such institutions may have been connected with the reform of crown pensions, which began in the late eighteenth century and gradually reduced the number of well-connected pensioners on the government payroll. By the mid-nineteenth century scores of pension and benefit societies existed in London alone and catered to genteel applicants, from artists to old Etonians. Aged and incapacitated 'ladies' made a particularly powerful call on public sympathy; and by the First World War seventy convalescent and rest homes, many by the seaside, joined the long list of pension and benefit societies which specialised in their needs.

[. . .]

Philanthropy was prominent as a recreation in the past, especially for children in communities cut off from the centres of culture. Among evangelicals generally and Quakers in particular, restrictions on entertainment and dress reduced the diversions available, highlighting charitable celebrations. Memoirs and devotional literature are rich in details on entertainments with philanthropic purposes, some of which may seem quaint and comical, but which were widespread and avoided only with difficulty by the respectable, whatever their station. Among the commonplace were children's bazaars, ladies' sales and jumble sales, charity balls, dinners and concerts, preparations for Boxing Day, Sunday school marches and outings, and the festivities surrounding the opening of collection boxes for one of the great London societies. In such popular activities benevolence helped to erode the distinctions between labour and love, seriousness and fancy, and gave the extra satisfaction of the performance of a duty. Like mothers' meetings and working parties they contributed to the development of a sense of community and the disposition to kindness in children and adults.

Given the pronounced religious training of children, the many millions of pounds which they contributed to various charities since the early nineteenth century become more comprehensible. To the missionary and Bible societies, the RSPCA and the NSPCC, the temperance movement and other causes, their donations, channelled through domestic meetings, Sunday schools and juvenile associations, became an important, in some cases an indispensable, source of funds. As time passed charities paid more and more attention to their contributions and kept up to date with the creation of new organisations and fundraising gimmicks. The League of Pity, founded in 1894 as the children's branch of the NSPCC, raised £290,000 in 1979 through such innovations as spell-ins. The success of the campaign to lighten the child's purse ensured that parents and teachers were assiduous in overseeing the charitable impulses that their training aroused. Quite naturally, they wished for their children to be like themselves. The future of their causes depended on a steady supply of subscribers and workers drawn from the ranks of youth. As the pennies dropped in the collection boxes, greater recognition was given to the child's personality and habits of benevolence passed from generation to generation.

[. . .]

Competitive and acquisitive, the charitable societies put the public under relentless pressure to contribute. Thriving on advertisement, they would form a large chapter in any history of publicity. Every effort was made to elicit favourable notice, to merge philanthropy and fashion. Thus institutions invited celebrities and public figures to be patrons and patronesses. As such people needed philanthropic attachments to give the respectability and opportunities for display, perhaps even a knighthood, such invitations were taken seriously. A 'royal' or an actress could be worth thousands of pounds a year to a society – a bishop or a Member of Parliament rather less. Parish charities, of course, had to make do with local worthies, the vicar's wife or a magistrate, perhaps. Patrons received backing from a host of administrators, writers, speakers and preachers [. . .] anxious to give publicity to their causes and geared to capitalise on it. The published subscription lists, the opulent offices and lavish dinners, the newspaper advertisements (*The Times* prospered on them) were all part of the marketing of philanthropy. At the doorstep were the countless charitable salesmen who invaded the nation's homes. In the Bible Society alone there were 15,000 agents, mostly women, raising funds from door to door by 1820. At the end of the century the NSPCC had 6,000 female collectors, using methods learned from district visiting.

[. . .]

As the number of publicists and fundraisers suggests, philanthropy looms large in any history of employment, though it has not been much studied in this context. Few occupations in the nineteenth century could match the labour force marshalled by the charitable societies. There were nearly twice as many paid workers in the 'domestic services' of the benevolent institutions and charity hospitals as there were employees in the poor law authority. Tellingly, there were more paid Scripture readers or missionaries than scientists. For women, opportunities for salaried employment in philanthropy were good by the end of the century. It was estimated in 1893 that 20,000 women worked as full-time paid officials in charities, excluding nurses and women in religious orders, making it one of the leading female professions. In the nineteenth century, of course, philanthropy was seen as the vocation for middle-class women, an outlet for their domestic skills and their much heralded characteristics of kindness and compassion. This helps to explain why roughly 500,000 women worked 'continuously and semi-professionally' as volunteers in philanthropic institutions by the end of the century. Only domestic service recruited larger numbers of females. The notion of the 'idle' Victorian woman, which stems from the view that only paid employment matters, may be seen largely as a fiction when charitable work is introduced.

Philanthropy's place in American history

Olivier Zunz, 2011

From Andrew Carnegie to Bill Gates, and from ordinary people who purchased Christmas seals to fight tuberculosis to those who wear pink ribbons to battle breast cancer, the nation has come to view philanthropy as both a quintessential part of being American and another means of achieving major objectives. Foundations originating in large private fortunes have collaborated with institutions of mass philanthropy in promoting scientific research, supporting educational institutions, and fighting for human rights. Together they have forged a philanthropic sector that donors, beneficiaries, and the state recognize as a critical source of ideas as well as of funding.

[. . .]

[P]hilanthropy in the United States is not simply the consequence of a universal altruistic impulse; it is also a product of the large organizational revolution that American managerial and financial capitalism orchestrated in the last century and a half. Adam Smith made the case for universalism in the opening of his classic *The Theory of Moral Sentiments* by observing:

> How selfish soever man may be supposed, there are evidently some principles in his nature, which interest him in the fortune of others, and render their happiness necessary to him, though he derives nothing from it except the pleasure of seeing it.

For this Scottish founder of modern political economy, this altruistic vision encompasses "the greatest ruffian, the most hardened violator of the laws of society" as well as the ordinary citizen. That American giving on a large scale reflects altruism, there is no doubt. But Americans of different wealth and culture have turned a universal desire to do good into a distinct brand of philanthropy. They have learned to turn market profits and market methods into a philanthropic engine powerful enough to influence the course of their history.

One way to appreciate the novelty of philanthropy in America is by turning to those pioneer anthropologists who, a century ago, observed giving in small surviving nonmarket societies in order to gain a glimpse of an alternative to profit-making. They generated an influential discourse on giving. Columbia University anthropologist Franz Boas investigated the potlatch among American Indians of the North Pacific coast. Bronislaw Malinowski contributed his studies of free and reciprocal giving (or *kula*) in the Trobriand Islands. Marcel Mauss, in a landmark synthetic essay he wrote in 1923 entitled *The Gift*, portrayed the ritualistic and reciprocal exchange of gifts his colleagues had discovered as the "total social fact" of archaic societies. Mauss went on to contrast this archaic giving with selling in modern market societies. After positing the gift as the main form of economic, social, and cultural exchange in a world very different from ours, Mauss explained that the Greeks and the Romans were first to distinguish between a sale and a gift, and to insist on treating a sale as a contract subject to the rule of law and a gift as a moral obligation. This dichotomy was adopted by Christianity and remained dominant in Western civilization until such time as the Americans invented modern philanthropy.

Americans have come to think of philanthropy not as a gift only, but also as an investment. Late nineteenth-century Americans who made large fortunes were the first to openly combine the ideas of managing the market and giving in a single mechanism geared for social progress. That money needs to be available before it can be given is obvious; the innovation lay in bridging the gap between a transaction in which you act for profit and a gift, in effect merging in various proportions the two activities. Having inherited a critical distinction between profit-making and giving, inscribed in law and custom, they have made the two behaviors organically dependent rather than outcomes of opposite impulses, as Adam Smith implied.

The innovation was not limited to rich philanthropists. Broad participation gave philanthropy its democratic imprint in America. While the wealthy have invested their fortunes in large foundations, Americans of modest means have financed their own institutions of philanthropy from surplus income, also the product of capitalism. These two kinds of institutions both oversee their endowments and manage their activities with techniques learned from for-profit corporations, a distinguishing mark of American philanthropy.

In other words, American philanthropy is not a matter of the rich helping people in need, but of people, rich or not, providing for their own future. American philanthropy contains a very important and motivating element of frank self-interest. Donors themselves gain when their contribution leads to a cure for a common disease or when it provides them access to better cultural amenities.

In attempting to characterize American philanthropy, Alexis de Tocqueville's grasp of the relationship between interest and altruism remains an essential starting point. Tocqueville saw in American life the application of Smith's humanity to market forces. Instead of merely concluding that all human beings have a generous impulse, he uncovered the means Americans have used time and again to turn generosity to their advantage. He labeled the mechanism "self-interest properly understood."

It took Tocqueville some time to establish a positive connection between "self-interest" and collective betterment. In his travels, he at first saw people fending only for themselves everywhere he turned. "Private interest rears its head here constantly, reveals itself openly, and proclaims itself to be a social theory," Tocqueville wrote disparagingly to his friend Ernest de Chabrol from New York in 1831. But he later changed his mind and posited instead an "enlightened love" of oneself that leads Americans to "sacrifice a portion of their time and wealth" to public affairs. Using language inherited from the political philosophy of the eighteenth century, Tocqueville speculated that in America, "interest" had replaced "virtue" as the motivation for working for the common good. Turning self-interest into a benefit for all, Tocqueville argued, was a positive development for civilization because as an impulse, it was in much greater supply than virtue. Tocqueville applied this concept to explain the development of associations in America. Here was a joint enterprise to which people could adhere freely, and help themselves while helping others.

Tocqueville's formulation may be even more applicable to philanthropy, as we have described it in this history, than to associations. Tocqueville could not anticipate it, but mass philanthropy, with its army of volunteers raising money in American neighborhoods year after year to help solve some of the larger problems of the country, is a constant re-enactment of self-interest properly understood. Individual Americans return to society some monetary gain with the motivation that it might benefit them in the long run. This same idea can also be applied to American philanthropy abroad. In participating in the vast expansion of American influence in the world, philanthropic institutions have been constrained by Realpolitik, especially in times of war, but they have explicitly invested in global welfare.

Although philanthropy operates on a much smaller scale than government, the resources available to foundations and broadly supported organizations are large enough that continual debate about the proper relationship of government to philanthropy has become a distinctive feature of American society. Generally speaking, the federal government wants to encourage philanthropy, but it also wants to control it, and this has repeatedly led to friction. The government feels most comfortable when philanthropy adheres to "charitable" purposes, an adjective still used in the tax code to characterize philanthropic and nonprofit institutions, not only because it is inherited from their early identification with the church but also because it reflects the lesser range of activities the state is willing to subsidize. The government is less at ease with philanthropy's entry into the realm of policymaking, and has proven most hostile to its efforts at advocacy, seeing its own prerogatives challenged directly. Given the sweeping goals of American philanthropy, this conflict has been played out over and over again.

In accordance with the constitutional separation of church and state, American philanthropy has also largely been ecumenical if not secular. Many Christians have had no trouble supporting a broadly defined philanthropy with aims that may even be at odds with their religious tenets. After John D. Rockefeller III, a liberal Protestant, created the Population Council to promote birth control around the world, Henry Ford II, who had converted to Catholicism when getting married, surprised Ford Foundation officers by authorizing its support. Churches have generally looked to find common cause with secular goals, adapting their activities to the secular philanthropic model, if only to benefit from grants from the US government. Catholic Relief Services and federated Protestant charities have acted not as missions but as humanitarian institutions combining taxpayer money with their own for carrying out modernizing projects in many theaters around the world. Conservative Christians, however, have resisted this trend; Howard Pew, a large donor to evangelical causes, participated in the politics of philanthropy at midcentury with the goal of stemming the secular tide. In his view and that of others since, proselytism and good works need to go hand in hand.

How much of a contribution to American democracy at home and abroad philanthropy is likely to make in the future is of course a matter of speculation. Before the 2008 collapse of financial markets, economists predicted a massive intergenerational transfer of wealth from the baby-boom generation in the coming years, much of it going to philanthropic causes. The amount of giving is now likely to be less. Economic setbacks always generate the fear that philanthropy may dry up or may be inadequate to the challenges faced. This was the case during the Great Depression when President Hoover unsuccessfully called philanthropy to the rescue, and it has been widely feared that the Great Recession might have the same result.

But philanthropy is deeply entrenched in the American political economy because it draws on values that Americans claim for themselves in otherwise compartmentalized parts of their lives: a commitment to profit-making but also to social justice; a respect for individual freedom and a strong sense of community.

The European roots of North American philanthropy

Thomas Adam, 2004

Throughout the nineteenth century, wealthy North Americans travelled to Europe to explore its lands, culture and society. After Henry E. Dwight had visited the northern part of Germany in 1825 and 1826, he jealously reported in his letters about the famous royal library and the art gallery of Dresden, which displayed more than 1,400 paintings "of the most distinguished artists of every school and age, since the revival of painting in Italy'. George Ticknor, who travelled to Italy, France, Great Britain and Germany between 1835 and 1838, spent a great deal of time in Dresden enjoying the advantages of the royal library, which possessed over 300,000 volumes, "among them the most complete collection of historical works in existence." After his return to Boston, Ticknor took an interest in establishing a similar library in his own town. When the founding of the Boston Public Library became feasible in the 1850s, Ticknor could contribute his knowledge of the structure and functionings of the Dresden library. Following Dwight and Ticknor, J. Bayard Taylor published his European travel notes in 1846, giving his fellow Americans an impressive description of the Grune Gweolbe (Green Vault), a gallery in Dresden, which he admiringly described as "a collection of jewels and costly articles, unsurpassed in Europe." Toronto mayor James Mavor brought knowledge of social housing projects from his native Glasgow to his adopted home; the Glasgow projects were, in fact, modeled on several important London foundations. During business trips to Europe, Mavor studied various social and cultural projects.

This transatlantic version of the Grand Tour was very important for US nouveaux riches after the Civil War. Insecure in their social status, they used the European experience to become more self-confident and to learn about European art and culture; their new knowledge gave them a basis for claiming "membership in a superior social class." As William W. Stowe notes, "European travel was a way of affirming the respectability of one's race, class, or gender." For Canadians, transatlantic travel began somewhat later, around the turn of the twentieth century. For example, after firmly establishing his career at the Canadian Bank of Commerce, Sir Edmund Walker started travelling abroad for business and pleasure – to Europe, Japan, the United States, and South America. Walker made a point of visiting churches, museums, private collections, commercial galleries, and artists' studios. It should come as no surprise that Walker was instrumental in the creation of the Art Gallery of Toronto, which opened in 1913.

After their return, wealthy Americans and Canadians attempted to recreate what they had seen and experienced in Europe. When New York's upper class decided to create its own museums, John Fiske Comfort reminded his fellow citizens of the cultural treasures of Europe and recommended art galleries and museums in Leipzig, Amsterdam, Gotha, Berlin, and Nuremberg as models for the Metropolitan Museum of Art. Museums, art galleries, and libraries in New York, Boston and Toronto were the result of this transatlantic transfer. The transfer of social and cultural models has remained a generally unexplored historical topic. In his pathbreaking book *Atlantic Crossings*, Daniel Rodgers has reminded us that "the Atlantic functioned . . . less as a barrier than as a connective lifeline – a seaway for the movement of people, goods, ideas, and aspirations." However, most of what now constitutes transatlantic history focuses on the premodern era – a time of exploration, migration, and the construction of the New World. Twice annually, Harvard University organizes a conference on Atlantic history but limits the historical survey to the time before 1800 (although it sometimes extends this date to 1825). Modern transatlantic history – the history of the interrelations and cultural exchanges between European and North American societies in the nineteenth and twentieth centuries – is an all-but-unknown field. As Rodgers points out, "Historical scholarship bends to the task of specifying each nation's distinctive culture, its particular history, its *Sonderweg*, its exceptionalism." For example, while Germany is assumed to have taken a special path of modernization – industrialization without democratization – which led to an authoritarian model of industrialized society, the United States is considered "special in starting from a revolutionary event" and has been described as the "most egalitarian nation in social relations and democratic in politics."

The historical research presented in this volume explores the differences and similarities among nineteenth- and twentieth-century US, British, Canadian, and German societies. Several chapters investigate the transatlantic transfer of ideas and concepts and undermine previously held assumptions about the distinctness of the countries under study. As Sven Beckhert has recently demonstrated, late-nineteenth-century bourgeois who travelled from Hamburg to New York did not feel as though they were entering an alien or distinct culture; rather, they felt at home because of a shared transatlantic bourgeois culture. In fact, German bourgeois life was imitated by New York's wealthy upper-class families, who copied the quasi-aristocratic behavior of the European bourgeoisie. In this volume, the term "bourgeoisie" will be based on the German concept of *Burgertum*, or wealth and the use of wealth. Berlin, London, Leipzig, and Dresden produced the blueprints for bourgeois philanthropic undertakings, which have been copied and implemented into North American urban society.

Nineteenth-century German society has been long described without reference to its philanthropic traditions. Historians have argued that German culture, educational, and social public institutions were established and funded by municipalities and the state. Despite extensive research about the German *Burgertum* (bourgeoisie), the most bourgeois behavior – philanthropy – has not been considered. Historians have assumed that the German bourgeoisie did not develop feelings of responsibility for German society; rather, they have argued, they expected the state to take responsibility for financing social and cultural public institutions. Philanthropy has thus been widely seen as an American invention and as a distinct American approach to modern life. This volume will show that nineteenth-century German society was organized along philanthropic lines – theatres, concert houses, art galleries, and even social housing projects depended on private financing schemes and the philanthropists who established and financed these institutions. Only after the turn of the twentieth century did German society shift from a philanthropic society toward a state-oriented society.

Reflections on philanthropy in China

Joanna Handlin Smith, 1998

Until the 1980s, most scholars considered the subject of Chinese charity an anomaly pertaining only to a few towns and cities in a predominantly agrarian society. If they noticed Chinese charitable activities at all, they dismissed their significance. The Chinese, it was commonly said, were charitable only to their kin; their benevolence lacked piety, was not altogether voluntary, and served the interests of the elite.

Discouraging Western scholars from taking a good look at Chinese charitable traditions was the legacy of nineteenth-century Christian missionaries, who, though copiously documenting Chinese charity, marshaled their findings to spotlight deficiencies in Chinese practices, thereby to pave the way for their own, presumably worthier activities. When the direst famine of the Qing dynasty struck North China from 1876 to 1879, Chinese at many levels of society valiantly sought to aid the starving. The emperor contributed funds; the governor of Shandong had grain imported for sale at reduced prices; local residents erected soup kitchens and orphanages; benevolent associations aided the needy and buried the dead; and gentry of other provinces, moved by the plight of victims in Shandong, reached across administrative boundaries to help. Yet missionaries, who were then enjoying the strengths of a prosperous, progressive industrialized West, found fault in these efforts. The assistance from the imperial coffers was "a mere pittance," they claimed, observing that the careless distribution of grain had provoked food riots and invited false claims on resources.

The missionaries' criticisms appeared to be substantiated by overwhelming evidence: the famine of the late 1870s took between 9.5 and 13 million lives. Surveying the disastrous outcome, the crusader Timothy Richard had grounds to conclude that the civilization of the West, with its science and Christianity, surpassed that of China. The West, he explained, had discovered "the workings of God in Nature," and had, "in applying the laws of science to the needs of man, . . . [developed] marvellous intentions that were little less wonderful than miracles." Fortified by the technological advancements of his own society, he intruded upon the Chinese scene to take over relief efforts. Confident in the superiority of his own civilization, he assumed a patronizing attitude toward the Chinese: he had those "dead idols" whom Chinese magistrates routinely supplicated for rain replaced with his own God. As he told it, he asked the Chinese to kneel so that he might "pray to God to look down in pity on them."

The missionary Arthur Smith, writing around 1894, called attention to what he perceived to be a huge discrepancy between Chinese theories about benevolence and actual practice. The Chinese had "foundling hospitals, refuges for lepers and the aged, and free schools," observed Smith; nonetheless, surveying China's enormous population, he concluded that "such establishments must be relatively rare." At every turn, he saw inadequacies in Chinese "benevolence." He discounted "the provincial clubs" that cared for the destitute away from home as conducting "an ordinary business transaction of the nature of insurance." He faulted the imperial government – which had, he acknowledged, responded with alacrity to famines and floods – for having nonetheless acted "in a makeshift way." He deprecated donors who distributed alms to beggars and migrants; they were, he claimed, essentially buying insurance against the possibility that marauders might raid their homes and warehouses, or they were encouraging migrants to be quickly on their way to other townships. Even the Chinese practice of keeping accounts of their good and bad deeds was, Smith thought, motivated by a self-interested desire to make a good case to the judge of the underworld. Castigating the Chinese for seeking from benevolent acts what he called a "relaxed benefit," Smith argued that the best palliative for their social ills was Christianity.

Likewise did Gabriel Palatre of the Catholic mission in Shanghai use information about Chinese charity to build the case that Western beliefs and practices were superior to those of the Chinese. Noting in 1878 that many Western travellers to China denied having ever witnessed cases of infanticide and therefore refused to support his orphanage, Palatre collected for his French audience an abundance of information about infanticide – imperial proclamations, didactic tales, and woodblock illustrations. These materials all warned against the evils of infanticide, but Palatre drew from them another lesson: Chinese laws were ineffective – unlike Catholicism, which, "by simply proclaiming to the faithful the single statement 'God is the creator of human life and no one on earth has the right to take the life of his fellow creatures,' will work miracles." Evidence that many Chinese opposed infanticide, though plentiful, did not shake his conceptual framework.

What Westerners saw of China in the twentieth century seemed to confirm the missionaries' grim assessments. The country, torn apart by civil war and foreign invasion, suffered overpopulation and food shortages with little sustained relief; moreover, by 1949 an authoritarian regime had arisen that would discourage individual, voluntary initiatives for the public good. China's deplorable conditions were vividly communicated to Westerners through photographs, one of which captured skeletal laborers harnessed like draft animals to a huge ship that they were tracking up the Yangzi River. Who after seeing this could trust talk of Chinese benevolence? Who could see back to a time when Chinese society had been guided by – and at times even lived up to – a human and life-nurturing rhetoric? That most twentieth-century Chinese themselves turned against their heritage as the creation of a self-serving elite further reinforced Western myopia. Thus in 1989 an op-ed piece in the *New York Times*, taking a cue from Deng Xiaoping's son, and sounding somewhat like Arthur Smith, made a statement that altogether ignored the centrality of the concept of humaneness (*ren*) in premodern Chinese thought: "The restraining philosophy of humanitarianism is absent or nearly absent in Chinese tradition." The journalist added, "China developed no great philosophy of charity, aid to the downtrodden or an obligation to help the less fortunate."

Weighing against such scepticism are China's historical records, which employ a large vocabulary for charitable activities. They speak of "liking to be charitable" (*haoyi, leshan haoshi, haoshan leshi, hoaxing shanshi*, and *cishan haoyi*), of "doing good" (*weishan, xingshan*), and of "good deeds" (*shanju* and *yixing*). They applaud "those who like to do good," or (without the pejorative and sarcastic overtones that the term has acquired in English) "do-gooders" (*haoshan zhe*). And they speak of "compassion" (*cishan*) for the poor, of "giving aid" (*shiji*), and, with a connotation of justice, of "aiding the weak and helping out in emergencies" (*yi*). They tell of benefactors who financed the construction of bridges, maintained free ferry services, and sponsored community schools for indigent village boys; and of compassionate men who provided the poor and needy with food, shelter, burials, and medicines. The list of good deeds continues but in itself is nearly meaningless, composed as it is of disconnected items randomly displayed. How does one go about weighing their significance? How might one navigate between two temptations, either to collect facts endlessly (as though the longer the list the more incontrovertible would be the proof of China's charitableness) or to bring quick closure by organizing those facts according to some preconceived theory?

What prompted me to write this was neither some conviction about the merits or flaws of Chinese charity in late imperial times, nor a fixed idea about what charity is or ought to be, but rather a chance to encounter with a type of voluntary charitable organization that emerged in the late sixteenth century and was the forerunner of institutions that would in the nineteenth century acquire the English label "benevolent societies." If, as has often been said, the Chinese focused charity on their kin, why, I wondered, did men who belonged to prominent lineages additionally establish these associations to serve the community at large?

The causes served by the benevolent societies had been encouraged by ancient Chinese texts and long pursued by various institutions whose main purpose was something other than charity. Emperors extended their governance to sponsor poorhouses (*yangji yuan*) and dispensaries for the "poor, sick, disabled, and lonely," thereby expressing their paternalistic care for the people. Buddhist monasteries, elaborating on their pious goals, provided shelters, medicines, and soup kitchens for the poor. Lineages occasionally used income from land trusts, or "charitable estates" – whose main function was to foster lineage prosperity and longevity by relieving kin of burdensome ritual and educational expenses – to aid the poor and needy beyond their kin. Unlike these institutions, in which charity had an ancillary role, benevolent societies *appeared* to have charity as their primary, defining purpose. Given these alternative routes for aiding the poor, why did members of the local elite (which this study defines broadly to include former officials, educated men, and wealthy residents) voluntarily sponsor and manage benevolent societies, and why did these institutions first arise in the late sixteenth century?

When benevolent societies were making their appearance, the topic of charity became increasingly visible in the written record, thus inviting the historian's scrutiny. Ancient political texts had counseled rulers to employ, feed, and clothe the dumb, the deaf, the crippled, and the lame, and to aid those who were widowed, orphaned, and socially isolated. Historical records had long spoken of rulers and officials who sponsored a host of welfare activities. Before the late Ming, however, discussions of routine welfare were rare and generally unrevealing. State regulations (*huiyao*), administrative handbooks, and ethical guides underscored an ideal of caring for the needy and exhorted readers to share their wealth with others (*fencai, quanfen*), yet they tended to be terse, impersonal, and abstract, floating high above everyday particularities. Seldom did they document whether plans were actually implemented, let alone the names of individual benefactors. Crises concerning food, especially from the Song dynasty on, were more likely to elicit comment than the routine needs of the poor. Still, with few exceptions – most notably, a Song-dynasty retired official who personally took responsibility for installing soup kitchens that enabled thousands of people to survive a famine – Song materials provide few links between abstract prescriptions and actual situations.

Documents are invariably more readily available for recent periods than for earlier ones; such is the result of war, natural disasters, and changing values concerning what is worth preserving. Even for the late Ming, one reads of numerous books and essays, not to mention such ephemeral materials as account books, physician case books, population surveys, and proclamations to residents, that no longer survive. Accelerating the use and circulation of written information in the late Ming were twin developments: the spread of literacy and an explosion in publishing. Yet, more important than the proliferation of written materials was the change in attitude that accompanied the expanded readership: before the late Ming, members of the literate elite had little interest in writing about charity and valued "hidden merit" (*yinde*) – that is, merit known to the self but not to others. They feared that others might view any public display of philanthropy as harboring nefarious political ambitions. So it was with the eleventh-century poet-statesman Su Shi: when he raised funds for a public hospital, bridge construction, and a program to discourage infanticide, he credited religious figures and friends and begged intimates to keep his role secret. Already in political disgrace, he wished to escape suspicion that he was trying to build up his political reputation. The record of Su Shi's good deeds has survived because he was a statesman and talented poet; the good deeds themselves did not bring him renown. The subject of philanthropy was peripheral to elite identity, and Su's philanthropy was unusual, according to a scholar writing a century later. Men were reluctant to take credit for charitable acts because they lacked a consensus about what such acts meant.

Late Ming benefactors, though they occasionally invoked the value of "hidden merit," more often strove to make their good deeds visible. They printed up pamphlets explaining the circumstances that had prompted their beneficence and listed the names of donors; they erected steles that explicated their fine goals and commemorated the sponsors. They wanted to be seen as do-gooders and were in full agreement that being so seen was respectable. The subject of charitable deeds thus gained a foothold in local gazetteers – records that districts (*xian*), subprefectures (*zhou*), and prefectures (*fu*) published once every few generations to preserve local lore and commemorate worthy residents. In contrast to earlier editions, district gazetteers that appeared soon after the Ming fall customarily reserved one section for biographies of men who had performed "charitable" or "just deeds" (*yixing*). (They relegated women to a separate section that celebrated chaste widow-hood and filiality, commenting only incidentally on their charitable contributions.) There, under the rubric "charitable deeds," countless exemplars of beneficence parade by in cramped succession. One benefactor paid clergy to perform funeral rites for thousands of corpses that had washed ashore in a flood of 1628; another burned the contract of a desperate debtor who was considering selling his son into servitude. And so forth. Therefore, where previously records of charitable activities had been most likely to survive when pertaining to men of great political or literary statute, such as Su Shi, some late Ming men, even illiterate ones, gained stature and lasting reputations simply because they had performed good deeds.

Generosity versus altruism

US versus UK

Karen Wright, 2002

International differences in giving levels are becoming increasingly well documented by a variety of sources. Less well explicated in both research and practice are the social understandings of the role and meaning of charitable giving in different countries and cultures. This article contributes a comparative analysis of giving ethos and behaviour in two countries, the United States and the United Kingdom, in particular the relationship of giving to civic life. It identifies differences in giving ethos and behaviour in the two countries, and postulates two models – generosity and altruism – for explaining those differences.

Obvious disparities between the two countries exist when overall levels of giving are considered. In the United States, individual giving as a percentage of Gross Domestic Product has consistently hovered around 2 per cent. By contrast, charitable giving in the United Kingdom has yet to reach 1 per cent of GDP. Various strategies, including those imported from the US, have not been able to move that percentage significantly higher, and giving levels were in fact declining in the mid-1990s as incomes were rising. Intriguingly, while the two countries differ dramatically in the total amounts given, rates of participation in giving are quite similar.

These kinds of figures have encouraged some analysts to conclude that the giving culture in the UK is simply less well developed than in the US. This conclusion, however, neglects the complexity of the differences between the political structures, social attitudes, and the role of charitable giving in the two countries. Other countries and cultures may also suffer similar simplistic assessments in an era when the export of American civic concepts and strategies has become increasingly popular.

Concepts of philanthropy and charity

The first of many cultural paradoxes to be found in a comparison of giving in the United States and United Kingdom is the question of what to call it. 'Philanthropy' – both the practice and the word itself – is very popular in the US. It is considered a positive and robust term and it is employed widely by both the left and the right. While giving to opposing causes, both ends of the political spectrum support wholeheartedly the value and importance of philanthropy. Lingering elite connotations are tempered by popular giving mechanisms such as United Ways, and by numerous 'social change' philanthropic efforts involving representatives of possible recipient groups in the decisions about the distribution of philanthropic resources.

In the UK, however, philanthropy has not been so popular. While it has enjoyed a very recent renewal of interest, spurred by modern visions of such things as e-philanthropy and social 'investment', for many in Britain it still carries disparaging connotations of Victorian 'do-gooderism' and is often seen as elitist, patronising, morally judgmental and ineffective, as well as old fashioned and out of date. It is perceived as an idea whose time came, was proved unworkable, and went – to be replaced by a universal, fair, and more efficient welfare state. Moreover, the classic distinction drawn by William Beveridge [the architect of the UK welfare state] between philanthropic and self-help organisations rests on a sharp delineation between altruistic and self-interested purposes and motivations, implying of course that philanthropy was – or at least should be – entirely selfless. In doing so, Beveridge both reflected and further reinforced public perceptions of philanthropy as an attitude of benevolent superiority. This distinction persists today; indeed, in many circles in modern Britain, philanthropy is the form of giving that 'dare not speak its name'. In the UK 'charity' and 'charitable giving' are the preferred terms; though not entirely free of baggage, they are seen as more modern, egalitarian and respectful.

A further irony of this paradox is that in many ways the negative connotations applied to the concept of philanthropy in the UK are very similar to the meanings that the term charity carries in the US. The terms are used almost as mirror opposites in the two countries. Moreover, philanthropy is viewed in Britain as a somewhat dubious *attitude* or *stance*; charitable giving on the other hand is a comparatively positive *act*. In the United States the situation is reversed. Philanthropy is an act, and an increasingly commanding one, while charity is dismissed as a patronising and somewhat out of date attitude.

[. . .]

Generosity versus altruism

The picture painted above is one of contrasting conceptions not only of why, how and to whom giving should take place, but also of whether or not private giving in itself is a good thing. This next section aims to pull together a comparative analysis of the social meaning and practice of philanthropy and charitable giving – a giving ethos – for the United States and the United Kingdom. It proposes two paradigms – generosity in the US and altruism in the UK – for understanding the cultural context in which charitable giving takes place in each country. Such an analysis may be able to provide a basis for understanding each country's 'giving culture' as well as for assessing which policies or institutions might likely be effective in each.

Generosity (US): 'Charity begins at home'

Generosity is an apt characterisation of the giving ethos in the United States. As used by Julian Wolpert in his extensive studies of giving in 83 US cities, it implies bounteousness but does not require altruism. US giving is heavily interlaced with self-interest, either directly through tax benefits, benefits from the supported charity, or social status; or indirectly through the achievement of social goals which one might desire, such as better child care, civil rights, better parks, etc. Moreover in America these self-interested motivations are not only acceptable, but are socially approved [. . .] The concept of 'enlightened self-interest' in which individual and community interests are seen to be in a reciprocal relationship, drives both individual and especially corporate giving. Giving is seen as an expression of personal and social identity and goals. For example, both the Jewish and sexual minority communities in the US are particularly generous givers, in part because they may see their gifts as supporting community institutions which are outside and even excluded from mainstream resources. In the US giving and volunteering are integral components to civic involvement; indeed they may be considered far loftier expressions than actual political involvement. Giving modes are predominately purposeful and planned, and yield relatively higher average gifts. Gifts are largely directed towards theoretically 'particular' causes, in which the giver may directly participate, such as a church or performing arts group, or ones where they may have received some direct benefit in the past, such as a college or university. Moral motivation rests on values of individual initiative and reciprocity.

Altruism (UK): 'Charity for all'

Altruism connotes pure selflessness, and for the most part, the British expect that giving should be altruistic, even self-sacrificing. They have traditionally rejected mixed motives for giving, and are quite suspicious – particularly of philanthropic giving – because it is so rarely able to live up to popular expectations of purely altruistic motives. Tax benefits reflect these altruistic principles with considerable popular support. However there is a subtle paradox here – people express increasing acceptance that their own giving may involve both altruistic and self-interested motives, but they must be seen as independent in order to preserve the 'genuineness' of their charitable intention. British corporate giving has been dominated incongruously in recent years by a 'business case' rationale, which justifies community involvement in terms of corporate interests in customer and employee loyalty. Giving is seen largely as a private decision, and peripheral to both social identity and civic responsibility, though new government initiatives aim to bring them closer together. 'Spare change' modes dominate giving, yielding small gifts, and making giving vulnerable to other demands on pocket change. In a pattern reflective of William Galston's 'cosmopolitan altruism', universal causes such as Oxfam and Save the Children, in which there is little direct or indirect benefit to the giver, receive the bulk of UK donations. Far fewer gifts go to organisations where the donor has had a direct association, such as a church or university. For the British, moral motivation is deeply rooted in collective duty, a concept that would be quite foreign to Americans, just as enlightened self-interest does not translate across the Atlantic in the other direction. While reason is the most socially legitimate ground for moral motivation, it has paradoxically been a powerful emotion, which has generated some of the most generous giving in recent years, most notably the £72 million donated by almost three million people to no specific aim or group in the wake of the death of Diana, Princess of Wales.

Conclusion

The United States and Britain are seen by many as relatively similar countries, sharing a history, many aspects of heritage, and some would say a common language. Politically, they continue to have a 'special relationship' despite changing fortunes and international roles. Basic philanthropic institutions – trusts and foundations, charity law, membership and subscription mechanisms have grown from the same (English) roots. And yet why and how they practise giving is, as we have seen, in many ways quite different. This has not stopped the interest in transferring institutions and policies from one country to another. The original transfer from England to the US has been succeeded by a reverse transfer of US charitable institutions to the UK.

There is currently world-wide interest in promoting the development of institutions and practices that contribute to a thriving civil society. Models for these institutions and practices have drawn heavily from the experiences of the United States. Policies and institutions are created – and are effective – within particular cultural contexts. Before assuming that similar policies or practices will meet with comparable success elsewhere, it is critical to assess the compatibility of relevant existing structures, norms and beliefs in the two cultures. In effect, such assessment means that institutions and policies, if desired and appropriate, must be translated, rather than simply transferred, into forms that reflect local cultural values and practices. To neglect to do so is to invite the failure of sometimes major efforts built on the best hopes and intentions.

2.3 Continuity and change across eras

Lessons from antiquity and the Middle Ages

Scott Davis, 1996

"Philanthropy," "charity," and related concepts were well known to late antiquity and the Middle Ages. Rulers, wealthy individuals and, early on, the Christian Church founded hospitals, distributed food, and established forms of relief for the needy of various sorts throughout the period. The problem comes in interpreting these activities, their motives, and their goals. Is the *philanthrôpía* of a pre-Christian philosopher of a piece with the *agape*, or Christian love, of a fourth-century bishop? When the Roman emperor provides bread and circuses, what does he intend and why does he do it? Does the twelfth-century nobleman intend the same? As with so many of our social, moral, and political concepts, placing "philanthropy" and its premodern cognates in their historical and intellectual context highlights our contemporary understanding of philanthropic work and its place in our moral world.

Consider two respected scholars in the field. Demetrios Constantelos, revising a major study of East Roman social welfare that he had published twenty-five years earlier, writes that in the intervening period he has come to believe "the Christian agape developed as a direct inheritance of ancient Greek *philanthrôpía*." And he adds that he now sees "more continuity in the social ethos of ancient Hellenism with Christian Hellenism than I was willing to acknowledge." On the other hand, the celebrated French historian Paul Veyne argues persuasively that the appearance of continuity between classical philanthropy and Christian charity "is an illusion," that the grand expressions of pagan benevolence, as opposed to the "pious and charitable works" of Christians, "differ in ideology, in beneficiaries and in agents, in the motivations of agents, and in their behaviour." Neither Veyne nor Constantelos denies that from late antiquity on there were hospitals and orphanages, poor relief and patronage. But knowing what happened is only part of the story. What we would like to know is why they were established and what they meant, how they fitted into the fabric of ancient and medieval moral thought and political life.

Unfortunately, this is easier said than done, for it is not entirely clear what we want to know, or how to discover it. In imperial Rome the doing of grand public works is reserved to the emperor, at least in the capital; is this intended to stamp out popular rivals or encompass the city in the godlike embrace of the first citizen? Are the foundations of hospitals and the like power plays, penance for evils done, acts to ingratiate the doer with the gods or expressions of compassion at the plight of the indigent? Is the patronage of Maecenas, so indispensable to Virgil and Horace, an instance of philanthropic support for the arts, the ostentatious display of a powerful aristocrat, or both? Veyne, reflecting on the family allowances instituted by Trajan, notes that "its humble beneficiaries thanked the Emperor for his liberality, while the political world praised him for ensuring the survival of the Italian race . . . whether it was beneficence or birth-rate policy, he had spent his money on a new and gracious task."

The point, of course, is that we have no clear way of determining whether these pensions were established for "philanthropic" purposes or for reasons of state, to secure a stable agricultural base. How could we tell?

[. . .]

I began with a dispute over the continuity of philanthropy from late antiquity into the Middle Ages. By and large I [side] with Veyne and his claim for the discontinuity of the classical with the late antique and medieval meanings of philanthropy. But there was still an important story to be told about philanthropy, charity, and their related vocabulary. This is the story I have tried to sketch, and it involved the spectrum of medieval thought, institutions, and common presuppositions. If there is a medieval consensus, St. Thomas represents it as well as anyone else, but it is important to recognize the continuing plurality of forms and understandings that underlie the medieval concept of philanthropy. While Thomas measured giving against the norms of nature and virtue, Benedict counseled his charges to climb the solitary ladder of humility. Francis left an example that stood in judgment against even Aquinas's analysis. Whatever the dictates of practical reason, the plight of the poor should inspire the total sacrifice of Francis, and while failure to go as far as the saint may not be a moral failure, it points nonetheless to our spiritual limits. To do at least something, even for the furthest Mysian, is not just a duty, it should be a desire.

Lessons from the nineteenth century

Gertrude Himmelfarb, 1995

"Gain all you can. . . . Save all you can. . . . Give all you can." For John Wesley, this trinity was one of the central tenets of Methodism. Max Weber cited it as the essence of the "Puritan ethic." More recently, Margaret Thatcher recommended it as the guiding precept of conservativism. It may also be taken as the perfect expression of the apparent paradox behind the Victorian ethos: the fact that the most individualistic of countries was also the most philanthropic-minded.

One of the many myths about Victorianism is that it was ruthlessly materialistic, acquisitive, and self-centered. The myth starts with the image of the hardheaded, hard-nosed Victorian employer who regarded his workers as instruments of production rather than as human beings, and who exploited them under the cloak of principle, invoking the natural, even divine, laws of political economy. The sole function of government in this laissez-faire system is said to have been the preservation of law and order, which in practice meant keeping the potentially lawless and disorderly lower classes in a state of docility and subjugation. Those who professed a concern for the poor are dismissed as eccentric do-gooders, condescending Lady Bountifuls, or officious philanthropists who pretended to help the poor for their own self-serving motives.

Part of this myth is easily disproved. Neither in principle nor in practice was political economy as rigidly laissez-faireist as this picture suggests. The first of the factory acts limiting the hours of work for children was passed in 1833; within a decade it was followed by laws limiting the hours of women, and somewhat later, the hours of men. In the course of the century, Parliament enacted scores of other reforms concerning health, sanitation, housing, education, transportation, even holidays, while the municipalities assumed responsibility for the water supply, sewage, public baths, street lighting, street cleaning, libraries, parks. All of these reforms coincided with a period of rapid economic growth, so that by the last quarter of the century the standard of living of the working classes had risen considerably, thus belying the Marxist theory of "immiseration": the idea that capitalism inevitably results in the growing misery and poverty of the proletariat.

Even more notable than the improvement in the conditions of the working classes was the enormous surge of social consciousness and philanthropic activity on the part of the middle and upper classes. This is not to say that there had been no such consciousness and activity in the previous century. When John Wesley preached "Gain all you can. . . . Save all you can. . . . Give all you can," he gave practical effect to those principles by taking up collections for the poor, setting up loan funds and work projects, and instructing his followers to pay "visitations" to the sick and to prisoners in jail. It is not surprising to find Methodists and Evangelicals prominent in the founding of orphanages, schools, hospitals, friendly societies, and charitable enterprises of every kind. By the late eighteenth century, the principle of "philanthropy" (still carrying with it its original meaning of "love of mankind") had given rise to full-time philanthropists like John Howard, who agitated for the reform of the prison system, and Jonas Hanway, who devised the "boarding out" system to remove infants from the poorhouses. Hannah More, preferring moral reformation to philanthropy, characterized this period, not altogether in praise, as the "Age of Benevolence." A London magistrate, deploring the corruption of "virtue" into "good affections," complained: "We live in an age when humanity is in fashion."

That magistrate would have had more to complain of in the nineteenth century, when the fashion for humanity expressed itself in a score of legislative and administrative reforms as well as a renewed burst of philanthropies and social activities. So far from supplanting private, voluntary efforts, as many people had feared, the government seemed to inspire them to greater exertions. For Hippolyte Taine, this was yet another of the peculiarities of the English. Citing an article in the *Edinburgh Review* in 1861, he noted that of the £13 million spent on public education in the preceding twenty-one years, only £4 million was contributed by the state; the rest came from private subscriptions. (Even after the institution of compulsory, publicly supported education in 1870, church-endowed and private schools continued to play a large part in the educational system.) And education was only one of the causes that drew upon private funds.

> There are swarms of societies engaged in good works: societies for saving the life of drowning persons, for the conversion of the Jews, for the propagation of the Bible, for the advancement of science, for the protection of animals, for the suppression of vice, for the abolition of tithes, for helping working people to own their own houses, for building good houses for the working-class, for setting up a basic fund to provide the workers with savings banks, for emigration, for the propagation of economic and social knowledge, for Sabbath-day observance, against drunkenness, for founding schools to train girls as schoolteachers, etc., etc.

What was even more remarkable, Taine observed, was that an Englishman regarded this kind of "public business" as "his business," feeling obligated to contribute to the "common good" and bringing to it the same conscientious attention as a Frenchman brought to his private business affairs.

Two decades later, Taine would have had still more societies to add to his roster and more reason for astonishment. The 1880s saw a veritable explosion of social concerns and activities. In 1884, the journal of the leading philanthropic association, the Charity Organisation Society, reported: "Books on the poor, poverty, social questions, slums and the like subjects, rush fast and furious from the press. The titles of some of them sound like sentimental novels." That same year, Beatrice Webb wrote in her diary: "Social questions are the vital questions of today: they take the place of religion."

There was, in fact, a religious, almost revivalist tone in this accession of social consciousness. Beatrice Webb has left a memorable description of what she called the "Time-Spirit" of this period. The spirit was a compound of two elements: the first, a religious dedication to the service of others, inspired not by orthodox religion or a belief in God but by a secular religion, the "Religion of Humanity;" the second, the faith in science, the idea that the welfare of society could best be promoted by scientific, rational, organized means.

To one degree or another, these elements manifested themselves in the multitude of philanthropic enterprises, reform movements, humanitarian societies, research projects, publications, and journalistic exposes that flourished in the last quarter of the century. Some were overtly religious, such as the Salvation Army and the Christian Social Union. But many more exhibited the kind of sublimated, secularized "religion" described by Beatrice Webb. In this respect, the time-spirit of late-Victorian England was in notable contrast to that of earlier periods. Most of the reformers earlier in the century, such as the Evangelicals who led the movement for the abolition of the slave trade, had been inspired by a firm religious creed; they were reformers, one might say, because they were devout Christians. Many of the later reformers were less devout, but no less ardent in pursuing worthy causes. Just as they redoubled their moral zeal to compensate for their loss of religious faith, so they redoubled their humanitarian zeal as well. Humanitarianism became, in effect, a surrogate religion. This quasi-religious spirit was evident even in socialist organizations like the Fabian Society, which was professedly secular, or the Social Democratic Federation, which was ostensibly Marxist.

The scientific aspect of the time-spirit also took many forms. For socialists (in the Fabian Society, Social Democratic Federation, and Socialist League), science meant the rational, planned organization of the economy and society. For social workers (in the Charity Organisation Society), it meant the rational, planned organization of charity and relief. For settlement-house workers (in Toynbee Hall), it meant the education and edification of the working classes. For social researchers (like Charles Booth or Seebohm Rowntree), it meant the systematic investigation and analysis of the different classes of the poor, their material and moral conditions, their problems and prospects of improvement.

It was this combination of religiosity and rationality that informed the social consciousness of the late Victorians. Critics at the time complained that the Religion of Humanity had the effect of diluting and distorting religion, replacing the old stern Puritanism with "a vapid philanthropic sentiment . . . a creed of maudlin benevolence." The new philanthropy, however, was neither vapid nor maudlin. The God of Humanity proved to be as stern a taskmaster as the God of Christianity. The Charity Organisation Society instructed its social workers that "scientific" charity should not be "indiscriminate" or "promiscuous," distributed without regard to need or worth, lest it contribute to the very evil it was designed to remedy, the pauperization and demoralization of the poor. True humanitarianism was said to be an exercise in doing good, not feeling good – doing good to others, even if it meant curbing one's own spontaneous, benevolent impulses.

The dispensers of charity, no less than the recipients, were held to high standards. They were expected to give generously of their time and resources and to have a sustained personal involvement in their work. This was not "check-book philanthropy," satisfied merely by the contribution of money (although such contributions were expected, in small amounts as well as large, since the organizations were entirely dependent on private funds). Nor was it the kind of "telescopic" philanthropy satirized by Dickens in the character of Mrs. Jellyby, in *Bleak House*, who was so preoccupied with the natives of Borrioboola-Gha that she neglected her own children. Nor was it professional philanthropy in the current sense, where everyone from the director of the charity to fund-raisers, social workers, and clerks is a salaried employee, paid to do a job quite like any other.

Victorian philanthropists, social workers ("visitors," as they were called), settlement house "residents," even researchers, were personally involved in the day-to-day lives of the poor with whom they were concerned. And while they brought to their work a spirit of professionalism, seeking to dispense charity or conduct their inquiries "scientifically," they also brought to it the dedication of unpaid, voluntary workers giving a good deal of their time, their energy, and their money to the welfare of those less fortunate than themselves.

Charles Booth's survey of London, the voluminous *Life and Labour of the People in London*, which today would have been financed by a government agency or a tax-exempt foundation and would have employed a full complement of project directors, supervisors, interviewers, writers, consultants, and accountants, was entirely organized and supported by Booth himself. The research was conducted by him personally with the help of a few assistants, and the seventeen volumes were written by him and his aides – all of this while he was actively engaged in his shipping business. It was a remarkable enterprise, not only for the massive amount of data and analysis that it produced, but for the massive contribution of time, effort, money, and personal dedication that it represented. Booth was the epitome of Webb's time-spirit, the very model of a Victorian philanthropist. A Unitarian turned Positivist, he undertook this vast project not only out of scientific interest and intellectual curiosity, nor simply as a means of developing well-informed social policies, but as his personal contribution to the public welfare, a way of discharging what he called, in a moving testament of faith, his "great debt to Humanity."

[. . .]

The Victorians were avowedly, unashamedly, incorrigibly moralists. They were moralists on their own behalf – they engaged in philanthropic enterprises in part to satisfy their own moral needs. And they were moralists on behalf of the poor, whom they sought not only to assist materially but also to elevate morally, spiritually, culturally, intellectually – and whom, moreover, they believed capable and desirous of such elevation. Just as it is demeaning to the working classes to suggest that work, thrift, prudence, sobriety, self-help, were middle-class values imposed upon them from above, so it is demeaning to the philanthropists to suggest that they promoted these values solely for their own ulterior motives. In any case, whatever their motives (and there were surely self-serving, self-aggrandizing, self-satisfied individuals among them), the values they commended to the poor were those that they cherished for themselves and for their own families. It was no small achievement that people of very different political and philosophical persuasions, engaged in very different philanthropic enterprises, should have agreed on this: that the poor had the will to aspire to these same values and the ability to realize them.

Elite philanthropy in contemporary Israel

Hillel Schmid and Avishag Rudich-Cohn, 2012

Philanthropy is a time-honored value in Israeli society, and the concept of charity (*tzedakah*) is deeply rooted in Jewish tradition. Israeli philanthropists are from families and social networks that emphasize ideological, moral, and emotional motives as well as motives aimed at promoting their own interests. As such, their activities are based on the premises of charity, altruism, and help for disadvantaged populations. The phenomenon of "new philanthropy" in Israel has developed over the past three decades, and refers mainly to people who made money in electronic and high-tech industries, and who want to make a difference in Israeli society.

[. . .]

Elite philanthropy in Israel includes "old" and "new" philanthropists. The old philanthropists are well-established, wealthy families who have made substantial contributions to major social causes, whereas the new philanthropists are those who became wealthy over the past three decades in high-tech industries, electronics, and venture capital. As mentioned, elite philanthropists can be distinguished from many other donors who contribute to various nonprofit and human service organizations. Hence, there is a need to explore the distinctive characteristics of this group of philanthropists, their motives for giving, their preferred areas of interest for contributions, and the scope of their donations, as well as their impact on promoting social and national programs. The importance of this research also lies in the attempt to shed light on the transition that has taken place in Israeli elite philanthropy in the process of seeking a distinctive identity. This transition is connected to the existing relationship between Jewish and Israeli philanthropy, as well as to the need to provide more incentives for Israeli philanthropists to establish new avenues for their activity such as family, community, and corporate foundations. Research on elite philanthropy is particularly important in light of the major changes that have been taking place in Israeli society. In recent years, Israeli society has been experiencing an ideological transition from a centralist, socialist ideology to a radical liberal ideology, which seeks to reduce the government's role and encourages privatization, contracting out, devolution, and competition. In response to this process, social groups have organized protests and expressed their opposition to the social gaps that have been growing as a result of this policy. In this turbulent context, elite philanthropists can have an impact on policy makers in governmental and non-governmental agencies, as well as on public activists who are concerned with remedying social ills and governmental inefficiencies.

[. . .]

[T]he decisions of elite philanthropists are based more on intuition, past experience with giving, a family tradition of giving, and interpersonal relations with the recipient than on rational, systematic considerations. In light of the results of previous studies, it is known that personal relationships and "chemistry" between the donor and the recipient of the donation play a key role in decisions about giving, above and beyond other factors.

In sum, elite philanthropy in Israel encompasses "old" and "new" philanthropists. In contrast to other philanthropists, these elite philanthropists have a relatively high level of education, and are characterized by a family tradition of giving. Their main motives for giving are a sense of obligation to give back to society in appreciation for being able to attain their status and wealth. Elite philanthropists in Israel also view themselves as playing an important role in the national effort to create a new society. Toward that end, they contribute substantial sums of money, which distinguish them from other philanthropists, who contribute to programs and initiatives that are limited in scope and social impact. The phenomenon of elite philanthropy has various implications for other philanthropists, and for their relationships with the governmental and nonprofit organizations that they contribute to. Elite philanthropy is a spearhead and role model for other philanthropists to increase their contributions and influence social causes in order to improve the well-being of populations at risk and underprivileged citizens. Regarding relationships with the government, because elite philanthropists control large amounts of capital and assets, they are well connected with policy makers at the national and local levels, and can influence them. The concentration of a relatively large share of capital in the hands of an elite group can also cause policy makers and third sector organizations to become dependent on the decisions and actions of those who possess the power.

Nonetheless, [our research] suggest[s] that Israeli elite philanthropists do not view themselves as a substitute for official state institutions, and they often voice criticism about the functioning of public and governmental agencies. The relatively generous contributions of Israeli philanthropists are no substitute for government budgets – nor are they intended as such. The statements of the participants in this survey indicate that Israeli elite philanthropists seek to supplement government activity, to contribute to society in areas where the government has had difficulty responding to the needs of the population, and to put processes in motion where the bureaucratic government encounters red tape.

Philanthropy in the building of modern India

Pushpa Sundar, 2013

One might be tempted to think that Indian philanthropy is either an import from the West or a recent consequence of globalization. In fact, it has played a vital part in the building of modern India, especially in the pre-independence era, and modern India owes much to the many wealthy men and women who were themselves visionaries or supported the visions of India's leaders with their money.

Indian philanthropy has its own unique organic evolution, shaped by its socioeconomic history, culture and political ideologies. Three major factors set it apart from the Western tradition. First, Indian business has its origins in merchant communities in pre-industrialized India, such as the Chettiars, Marwaris, Jains, Banias and Parsis, and has largely been synonymous with family business for much of its history. Second, India was under colonial rule when it industrialized and the struggle to free it from foreign domination left an indelible mark on philanthropy. And third, after independence the Indian state envisioned a mix of private and state enterprise to take it into the modern era. This meant that the state began to play a major role in the economy and in social provisioning but also left space for private players.

Modern Indian philanthropy is rooted in the pre-industrial philanthropic tradition, which was largely motivated by religion and still displays some of its characteristics. It also owed its existence to other drivers, such as the concept of *noblesse oblige* and the fact that there were fewer outlets for wealth at the time. Though wealth was invested in real estate or in good living in ornate houses and a little was spent on secular display, giving to charity offered several benefits.

Charitable giving allowed people to accumulate merit in the life hereafter and was also a good business strategy because of the importance placed on *abru* (reputation, goodwill). Since all transactions were based on oral agreements, building an image as a trustworthy person was very important. There was a saying in the Marwari community: *gayi sakh, rahi rakh* – "If a reputation is lost, then all is lost." Finally, in a society where certain castes could not aspire to higher status in any other way, philanthropy offered a way of gaining social status. Each community, therefore – but especially business communities – had a tradition of setting aside a percentage of income or profits for charity. However, most charity was confined to one's own community, caste or religion, and was ad hoc and ameliorative.

This tradition saw a shift in the middle of the 19th century, with industrialization and the freedom struggle acting as catalysts. This period marks the beginning of modern philanthropy in India.

Industrialization and modernization – new impulses for philanthropy

Industrialization influenced Indian philanthropy in several ways. First, it created fortunes far surpassing any made before, so the economic surplus available for public welfare was on a scale hitherto unmatched. Second, several of the business dynasties established at the time laid the foundation of a philanthropic tradition which was adhered to and enhanced by succeeding generations. Third, by extending business activity to several locations beyond the home city, industrialization extended philanthropic giving beyond the traditional boundaries of city, caste, community and religion.

This period also saw a change in the causes philanthropy addressed. Industrialization was the outcome of a vision of creating an India radically different from the one the industrial pioneers had known and of a desire to assert the Indian potential. They asked what deficiencies in Indian society had led to India's subjugation by the British and concluded that modern science and technology had given the West an edge. Their philanthropic activities accordingly became a means of making good this deficit.

Finally, this period also changed the underlying motivations for philanthropy. The activities of Christian missionaries and the introduction of Western education exposed Indian society to new ideas which changed the values and outlook of Indians. The ideal of a democratic society that would ensure the welfare of all its members replaced religious motivation as the basis for legal and social reform.

Social reform included campaigns for the abolition of *sati* [a tradition among certain Indian communities which would see widows immolate themselves as their husband was cremated] and dowry, widow remarriage, women's education, intermarriage between castes, Hindu-Muslim unity, and improvement of the lot of untouchables. Simultaneously, there was a revival of pride in Indian culture which led to an interest in development of vernacular literatures, revival of Indian art, research into Indian history, study of classical languages, and promotion of classical music.

There was also a spurt in the growth of an associational culture in the form of Western-style societies (e.g. the Bombay Native Education Society and the Servants of India Society) and institutions such as the Benaras Hindu University. The organizations which emerged needed funds and offered the wealthy new opportunities for charity. Simultaneously, British rulers of the 19th century believed that progress lay in Indians adopting English-style institutions – schools, colleges, hospitals, public libraries and museums – and encouraged philanthropy for these causes by offering titles and light taxation.

The early pioneers of industry took an active interest in this associational culture and in public life. The outcome was that charity became more substantial, more secular, more institutionalized and more inclusive. Thus encouraged, India's philanthropists went about building some of the country's most important institutions.

Education was a favored cause, especially education for girls. For instance, Jagannath Shankarshet (1803–65) started many schools for girls and campaigned for female education against great opposition from the conservative members of his community. He was responsible for founding the Native School of Bombay in 1824, a direct precursor to the Elphinstone College (of which Jamsetji Tata was an alumnus), and also made large contributions to modern institutions such as the Grant Medical College and the Victoria Museum and Gardens (one of the oldest zoos in India).

Other businessmen gave large donations too. Kavasji Jehangir Readymoney (1812–78) gave donations for Mumbai University and hospitals totaling INR 14 lakhs. Premchand

Roychand (born 1831) gave handsomely, to the tune of INR 60 lakhs, and helped fund Mumbai University and Kolkata University, the Gujarat vernacular College at Ahmedabad, and the Rajabai clock tower, later annexed to the Mumbai University library.

One of the most renowned philanthropists and self-made merchants of Mumbai at the time was Jamsetji Jeejeebhoy, or "J. J." (1783–1859), who is estimated to have donated over GBP £230,000 to charity by the time of his death. Sir J. J. endowed the first civil hospital (the Sir J. J. Hospital), the first obstetric institution, and the first arts college (the J. J. School of Art). At the insistence of Lady Jamsetji, he built the Lady Jamsetji (or Mahim) Causeway in 1845, after many lives were lost as a result of boats capsizing while crossing the Mahim creek during the rains. Until the Bandra-Worli Sea Link opened in 2009, the Mahim Causeway was, for over 150 years, the only road connecting the western suburbs to Mumbai's central district.

In Chennai, one of the greatest of the early philanthropists was Pachaiyappa Mudaliar (1754–94), whose bequest was used to set up the first private college in Chennai – Pachaiyappa's College. Rajah Sir Annamalai Chettiar gave a new direction to the charitable activities of his community, which hitherto had been largely religion-oriented, by establishing hospitals, schools, dispensaries and colleges throughout Chettinad and in Chennai.

This period also saw a change in the way charity was dispensed. Like their counterparts in the West, the newly rich business families began to set up and use trusts for their charitable programmes. One of the first foundations in India, pre-dating most large modern Western foundations, was the N. M. Wadia Foundation, set up in 1909 for the benefit of all, irrespective of creed or community – a fact for which he incurred the displeasure of his Parsi community.

The man who is credited with having made the most lasting contribution of all was Sir Jamsetji Tata. Tata was exercised about the use of wealth at the same time as Carnegie and Rockefeller and voiced opinions remarkably similar to Carnegie's:

> What advances a nation or community is not so much to prop up its weakest and most helpless members as to lift up the best and most gifted so as to make them of the greatest service to the country. I prefer this constructive philanthropy which seeks to educate and develop the faculties of the best of our young men.

Tata launched the J. N. Tata Endowment Scheme in 1892, long before the first major foundation appeared in America. In 1894 he set aside 14 of his large buildings and four landed properties to create an endowment for a postgraduate university of science and technology. His offer was taken up only after his death and used to create the Indian Institute of Science in Bangalore, on the lines of the Johns Hopkins University in Baltimore. It pioneered advanced scientific education in India.

Later, Tata's sons continued this tradition and set up their own foundations, which in turn endowed many modern institutions. The Sir Dorabji Tata Trust created the Tata Memorial Centre for Cancer Treatment and Research, which in 1966 was merged into the national government's Tata Memorial Centre; and in 1936 it created the Sir Dorabji Tata Graduate School of Social Work, India's oldest social sciences institute [now known as the Tata Institute of Social Sciences]. In 1945, after Sir Dorabji's death, his trust helped set up the Tata Institute of Fundamental Research (TIFR) for work on atomic energy, another institution that was later taken over by the government.

Freedom and the building of modern India

The freedom struggle, and Gandhi's leadership of it, in the early 20th century was another turning point. It was at this period that philanthropists began to extend their focus beyond endowing institutions to changing mindsets and promoting skills, especially with a view to uplifting the rural masses. Gandhi's theory of trusteeship influenced many of the leading businessmen to give for public causes.

Inaugurating the annual session of the Federation of Indian Chambers of Commerce and Industry in 1931, Gandhi exhorted businessmen: "You should regard yourself as the trustees and servants of the poor. Your commerce must be regulated for the benefit of the toiling millions and you must be satisfied with earning an honest penny." In the following years he would caution them further: "Earn your crores by all means. But understand that your wealth is not yours; it belongs to the people. Take what you require for your legitimate needs, and use the remainder for society."

The richest of India's mill-owners came under the spell of Gandhi, and heeding his call for trusteeship of wealth, they opened their purse strings for his myriad causes. Jamnalal Bajaj and G. D. Birla, two of the country's foremost industrialists of the time, were particularly influenced. They put themselves and their wealth at the disposal of Gandhi not only for the freedom movement but also for his constructive programme of removal of untouchability, popularization of *khadi* [handspun cloth promoted by Gandhi as a means for generating self-employment and self-reliance] and village industries, promotion of basic education and Hindu-Muslim unity.

G. D. Birla initiated a philanthropic programme unmatched by any one business individual in its breadth, catholicity, holistic vision and geographical outreach. The best known of the institutions founded by him is the Birla Institute of Technology (now a university) at Pilani, modeled on the Massachusetts Institute of Technology. He gave both to the Aligarh Muslim University and to the Benaras Hindu University. The exact amount donated by Birla for Gandhi's causes has never been calculated but, according to his biographers, the amount ran into millions of rupees.

When India became free, the independent state looked to the business community to propel the country to a prosperous future, and in the euphoria of independence the business class responded both by creating more wealth and by utilizing it for non-business purposes. Whereas in the earlier period only a few large Western-style trusts had been set up, the immediate post-independence period witnessed a proliferation of trusts, foundations and other charitable institutions.

Kasturbhai Lalbhai of Ahmedabad contributed to the establishment of the Physical Research Laboratory, the "cradle of space sciences" in India and today a national research institute for space and allied sciences. He also supported the setting-up of the Indian Institute of Management, Ahmedabad, consistently ranked as one of the best business schools in India and Asia. In Delhi, Lala Shri Ram, the founder of the DCM Group and nicknamed the College King, set up some of the most important colleges for technical education and for women that still stand, including the Shri Ram College of Commerce and, in memory of his wife, the Lady Shri Ram College for Girls. He set up the Commercial Education Trust (CET) in 1920 with a corpus of INR 2 lakhs, and the Shri Ram Charitable Trust in 1932, by contributing INR 12 lakhs initially, followed by an annual contribution of INR 1 lakh.

Constraints of space forbid fuller coverage of all the other great philanthropists who laid the foundation for a modern India, but among them mention should be made of

Kuppuswamy Naidu and the Murugappa Group in the south; Kamalapat and Lakshmipat Singhania and Gujarmal Modi in the north; and P. D. Agarwal, Goenkas and Kanorias in Kolkata. All contributed to the institutional efflorescence of the time.

A final thought

Today we tend to forget that philanthropy played a vital role in building modern India, whether in terms of ideas, institutions or innovations, but one has only to look at the physical and institutional facilities of most cities – parks, drinking-water stands, auditoria and halls, planetariums, hospitals, museums and art galleries – to appreciate this contribution. Private philanthropy also led the way in supporting new fields of endeavor – girls' education, art, engineering, commercial and technical education, textile technology, management, and scientific and medical research. The state later used the experience and expertise so gained to widen the field and disseminate the gains more widely. This contribution of philanthropy should be celebrated.

Philanthropy in Latin America

Cynthia A. Sanborn, 2005

Persistent poverty amidst great wealth, denial of basic rights amidst formal democracy, profound and morally intolerable inequality: these conditions characterize much of Latin America today. For this reason, numerous leaders in global philanthropy have argued that closing the gap between rich and poor, and empowering the latter, are the more important challenges for this sector in the 21st century. But does this not pose a fundamental contradiction? Is it realistic to expect that those who have benefited from the unequal distribution of wealth and rights are going to promote, or even permit, a change in this situation?

In fact, giving and volunteering to help the needy and advance the common good is nothing new in Latin America. The cultural diversity of the region's more than 500 million people is reflected in their many traditions of reciprocity and community self-help, religious and immigrant solidarity, as well as in trade unionism and grassroots movements to challenge the status quo. Furthermore, since the early 1990s, there have been increased efforts in the region to promote new forms of organized philanthropy aimed at achieving lasting social change. Such efforts are being led by international donors and aid agencies, religious organizations and educational institutions, as well as local government and corporate figures.

[. . .]

Existing research does indeed show that new private giving has been aimed at addressing some priority social problems in Latin America, including education and community development. The persistence of religious charity and *asistencialismo* (or basic service provision), understandable in a region where states alone are incapable of meeting basic needs, has been joined by growing interest among some members of the economic elite in finding longer-lasting solutions to hunger, poverty and violence.

At the same time, much of the new philanthropy in Latin America is still scattered and limited in its impact and capacity to achieve its proposed objectives. Additionally, an important share of private giving remains directed toward activities that primarily benefit – and reproduce – social elites themselves, including support for private schools and universities, wealthy parishes, fine arts institutions, and scientific and cultural events. Such patterns of giving are similar to those in developed countries, and undeniably support worthy initiatives. Nevertheless, in societies with profound social gaps and serious limitations in public resources and capacity, these patterns provoke the suspicions of government authorities regarding the civic virtues of philanthropy, and explain their reluctance in many cases to promote it thorough public policy, tax or legal or tax initiatives.

[. . .]

Charity and solidarity: philanthropic traditions in Latin America

The inhabitants of this region have longstanding and diverse traditions of charity and solidarity, making it difficult to speak of "Latin American philanthropy" as though it were a homogeneous block. Nonetheless, it is possible to identify some tendencies and experiences common to a large part – if not all – of this region.

The Catholic Church and Christian charity

It is not surprising that the Catholic Church has played a central role in the history of philanthropy, given that between 80 and 95 percent of Latin Americans consider themselves of the Catholic faith. During the Colonial period, the Church was the principal provider of education, health and social welfare services, and it controlled virtually all of the existing charitable entities. Financed by the colonial government and wealthy elites, Church-provided social assistance was for centuries provided to groups of the poor, in a paternalistic manner and in explicit support of the colonial power structure.

The predominance of the Church in the charitable sphere lasted through the 19th century and the greater part of the 20th. Nevertheless, it would be incorrect to consider the Church's varied activities as a continuum of the colonial model. During the 20th century in particular, the stance of the Catholic Church in Latin America on social issues evolved from a conservative and elitist position toward a preferential identification with the poor and a defense of equitable development and social justice. This turnaround in focus was also reflected in the methods of the different educational and social welfare entities associated with the Church. Furthermore, during the 20th century, important social movements were inspired by the ideals of the new Liberation Theology, and a considerable number of Catholic activists were founders and members of grassroots organizations, NGOs and human rights groups. Although there have always been divisions within the Church concerning the scope and objectives of religiously inspired social work, at the end of the 20th century almost all doctrinal positions within the Church were reflected in hands-on initiatives with preferential concern for the poor.

The state and central governments

While predominance of the Catholic Church is a historical characteristic of Latin American philanthropy, another is the controlling role played by the state and central governments. During the 19th century, an important component in the creation of new national states was the effort of governments to centralize power and take control over social services. In Argentina, Brazil, Uruguay and Mexico, a formal separation between state and church took place, and in most countries the state progressively assumed various social functions that had previously been assigned to religious authorities.

Nonetheless, with the exception of Uruguay, the Church maintained considerable power and a notable presence in the social arena as an ally of the state and the local (*criolla*) elite. Yet this was not the case with other forms of private organization. Despite the existence of associative experiences with longstanding traditions, many analysts contend that the creation of organized and consolidated civil societies was subsequent to the creation of independent states in this region, and was strongly conditioned by the same. Moreover, there are those who argue that "modern" civil society in Latin America has developed principally in reaction to the actions and policies of the state.

In regard to the 20th century, the formulation and implementation of diverse social policies on the part of national states must be understood in the context of the general development models that were introduced. While considerable variation existed between countries, for the most part, between the 1930s and 1960s Latin American governments promoted forms of industrialization through protectionist trade policies and the substation of imports by locally produced goods (known as ISI). These actions privileged and protected the growth of a national industrial sector and internal markets, and motivated the creation of urban interest groups made up of working- and middle-class members interested in promoting diverse forms of social services. In this respect, expanded public health and education systems allowed for greater coverage and entailed centralization control and administration. Even today, in the wake of neo-liberalism, the education and health services provided by private entities in most countries cover only a reduced segment of the total population. Of the latter, however, the Catholic Church continues to be the privileged partner of the state in the administration of services for the poor.

The economic and social elite

If the state and the church dominated the realm of social welfare, what has been the role of the region's social and economic elites? The involvement of the wealth in charitable activities during colonial rule and for much of the Independence period was characterized by a paternalistic style inspired by religious motivations and self-interest. The Societies of Public Benefit (*Sociedades de Beneficiencia Pública*) were a leading form of private involvement in social welfare, in which conspicuous members of the upper classes managed the provision of various welfare services. Subsequently, during the ISI period, modernizing sectors of the bourgeoisie became the force behind the creation of new private universities, technical institutions and foundations aimed at promoting national development. Encouraged by the US-sponsored Alliance for Progress in some cases, these private sector initiatives also included diverse campaigns in benefit of the poorer and more excluded sectors of the population. Nevertheless, in societies marked by longstanding discrimination and social exclusion, the generosity of the elite did not always extend to the acceptance of universal suffrage and full citizenship rights for the broader population.

Migrants and immigrants

In the late 19th and early 20th centuries, two trends had a significant impact on both civil society and philanthropy in this region: new waves of immigrants from Europe and Asia, and the accelerated flow of migrants from rural areas to the cities. Fleeing from economic poverty and from political or ethnic persecution, waves of Italian, Spanish, Chinese and Japanese immigrants arrived in Latin America, as well as important numbers of European Jews. Each immigrant group established diverse types of mutual aid societies, schools, hospitals and charitable organizations, aimed at providing collective assistance and preserving their cultural traditions. European immigrants also encouraged the creation of trade unions and mass-based political parties in the region.

Weak liberal political traditions

Another factor that bears on the nature of philanthropy is the weakness of liberal political tradition in this region. Although Latin American countries vary in their political histories, and limited forms of democracy flourished early in some societies, authoritarian and populist regimes have been the predominant conduits for exercising state power. These types of regimes have tended to combine the creation or co-option of officially sanctioned social organizations, with the direct repression or indirect control of more autonomous forms of civic association. In some cases, these regimes have achieved important advances in income distribution and social welfare benefits, especially toward better-organized urban labor and professional groups (Peronism in Argentina and the PRI in Mexico are cases in point). Nevertheless, these schemes also involved strict state regulation of society, still partial degrees of political citizenship and social inclusion, and few incentives for – or outright suspicion of – philanthropic initiatives from outside a narrow religious ambit.

The role of international cooperation

Between the 1960s and the 1980s, a wave of new military dictatorships arose in South America, characterized not only by their radical suppression of popular uprisings and armed opposition groups, but also by their modernizing projects for development and state reform. In this context, new organizations for the defense of human rights and social justice also emerged, with strong support in some countries by Catholic Church authorities, including Brazil and Chile, in open confrontation with the authoritarian regimes. The existence of international humanitarian aid and development assistance was also essential for sustaining these activities, because in many cases the local philanthropic elite supported these regimes and looked the other way during the worst periods of state violence. It is important to highlight the role played by international religious agencies of different faiths, such as Catholic Relief Services, Misereor, World Relief and World Vision (the latter two being Protestant) and the World Council of Churches. The Ford Foundation, the Inter-American Foundation and diverse European donors provided significant international aid to refugees and victims of military dictatorships during the 1970s and 1980s.

With the return of civilian rule in most of the region by the late 1980s, international donors continued to be a fundamental source of support for those civil society organizations that defended the consolidation and expansion of democracy, social justice for the poor, and the extension of equal rights and opportunities to women, ethnic minorities and other excluded groups. With few exceptions, for the most part these were objectives that the economic elite were not ready to support and from which most national donors maintained a prudent distance [. . .] [I]nternational aid also remained a key source of support for the social programs sponsored by the Catholic Church in Latin America from the 1980s onward, replacing or complementing available public sudsidies.

As the decade of the 1990s began, therefore, the philanthropic panorama of Latin America included a variety of actors and institutional forms that ranged from the traditional religious charity to new forms of solidarity and support for social justice. Also evident was the persistence of the central state as the predominant provider of basic services, the role of the Catholic Church as the privileged ally of the state in various social tasks, and a still incipient presence of private elites in the philanthropic sphere.

[. . .]

Final reflections

Latin American philanthropy has increased in scope, scale and ambition in recent years, attempting to address a wide variety of public and private concerns. As discussed, much of this activity remains scattered and relatively ineffective at bringing about significant social change – and much of it does not even attempt to do so. Yet encouraging examples continue to emerge. Today there are private foundations supporting peace in war-torn Colombia, and waging war on child exploitation in Brazil. There are business leaders who advocate for education policy reform, as well as supporting poor schools and giving scholarships to promising youths. There are large companies that invest in the long-term development – and political empowerment – of the communities in which they operate. We also find wealthy individuals who look beyond their immediate families and endow organizations that aim to change society on a broader scale, and middle-class professionals who pool their savings to support the causes they believe in. These are all exceptions. Yet through study and dissemination of such efforts, we can identify best practice and draw lessons for others to follow.

How can such efforts be more effective? Research and practice in Latin America suggest that in order to strengthen those philanthropic initiatives that aim to close the social gap, it is necessary to build alliances in which the public sector can participate as an active and legitimate partner. Likewise, it is indispensable that wealthy donors be willing to reflect on the causes of the social problems plaguing Latin America, and to seek greater coherence and effectiveness in their efforts to resolve such problems. It is also fundamental to strengthen other groups in civil society, especially among the poor and marginal, and convert their members into citizens who are carriers of rights and responsibilities, not just recipients of charity. It is only through these means that the beneficiaries of philanthropy will become active partners, capable of making their voices heard on public agendas and participating in alliances for lasting change.

2.4 The role of religion, race, gender and geography

Philanthropy in the world's traditions

Warren F. Ilchman, Stanley N. Katz and Edward L. Queen II, 1998

[Note from the editors: As this reading is the introduction to an edited collection of chapters on "philanthropy in the world's traditions," it makes reference to the overall book and to the authors and contributions therein.]

This book represents a significant addition to the comparative study of philanthropy and culture. In no other volume have a variety of area specialists been asked to turn their attention to the role of philanthropy – of giving and sharing beyond the family – in the life of a particular culture at a particular time. That so little attention has been paid to this subject is surprising. One need only consider the role that philanthropy has played in defining and sustaining numerous religious traditions, e.g., Buddhism, in the establishment of a wide range of educational and cultural institutions, and, perhaps most visibly, the construction of innumerable public buildings and facilities – roads, khans, fountains, etc. The sheer magnitude of this construction undertaken throughout history should have made that activity a prime candidate for study. However, such has not been the case.

The presumption at the outset of this work was that something called "philanthropy" – rooted in the ethical notions of giving and serving to those beyond one's family – probably existed in most cultures and in most historical periods, and that it often was driven by religious traditions. In making this presumption, however, we recognized the difficulty in choosing an appropriate generic term for the activities we hoped to examine. In dealing with many cultures in a variety of historical periods, the editors realized that we would run up against the problem of overidentifying what was culturally possible. Just as it would be inappropriate to condemn those in the fourteenth century for failing to make the necessary hygienic responses to the outbreak of the Black Death, so it would be inappropriate to look for nineteenth-/twentieth-century North Atlantic understandings of philanthropy in other times and places. For that reason, we have dispensed with the charity/philanthropy distinction. The distinction is of recent invention, linked with a belief in instrumental rationality, progress, and professionalization. Absent these realities, as well as the existence of the modern state, either the distinction makes no sense, or there can be no philanthropy. All that would be left for the subject matter of these essays would be charity, good deeds, and beneficence. This may be a valid way of approaching the issue, but it leaves open the question of what generic term identifies these seemingly related activities. We decided, therefore, to retain "philanthropy" as the most useful term to connect this set of behaviors and activities sharing marked family resemblances. Certainly in many ways it is a vague abstraction, but so are "the state," "the law," and "religion" and we find ways to talk about them.

Although there remain ragged edges where clarity eludes us, we usually find these concepts understandable and useful both in ordinary language and in academic discourse. There is no reason why philanthropy should be any less useful.

In this volume "philanthropy," understood primarily as activities of voluntary giving and serving to others beyond one's family, is the collective term. In using it we owe a debt to Robert Payton's definition of philanthropy as "voluntary action for the public good." Encompassing as it does the activities of voluntary giving, voluntary service, and voluntary association, this definition helps us analyze the role philanthropy plays in different cultures and in people's attempts to realize their understandings of the good through actions or donations. One of the significant results is that philanthropic acts become the preeminent means by which people attempt to realize their understanding of cultural values, to practice what their culture preaches.

People's attempts to realize these values through giving and serving often can be fraught with controversy and peril, especially when others view them as "factional" or when rulers interpret the activities as assaults upon the legitimacy or adequacy of their rule or as attempts to elevate oneself at the ruler's expense. These issues serve as a clear reminder that philanthropy as a public phenomenon is not always viewed as good by everyone.

The task assigned to the various authors as specialists was to discern the distinctive form that philanthropy took in different historical periods and in different cultures, to describe the ways in which it worked, to articulate why it was formed this way or these ways, and, if possible, to address the relative importance of philanthropy within the culture and its predominant religious tradition. As these latter sentences suggest, we assumed that philanthropy was not a free-floating activity separated from the complex elements of the societies in which it resided, but was influenced, indeed structured, by the specificity of particular cultures.

In making this assumption we acted upon a particular set of understandings about culture, namely that culture is not primarily "complexes of behavior patterns," but "a set of control mechanisms – plans, recipes, rules, instructions – for the governing of behavior." Members of particular cultures internalize these rules and then live their lives through them so that, to a great extent, culture becomes learned behavior or, perhaps more precisely, the learning of rules for determining behavior. This assumption made it imperative that the beginning of a study of the ways in which philanthropy operated in different cultures required a strong grounding in their specificity.

By focusing on philanthropy as socially and historically conditioned, we believed that the collection of essays could help us get a better handle on how to talk about philanthropy cross-culturally. Additionally, it would give us a deeper and more nuanced understanding of philanthropy as a phenomenon and make us more capable of seeing it in both its universal and particular aspects. Emphasizing the social and cultural roots of philanthropy enables us to see how philanthropic activities are related to people's conceptions of a good society, or a good life, making it possible to ask questions about what activities people undertake, absent state coercion or familial obligation, to effect some goal or purpose they believe is necessary for the achievement of a good society or a good life. The answers to those questions illuminate how the specific conditions of given societies call forth different philanthropic responses or, at least, color how philanthropic activities are perceived. Knowing this enables us to deal seriously with the fact that significant philanthropic activities in some societies might look fairly peculiar to people from other societies. A possible example of this is the voluntary association for the saving of animals.

These organizations emerge from a particular vision of how society ought to be, in this instance a place where animals are not killed and are treated well. These activities rooted in the doctrine of *ahimsa*, would be major philanthropic activities in cultures deeply influenced by Hinduism and Buddhism.

Centering on the values of a society or culture also can help us to understand why, for example, the establishment of madrasas – teaching academies – was a preeminent purpose of the various *waqfs*, or foundations in Islamic societies. *Madrasas* helped to realize a basic good central to social identity, the strengthening of Islam. One can easily see how the understanding of what philanthropy can be is rooted in a particular cosmological vision, a point suggested in many of the essays and one which John A. Grim's essay argues directly. This point also explains the centrality of religion.

[. . .]

As a preeminent source of rules and principles for the living of lives, the religious constructions of philanthropy appear to have a particularly powerful resonance that manifests itself across cultures.

Although some have written about the role of philanthropy, of giving and serving, in the lives of various cultures – of their attention to the needs of the weak, the poor, and the stranger – little sustained attention has been devoted to the issue. Certainly some scholars have addressed the issues of giving, serving, and patronage, but few have struggled to understand a particular culture's understanding of philanthropy itself and its role in the culture. In this volume the various authors have undertaken that struggle – trying to understand the role of philanthropy in particular cultures at particular times and attempting to understand it as an integral part of the culture while describing the ways in which its forms reflected that culture's values.

What is reflected, however, varies immensely depending upon the mirror's direction. In Said Arjomand's essay it reflects the multiple goals of certain local elites who worked to maintain their status by donating funds to a culturally valued purpose – the support of Islam – and to do so in a manner that furthered their preferred method, legal interpretation, or instruction. This was done through a culturally and legally sanctioned form, the *waqf*, that received its status because of its prescription by the founder of Islam as the preferred method of supporting charitable activities.

Another issue that figures in several of the essays is the problem, both factually for the donors and conceptually for scholars, that emerges in states where the donative activities of elites are nearly inseparable from their governance functions as allocators of resources. For the donors this means that little could be done to protect their gifts from the predations of those regimes or individuals who succeeded them, especially through violence or conquest. The continuation of those institutions would have attested to the validity and even success of their predecessors, a situation that many successors found unacceptable.

For scholars of philanthropy it forces them to be clear, conceptually, on the fact that such contemporary distinctions as private, as opposed to government or dynastic, monies are fairly recent. As many of the authors struggled with a working definition of philanthropy, one element that presented itself was the inordinate emphasis placed upon the distinction between public and private or, more correctly, state and non-state in most contemporary discussions of philanthropy. Since many of these authors focused on dynastic or patrimonial states, where the issue of what belonged to the ruler as an individual and what as a sovereign is murky, the relativity of this distinction became quite evident. While the inadequacy of the public/private distinction for the pre-modern period should have been clear to anyone who worked in the history of medieval or early modern Europe, the fact was highlighted by bringing in the comparative dimension.

The mirror also tends to reflect powerful underlying cultural assumptions, many of which are not and often cannot be directly articulated. This comes out quite vividly in Adele Lindenmeyr's essay when she discusses the Russian term for objects of charity. The word, *neschastnye*, generically meaning unfortunates and applied specifically to beggars, criminals, convicts, and the poor as a whole, suggests a particular cultural understanding about misfortune – namely that it is random, undeserved, and likely to afflict anyone. Additionally, the existence of prisoners as appropriate objects of philanthropy, both under the tsars and the Communists, while undoubtedly owing much to the particular Orthodox understandings of duty and to a historical context in which the ransoming of prisoners taken in war or by pirates still had some vitality, seems also to argue for a general cultural view that imprisonment was not (necessarily) deserved but a random event that, like impoverishment, could strike anyone at any time. Charity/philanthropy toward prisoners, therefore, often could be seen as a challenge to the fundamental legitimacy of the state in imprisoning these people. Certainly the prison narratives of many political prisoners saw it that way as did the state, especially during the Soviet terror when any act of compassion toward an "enemy of the people" was punished severely.

These essays also show that philanthropy does not simply reflect a culture but the struggles and contexts in which a culture finds itself and of struggles between cultures. Like many other arenas it becomes a location where cultural values and norms are contested. The way philanthropy is done, the way it is structured, and its preferred objects often become battlegrounds for other issues. This becomes clear in several of the essays. In Derek J. Penslar's essay the theme is the way philanthropy becomes a process by which donors to and administrators of philanthropic enterprises attempt to transform, in a substantive way, the existing cultural reality. In the essay by Mark Juergensmeyer and Darrin M. McMahon we read how individuals attempting to act on certain personal values and goals find themselves caught up in conflicts in which they have no interest and identified as aiding people and purposes with whom they have no shared interests or concerns. This is extended in Gregory C. Kozlowski's and Amanda Porterfield's essays as they show how philanthropy can further certain purposes outside of particular cultures often taking on a transnational reach, by attempting to transform other peoples and other cultures or to bring certain cultural practices more in line with the desires of the donors.

A further element that permeates many of these essays and which deserves significantly more attention is the conception of the autonomy of the individual that lies behind the idea that individuals can choose those activities and organizations to which they give their money and their attention. Additionally, the presumption of inviolability of gifts that exists in several of these cultures, despite this often being factually violated, presents some idea about limitations on state power and the significance of the wishes of the individual. These facts imply something important about the role of philanthropy as the means by which individuals realize their values. The conflict between the attempts of individuals to do this and the ruling powers, between individuals and the state, suggests that philanthropic activities might play a significant role in the formation of civil society. Civil society here must be understood as that place where and those activities which individuals undertake to realize values and goals of importance to them. These activities also suggest some fundamental limitations or gaps in the state's abilities or its right to interfere with these activities, although this limitation historically has been recognized mostly in the breach. If these interpretations are valid, there remains significant work to be done on the relationship between a religious tradition's understandings of philanthropy and the ease with which the culture where it is predominant can develop a full-blown civil society. Linked with these ideas is the idea of accepting unknown others as legitimate. If civil society is the place where people struggle to realize their understandings of the good there must be the acceptance of others and their ability to pursue their values if the society is not to be constantly rent by violence. This giving of trust and acceptance, whether through necessity or conviction, constitutes a major basis of civil society as the realm or sphere where individuals undertake voluntary actions in concert with others to realize their vision of the public good.

Certainly this constitutes a subtext in many of these essays. As one reads through them it becomes obvious that the ways in which people try to realize certain values occasionally constitutes a contestation about the way in which the world should be constructed. People often must undertake these activities in the face of opposition by the ruling powers. The ways in which state apparatuses have acted to hinder and limit these activities or to control and channel them well demonstrates the truth of this claim. This suggests a need for more extended and detailed pursuit of these questions within specific traditions. Can one ask whether it has been the very pluriformity of Hinduism that has helped make India a relatively well-functioning democracy despite its innumerable difficulties and problems? Has not the history of multiple answers to religious questions constructed an ethos that enables Indians to live with the plurality and ambiguity that liberal democracy demands in a way that the Confucian tradition in China has perhaps helped to mitigate against? Certainly questions like this often make scholars apoplectic, especially when they seem to suggest failings in cultures and traditions for which long hours of study and reflection have generated much affection. If comparative studies are to have any value, however, they must indeed begin to address the significant question of what difference does difference make? Do certain traditions have a more expansive view of philanthropy than others? Is philanthropy more central, more defining, to certain traditions? Do particular cultural understandings lead more directly to institutionalization of philanthropy? How distinctive are the rationales and rhetoric within different traditions? This book, we believe, can begin to make it possible to ask such probing questions and to suggest directions for future research. This book, therefore, must in the end be seen not as the final word, but as the first word. The essays by grounding the study of philanthropy and culture in specific times and places serve to illuminate and expand our understandings of philanthropy and the activity of studying it. In doing this, however, they raise for all of us new and exciting questions which we hope these and other scholars will pursue more fully in the future.

Race and philanthropy

Sudhir Alladi Venkatesh, 2002

In Spring 2001, the Institute for Research in African-American Studies at Columbia University sponsored a two-day conference on the relationship of American philanthropy to communities of color. As the Race and Philanthropy event wore on, it became clear that there is little widespread understanding of the ways in which philanthropic practice is, and has been, a deeply politicized practice. Foundation program officers, progressive funders, staffers at community-based organizations, and policymakers debated vigorously about the impact of philanthropy on race relations, community empowerment, and civic responsibility. Many who visited the sessions remarked that they had no idea that the practices of helping and giving money could be so contested – and so racially motivated.

Is this naiveté? Hardly. Think back to the days before September 11, 2001. Until that date, notwithstanding the hard work of the National Center for Responsive Philanthropy, the National Center for Black Philanthropy, and other critical voices, public perceptions of philanthropy tended to focus on the generosity of (typically white male) captains of industry. With the need to assist families, workers, and businesses deeply affected by the World Trade Center attacks, there has now emerged critical dialogue about who is authorized to allocate the charitable resources. Which persons (displaced workers, widows, orphans, small businesses, etc.) should receive what type of support? Why should certain recipients (e.g., the airlines and pharmaceutical industries) benefit from public largesse, while others (undocumented and displaced workers, less politically powerful businesses) should be neglected, or worse, suffer harassment. Race and ethnicity are emerging as central in this drama: Governments rescue industries, most controlled by powerful whites with tax credits and direct aid; but countless stories of (nonwhite) immigrant-owned businesses closing because of inadequate assistance pepper the media. The missing and deceased came from more than 100 countries, and there are many who are working in this country without proper documentation, typically from Central American countries, and without adequate wages and health care. One of our greatest challenges will be to allocate public, charitable, and philanthropic resources in a way that both acknowledges the racial and ethnic dimension of the tragedies, but does not invidiously privilege the tolls taken by members of one or another segment of the populace.

This present moment is serving as a period of reflection, questioning, and assessment of many of our cherished social institutions, ranging from civil and constitutional rights to immigration policies and public health systems. It should also serve as a period in which to critically examine the practice of philanthropy, particularly how our charity and not-for-profit institutions are shaped by and, in turn, shape our understanding of race and ethnicity.

Historically, the role of philanthropy in communities of color has been complex and at times contentious. This is to be expected since, for any group or community, the practice of giving fosters a wide range of relationships, not all of which are benevolent. Philanthropic intent may be directed by the laudable motives of promoting empowerment and providing basic goods and services to those in need. Yet, it can quite easily lead to the loss of self-determination on the part of the recipient and/or the receiving community. Short-run assistance may, in the long run, undermine personal and collective capacities for self-sustenance and self-determination.

The Race and Philanthropy conference examined many of the present conundrums and pitfalls of philanthropic practice, while suggesting new and innovative directions that foundations, donors, and advocates and policymakers could take to ensure a more responsive and responsible posture in relation to those in need. Most presentations were made by individuals who are working in the not-for-profit sector and who are thinking critically about the role of race in philanthropy. Not all are academics, in the strict sense of individuals working in institutions of higher education. But, even the members of the professoriate, like John Powell and Alice O'Connor, speak from years of tireless work with foundations and donors to ensure that race relations remains at the forefront of their thinking.

For many, the term "philanthropy" tends to conjure up images of the modern, beneficent, and bureaucratic not-for-profit organization bestowing its riches on the poor and needy. It is rarely thought of as a conflictual or troubled field. For persons of color, however, philanthropy has a long and deeply politicized history. Consider, as one example, black Americans. For several hundred years, there has been a strong, well-documented tradition of sharing and collective action within African-American circles aimed at redressing needs, fostering advancement, and promoting liberty and equality. In fact, in most cases, these initiatives have been outside the scope of a formal organizational entity – like a government agency, charity, or foundation. Instead, benevolent societies and secretive associations, surreptitious and clandestine networks, all indigenous to the black community and under the radar of landowners, state officials, and whites generally, have been under charity's auspices. Indeed, until the mid-twentieth century, whether by custom or law, black Americans were excluded from numerous social institutions, ranging from marriage and commerce to electoral politics. In this context, philanthropy became a complex practice, at once charitable, deeply politicized, and often in a climate of opposition and resistance. The Underground Railroad, funeral associations, religious and healing societies, and various forms of extended kin and peer networks are some of the best-known examples of self-help collectives that thrived in slave and free communities.

Much of contemporary thought on philanthropy may be traced to the germinal period between World War II and the 1960s. During this time, philanthropic actors forged a relationship to communities of color, the spirit of which remains in place. Perhaps most important, the organization of charity and giving had a contradictory relationship with political action and social advancement. Philanthropists and foundations that gave willingly in the black community (and the sympathetic leaders who worked with them) tried to adopt a politically neutral stance; they preferred to frame their work as charity instead of participatory in social movements. Indeed, they often explicitly refused to support outright "political" initiatives. As the demands of black communities grew louder and more militant, the refusal of larger philanthropists to support grassroots efforts spoke loudly to philanthropy's alignment with liberal and corporate America.

Other significant developments during this time period included the formation of a "brokerage" class, typically conservative persons of color who mediated between the predominantly white world of government and foundations and the dispossessed communities of color whose interests they were supposed to represent. Instead of funding outright political movements, foundations recruited so-called grassroots or community-based leaders who could legitimize their wish to support more liberal, reformist initiatives. The dampening of politics and the need for philanthropists to recruit "brokers" qua voices of legitimation within communities of color remain two of the most pressing obstacles in the struggle to make philanthropy more effective.

Today, a renewed spirit of "collaboration" and "reform" has invested in philanthropic practice in relation to communities of color. As America witnesses the pullback of government services and, correlatively, the increased reliance on charity, volunteerism, and grant making as a means to respond to social hardships, it is imperative to understand the role that philanthropic and not-for-profit actors will play in attempts to promote social betterment. Their influence, historically, in shaping the discourse on American race relations has been clear, and, as the country continues to grow more heterogeneous, it is likely that influence of not-for-profit actors on our understanding of race will only expand.

Women in philanthropy

Kathleen D. McCarthy, 2001

[Note from the editors: As this reading is the introduction to an edited collection of chapters on "women, philanthropy and civil society," it makes reference to the overall book and to the authors and contributions therein.]

The growing interest that scholars have shown in women's political culture – the ways in which women built institutions and influenced public policymaking from beyond the electoral arena – is perhaps not surprising. During the 1990s, innovative work on theories of the role of the state, maternalism, women's roles in political processes and nation-building, and the economic roles organizations play has expanded our understanding of the scope and nature of civil society and mapped a direction for future research. To date, much of this work has focused on the United States and Western Europe, raising important questions about the representativeness of the experiences of women in industrialized nations.

This volume, which grows out of a research project on women and philanthropy sponsored by the Center for the Study of Philanthropy at the Graduate Center of The City University of New York, expands our understanding of female beneficence in shaping diverse political cultures. The contributors examine the role of philanthropy – the giving of time, money, and/or valuables for public benefit – in shaping nongovernmental organizations (NGOs), civil society, and women's political culture world-wide. As in the US, this often enabled them to create "parallel power structures" that resembled, but rarely precisely replicated, the commercial and political arenas of men. From nuns who managed charitable and educational institutions to political activists demanding an end to discriminatory practices against women and children, many of the women whose lives are documented on these pages claimed distinctive public roles through the nonprofit sphere.

The authors in this volume are from Europe, the United States, Latin America, the Middle East, Egypt, India and Asia. Their essays cover nations on every continent, representing a variety of political and religious systems.

In approaching the subject of women as shapers of civil society through their donations of time and money, each of the contributors shares certain basic understandings of the environment in which civil society is formed, much of their perspective being drawn from contemporary discourses on women's political culture. For example, historians have argued that women's organizations have tended to have more policymaking authority in weak (i.e., decentralized, as in the United States) rather than strong states, such as Bismarkian Germany. However, the authors in this volume have discovered that public-private partnerships between governments and women's organizations were pervasive in both weak and strong states.

In the nineteenth century, middle-class and elite women coupled their private donations and their work as volunteers with public funding to foster an invisible – but often highly significant – form of political activity. In effect, female philanthropy helped to subsidize state programs. Several of the articles in this collection show clearly that the roots of state welfare organizations lie in volunteer and religious institutions – in France, for example – and that women (including nuns) acted on behalf of the state, at least implicitly, by cutting the public costs of caring for those in need.

Colonialism may have helped to foster separatist (i.e., single sex) organizations and female voluntarism in some areas, as local needs were identified and addressed in the community rather than at the level of the state government. The consolidation of nation-states, on the other hand, often had a chilling effect on self-help organizations, curtailing advocacy, and encouraging service delivery in those areas of need approved by the state. In other words, some strong state systems worked, and in many places continue to work, to suppress the activities of volunteer or nongovernmental organizations.

In the 1980s and '90s, however, there has been a significant resurgence of civil society and NGOs around the world. This "association revolution" has been fuelled, in part, by women's organizations and the rise of feminist agendas, trends vividly illustrated in the United Nations' conference on women in Beijing and the UN population meeting in Cairo. The growing visibility of NGOs is related to the downsizing of government in many regions and the declining faith in the state's ability to do everything. The weakening of centralized nation-states has opened the door to nongovernmental organizations, and women have been quick to seize the initiative. These women's organizations are influential well beyond their levels of staffing and funding. Simply in terms of presence they have a substantial impact on the formation and implementation of government policy.

Moreover, although we still lack reliable data, anecdotal information suggests that women probably comprise a majority of volunteers and NGO workers in many, if not most, countries. Certainly, the essays in this book suggest that their influence is pervasive.

There are economic implications as well. Research on the economic impact of women's nonprofit entrepreneurship and market activities carried out through voluntary associations reveals the previously invisible roles played by elite and middle-class women in creating wealth to sustain their services. In the process, they often helped to create a parallel, "subterranean economy" for the production, marketing and sale of artifacts produced by and for women.

Frequently, women's philanthropic contributions to the state – their unacknowledged subsidies for social services – were delivered through religious organizations. Certainly, such organizations and the ethical behaviors they encouraged through religious teachings affected the ways in which women participated in social and political arenas. Catholicism, Islam, Hinduism, and Judaism all emphasize giving as a social and religious good. Islamic law and Hindu customs in particular enabled women to control some of their own wealth. Protestantism and English common law encouraged women to volunteer their time as well as donate funds. Many of the activities undertaken by women on behalf of the social and political economy can only be described as entrepreneurial. Such efforts can be found in many countries – in seventeenth-century French convents, nineteenth-century Irish lacemaking projects, and schools for teaching carpetmaking skills in twentieth-century Egypt. The role of women as entrepreneurs on the margins is clearly an area that merits further research across cultures.

Religion played a particularly important role in determining the contours of women's philanthropic activities in different cultures. Questions concerning the place of religious institutions within the nonprofit sector have reverberated through many of the discussions about the sector's scope and nature in recent years. While some scholars sought to include only the non-sacramental services delivered by religious groups, others argued that religious institutions were a vital part of the sector in and of themselves; these debates have profound implications for our understanding of the sector's scale and aims.

In the United States, religious groups were legislated into the voluntary sphere beginning in the 1780s, as state after state followed Virginia's lead in disestablishing state churches and severing them from public support. The upshot was that every church had to compete for parishioners and funds, efforts that led not only to the exponential growth of the country's denominational networks, but also to expand public roles for the women who collectively helped to underwrite this organizational explosion with their money and time.

In the US, as in many countries, different religious groups fostered distinct cultures of giving. During the nineteenth century, Protestant laywomen gave money and time, and were often active politically. They tended to be involved in social advocacy and organized charities. Similarly, the role of Protestantism in promoting voluntarism and female civil society in other countries has frequently been important (one of the most Christianized countries in East Asia, Korea, is a key example, as Lee's paper demonstrates). Jews also give and volunteer, but particularly in the nineteenth century the emphasis was on the delivery of services within the Jewish community. Certainly, the roots of Jewish philanthropy remain there.

Catholics tended to emphasize the delivery of charitable and educational services, for example through hospitals and schools. Laywomen tended to participate as funders, while nuns managed the charities.

These service systems provided important power bases for women who sought to remain independent actors, particularly within the Catholic hierarchy. Nuns have traditionally been effective in funding convents through dowries and in generating income through services and the skills of individual nuns and the dependents and deviants entrusted to their care. In time, the behavior of women religious was politicized with the rise of Liberation Theology and the liberization of the church following Vatican II. A new emphasis on voluntarism in more open structures has freed many women to be more active in the arena between church and state. In some countries, particularly in Latin America, these activities have highlighted church-state conflicts and invited suppression by both the state and church hierarchies.

Hinduism and Islam tended to emphasize the roles of women as donors. In the twentieth century, however, organizations such as the Muslim Sisterhood, and Gandhian protests, encouraged the rise of women's voluntarism. Conversely, Confucianism offered no public space for women, nor opened prospects for women to control funds for services.

Research hypotheses

The Center for the Study of Philanthropy initiated a research project in 1994 to elucidate the role of women in building civil society through their gifts of money and time in a variety of countries. These papers come out of that initial project. All of the writers worked with a common set of seven hypotheses that guided their inquiries. The papers included in this book all address some or all of these hypotheses to a greater or lesser degree, providing a useful ground for comparing the authors' findings.

> *Hypothesis #1: Religion was the most important factor in shaping women's philanthropy and civil society.*
>
> *Hypothesis #2: Women's organizations made their greatest impact on public policymaking agendas through "maternalist" programs for mothers and children.*
>
> *Hypothesis #3: Women's organizations historically had more authority in weak, decentralized states than in strong, highly centralized ones.*
>
> *Hypothesis #4: Women's nonprofit organizations were heavily dependent on public funding.*
>
> *Hypothesis #5: Participation in voluntary associations enabled women to build "parallel power structures" to those of men.*
>
> *Hypothesis #6: The type of strategies that women's groups adopted [e.g., as separatist organizations, or in "assimilationist," mixed-sex groups] had a profound impact on the degree of authority and autonomy that they wielded.*
>
> *Hypothesis #7: Transnational philanthropy played a crucial role in opening a "space" for indigenous women's civil society activities.*

These hypotheses play through the essays in this volume in various, often subtle ways. In one way or another, all prove to have at least some validity in the countries studied. Organized according to the factors mentioned earlier that shape civil society – government, market, and religious structures – one can see in these studies significant variations on the themes, as the following summaries suggest.

In terms of government structures, for example, Maria Luddy's paper on Ireland shows how women's philanthropy aided the development of a conservative Catholic state, where Catholic laywomen had only a limited tradition of social activism and reform. Women in Australia were politically marginalized, as Shurlee Swain explains. The strong centralized state church in France, and the strong centralized state, blurred the lines between private and public activities, as discussed by Evelyne Diebolt. The comparison between France and Brazil in this respect is instructive, as Leilah Landim demonstrates, although the Brazilian church and state were legally separated in 1889. The strong central state in Egypt created tensions for the development of civil society, but as Amani Kandil shows the 1970s and '80s witnessed a re-emergence of independent women's groups. Ghada Hashem Talhami's paper examines the interesting development of hybrid women's organizations that mixed politics and social work in Palestinian areas. In Korea, NGOs re-emerged as vehicles for active citizen participation after the end of the authoritarian regime in 1987.

Religion plays a central role in all of these essays. Certainly, in the United States, Australia and Norway, Protestantism has been a vital factor in the growth of women's organizations. Religion was also central in Ireland, although there was little cooperation between Protestants and Catholics and substantial differences in the way the two groups worked. Protestant groups were often auxiliaries to Bible societies; there were few Catholic laywomen's organizations after 1850. There was a similar divide between Protestants and Catholics in Australia, where evangelical Christianity helped to spur voluntarism.

Religion was central to the rise of women's philanthropy in Brazil, providing legitimation and access to funds, for example. But as in France, the professionalization of social work broke the hegemony of the church in providing social services. In Egypt, the concept of philanthropy was tied to Christian and Islamic charity. Both Hinduism and Islam have strong doctrinal sanctions – Islam for giving via zakat and Hinduism for service via the Bhagavad Gita. The earliest female-controlled charities in India focused on women's rights and the abolition of traditional customs, such as purdah. Voluntarism came with secularization and the advent of Christianity.

The patriarchal culture of Korea and Confucianism combined to keep women from controlling money or even their own decisions. Women's philanthropy was a revolutionary idea in Korea, where Christianity had a powerful influence through its emphasis on education. Christian women leaders became the cornerstone of the Korean church – and formed the heart of the anti-Japanese movement during the period of occupation.

The articles in this book illustrate the extent to which government, the market, and religion have shaped the role of female philanthropy and philanthropists in different national settings. By shifting the focus from organizations to donors and volunteers, we can begin to assess the relative importance of each of these factors in creating opportunities for citizen participation.

Geography matters

The case of English almshouses

John R. Bryson, Mark McGuinness and Robert J. Ford, 2002

It is a well-known cliché that charity begins at home. This is one of charity's advantages and disadvantages. It is also one of the rationales for the establishment of the State Welfare System. Commenting on one of the earliest studies of London's charities undertaken by Sampson Low in 1872, Charles Loch noted that London's charities

> stand, one by one, isolated like light-houses; but unfortunately not, like lighthouses, placed with care precisely on those points of the dangerous coastline of pauperism, where their lights will save from shipwreck the greatest number of distressed passers-by.

From 1948, the emphasis shifted from charity to a focus on the state as the means for securing social well-being. New Labour's [the UK government in power from 1997 to 2010] identification with a 'Third Way' for welfare provision, and the resultant emphasis that this places on the third sector, revives a series of arguments concerning the role of charity that were well rehearsed during the nineteenth century, as well as by William Beveridge [considered to be the architect of the UK welfare state] in 1948. Social reformers in the nineteenth century considered charities to be an uncoordinated and localized form of welfare support. Beveridge, in a little discussed sequel to his report which established the UK's welfare state, noted that voluntary action 'is needed to do things which the State is most unlikely to do. It is needed to pioneer ahead of the State and make experiments'. New Labour's 'Third Way' represents a return to Beveridge's conceptualization of the role of charity in the welfare system. Charities should play an important role, but it is one that should supplement rather than replace state provision. A welfare system heavily dependent on charity is undermined by the localized and uneven geography of much charitable activity.

Almshouse charities are locally embedded on multiple levels, in terms of the clients they serve, the management that directs the organization and the legal frameworks in which they operate. Local geographies are implicitly and explicitly constructed by the functioning of the charity. All charities are governed by a deed of foundation which enshrines the founder(s)' wishes and usually regulates the geographical extension of the charity's activities ('Area of Benefit'). This is most often intended as a means of determining those who may (or may not) benefit. The deed of foundation for Yardley Great Trust, an almshouse charity based in the West Midlands, is typical of this type of close geographical language. The foundation deed determines that the charity's:

> Area of Benefit shall mean the wards of Hodge Hill (south of the river Cole), Shard End (south of the river Cole to the west of Wychbold Crescent), Yardley, Acocks Green, Fox Hollies, Sheldon (north of the Coventry Road and west of Barrows Lane), Small Heath (south of Sparkbrook), Sparkhill (east of Stoney Lane and east of Belle Walk), Moseley (to the east of Billesley Lane-Barn Lane), Billesley, Hall Green, Sparkbrook (south of Walford Road and east of Stoney Lane) and Brandwood (east of Warstock Lane), all in the City of Birmingham, in the county of West Midlands.

The legal requirement to define potential beneficiaries is often pursued through this style of precise geographical statement. This limits access to finite resources, whilst meeting the legal requirement to define a public that will benefit, rather than any private interest group. The ways in which the wishes of the founder(s) are so clearly preserved and operationalized in specific places suggests that the geography of charity may be the product of a form of 'sentimental space' that represents founders' attachments to particular places. These attachments become fixed in space with little regard for actual need. The 'sentimental space' of Yardley Great Trust manages to exclude applications from residents of five contiguous wards that are amongst the 'most deprived' wards in England. This geography certainly differs radically from geographies of local government and administration that might otherwise limit access to resources. It is a geography unique to this particular institution. Certainly, such geographical articulations offer an opportunity to construct an historical geography of charity, following the establishment of charities with particular functions in particular places.

It has become almost a cliché to suggest that geography is malleable and ever changing. This applies as much to the geographies of charities where, despite the detailed cartographic precision of many charity schemes, the actual boundaries of the charity become difficult to identify in the face of changing administrative and physical geographies. Contemporary interpretations of a charity's space – and hence a potential client group – may be difficult to identify. The following example, from an interview with an almshouse administrator in south-east England, illustrates this problem. The charity's area of giving was clear to the eighteenth-century lawyers who drafted the deed of foundation, but today the trustees have found it difficult to delimit the charity's geographical identity:

> some of the edges have been blurred, though it's easy on one side for example, which is the canal is straight-forward. But we also have 'the old oak tree, down Fairwood Road' – the oak tree is still there but it's on the golf course now. There is another oak tree down the other end, opposite the Shell petrol station and I've seen it's still there, but is it the right one? [We've] pored over these maps for many, many hours and we're in fact just going to decide and have [the map] laminated and that will be it. But one of the things I have very much in mind [is that] the real poor nowadays in this area are not actually in this parish, but just outside the parish, where there wasn't a parish before, but half a mile on . . .
>
> (interview with trustee)

Charity administrators, through a geographical–legal articulation, (re)construct the notion of 'local community' through a complex interlacing of founders' wishes and contemporary interpretations, but are also mindful of modern urban and social developments and, of course, charity law. In this case, the changing perceptions of locality produce historically and socially differing notions of the 'local'. It clearly demonstrates how shifting broader geographies over time can heighten the need for some charitable functions whilst rendering others redundant. The geography of need and the geography of charity established to meet that particular need do not necessarily coincide. They may even run counter to each other.

For charities, geography matters, or more importantly precise local geographies matter, as these are one of the barriers imposed by founders on the community included in a charity's area of giving. For charity, it matters on which side of a street one lives or whether a house was to the left or right of an oak tree that existed in the seventeenth century. The geography of almshouse charity is closely related to the historical and localized accumulation of capital. Almshouses were founded by wealthy individuals and families and their location mirrors former geographies of private wealth. In some respects, the uneven distribution of charitable organizations in the UK reflects Massey's well-known geological metaphor of historical accumulation of layers of capital investment. The distribution of charities reflects previous rounds of capital investment as well as forms of patronage ranging from old established families to royalty. The earliest English almshouses were closely linked to the church, but were also founded during the feudal period by the Lord of the Manor and quite frequently by women of high rank. The majority of pre-reformation almshouses were closed by 1540, as a consequence of the dissolution of the monasteries.

From the sixteenth century, almshouses continued to be established by the aristocracy, by members of the new merchant class as well as by individual companies. These trends help explain the concentration of almshouses in London and the South East (36.3 percent), the South West (14.8 percent) and the East and West Midlands (11.4 percent and 10.2 percent).

The relationship between the geography of charities and the historical accumulation of wealth and its investment in pre-defined localities results in a very odd geography of charity; odd because some studies suggest very crudely that charity is available in an inverse relation to need. For example, a study by Knight found that the number of charities per head of population differed widely from one organization to every 165 people in a Scottish town to one to 361 people in an inner-city area. This study builds on the work of Hatch and Abrams *et al.*, who show that there is more charitable and voluntary action in areas where apparently there is less need. Additionally, charities may remain active in areas in which the need for that service has long since been met or removed. The consequence is the deepening of uneven geographies of welfare, where service provision may not reflect welfare need but historical layers of wealth accumulation and charitable foundation. The uneven geography of charitable organizations in the fields of health, social care and housing makes service availability and quality to some extent a spatial lottery.

Section 3

BEING A PHILANTHROPIST: CALLINGS AND CRITIQUES

Editors' introduction

Overview

People are called to become philanthropists for many reasons. Some heed a religious call; some have secular motives. Some explain their giving with universalising philosophical justifications, saying they are acting on the logic that all humans are equal or the obligation to achieve "the greatest good for the greatest number." Others explain their giving with intensely personal accounts, including stories of good fortune or help they have received in the past that they feel called now to "give back" in some way. Most accounts of philanthropic callings include mixed motives, and a complicated mix of free choice and felt obligation. The idea of a "calling" as explored in this section reflects both motives and obligations. It captures the reasons why people *should* give, and why they say they actually *do* give.

The explanations offered by philanthropists, and what their callings lead them to do with their giving, are also often the subject of critiques. This is particularly true for the elite donors whose reasoning and actions are most intently scrutinised. Classic critiques of big donors such as John D. Rockefeller claimed they were "really" just becoming philanthropists to either assuage their guilt from being such ruthless businessmen, or were "really" just looking to improve their tarnished reputations and get good press from their giving. Later critiques continue to question philanthropists' motives, but also raise more fundamental issues about philanthropic values and the role of philanthropy in a democracy. Donors today are critiqued for perpetuating the status quo, for giving only to serve their own interests and for giving primarily to attain prestige or social status. But they are also critiqued for using philanthropy to exert special influence on policy and wield undue power over social outcomes. Paying attention to such critiques reveals a lot about how philanthropy is perceived and understood.

As critiques extend to include challenging the enterprise of philanthropy itself, further core questions about the role of philanthropy come to the surface. These critiques against philanthropy come from both the political Left and Right. While many from the Right advocate for philanthropy as a much more effective and less wasteful alternative to government, philanthropy is also criticised from the Right for not being as effective as capitalism. From the Left, philanthropy is criticised for being too small and fickle to be trusted to solve major problems, and for wielding great power without being accountable or representative, as ideal government programmes are expected to be. Still others transcend the apparent choice of "philanthropy or government or capitalism" and argue for newer alternative methods, such as "social entrepreneurship," to meet human needs and achieve shared aspirations.

The readings here on callings and critiques are grouped into the following four subsections.

Why should people give?: religious and secular calls

Religions around the globe and across time have called people to be generous and to give for the good of others. Believers are taught to give for the glory of their gods, in gratitude for the gift of life or other blessings, and to ensure one's place in the afterlife. This religious duty to give is, of course, not limited only to the well-known Western religions, represented here by John Wesley's famous sermon exhorting Christians to be hard-working and faithful stewards of money, to "gain all you can" and "save all you can" but then also "give all you can" in useful ways. Eastern religions also have ancient teachings about giving with a generous spirit and being charitable, as shown in the piece by the Dalai Lama on the many benefits – social and spiritual – of showing empathy, love and compassion toward other sentient beings.

Nor do the calls to be philanthropic only come from religious sources. There are numerous arguments and encouragements from a secular point of view, and these calls make no less universal claims that giving is a human obligation and that sacrificing in order to meet the needs of others is logically justified. Recently, the most popular type of secular call to give has come out of the utilitarian tradition, and the Australian philosopher Peter Singer has provided a well-known version of this argument. Singer's logic is presented simply: you wouldn't refuse to save a drowning child if you had the chance, so you shouldn't refuse to save the life of a child (or anyone else) if you can give money to do so. In fact, so this argument goes, the "haves" of the world – which includes most of the population in developed countries – have a special moral imperative to save as many lives as they can, not least because they can do so without giving up much of the comfort they enjoy. Michael Ignatieff shares Singer's focus on the inherent value of all human lives, be they friends or strangers, and bases his broader call for humanitarian assistance on the idea that human needs – including the need for respect and to flourish, not just survive – are not adequately met by market mechanisms or collective social provision.

Why do wealthy people give?: elite donor statements

Note that the religious and secular callings described so far are meant to apply to all humans, not just those with an exceptional amount of resources they might use for philanthropy. This is important to remember because it is elite-level philanthropists who are asked most often to explain – and often defend – their own reasons for giving. The statements from elite donors in which they respond to this demand are important because major givers have a disproportionate influence due to the scale of their giving and their ability to lead innovation in this field.

This subsection provides statements from a varied sample of elite donors about why they feel called to give – including some written by the donors themselves and others collected in secondary analyses. As Paul Schervish notes, some of the motives expressed by the wealthy are very similar to those expressed by all levels of giver – such as identification with the cause or perceived connection to the person being helped – while other motives are distinctive to the rich – such as limiting transfers to heirs or the sense that "hyperagency" status goads them to try to "make history."

Like all philanthropists, wealthy donors come to philanthropy from the context of what Schervish calls their "moral biography," by which he means a conscious combination of personal capacity and moral compass. We can see several versions of this moral compass in the first-person statements from Andrew Carnegie (1835–1919), Bill Gates (1955–), Xin Zhang (1965–) and Victor Pinchuk (1960–). Carnegie's famous "Gospel of Wealth" was in fact a non-religious declaration of philanthropic purpose, targeted squarely at other wealthy capitalists of his day. Carnegie warns the rich that "the man who dies thus rich dies disgraced" and argues strongly for giving one's wealth wisely during one's lifetime rather than leaving it to heirs. This call remains famous despite Carnegie's other arguments here that are less popular with modern audiences, such as the claim that capitalism has allowed the wealthy to prove themselves the "fittest" and they should therefore be in charge of "administering" charitable wealth for the good of those less fit. Carnegie's modern-day American counterpart, Bill Gates, shares the belief that being wealthy carries with it the clear obligation to be philanthropic, and shares Carnegie's disappointment at how little is done to help the unfortunate. Gates provides a different sort of explanation for his obligation to give, though, one that echoes Singer and Ignatieff. Put simply, he gives because "every life has equal value."

Carnegie and Gates also share the belief that the wealthy must be diligent to give in the most effective way possible, especially when trying to solve very complex global problems. And they both actively seek to encourage other wealthy people to be more philanthropic. For Gates, this has included efforts – along with his wife, Melinda, and close philanthropic ally, Warren Buffett – to encourage wealthy individuals around the globe to publicly commit more wealth for charitable purposes. This global spread of philanthropy is represented in this section by statements from two philanthropists on the world stage, both of whom come from non-Western countries transitioning to the sort of market economy that fosters elite philanthropy. Xin Zhang offers a moving personal story to explain why she has stepped up her philanthropy – giving mainly to provide educational opportunities for others in China who, like her, can have their lives transformed by such an opportunity. Victor Pinchuk echoes this call to "give back," describing how he wants to use philanthropy to empower the next generation in Ukraine.

Threaded into the accounts of all of these wealthy donors is the view that philanthropy can and must play a role alongside capitalism and the state to meet pressing human needs or foster social development and broader opportunity. Ilana Silber adds a twist to this view in her research on why major Israeli philanthropists say they give. While she found the usual mix of personal and social motives, Silber also identified a powerful undercurrent of negative emotions in the donors, a sense of "civic anger" aimed at the state and government for being too indifferent to needs and doing too little to address social ills. This tension between philanthropic and capitalistic and governmental responses is something we return to again at the end of this section.

Critiques of elite donors

Just as elite donors are often asked to explain their calling to give, they are also often critiqued for both their giving and their explanation of it. Regardless of whether one considers the philanthropists' accounts as sincere and heartfelt or not, it is important to pay attention to these critiques, especially when they focus on perceived problems with elite philanthropy itself rather than individual major donors. These critiques reveal a lot about our shared expectations for philanthropy and the values that surround it. Critiques can be revealing of assumptions about the "proper role" that philanthropy should play, and can raise complex questions about power, transparency, inclusion and obligation.

One sort of critique of elite philanthropy sees wealthy mega-donors as using their philanthropy to advance their own interests and to support causes that benefit the rich rather than the truly needy. A classic book by Teresa Odendahl, excerpted here, argues that there is a "culture of philanthropy" among elite donors that keeps them insulated in a world of affluent institutions, board meetings and fundraising galas, and that perpetuates an ideology justifying their own elite status. Further, the giving by these elites largely serves their own interests through supporting "high culture," "high education" of Ivy League institutions, "high medicine" of private hospitals, and so on.

Another sort of critique of elite donors focuses more on their reasons for engaging in philanthropy, specifically pointing to the personal benefits they receive from an activity that is supposed to be about benefitting others. The reading from Francie Ostrower includes a similar finding to Odendahl about the self-serving causes supported by elite donors, but frames the analysis of these elites more in terms of the prestige and status they get from philanthropic activities. Philanthropy for the donors that Ostrower studied is a path to social status, a means of "social climbing," even a mandatory "accoutrement" to demonstrate one's social rank.

A final critique covered in this section focuses on the undemocratic nature and undue power and influence of philanthropy. This argument warns of the dangers of what Schervish labelled the "hyperagency" tendencies of major donors, and their very real level of influence over public policy – influence that is exercised without the attendant transparency and accountability that democratic society demands of those with such power. Benjamin Soskis makes this sort of argument, asserting that criticising philanthropy is even more essential when big donors set out to affect public policy. What is more, as Odendahl and Ostrower note, elites are likely to exercise this power over policy or other social outcomes in ways that perpetuate the status quo rather than change it. This makes paying attention to the critiques all the more important.

Philanthropy versus the alternatives

As we have seen, very often both the callings and the critiques of philanthropy presented in this section assess philanthropy in contrast to government and to capitalism as alternative ways that people in societies come together to pursue their goals and further social progress. We have seen how philanthropy is called for because of the inadequacies of the state to meet needs, or because it should be a natural complement to capitalist development and wealth creation. We have also seen how philanthropy is sometimes seen as misusing its power to influence government, or perpetuate the inequalities created by capitalism.

The readings in this section turn to this critical comparison of philanthropy versus the alternatives. We consider four specific arguments – two from the political Right and two from the political Left. This range of views is evidence that there is no single ideological position about philanthropy on either side of the proverbial aisle. Taken together, these arguments again reveal the complexity of philanthropy and the fundamental issues we need to consider when deciding its proper place.

From the Right, a short piece by Jim Lacey asserts that successful businessmen should focus more on business and less on philanthropy, that they can do more good for society by sticking to generating new wealth and jobs through capitalism rather than storing up their existing wealth into perpetually endowed foundations. Marvin Olasky presents another common but somewhat opposing view from the Right, that philanthropy – especially in its traditional form of local charity – can do more good, more effectively for those in need than wasteful government welfare state programmes ever can.

The British political commentator Polly Toynbee, writing from the Left, offers the directly opposite view to Olasky. She argues that philanthropy is fickle, random and often eccentric, and cannot (indeed should not) ever be big enough to solve problems in the way that the welfare state can. The selection from Gara LaMarche then echoes many of the critiques of elite donors given earlier – e.g., from Odendahl, Ostrower, and Soskis – pointing to the tremendous power of major philanthropy to influence how we try to solve our social problems. While philanthropy can accomplish good things, it is also troubling that such a powerful – and tax-exempt – force is also not transparent, not democratically accountable and not representative of the diversity of society.

Note that these arguments offer differing views – even from the same general political perspective – on whether there should be more philanthropy or less compared to government or capitalism. Other commentators transcend those alternatives by arguing for new alternatives. One of the most popular emerging alternatives is social entrepreneurship, and the J. Gregory Dees reading provides a classic definition and defence of that method. Pointing to the limitations of both government and charity, Dees presents social entrepreneurs – people and institutions who "bring to social problems the same kind of determination, creativity, and resourcefulness that we find among business entrepreneurs" – as a more promising path to dealing with our most difficult social challenges. We will read more about emerging alternatives such as this in Sections 5 and 6 of this reader.

Discussion questions

- How do the reasons given by elite donors for why they give compare to the reasons you would give? How are they similar or different? Do your own reasons line up with the religious or secular calls for giving in the first set of readings?
- Should we believe what wealthy donors say about why they give? Are the critics of elite donors too critical? What is the danger of criticising donors, if any, and what are the benefits?
- Do elite donors have too much power in a democratic society? How can we ensure that philanthropy contributes in positive ways but avoids the problems that the critics in these readings point out?
- Is defence of philanthropy a defence of capitalism? Why or why not? Is philanthropy best seen as an alternative to government, or a partner with government?
- To what extent does the idea of "social entrepreneurship" resolve or aggravate some of the criticisms made of philanthropy? Think of an example of someone you would consider a social entrepreneur and describe what qualities they bring to the hard job of solving social problems.

3.1 Why should people give?: religious and secular calls

Give all you can

John Wesley, 1760

An excellent branch of Christian wisdom is here inculcated by our Lord on all his followers, namely, the right use of money – a subject largely spoken of, after their manner, by men of the world; but not sufficiently considered by those whom God hath chosen out of the world. These, generally, do not consider, as the importance of the subject requires, the use of this excellent talent. Neither do they understand how to employ it to the greatest advantage; the introduction of which into the world is one admirable instance of the wise and gracious providence of God. It has, indeed, been the manner of poets, orators, and philosophers, in almost all ages and nations, to rail at this, as the grand corrupter of the world, the bane of virtue, the pest of human society.

[. . .]

But is not all this mere empty rant [. . .] The fault does not lie in the money, but in them that use it. It may be used ill: And what may not? But it may likewise be used well: It is full as applicable to the best, as to the worst uses. It is of unspeakable service to all civilized nations, in all the common affairs of life: [. . .] in the present state of mankind, it is an excellent gift of God, answering the noblest ends. In the hands of his children, it is food for the hungry, drink for the thirsty, raiment for the naked: It gives to the traveler and the stranger where to lay his head. By it we may supply the place of an husband to the widow, and of a father to the fatherless. We may be a defense for the oppressed, a means of health to the sick, of ease to them that are in pain; it may be as eyes to the blind, as feet to the lame; yea, a lifter up from the gates of death!

It is therefore of the highest concern that all who fear God know how to employ this valuable talent; that they be instructed how it may answer these glorious ends, and in the highest degree. And, perhaps, all the instructions which are necessary for this may be reduced to three plain rules, by the exact observance whereof we may approve ourselves faithful stewards of "the mammon of unrighteousness."

[. . .]

[I]t is the bounden duty of all who are engaged in worldly business to observe that first and great rule of Christian wisdom with respect to money, "Gain all you can." Gain all you can by honest industry. Use all possible diligence in your calling. Lose no time. If you understand yourself and your relation to God and man, you know you have none to spare. If you understand your particular calling as you ought, you will have no time that hangs upon your hands. Every business will afford some employment sufficient for every day and every hour. That wherein you are placed, if you follow it in earnest, will leave you no leisure for silly, unprofitable diversions. You have always something better to do, something that will profit you, more or less. And "whatsoever thy hand findeth to do, do it with thy might." Do it as soon as possible: No delay! No putting off from day to day, or from hour to hour! Never leave anything till to-morrow, which you can do to-day. And do it as well as possible. Do not sleep or yawn over it: Put your whole strength to the work. Spare no pains. Let nothing be done by halves, or in a slight and careless manner. Let nothing in your business be left undone if it can be done by labour or patience.

[. . .]

Having gained all you can, by honest wisdom and unwearied diligence, the second rule of Christian prudence is, "Save all you can." Do not throw the precious talent into the sea: Leave that folly to heathen philosophers. Do not throw it away in idle expenses, which is just the same as throwing it into the sea. Expend no part of it merely to gratify the desire of the flesh, the desire of the eye, or the pride of life.

[. . .]

But let not any man imagine that he has done anything, barely by going thus far, by "gaining and saving all he can," if he were to stop here. All this is nothing, if a man go not forward, if he does not point all this at a farther end. Nor, indeed, can a man properly be said to save anything, if he only lays it up. You may as well throw your money into the sea, as bury it in the earth. And you may as well bury it in the earth, as in your chest, or in the Bank of England. Not to use, is effectually to throw it away. If, therefore, you would indeed "make yourselves friends of the mammon of unrighteousness," add the Third rule to the two preceding. Having, First, gained all you can, and, Secondly saved all you can, Then "give all you can."

In order to see the ground and reason of this, consider, when the Possessor of heaven and earth brought you into being, and placed you in this world, he placed you here not as a proprietor, but a steward: As such he entrusted you, for a season, with goods of various kinds; but the sole property of these still rests in him, nor can be alienated from him. As you yourself are not your own, but his, such is, likewise, all that you enjoy. Such is your soul and your body, not your own, but God's. And so is your substance in particular. And he has told you, in the most clear and express terms, how you are to employ it for him, in such a manner, that it may be all an holy sacrifice, acceptable through Christ Jesus. And this light, easy service, he has promised to reward with an eternal weight of glory.

The directions which God has given us, touching the use of our worldly substance, may be comprised in the following particulars. If you desire to be a faithful and a wise steward, out of that portion of your Lord's goods which he has for the present lodged in your hands, but with the right of resuming whenever it pleases him, First, provide things needful for yourself; food to eat, raiment to put on, whatever nature moderately requires for preserving the body in health and strength. Secondly, provide these for your wife, your children, your servants, or any others who pertain to your household. If when this is done there be an overplus left, then "do good to them that are of the household of faith." If there be an overplus still, "as you have opportunity, do good unto all men." In so doing, you give all you can; nay, in a sound sense, all you have: For all that is laid out in this manner is really given to God. You "render unto God the things that are God's," not only by what you give to the poor, but also by that which you expend in providing things needful for yourself and your household.

[. . .]

You see then [. . .] the nature and extent of truly Christian prudence so far as it relates to the use of that great talent, money. Gain all you can, without hurting either yourself or your neighbor, in soul or body, by applying hereto with unintermitted diligence, and with all the understanding which God has given you; – save all you can, by cutting off every expense which serves only to indulge foolish desire; to gratify either the desire of flesh, the desire of the eye, or the pride of life; waste nothing, living or dying, on sin or folly, whether for yourself or your children; – and then, give all you can, or, in other words, give all you have to God. [. . .] "Render unto God," not a tenth, not a third, not half, but all that is God's, be it more or less; by employing all on yourself, your household, the household of faith, and all mankind, in such a manner, that you may give a good account of your stewardship when ye can be no longer stewards; in such a manner as the oracles of God direct, both by general and particular precepts; in such a manner, that whatever ye do may be "a sacrifice of a sweet-smelling savour to God," and that every act may be rewarded in that day when the Lord cometh with all his saints.

Brethren, can we be either wise or faithful stewards unless we thus manage our Lord's goods? We cannot, as not only the oracles of God, but our own conscience beareth witness. [. . .] I entreat you, in the name of the Lord Jesus, act up to the dignity of your calling! No more sloth! Whatsoever your hand findeth to do, do it with your might! No more waste! Cut off every expense which fashion, caprice, or flesh and blood demand! No more covetousness! But employ whatever God has entrusted you with, in doing good, all possible good, in every possible kind and degree to the household of faith, to all men! This is no small part of "the wisdom of the just." Give all ye have, as well as all ye are, a spiritual sacrifice to Him who withheld not from you his Son, his only Son: So "laying up in store for yourselves a good foundation against the time to come, that ye may attain eternal life!"

The ethic of compassion

Dalai Lama, 1999

We noted earlier that all the world's major religions stress the importance of cultivating love and compassion. In the Buddhist philosophical tradition, different levels of attainment are described. At a basic level, compassion (*nying je*) is understood mainly in terms of empathy – our ability to enter into and, to some extent, share others' suffering. But Buddhists – and perhaps others – believe that this can be developed to such a degree that not only does our compassion arise without any effort, but it is unconditional, undifferentiated, and universal in scope. A feeling of intimacy toward all other sentient beings, including of course those who would harm us, is generated, which is likened in the literature to the love a mother has for her only child.

But this sense of equanimity toward all others is not seen as an end in itself. Rather, it is seen as the springboard to a love still greater. Because our capacity for empathy is innate, and because the ability to reason is also an innate faculty, compassion shares the characteristics of consciousness itself. The potential we have to develop it is therefore stable and continuous. It is not a resource which can be used up – as water is used up when we boil it. And though it can be described in terms of activity, it is not like a physical activity which we train for, like jumping, where once we reach a certain height we can go no further. On the contrary, when we enhance our sensitivity toward others' suffering through deliberately opening ourselves up to it, it is believed that we can gradually extend out compassion to the point where the individual feels so moved by even the subtlest suffering of others that they come to have an overwhelming sense of responsibility toward those others. This causes the one who is compassionate to dedicate themselves entirely to helping others overcome both their suffering and the cause of their suffering. In Tibetan, this ultimate level of attainment is called *nying je chenmo*, literally "great compassion."

Now I am not suggesting that each individual must attain these advanced states of spiritual development in order to lead an ethically wholesome life. I have described *nying je chenmo* not because it is a precondition of ethical conduct but rather because I believe that pushing the logic of compassion to the highest level can act as a powerful inspiration. If we can just keep the aspiration to develop *nying je chenmo*, or great compassion, as an ideal, it will naturally have a significant impact on our outlook. Based on the simple recognition that, just as I do, so do all others desire to be happy and not to suffer, it will serve as a constant reminder against selfishness and partiality. It will remind us that there is little to be gained from being kind and generous because we hope to win something in return. It will remind us that actions motivated by the desire to create a good name for ourselves are still selfish, however much they may appear to be acts of kindness. It will also remind us that there is nothing exceptional about acts of charity toward those we already feel close to. And it will help us to recognize that the bias we naturally feel toward our families and friends is actually a highly unreliable thing on which to base ethical conduct. If we reserve ethical conduct for those whom we feel close to, the danger is that we will neglect our responsibilities toward those outside this circle.

[. . .]

Consider, too, that habitually our feelings toward others depend very much on their circumstances. Most people, when they see someone who is handicapped, feel sympathetic toward that person. But then when they see others who are wealthier, or better educated, or better placed socially, they immediately feel envious and competitive toward them. Our negative feelings prevent us from seeing the sameness of ourselves and others. We forget that just like us, whether fortunate or unfortunate, distant or near, they desire to be happy and not to suffer.

The struggle is thus to overcome these feelings of partiality. Certainly, developing genuine compassion for our loved ones is the obvious and appropriate place to start. The impact our actions have on our close ones will generally be much greater than on others, and therefore our responsibilities toward them are greater. Yet we need to recognize that, ultimately, there are no grounds for discriminating in their favor. In this sense, we are all in the same position as a doctor confronted by ten patients suffering the same serious illness. They are each equally deserving of treatment. The reader should not suppose that what is being advocated here is a state of detached indifference, however. The further essential challenge, as we begin to extend our compassion toward all others, is to maintain the same level of intimacy as we feel toward those closest to us. In other words, what is being suggested is that we need to strive for even-handedness in our approach toward all others, a level ground into which we can plant the seed of *nying je chenmo*, of great love and compassion.

If we can begin to relate to others on the basis of such equanimity, our compassion will not depend on the fact that so and so is my husband, my wife, my relative, my friend. Rather, a feeling of closeness toward all others can be developed based on the simple recognition that, just like myself, all wish to be happy and to avoid suffering. In other words, we will start to relate to others on the basis of their sentient nature. Again, we can think of this in terms of an ideal, one which it is immensely difficult to attain. But, for myself, I find it one which is profoundly inspiring and helpful.

Let us now consider the role of compassionate love and kind-heartedness in our daily lives. Does the ideal of developing it to the point where it is unconditional mean that we must abandon our own interests entirely? Not at all. In fact, it is the best way of serving them – indeed, it could even be said to constitute the wisest course for fulfilling self-interest. For if it is correct that those qualities such as love, patience, tolerance, and forgiveness are what happiness consists in, and if it is also correct that *nying je*, or compassion, as I have defined it, is both the source and the fruit of these qualities, then the more we are compassionate, the more we provide for our own happiness. Thus, any idea that concern for others, though a noble quality, is a matter for our private lives only, is simply short-sighted. Compassion belongs to every sphere of activity, including, of course, the workplace.

[. . .]

Some people may object to this ideal on the grounds that by entering into others' suffering, we bring suffering on ourselves. To an extent, this is true. But I suggest that there is an important qualitative distinction to be made between experiencing one's own suffering and experiencing suffering in the course of sharing in others'. In the case of one's own suffering, given that it is involuntary, there is a sense of oppression: it seems to come from outside us. By contrast, sharing in someone else's suffering must at some level involve a degree of voluntariness, which itself is indicative of a certain inner strength. For this reason, the disturbance it may cause is considerably less likely to paralyze us than our own suffering.

Of course, even as an ideal, the notion of developing unconditional compassion is daunting. Most people, including myself, must struggle even to reach the point where putting others' interests on a par with our own becomes easy. We should not allow this to put us off, however. And while undoubtedly there will be obstacles on the way to developing a genuinely warm heart, there is the deep consolation of knowing that in doing so we are creating the conditions for our own happiness. As I mentioned earlier, the more we truly desire to benefit others, the greater the strength and confidence we develop and the greater the peace and happiness we experience. If this still seems unlikely, it is worth asking ourselves how else we are to do so. With violence and aggression? Of course not. With money? Perhaps up to a point, but no further. But with love, by sharing in others' suffering, by recognizing ourselves clearly in all others – especially those who are disadvantaged and those whose rights are not respected – by helping them to be happy: yes. Through love, through kindness, through compassion we establish understanding between ourselves and others. This is how we forge unity and harmony.

Compassion and love are not mere luxuries. As the source both of inner and external peace, they are fundamental to the continued survival of our species. On the one hand, they constitute non-violence in action. On the other, they are the source of all spiritual qualities: of forgiveness, tolerance, and all the virtues. Moreover, they are the very thing that gives meaning to our activities and makes them constructive. There is nothing amazing about being highly educated; there is nothing amazing about being rich. Only when the individual has a warm heart do these attributes become worthwhile.

So to those who say that the Dalai Lama is being unrealistic in advocating this idea of unconditional love, I urge them to experiment with it nonetheless. They will discover that when we reach beyond the confines of narrow self-interest, our hearts become filled with strength. Peace and joy become our constant companion. It breaks down barriers of every kind and in the end destroys the notion of my interest as independent from others' interest. But most important, so far as ethics is concerned, where love of one's neighbor, affection, kindness, and compassion live, we find that ethical conduct is automatic. Ethically wholesome actions arise naturally in the context of compassion.

The rich should give

Peter Singer, 2006

What is a human life worth? You may not want to put a price tag on it. But if we really had to, most of us would agree that the value of a human life would be in the millions. Consistent with the foundations of our democracy and our frequently professed belief in the inherent dignity of human beings, we would also agree that all humans are created equal, at least to the extent of denying that differences of sex, ethnicity, nationality and place of residence change the value of a human life.

[. . .]

For Bill Gates, the founder of Microsoft, the ideal of valuing all human life equally began to jar against reality some years ago, when he read an article about diseases in the developing world and came across the statistic that half a million children die every year from rotavirus, the most common cause of severe diarrhea in children. He had never heard of rotavirus. "How could I never have heard of something that kills half a million children every year?" he asked himself. He then learned that in developing countries, millions of children die from diseases that have been eliminated, or virtually eliminated, in the United States. That shocked him because he assumed that, if there are vaccines and treatments that could save lives, governments would be doing everything possible to get them to the people who need them. As Gates told a meeting of the World Health Assembly in Geneva last year, he and his wife, Melinda, "couldn't escape the brutal conclusion that – in our world today – some lives are seen as worth saving and others are not." They said to themselves, "This can't be true." But they knew it was.

Gates's speech to the World Health Assembly concluded on an optimistic note, looking forward to the next decade when "people will finally accept that the death of a child in the developing world is just as tragic as the death of a child in the developed world." That belief in the equal value of all human life is also prominent on the website of the Bill and Melinda Gates Foundation, where under Our Values we read: "All lives – no matter where they are being led – have equal value."

We are very far from acting in accordance with that belief. In the same world in which more than a billion people live at a level of affluence never previously known, roughly a billion other people struggle to survive on the purchasing power equivalent of less than one US dollar per day. Most of the world's poorest people are undernourished, lack access to safe drinking water or even the most basic health services and cannot send their children to school. According to UNICEF, more than 10 million children die every year – about 30,000 per day – from avoidable, poverty-related causes.

Last June the investor Warren Buffett took a significant step toward reducing those deaths when he pledged $31 billion to the Gates Foundation, and another $6 billion to other charitable foundations. Buffett's pledge, set alongside the nearly $30 billion given by Bill and Melinda Gates to their foundation, has made it clear that the first decade of the 21st century is a new "golden age of philanthropy." On an inflation-adjusted basis, Buffett has pledged to give more than double the lifetime total given away by two of the philanthropic giants of the past, Andrew Carnegie and John D. Rockefeller, put together. Bill and Melinda Gates's gifts are not far behind.

Gates's and Buffett's donations will now be put to work primarily to reduce poverty, disease and premature death in the developing world. According to the Global Forum for Health Research, less than 10 percent of the world's health research budget is spent on combating conditions that account for 90 percent of the global burden of disease. In the past, diseases that affect only the poor have been of no commercial interest to pharmaceutical manufacturers, because the poor cannot afford to buy their products. The Global Alliance for Vaccines and Immunization (GAVI), heavily supported by the Gates Foundation, seeks to change this by guaranteeing to purchase millions of doses of vaccines, when they are developed, that can prevent diseases like malaria. GAVI has also assisted developing countries to immunize more people with existing vaccines: 99 million additional children have been reached to date. By doing this, GAVI claims to have already averted nearly 1.7 million future deaths.

Philanthropy on this scale raises many ethical questions: Why are the people who are giving doing so? Does it do any good? Should we praise them for giving so much or criticize them for not giving still more? Is it troubling that such momentous decisions are made by a few extremely wealthy individuals? And how do our judgments about them reflect on our own way of living?

Let's start with the question of motives. The rich must – or so some of us with less money like to assume – suffer sleepless nights because of their ruthlessness in squeezing out competitors, firing workers, shutting down plants or whatever else they have to do to acquire their wealth. When wealthy people give away money, we can always say that they are doing it to ease their consciences or generate favorable publicity. It has been suggested – by, for example, David Kirkpatrick, a senior editor at *Fortune* magazine – that Bill Gates's turn to philanthropy was linked to the antitrust problems Microsoft had in the US and the European Union. Was Gates, consciously or subconsciously, trying to improve his own image and that of his company?

This kind of sniping tells us more about the attackers than the attacked. Giving away large sums, rather than spending the money on corporate advertising or developing new products, is not a sensible strategy for increasing personal wealth. When we read that someone has given away a lot of their money, or time, to help others, it challenges us to think about our own behavior. Should we be following their example, in our own modest way? But if the rich just give their money away to improve their image, or to make up for past misdeeds – misdeeds quite unlike any we have committed, of course – then, conveniently, what they are doing has no relevance to what we ought to do.

A famous story is told about Thomas Hobbes, the 17th-century English philosopher, who argued that we all act in our own interests. On seeing him give alms to a beggar, a cleric asked Hobbes if he would have done this if Christ had not commanded us to do so. Yes, Hobbes replied, he was in pain to see the miserable condition of the old man, and his gift, by providing the man with some relief from that misery, also eased Hobbes's pain. That reply reconciles Hobbes's charity with his egoistic theory of human motivation, but at the cost of emptying egoism of much of its bite. If egoists suffer when they see a stranger in distress, they are capable of being as charitable as any altruist.

Followers of the 18th-century German philosopher Immanuel Kant would disagree. They think an act has moral worth only if it is done out of a sense of duty. Doing something merely because you enjoy doing it, or enjoy seeing its consequences, they say, has no moral worth, because if you happened not to enjoy doing it, then you wouldn't do it, and you are not responsible for your likes and dislikes, whereas you are responsible for your obedience to the demands of duty.

Perhaps some philanthropists are motivated by their sense of duty. Apart from the equal value of all human life, the other "simple value" that lies at the core of the work of the Gates Foundation, according to its website, is "To whom much has been given, much is expected." That suggests the view that those who have great wealth have a duty to use it for a larger purpose than their own interests. But while such questions of motive may be relevant to our assessment of Gates's or Buffett's character, they pale into insignificance when we consider the effect of what Gates and Buffett are doing. The parents whose children could die from rotavirus care more about getting the help that will save their children's lives than about the motivations of those who make that possible.

Interestingly, neither Gates nor Buffett seems motivated by the possibility of being rewarded in heaven for his good deeds on earth. Gates told a *Time* interviewer, "There's a lot more I could be doing on a Sunday morning" than going to church. Put them together with Andrew Carnegie, famous for his freethinking, and three of the four greatest American philanthropists have been atheists or agnostics. (The exception is John D. Rockefeller.) In a country in which 96 percent of the population say they believe in a supreme being, that's a striking fact. It means that in one sense, Gates and Buffett are probably less self-interested in their charity than someone like Mother Teresa, who as a pious Roman Catholic believed in reward and punishment in the afterlife.

More important than questions about motives are questions about whether there is an obligation for the rich to give, and if so, how much they should give. A few years ago, an African-American cabdriver taking me to the Inter-American Development Bank in Washington asked me if I worked at the bank. I told him I did not but was speaking at a conference on development and aid. He then assumed that I was an economist, but when I said no, my training was in philosophy, he asked me if I thought the US should give foreign aid. When I answered affirmatively, he replied that the government shouldn't tax people in order to give their money to others. That, he thought, was robbery. When I asked if he believed that the rich should voluntarily donate some of what they earn to the poor, he said that if someone had worked for his money, he wasn't going to tell him what to do with it.

At that point we reached our destination. Had the journey continued, I might have tried to persuade him that people can earn large amounts only when they live under favorable social circumstances, and that they don't create those circumstances by themselves. I could have quoted Warren Buffett's acknowledgment that society is responsible for much of his wealth. "If you stick me down in the middle of Bangladesh or Peru," he said, "you'll find out how much this talent is going to produce in the wrong kind of soil."

[. . .]

In any case, even if we were to grant that people deserve every dollar they earn, that doesn't answer the question of what they should do with it. We might say that they have a right to spend it on lavish parties, private jets and luxury yachts, or, for that matter, to flush it down the toilet. But we could still think that for them to do these things while others die from easily preventable diseases is wrong. In an article I wrote more than three decades ago, at the time of a humanitarian emergency in what is now Bangladesh, I used the example of walking by a shallow pond and seeing a small child who has fallen in and appears to be in danger of drowning. Even though we did nothing to cause the child to fall into the pond, almost everyone agrees that if we can save the child at minimal inconvenience or trouble to ourselves, we ought to do so. Anything else would be callous, indecent and, in a word, wrong. The fact that in rescuing the child we may, for example, ruin a new pair of shoes is not a good reason for allowing the child to drown. Similarly if for the cost of a pair of shoes we can contribute to a health program in a developing country that stands a good chance of saving the life of a child, we ought to do so.

Perhaps, though, our obligation to help the poor is even stronger than this example implies, for we are less innocent than the passer-by who did nothing to cause the child to fall into the pond. Thomas Pogge, a philosopher at Columbia University, has argued that at least some of our affluence comes at the expense of the poor. He bases this claim not simply on the usual critique of the barriers that Europe and the United States maintain against agricultural imports from developing countries but also on less familiar aspects of our trade with developing countries.

[. . .]

In this light, our obligation to the poor is not just one of providing assistance to strangers but one of compensation for harms that we have caused and are still causing them. It might be argued that we do not owe the poor compensation, because our affluence actually benefits them. Living luxuriously, it is said, provides employment, and so wealth trickles down, helping the poor more effectively than aid does. But the rich in industrialized nations buy virtually nothing that is made by the very poor. During the past 20 years of economic globalization, although expanding trade has helped lift many of the world's poor out of poverty, it has failed to benefit the poorest 10 percent of the world's population. Some of the extremely poor, most of whom live in sub-Saharan Africa, have nothing to sell that rich people want, while others lack the infrastructure to get their goods to market.

[. . .]

The rich, then, should give. But how much should they give? Gates may have given away nearly $30 billion, but that still leaves him sitting at the top of the Forbes list of the richest Americans, with $53 billion. His 66,000-square-foot high-tech lakeside estate near Seattle is reportedly worth more than $100 million. Property taxes are about $1 million. Among his possessions is the Leicester Codex, the only handwritten book by Leonardo da Vinci still in private hands, for which he paid $30.8 million in 1994. Has Bill Gates done enough? More pointedly, you might ask: if he really believes that all lives have equal value, what is he doing living in such an expensive house and owning a Leonardo Codex? Are there no more lives that could be saved by living more modestly and adding the money thus saved to the amount he has already given?

Yet we should recognize that, if judged by the proportion of his wealth that he has given away, Gates compares very well with most of the other people on the Forbes 400 list, including his former colleague and Microsoft co-founder, Paul Allen. Allen, who left the company in 1983, has given, over his lifetime, more than $800 million to philanthropic causes. That is far more than nearly any of us will ever be able to give. But *Forbes* lists Allen as the fifth-richest American, with a net worth of $16 billion. He owns the Seattle Seahawks, the Portland Trailblazers, a 413-foot oceangoing yacht that carries two helicopters and a 60-foot submarine. He has given only about 5 percent of his total wealth.

Is there a line of moral adequacy that falls between the 5 percent that Allen has given away and the roughly 35 percent that Gates has donated? Few people have set a personal example that would allow them to tell Gates that he has not given enough, but one who could is Zell Kravinsky. A few years ago, when he was in his mid-40s, Kravinsky gave almost all of his $45 million real estate fortune to health-related charities, retaining only his modest family home in Jenkintown, near Philadelphia, and enough to meet his family's ordinary expenses. After learning that thousands of people with failing kidneys die each year while waiting for a transplant, he contacted a Philadelphia hospital and donated one of his kidneys to a complete stranger.

After reading about Kravinsky in *The New Yorker*, I invited him to speak to my classes at Princeton. He comes across as anguished by the failure of others to see the simple logic that lies behind his altruism. Kravinsky has a mathematical mind – a talent that obviously helped him in deciding what investments would prove profitable – and he says that the chances of dying as a result of donating a kidney are about 1 in 4,000. For him this implies that to withhold a kidney from someone who would otherwise die means valuing one's own life at 4,000 times that of a stranger, a ratio Kravinsky considers "obscene."

What marks Kravinsky from the rest of us is that he takes the equal value of all human life as a guide to life, not just as a nice piece of rhetoric. He acknowledges that some people think he is crazy, and even his wife says she believes that he goes too far. One of her arguments against the kidney donation was that one of their children may one day need a kidney, and Zell could be the only compatible donor. Kravinsky's love for his children is, as far as I can tell, as strong as that of any normal parent. Such attachments are part of our nature, no doubt the product of our evolution as mammals who give birth to children, who for an unusually long time require our assistance in order to survive. But that does not, in Kravinsky's view, justify our placing a value on the lives of our children that is thousands of times greater than the value we place on the lives of the children of strangers. Asked if he would allow his child to die if it would enable a thousand children to live, Kravinsky said yes. Indeed, he has said he would permit his child to die even if this enabled only two other children to live. Nevertheless, to appease his wife, he recently went back into real estate, made some money and bought the family a larger home. But he still remains committed to giving away as much as possible, subject only to keeping his domestic life reasonably tranquil.

Buffett says he believes in giving his children "enough so they feel they could do anything, but not so much that they could do nothing." That means, in his judgment, "a few hundred thousand" each. In absolute terms, that is far more than most Americans are able to leave their children and, by Kravinsky's standard, certainly too much. (Kravinsky says that the hard part is not giving away the first $45 million but the last $10,000, when you have to live so cheaply that you can't function in the business world.) But even if Buffett left each of his three children a million dollars each, he would still have given away more than 99.99 percent of his wealth. When someone does that much – especially in a society in which the norm is to leave most of your wealth to your children – it is better to praise them than to cavil about the extra few hundred thousand dollars they might have given.

Philosophers like Liam Murphy of New York University and my colleague Kwame Anthony Appiah at Princeton contend that our obligations are limited to carrying our fair share of the burden of relieving global poverty. They would have us calculate how much would be required to ensure that the world's poorest people have a chance at a decent life, and then divide this sum among the affluent. That would give us each an amount to donate, and having given that, we would have fulfilled our obligations to the poor.

[. . .]

If we are obliged to do no more than our fair share of eliminating global poverty, the burden will not be great. But is that really all we ought to do? Since we all agree that fairness is a good thing, and none of us like doing more because others don't pull their weight, the fair-share view is attractive. In the end, however, I think we should reject it. Let's return to the drowning child in the shallow pond. Imagine it is not 1 small child who has fallen in, but 50 children. We are among 50 adults, unrelated to the children, picnicking on the lawn around the pond. We can easily wade into the pond and rescue the children, and the fact that we would find it cold and unpleasant sloshing around in the knee-deep muddy water is no justification for failing to do so. The "fair share" theorists would say that if we each rescue one child, all the children will be saved, and so none of us have an obligation to save more than one. But what if half the picnickers prefer staying clean and dry to rescuing any children at all? Is it acceptable if the rest of us stop after we have rescued just one child, knowing that we have done our fair share, but that half the children will drown? We might justifiably be furious with those who are not doing their fair share, but our anger with them is not a reason for letting the children die. In terms of praise and blame, we are clearly right to condemn, in the strongest terms, those who do nothing. In contrast, we may withhold such condemnation from those who stop when they have done their fair share. Even so, they have let children drown when they could easily have saved them, and that is wrong.

Similarly, in the real world, it should be seen as a serious moral failure when those with ample income do not do their fair share toward relieving global poverty. It isn't so easy, however, to decide on the proper approach to take to those who limit their contribution to their fair share when they could easily do more and when, because others are not playing their part, a further donation would assist many in desperate need. In the privacy of our own judgment, we should believe that it is wrong not to do more. But whether we should actually criticize people who are doing their fair share, but no more than that, depends on the psychological impact that such criticism will have on them, and on others. This in turn may depend on social practices. If the majority are doing little or nothing, setting a standard higher than the fair-share level may seem so demanding that it discourages people who are willing to make an equitable contribution from doing even that. So it may be best to refrain from criticizing those who achieve the fair-share level. In moving our society's standards forward, we may have to progress one step at a time.

The needs of strangers

Michael Ignatieff, 1984

I live in a market street in north London. Every Tuesday morning there is a barrow outside my door and a cluster of old age pensioners rummage through the torn curtains, buttonless shirts, stained vests, torn jackets, frayed trousers and faded dresses that the barrow man has on offer. They make a cheerful chatter outside my door, beating down the barrow man's prices, scrabbling for bargains like crows pecking among the stubble.

They are not destitute, just respectably poor. The old men seem more neglected than the women: their faces are grey and unshaven and their necks hang loose inside yellowed shirt collars. Their old bodies must be thin and white beneath their clothes. The women seem more self-possessed, as if old age were something their mothers had prepared them for. They also have the skills for poverty: the hems of their coats are neatly darned, their buttons are still in place.

These people give the impression of having buried their wives and husbands long ago and having watched their children decamp to the suburbs. I imagine them living alone in small dark rooms lit by the glow of electric heaters. I came upon one old man once doing his shopping alone, weighed down in a queue at a potato stall and nearly fainting from tiredness. I made him sit down in a pub while I did the rest of his shopping. But if he needed my help, he certainly didn't want it. He was clinging on to his life, gasping for breath, but he stared straight ahead when we talked and his fingers would not be pried from his burdens. All these old people seem like that, cut adrift from family, slipping away into the dwindling realm of their inner voices, clinging to the old barrow as if it were a raft carrying them out to sea.

My encounters with them are a parable of moral relations between strangers in the welfare stare. They have needs, and because they live within a welfare state, these needs confer entitlements – rights – to the resources of people like me. Their needs and their entitlements establish a silent relation between us. As we stand together in line at the post office, while they cash their pension checks, some tiny portion of my income is transferred into their pockets through the numberless capillaries of the state. The mediated quality of our relationship seems necessary to both of us. They are dependent on the state, not upon me, and we are both glad of it. Yet I am also aware of how this mediation walls us off from each other. We are responsible for each other, but we are not responsible to each other.

My responsibilities towards them are mediated through a vast division of labour. In my name a social worker climbs the stairs to their rooms and makes sure they are as warm and as clean as they can be persuaded to be. When they get too old to go out, a volunteer will bring them a hot meal, make up their beds, and if the volunteer is a compassionate person, listen to their whispering streams of memory. When they can't go on, an ambulance will take them to the hospital, and when they die, a nurse will be there to listen to the ebbing of their breath. It is this solidarity among strangers, this transformation through the division of labour of needs into rights and rights into care that gives us whatever fragile basis we have for saying that we live in a moral community.

Modern welfare may not be generous by any standard other than a comparison with the nineteenth-century workhouse, but it does attempt to satisfy a wide range of basic needs for food, shelter, clothing, warmth and medical care. The question is whether that is all a human being needs. When we talk about needs we mean something more than just the basic necessities of human survival. We also use the word to describe what a person needs in order to live to their full potential. What we need in order to survive, and what we need in order to flourish are two different things. The aged poor on my street get just enough to survive. The question is whether they get what they need in order to live a human life.

[. . .]

It is because money cannot buy the human gestures which confer respect, nor rights guarantee them as entitlements, that any decent society requires a public discourse about the needs of the human person. It is because fraternity, love, belonging, dignity and respect cannot be specified as rights that we ought to specify them as needs and seek, with the blunt institutional procedures at our disposal, to make their satisfaction a routine human practice. At the very least, if we had a language of needs at our disposal, we would be in a better position to understand the difference between granting people their rights and giving people what they need.

I am saying that a decent and humane society requires a shared language of the good. The one our society lives by – a language of rights – has no terms for those dimensions of the human good which require acts of virtue unspecifiable as a legal or civil obligation.

A theory of human needs is a particular kind of language of the human good. To define human nature in terms of need is to define what we *are* in terms of what we *lack*, to insist on the distinctive emptiness and incompleteness of humans as a species. As natural creatures, we are potential only. There is nothing intrinsic to our natures which entitles us to anything. Yet we are the only species with the capacity to create and transform our needs, the only species whose needs have a history. It is the needs we have created for ourselves, and the language of entitlements we have derived from them, which give us any claim to respect and dignity as a species, and as individuals. Needs language, therefore, is a distinctively historical and relative language of the human good.

[. . .]

Questions about human needs are questions about human obligations. To ask what our needs are is to ask not just which of our desires are strongest and most urgent, but which of our desires give us an entitlement to the resources of others. This natural pairing of the idea of need with the idea of duty and obligation is what distinguishes need from desire. Need is bounded by the idea of utility. It is possible to specify the duties which would follow from an obligation to meet someone's need. But the duty would be boundless, and therefore meaningless, if it extended to a person's desires.

Need is a vernacular of justification, specifying the claims of necessity that those who lack may rightfully address to those who have. Without a language of need, and the language of right that derives from it, the human world would scarcely be human: between powerful and powerless only the law of hammer and anvil, master and slave would rule. The pathos of need, like the pathos of all purely verbal claims to the justice or mercy of another, is that need is powerless to enforce its right. It justifies an entitlement only if the powerful understand themselves to be obliged by it.

What is it then which binds those who have more than enough and those with less than enough in the ties of obligation? For most people, obligations are a matter of custom, habit and historical inheritance as much as a matter of explicit moral commitment. But might there not be something more than custom, habit and inheritance? Whatever the customs of a country, it would seem 'unnatural' for a father to deny his duty towards the needs of his children, unnatural for a daughter to refuse her homeless father. Beneath all these, there is nature: the natural feeling which ought to exist between father and children and more mysteriously between human beings as such.

The language of human needs is a basic way of speaking about the idea of a natural human identity. We want to know what we have in common with each other beneath the infinity of our differences. We want to know what it means to be human, and we want to know what that knowledge commits us to in terms of duty. What distinguishes the language of needs is its claim that human beings actually feel a common and shared identity in the basic fraternity of hunger, thirst, cold, exhaustion, loneliness or sexual passion. The possibility of human solidarity rests on this idea of natural human identity. A society in which strangers would feel common belonging and mutual responsibility to each other depends on trust, and trust reposes in turn on the idea that beneath difference there is identity.

Yet when one thinks about it, this is a puzzling idea. For who has ever met a pure and natural human being? We are always social beings, clothed in our skin, our class, income, our history, and as such our obligations to each other are always based on difference. Ask me who I am responsible for, and I will tell you about my wife and child, my parents, my friends and relations, and my fellow citizens. My obligations are defined by what it means to be a citizen, a father, a husband, a son, in this culture, in this time and place. The role of pure human duty seems obscure. It is difference which seems to rule my duties, not identity.

Similarly, if you ask me what my needs are, I will tell you that I need the chance to understand and be understood, to love and be loved, to forgive and be forgiven, and the chance to create something which will outlast my life, and the chance to belong to a society whose purposes and commitments I share. But if you were to ask me what needs I have as a natural, as opposed to a social being, I would quickly find myself restricted to those of my body. I would abandon the rest as the work of my time and place, no less precious for all that, but not necessarily a universal human claim or entitlement. Yet even the natural identity of my body seems marked by social difference. The identity between such hunger as I have ever known and the hunger of the street people of Calcutta is a purely linguistic one. My common natural identity of need, therefore, is narrowed by the limits of my social experience here in this tiny zone of safety known as the developed world.

Why bother with the natural then, so long as the social tells what we ought to do? The problem, of course, is that the social does not always tell us what to do. We may know what our obligations are to our families and friends and our fellow citizens, but what are our obligations to those strangers at our gates? Take one step outside our zone of safety – the developed world – and there they are, hands outstretched, gaunt, speechless or clamouring in the zone of danger. There is no claim of kith and kin to connect us together: there is only the indeterminate claim of one human being helping another.

What these claims from strangers make so painfully clear is the asymmetry between natural and social obligation. The lives of a father, a daughter, a son are precious to us; the lives of strangers count for little. If we have the same needs, the same natural identity, this should not be so. Why does our natural identity count for so little, why does difference count for so much?

3.2 Why do wealthy people give?: elite donor statements

Why the wealthy give

Paul G. Schervish, 2007

Introduction

Why the wealthy give is both a commonplace and a distinctive matter. It is commonplace because the motives that generate philanthropic giving are for the most part what prompt people across the economic spectrum. Inquire of any individual, rich or poor, just why he/she gives and we will hear a similar array of factors that inspire his/her philanthropy, mainly identification or empathy with the fate of others, and gratitude for blessings in his/her life. There is, too, for all people the deep and reinforcing satisfaction that accompanies meeting directly the true needs of others.

Why the wealthy give is also a distinctive matter, for there are several factors that mobilize philanthropy, which are particular to those with substantial means. In particular are the motives of financial security, a desire to limit the amount of inheritance to heirs, and what I call hyperagency. The truly wealthy are those who are financially secure, having settled the economic problem of achieving indefinitely a desired standard of living for themselves and their heirs, and are now looking for an additional outlet for the productive use of their money. They, of course, provide substantial inheritances to their heirs, but have in mind a plan to allocate only an amount that will be a positive force in the life of their heirs, rather than the goal of simply transferring to heirs as much as possible. Hyperagency is the combination of psychological and material capacity to not just contribute to or support causes, but to relatively single-handedly produce new philanthropic organizations or new directions in existing ones.

There are, of course, many other motivations which are important, but I do not address them here. First there are tax incentives – which may, but not necessarily, affect wealth holders more, but advance giving by the non-wealthy, as well. There are also religious and spiritual obligations, family traditions, guilt and prestige to name just a few. Name any motivation and it will induce philanthropic giving by someone, somewhere, in some circumstance. A book by Theresa Lloyd, *Why Rich People Give* covers some of the same ground I review here and should also be useful for those interested in her focus on giving by wealth holders in the UK.

In the end, all giving is motivated by an array of factors, some of which we might consider nobler than others. But I have learned that it is rarely possible for people who do not intimately know the hearts of others to draw hard conclusions about what compendium of motives are in play and which determine any gift. We may be able to criticize attitudes and behaviors. But when it comes to motives, it is far more difficult to discern from the outside whether any individual is imbued with nobler or baser ones. In order to avoid as much as possible the notion of motivation as an ultimate inner disposition which is either lofty or low, I will speak of motivations and motives in the sense of their Latin root, *movere* – to move. As such, motives are the mobilizing forces of purpose and aspiration that animate activity.

[. . .]

The moral biography of wealth

The context for discussing the motivations for charitable giving among wealth holders is what I call the moral biography of wealth. The term moral biography refers to the way that individuals conscientiously combine in daily life two elements: personal capacity and moral compass. Capacity is simply the set of resources we have at our disposal to accomplish our goals, and includes our financial assets, intellectual capital and physical talents. Moral compass is the array of purposes or aspirations to which we devote our capacity. Living a moral biography is something as simple as leading a good life and something as profound as following Aristotle's teaching that happiness comes from making wise decisions in our daily life. What creates a moral biography is not merely the existence of financial, intellectual, physical, creative or other personal capacities, but the presence of a moral compass which identifies and strives to accomplish the nobler aims of life for which finances – and one's other capacities – serve as instruments; that is, to combine prosperity and purpose in a spiritually fulfilling, culturally formative and socially consequential way.

[. . .]

Philanthropy is one of the primary ways that individuals pursue care. As such, philanthropy is also a central dimension of the moral compass, by which wealthy individuals allocate their financial resources for the care of others. In carrying out philanthropy, wealth holders carry out their moral biography imbued with substantial financial capacity. To explore the motivations of philanthropy, then, is to examine the motivations of care and, more broadly still, to examine some of the key motivations for living a moral biography.

Before turning to the motivations that generate a commitment to philanthropy as part of one's moral biography, I review what I call the new physics of philanthropy as a second context for understanding just why the wealthy give.

The new physics of philanthropy

The distinctive trait of wealth holders in all eras is that they enjoy the fullest range of choice in determining and fulfilling who they want to become and what they want to do for themselves, their families and the world around them. Today, increasing numbers of individuals are approaching, achieving or even exceeding their financial goals with respect to the provision for their material needs, and doing so at younger and younger ages. A level of affluence which before this time was the province of a scattering of rulers, generals, merchants, financiers and industrialists has come to characterize large groups and even whole cultures. For the first time in history, the question of how to align broad material capacity of choice with spiritual capacity of character has been placed before so many of a nation's people.

Today, many changes in capacity and purpose are taking place on the supply (or donor) side of philanthropy and on the demand (or beneficiary and fundraising) side. Taken together, the financial and personal factors we have uncovered in the course of research constitute what I call the new physics of philanthropy. The new physics entails an innovative way of thinking, feeling and acting in regard to philanthropy. In the new physics, wealth holders:

- are becoming more numerous, have higher net worth at a younger age, and increasingly recognize their financial security;
- seek out rather than resist greater charitable involvement;
- approach their philanthropy with an entrepreneurial disposition;
- move their giving towards *inter vivos* involvements;
- plan to limit the amount of inheritance for heirs;
- understand that caring for the needs of others is a path to self-fulfillment;
- make philanthropy a key and regular ingredient of the financial morality that they observe and impart to their children; and
- view philanthropy as a way to achieve simultaneously the happiness of themselves and others.

When speaking about motivations for philanthropy by wealth holders, we are addressing more and more what motivates individuals to carry out the new physics of philanthropy as a moral biography.

Motives for philanthropy

The next question is just what motivations mobilize wealth holders to carry out the new physics of philanthropy and to make charitable giving an important dimension of a moral compass of care? What factors motivate high net-worth individuals to allocate substantial portion of their wealth to philanthropy rather than to other worthwhile endeavors? As stated, the motivations of identification, gratitude and strategic friendship, which are common to all who engage in philanthropy, join financial security, a desire to limit bequests to heirs and hyperagency as motivations which are distinctive to wealth holders. I discuss the motivation of identification most at length because it is the cornerstone of all care.

Identification

The key to care and philanthropy, as I have written elsewhere, is not the absence of self that motivates charitable giving, but the presence of self-identification with others. This is what Thomas Aquinas teaches as the convergence of love of neighbor, love of self and love of God. In its civic expression, it is what de Tocqueville meant by "self-interest properly understood," and what Harriet Martineau, a contemporary of Tocqueville who wrote six volumes on her travels in the USA, calls the "spirit of fraternity." Such a spirit of fraternity, she maintains, arises "from the movers feeling it their own concern that any are depressed and endangered as they would themselves refuse to be."

[. . .]

Given the strength of identification as the wellspring of charitable giving, it is not surprising that donors contribute the greatest bulk of their charitable dollars to causes from whose services the donors directly benefit. It is not by coincidence that schools, health and arts organizations, and especially churches attract so much giving. For it is here that donors, because they are also recipients, most identify with the individuals –

namely themselves, their families and people much like them – whose needs are being met by the contributions. Although, describing this form of giving as consumption philanthropy may seem to discount its value, my intention is just the opposite. Within the identification model, consumption philanthropy is an honorable prototype of motivation to be emulated rather than a regrettable stereotype to be eschewed. Consumption philanthropy mobilizes charitable giving so formidably because it is here that identification between donor and recipient is strongest.

[. . .]

Taking a gift with gratitude

The motivation of identification is complemented by a particularly strong sense of gratitude for unmerited advantages or, as some say, "blessings" in reaching financial success. Over the course of two decades, my colleagues and I have interviewed over 250 individuals from across the economic spectrum about their motivations for care. A virtually universal disposition which we encountered is the propensity that many summarize by the simple yet heartfelt phrase "to give back." It turns out, however, that upon probing we unearth an impetus that is even more vital than this salutary phrase suggests. Invariably, beneath the desire to give back is a sense of gratitude, and behind that gratitude is an appreciation of blessing, grace, gift, luck or fortune. Gratitude is an active, mobilizing sentiment; a discerning encounter with blessing animates a response of care for others.

[. . .]

In a perceptive way, this brings us back full circle to identification. Those who experience such blessing and gratitude also formulate the moral logic by which a spiritual experience of blessing engenders a pragmatic practice of care. The most consequential corollary of apprehending one's life as imbued with gift is the generative recognition that just as my fortune is not due entirely to my own merit, others' misfortune may not be completely attributable to their own failure. Such an insight forges identification between donors and recipients as the offspring of a common heritage of unmerited positive and negative fortune, and as the source of a common destiny. Those who have been dealt a friendly hand care for those who have been dealt an inauspicious one. Blessing breeds gratitude and gratitude breeds identification and, again, identification breeds generosity. There is one other mobilizing factor that affects all givers – namely, the satisfaction of directly caring for others. I will discuss this factor below as the motivation that leads those who are financially secure to focus on philanthropy rather than other productive uses for their wealth.

Financial security

In addition to identification and gratitude, which motivate all givers including the wealthy, key mobilizing forces that lead major wealth holders to make major gifts include the mobilizing factors of financial security, a desire to limit the amount of bequests to heirs, and the world-constructing disposition of hyperagency.

Financial security is the self-perceived ability, despite general financial downturns, to provide a desired standard for oneself and one's family. Our research has offered some suggestive empirical evidence which indicates a positive relation between financial wealth and both *inter vivos* giving and charitable bequests. For every category of high net worth, controlling for income, those who understand themselves as financially secure contribute a higher percentage of their wealth, a higher percentage of their income and a higher dollar amount to charity. For the non-wealthy, those who express economic confidence in the future, controlling for income, contribute a higher dollar amount and a higher percentage of income to charity.

[. . .]

Limiting transfers to heirs

For the high net-worth individuals, the allocation of wealth to heirs is regularly limited by considerations such as the potentially negative effects of large inheritances on children; and allocations to philanthropy are more frequently occurring via a family foundation or through the involvement of the wealth holder and heirs in philanthropy, as a good way to resolve the moral dilemmas that surround the best use of excess wealth.

[. . .]

The satisfactions of philia

Even with financial security and a disposition to limit the inheritance to heirs, the question remains, just why philanthropy is such an attractive venue for allocating wealth instead of, say, to more investments. Why is philanthropy such an appealing outlet for allocation of wealth? The beginning to the answer is found in Aristotle's discussion of *philia*.

For Aristotle, the essence of philanthropy is to be found in friendship love or *philia*, which in turn is the basis for community. *Philia* is first encountered in the family where family members learn to love others as they love themselves. Friends become "a sort of other selves." A person is "related to a friend as he is to himself (since the friend is another self)." The upshot is that "Every sort of friendship, then, is in a community." It extends beyond the family to companions, fellow citizens, and so forth, wherever the relationship is extended towards "something good and superior." It is for this reason that I have now come to refer to philanthropy as strategic friendship, and strategic friendship as the foundation of civil society, or what I call the moral citizenship of care.

In commercial and political relations, the goal to achieve "something good and superior" may be actively present. But it is subordinated to market relations wherein the provision of goods and services to meet the needs of others occurs only to the extent that others voice their needs through dollars for purchases, in the commercial realm, and campaign contributions and votes in the political realm.

In the philanthropic realm of strategic friendship and the moral citizenship of care, the *telos* of the moral biography is oriented directly to the well-being of the other as a friend (even at a distance). A friend, says Aristotle, is "someone who wishes for and does good things . . . for the sake of the other person, or who wants the friend to be and to live for the friend's own sake." The moral vision that directs philanthropy is the recognition that "life is difficult for one who is alone," and that "a human being is meant for a city and is such a nature as to live with others," that "it is necessary for a happy person to have friends" because happiness is an activity that requires contact with others. The content of that contact is the mutual benefit of friendship which when extended to broader horizons of kinship, time and space, makes strangers into friends. "A friend, who is another self," says Aristotle, "supplies what someone is incapable of supplying by himself" and, conversely, "the excellent person will need people for him to benefit."

[. . .]

The moral compass of a moral biography, then, is one that is inherently communal and attends directly, and not just through the market, to the needs of others. Such a moral biography is the building block of the moral citizenship of care, that array of intersecting relationships of care by which individuals respond to the needs of others, not through commercial or political markets, but directly because of the tie of *philia*, or friendship love, that one wishes to carry out effectively and strategically.

[. . .]

Hyperagency: the capacity and great expectations to be world-builders

In one of his more famous statements, Marx argued that while people do indeed make their own history, they are not able to choose the conditions under which they do so. Although Marx was referring to collective action, the same dictum holds for individual actors as well. However, the capacity to "make history" is not equally distributed. Some, including wealth holders, make more history than others. I call this history-making capacity of individuals "hyperagency." For sure, not every hyperagent is wealthy. Some financially common folk make history by virtue of being profound, creative or spiritual. But in the material realm, every wealth holder is at least potentially a hyperagent, and all of those who start businesses or set directions in philanthropy certainly are.

The desire to make a difference in philanthropy is one outlet for exercising the entrepreneurial disposition of hyperagency. Coupled with the motives of identification, gratitude, financial security, the desire to limit inheritances to successors and the attractive call of *philia*, the ability to exercise hyperagency and change the world becomes an especially strong motivation for philanthropy.

Hyperagency refers to the enhanced capacity of wealthy individuals to establish or control substantially the conditions under which they and others will work and live. For most individuals, agency is limited to choosing among and acting within the constraints of those situations in which they find themselves. As monarchs of agency, the wealth holders can circumscribe such constraints and, for good or for ill, create parts of the world according to their own design. As everyday agents, most of us strive to *find* the best possible place to live or job to hold within a given field of possibilities. As hyperagents, the wealthy – when they choose to do so – can *found* a broad array of the field of possibilities within which they and others will live and work.

[. . .]

The definition of wealth holders as hyperagents with personal determination and institutional dominion directly applies to their activity in the realm of philanthropy. Self-construction and world-building do not stop at the doors to their homes or their businesses. It extends to all of their involvements including, for those who choose, politics, community, religion and philanthropy. The wealthy are by dint of personality no more egoistically myopic or socially responsible than anyone else. Great expectations and grand aspirations occupy people across the financial spectrum. What is different for wealth holders is that they can legitimately be more confident about actualizing their expectations and aspirations because they are able to directly effect the fulfillment of their desires. It's a matter of realizing "how much a little money can make a difference," as Californian Francis Toppler puts it.

The gospel of wealth

Andrew Carnegie, 1889

The problem of our age is the proper administration of wealth, so that the ties of brotherhood may still bind together the rich and poor in harmonious relationship.

[. . .]

The price which society pays for the law of competition, like the price it pays for cheap comforts and luxuries, is also great; but the advantages of this law are also greater still, for it is to this law that we owe our wonderful material development, which brings improved conditions in its train. But, whether the law be benign or not, we must say of it, as we say of the change in the conditions of men to which we have referred: It is here; we cannot evade it; no substitutes for it have been found; and while the law may be sometimes hard for the individual, it is best for the race, because it insures the survival of the fittest in every department. We accept and welcome therefore, as conditions to which we must accommodate ourselves, great inequality of environment, the concentration of business, industrial and commercial, in the hands of a few, and the law of competition between these, as being not only beneficial, but essential for the future progress of the race. Having accepted these, it follows that there must be great scope for the exercise of special ability in the merchant and in the manufacturer who has to conduct affairs upon a great scale. That this talent for organization and management is rare among men is proved by the fact that it invariably secures for its possessor enormous rewards, no matter where or under what laws or conditions.

[. . .]

It is a law, as certain as any of the others named, that men possessed of this peculiar talent for affair, under the free play of economic forces, must, of necessity, soon be in receipt of more revenue than can be judiciously expended upon themselves; and this law is as beneficial for the race as the others.

Objections to the foundations upon which society is based are not in order, because the condition of the race is better with these than it has been with any others which have been tried.

[. . .]

We start, then, with a condition of affairs under which the best interests of the race are promoted, but which inevitably gives wealth to the few. Thus far, accepting conditions as they exist, the situation can be surveyed and pronounced good. The question then arises – and, if the foregoing be correct, it is the only question with which we have to deal – What is the proper mode of administering wealth after the laws upon which civilization is founded have thrown it into the hands of the few? And it is of this great question that I believe I offer the true solution.

[. . .]

There are but three modes in which surplus wealth can be disposed of. It can be left to the families of the decedents; or it can be bequeathed for public purposes; or, finally, it can be administered during their lives by its possessors. Under the first and second modes most of the wealth of the world that has reached the few has hitherto been applied. Let us in turn consider each of these modes. The first is the most injudicious.

[. . .]

Why should men leave great fortunes to their children? If this is done from affection, is it not misguided affection? Observation teaches that, generally speaking, it is not well for the children that they should be so burdened.

[. . .]

As to the second mode, that of leaving wealth at death for public uses, it may be said that this is only a means for the disposal of wealth, provided a man is content to wait until he is dead before it becomes of much good in the world. Knowledge of the results of legacies bequeathed is not calculated to inspire the brightest hopes of much posthumous good being accomplished. The cases are not few in which the real object sought by the testator is not attained, nor are they few in which his real wishes are thwarted. In many cases the bequests are so used as to become only monuments of his folly.

[. . .]

Men who leave vast sums in this way may fairly be thought men who would not have left it at all, had they been able to take it with them.

[. . .]

There remains, then, only one mode of using great fortunes; but in this we have the true antidote for the temporary unequal distribution of wealth, the reconciliation of the rich and the poor – a reign of harmony – another ideal, differing, indeed, from that of the Communist in requiring only the further evolution of existing conditions, not the total overthrow of our civilization. It is founded upon the present most intense individualism, and the race is projected to put it in practice by degree whenever it pleases. Under its sway we shall have an ideal state, in which the surplus wealth of the few will become, in the best sense the property of the many, because administered for the common good, and this wealth, passing through the hands of the few, can be made a much more potent force for the elevation of our race than if it had been distributed in small sums to the people themselves. Even the poorest can be made to see this, and to agree that great sums gathered by some of their fellow-citizens and spent for public purposes, from which the masses reap the principal benefit, are more valuable to them than if scattered among them through the course of many years in trifling amounts.

[. . .]

Poor and restricted are our opportunities in this life; narrow our horizon; our best work most imperfect; but rich men should be thankful for one inestimable boon. They have it in their power during their lives to busy themselves in organizing benefactions from which the masses of their fellows will derive lasting advantage, and thus dignify their own lives. The highest life is probably to be reached, not by such imitation of the life of Christ as Count Tolstoi gives us, but, while animated by Christ's spirit, by recognizing the changed conditions of this age, and adopting modes of expressing this spirit suitable to the changed conditions under which we live; still laboring for the good of our fellows, which was the essence of his life and teaching, but laboring in a different manner.

This, then, is held to be the duty of the man of Wealth: First, to set an example of modest, unostentatious living, shunning display or extravagance; to provide moderately for the legitimate wants of those dependent upon him; and after doing so to consider all surplus revenues which come to him simply as trust funds, which he is called upon to administer, and strictly bound as a matter of duty to administer in the manner which, in his judgment, is best calculated to produce the most beneficial results for the community – the man of wealth thus becoming the mere agent and trustee for his poorer brethren, bringing to their service his superior wisdom, experience and ability to administer, doing for them better than they would or could do for themselves.

[. . .]

The best uses to which surplus wealth can be put have already been indicated. These who, would administer wisely must, indeed, be wise, for one of the serious obstacles to the improvement of our race is indiscriminate charity. It were better for mankind that the millions of the rich were thrown in to the sea than so spent as to encourage the slothful, the drunken, the unworthy. Of every thousand dollars spent in so called charity to-day, it is probable that $950 is unwisely spent; so spent, indeed as to produce the very evils which it proposes to mitigate or cure. A well-known writer of philosophic books admitted the other day that he had given a quarter of a dollar to a man who approached him as he was coming to visit the house of his friend. He knew nothing of the habits of this beggar; knew not the use that would be made of this money, although he had every reason to suspect that it would be spent improperly. This man professed to be a disciple of Herbert Spencer; yet the quarter-dollar given that night will probably work more injury than all the money which its thoughtless donor will ever be able to give in true charity will do good. He only gratified his own feelings, saved him-self from annoyance – and this was probably one of the most selfish and very worst actions of his life, for in all respects he is most worthy.

In bestowing charity, the main consideration should be to help those who will help themselves; to provide part of the means by which those who desire to improve may do so; to give those who desire to use the aids by which they may rise; to assist, but rarely or never to do all. Neither the individual nor the race is improved by alms-giving. Those worthy of assistance, except in rare cases, seldom require assistance. The really valuable men of the race never do, except in cases of accident or sudden change. Every one has, of course, cases of individuals brought to his own knowledge where temporary assistance can do genuine good, and these he will not overlook. But the amount which can be wisely given by the individual for individuals is necessarily limited by his lack of knowledge of the circumstances connected with each. He is the only true reformer who is as careful and as anxious not to aid the unworthy as he is to aid the worthy, and, perhaps, even more so, for in alms-giving more injury is probably done by rewarding vice than by relieving virtue.

[. . .]

[T]he best means of benefiting the community is to place within its reach the ladders upon which the aspiring can rise – parks, and means of recreation, by which men are helped in body and mind, works of art, certain to give pleasure and improve the public taste, and public institutions of various kinds, which will improve the general condition of the people – in this manner returning their surplus wealth to the mass of their fellows in the forms best calculated to do them lasting good.

Thus is the problem of Rich and Poor to be solved. The laws of accumulation will be left free; the laws of distribution free. Individualism will continue, but the millionaire will be but a trustee for the poor; intrusted for a season with a great part of the increased wealth of the community, but administering it for the community far better than it could or would have done for itself. The best minds will thus have reached a stage in the development of the race in which it is clearly seen that there is no mode of disposing of surplus wealth creditable to thoughtful and earnest men into whose hands it flows save by using it year by year for the general good. This day already dawns. But a little while, and although, without incurring the pity of their fellows, men may die sharers in great business enterprises from which their capital cannot be or has not been withdrawn, and is left chiefly at death for public uses, yet the man who dies leaving behind many millions of available wealth, which was his to administer during life, will pass away "unwept, unhonored, and unsung," no matter to what uses he leaves the dross which he cannot take with him. Of such as these the public verdict will then be: "The man who dies thus rich dies disgraced."

Such, in my opinion, is the true Gospel concerning Wealth, obedience to which is destined some day to solve the problem of the Rich and the Poor, and to bring "Peace on earth, among men Good-Will."

Caring and complexity

Bill Gates, 2007

I left Harvard with no real awareness of the awful inequities in the world – the appalling disparities of health, and wealth, and opportunity that condemn millions of people to lives of despair.

I learned a lot [. . .] at Harvard about new ideas in economics and politics. I got great exposure to the advances being made in the sciences.

But humanity's greatest advances are not in its discoveries – but in how those discoveries are applied to reduce inequity. Whether through democracy, strong public education, quality health care, or broad economic opportunity – reducing inequity is the highest human achievement.

I left campus knowing little about the millions of young people cheated out of educational opportunities here in this country. And I knew nothing about the millions of people living in unspeakable poverty and disease in developing countries.

It took me decades to find out.

[. . .]

Imagine, just for the sake of discussion, that you had a few hours a week and a few dollars a month to donate to a cause – and you wanted to spend that time and money where it would have the greatest impact in saving and improving lives. Where would you spend it?

For Melinda and for me, the challenge is the same: how can we do the most good for the greatest number with the resources we have.

During our discussions on this question, Melinda and I read an article about the millions of children who were dying every year in poor countries from diseases that we had long ago made harmless in this country. Measles, malaria, pneumonia, hepatitis B, yellow fever. One disease I had never even heard of, rotavirus, was killing half a million kids each year – none of them in the United States.

We were shocked. We had just assumed that if millions of children were dying and they could be saved, the world would make it a priority to discover and deliver the medicines to save them. But it did not. For under a dollar, there were interventions that could save lives that just weren't being delivered.

If you believe that every life has equal value, it's revolting to learn that some lives are seen as worth saving and others are not. We said to ourselves: "This can't be true. But if it is true, it deserves to be the priority of our giving."

So we began our work in the same way anyone here would begin it. We asked: "How could the world let these children die?"

The answer is simple, and harsh. The market did not reward saving the lives of these children, and governments did not subsidize it. So the children died because their mothers and their fathers had no power in the market and no voice in the system.

But you and I have both.

We can make market forces work better for the poor if we can develop a more creative capitalism – if we can stretch the reach of market forces so that more people can make a profit, or at least make a living, serving people who are suffering from the worst inequities. We also can press governments around the world to spend taxpayer money in ways that better reflect the values of the people who pay the taxes.

If we can find approaches that meet the needs of the poor in ways that generate profits for business and votes for politicians, we will have found a sustainable way to reduce inequity in the world.

This task is open-ended. It can never be finished. But a conscious effort to answer this challenge will change the world.

I am optimistic that we can do this, but I talk to skeptics who claim there is no hope. They say: "Inequity has been with us since the beginning, and will be with us till the end – because people just . . . don't . . . care."

I completely disagree. I believe we have more caring than we know what to do with.

All of us [. . .],at one time or another, have seen human tragedies that broke our hearts, and yet we did nothing – not because we didn't care, but because we didn't know what to do. If we had known how to help, we would have acted.

The barrier to change is not too little caring; it is too much complexity.

To turn caring into action, we need to see a problem, see a solution, and see the impact. But complexity blocks all three steps.

Even with the advent of the Internet and 24-hour news, it is still a complex enterprise to get people to truly see the problems. When an airplane crashes, officials immediately call a press conference. They promise to investigate, determine the cause, and prevent similar crashes in the future.

But if the officials were brutally honest, they would say: "Of all the people in the world who died today from preventable causes, one half of one percent of them were on this plane. We're determined to do everything possible to solve the problem that took the lives of the one half of one percent."

The bigger problem is not the plane crash, but the millions of preventable deaths.

We don't read much about these deaths. The media covers what's new – and millions of people dying is nothing new. So it stays in the background, where it's easier to ignore. But even when we do see it or read about it, it's difficult to keep our eyes on the problem. It's hard to look at suffering if the situation is so complex that we don't know how to help. And so we look away.

If we can really see a problem, which is the first step, we come to the second step: cutting through the complexity to find a solution.

Finding solutions is essential if we want to make the most of our caring. If we have clear and proven answers anytime an organization or individual asks "How can I help?," then we can get action – and we can make sure that none of the caring in the world is wasted. But complexity makes it hard to mark a path of action for everyone who cares – and that makes it hard for their caring to matter.

Cutting through complexity to find a solution runs through four predictable stages: determine a goal, find the highest-leverage approach, discover the ideal technology for that approach, and in the meantime, make the smartest application of the technology that you already have – whether it's something sophisticated, like a drug, or something simpler, like a bed net.

The AIDS epidemic offers an example. The broad goal, of course, is to end the disease. The highest-leverage approach is prevention. The ideal technology would be a vaccine that gives lifetime immunity with a single dose. So governments, drug companies, and foundations fund vaccine research. But their work is likely to take more than a decade, so in the meantime, we have to work with what we have in hand – and the best prevention approach we have now is getting people to avoid risky behavior.

Pursuing that goal starts the four-step cycle again. This is the pattern. The crucial thing is to never stop thinking and working – and never do what we did with malaria and tuberculosis in the 20th century – which is to surrender to complexity and quit.

The final step – after seeing the problem and finding an approach – is to measure the impact of your work and share your successes and failures so that others learn from your efforts.

You have to have the statistics, of course. You have to be able to show that a program is vaccinating millions more children. You have to be able to show a decline in the number of children dying from these diseases. This is essential not just to improve the program, but also to help draw more investment from business and government.

But if you want to inspire people to participate, you have to show more than numbers; you have to convey the human impact of the work – so people can feel what saving a life means to the families affected.

I remember going to Davos some years back and sitting on a global health panel that was discussing ways to save millions of lives. Millions! Think of the thrill of saving just one person's life – then multiply that by millions . . . Yet this was the most boring panel I've ever been on – ever. So boring even I couldn't bear it.

What made that experience especially striking was that I had just come from an event where we were introducing version 13 of some piece of software, and we had people jumping and shouting with excitement. I love getting people excited about software – but why can't we generate even more excitement for saving lives?

You can't get people excited unless you can help them see and feel the impact. And how you do that – is a complex question.

Still, I'm optimistic. Yes, inequity has been with us forever, but the new tools we have to cut through complexity have not been with us forever. They are new – they can help us make the most of our caring – and that's why the future can be different from the past.

I never dreamed I'd be a philanthropist

Xin Zhang, 2014

I never dreamed that one day I would become a philanthropist. I was born in Beijing in 1965, and spent my teenage years working long hours as a factory girl, sewing collars and buttons onto dress shirts in Hong Kong. Today, I am the chief executive of SOHO China, the country's largest prime office property developer.

China has seen rapid economic growth over the past three decades, and it is now one of the world's fastest growing producers of billionaires – 242 and counting, according to *Forbes* – which is extraordinary considering that just over a decade ago, there were none.

Though many Chinese have grown wealthy, few have embraced the practice of philanthropy in a manner and scale that is comparable with their counterparts in the West. But I believe we are on the cusp of change. With a new generation of Chinese who feel grateful for the opportunities the country's growth has provided, social consciousness is rising, contributing to a growing urge to give back in innovative ways and to contribute to the nation's future and to the betterment of our society.

My generation's success stories are unique. We were born into Communist China, at a time when almost nobody had access to material wealth. The guiding philosophy was to "serve the people," but no one had the economic means to give back to society, nor were there many philanthropic foundations. It was an impossible time to have a culture or tradition of philanthropy nurtured by the generous individuals and families like the Rockefellers or the Carnegies. There were no philanthropic role models under communism. China was completely insulated from the rest of the world, with very little access to outside information. As children of that society, we could not have imagined the possibility of becoming a philanthropist.

But in 1978, Deng Xiaoping opened China's doors to economic reform and capital markets. China's entrepreneurial spirit was reborn and my generation blossomed. We studied abroad, we started businesses and many of us prospered in unprecedented ways.

For many Chinese of my generation, our first point of contact with Western philanthropy was the financial aid we received when we studied abroad. Very few of us had money – most only had raw ambition. We were "PHDs:" poor, hungry and determined. Financial aid transformed our lives.

I studied in the United Kingdom on a full scholarship in the 1980s, earning a bachelor's degree from Sussex University and a master's from Cambridge University. My education would eventually lead to a job on Wall Street, and then in 1995 I returned to China and founded SOHO China with my husband, Pan Shiyi, who grew up in rural western China. He had also attended university, which carried him away from village life and into our growing and changing nation's business community.

That opportunity to study was the most dramatic turning point in my life. My education opened my eyes to the world, provided me with the academic grooming necessary to pursue an international career, and gave me the courage to return to China, build an enterprise and innovate. Without financial aid, I, and so many other Chinese who have played various roles in advising, consulting and building the modern China we know today, may have never had the chance to attend university.

In the decade after I returned to China, many of my peers returned as well. China became increasingly globalized, joining the World Trade Organization in 2001 and preparing for the 2008 Summer Olympics in Beijing. The economy boomed. At the same time, the Internet and social media gained remarkable momentum. There was a push for increasing transparency and pressure mounted on businesses and the government to become more socially responsible now that China was on the world stage.

In those early days of post-economic-reform, most philanthropic giving went to disaster relief and to the construction of schools in remote areas of China. My husband and I joined that philanthropic wave, giving to aid victims of the Asian tsunami disaster in 2004. We then started donating funds to help build schools in China's highly impoverished western provinces of Qinghai and Gansu, where my husband was born and raised. We also gave to the Sichuan earthquake relief efforts in 2008 – a disaster that took the lives of nearly 70,000 people, devastating communities in southwestern China. The suffering of those affected prompted an outpouring of donations from the public, and philanthropy became a topic that people understood, discussed and debated.

At that point, the giving my husband and I were involved in was sporadic and focused on dire need and immediate solutions. It became clear that this Band-Aid approach did not work, since many communities required long-term aid to deal with chronic problems. We needed a cause that would capture our long-term philanthropic aspirations. Looking back on how my education had opened new doors for me, I knew that was the cause closest to my heart: I believe that education is the primary factor in improving social mobility.

My husband and I founded the SOHO China Foundation in 2005, which focuses on improving the quality of education in underprivileged communities. Our first project was a teacher-training program in rural western China. Over the course of five years we brought more than 1,700 teachers from rural communities to Beijing for summer training, improving the level of education provided to more than 80,000 primary school students. When we learned of the poor sanitary conditions at the schools, we also built 45 school toilets, impacting more than 35,000 students.

As I worked with the rural schools, I saw that these students have few opportunities. China's growth has been accompanied by an intensified divide in income distribution, with large cities prospering much more than smaller cities and rural areas. Many wealthy Chinese send their children abroad to study, but countless outstanding rural students lose out on such opportunities due to a lack of financial means. There is a danger that the chance for Chinese youth to study abroad will become purely privilege-based instead of merit-based. Some of our best students are now so intimidated by the economic burden of pursuing a world-class education that they don't even apply to top universities.

It is with this understanding that we decided to create the SOHO China Scholarships, pledging to endow $100 million in financial aid scholarships for Chinese undergraduate students attending leading international universities. Our first gift agreement of $15 million was signed with Harvard University and our second gift agreement of $10 million was signed with Yale University.

This instantly created controversy in China. On the one hand, we received overwhelming encouragement, while on the other our decision to partner with international institutions instead of with domestic universities was heatedly questioned. Philanthropy became a hot topic online and across social media.

My answer to those questioning our choice: The most striking feature of our time is globalization. It is important for China to be integrated with the rest of the world. Our aim is to enable China's best and brightest to act as a bridge between China and other nations – an important tool for modernizing the Middle Kingdom.

When I look back at our decision to create the scholarships in 2014, I recall the time I met Warren Buffett and the deep impression he left on me. Buffett and Bill Gates had traveled to China in 2010 to encourage high-net-worth Chinese to think about philanthropy. Buffett explained that he had always given, and then one day he realized that the rate at which he was giving was slower than the rate at which he was earning money. He was 80 years old at the time, so he decided to entrust a large part of his fortune to the Bill and Melinda Gates Foundation. I walked away inspired by the vision behind his large-scale, highly impactful giving, and ultimately thought, "Don't wait until it's too late."

Soon after the announcement of our SOHO China Scholarships, I heard that my friend the Hong Kong property developer Ronnie Chan and his family made a $350 million gift to Harvard's School of Public Health, and a $20 million gift to his alma mater, the University of Southern California. I have also heard that Jack Ma of Alibaba, the e-commerce giant, along with co-founder Joe Tsai, have said that they will commit 2 percent of Alibaba's equity to a charitable trust.

I believe that the year 2014 is a turning point in Chinese philanthropy. This tradition is finally getting the impetus it needs to flourish because of an emerging group of Chinese entrepreneurs who are socially conscious, globally engaged and hoping to make a positive and lasting impact on China and the world – they're not looking for quick fixes. They feel responsible.

With the help of financial aid, I went from factory worker to university student, then became an entrepreneur and eventually, chief executive of my own company. But of my achievements, I am most proud of my work as a philanthropist, and I hope to continue with it for the rest of my days. The world is waiting to see what Chinese philanthropists will do next.

Giving back for the next generation

Victor Pinchuk, 2013

Blessed with success, one has a responsibility to give back. In today's world, where all rules are constantly changing, social investments can have a greater impact than ever before. By helping to create a more level and a more just playing field with more equal access for all. There has never been a better time for giving.

In times of crisis, giving becomes even more important. Governments have both fewer means and greater spending needs. Time for those who have been successful in building their businesses to step up and help societies become more just.

My goal in my social investments is to empower the next generation to change their country and the world. To enable them to build a new country based on openness and an understanding of the world of today and tomorrow. My focus is on using innovative approaches to provide access to education, healthcare, and the inspirational power of contemporary art. Combined with modern and innovative business projects, I believe this constitutes a powerful formula for change. I have taken my first steps, with large-scale scholarship programs, opening a museum of contemporary art with free admission, and establishing a network of neonatal clinics – but this is just the beginning.

I have a particular focus on my own country, Ukraine, and its integration with the world. As a post-Soviet society, Ukraine needs the support of "social investors" in order to implement reforms and to promote ideas like the rule of law. We face a long road ahead compared to the Western countries, and we who have already benefited from change must help more. And Western countries have not only developed infrastructure, but have also established strong reputations around the globe. Successful business leaders in Ukraine and our region have an important role to play in promoting their own countries to the rest of the world.

My personal history guides my understanding of my future responsibilities. I achieved my first significant business successes with innovations in industrial production and used this to acquire assets, which turned profitable and allowed me to expand my business further. Old factories in a disintegrating economy requiring fast and fundamental changes in management structures – this was risky business, but it paid off. I was one of a relatively small group that was able to turn huge risks into huge profits. Our generation – the first businessmen in Ukraine to emerge after the collapse of the Soviet Union – made some misjudgments, a fact that I am well aware of. We were pioneers of this path and we had no role models. But we managed to breathe new life into Ukrainian industry, and contributed to building the foundations of a new, market-based economy.

Those were times of great opportunity for me. This makes me feel a special responsibility to give back to my country and society. The transformation process was very painful for Ukraine and other post-Soviet countries. Many people feel this era was unfair for society. Some of us had the chance to use the opportunities that arose to make our fortunes. It is time to give back, so that as many citizens as possible can benefit, and hopefully make their peace with this period of our history.

In our part of the world the legacy of communism has made many people more skeptical of the wealthy than in Western countries. I want to convince some of them that successful entrepreneurs and business leaders can be constructive, inventive, and active contributors to making everyone's life better.

Joining a group of dedicated people, and with the opportunity to learn from them, I look forward to my giving becoming more impactful. Investing half or more of my fortune in my lifetime and beyond into areas like education, healthcare, access to contemporary art, and the promotion of my country, I will be investing in the next generation, those who will build the Ukraine and the world tomorrow.

Civic anger among major donors

Ilana F. Silber, 2012

This article focuses on a distinctive cluster of negative emotions, termed here 'civic anger', found to emerge as a salient discursive theme in interviews conducted with 26 mega-donors in the specific context of Israel.

[. . .]

A first feature that emerged from donors' accounts of their own biographic philanthropic trajectory is that heavy engagement with giving was always presented as a highly personal and voluntary option, yet also usually facilitated by exemplary influences in donors' proximate social surroundings. Nearly all donors interviewed thus mentioned the impact of a family background where one or both parents, or a very close relative (most often one or more grandparents) offered an influential precedent of either charitable generosity and/or high involvement in public affairs. Quite independently of any precise level of wealth, moreover, this family precedent was often described as anchored in a traditional pattern of Jewish charity and communal solidarity.

[. . .]

Yet far from being understood as the automatic result of such surrounding influences, be they local or translocal, philanthropy was also conceived as a highly personal and voluntary, as well as reflexive and deliberated matter. Most donors thus reported having devoted systematic thought to the topic of giving and reached a range of highly conscious choices, as well as experienced serious dilemmas. It is also as a result of such reflexive deliberation, that most reported having chosen to focus on problems of welfare and/or education, rather than the arts and culture. Nearly all, moreover, are not only donors, but also active fundraisers, expending much effort convincing others to give. Some even operate as philanthropic entrepreneurs, devoting much time to the management of the organizational structures and projects they are involved with. For all interviewees, moreover, giving is not only a highly personal and time-consuming activity, but also one that gives them much satisfaction, a sense of accomplishment ('getting things done', 'making a difference', 'promoting change').

[. . .]

Yet one of the most striking and repeated findings, on that collective and civic plane precisely, is a bitter criticism and intensely negative feelings, often reaching the point of anger, emerging with regard to the 'state' and its government. This anger is so common as to cut across donors' differences in biographical background characteristics. Mixing instrumental and moral grounds of indictment, it is chiefly turned against what is perceived as a lack of competence and efficiency on the part of the state and of governmental staff, compounded by an attitude of 'indifference' and 'failure to assume responsibility' in the face of the expanding scope of social ills and poverty.

[. . .]

Criticism and anger were also extended at times to what was seen as the undue politicization of fields that should have remained domains of pure managerial and professional expertise immune to the encroachment of politics. Relatedly, most donors denied any relation between their philanthropic involvement and their specifically partisan, political views, and several were intent to present their involvement with philanthropy as the expression of a 'social', rather than 'political' form of Zionism.

However, I do not mean to argue that anger is the one and most determinant ingredient of all elite philanthropic involvement in the Israeli context. Among the sample of mega-donors interviewed in the present study at least, it was never the only and not always the dominant emotion expressed. Rather, it always combined with a variety of positive, benevolent motives of the kind more ordinarily associated with charitable or philanthropic giving. Feelings of solidarity and compassion, and the drive to help the needy out of a sense of concern, involvement and care (in the sense of 'caring about', or *ekhpatiut* in Hebrew) were thus also often expressed, besides, as already noted, a sense of individual efficacy and satisfaction at being able to help; and in a few cases at least, explicit feelings of post-materialist dissatisfaction with highly successful business activity were also voiced. If one also recalls the impact of family precedents and other facilitating influences reported by nearly all donors, there is thus certainly no ground to see civic anger as the all-determinant cause, or trigger for philanthropic giving. Indeed, donors themselves never presented their philanthropic giving as a result, either direct or indirect, of anger.

Moreover, there is need to further qualify the very notion of anger. In the cases at hand, the anger expressed was intense, sometimes even very intense indeed but certainly not one to convey a state of wild emotion, or uncontrolled rage or 'irrational' fury. Neither was it expressed in a monolithic fashion, and only by the sole wording of the term 'anger' (or angry) as such. Rather, the term anger is used here to regroup the expression of a wider range of strongly negative and critical feelings, which included indignation, being upset, deep sadness, criticism, outrage, appal, bitterness, contempt, disappointment, disgust, or even in one extreme case, in that donor's extreme terms, 'feeling like I could explode'. These negative feelings were identified not only on the basis of verbal, discursive statements, but also changes of voice, vehement insistence, facial expressions or body movements indicative of a heightened and negative pole of feelings that stood in rupture relatively to a baseline style and tone of speech in the rest of the interview and made it clear that these were not just expressions of detached criticism, otherwise also occasionally expressed on various matters. In fact, if certainly never reaching a state of uncontrolled rage or fury, no other cluster of themes reached a same level of expressive intensity, either verbally or non-verbally stated, in the context of these interviews.

3.3 Critiques of elite donors

Philanthropy, prestige and status

Francie Ostrower, 1995

[P]hilanthropy clearly remains a sign of prestige among the elite. We have seen that donors view giving as an obligation of the privileged. Philanthropy, however, is not merely something that members of the elite do, nor is it isolated from other aspects of upper-class life. Rather, philanthropy is itself a mark of privilege and high social status. It is a part of elite standing, which is perceived as one of the very defining characteristics of being upper class. Thus, one donor wryly described nonprofit board membership as virtually mandatory "accoutrement." Said he, "I am a trustee of a hospital. You have to be a trustee of a hospital if you're wealthy. It's required . . . But I know nothing about hospitals." Another donor observed,

> Part of the activity of a certain class of people is to be philanthropic . . . I don't know if people do it more out of obligation or that's their way of being part of society. Everybody wants to belong. In our culture, in our way of doing things, that is the role of the wealthy . . . And poor people go to the local church or temple, right? Make suppers, cake sales.

Her comparison with the local church is appropriate, for it highlights donors' involvement with recipient organizations. Nonprofit organizations are focal points around which upper-class life revolves. Through their philanthropy, wealthy donors come together with one another and sustain a series of organizations that contribute to the social and cultural coherence of upper-class life.

The association between philanthropy and privilege means that philanthropic involvements are viewed as symbolic of the donors' personal success and affluence. Speaking of why he agreed to head the alumni fundraising drive among his classmates, one person confessed, "Honestly, I was well motivated by about 80 to 90 percent, but certainly there was a factor in there that it improved my visibility . . . Just among my classmates, because everybody knows that someone who takes on the chairmanship of a class reunion is prepared to give, and has the time and interest to give, and as you say, that's a luxury in society."

While some expressed regret that prestige and even snobbery are influential, donors also emphasized their usefulness in raising money. Said one, "If an organization is going to exist, I suppose it has to have a certain amount of snobbery." Another observed that "social snobbery is a device of fundraising."

At one level, the sheer display of wealth through giving indicates one's success. The connection between prestige and philanthropy, however, involves far more than giving money, and extends to identification and involvement with prominent nonprofits and the elite networks with which they are associated. One man, for instance, acknowledged that "there are some aspects of philanthropic work which are connected with social snobbery. I recognize it myself." Thus, he was "thrilled" when asked to join the board of one prestigious arts organization. Said he, "Naturally I want to be known as an expert on [the organization]. That may be a form of social snobbery, but I'm delighted that this is happening!"

[. . .]

Being identified with prestigious nonprofits serves as a symbol of "having arrived" socially. One respondent observed that "someone or his wife gets very concerned about their status in society" and will try to get involved with organizations so that "they can take their – as the British would say – 'rightful place in Society.'"

Prestigious nonprofits and charity benefits become the target of "social climbing" and networking. As one donor put it, philanthropy "is one of the avenues by which Society makes its connections." Charity benefits, for instance provide exclusive settings for elite interaction. Donors viewed benefits as a prominent component of New York social life, which 89 percent said they attend. As one respondent explained, he enjoys himself at benefits because "there are a lot of people like me there." Another brought up benefits during a discussion of social snobbery and philanthropy, saying, "I will admit I'm partially guilty . . . I very much like the black tie . . . dance at [Organization X] . . . It's an opportunity to meet some people and do some things, which in my mind is more networking than anything else." One donor volunteered that he knew someone who attended benefits for "purely social reasoning – she wanted to meet people and marry a wealthy husband." More generally, he observed that "in some of these organizations there is complete social snobbery. Pick an organization and it has benefits, and people go. And those who can't afford to go, can't go. Also, it's a way of meeting people. It is an important part of social life."

As these quotes suggest, charity benefits further illustrate the closure characterizing elite philanthropy. Here, we often find elites giving at the request of other elites to attend functions with other members of the elite, often in support of organizations that are used by and have prestige in the eyes of the elite.

[. . .]

Implicit in the discussion to this point is that a good deal of elite philanthropy takes place within the same generally well-to-do ambiance that characterizes the work and social environment of these donors. Indeed, privileged access to prestigious settings represents another return to donors for philanthropic contributions, as seen, for instance, in charity benefits and private performances. The lavish backdrop against which philanthropy occurs, in turn, contributes to retaining the identification between philanthropy and prestige. Many donors, who are also fundraisers for causes, stressed the importance of this. Discussing whether too much money is generally spent enhancing the setting of charity benefits, a donor who organizes such benefits emphasized the importance of surroundings as follows: "I think it's money well spent. When a charity becomes attractive to people, they're going to raise more money . . . One time we used to say, 'People are paying a hundred dollars for dinner.' Now they're paying a thousand dollars for dinner! You have to give them flowers. You have to give them a decent meal."

[. . .]

Considerations of organizational prestige are influential in channeling largest gifts as well. As some of the above quotes indicate, nonprofits do not enjoy equal stature among the elite. Rather, philanthropy is structured by a prestige hierarchy. One factor influencing an institution's position in that hierarchy is the area of activity in which it is engaged, as illustrated by the distribution of largest gifts made by donors. With striking frequency, these gifts went to precisely the kinds of educational and cultural organizations that are used by, and have prestige among, the elite. Education received largest gifts from the greatest number of donors, followed by culture. Indeed, these two areas alone received fully 58.6 percent of all (244) largest gifts made, with the remainder divided among six areas. The particular organizations within these areas, in turn, were among the most prestigious in their fields. For instance, most gifts in education went to universities and colleges. Of these 63 gifts, in turn, fully 42.9 percent went to Ivy League schools, with many others going to competitive smaller colleges. In both education and culture, moreover, we find a concentration of giving whereby certain organizations received gifts from multiple donors. In the case of education, this reflected gifts made to particular Ivy League schools; in the case of culture, these were arts institutions described by various donors as among the most prestigious, prominent, and "chic" nonprofits in New York.

[. . .]

An analysis of variation in giving to education further demonstrates that prestige is one factor channeling gifts to certain organizations. Among college graduates, donors who attended more prestigious schools were also more likely to have made one of their largest gifts to their alma mater. This finding also reveals the importance of prestige hierarchies within, as well as between, areas. It indicates as well that even when a donor has familiarity with an organization, its prestige will still be a factor in eliciting largest contributions.

Taken together, the results we have been considering reveal that it is not only giving money or organizational involvement that makes philanthropy prestigious. It is also a question of where that money or involvement is directed. Particular organizations, like philanthropy itself, carry symbolic status values, which influence the distribution of donors' gifts.

Donors themselves expressed an awareness that a status hierarchy exists among nonprofits, and that culture and education are privileged in this regard. When deciding about whether to attend various benefits, one donor is influenced by the involvement of friends, whether the events sound like fun, "or if they're very prestigious, let's be honest." Another donor said, "There are certain institutions, that if you're a volunteer for them, then you're a big deal. If you are on the board of something else, nobody's heard of it. People don't tend to come to meetings." She added that while volunteers are hard to get elsewhere, "they line up by droves" to volunteer for a prestigious arts organization with which she is familiar.

Philanthropy serves the interests of the rich

Teresa Odendahl, 1990

Elite American philanthropy serves the interests of the rich to a greater extent than it does the interests of the poor, disadvantaged, or disabled. [. . .] Voluntary organizations supported and directed by the wealthy philanthropists divert decision-making in the arts, culture, education, health, and welfare from public representatives to a private power elite.

Paradoxically, although people of all classes participate in nonprofit groups, most of these organizations are controlled by a few, and many charities benefit the rich more than they do the poor. The vast majority of nonprofit agencies and programs do not primarily serve the needy. Many elite philanthropists are civic-minded and sincere, but the system they help to maintain may actually reduce the extent to which basic human services are provided on a democratic basis.

By studying rich people and their charitable endeavors, I have identified a nationwide "culture of philanthropy." Those who inherited "old money" and the richest Americans, usually with "new money," tend to be the most involved in voluntary activities. But they contribute disproportionately to clinics, legal aid programs, or other projects for the poor. There are thousands of good causes in which millionaires have little interest.

[. . .]

Not all millionaires in the United States are serious philanthropists. My guess is that fewer than half of the wealthy are charitably minded. Those who regularly contribute large sums of money to nonprofit organizations, serve on several volunteer boards of directors, and spend much of their time raising additional resources for charity from colleagues, friends, and relatives belong to a select social group.

[. . .]

In addition, and of great importance, is the fact that through their charitable activities wealthy philanthropists and their advisers sponsor what we think of as "high culture" – ballet, opera, symphony, theater, and the visual arts. Rich children learn to value these "serious" cultural forms that on the whole are produced by nonprofit organizations. But there is more to philanthropic culture than breeding and taste.

Through their donations and work for voluntary organizations, the charitable rich exert enormous influence in society. As philanthropists, they acquire status within and outside of their class. Although private wealth is the basis of the hegemony of this group, philanthropy is essential to the maintenance and perpetuation of the upper class in the United States. In this sense, nonprofit activities are the nexus of a modern power elite.

The culture of philanthropy is manifest in the common behavior and manners, economic status, and sociocultural institutions, as well as in the shared attitudes, ideas, perceptions, tastes, and values of this group whose members frequently interact with one another. The "established" wealthy are socialized in the family and by exclusive preparatory schools and private colleges. Their interaction continues throughout adulthood as business associates, friends, leaders of local and national voluntary organizations, and relatives by birth and marriage. Elite culture is passed from generation to generation, and from those with old money to the newly rich.

[. . .]

My use of the term culture in connection with philanthropy is intentional: the word carries so many subtle applicable meanings. The rich are integral members of the wider society. In certain respects the charitable elite are so aware of prevalent middle-class cultural norms that they deny their affluence and privilege and do not present or even think of themselves as being upper class.

[. . .]

In general, the charitable wealthy live well below their means. They are conspicuous contributors rather than conspicuous consumers. Nonprofit work, more than anything else, engages them, giving them a sense of identity and meaning. This is particularly true for rich women, who view themselves as having fewer options than wealthy men owing to a relatively rigid division of labor by gender in the upper class. Historically, charity work has been a meaningful activity allowed but not limited to wealthy women.

[. . .]

This is not a psychoanalytic study, but it is clear that many elite philanthropists have psychological "complexes:" anxiety about their place in the world, denial that they are rich, and fear that people or the government are after their money, along with a lack of self-confidence or its counterpart – arrogance. Like everyone else, the wealthy harbor prejudices and stereotypes about themselves and others. Their world is framed by a "we" and "they" perspective.

"They" are government officials who are not of the upper class, as well as the masses, who might take away private wealth through misappropriation, taxation, welfare, or revolution. In contrast, the "social change funders," a young minority group who are sometimes known as the "rich kids," think that the other "they" are conservative, mainstream, or traditional grant-makers. In many cases, then, "they" may be the parents of these younger philanthropists.

For the charitable wealthy of all ages, giving and volunteering is the "proper" thing to do. The improper, other rich are also "they," who spend too lavishly on themselves. Feeling self-conscious about having so much wealth but wanting to retain it, the philanthropic rich assuage their guilt by living relatively modestly and contributing some of their income to "good causes."

[. . .]

I consistently learned that the charitable wealthy and their institutions encourage personal social responsibility, or noblesse oblige. In addition, they consider themselves virtuous in comparison to other wealthy people who do not give. They have a vision of the world that they want to promote, not just to their families, but to others. They see themselves as upholders of an American democracy in which they are the natural leaders. They believe they set an example in their local communities and nationally. In this regard, much of their charity work is paternalistic.

Furthermore, the philanthropic elite think that they have greater knowledge than the average citizen. This is mirrored by a perception on the part of the middle and working classes that the wealthy are in fact the bearers of high culture and sophistication.

Fundamentally, the ideology of the elite concerning their legitimate role in society depends on this perception of the middle and working classes – that the wealthy deserve their status. Conversely, the belief of the mass of citizens that a special minority must have special authority depends on the elite maintaining a posture of noblesse oblige. These complementary ideologies help explain the perennial fascination with wealth and the wealthy that is so notable a part of the attitude of the American people.

[. . .]

Whether it be high culture, "high education," such as that provided at Ivy League universities, the "high philanthropy" of foundations, or the "high medicine" of private nonprofit hospitals, the rich fund and make policy for these institutions, while on the whole the middle class produce the cultural and intellectual products and services. There has always been a tension between wealthy philanthropists and professionals. Just who are the experts and who is or should be running the shows? Ultimately, and according to the law, the trustees are responsible, and even the chief staff officer serves at the pleasure of the board.

[. . .]

What about the neediest citizens, those who are generally thought to be the beneficiaries of charity? It could be argued that philanthropy as currently practiced creates an unequal reciprocity between the upper and lower classes that may stifle rebellion or reform. A system of private charity is not in the interests of the disadvantaged.

[. . .]

The charity system as organized today warrants investigation not only because it benefits the rich to a greater extent than others but also because of the frequency with which philanthropy is invoked by its proponents as an argument against redistributions of wealth by the government. Public policy, enacted through tax codes, allows and encourages a relatively small group of rich people and their advisers to hold much more power over the shape of society than the vast majority in the middle and lower classes.

The importance of criticizing philanthropy

Benjamin Soskis, 2014

Last month, readers of the *Chronicle of Philanthropy*, the trade journal of the nonprofit world, were treated to a memorable op-ed. It was written by John Arnold, a 40-year-old former Enron natural-gas trader and hedge-fund founder who, with his wife, ranked third on the 2013 list of the nation's most generous benefactors. "Attacks and Vitriol Will Not Deter Me From Supporting Fixes to Public Policy," the piece's headline announced, and it went on to document the "intensely personal public attacks" Arnold had endured in retaliation for his contributions to the causes of education, criminal justice, and pension reform. He was falsely charged with attempting to make his donations surreptitiously, he claimed, and had been the target of "selective reporting" regarding his partisan sympathies (smeared, for instance, as a "right-wing ideologue," without a mention of the fact that he raised money for Obama). And he's been subjected to a steady stream of "juvenile insults" (one critic quipped that he had the "jug-eared face of a Division III women's basketball coach"). That last one, evidently, stung.

[. . .]

It's always a bit uncomfortable to see a private citizen taking his knocks in the public square. We probably shouldn't take much pleasure in the spectacle. Yet in the midst of this latest Gilded Age, as the prerogatives of concentrated wealth march onwards with little resistance, an aggressive – even at times an antagonistic – engagement between the public and their benefactors shouldn't be considered a mark of incivility. It should be considered a democratic imperative.

For much of the 20th Century, philanthropists could expect a less-than-welcome reception from much of the public. When Standard Oil-founder John D. Rockefeller attempted to secure a federal charter for his Foundation, politicians and progressive journalists competed with one another to denounce his project. (Congress rejected the request and Rockefeller settled for incorporation in New York.) According to critics, these new foundations, unprecedented in their scale and scope, posed a direct challenge to federal authority; as the head of a Progressive-era congressional investigation into their practices declared, they represented "a menace to the future political and economic welfare of the nation." The debate about the legitimacy of large benefactions became so heated that in 1909 one New Orleans newspaper quipped that philanthropy had become "the recognizable mark of a wicked man."

At mid-century, Americans witnessed another surge in the suspicions directed toward philanthropy and yet another series of Congressional investigations into foundations. This time the ill-winds blew mostly from the right; these latest, populist, and often reactionary assaults associated foundations with the liberal and internationalist political orientations of the Eastern establishment. Philanthropy, these critics charged, engaged in "thought control" by determining the information the public had access to; abetted tax evasion and perpetuated dynastic wealth; and posed a threat to small businesses, and, more generally, to the traditional American way of life. As the chief counsel of that first Progressive-era congressional investigation explained, while its work was grounded in the concern that "foundations would be the tool of reaction," by midcentury, "the most articulately expressed fear has been that the foundations have swung from that position far to the left, and now they are endangering our existing capitalistic structure." Yet whether issuing from the left or the right, these attacks converged around a recognition of the threat that great private wealth posed to American democracy. Philanthropists came to take this suspicion for granted, especially when they were compelled to make public justifications of the tax privileges they enjoyed; public ambivalence to their vocation was one of the burdens of the great wealth they bore.

Then, for a brief, balmy season at the closing decades of the century and at the opening of the new one, something changed: Philanthropy began to enjoy the benefit of the doubt. As the public's faith in the efficacy of government to address the nation's most pressing problems began to plummet, a faith in philanthropy received a compensatory boost. The increased favor also stemmed from the fact that, as the rich got richer, there was more to give.

Charitable giving in the United States jumped from $13 billion in 1996 to nearly $32 billion a decade later. Although it only accounted for a relatively small fraction of the total, a few major benefactions issuing from the emerging tech and financial industry titans grabbed the public's attention. The media's fascination with the promise of philanthropy peaked in June 2006, when investor Warren Buffett pledged more than three-quarters of his massive fortune, some $31 billion in all, to the Bill and Melinda Gates Foundation. The news, declared Princeton ethicist Peter Singer in the *New York Times*, heralded a "golden age of philanthropy." The media coverage philanthropy received tended to reflect this enthusiasm: According to an analysis by Foundation Works, 99 percent of all stories about philanthropy published between 1990 and 2004 were positive in their orientation.

It is safe to say that the golden age is over. Not that philanthropy has lost all its luster – there are still plenty of folks who consider it the best hope for, in the words of the Rockefeller Foundation charter, "promot[ing] the well-being of mankind throughout the world." But there is now, once again, a significant and vocal faction willing to call those ambitions into question. In part, the pushback can be traced to the nation's mounting uneasiness with income inequality and to the spread of an economic populism that refuses to regard the concentration of wealth charitably.

Trends in philanthropic practice have also had a hand in courting these suspicions. Over the last several decades, an increasing number of philanthropists have sought to leverage the funds at their disposal to tap into the much vaster resources of the federal and state governments. Shaping public policy has become a central preoccupation with many of the nation's leading funders. As Steve Teles, Heather Hurlburt and Mark Schmitt point out in the most recent issue of *Stanford Social Innovation Review*, while philanthropy has achieved notable successes in this arena over the last quarter-century, the political terrain has changed over that time to make the enterprise considerably more perilous. Whereas once philanthropy could comfortably pose as a disinterested provider of expertise and analysis, holding itself at a safe and decorous remove from the partisan fray, the hyper-partisanship that has infected politics in the recent decade has made that self-image impossible to sustain. The public has now been primed to view philanthropists as ideological combatants in a messy, brutal battle for political power over the instruments of governance. If philanthropy is not now "the recognizable mark of a wicked man," it is often the mark of an ideologically driven, partisan one.

This is the new – or in some ways, the return of the old – dispensation that has vexed Arnold's giving. The Foundation's efforts to reform the underfunded state-based public pension system (largely by cutting the benefits pensions would offer to public employees), has attracted the most controversy.

[. . .]

Arnold's *Chronicle* op-ed served as a response to these attacks. In it, he styled himself a brave and impartial do-gooder, committed to the dispassionate analysis of the "nuanced and complex problems" facing the nation. He could have chosen to give his money away the old-fashioned way, he wrote, and endowed a hospital or a museum. Instead, he followed the more difficult path of policy reform. This sort of work, he noted ruefully, "makes you no friends." But it was necessary to counterbalance the power of the entrenched "special interests groups" (in this case, public sector unions and their allies) who had "become experts in the world of lobbying, influence-peddling, and ad hominem attacks against those who stand for reform."

[. . .]

There are a few reasons to suspect these claims to scrappy underdog status. First, as Sirota has pointed out, the business sector (which supports pension reform) has spent vastly greater sums of money pushing public policy than has labor. And if the other reform campaigns undertaken by Big Philanthropy are any indication, the contest doesn't exactly seem like a fair fight. Take, for instance, the drive for education reform based on market-based principles – the expansion of charter schools, merit pay for teachers pegged to student test scores; greater freedom to fire teachers in low-achieving schools, among other policies. Up until the last few years, the contest has been a rout. The "special interests" (the teachers unions, in this case) have been able to muster only a perfunctory defense against the efforts of a number of leading philanthropies (the Gates, Walton, and Broad Foundations, with the Arnold Foundation now muscling its way into the triumvirate) committed to ed[ucation] reform. These foundations offer grants to cash-strapped school-districts contingent on schools following reform-based prescriptions. And they have also devoted millions to generate sympathetic press treatment and to seed research institutions and advocacy groups committed to the cause. Meanwhile, as individuals, the founders of these foundations have poured vast sums of money into local and state elections to secure victory for reform-friendly candidates. As Joanne Barkan, a leading critic of philanthropy-backed ed[ucation] reform, explains, the reform movement "is such a juggernaut that the unions haven't really been able to exert any pushback."

None of this is to say that Brookings and Pew erred in accepting funding from the Arnold Foundation, or that either organization's analysis was swayed by the preferences of their deep-pocketed funder. There need not be anything deliberately sinister in the Arnold Foundation's giving for it to demand our scrutiny. For given the power that private philanthropy can wield over public policy, a spirited, fully informed public debate over the scope, scale, and nature of that influence is a democratic necessity. It's our closest approximation of holding our mega-donors accountable.

Of course, spirited doesn't have to mean nasty; the debate serves civic purposes best when it doesn't descend into ad hominem attacks. It also requires critics of Big Philanthropy to be upfront about one crucial distinction that is often obscured in the contemporary discourse on philanthropy. They must determine whether it is the practice of philanthropy shaping public policy itself that they fear, or the particular policies in play. Often, critics wrap themselves in the noble – and consistent – absolutism of the former while really taking aim at the latter. Disentangling these two strands and grappling hard with each is one of our most pressing civic challenges. It's one that's worth a little vitriol. But Arnold's op-ed is absolutely right about one thing. Let's make this a clean fight: Stay away from the face.

3.4 Philanthropy versus the alternatives

Business is better than endowed foundations

Jim Lacey, 2011

Nothing grates on me more than hearing that Bill Gates or some other successful person needs to "give back" to society. I would say that building a company that employs tens of thousands and creates products that underpin millions more jobs around the world qualifies as one heck of a contribution to society. Having made billions doing so, Mr. Gates is perfectly within his rights to spend it any way he wishes. Still, we should recognize that the billionaire who opts to place his money into a venture-capital firm that may finance the Microsofts of tomorrow is making a contribution to human well-being at least as large as that of the billionaire who gives his money to charity. And if he makes more billions in the process, more power to him. He now has even more money to give away or, if he chooses, to invest in creating new businesses.

Until someone sends me a canceled paycheck he received from a poor man, I will go on believing that capitalists, who are building businesses that provide most of us with a standard of living unimaginable in any previous era, walk with the angels. I have nothing but praise for the Peace Corps volunteers who bring clean drinking water and possibly a bit of locally generated electricity to a poor village. At the same time I recognize that such a contribution pales in comparison to what a capitalist who invests in and profits from building a power plant, providing water and power to a million persons, contributes to the greater good of humanity.

Still, as so many billionaires are already committed to giving away sizable portions of their wealth, I have some concerns and thoughts to share with them.

[. . .]

Foundations are not risk takers. The impulse of any foundation's board is to park its endowment in the safest investments available.

Unfortunately for society, this is often the worst use of excess capital. No great or even small business is built unless someone decides to risk some portion of his capital building it. Risk-averse foundations will only rarely invest their endowments in ways that drive general economic growth. As a result, locking up hundreds of billions of dollars in the "dead hand of the foundations" retards economic growth and keeps millions of people significantly poorer than they otherwise would be. All of society would benefit if foundations had a drop-dead date by which their entire endowment had to be spent.

[. . .]

Moreover, the world has plenty of problems and crises right now. If AIDS in Africa is at pandemic proportions, what sense does it make for a $30 billion foundation to combat this crisis a few hundred million at a time? New research shows that an anti-viral drug cocktail dramatically reduces transmission rates. That means the time to win this battle is now. If the entire $30 billion is spent in one great effort, the tide can possibly be turned and victory declared in 2012. If such a dramatic outcome is possible, why opt to glory in small improvements spread out over decades?

[. . .]

In the years immediately after World War I, Julius Rosenwald, the man who made Sears Roebuck great, used much of his fortune to build 5,400 schools for black children in the South. By some estimates, 60 percent of American blacks who completed primary-level education in that period attended a school built by Mr. Rosenwald. As he said, "Permanent endowments tend to lessen the amount available for immediate needs, and our immediate needs are too plain and too urgent to allow us to do the work of future generations."

Today, there is over $500 billion available in various foundations. Development economist Jeffrey Sachs believes that a $250 billion "big push" in Africa would propel that continent onto a permanently high growth trajectory that would greatly improve the lives of billions yet unborn. If he is right, then the foundations have it in their power to immediately save a huge segment of humanity from poverty and disease.

Charity is better than government

Marvin Olasky, 1996

The tragedy of America's underclass is chronicled daily in our newspapers and on the nightly news. Today we watch, seemingly helpless, as generation after generation of children are condemned to lives of squalor, violence, and, all too often, premature death. We know it is wrong – deeply, fundamentally, morally wrong. But we seem powerless to do anything about it.

Why are we failing? Some argue that the government has not spent enough on antipoverty programs. And yet, the trillions of dollars we've spent on welfare programs over the past thirty years have failed to alleviate poverty. Indeed, the big government approach appears to have made many of our most pressing problems, from joblessness to family disintegration, even worse. The destruction of bonds among givers, receivers, and mediating organizations has laid waste to once productive communities of helpers and helped.

Some reformers call for private charities to step in and shoulder more of the burden. That's the right idea, but much of our private assistance network – like a muscle that's too long been unused – has begun to atrophy. Fundraisers for charities complain of "compassion fatigue" – dwindling donations from people who are either overwhelmed by the size of our problems or assume that they're the government's responsibility. (What else are they doing with my taxes? They figure.) The understanding that people should make charitable contributions to organizations in which they volunteer or about which they are knowledgeable has often been lost.

It's time to transform the way we help those in need. On one point the country has reached consensus; we need a major overhaul of the welfare system. And yet, we must be clear about the reasons for reform. Governmental welfare programs must be confronted not because they are too expensive – although, clearly billions are being wasted – but because they are inevitably too stingy in what only individuals can give: time, love, and compassion.

The welfare state should be abolished not out of fiscal responsibility, but out of moral responsibility. The casualties of America's war on poverty have been the poor themselves. The evidence of history can no longer be ignored: the welfare state is cruel, not merely misguided. As Americans, we can and must do better.

Private charities can do a better job than government. The history of American philanthropy is one of our country's greatest legacies. And yet, some private programs or partnerships do a pale impersonation of the government initiatives that have so dismally failed. Some private charities also suffer from bureaucratization, centralization, the mass production of benefits, and an exclusive focus on the material nature of poverty. We need to focus once again on moral questions, on the processes that build character. Charity that treats the capable as incapable robs people of capacities.

[. . .]

Americans can be proud of our nation's long history of compassion for those in need. But the condition of our cities, the epidemic of drug addiction and violent crime, the crisis of teen pregnancy, the crushing poverty and endemic homelessness – these are all causes for shame.

In recent decades, we have allowed true caring to be replaced by the myth of institutional compassion – the idea that we can fulfill our sincere desire to help those in need by writing a check to some institutional charity (government or private) that will do the rest for us. The cost of that myth is measured daily in the lives of three generations of children who have grown up in a culture of poverty.

It is time to dispense with the myth and substitute for it the principles of effective compassion that Americans long have known. For more than two centuries, those principles guided our efforts to provide opportunity for those in need. It is time to reclaim wisdom only recently forgotten. The renewal of American compassion will not occur immediately, and I know that revitalization will not be easy. But each year of delay is a year of increased suffering.

The good news is that the revolution has begun. Individuals, church groups, and volunteer associations are rediscovering the principles of effective compassion that have historically made American generosity a shining example for all the world. People have caught on to the folly of relying on arbitrary benchmarks of spending or numbers served and have begun to count compassion the only way that really matters: one person, one family at a time.

Thank goodness the poor don't rely on philanthropy

Polly Toynbee, 2009

At the height of the boom the BBC led with the good news that the businessman Sir Tom Hunter was pledging to give away £1 billion. "With great wealth comes great responsibility," he said. "I am not going to hide it under a bushel."

This heralded, many said, the new age of philanthropy, when the mega-rich would redistribute their wealth voluntarily. No need for higher taxes: once they had every mansion, super-yacht and jet they could ever use, their excess wealth would buy glory with patronage to match the Rockefellers, Carnegies and Medicis. There was much pressure on the Treasury to give even bigger tax breaks for donations to charity.

But that was then. This week Sir Tom Hunter said he would not be giving away £1 billion, following losses in his investment empire. Last year Hunter was 68th in the *Sunday Times* rich list: this year he is expected to have dropped a few places, but not to drop out altogether. He has given over £35 million for business enterprise lesson in schools and to projects in Africa.

[. . .]

Charity is the battle cry of the Conservatives, the answer to everything, the gentle face of their shrink-the-state rhetoric. Last June David Cameron launched a policy on the voluntary sector that "will provide many of the solutions to tomorrow's problems". The document on cities by the Tory MP Chris Grayling stresses that the "potential of our voluntary sector to tackle the difficult social problems in our most deprived areas is huge." Iain Duncan Smith concludes that small, local voluntary organisations are the best answer to his "broken Britain", lavishing praise on amateur community voluntarism.

[. . .]

And consider where charitable money from the public flows. This year, for the first time, religious institutions received most money – churches, mosques, synagogues and the like. Although only 7 per cent of donors give to the religions, it is the small number of big donors who raise so much for religion. Next comes medical research – cancer mostly – and then children, followed by hospitals/hospices, overseas aid and animals.

Looking at those priorities, it's worth remembering that every time someone gives to charity, the taxpayer is obliged to donate too. When, for instance, someone gives to the tiny Odinist Fellowship (which seems to take five times more money than it spends on Odin worship), we taxpayers put in up to another 28 per cent, willy-nilly.

The randomness of charity is part of its charm, adding to the rich texture of society. How bleak were communist societies with no charitable tradition, no volunteering, no civil society. How desolate life would be without the impulse to give and volunteer – from raffles to sponsored runs, fetes to balls, tin-rattling poppy sellers to hospital friends' trolleys – for good or eccentric causes.

Charity is mostly a social good in itself, but it is no substitute for the state. It's an add-on: free-wheeling, often innovative, sometimes a beacon showing how to do things better, with ideas to lead the state sector. But it is minute compared to the welfare state. Right-wing thinktanks that claim the welfare state has stunted Victorian voluntarism conveniently forget how little health, welfare or education charities ever delivered. The voluntary sector has only become more important by taking welfare state contracts to do things a democratically elected government chooses. The money is accountable – whereas random funds from philanthropists take a taxpayers' subsidy unaccountably.

As donors turn off the taps in a recession, what a disaster if the welfare state were seriously dependent on haphazard generosity. In the boom time, when I researched attitudes of high earners for the book *Unjust Rewards*, time and again the rich justified their extreme pay by citing philanthropy. It was a thin excuse as the top 10 per cent give proportionally less of their income than the bottom 10 per cent – so philanthropy should be a reason to pay more to low earners and less to the rich. But imagine if all those powerful philanthropists devoted their energy to persuading fellow plutocrats to pay all their due taxes without resorting to avoidance. That would raise billions more – and do immense civic good.

Democratic critiques of big foundations

Gara LaMarche, 2014

I do wonder [. . .] about my progressive friends. They believe in a strong government, in a fair tax system, in a robust social-welfare system, and in a vibrant democracy where all voices count equally. Why are they are not more concerned about the undemocratic and largely unaccountable nature of philanthropy? Why are we – since I too have failed, for years, to ask these big questions – hypersensitive to the dangers of big money in politics, and the way it perpetuates advantage and inequality, but blind, it seems, to the dangers of big philanthropy in the public sphere?

It wasn't always so in our history. When the titans of their day, Andrew Carnegie and John D. Rockefeller, sought to set up trusts to spend some of their vast wealth for charitable purposes, Frank P. Walsh, a progressive lawyer who chaired a congressional inquiry into industrial relations, called the new Rockefeller Foundation and Carnegie Corporation "a menace to the future political and economic welfare of the nation." In that period, 100 years ago, the foundations' endowments surpassed what the federal government, in the pre-New Deal era, spent on education and public health. Walsh called for the "democratization of private benevolence" through more progressive taxation.

In testimony before the Walsh Commission, Morris Hillquit, the labor lawyer and Socialist Party leader, said that large foundations like Rockefeller, Carnegie, and Russell Sage "represent in the domain of philanthropy just what trusts represent in the industrial field." Edward P. Costigan, who would later represent Colorado in the Senate, called the Rockefeller Foundation "a supreme example of the philanthropy which deadens, by its large benefactions, a public criticism which otherwise would be as formidable as inevitable." Even feudalism and slavery, Costigan went on, "boasted of their occasional generosity." The Reverend John Haynes Holmes of the New York Church of the Messiah, who would serve for two decades as chair of the board of the American Civil Liberties Union, called foundations "essentially repugnant to the whole idea of a democratic society."

In 2013, you'd be hard-pressed to find anyone close to the mainstream of American civic life and political thought raising those kinds of fundamental concerns. Is it because 100 years of practice has erased them? Or because philanthropy has deadened criticism, as Costigan warned, with its "large benefactions?"

The closest we come today is the emerging critique of the Gates Foundation, with its $3 billion-a-year spend rate that is at least four times as big as the next largest philanthropy. Gates is in a class by itself when it comes to size, but its influence in the few areas it has identified for strategic investment is even greater than it might be precisely because it is not scattered, but quite focused on particular approaches to education reform in the United States and public health abroad. When Dean Rusk was running the Rockefeller Foundation, he reportedly said he kept an eye on the Ford Foundation because what the "fat boy in the canoe does makes a difference to everybody else." If Ford, then the largest foundation, was the fat boy in the canoe, then Gates is the blue whale in the toy sailboat. Not only does what it does make a difference to others in the fields it engages in – it can virtually define the fields and set the policy agenda for government as well as philanthropy.

Laurie Garrett of the Council on Foreign Relations has argued that in focusing on a few big diseases in the developing world, Gates has drawn dollars away from more basic and vital investments in health systems and primary care. A 2007 *Los Angeles Times* article raised similar concerns, asserting that "the focus on a few diseases has shortchanged basic needs such as nutrition and transportation" and that "Gates-funded vaccination programs have instructed caregivers to ignore – even discourage patients from discussing – ailments that the vaccinations cannot prevent."

[. . .]

So the rise of very large philanthropies that are not shy about playing for big stakes in the public sphere raises crucial questions about philanthropic power and to whom it is accountable.

[. . .]

[T]he favored tax status that philanthropy enjoys in the United States makes sense only when it serves an unalloyed public good and only when it does so with integrity, transparency, fairness, inclusion, and effectiveness. Philanthropy has accomplished many good things for society in the last 100 years, and its favored tax treatment might be justified by an argument that it encourages foundations to take risks that corporations and the public sector, for different reasons, don't usually take. Foundations don't have to run for office, or satisfy shareholders, or attract customers, or win popularity contests. They can take the long view, and undertake bold initiatives that make it safer for government and other private capital to come in later on.

That's a plausible argument, and certainly one foundations and their advocates make for themselves all the time, citing, for instance, Carnegie's role in laying the groundwork for public television, or the Rockefeller Foundation's support for the Green Revolution.

But few bother to examine these claims about the agency of foundations with much rigor, and the same list of philanthropy's "greatest hits" appears again and again. Courageous risk-taking is not what most people associate with foundations, whose boards and senior leadership are often dominated by establishment types. If tax preference is meant primarily to encourage boldness, it doesn't seem to be working. The question is not whether many good things are accomplished with the money excluded from taxation for philanthropy. The standard is whether the record of philanthropy justifies the foregone tax revenue that in our current dire fiscal state could be used to keep senior centers and libraries and after-school programs open, hold tuition within reach at public colleges and universities, expand Internet access in rural communities, and on and on.

The precise level of the charitable deduction (like the fact of the deduction itself) did not come down on tablets from Mount Sinai. It is a choice that a democratic society makes, weighing competing interests and values. One of these is donor independence and philanthropic pluralism. These are not fleeting values. But neither is the responsibility of citizens in a democracy, acting together through government, to strengthen social protections.

[. . .]

[T]he sector is not sufficiently reflective of the rich diversity of this country and globe, and in particular does not reflect the voices of the most marginalized. Fully 85 percent of foundation board members are white, while just 7 percent are African American and only 4 percent are Hispanic, in a country where 92 percent of the population growth in the last decade, according to *The Economist*, came from people of color. Nearly three-quarters of foundations have no written policy on board diversity, and fewer than 10 percent of board members are under 40.

An emerging alternative

Social entrepreneurship

J. Gregory Dees, 2007

A cursory look at world affairs should convince any thinking and caring person, regardless of political ideology, that we have considerable room for improvement. Despite the tremendous strides in the quality of life that humankind has made in the past two centuries, many persistent problems remain and new ones have emerged.

[. . .]

One potentially promising strategy for improvement is to encourage and support social entrepreneurs, individuals, and organizations that bring to social problems the same kind of determination, creativity, and resourcefulness that we find among business entrepreneurs. One prime example is the 2006 Nobel Peace Prize winner Muhammad Yunus, who founded the highly successful Grameen Bank in Bangladesh to provide credit to the poor to help them move out of poverty. Two of the 2006 MacArthur Fellowship winners were also leading social entrepreneurs. Victoria Hale founded the Institute for OneWorld Health, a nonprofit pharmaceutical company that develops safe, effective, affordable medicines for developing countries, and Jim Fruchterman is a Silicon Valley engineer who created Benetech to craft technological solutions to social needs, ranging from literacy to human rights and landmine detection.

The concept of "social entrepreneurship" emerged in the 1980s from the work of Bill Drayton at Ashoka, funding social innovators around the world, and Ed Skloot at New Ventures, helping nonprofits explore new sources of income. It has come into its own in the last decade, capturing the imaginations of many thoughtful observers. [. . .] The embrace of this concept cuts across political and national boundaries, with activities and interest cropping up around the world.

Is this attention and excitement warranted? Does social entrepreneurship have the potential to create sustainable and scalable impact in arenas where government efforts have been ineffective? After studying this activity for over a decade, I am convinced that social entrepreneurs, operating outside of the constraints of government, significantly enhance our ability to find and implement effective solutions to social problems. Of course, the real test of any thesis of this sort lies in action and results.

[. . .]

Government as problem-solver

[. . .]

Over the course of the past two centuries, the world has witnessed a variety of experiments in government-based efforts to tackle poverty, as well as other social and environmental problems. Over this period, a mixed religious and secular civil society continued to evolve and play a complementary role, but the hope for social problem-solving has largely been on government.

While this focus on government as social problem-solver led to some notable successes, such as increased access to education and health care for many, the experience also revealed the limits of government as the vehicle for social problem-solving. It has become clear that large-scale, top-down government programs have serious drawbacks [. . .] Communism, socialism, and the welfare state have been subjected to the same kind of criticism that was leveled against the charity of old. They, too, run the risk of creating dependency, perhaps even more so because of the sense of entitlement they can create.

Government service delivery, including in the relatively successful arenas of education and health care, has been criticized as bureaucratic, ineffective, wasteful, too political, and antithetical to innovation. Because of the risks of fraud, waste, and abuse of power, bureaucracy became the dominant organizing method for government agencies. This is not an organizing mode that is conducive to creative problem-solving. In hindsight, these shortcomings are not surprising given the incentives and decision mechanism common to governmental organizations. Government alone is clearly not the answer. After two centuries of aggressive experimentation with different forms of government, we have learned, at the very least, that government is a tool that is effective for some kinds of social interventions but not as effective for others. We do not need to enter the ideological debates about the appropriate role and size of government to recognize the potential value of bringing private initiative, ingenuity, and resources to the table.

Through various government efforts to solve social problems, we have learned that with all our scientific knowledge and rational planning, we still do not know in advance what will work effectively. Thus, progress in the social sphere depends on a process of innovation and experimentation akin to entrepreneurship in the business world. When the Austrian economist Joseph Schumpeter formulated his theory of economic development, he saw entrepreneurs playing a central role. They drove development by "carrying out new combinations." They could modify existing products or services, develop new ones, improve production and marketing processes, find new sources or supply, take existing products into new markets, or create new forms of organization. In so doing, as he later put it, they "reform or revolutionize the pattern of production." And they shift resources into areas of higher yield and productivity, to paraphrase J. B. Say, the eighteenth-century French economist who popularized the term "entrepreneur." To be sure, large firms engage in incremental innovations, but as Carl Schramm and Robert Litan of the Kauffman Foundation recently put it, "Radical breakthroughs tend to be disproportionately developed and brought to market by a single individual or new firm." Social entrepreneurs are needed to play the same innovating role with regard to social needs and problems.

Social and business entrepreneurs uncover or create new opportunities through a process of exploration, innovation, experimentation, and resource mobilization. This is an active, messy, highly decentralized learning process. Decentralization is critical because finding what works depends on having the right knowledge, being able to envision new combinations, and having the freedom to test ideas through action. The necessary knowledge cannot easily be centralized; much of it is local and dispersed among the population. As a result, some people will see opportunities and conceive of promising new combinations that others could not envision. Because of the creative nature of this process, centralizing social problem-solving makes about as much sense as centralizing art production. Finally, since independent entrepreneurs must mobilize resources to continue to pursue their visions, they have to persuade financiers who are putting their money behind the idea and talented employees who are devoting their time and skills that this venture is worthwhile. This selection process provides a discipline, albeit imperfect, that helps narrow the funnel to those ideas that have better chances of working. When it works well, this decentralized process allows bad ideas to fall by the wayside, encourages lessons to be learned, and provides an incentive for continuous improvement of the more promising ones.

[. . .]

Why can't government agencies do this? When compared to government agencies, independent social entrepreneurs have several distinct advantages. They have greater freedom of action and can usually move more quickly than public officials. They can explore a wider range of alternatives, largely because they are not as constrained by bureaucratic rules, legislative mandates, political considerations, and a fixed budget. Social entrepreneurs can tailor their efforts to different communities or markets in ways that would be difficult for government programs. Moreover, independent social entrepreneurs have access to private resources, while private contributions to government are relatively rare. Thus, social entrepreneurs are able to attract voluntary gifts of money, time, and in-kind donations, leveraging public money devoted to the same problem with philanthropy, social investment, or earned income from their business ventures.

The reliance on independent social entrepreneurs also provides society with greater opportunities to learn with less risk. Government programs usually represent relatively large bets on fairly standardized interventions with commitments to a certain course of action that can be very hard to modify once announced. As economists Douglas North and Robert Thomas observed, "government solutions entail the additional cost of being stuck with the decision in the future – that is, withdrawal costs are higher than those related to voluntary organizations." With social entrepreneurs we have more and smaller bets on varied efforts to tackle the same social problem. When we have high levels of uncertainly about the best approach, diversification and experimentation increase the opportunities for learning and success. Diversification of activity has the added benefit of reducing the costs of failure during this learning process. If some of the small bets fail, the impact will be far less than the failure of a large-scale government program. To the extent that these experiments are privately funded, this learning process does not come at great public expense.

Furthermore, some social innovations are unlikely to be very effective if they are carried out by governmental organizations. The private nature of social ventures can be a distinct advantage. Consider Planned Parenthood, Alcoholics Anonymous, the Sierra Club, Habitat for Humanity, or community foundations. Could these work as well as branches of government? It seems unlikely. Boy and Girl Scouts would certainly take on a very different connotation if the government ran these programs. A rape crisis center might be effective in large part because it is run and staffed by volunteers who have been victims of rape themselves. Would victims of rape trust the center as much if it were government-run? Additionally, in some cases, it is important to work across governmental levels and jurisdictional boundaries. The Nobel Prize winning organization, Médecins Sans Frontières (Doctors Without Borders) captures this notion in its very name. It is much harder for government agencies to work effectively across boundaries. Since many social and environmental issues cut across these boundaries, it makes sense for the organizations tackling them to be organized accordingly. Thus, many innovative approaches to social problems are not only best started outside government, they are best kept outside government.

Social entrepreneurs have an important role to play, whether it is to complement or supplant government efforts. They are better positioned to innovate and experiment than government agencies. They have flexibility in how they serve their missions that should allow them to be more efficient and effective. They increase our chances of learning, and they bring private resources to the table. Unfortunately, until recently, they were not taken as seriously as they should be as an important driver of social progress. People tended to focus on government and markets as the main social forces, treating the "third sector" as marginal, rather than as a potential major engine for progress. Yet, independent social entrepreneurs have the potential to play the same role in addressing social needs that business entrepreneurs play in what economic Nobel Laureate Edmund Phelps calls "dynamic capitalism." Social entrepreneurship engages the problem-solving skills and local knowledge of many individuals and organizations in search of innovative solutions. As a result, it has some powerful advantages over centralized policy analysis and planning.

Charity and problem-solving

The recent rise of interest in social entrepreneurship is definitely not a case of the pendulum swinging away from government, back to charity, as much as some political commentators, such as Marvin Olasky, might like to see. Today's social entrepreneurs do not see themselves as engaged in "charity" in the traditional, alms-giving sense. They recognize its limits and weaknesses, as did the Enlightenment critics. Muhammad Yunus makes the point forcefully: "When we want to help the poor, we usually offer them charity. Most often we use charity to avoid recognizing the problem and finding a solution for it. Charity becomes a way to shrug off our responsibility. Charity is no solution to poverty. Charity only perpetuates poverty by taking the initiative away from the poor. Charity allows us to go ahead with our own lives without worrying about those of the poor. It appeases our consciences."

Other social entrepreneurs may not object as strongly to charity. However, even those who acknowledge a need for temporary relief tend to view their own work as fundamentally different. They aim to create sustainable improvements and are willing to draw on self-interest, as well as compassion to do it.

Social entrepreneurship represents another step in the continuing reinvention of the "third sector" over the past one hundred and fifty years. The Enlightenment brought not only a shift in political philosophy; it also changed private charitable institutions. Many of them embraced the new rationality leading to the rise of what historian Gertrude Himmelfarb calls "scientific charity." This shift generated a relative boom of new organizations in the later nineteenth and early twentieth centuries. The movement included new religious charities with more "scientific" approaches, the creation of secular charitable institutions, professionally run philanthropic foundations, and the establishment of new helping professions, such as social work. The Salvation Army, YMCA, Boys and Girls Clubs, and many prominent third-sector organizations and major foundations trace their roots to this era.

Leading social entrepreneurs today are most aptly described as pragmatists. They are focused on achieving sustainable results and will use whatever tools are most likely to work. They embrace innovation, value effective management, and are open to a wide range of operational and business models. They are willing to adapt ideas and tools from business when these will help. They are even willing to use for-profit forms of organization or hybrid structures that include for-profit and nonprofit elements. When it is possible, social entrepreneurs will happily craft market-based solutions that rely only on self-interest, allowing scarce philanthropic or government resources to flow to areas that genuinely need subsidy. If they can find an overlooked market opportunity that also improves social conditions, they will gladly pursue it. Yunus's Grameen Bank is legally a for-profit institution owned by its borrowers and is now financially self-sustaining.

Recognizing that for-profit or hybrid organizations may have an important role in creating better social conditions, some new philanthropists are disregarding old sector boundaries. When Silicon Valley venture capitalists Brook Byers and John Doerr started the New Schools Venture Fund, they decided to use it to fund both nonprofit and for-profit ventures that have the potential to create major improvements in K-12 education. Recently, the giant Internet search company Google decided that instead of creating the typical nonprofit company foundation, it would create its philanthropic arm as a for-profit capable of investing in nonprofit or for-profit ventures with a social purpose, such as more fuel-efficient vehicles. The lines between for-profit and nonprofit are breaking down as social entrepreneurs and entrepreneurial philanthropists look for new ways to tackle a range of social issues from alternative energy to improvements in health care.

Today's social entrepreneurs are building on the tradition of Ben Franklin. When Franklin saw opportunities to improve life for his fellow citizens in Philadelphia, he pursued them in whatever form seemed most sensible. He created for-profit printing and publishing businesses to keep citizens informed, a voluntary firefighting association to protect the homes of members, a subscription-based lending library, and a philanthropically supported academy that became the University of Pennsylvania, just to mention a few examples. For each entrepreneurial venture Franklin adopted an economic, operating, and legal structure that was suitable given the circumstances. Social entrepreneurs operating today embrace this legacy of pragmatic private initiatives to improve social conditions. They do not see themselves as "charities" or even as "nonprofits," though they often use that legal form of organization. They are entrepreneurs who move comfortably across sector boundaries in search of the best ways to achieve sustainable impact.

Section 4

PHILANTHROPISTS AND BENEFICIARIES: A COMPLEX RELATIONSHIP

Editors' introduction

Overview

The philanthropy sector differs from the other main sectors of society – the market and the state – by being supply-driven. Whereas the demands of customers and voters propel action in those other sectors, it is donors' supply of philanthropic resources, rather than the claims of beneficiaries, that usually animates outcomes in philanthropy. Yet philanthropic transactions are often understood to generate mutual benefits, and many donors aspire to be responsive to the needs and wants of others, so the relationship between philanthropists and beneficiaries is more complex than that between the parties involved in commercial or electoral transactions.

Questions about the "right relationship" between those who give and those who receive have been a concern of philosophers throughout the ages. Their ruminations, as well as instructions contained in many different religious texts, create somewhat conflicting advice on how best to manage gift interactions:

- Is it better to make gifts publicy, personally or anonymously? How should we weigh the merits of inspiring others and creating prosocial norms against acting with humility and respecting the privacy of recipients?
- Should gifts be assessed by their tangible value or by the spirit in which they are given? Would someone in need prefer a larger gift given reluctantly or a smaller gift given willingly?
- Is the suggestion that it is better to give than to receive a moral evaluation, or an acknowledgement of the substantial "returns" achieved by donors?
- What freedom actually exists in philanthropic transactions? Are those with surplus resources obliged to share? Are their intended beneficiaries compelled to accept?

The crux of the complexity in the donor-recipient relationship lies in concerns about power: those with resources to bestow are usually viewed as inevitably holding most – or indeed all – of the cards. The power of givers extends beyond determining the timing and size of their gift, to include other consequential decisions, including which people and organisations will benefit, and what it can – and cannot – be spent on (e.g., core costs, project expenses or endowment). Donors making significant gifts often also shape the recipients' response by specifying in advance how their contribution will be recognised and stewarded, such as through naming opportunities and reporting requirements.

Despite this reality of donor control, it is not absolute. Giving and getting may appear to be examples of archetypal opposites, but in fact they are mutually dependent as one cannot occur without the other. Donors need recipients, both to create giving opportunities and to generate the various benefits and satisfactions that they seek. A "successful" philanthropic act requires the existence and cooperation of recipients, whose interests therefore need to be understood and accomomodated in order to achieve a successful rendering of a gift transaction. The history of philanthropy includes many examples of unwanted gifts, ungrateful recipients, and gifts that otherwise go wrong, serving as a cautionary tale for those who believe that philanthropists call all the shots. The presence and absence of power on both sides of the gift relationships is what makes it so complex and worthy of close attention.

The picture is further complicated by the fact that society is not divided into permanently fixed or mutually exclusive groups of "donors" and "recipients" as most of us wear both hats simultaneously. The embedded nature of philanthropy means that we constantly – if unconsciously – benefit from the efforts of past and present donors. Medical discoveries, legislative advances and community facilities are just some of the more obvious examples of philanthropic benefits that impinge on our lives on a daily basis. More prosaically, people who attend a theatre they support, or worship in a religious building to which they contribute, further exemplify the lack of clear distinctions between those who give and those who get. Less obviously – but no less real – are deferred and latent benefits, such as those achieved by supporting healthcare or rescue organisations on which the donors or their loved ones eventually need to call. No calculation is necessarily required or assumed as people can become "accidental beneficiaries," but nonetheless the status of being a donor or a recipient is fluid, not fixed.

A final dimension of note in this section is that the relationship between philanthropists and beneficiaries is not the same the world over. The diversity of donor-recipient transactions is evident in discussions of philanthropy across the globe, where different structures of economic and social relations result in more nuanced accounts of who should – and who does – help whom.

Fourteen readings concerned with many different aspects of the complex relationship between philanthropists and beneficiaries are organised into five sections, as follows.

Giving and receiving

The nature of benefits and the implications of benefiting from the acts of others have long attracted the attention of profound thinkers and led them to provide guidelines for good giving and receiving that still resonate today. We therefore begin by reviewing the writing of Aristotle (384–322 BC), Seneca (4 BC–AD 65) and Maimonides (1135–1204) as they wrestle with the age-old question of benefits and being a benefactor.

Aristotle famously made the case that being philanthropic is essential for full human flourishing. In this extract, he reflects on how the value of philanthropy weighs differently for the parties involved, arguing that "Benefactors seem to love their beneficiaries more than the beneficiaries love those who have benefited them." He does not attribute this fact to any power imbalance but rather to the greater satisfaction gained by those who labour and invest, over the more passive act of receiving. Seneca's reflection on the nature of benefits prioritises the spirit in which a gift is given, defining a benefit as "the art of doing a kindness which both bestows pleasure and gains it by bestowing it." In his view, what matters to recipients is the spirit of "kindness" that outlasts the tangible gift, and what matters to donors is the act of bestowing gifts, not any potential return.

The extract from Moses Maimonides is focused on providing guidelines for the act of giving, describing "eight levels of *tzedakah*," a Hebrew word commonly equated with "charity" and "righteousness." This famous argument has become known as the "ladder of giving" as it sets out, and ranks, a range of potential relationships between donors and beneficiaries, from the least impressive levels of giving "begrudgingly" and publicly, to intermediate levels involving greater anonymity, to the highest and most admirable level of making a personal gift or loan that results in the independence of the recipient.

Philanthropy as a type of gift

While philanthropy was long viewed as a one-way transaction, it is increasingly understood as a type of gift that involves a threefold process of giving, receiving and giving back. The extracts in this subsection build on this classic idea, first set out by Marcel Mauss, which implies that gift relationships therefore make demands of both donors and recipients, and are far more complicated than they might initially seem.

David H. Smith notes that gifts mean different things to different people, but a common thread is their role in helping to solidify social relations and the engagement of the self, which stand in contrast to market exchanges. James Allen Smith argues that ancient lessons about the manner and method of gift giving remain relevant to modern grantmaking, despite its recent professionalisation. Timeliness – both in terms of the speed at which decisions are made and the duration of funding commitments – is described as an issue that profoundly affects the nature of the gift relationship and is therefore worthy of more attention by today's philanthropists. This reading raises other profound issues, including the rightness of placing expectations on recipients, assuaging disappointment and ingratitude, and the question of what intellectual deference is due to grantees.

When philanthropic gifts go wrong

Despite philanthropy being often viewed as a synonym for "good works," it has the potential to do harm as well as good. The extracts in this subsection list and illustrate the dark side of philanthropy. The discipline of philosophy has the most to say on this topic, so we begin with a brief extract from Mike W. Martin's reflection on the relationship between philanthropy and the autonomy of recipients, which concludes with the suggestion that philanthropists should heed Hippocrates' advice to physicians: Seek to do good, but do no harm. This challenge is taken up in Michael Moody's discussion of how the Hippocratic oath could be applied in a philanthropic context, including a systematic summary of the types of harm that donors can – usually unwittingly – do.

This subsection ends by jumping back over 100 years to the thoughts of Jane Addams, the Nobel Peace Prize-winning founder of Hull House, who reflects on the "subtle problems" inherent in charitable activity, such as the lack of recognition of mutual aid among recipients, "withholding" and "calculating action" by donors, and imposition of benefactors' preferences, which collectively make questions about who and how to help even more perplexing.

Being a giver, being a recipient

Philanthropy needs two parties: those who give and those who get, but the focus is most often on the former. Here, we explore and contrast the experience of being on either side of this transaction, historically and contemporaneously. Questions about power lie behind much thinking on this issue, but assumptions that donors inevitably have (and have always had) greater power are increasingly being questioned.

We begin with Ellen Ross' description of the experience of receiving charity in Victorian and Edwardian London, in which she notes that donor distrust and recipient cheating coexisted to undermine the apparent moral simplicity of the charitable relationship. Susan A. Ostrander and Paul G. Schervish further complicate the picture by challenging the idea that philanthropy ever was, or should be, a one-way relationship, because "donors have needs to be fulfilled as well as resources to grant," which makes the social relation between donors and recipients the most "fundamental fact" about philanthropy.

To illustrate what this might mean in practice today, we end this subsection with Julie Salamon's description of a "human exchange of equals" on the streets of New York, in which the residents of a homeless shelter – normally perceived as unambiguous recipients of help – were able to perform charity in the aftermath of the mass disruption caused by the 9/11 terrorist attacks.

What is the right relationship between those who give and those who get?

The question of the right relationship between donor and recipient has been explored for millennia, and continues to vex today. Commentary and advice on how best to arrange relationships in different eras and in different geographical locations are the focus of this final subsection.

Marco H. D. Van Leeuwen's review of major gifts made in Amsterdam in the seventeenth and eighteenth centuries points to the role of salvation and status as key motives, which animate the interdependent relationship between donors and recipients, because the latter hold power in realising their benefactors' wishes. Even secular donors' desire to use their resources to strengthen the community relied on grantees responding in a manner that strengthened rather than weakened the social fabric.

Alan Fowler and Susan Wilkinson-Maposa's description of "horizontal philanthropy" in southern Africa recasts the power imbalance found in modern Western giving relationships to one of equals, recognising that people with similar wealth (or, in this case, similar poverty) often provide help to one another. This reading also confirms the intangible but powerful return exchange – "the one that gives is also given to" – such that the recipient confirms the donor's humanity, because "denying help to another is to deny one's own identity as a human."

The final reading in this section builds on the preceding piece to insist that philanthropy must be understood in context. Halima Mahomed and Bhekinkosi Moyo argue that the narrative of philanthropy in Africa has long been dominated by a "Global North" perspective, which is often far from the reality. Assumptions about the relationships between philanthropic actors have exacerbated power imbalances that shape development agendas in Africa. We return in Section 6 to consider more closely the relationship between philanthropy and development issues.

Discussion questions

- In what ways can we say that donors need beneficiaries? Does this mean that donors should pay closer attention to what beneficiaries need or want, and change their giving accordingly? Do donors have too much control over philanthropy?

- Are the guidelines for good giving and good receiving as laid out long ago by Seneca and Maimonides still valid today? Why do you think Maimonides favoured anonymity in the gift relationship so much, and is that belief still held today? How might our modern giving practices change if we followed the advice of Seneca or Maimonides?
- What role does power play in the relationship between those who give and those who receive? Are donors always in the more powerful position? What are some practical steps we can take to address these power dynamics in the gift relationship?
- Despite meaning "love of mankind," philanthropy also has a "dark side" – it can do harm as well as good. Come up with some examples of philanthropic harm and reflect on how we might mitigate these harms. Does it make a difference whether the philanthropist meant to do harm, or if this happened unintentionally?
- If Aristotle is correct that being philanthropic is essential for full human flourishing, what is the right relationship between those who give and those who get? How might this "right relationship" change as the donors and recipients involved change – e.g., if the donor is rich and the recipient poor, versus if both donor and recipient are poor? Should the relationship be different if the donor and recipient come from different parts of the world?

4.1 Giving and receiving

On benefactors and beneficiaries

Aristotle, 350 BC (translated by Leon Kass, 2008)

Benefactors seem to love their beneficiaries more than the beneficiaries love those who have benefited them. As this seems unreasonable, it should be investigated. Now for the majority, the explanation is plain: beneficiaries (like debtors) owe, but benefactors (like creditors) are owed. In the case of loans, debtors wish that their creditors would die, but creditors will even take care of the safety of their debtors. Similarly, so it is thought, benefactors wish their recipients continued existence so that they will receive back favors, whereas the recipients do not care to make a return. Now Epicharmos probably would say that those who say such things are looking at life from the seamy side; but it seems to be human. For the many do not remember kindnesses, but seek rather to receive well than to do well.

But it would seem that the cause is more natural, and, in fact, the case of the benefactor is different from that of the creditor. For creditors feel no affection for their debtors; they wish only for their safety, and then only so that the debts will be paid. In contrast, benefactors love and are fond of those they have treated well, even though they are neither useful to them now nor likely to become so later on.

The same thing also happens with craftsmen; for every craftsman loves his own work more than he might be loved by that work were it to become alive. This is especially true, perhaps, with poets, for they love exceedingly their own poems, loving them as children. This is in fact also the case with the benefactor, for the beneficiary is the work of the benefactor; thus, the benefactor is fond of him more than "the work" is of its maker. The cause of this is that being is desirable and loveable for all, and we are most emphatically when we are-at-work, when we are in activity (in living and acting). But any deed is, in a sense, the doer-at-work. So he loves his work, because he also loves being.

[. . .]

At the same time, in addition, the benefactor also has the nobility of his action, so that he rejoices in the person for whom the action was done. For the recipient, however, there is nothing noble in the benefaction, but, at most, something profitable; and the profitable is less pleasant and loveable than the noble. Now for the doer, his deed abides, for the noble is long lasting, but for the recipient, the useful passes away. Pleasant are the activity of the present, the hope of the future, and the memory of the past; but pleasantest is the pleasure of actively being at-work, and it is similarly also the most loveable.

[. . .]

Moreover, all love more those things that come-to-be laboriously, for example, those making their own wealth love it more than those inheriting it. Yet it seems that receiving-well is trouble-free, whereas doing-well is troublesome. (On account of this, also, mothers love their children more than fathers; for their genesis is more labored for mothers, and they know that they are their own.) It would seem that also this is true of benefactors.

On benefits

Seneca, AD 63 (translated by Aubrey Stewart, 1887)

Among the numerous faults of those who pass their lives recklessly and without due reflection, my good friend Liberalis, I should say that there is hardly any one so hurtful to society as this, that we neither know how to bestow or how to receive a benefit . . . As it is, virtue consists in bestowing benefits for which we are not certain of meeting with any return, but whose fruit is at once enjoyed by noble minds. So little influence ought [the anticipation of return] have in restraining us from doing good actions, that even though I were denied the hope of meeting with a grateful man, yet the fear of not having my benefits returned would not prevent my bestowing them.

[. . .]

The book-keeping of benefits is simple: it is all expenditure; if any one returns it, that is clear gain; if he does not return it, it is not lost, I gave it for the sake of giving. No one writes down his gifts in a ledger, or like a grasping creditor demands repayment to the day and hour. A good man never thinks of such matters, unless reminded of them by some one returning his gifts; otherwise they become debts owing to him.

It is a base usury to regard a benefit as an investment. Whatever may have been the result of your former benefits, persevere in bestowing others upon other men; they will be all the better placed in the hands of the ungrateful, whom shame, or a favorable opportunity, or imitation of others may some day cause to be grateful. Do not grow weary, perform your duty and act as becomes a good man. Help one man with money, another with credit, another with your favor; this man with good advice, that one with sound maxims.

[. . .]

These, however, are but the outward signs of kindnesses, not the kindnesses themselves. A benefit is not to be felt and handled, it is a thing which exists only in the mind. There is a great difference between the subject-matter of a benefit, and the benefit itself. Wherefore neither gold, nor silver, nor any of those things which are most highly esteemed, are benefits, but the benefit lies in the goodwill of him who gives them. The ignorant take notice only of that which comes before their eyes, and which can be owned and passed from hand to hand, while they disregard that which gives these things their value. The things which we hold in our hands, which we see with our eyes, and which our avarice hugs, are transitory, they may be taken from us by ill luck or by violence; but a kindness lasts even after the loss of that by means of which it was bestowed; for it is a good deed, which no violence can undo. For instance, suppose that I ransomed a friend from pirates, but another pirate has caught him and thrown him into prison. The pirate has not robbed him of my benefit, but has only robbed him of the enjoyment of it. Or suppose that I have saved a man's children from a shipwreck or a fire, and that afterwards disease or accident has carried them off; even when they are no more, the kindness which was done by means of them remains. All those things, therefore, which improperly assume the name of benefits, are means by which kindly feeling manifests itself. In other cases also, we find a distinction between the visible symbol and the matter itself, as when a general bestows collars of gold, or civic or mural crowns upon any one. What value has the crown in itself? or the purple-bordered robe? or the fasces? or the judgment-seat and car of triumph? None of these things is in itself an honor, but is an emblem of honor. In like manner, that which is seen is not a benefit – it is but the trace and mark of a benefit.

What, then, is a benefit? It is the art of doing a kindness which both bestows pleasure and gains it by bestowing it, and which does its office by natural and spontaneous impulse. It is not, therefore, the thing which is done or given, but the spirit in which it is done or given, that must be considered, because a benefit exists, not in that which is done or given, but in the mind of the doer or giver. How great the distinction between them is, you may perceive from this, that while a benefit is necessarily good, yet that which is done or given is neither good nor bad. The spirit in which they are given can exalt small things, can glorify mean ones, and can discredit great and precious ones; the objects themselves which are sought after have a neutral nature, neither good nor bad; all depends upon the direction given them by the guiding spirit from which things receive their shape. That which is paid or handed over is not the benefit itself, just as the honor which we pay to the gods lies not in the victims themselves, although they be fat and glittering with gold, but in the pure and holy feelings of the worshippers.

Eight levels of giving

Moses Maimonides, 1170–1180 (translated by Judah Mandelbaum, 2002)

1. There are eight levels of *tzedakah*, one better than the next. A high level, of which none is higher, is where one takes the hand of an Israelite and gives him a gift or loan, or makes a partnership with him, or finds him employment, in order to strengthen him until he needs to ask help of no one. Concerning this it says, "And you will give strength to the resident alien, so he may live among you," as if to say, strengthen him until he will not falter or need.
2. Below this is one who gives *tzedakah* to the poor, not knowing to whom he gives, while the poor person does not know from whom he takes. For this is [fulfillment of a] commandment for its own sake. And for such there was a Chamber of Secrets in the Temple, whereunto the righteous would contribute secretly, and wherefrom the poor of good families would draw their sustenance in equal secrecy. Close to such a person is he who contributes directly to the alms fund. One should not, however, contribute directly to the alms fund unless he knows that the person in charge of it is trustworthy, is a Sage, and knows how to manage it properly . . .
3. Below this, the giver knows to whom he gives, and the poor person does not know from whom he takes. For example: the rabbinic sages who went in secret, tossing coins in the door openings of the poor. In this case, it is proper and good [to do this] if the alms officers do not behave precisely [i.e. conduct themselves as they should].
4. Below this, the poor person knows from whom he takes, and the giver does not know: as per example of the greatest of the sages who would bundle small change in their sheets, and throw them over their shoulders, in sight of the poor, who took, so they would have no shame.
5. Below this, one puts into another's hand before [the latter] asks.
6. Below this, one gives another after [the latter] asks.
7. Below this, one gives another less than is appropriate, in a pleasant manner.
8. Below this, one gives begrudgingly (sorrowfully, reluctantly, or with regret).

4.2 Philanthropy as a type of gift

What is a gift?

David H. Smith, 2005

Giving is a much studied term that means different things to different people. In our ordinary usage we think of a gift as spontaneous, a surprise and unnecessary. When I was a Divinity School student at Yale in the early 1960s, my wife and I had little money. One cold December night we stood in line outside Woolsey Hall hoping to buy balcony tickets for a recital by the great cellist Rostropovich. A large man in a huge coat and wearing a Russian hat approached us, asked us if we hoped to buy tickets to the recital, and – when we said we did – gave us two tickets – indeed two of the best seats I have ever had in a major hall. It was the then Yale Chaplain William Sloane Coffin.

That remarkable act beautifully illustrates our usual concept of the gift. The gift is contrasted with what we are obliged to provide. Think of the statement "I will give you my basketball tickets." That means I choose to give them; I did not "have to" or owe them to you, and I am not selling them to you. On these terms, what we might call the pure *gift* is spontaneous, uncoerced, and for those reasons often received with surprise. The essence of the gift is its voluntariness, the freedom with which it is offered. The gift is unexpected by the recipient, completely voluntary and unnecessary by the giver. It is a Romantic notion of gift, nurtured in an individualist society.

In contrast to this stands a more classical concept of gift as a distinctive form of social relation, a relation insightfully studied by Marcel Mauss, Lewis Hyde, and others. These writers identify a form of social exchange that contrasts with market exchanges. On these terms gift giving is obligatory, not optional. Gifts are transactions that knit a social group together; they establish personal relations; not giving a gift can cause a major social rupture. We are all familiar with this form of giving as well as the more romantic and individualistic gift. Failing to provide a gift for an anniversary, birthday, Christmas, or bar mitzvah is to default on an obligation. This kind of gift is expected, and so is reciprocation of some sort.

This form of giving is the lifeblood of traditional societies. I receive a gift and am expected to pass it on; if I cannot literally pass it on, then I should give something else. In its most rigorous form, the notion that many, if any, items are my personal and private possession is called into question. Provision of such gifts is a very important component in sustaining the web of social relations that holds a society together.

For us, a gift "economy" parallels the market economy of buying and selling. Though we distinguish the two kinds of transactions sharply, we tend to de-value the obligatory nature and importance of our own gift economies, perhaps because they seem less tangible and quantifiable than market exchanges. In fact, they are not really optional or voluntary; the omission of a wedding or birthday gift makes a statement, whether one wants it to or not. To be sure, the form of coercion involved is not the long arm of the law. It is internalized and socially reinforced. But the social force is nevertheless real and powerful.

Other characteristics of gifts come to mind. Jesus praises what is often called the "widow's mite." The penurious widow makes a small contribution, but Jesus says that her gift has greater value than the larger contributions of others who are wealthier. Her giving represents a larger fraction of what she has than the others have offered. It holds more consequences for her than their larger donations hold for them. Whether the gift is customary or free, we think of gifts as more valuable if they are precious or close to the self or identity of the giver; indeed, their value increases as they approximate or symbolize a gift of oneself.

The social or moral compulsion associated with gifts reflects the extent to which they are perceived as gifts of self, or gifts that establish or seal a relationship between selves. After the tragedy of September 11 [2001, a day of terrorist attacks in the US], many people felt that they had no choice but to give after they had seen what they had seen. Of course, in one sense they had a choice; no one was forcing them. In that sense, their contributions were pure gifts. But in a more profound sense they had to give out of a sense of identification with victims and a need to identify with those who were heroically helping. They gave because of who they were and wanted to be.

Thus on the surface, it seems that at least three types of exchange exist: buying and selling in the market, providing the free or pure gift, and offering the customary or obligatory gift. The difficult issue is to assess how many of the apparently spontaneous gifts are – from the standpoint of the giver – matters of obligation, conscience, or a search for meaning. In any case, gifts seem closer to the self, more a reflection of someone's identity than the demands of justice. We can be just for diverse reasons and without really committing ourselves in heart and mind. But giving requires an engagement of the self, no matter how much we may wish it didn't.

In search of an ethic of giving

James Allen Smith, 2006

To understand why the gift relationship is so complex, so fraught with potential harms, we must first ask what makes gifts so powerful. Gifts have always enabled individuals to reinforce their personal relationships, solidifying friendships and strengthening social or political affiliations. But a gift's power can reach beyond the individuals directly involved; it can extend in many different directions. Gifts are able to exercise their force across time and generations, as in the *Iliad* when Glaukos and Diomedes ended their combat upon suddenly realizing that many years earlier their grandfathers had enjoyed a hospitable relationship, eating and drinking together and exchanging gifts. Gifts also have the power to operate across geographical and political boundaries, ending violence and promoting amicable relations between hostile tribes, cities, and great empires.

[. . .]

Gift versus grant

The ancient philosophers always offered their advice on gift-giving with the understanding that giving and receiving took place within a thick web of personal obligations. Exchanges of gifts and favors sustained familial ties, solidified friendships, shaped patron-client relationships, and maintained political allegiances. Today, while friends still exchange gifts, individual patrons still support many good works, and politically active citizens donate to various causes, these practices occur in a very different, often much less personal, context. And while our highly organized (some might even say overly bureaucratized) modern philanthropy can trace its distant origins to the charitable institutions of the ancient and medieval world and to the spirit of magnanimity that accomplished great public works, our contemporary philanthropic institutions function in a legal and professional environment that leaves little space for thinking about grant-making as an activity that might still bear some relationship to the older forms of gift-giving.

Many of the things that once made gift-giving such a personal matter have been shunted aside in the organized philanthropy of our own times. Some of this is clearly to good effect. Fiduciary responsibilities and charitable purposes have been explicitly defined in law. This framework of law and regulation helps assure that modern philanthropy will seek to pursue the public benefit rather than being used exclusively for personal advantage. Since the late nineteenth and early twentieth centuries, philanthropy has also become an increasingly professional affair or, at the very least, has drawn professionals from other domains into the philanthropic orbit. There are now widely accepted procedures and practices that govern many aspects of grant-making, especially in the largest foundations. In those foundations we can sometimes find external peer review processes, and almost certainly we can count on an array of internal procedures to assure careful evaluation of proposals and systematic decision-making. Policies have also been implemented to forbid conflicts of interest and overt favoritism in grant-making. Formal grant agreements are also routinely required, specifying conditions for payment and performance. These practices now define the grant relationship.

But these institutional practices do not necessarily define or promote a professional ethos. They might even deter us from looking to the past – to what we have come to understand about the gift relationship – as we seek to create professional norms for modern philanthropy. Perhaps it is these bureaucratic formalities that led Mary Douglas to remark on her experience of working in a foundation that "newcomers to the office quickly learnt that the recipient does not like the giver, however cheerful he be." Why should this be so? Perhaps it is because we have ceased to think about the aspects of the gift relationship that remain deeply embedded in our grant-making activities. Douglas cautions us that foundations should never confuse their donations with *free* gifts: "There are no free gifts; gift cycles engage persons in permanent commitments that articulate the dominant institutions." If even the most successful grantees do not like donors (and certainly unsuccessful grant-seekers like them even less), it is because of the substantial imbalance of resources, power, and control in the grant relationship.

Complaints by today's grantees resound in familiar ways to any reader of Aristotle, Cicero, or Seneca. Modern grant-seeking processes can be as drawn out and humiliating as anything faced by a poor person pleading for assistance in antiquity. Indeed, speedy responses and timely help may be even more difficult to win in the modern foundation world with its well-defined grant cycles and diligent review processes. The burdens placed upon the grantee in describing a project and assessing results can be as heavy as any obligation that weighed down an ancient beneficiary. Clearly, a species of gift relationship is created when a foundation and its grantees interact. In refracting our current grant-making practices through the lens of antiquity, perhaps we can recover insights – or at least a set of relevant questions – that will prove helpful in constructing professional norms that might govern modern philanthropic conduct. However different the contexts, a few large questions might still be framed in terms that echo the language of Aristotle, Cicero, and Seneca: What now threatens to poison the gift relationship? What are the wellsprings of ingratitude?

Certainly ancient lessons about the manner and method of giving ought to be absorbed by modern grant-making institutions. The philosophers wrote often about the timing of the gift and the need to avoid hesitation and delay. This hesitancy, the seeming reluctance to give, was frequently the reason for the recipient's ill will toward the donor. Today, dilatory foundation procedures, inexplicable delays, and deferrals in making a grant are among the most annoying feature of institutionalized and professionalized philanthropy. Diligence in evaluating proposals, attention to fiduciary responsibilities, and sound evaluation processes are important – much as careful deliberation about the gift was to Seneca – but too often they can become excuses for delay. They do not necessarily lead to better or more disciplined decisions. They allow staff and boards to justify their hesitation and they show little regard for meeting the needs of the potential beneficiary in a timely manner. While donors waver and delay, grantees grow uncertain and resentful. Time and timeliness in gift-giving were subjects of keen interest to the ancients; rarely is it a significant topic of conversation today. How should those involved in modern philanthropy think about time – the timeliness of decisions, the duration of their commitments?

The ancients also were concerned about the expectations that benefactors were liable to place upon their beneficiaries. Donors were advised not to dwell upon their own expectations for gratitude or return favors; they were urged not to make their beneficiaries shoulder undue burdens. Too often a gift came with heavy expectations. Today, those expectations might take the form of detailed performance measures, the need to obtain speedy results, and prompt project evaluation. A philanthropic ethic would certainly ask what burdens ought to be born by a grantee. How should donors limit the burdens their expectations place upon a beneficiary? In this same context, ancient donors were cautioned about conveying their gifts with excessive advice or criticism, knowing that words delivered by a donor have a power, for better or for worse, that is different from counsel between equals. A donor's words can often be taken not as advice but as an order. And this advice sometimes comes from someone who has no detailed knowledge or understanding of the recipient's circumstances. This, too, is a subject rarely discussed in modern philanthropy (and when it is, it is often cast in the sterile language of technical assistance). The ancients were sensitive about offering advice. How and when is advice best conveyed? What intellectual deference is due the grantee? In what ways should knowledge become a part of the philanthropic exchange?

Aristotle was emphatic that the gift should be the right amount. In part, it had to be right in proportion to the donor's resources. More important, it had to be right given the needs of the beneficiary. A discussion of the "right" amount for a modern foundation leads in many different directions: payout levels, average grant sizes, duration of support, contributions to endowment or capital projects versus project support, loans or venture capital-style investments, among other subjects. These topics are a matter of almost constant discussion by foundation staff and board members. And they are perhaps the greatest source of tension between donor and recipient. The amount will never seem to be enough to the recipient. How can disappointment or ingratitude be assuaged? Perhaps it can be tempered when, in conveying the gift or grant, the donor demonstrates a true understanding of the recipient's needs and if the donor has responded in ways that are not merely a token show of support or sympathy. The ancients remind us that discussions of the right amount must always ask the question from both the donor's and the recipient's perspectives. In viewing the gift relationship from both vantage points, they also remind us of the importance of adhering to simple civilities.

Finally, it is by reminding us to carefully consider why we give that the ancients, especially the Stoics, have the most to teach us. The ancients focused on motivation, offering advice that tempers our impulses to be poorly motivated or unreflective about the purposes of gift-giving. They understood that a gift should be motivated not by the expectation of a return favor, not by a desire to control the beneficiary, not merely to obtain praise (though giving was certainly deemed to be praiseworthy), and most certainly not to bestow a gift that would create ingratitude. Indeed, it was ingratitude they most often sought to avoid. The gift relationship itself is harmed – gratitude suffers – when motivations are self-serving or thoughtless. And it is because the gift is such a powerful instrument that we must constantly ask ourselves why we give. We must continually subject our motives to hard scrutiny. Whether an ancient patron or a contemporary program officer, the intent of the donor ought always be to bestow a benefit that will in some manner sustain cohesive social relationships. Gifts and grants are both about human solidarity. Donors should be ever mindful of how they are sustaining the habit of giving and returning.

4.3 When philanthropic gifts go wrong

The harms philanthropy can do

Mike W. Martin, 1994

Philanthropy can be ineffective for many reasons: bad luck or poor judgment, unrealistic faith or lack of hope, excessive generosity or insufficient courage. When philanthropy is ugly and demanding, however, as well as ineffective, usually the primary cause is a failure to respect persons.

In this context, respect is recognition of the moral worth of all people, rather than admiration for exceptional individuals. Kant suggested that to respect persons is to respect their autonomy – their rational and moral self-governance. Difficulties arise concerning how he developed this suggestion. For one thing, in exalting reason he downplayed other value-bestowing aspects of human life, such as capacities for sympathy and loyalties to communities. This is part of a wider failure to understand respect in more personal terms which take into account individual differences and particular contexts, rather than to treat persons as instances of an abstract rational being. For another thing, he relied on a simplistic view of moral reasoning as grounded in absolute or exceptionless moral principles, failing to appreciate how often rules conflict in ways that force exceptions. Nevertheless, Kant's emphasis on autonomy has fundamental importance in understanding respect for persons.

Autonomy has three aspects: rights, capacities, and competencies. *Rights autonomy* is possessing moral rights to pursue one's legitimate interests without unjust interference from others. People are morally equal in the sense that they all have these rights. *Capacity autonomy* means having the general capacities to reason, exercise self-control, identify with and affirm healthy desires, and care for persons, practices, and organizations. Infants, young children, and some adults lack these capacities in varying degrees. *Competence autonomy* means exercising these capacities skillfully so as to meet morally permissible goals. Competence autonomy is a moral achievement, at least when it becomes a steady pattern.

Respect for autonomy, accordingly, implies respect for rights and respect for people's efforts at self-determination. In philanthropy, failures of moral respect take many forms: Freedom to Harm, Tyranny of Gifts, Manipulation of Givers, Exploitation of Women, and Incentives to Give. Taken together, these examples suggest that as philanthropists we do well to heed Hippocrates' advice to physicians: Above all, do no harm.

Seek to do good, but do no harm

Michael Moody, 2011

Most people probably have some vague familiarity with what has come to be called the "Hippocratic Oath," and might know that newly minted doctors commit to this ethical pledge in some way.

[. . .]

The primary principle that guides ethical doctors is best summarized as "seek to do good, but do no harm." And it is not just the individual patient who benefits from doctors following ethical guidelines such as this. Principled medical work, whether by a cadre of trained professionals or indigenous healers, is necessary for the greater good of any society – a point we are reminded of whenever we debate our national health care policy. Doctors play an essential social role, and anyone playing such a role should, in a good society, take that role seriously and agree to uphold principles like the Hippocratic Oath.

Applying the oath to philanthropists

Robert Payton and I have suggested elsewhere that this maxim of "seek to do good, but do no harm," might also serve as an ethical guideline for philanthropists, for those who seek to heal our society's ills instead of our physical ones.

[. . .]

Like with doctors who work for the good health of their patients, we want philanthropists to be focused on the good they seek (and the harm they deter) for others, not on themselves. Philanthropy can still be personally rewarding just as medical practice is – e.g., through warm fuzzy feelings, or your name on a building – but philanthropy is distinguished and heralded for its intention to enact some vision of the public good, some way of healing others or improving the health of society.

Philanthropy by this definition is moral action, and philanthropists can be seen as moral leaders by virtue of their actions to pursue a vision of the good. Of course, moral visions of the good often differ from philanthropist to philanthropist and nonprofit to nonprofit; and again, this vision of the good is not the only motive for philanthropic work. Taken together, though, these voluntary interventions in service of the public good are responsible in large part for shaping and advancing any society's moral agenda, and for doing a great amount of good. This is why clarifying the ethical prescriptions that philanthropists follow is crucial.

As this paper explores applying the Hippocratic Oath to philanthropy, it will become clear that both parts of the primary principle, as stated above, require close attention – being an ethical philanthropist, like an ethical doctor, is not just a matter of "do no harm." Applying the oath to philanthropy will also prove to be much more difficult than in medicine, because there is no generally agreed upon definition of "good" and "harm" like there is (in most cases) with medicine. But exploring these questions is a good way to highlight the promise as well as the potential peril of philanthropy. It reminds us that intervening philanthropically in other people's lives – in our own communities or in the earthquake zone in Haiti – is both inherently dangerous and absolutely essential to a good society.

"Seek to do good" is an admonition to be philanthropic, something we find in some form in every society and tradition. "Do no harm" is a reminder that doing good through philanthropy is not always easy, that good results do not always follow from good intentions.

[. . .]

Seek to do "good"

We must remember that the Hippocratic maxim calls for philanthropists to *seek* to do good, not necessarily to "do good by everyone's definition." For many, using the term "public good" suggests that there is something close to an absolute, correct, objectively determined and universally agreed public good out there, and our job is to discover it and implement it. But the reality, as Craig Calhoun puts it, is that the public good is "forged" not "found;" it is "created in and through the public process, it does not exist in advance of it." The public good is constantly contested and debated, and philanthropists engage in this debate when they intervene in others' lives to enact their own view of what is good. This can lead to problems, of course, such as when a philanthropist's definition of "good" is reprehensible to the majority, or prioritizes certain needs or goals over what seem to be much more urgent ones. A notable recent example of the latter was when the famously caustic and eccentric New York hotel magnate Leona Helmsley left the bulk of her multibillion-dollar fortune, upon her death, to a charitable trust with (somewhat vague) instructions that the money be used chiefly to support the care and welfare of dogs. While leaving money to help animals was laudatory, many felt that leaving all of the money to this purpose – especially when this would be one of the largest philanthropic grantmakers in the country – was problematic. Critics essentially questioned her definition of the public good. Less striking disagreements over what is "good" include which diseases deserve priority funding, and which solutions to teacher shortages will have the most impact.

The point is that honoring the first part of a Hippocratic Oath for philanthropists involves making choices about the definition of the public good you seek, and that these choices might be called into question. This is part of trying to follow an ethical principle.

[. . .]

Types of potential harm

The second part of the Hippocratic Oath as applied to philanthropy certainly makes doing good even more uncomfortable and challenging. Again, history provides too many examples of how doing harm can result from trying to do good through philanthropy; we might even know this from our own experiences of good deeds going bad. There is risk whenever we intervene in other people's lives.

[. . .]

So far, though, there have been few systematic attempts to summarize the range of types of potential harm from philanthropic interventions. Below I offer an initial list, in the hopes that others will then refine and expand it.

[. . .]

Malfeasance, corruption, fraud

This is the most blatant form of harm and can take many forms, which legal scholars have reviewed. Funds donated to a nonprofit can be misappropriated or embezzled for personal gain. Volunteers can commit crimes while on site. Board members can fail to report conflicts of interest or funnel contracts to friends. Scammers can raise money for a fake charity. Food donated to Haitian earthquake victims can be hoarded and sold for profit.

Lack of transparency

In the worst cases, this sort of harm involves outright deception by philanthropic actors in a way that approaches fraud but remains legal, such as when nonprofit organizations with secret ties to politicians raise money as a way to get around campaign finance laws, or when multinational corporations make a rash of new donations in countries where they are vying for a government contract. In more subtle instances, this involves cases of intentional non-disclosure, such as nonprofits who make their major sponsors hard to decipher, or cases in which decisions about grants are made behind closed foundation doors in ways that seem to favor certain recipients [. . .]

Diversion of resources

[. . .] This is harm by omission and opportunity cost, by diverting scarce resources (time, talent, treasure) from a more effective or efficient solution, or from a more pressing or widespread need. In the recent response to the Haiti crisis, for example, some aid organizations were criticized for soliciting and distributing donations of clothing in the first few days, when medical supplies should have been the priority. Critiques of wealthy donors giving to elite universities or arts organizations often make this claim of harm. [. . .]

Short-term band-aids

Philanthropic interventions can do harm by merely addressing the symptoms of a problem with band-aid solutions, while ignoring the persistent and systemic causes and more permanent solutions. Philanthropy can create short-term good but in doing so perhaps expand the long-term harm. [. . .] [T]his classic criticism is sometimes made against foundations or individual donors who support service delivery programs but not advocacy efforts. And clearly in disaster response situations such as Haiti, observers often warn of the potential for an over-emphasis – e.g., in donor appeals – on short-term "relief" instead of long-term "development."

Faulty or inefficient strategy

The two previous types can both be seen as forms of a more general category of potential harm, when a philanthropist's faulty strategy causes well-meaning efforts to fail – or, at least, to be less effective or efficient than they could be. [. . .] [Some] foundations might not give large enough grants, or might abandon a solution before it has a chance to work, or might have a "theory of change" that ignores a major cause of the problem, or might ignore the need to build an inclusive coalition to create lasting reforms. Some strategy problems that lead to harm arise from philanthropists going too slow, or too fast. In crisis situations like the Haiti aftermath, the impulse is often to deploy relief too quickly – e.g., to create "tent cities" for survivors before adequate food supply chains and sanitation facilities can be arranged, which can then create new problems for victims. On the other hand, withholding relief supplies while proper plans are drawn up can lead to harsh criticism and the classic "paralysis by analysis" problem. [. . .]

Faulty or inefficient implementation

Sometimes the negative consequences of philanthropy come not from a faulty strategy, but a faulty implementation of strategy. This has long been a critique made of international humanitarian and development organizations, that their lack of coordination, bureaucratic bottlenecks, and ineffective systems of information sharing lead to failed programs on the ground. A report from the International Red Cross following the tsunami disaster [in December 2004] acknowledged that the lack of reliable information dissemination caused resources to pile up in areas that did not need them, while other areas got little help. In some cases, the failure of implementation comes from a failure to adapt in the face of new information or altered circumstances.

Lack of measurable impact

This is the primary type of potential harm that concerns many thought leaders in the philanthropic field at the moment. The issue here is one of uncertainty about whether good or harm is resulting from a philanthropic action. A community's cherished youth literacy program might be producing real, sustainable outcomes for the kids involved, but if this cannot be demonstrated and measured its supporters cannot know if the program is in fact achieving good or not. Without impact measures, the argument goes, we cannot optimally direct our philanthropic investments to those solutions that do the most good and the least harm. We cannot know whether to tweak our strategy or improve our implementation.

Unintended consequences

There are myriad reasons why good intentions can lead to unexpected bad outcomes, and the likelihood of this increases as problems and solutions become more complex. [. . .] [S]ometimes helping one person can end up hurting a lot of other people. In Great Britain the popular charity Oxfam has solicited used book donations and opened a number of local bookstores to generate revenue for their programs, but these fundraising efforts have had the unfortunate effect of hurting independent booksellers in those same towns. In Haiti, the huge influx of donated clothing and food has the potential to force some food and clothing merchants to close up shop.

Dependency

Another sort of unintended consequence – that philanthropy creates dependency on the part of recipients – has been the source of an enduring critique of philanthropy. Critics have long claimed that charity causes harm by discouraging self-reliance. This view persists today in arguments for microfinance loans or for foreign assistance directed at market development instead of mere "handouts." We see it also in arguments that anti-poverty nonprofits should focus on job skills training instead of grocery vouchers. A version of this problem also arises at the level of interpersonal philanthropic interaction. We know that individuals who receive a philanthropic gift often feel indebted to their benefactor, and feel an obligation to repay them somehow. And when they cannot find a way to repay adequately – they often cannot – these recipients sometimes feel resentful, or avoid contact, or otherwise suffer from the weight of their burden.

Reinforcing status quo

In both subtle and obvious ways, philanthropy can perpetuate dominant power relations and neglect to support truly disadvantaged groups, or groups that seek more systemic social change. In a way, this is a specific form of the diversion of resources problem. [A] recent National Committee for Responsive Philanthropy report claimed that institutional philanthropy was guilty of reinforcing the status quo and underfunding social change. They called on foundations to correct this by giving half of their grant money to benefit low-income groups or those representing communities of color, and at least 25 percent to support social justice advocacy and organizing. This type of harm can take a more nefarious tint, such as when humanitarian aid to the developing world reinforces tyrannical governance structures, or even funds warlords.

Paternalism and cultural insensitivity

[. . .] "Do-gooders" can cause harm by taking what some consider a condescending, paternalistic attitude, believing they know what is "good" for the targets of their interventions, and by imposing their own values instead of being sensitive to the values and situation of those they seek to help. This sort of argument was often made against Victorian-era social reformers, such as the elite students involved in the settlement house movement, and "friendly visitors" who sought to "civilize" the poor by bringing high culture into their homes.

Favoring philanthropists' needs over recipients

As those last examples suggest, many people consider it harmful when philanthropy seems overly driven by the donor's interests and needs, especially when these are out of synch with what recipients or communities really need. Individual donors might be attracted to a particular solution or favorite organization, ignoring evidence that another solution or group is more effective. Foundations might stick to safe, familiar giving guidelines instead of listening to what their grantees really need. Or too much attention can be paid to helping donors feel good about themselves or ensuring they have a good experience. [. . .]

Teleopathy

This is a term coined by Goodpaster to refer to the unbalanced pursuit of non-essential goals in organizations. In philanthropic organizations defined by the pursuit of a mission, teleopathy occurs when people lose sight of that mission as the primary goal, and let other concerns (e.g., organizational politics, career goals) determine their action. [. . .] Perhaps the most common illustrations of teleopathy are those organizations that spend nearly every dollar they raise on internal administrative expenses instead of programs – exposés often focus on these groups with unacceptable "fundraising ratios."

Risks for philanthropists

Finally, harm can come to the philanthropists themselves as a result of their interventions for the public good. The risks of harm can be minor, as with the everyday Good Samaritans who provide a helping hand, or extraordinary, as with Holocaust rescuers, or volunteer searchers clamoring into collapsed buildings to save someone trapped inside. The potential harms can be physical, emotional, or even social and political – e.g., when a donor chooses to remain anonymous to avoid unwanted attention or potential social backlash for their giving choices.

This litany of types of potential harm is certainly incomplete. And the types of harm, as well as their perceived importance or prevalence, will change over time and vary across cultures. For instance, concerns about the paternalism of philanthropists grew much more common after the Victorian period, and critiques of philanthropy's support for the status quo intensified in the 1970s.

This list is also sobering, especially when we consider how many types might result from causes outside of our control. It might be the case that we will never be able to do *no* harm at all, but we can certainly work to minimize the harm we might cause. This vigilance and care is what applying the Hippocratic Oath to philanthropy requires.

The subtle problems of charity

Jane Addams, 1899

Probably there is no relation in life which our democracy is changing more rapidly than the charitable relation – that relation which obtains between benefactor and beneficiary; at the same time there is no point of contact in our modern experience which reveals so clearly the lack of that equality which democracy implies. We have reached the moment when democracy has made such inroads upon this relationship, that the complacency of the old-fashioned charitable man is gone forever; while, at the same time, the very need and existence of charity, denies us the consolation and freedom which democracy will at last give.

It is quite obvious that the ethics of none of us are clearly defined, and we are continually obliged to act in circles of habit, based upon convictions which we no longer hold. Thus our estimate of the effect of environment and social conditions has doubtless shifted faster than our methods of administrating charity have changed. Formerly when it was believed that poverty was synonymous with vice and laziness and that the prosperous man was the righteous man, charity was administered harshly with a good conscience; for the charitable agent really blamed the individual for his poverty, and the very fact of his own superior prosperity gave him a certain consciousness of superior morality. We have learned since that time to measure by other standards, and have ceased to accord to the money-earning capacity exclusive respect; while it is still rewarded out of all proportion to any other, its possession is by no means assumed to imply the possession of the highest moral qualities. We have learned to judge men by their social virtues as well as by their business capacity, by their devotion to intellectual and disinterested aims, and by their public spirit, and we naturally resent being obliged to judge poor people so solely upon the industrial side. Our democratic instinct instantly takes alarm. It is largely in this modern tendency to judge all men by one democratic standard, while the old charitable attitude commonly allowed the use of two standards, that much of the difficulty adheres. We know that unceasing bodily toil becomes wearing and brutalizing, and our position is totally untenable if we judge large numbers of our fellows solely upon their success in maintaining it.

A very little familiarity with the poor districts of any city is sufficient to show how primitive and genuine are the neighborly relations. There is the greatest willingness to lend or borrow anything, and all the residents of the given tenement know the most intimate family affairs of all others. The fact that the economic condition of all alike is on a most precarious level makes the ready outflow of sympathy and material assistance the most natural thing in the world. There are numberless instances of self-sacrifice quite unknown in the circles where greater economic advantage make that kind of intimate knowledge of one's neighbors impossible. An Irish family in which the man has lost his place, and the woman is struggling to eke out the scanty savings by day's work, will take in the widow and her five children who have been turned into the street, without a moment's reflection upon the physical discomforts involved. The most maligned landlady who lives in the house with her tenants is usually ready to lend a scuttle full of coal to one of them who may be out of work, or to share her supper.

[. . .]

The evolutionists tell us that the instinct to pity, the impulse to aid his fellow, served man at a very early period, as a rude rule of right and wrong. There is no doubt that this rude rule still holds among many people with whom charitable agencies are brought into contact, and that their ideas of right and wrong are quite honestly outraged by the methods of these agencies. When they see the delay and caution with which relief is given, it does not appear to them a conscientious scruple, but as the cold and calculating action of a selfish man. It is not the aid that they are accustomed to receive from their neighbors, and they do not understand why the impulse which drives people to "be good to the poor" should be so severely supervised. They feel, remotely, that the charity visitor is moved by motives that are alien and unreal. They may be superior motives, but they are different, and they are "agin nature."

Even those of us who feel most sorely the need of more order in altruistic effort and see the end to be desired, find something distasteful in the juxtaposition of the words "organized" and "charity." We say in defense that we are striving to turn this emotion into a motive, that pity is capricious, and not to be depended on; that we mean to give it the dignity of conscious duty. But at bottom we distrust a little a scheme which substitutes a theory of social conduct for the natural promptings of the heart, even although we appreciate the complexity of the situation. The poor man who has fallen into distress, when he first asks aid, instinctively expects tenderness, consideration, and forgiveness. If it is the first time, it has taken him long to make up his mind to take the step. He comes somewhat bruised and battered, and instead of being met with warmth of heart and sympathy, he is at once chilled by an investigation and an intimation that he ought to work. He does not recognize the disciplinary aspect of the situation.

The first impulse of our charity visitor is to be somewhat severe with her shiftless family for spending money on pleasures and indulging their children out of all proportion to their means. The poor family which receives beans and coal from the county, and pays for a bicycle on the installment plan, is not unknown to any of us. But as the growth of juvenile crime becomes gradually understood, and as the danger of giving no legitimate and organized pleasure to the child becomes clearer, we remember that primitive man had games long before he cared for a house or regular meals.

[. . .]

In the first year of their settlement the Hull-House residents took fifty kindergarten children to Lincoln Park, only to be grieved by their apathetic interest in trees and flowers. As they came back with an omnibus full of tired and sleepy children, they were surprised to find them galvanized into sudden life because a patrol wagon rattled by. Their eager little heads popped out of the windows full of questioning: "Was it a man or a woman?" "How many policemen inside?" and eager little tongues began to tell experiences of arrests which baby eyes had witnessed.

The excitement of a chase, the chances of competition, and the love of a fight are all centered in the outward display of crime. The parent who receives charitable aid and yet provides pleasure for his child, and is willing to indulge him in his play, is blindly doing one of the wisest things possible; and no one is more eager for playgrounds and vacation schools than the conscientious charity visitor.

[. . .]

Just when our affection becomes large enough to care for the unworthy among the poor as we would care for the unworthy among our own kin, is certainly a perplexing question. To say that it should never be so, is a comment upon our democratic relations to them which few of us would be willing to make.

Of what use is all this striving perplexity? Has the experience any value? It is certainly genuine, for it induces an occasional charity visitor to live in a tenement house as simply as the other tenants do. It drives others to give up visiting the poor altogether, because, they claim, it is quite impossible unless the individual becomes a member of a sisterhood, which requires, as some of the Roman Catholic sisterhoods do, that the member first take the vows of obedience and poverty, so that she can have nothing to give save as it is first given to her, and thus she is not harassed by a constant attempt at adjustment.

Both the tenement-house resident and the sister assume to have put themselves upon the industrial level of their neighbors, although they have left out the most awful element of poverty, that of imminent fear of starvation and a neglected old age.

The young charity visitor who goes from a family living upon a most precarious industrial level to her own home in a prosperous part of the city, if she is sensitive at all, is never free from perplexities which our glowing democracy forces upon her.

[. . .]

In our charitable efforts we think much more of what a man ought to be than of what he is or of what he may become; and we ruthlessly force our conventions and standards upon him.

[. . .]

The young woman who has succeeded in expressing her social compunction through charitable effort finds that the wider social activity, and the contact with the larger experience, not only increases her sense of social obligation but at the same time recasts her social ideals. She is chagrined to discover that in the actual task of reducing her social scruples to action, her humble beneficiaries are far in advance of her, not in charity or singleness of purpose, but in self-sacrificing action. She reaches the old-time virtue of humility by a social process, not in the old way, as the man who sits by the side of the road and puts dust upon his head, calling himself a contrite sinner, but she gets the dust upon her head because she has stumbled and fallen in the road through her efforts to push forward the mass, to march with her fellows. She has socialized her virtues not only through a social aim but by a social process.

The Hebrew prophet made three requirements from those who would join the great forward-moving procession led by Jehovah. "To love mercy" and at the same time "to do justly" is the difficult task; to fulfill the first requirement alone is to fall into the error of indiscriminate giving with all its disastrous results; to fulfill the second solely is to obtain the stern policy of withholding, and it results in such a dreary lack of sympathy and understanding that the establishment of justice is impossible. It may be that the combination of the two can never be attained save as we fulfil still the third requirement – "to walk humbly with God," which may mean to walk for many dreary miles beside the lowliest of His creatures, not even in that peace of mind which the company of the humble is popularly supposed to afford, but rather with the pangs and throes to which the poor human understanding is subjected whenever it attempts to comprehend the meaning of life.

4.4 Being a giver, being a recipient

The meaning of charity for donors and recipients

Ellen Ross, 1996

Charitable activity in nineteenth- and early twentieth-century England occupied a central place in the cultures both of its upper-class purveyors and of the needy people who were its objects. The commercial and industrial middle-classes of the late eighteenth and nineteenth centuries claimed and maintained their place in Britain's political sun in large measure through their voluntary charitable organizations, which also provided generations of middle-class men and women with pleasure, interest, and occupation. As for the poor, household survival was often postulated on charitable donations, offerings which, in one form or another, surely made up an element in the household budgets of a majority of Britain's poor and near-poor households. The social status and personal fulfillment achieved by charity giving, of course, had only a tangential relationship to the recipients' view of charity as one among many inadequate survival resources which, if pieced together carefully, could add up to security or even modest comfort.

[. . .]

My purpose is to urge a view of charity as all parties in the project, including the working-class wives and mothers who were its main objectors, found it. Making them actors in this drama of giving and receiving gifts provides a fresh way of evaluating the charities of the Victorian and Edwardian eras. By watching charities in their daily work with their clients we can begin to judge their significance both in helping the poor materially, and in shaping the experiences and views of the philanthropists themselves. My research was originally intended to challenge both the naive view of nineteenth-century philanthropists as generous and disinterested, and the more skeptical position pervasive in historical scholarship until quite recently which viewed philanthropy primarily as a nexus in which the rich controlled and scrutinized the poor.

[. . .]

The poor and charity

The poor were by no means exclusively *receivers* of charity. Working men collected money informally when co-workers were ill or needed money in emergencies, and there were more formal trades union or workmen's benefit clubs. The great private hospitals in and outside London collected thousands of pounds in tiny donations from working people. Working-class women taught Sunday school and did parish visiting in their own neighborhoods. The poor also, as a normal element of their existences, gave help, goods, and money to their neighbors and relatives, so much so that, as observers began to register the extent of this "unstinted and abounding charity of the poor to the poor" they had to recognize its significance in the survival of the one-third of households in London classed as poor.

[. . .]

Meant by the givers to bridge the chasm between the classes, charity was invariably distorted as it travelled from one side to the other: recipients lied, cheated, and used donations in ways charity givers did not intend. The enormous influence of Levi-Strauss's stress on the "laws" of reciprocity has obscured the fact that with all gift giving, there is always the possibility of non-reciprocation, rejection, and ingratitude. To dispel their chronic suspicion of "charity mongering" many charities carried out endless extra casework: middle-class female time, the foundation on which the Charity Organisation Society method of "thorough investigation" of cases was built, was plentiful in the nineteenth century. Charity in Victorian and Edwardian Britain was based on two dilemmas which made cheating on the part of the users and distrust on the givers' side inevitable. First, the rich seldom gave the poor what they most wanted: cash to use as they pleased – to pay the rent, redeem the bedding from pawn, buy the "pieces" from the butcher, or even send for a pint of stout from the pub. Second, charities frequently gave to individuals, but most working-class individuals had powerful family obligations, and resources flowed in the direction of those obligations. Thus gifts from rich to poor were, as a matter of course, "deformed" (to use Stedman Jones' useful misreading of Marcel Mauss).

[. . .]

Children's school meals

Schoolchildren's breakfasts and noon dinners are a deceptively mundane form of London charity. No one who has read Charles Morley's vivid account of hundreds of hungry children in the Borough sitting down to rapidly devoured hot meals supplied by the *Referee* (a London daily newspaper) Free Dinners Fund will dismiss the school feeding projects as bland exercises of upper-class benevolence. Because they involved the highly charged issue of feeding hungry children – a mother's job, after all – school meals were the object of hopes, fears, accusations, and fantasies for both the givers and the receivers, all the more so because the uncertainties about the meanings of reciprocity when services were offered across classes were still greater when their objects were children often too young to be expected to exhibit gratitude. For the study of charity as a social issue, the London meals provide a striking case study in the gift relationship, its meaning for both parties, and its concrete results for children's nutrition, mothers' budgets, and even party politics. From the vantage point of charity practice and policy, school meals serve as a good case study of the way in which donors' ambivalence about their project and suspicion of recipients distorted their gift even before it reached its object.

Throughout the period 1870–1918 the providers of the meals were volunteers (the kitchen workers and a few administrators were paid after 1907), whose impulses were on the whole generous, even loving, toward the poor, especially toward their children. Their soaring hopes for the feeding had sacramental overtones; volunteers spoke of the "spiritual beauty" of the feeding and of the meals as moments of "human communion." But these ideals came into thudding contact with the ideological outlines of Victorian and Edwardian charity with its suspicions of charity mongering and fears of "demoralizing" the poor. The caregivers' colorful fantasies also clashed with the gray hues of the mothers' (and occasionally fathers') highly practical approach to the meals; the parents simply wanted decent food for their offspring at some saving to themselves. To them, the meals represented no sacramental linking of the classes involving reverence and gratitude but a household resource.

[. . .]

Although all adults involved agreed on the rightness of feeding children, political chasms divided their views on the significance of the meals. For the Left, school meals were a foot in the door of state-funded universal social services available as entitlements. Many non-leftists, on the other hand, while responding warmly to the obvious hunger of the children, worried about the implications of feeding them: were they not taking on a responsibility that properly belonged to parents? The issues were sharpest for the hundreds of Charity Organization Society [COS] members who participated in meals programs. As an organization, the COS always opposed free feeding and maintained that position well past the point when the meals had begun to receive funding through local taxes. It was this ambivalence about the legitimacy of the feeding programs that generated so many of the obstacles the committees placed between the dinners and the children, obstacles we label, collectively, their stigma.

[. . .]

Meals providers often offered the dinners in unpalatable forms, both gastronomically and socially. The Charity Organization Society's commitment to thorough investigation of home circumstances – interviews, home visits, papers to fill out – even when only small donations like boots or meals were at stake, and which was especially well entrenched in several East London districts, was only one of many barriers between the child and the meals, barriers "calculated to deter all self-respecting parents from making an application [for meals] on behalf of their children," as an Independent Labour Party pamphlet put it in 1909. Even with the more formal and publicly financed operation of the school dinner machinery in the 1900s, at least some of the basic elements of stigma were enforced by most of the committees: careful investigation of the receivers; unattractive food or surroundings for the meals; public identification of the children in their classrooms; attempts to extract repayment from parents when their circumstances improved.

[. . .]

Separated from us in time and place and by its outmoded language, the British practice of charity a hundred years ago with its successes and failures leaves us with some more permanent insights perhaps by virtue of its very distance from our own world. The British charity givers' lack of control over the ultimate use to which recipients put their donations certainly offers one permanent cautionary tale for philanthropists today, as does the futile and ungenerous accumulation of punitive methods designed to control the destination of their gifts. And, as the administration of stigma along with London school dinners demonstrates, ambivalence about the justice of the cause or the worthiness of the recipients distorts the offer of charity as much as material obstacles in the form of funds and personnel.

Giving and getting

Susan A. Ostrander and Paul G. Schervish, 1990

An exclusive focus on donors runs the risk of obscuring issues that are of concern to recipients and therefore to philanthropy as a whole. The common language of giver and receiver used to characterize philanthropy suggests a one-way relationship in which valued goods and services move only in one direction, a point of view we challenge here. A donor focus also ignores the ways in which recipients actively take part in defining what goes on in the world of philanthropy, ways in which recipients are agents in creating philanthropic institutions and relations.

Attention tends to be diverted from the social needs that recipients have and that donors seek to address, and from what gifts actually accomplish from the perspective of those who receive them. Strategies that recipients and their advocates use to obtain support are generally left unexplored and unspecified.

Of greatest concern to us here is that the relatively exclusive focus on donors obscures the most fundamental sociological fact about philanthropy; namely, that philanthropy is a social relation of giving and getting between donors and recipients. The major aim of this chapter is to conceptualize and explore philanthropy in this way. This relational understanding of philanthropy elevates the position and priority of the recipient. It brings the recipient into theory, research, and practice in the field. Conceptualizing philanthropy as a social relation has the potential, we believe, for contributing to the making of a better match between the resources and needs of donors and the resources and needs of recipients. It can therefore help to improve philanthropic practice by developing a philanthropy that is more responsive to social need.

[. . .]

Like other social relations, that between donor-side and recipient-side actors contains identifiable patterns of interaction. Like other social relations, it is a transaction in which both parties get and give as a condition for establishing and maintaining the relation. At the same time, in this and many other social exchanges, the relation between the two parties is not an equal one. For a number of reasons a power difference between donor and recipient emerges from the current character of philanthropy as a social relation. The general tendency is for donors to occupy positions that give them substantially more active choice than recipients about how to define the philanthropic transaction and how to take part in it. Recipients also can and do make choices that affect what happens to themselves and to donors and shape the way philanthropy is organized.

This relative inequality between donors and recipients and the disparity in the extent of active choice available to each party derive from the larger societal context in which philanthropy occurs. We conceptualize this context by drawing on social theory about human agency and societal structure. Social structure both creates and is created by human action and choice in an iterative process. Once created, social structure defines the terms and boundaries of choice, presenting both obstacles and possibilities for action. Donors and recipients, then, are both constrained and facilitated by the structure of philanthropy in what they do and how they think. At the same time, both donors and recipients participate as agents in reinforcing or changing this structure of philanthropy – the structure that then in turn forms the context for their own thinking and acting in the philanthropic world.

Commercial transactions, electoral politics, and philanthropy

If it is not an institutional or legal boundary that separates philanthropic relations from commerce and politics, then what is it? What distinguishes philanthropy as a particular kind of social relation? The most important distinction we make between philanthropy and commercial and electoral relations revolves around the media of communication through which needs are put forth in each case. Each type of relation differs in how a request or demand is made and in how such demand elicits a response. Commercial appeals or demands are made in terms of dollars, while electoral appeals or demands are made in terms of votes. Philanthropic appeals are made in normative or moral or value terms.

[. . .]

The tendency of philanthropy to be donor-led

The major consequences for the way that philanthropy works as a social relation arises from its governance more by moral than by material or electoral claims. Because normative appeals do not carry the same kinds of rewards or sanctions as money or votes, philanthropy (unlike commercial transactions or electoral politics) tends to be driven more by the supply of philanthropic resources than by the demand for them based in recipient needs. Because philanthropic appeals are normative or morally based, they tend therefore to be "weaker" and less compelling than when the currency is votes or money. This means that attention to recipient needs may not always remain prominent or determinant in the minds of those providing donor resources or in the minds of those who seek funding on behalf of ultimate beneficiaries.

[. . .]

Donor ascendancy and recipient influence

Because normative appeals offer little, if any, immediate extrinsic reward or sanction to a potential donor, any single appeal can be refused without any direct negative material consequence. It is, of course, true that donors are not exempt from pressures to give money to "charitable" causes as a part of their climb to success in the corporate world or as a result of belonging to certain social networks. Still, for the most part, the obligation to give money is essentially based on moral grounds – because it is the right and good and sincere gesture to be made – without direct material censure or reward. Normative claims impose this obligation only to the extent that donors recognize and heed them. So recipient groups find themselves dependent on donors not only for funds. Ironically, they depend as well on donors for the very recognition of the legitimacy of the appeals by which recipients make claims on donors in the first place.

The structural tendency in philanthropic relations is, therefore, to grant more power to the donor than to the recipient.

[. . .]

Although donors certainly cannot be said to depend on recipients for their actual and material existence, it could be said that donors depend on recipients for the moral and normative and perhaps social meaning of their existence. Recipients have their own influence and their own set of resources to give to donors. In recipient appeals to potential donors, the moral currency that is used is not without value and command. As will be seen in our discussion of philanthropic strategies, donors respond to a whole array of non-material incentives, ranging from making a sincere effort to meet social needs to fulfilling a moral duty, obtaining psychic satisfaction, achieving social and personal legitimation, gaining status in the community, or achieving a social agenda.

Although philanthropy as currently constituted tends toward donor ascendancy, in actual practice the balance of power does not always remain firmly established on the side of the donor. Whenever recipients or their advocates introduce and enforce normative claims or incentives that affect donors, the balance of power begins to shift toward recipients. It is, then, not always the case that philanthropy is governed by the supply of donor resources though this does not refute the structural tendencies we have noted here. Framing the issue in this way does call for a specification of the conditions under which the structural tendencies get modified so that recipients have more influence. The strategies we next consider differ in the extent to which they contain possible directions for creating and strengthening such conditions. As we will show, it is not simply a matter of the degree to which recipients and their needs are taken into account by donors. It is also a matter of the qualitatively different ways in which this comes about.

[. . .]

Donor-side philanthropic strategies

In previous research, Schervish and Herman identified sixteen qualitatively different strategies or "logics" of philanthropy that are carried out by donors, distinguishing them according to differences in goals, modes of consciousness, and modes of practice. Here we discuss nine of those strategies, locating them within three broad approaches by which donors understand and carry out their relation to recipients. The three general donor-side approaches we will consider here are the personal-engagement, mediated-engagement, and donor-oriented strategies:

Personal-engagement strategies: direct personal contact and exchange of information between donors and beneficiaries, with priority given to recipient needs.

1. *Consumption*: donor is also beneficiary of gift.
2. *Therapeutic/empowering*: donors seek simultaneously to enhance their own sense of self-empowerment and to give over some active organizational control to beneficiaries.
3. *Adoptive*: donors attend personally to recipient needs in an ongoing and multifaceted relationship.

Mediated-engagement strategies: contact between donors and recipients mediated by organizations or other individuals, though knowledge and concern for recipient needs may be high.

1 *Contributory*: donor gives to a cause with no direct contact with recipients.
2 *Brokering*: donors solicit other key donors in their own network.
3 *Catalytic*: organizers donate time to mobilize large number of other donors in a mass appeal.

Donor-oriented strategies: donors governed and mobilized by their own circumstances rather than by those of recipients.

1 *Exchange*: giving propelled by mutual obligation within a network of donors.
2 *Derivative*: giving based on obligations associated with job expectations or family responsibilities.
3 *Noblesse oblige*: philanthropy grows out of decision to designate part of family money for social involvement.

[. . .]

Recipient-side philanthropic strategies

We have developed three strategies that recipient organizations can use to gain the attention and favorable response of donors and potential donors. They are needs-based, opportunity-based, and agenda-based strategies.

Needs-based strategy: needs of beneficiaries are presented forthrightly to donors as the sole basis for mobilizing contributions; these needs may be presented either by the benficiaries themselves or by recipient organizations or groups on their behalf.

- Recipient frames need as inherently worthy of attention.
- Recipient poses relationship to donor as a collaboration around a shared responsibility.
- Recipient appeals revolve around efforts to communicate information about beneficiaries and their needs.

Opportunity-based strategy: needs of beneficiaries are recast and expressed as donor opportunities representing social or political benefit for the donor beyond simply responding to the needs themselves.

- Recipients' appeals are formulated to persuade donors that responding to the needs of beneficiaries simultaneously provides donors with valued rewards.
- Recipients may present the proposed project or program as an opportunity for the donors to make an innovative or distinctive contribution to the community, to enhance their own status or influence, to make a good investment, or to enter a prominent donor network.
- Recipients may offer donors reduced costs or special access to programs or activities of recipient organizations.

Agenda-based strategy: needs of beneficiaries are submerged and even compromised as recipients offer donors the chance to fulfill interests arising from events or circumstances in the donors' personal, family, or professional life.

- Recipients cultivate personal relationships with current and prospective donors by focusing on what donors want or need as the condition or incentive for making a gift.
- Recipients remain alert to new and emerging donor agendas as old agendas are fulfilled or fade in importance.
- Recipients often maintain and update detailed prospecting files on individual donors.

Implications for the practice of philanthropy

As we have discussed, philanthropy typically is mobilized and governed more by availability of donor resources than by the existence of recipient needs. The implications of what we have had to say here about reconceptualizing philanthropy as a social relation between donor and recipient and about developing and applying philanthropic strategies that represent the interests and concerns of donors and recipients flow from this tension that is generated by a supply-led or donor-led process. As a counterbalance to the structural tendency of philanthropy to be supply-led – and therefore for donors to have more power in the relation than recipients – conditions need to be specified under which recipients can and do have influence in the philanthropic relation. As we have said, it is our belief that this counterbalance – that bringing recipients in – will improve the quality and performance of philanthropy for donors and recipients.

One principle in particular seems to derive from the arguments we have made here: donors have needs to be fulfilled as well as resources to grant, and recipients have resources to give as well as needs to be met. In other words, *donors and recipients both give and get in the social relation that is philanthropy*. In consumption philanthropy, where donors and recipients are one and the same, we see recipient needs are the most heeded. We think it is not accidental that such consumption philanthropy turns out to be the largest form of philanthropy in terms of size of contributions. What can be learned from this is not that consumptive philanthropy itself should be extended but rather that contributions are mobilized most strongly when donors see their interests and concerns to be the same as those of recipients or closely identified with them. This is counter to the more traditional view of philanthropic relation in which givers and receivers are socially distant and hierarchically arranged.

In each of the strategies we have laid out here, donors and recipients can be seen both as wanting something from each other and as having something to give that the other values. If recipients could be clearer about this, it would counter their tendency to go "hat in hand" to potential donors. It seems to us that recipients could use the needs-based strategy more often than our review of the fundraising literature would suggest they do, or at least are advised by that literature to do. A fundamental assumption made over and over in this literature is that donors will not give to a project simply because it is presented as an effective way to address an important community need or interest. The desire on the part of a donor to be a part of a community effort, the satisfaction of being an active participant in creating one's own community and being connected to others in a collaborative project, the enlightened self-interest on the part of donors who recognize that they might benefit directly or indirectly from some philanthropic project – these are not seen as sufficient to motivate donors to give. In *Proven Tips and Secrets for Winning Grant $$*, for example, grant seekers are advised that while they "must present a clear picture of why [their] program is necessary" and they must "solicit community involvement in the grantsmanship process," the most important factor is the ability to "tailor each proposal to the individual requirements of funders." Grant seekers are urged to keep the donors' wants constantly in mind and to "appeal to them often" in the proposal. Even more bluntly, *Grantsmanship: Money and How to Get It* advises, "Tailor the letter [of inquiry] to the [funding] organization's opportunity, not the applicant's need."

This kind of advice, repeated frequently and, as the above quotations illustrate, in very similar language, seems to advocate the use of what we have conceptualized here as the opportunity-based and agenda-based recipient-side strategies of grant seeking. Although these strategies may be effective in one sense, they are the most donor-centered, and they require the largest investment and effort on the part of recipients. The agenda-based strategy in particular requires that recipient groups have a substantial amount of information about donors in order to find out what donors want and how they as recipients might satisfy those wants as a condition of "winning" the gift. The fundraising techniques that are applied, again, especially in the agenda-based approach, often require the counsel of "experts" who constitute a whole new industry that can be called the fundraising business. Clients and consumers, along with the needs and interests they carry, are the least visible in these strategies and the appeals and practices that derive from them.

The needs-based strategy that we have conceptualized here places the concerns and interests of the grant-seeking organization and the clients and consumers it serves at the center. It is less costly to carry out. It empowers recipients because they are the ones who define the need and the program, ideally in collaboration and in dialogue with clients and consumers and with donors. The depth and scope of the need and the interest in all parties in addressing that need with an effective program are seen as sufficient to win the gift. Donors are envisioned as members of the community who have resources that they are willing to contribute in return for the satisfaction of community involvement and participation. While individual donors may indeed use their philanthropic activities to create opportunities for themselves or to carry out their own personal or professional agendas, these are not the focus of the grant-seeking organization's appeals. They are seen as individual matters not at the center of the social relation that is philanthropy.

Our call for a recipient movement toward the needs-based strategy corresponds to a parallel call for a donor movement away from donor-oriented strategies and toward mediated-engagement, especially personal-engagement, philanthropy. From the point of view of donor strategies, the implication is to encourage increased donor engagement – both personal and psychological – in the needs and interests of recipients. Such engagement may well lead to increased monetary contributions by donors, but this is not the only or even the most important consequence. Engagement between donors and recipients has the potential for transforming the practice of philanthropy in a more profound way. The projects funded may become more in line with what people need and less with what they can get funded. As the hierarchical and nonreciprocal distinction between donor and recipient becomes replaced with more collaborative approaches, philanthropy has the potential of becoming more innovative and creative, not only in regard to types of social projects that it initiates but in regard to the interactive quality of social relations that it exemplifies. A philanthropic practice that emphasizes a personal-engagement strategy for donors and a needs-based strategy for recipients would be organized around the values of reciprocity, cooperation, mutual respect, accountability, and commitment.

By conceptualizing philanthropy as a social relation rather than as an institution, sector, or organization, we have attempted to locate in a positive way the distinctive attribute of philanthropy. What constitutes philanthropy is not the legal tax status of an organization or the deductibility of a contribution. Rather, it is an interaction between donors and recipients that revolves around an effort to match what donors have to give to recipients with what recipients have to give to donors. Much of this matching tends to be talked about as donors giving concrete resources to recipients and recipients giving nonmaterial or intrinsic rewards to donors. This is true enough for much of the current practice of philanthropy. However, our definition of philanthropy as a social relation and how it gets carried out in the more mutual donor and recipient strategies indicates that there is more to it than this. When philanthropy is practiced at its best, donors are material opportunities – and not just psychic rewards – through their relation to recipients. In turn, recipients are given various kinds of nonmaterial resources – in addition to material support – such as respect, empowerment, and esteem when philanthropy is recognized and carried out as a reciprocal social relation.

A human exchange of equals in New York

Julie Salamon, 2003

I don't remember when I first noticed him, but it seems to me that he had been panhandling outside the corner grocery for at least a year. He appeared to be in his late thirties, but since he was one of those ageless souls, I could have been off by a dozen years in either direction. He was a pleasant-looking man, African American, medium height but thin – too thin. He had a sweet face and warm smile and favored brightly colored T-shirts. When I walked by he would say, "How are you doing, sister?" He would make his pitch, almost as an apologetic afterthought. Then he'd say, "Have a nice day," even though I had responded, also apologetically, not with money but with advice.

"Go to the Bowery Residents' Committee," I would tell him. I had been a volunteer at the agency for a long time, and had become chairman of its board. I had never questioned the agency's disapproval of panhandling: "Giving money, food or blankets directly to the homeless," its brochures spell out, "encourages them to stay on the street and avoid confronting their needs in a more constructive manner." In other words, the goal and essential philosophy of the Bowery Residents' Committee (BRC) is to help a person become self-sufficient.

That was my rationale each time I said to the man on the corner, "You can get help there," and then handed him a card with the BRC's address and phone number on it.

Always polite, he would respond to my unsolicited advice in different ways. He would tell me he wasn't interested in going to a program – guessing correctly that the BRC staff would encourage him to go into detox. Sometimes he would nod and say, "Oh yes, I'll do that," both of us knowing he was just trying to get me off his back. Each time, he would examine the card and put it in his pocket.

That was the extent of our relationship, if these exchanges could be called that, for several months. I felt a friendly surge of recognition when I saw him, and then my body would tighten, sending warning signals that I shouldn't be supporting his self-destructive habits. It was at those times that I would cross the street to avoid him.

Toward the end of a warm winter came one bitterly cold day. I was walking home and saw David – though I wouldn't learn his name for some months – shuffling toward me. The shuffle was new.

It had taken me a minute to recognize him. He was not in what I thought of as his usual place, but out of context, a few blocks from his post by our corner store. I stopped and asked what was wrong with his leg. He told me he had taken a fall. He looked miserable, although, as usual, he was neatly dressed.

My earlier reservations about helping him vanished. I asked him if he had had anything to eat yet that day. It was close to 1pm. He said no. I told him to come with me to the grocery store, where they also made sandwiches, and I would get him some food.

David looked surprised – he hadn't hit me up for money – but adapted deftly to this happy change in circumstance. He limped and I walked slowly up the street, past stores where $400 shoes are readily available; likewise $200 jeans, pre-ripped. He told me, unsolicited, that he had stopped drinking. "Did you go into a program?" I asked him. He waved his hand dismissively. "I don't like programs," he said. "My body told me it was time when I woke up throwing up or everything I had tasted like beer. It's been a month since I had a drink."

I asked him where he slept and he said sometimes in shelters, sometimes in his "lady girlfriend's" apartment in Brooklyn, and often outside. He spoke with some poetry about the pleasures of sleeping outdoors on warm nights up in the Bronx, where he was from, and about how he enjoyed looking at the stars. I considered the possibility that I was being hustled, and suspected – no, knew – that there were grim stories being withheld. But he seemed happy talking about the stars in the Bronx.

Inside the store, the woman behind the register looked disapproving, or so I imagined. Back at the deli counter, David ordered a hearty lunch: a sandwich with meat and cheese, some milk, a banana, some cookies, and chips. The bill came to $6.50.

"That's a good deal," David observed.

He thanked me and then we shook hands and went our separate ways.

I washed my hands when I got home.

I continued to see him on an irregular basis. He thanked me a few times more for the sandwich and then I found myself crossing the street again to avoid the old dilemma of whether to give him money. After about a month of this, on another spirit-chilling day, I saw him standing at his usual corner. This time I crossed the street in his direction, pulled five dollars from my pocket and just handed the money to him. After that I routinely gave him money before he asked, breaking one set of rules but conforming to another. At the time, I didn't know that I had moved up a notch on the ladder [Maimonides' eight levels of giving], where you give the poor man less than what is proper, but with a smile. Seeing David, reaching into my pocket, handing him money made me feel good. But now another question was left begging: Who was giving to whom?

[. . .]

When I met Patti she had already been in a wheelchair for three years; her son Jack was nine months old when she fell in front of a subway and was left paralyzed.

Patti always arouses much curiosity as she sails around in her wheelchair, a pretty woman wearing an Issey Miyake dress or something she picked up at a bargain store, stylish either way. Though she is in her early forties, she has the naughty smile of a subversive teenager and, despite her accident, remains slightly reckless, racing against traffic, popping wheelies on curbs. When Patti is around, things happen. She approaches life as an experiment, constantly testing new hair colors and new theories. I'd come to learn that she dispenses wisdom in most unusual ways. So when she told me to meet her at Bruno's Bakery for coffee because she had something to say about charity (she knew I was writing a book on the subject), I left home immediately.

On my way to Bruno's I saw "my" homeless man standing at the corner of a busy intersection. I began to veer in another direction, hoping he wouldn't see me, in part because I was eager to see Patti but also to avoid the guilty feelings he stirred up in me. My attempt at circumvention was hopeless and ridiculous. There was too much traffic to get very far.

"Hey there," he called out. "You don't have to walk away if you don't want to give me money."

Caught! Sheepishly I walked over and retrieved a small shred of dignity by not protesting.

"Look at this," he said with a smile, showing no sign of insult. He pulled a coin out of his pocket and made it disappear out of one hand and reappear in the other. He pulled a quarter from behind my ear and grinned.

"You know my name," he said, as if he was taunting me with the ladder of charity itself, which affords high ranking to anonymity between giver and receiver.

"David," I said. By then we had introduced ourselves.

He nodded. "That's right." And then he told me his entire name – first, middle, last.

So much for anonymity, though my cheeks were indeed burning with shame.

"My name is Julie," I said, thinking he had forgotten.

"I know," he replied, and then wished me a Happy Day, Darling, and waved good-bye. No money changed hands.

Patti was waiting for me at Bruno's. Her hair was an exuberant red that day. When I told her about my encounter with David she generously offered a parallel story. She told me about a man named Matthew who hangs out in her neighborhood in a wheelchair, selling batteries and audiotapes. He is a street person; she is married to an advertising executive and had a career in the fashion business. But because they are both disabled, Matthew has felt comfortable talking to her about their common experience, and she feels obligated to him for similar reasons. Now, even if she's in a rush or not in the mood, she finds it difficult to avoid him.

For Patti, giving (and taking) has become not so much a matter of choice or ethics but of necessity. There are too many sidewalks without graduated curbs at street crossings; unwieldy door entrances to negotiate; items placed beyond her reach in stores. Sometimes, because she is self-reliant and refuses to acknowledge these obstacles, she tries to manage by herself, falls out of her wheelchair, and then needs help getting back in. She doesn't have the freedom to choose anonymity; she has become a public person, an object of curiosity, concern, and fear. How did someone who looks so insouciant, so *normal*, end up in a wheelchair? She knows she has no reason to feel ashamed, but it's almost an inevitable reaction in a culture that places a premium on independence and fortitude.

"When I'm out on the street, I represent this thing that has been damaged, this life that has been damaged. For a while I was angry that I needed help and didn't want to rely on other people or to be their good deed for the day," said Patti. "I worried that maybe they'd done mean stuff to people or evil things at their job and then helping this woman in a wheelchair would bring them good karma. People actually say to me, 'That'll be my good deed for the day.' That made me feel like they were using me in some way."

For Patti, the corruption of charity, and the shame in it, isn't monetary but personal, most dangerous to the recipient when a gift is used as leverage. "If someone gives you help financially or physically, the next step can be that maybe you owe them something. You have to be very careful of that and don't want to put yourself into that position even if you are able to accept the fact that you need help," she told me.

If Maimonides was bent on reconciling faith and reason in his quest for righteousness, Patti has been determined to find symbiosis between the giving and the taking. This seemed to me the most viable interpretation of the fourth level [of Maimonides' eight levels of giving], where the poor person doesn't have to ask for help. Putting a shield of anonymity between giver and recipient is another. "You have to take those moments when you can make someone's day or life or situation a little better without having an ulterior motive," she said. "The more our collective consciousness sees things that way the better we will get at doing random acts of kindness."

[. . .]

Ronald Williams learned long ago not to make easy assumptions. Williams is program director for the Adult Day Health Care Program, which operates the crisis center for the Bowery Residents' Committee. The BRC offers services to homeless people, many of whom are mentally ill, many of whom rely heavily on drugs and alcohol. On a regular day at the crisis center some people are in detox programs, others are deciding whether they want treatment, others are moving from detox into other BRC programs. Some people just drop in for a shower and a safe bed for the night.

Early morning is an especially busy time, when people are being admitted and discharged. For some reason, Tuesday mornings are especially busy and September 11, 2001, was a Tuesday morning. Williams was in his office on Lafayette Street that morning. The crisis center is just below Houston Street, a mile north of New York's downtown financial district. When one of his homeless clients came running from Prince Street where he usually hangs out, a couple of blocks from the crisis center, he tapped on the window and said, "Mr. Williams, I think something is wrong."

Williams had a special relationship with this client, who'd been his first when he came to the BRC fourteen years earlier as a nurse with plans to stay only a few months.

The man had told Williams something that had become his guiding principle: "If you let a drunk come into your unit for one night, you've saved his life." Williams felt fondly toward this man, now in his late fifties, mentally ill and often disoriented.

But that morning the program director sensed that extra fear and confusion were in the mix. Something was terribly wrong. He brought the man inside to the main room, where the television was on. "There's a news flash," one of the clients said. Listening but not comprehending, staff and clients froze into silence.

Williams is a powerful-looking African American man in his fifties, with a graying beard and the hard-won experience to match, beginning with a segregated upbringing in Tulsa, Oklahoma, and including a tour of duty in Vietnam, where he was a medic.

"It reminded me of Vietnam, right before an offensive, when everyone is pensive," Williams told me. "You don't even know what's going to happen, what's going to transpire, but you know something is going to happen and it's going to be dramatic."

Soon enough the streets began to fill with groups of people coming up from lower Manhattan, walking fast. The first group looked as normal as terrified people can look. The next batch was covered in debris, and some also in blood.

What followed surprised Williams, who thought he was beyond surprise.

"My clients, people who were homeless, people at the lower end of society, were making suggestions to the staff. We put chairs outside, we had a hose attached to a faucet, a nurse came out with what first aid we could muster. When people started coming by covered in stuff, we hosed them off. A lot of people just wanted to sit down and get a drink of water. My clients were the ones doing this. They were out offering water, offering help. The clients just pitched in as if they were staff. They were sad because of what was going on, but they were glad to be part of something, to be doing something. They were there."

[. . .]

The homeless people on Lafayette Street found themselves, through their charity, part of the community that day. Usually ignored or avoided, or recipients of aid, they had been invited, through disruption of the normal order, to participate in the human exchange as equals. They had, momentarily, dropped the anonymity imposed on them by circumstance and been noticed for their good work. One woman they helped later returned to the center with a tray of cookies she'd baked, not out of pity but in thanks. Gifts had arrived before, but dispensed as charity, not in return for a favor, and that distinction was huge.

4.5 What is the right relationship between those who give and those who get?

Amsterdam in the Golden Age

Marco H. D. Van Leeuwen, 2012

Philanthropy is easier to describe than to explain, but when explaining it is less difficult to uncover the reasons why large donations were made. Large donations leave more traces than small ones, in the form of celebratory poems, speeches, contemporary accounts, paintings, coats of arms, obituaries and wills. Records of this kind are less likely in the case of small donations.

Wills provide only indirect pointers to the motives of testators. In Amsterdam none of the eighteenth-century Catholic wills examined contained a reference to the Virgin Mary, the Holy Spirit or a patron saint. However, recommending one's soul to God's mercy was a standard formula. In 1726 the distiller Cornelis de Lange began his will by 'commending his immortal soul to the inconceivable mercy of God'. A decent burial – to be arranged by the Catholic Charity – was often requested in wills.

Catholic testators often directed that after their death a priest should hold masses for the purification of their soul, again under the auspices of the Catholic Charity. Indeed, masses for the souls of the deceased were common. It was a case of *quid pro quo*. A good example of this is provided in the handwritten will of Neeltje Bijtebier, drawn up in 1736. She wished:

> For my body an honest funeral, for my soul three masses at that church at which extreme unction was administered. And then also two masses at other churches, and for the service Gouda candles on the altar and after a month at that church at which I received extreme unction. And on the first anniversary, new candles again, as at the funeral service, and twenty-five guilders for the perpetual memory [a fund out of which the cost of masses for the souls of the dead was paid].

Consider too the example of the merchant Octavio Francisco Tensini. In 1675 he left 60,000 guilders to the poor on condition that a mass for his soul be read every day until the Day of Judgement. His wish did not quite reach that far; the masses were said until 1945, paid for by the foundation managing his state, but then they stopped.

Catholics in Amsterdam tried, for that matter, to ensure their soul's salvation by giving to the poor before their death as well. An administrator of one Catholic charity noted in 1671: 'the ship's master when first leaving port took this box [i.e. collection box for the poor] with him on his journey to Smyrna. May God protect and save him so that he can return the box to us'. This is part of an old and rich tradition of votive offerings made by sailors on long and dangerous journeys. At this time, Amsterdam charities supported many sailors' wives and widows, and so sailors would have special reasons for giving to those organisations.

Descriptions of almshouse foundations also give us an insight into the motives of charitable benefactors. Verses explaining their good works are illuminating, whether they were written by the benefactors themselves or at their suggestion, or whether it was simply assumed they would like the text. The childless and the unmarried, and those who had fallen out with their spouse or descendants, saw themselves bereft of the usual ways of distributing their estate and had special reason to contribute to the common good. For example, after quarrelling long and bitterly with her daughter-in-law, in 1695 Agneta Deutz made a bequest to found an almshouse to be named after her. An added bonus was that the foundation would act as a concrete example of her good conduct and ensure that her name lived on: 'Here Agneta Deutz expressed her love and religious faith, as a comfort to the poor and as an example to the rich'. Another example is that of Ferard van de Rijp, who had separated from his wife and even took her to court at one stage. The unhappiness of his married life caused him to leave his estate to his sister's sons, on condition that they spent 20,000 guilders to found an almshouse in his name. That almshouse opened in 1748. Christoffel van Brants, a merchant who had built up a fortune of more than two million guilders from nothing and had become a member of the Russian aristocracy, acted as host to Peter the Great when he visited Amsterdam. Van Brants was probably right in thinking that his worldly fame, though certainly impressive, would not be sufficient to ensure that his name would live on forever. Just 260 years later – a fairly short period compared with eternity – hardly anyone remembers him as a celebrated man of arms. He did, however, escape from obscurity by giving 250,000 guilders to create an almshouse in his name in 1733.

Another almshouse, the Grill almshouse, was set up in 1721 by a childless Lutheran couple, Anthony and Elizabeth Grill, who explained the reasons for their good work: 'Anthony Grill with his wife created me and teach us even after their death how every member of the Christian Church should express their faith in their deeds'. Going a step further, the motive of salvation is found in a charitable donation made by Johanna van Mekeren, née Bontekoning, who gave 30,000 guilders to the Reformed Charity in 1789. The gift was recognised in these words: 'The generous love of Johanna Bontekoning gave this house for the use of Jesus' poor [. . .] Now resting after her labour, she sees her love rewarded. Her work out of mercy, rewarded with eternal salvation'. A century earlier, in 1684, a home for the elderly run by the Reformed Church was founded thanks to a donation from Mr Helleman:

> Give thanks, God-fearing people, by whom this House here stands,
> for the generous bequest of the high mighty magistrate
> for the money given, and for Helleman who by dying
> To the fund did bequeath at the right time no small sum
> the brethren for their care, for loss of time and for industry,
> All await of their Talent the Interest in time to come.

These examples indicate that, in addition to considerations of status, issues of religion, and in particular the idea of salvation for one's immortal soul or at least a reward in the afterlife, were fundamental in charitable giving, and that this was so not only for Catholics but also for Amsterdam's Protestant denominations, as, for that matter, for Sephardic Jews. That this is the case for Protestants is a surprising finding that will be addressed later.

The motives behind small donations are more difficult to ascertain than is the case with the bequests and almshouse foundations examined above. Dropping a coin into an offertory bag is an anonymous act. However, one can consider charitable appeals in order to find out what people making small donations regarded as valid reasons for giving. This approach provides more information than an analysis of policy documents relating to philanthropy because those relate to individuals of a higher social status. The underlying assumption here is that the reasons for giving will be reflected in the 'begging letters' written by charities to persuade people to support them. If those letters are to be effective, they must appeal to the views of potential donors. Fairchild expressed this assumption as follows:

> Because these pamphlets were designed for the purpose of fundraising, it is probable that the arguments they present were calculated to appeal to the assumptions of their audience – the pamphlets would have been ineffective otherwise. We can therefore assume that the ideas they elaborate were actually held by the people [. . .] The ideas found in these pamphlets are as near to truly "popular" attitudes as the historian is likely to get – much nearer at least, than the analyses of royal legislation and the writings of individuals which are usually employed as sources for "attitudes" about the poor.

Letters sent out by the Amsterdam Catholic Charity in 1738 to raise funds for the construction of a new Girls Orphanage, and in 1800 and 1807 to raise money for general purposes, show what tactics were used to kindle benevolence. What a primer does for paint, the begging letters do for giving. The letters would open with an appeal to the general compassion of their readers. They mentioned innocent victims such as 'suffering motherless children, begging for help [. . .] many elderly grey-haired folk and simple, gentle babes [. . .] with their parents [who] all need our help: look down on us with merciful eyes; take care of us or we will perish'. The affected reader is reminded that people are suffering through no fault of their own. The orphan girls were living in an overcrowded old building, forced 'to breathe in the seeds of sickness and disease, and [. . .] almost to suffocate in the bad air'. The poor in general were suffering as a result of the harsh winter, high unemployment in shipping, trade and industry, and the high cost of food. Once the suffering had been described and the reader's sympathy awakened, it was time to get them to open their purse. The first argument for giving was that of compassion. A second reason was force of habit: you gave in the past, nothing has changed, so we are counting on you to be generous once again. A third argument related more to insurance than to sympathy: the same might happen to you; giving now affords protection against misfortune in the future. Misplaced economy, so the reader is told, throws a shadow over what is to come. The governors of the Girls Orphanage wrote as follows:

> Consider those who are dearest to you, your children, your relations, your friends! Who among us is so far removed from human disaster that he can be sure that none of these people, or their descendants, will ever have to seek refuge in this establishment? There is a way to escape this fate, because sparse sowing, sparse reaping; sow bountifully and you will reap bountifully: he is ever merciful and lendeth and his seed is blessed.

Here, the appeal referred to the Catholic doctrine of Good Works and the doctrine of the Care by the Living of the Dead, promising that the grateful orphan girls would later 'send their sighs from a grateful heart to heaven, for your salvation and that of your family'. This brings us to the fourth and last argument for giving: obtaining salvation for the soul. The God of Mercy, the Father of the Orphans, gives his 'solemn promise: he hath dispersed, he hath given to the poor; his righteousness endureth for ever, his horn shall be exalted with honour'. In other letters, the charity claimed that benefactors 'will earn their reward for their generosity, both here and in the eternal bliss!' Looking at it from that point of view, a gift to the poor was a high-interest loan to God. Charity brought benefits to benefactors both here on earth and in the hereafter: 'In this way the charitable gifts of the wealthy and well-off [. . .] will rise up to the Lord [. . .] and then rain down on us a hundred fruits that will not perish now or in all eternity'.

That argument was used by Protestant charities too. The Lutheran Charity displayed the coats of arms of Abraham Cromhuysen and his sister Johanna Maria, who gave it large sums in 1751 and 1763. Abraham's gift was commemorated in the following:

> Here stands his immortal escutcheon,
> That stands for his joy and salvation;
> Blessed be those who, like him, have faith in the Saviour,
> And give their treasure to the service of God's Church, to earn their Heavenly Interest.

Mennonites also understood the Heavenly Interest argument. A governor of the Mennonite orphanage wrote: 'Give generously from what you have, as the money you invest in our poor orphans will not be lost. God will return it with interest, both now and in the life to come'.

The Heavenly Interest motif was found too among Calvinists, as can be seen in a letter from the Reformed Charity. This appeal for funds ends with the promise that giving to those in need will earn eternal reward:

> How many fatherless children, unhappy widows, old people, parents of large families, will not recommend you, your family, and all that is dear to you the Almighty in their daily prayers, and ask blessings for you, your spouse and your children; they will tell their children of your good deeds; and your generosity will still be praised after your death. And if you give [. . .] purely out of charity [. . .] then the same [charity] will be shown to you on the Day of Judgment [. . .] and you will enjoy heavenly treasure for all eternity.

This was not an isolated case. There are many other instances of Protestants being promised their reward in heaven. The prospect of such reward was an important reason for giving in Amsterdam, both for Protestants and Catholics, alongside considerations of enhancing the status and reputation of the donor.

[. . .]

In Amsterdam in the Golden Age there were opportunities for everyone, irrespective of their wealth or generosity, to give to good causes: people put money into collection boxes placed all over the city, they gave during church services, to door-to-door collections, through their wills or by making large donations during their lifetime.

The considerable variation in type and size of gift and the many opportunities for giving strongly suggests that people from all social classes gave to charity. The laudatory verses, public begging letters and gable stones stressing the importance of giving could, in any case, only have been missed by the blind and mute.

Not all those who made testamentary dispositions were necessarily members of the elite; they included members of craft guilds, shopkeepers, and, on rare occasions, even servants. Their income ranged from the seriously modest to the vast fortunes of the super-rich. Not all bequests were large. People from many different social backgrounds and income groups made charitable gifts in their wills. The testators often expressed a desire to make proper provision for the distribution of the property entrusted to them during their lifetime. They thought of the poor more as death on earth and eternal life in heaven approached. There were many mundane reasons why people gave to charity: they may have become estranged from their relatives and wished to leave money to the poor instead of to a disliked relation; perhaps they had no relatives to leave money to; and they may have wished to enhance their reputation by making charitable bequests. Religion in general was important, and the wish to earn Heavenly Interest particularly so. A secular system of trust based on the reputation of the charities and their administrators, together with supervision by civic authorities, provided a reasonable guarantee that the benefactors' religious and other wishes would be respected. Philanthropy certainly was an expression of faith, in a mundane sense as well as a religious one.

The religious foundation of charitable giving was an important factor in encouraging donations. The broad social support for charity was one consequence of the fact that charity was firmly anchored in religion, which itself was not limited to just one social group in society. Donations were made primarily to charities which shared the religion and community of the benefactor. Catholics could believe that charity would lead to salvation for the soul, as prescribed by the doctrine of Good Works and the Care by the Living of the Dead. But Protestant pastors also stressed that charity was a Christian duty. The idea of earning a reward in heaven was even expressed by Reformed, Lutheran and Mennonite charities, and people who gave funds to set up almshouses shared that idea too. Parents taught this view to children, and the poor themselves reminded the rich of their duty to help them, a duty that would be rewarded in perpetuity. How exactly Protestants were able to synthesise the Protestant rejection of the notion of Good Works as leading to salvation with widespread popular notions seemingly to the contrary is somewhat of a paradox: to strengthen Protestant communities the notion of Heavenly Interest was evoked in a way difficult to reconcile with the tenets of the various Protestant creeds.

Philanthropy was indeed as much an attempt to strengthen a community as it was an expression of belonging to it. It was an attempt to soften social divisions and to keep the social fabric intact. In the process of expressing a sense of community via philanthropy the sense of belonging together was strengthened, perhaps illustrated best through the growth of the capital of charities over time. Most citizens and authorities, be they secular or ecclesiastical, Catholic, Protestant or Jewish, elites, middle classes or the common civilian, women or men, were bound together by a pervasive culture of private giving. The fact that charity was almost always only one of the survival strategies of the poor, and the fact that elites and middle classes, sometimes quite candidly, spoke of it as a means of social control should not cloud the main issue here: the endurance of private voluntary giving, of benefactors and benefactions, in early modern history.

Horizontal philanthropy in southern Africa

Alan Fowler and Susan Wilkinson-Maposa, 2013

[In southern Africa we find the following features and patterns:] help is a daily lived reality and necessity, not an exceptional event. Asking for help brings *no stigma*. *Offering help* without being asked is commonplace. No matter how little you have you give – *the act is as important as the quantum involved*. Helping brings positive feelings that can be its own (spiritual or moral) reward. To qualify as 'help' *assistance cannot be exploitive or demeaning*. A recipient must *be deserving*. This attribute is principally judged by an individual's helping behaviour within their possibilities. Preference is given for seeking help from people who understand one's situation by virtue of a *shared condition or experience*, rather than from outsiders.

[. . .]

Within respondents' livelihood, survival and coping strategies, helping is more often exhibited as reciprocal exchange. Local idioms illustrate that reciprocity brings its own reward: *Lokwooko ohali shikula lokuulu* – The one arm follows the one of the leg – i.e. the one that gives is also given to. Reciprocity means that payback can be spread over time – effectively redistributing a giver's assets. If the receiver behaves as required, vulnerability is reduced because risk is spread, making reputation central in decision-making described below. However, reciprocity does not necessarily increase assets. It acts as a form of 'welfare', preventing slippage further into deprivation.

[. . .]

Assistance spans a broad typology. Examples are: 1) a donation, such as time for supporting orphans; 2) a subsidy, where a normal, expected return is forgone; 3) a fee for service, typically a token of appreciation; 4) a loan, where return is required; 5) a sharing, such as information or application of a skill, neither of which is depleted by the act of giving; 6) redistribution from a public asset, like a chief's grain store; 7) a collaborative endeavour for joint, even if unequal, gain; and 8) as intervention or intercession on someone's behalf.

[. . .]

The system, defined as philanthropy of community (PoC), has five dimensions, each with different properties and functions. [. . .]

Dimension 1: interplay of needs and networks

Unmet needs or unresolved problems are a quintessential aspect of poverty that drive people to seek and provide help to each other. Poor people differentiated help in terms of needs that are 'normal' or those that are 'urgent'. Normal needs are typically small, regular and frequent, including daily use, short term and gap filling. These demands can be planned for and anticipated and the size is manageable in terms of a drain on assets. Such needs are often satisfied through individual reciprocity and the return is quick.

Urgent needs are immediate and unplanned for or unanticipated. They are usually generated by emergencies such as fire, flooding, death, accidents and drought. The poor also see urgency in terms of dangerous levels of debt or financial constraints that, for example, prevent marriage because of an inability to meet a brideprice. While perhaps lower in frequency and more ad hoc, urgent needs require a rapid response and can demand a significant contribution in relation to available resources. The size of demand in proportion to an individual's asset base may require a group or collective response that can be spontaneous or premeditated. Typical in the latter case is collective creation of a risk-reducing strategic reserve – e.g. a burial society, or a savings and credit group with jointly managed resources that can be called upon under agreed conditions. [T]he degree to which such collective arrangements feature in help patterns and the associational modality involved varies [between countries in southern Africa]. The formalization of help relationships tends to correspond to purposes that should improve life circumstances rather than prevent deterioration in well-being: a spectrum explained in more detail later.

Both individual giving and pooling draw on and co-create help circuits. Access to assistance is gained through a personal set of connections or networks that mobilize resources and address needs. The network involved is shaped by the interplay between the type of need and the nature of affinity – blood and social identity or physical proximity between the actors – as well as individual reputation. In other words, help networks are needs-based and multiple. They may or may not include more institutionalized sources of assistance, such as informal associations and more formal organizations. In this respect, depending on the nature of the need, networks may be simple arrays of individual connections or contain complex combinations of actor types.

Dimension 2: range of capitals

A further aspect of needs and their network-generating effects are the importance that people who are poor attribute to non-material assistance described previously. While less frequent in terms of transactional content, the value attributed to knowledge, contacts, information, physical and manual assistance and moral/emotional support must not be underestimated. Such assets are not necessarily depleted, lost or foregone through use. In this sense, they help poor people satisfy a reputational requirement to give no matter how little – the act is as important as the content value – which maintains eligibility for assistance, social cohesion and network access.

Dimension 3: maintenance to movement

Poor people involved in [our] study judge help in many ways. An oft-cited criterion is whether or not the help is expected to maintain current living status, conditions and prospects – i.e. to prevent slippage into deeper deprivation – or to create movement, that is to increase the possibilities for escaping poverty and better countering adversity. Where political or economic forces and pandemics like HIV/AIDS are a continual source of livelihood insecurity and downward pressure on assets, the developmental significance and impact of maintenance-oriented help is often overlooked.

More readily treated (by outsiders) as developmental behaviour are help transactions that carry the potential for increasing or diversifying economic assets or other capitals and widening the scope of life to increase people's opportunities. The inclination of poor people to allocate resources in this way is mediated by their experience of returns on doing so. A case in point for many respondents was the diminishing value of investment in children's education that did not generate a benefit though improved access to employment or other sources of livelihood.

Dimension 4: conventions, rules and their application

People who are poor help each other and are helped according to unwritten yet widely understood conventions, customs, rules and sanctions. They are not static, but continually updated transaction by transaction. The help system is premised on the axiom 'no matter how little you have you give', which itself rests on a moral philosophy described in Dimension 5. It functions by means of experiential feedback that co-determines the reinforcement or attrition of a network's value to those within it.

In operation, the horizontal help system rests on a decision-making process. First, a trigger arises and a potential transaction is initiated – help is asked for or offered. A request is screened for appropriateness and actor eligibility. If the result of this screening is positive, informed by a motivational principle, a help transaction is selected [. . .] In a fourth step, actors establish an agreement on the terms or conditions that will apply. Finally, over time there are reputational rewards for conforming to conventions and rules and there are sanctions for not doing so. Sanctions may be individual in terms of decreased eligibility for assistance from the chosen source in the future. When a person's non-compliance becomes systematic or has wider effects, such as threatening social cohesion, they can be corrected by an acknowledged authority – such as elders or age cohorts – and in the extreme isolated, excluded or rejected.

Dimension 5: moral philosophy of the collective self

> You can fail to give because you don't have anything to offer; you are poor. But when you can't give you feel pained by the fact that you don't have something to offer to make you *a human being among others*.
>
> (Emphasis added)

The above quotation, and similar expressions to be found in the narratives, point towards a moral philosophy among respondents that requires re-calibration of Western metrics of selfless or selfish behaviour that are premised on Durkheim's 'anomie' and individualistic choice. The philosophy of *ubuntu* – I am because you are – rather than the Descartian axiom of I think therefore I am, provides a different behavioral proposition and interpretation of help among the poor in southern Africa.

Essentially, *ubuntu* is a theory and philosophy of collective self with strong spiritual and symbolic connotations. Denying help to another is to deny one's own identity as a human.

[. . .]

A further, fundamental, aspect of a conversation about African philanthropy is to unpack the concept of a 'gift'. In a Western world view, axiomatic to a 'gift' is the *voluntary transfer without condition or compensation* of an asset or capital that is valued by the recipient. The associated act of 'giving', however, does not necessarily comply with this condition. Rather, elision of 'giving' with a 'gift' – the term 'gifting' is seldom used in philanthropic discourse – sows confusion as to intent, implying that nothing is expected in return. [G]iving [does not] necessarily translate into self-sacrifice [and is not a] negative sum game [. . .] Zero and positive sum outcomes are also possible, meaning some form of 'compensation' is in play. There is always an aspect of 'utility' in giving. But our research provide[s] a more 'Africanized' analysis of the concept of altruism.

With caveats, horizontal philanthropy is an expression of *ubuntu*, as philosophy of common humanity.

Power and philanthropy in Africa

Halima Mahomed and Bhekinkosi Moyo, 2013

> The dilemma of the poor is not about resources. It is about power. If the poor have power, they will leverage the resources needed.
>
> (Adam Habib, Vice Chancellor, University of Witwatersrand)

Adam Habib's remark, made at the 2012 African Grantmakers Network Assembly on The Role of African Philanthropy in Shifting Power from North to South, is a stark reminder to us of the need to change the way we view the relationship between resources and power. In our philanthropy world, too often power is equated with money, and the one who holds the money dictates the agenda. For philanthropic agencies, the dilemma is how to ensure that their resources are not used as tools of power and control.

Any discussion of power has to be situated within context. In Africa, there are glaring power imbalances at all levels of society and they take many different forms – gender relations, asset ownership and resource rights, patriarchal systems, political decision-making, age, race and ethnicity, among others. The ways in which our societies choose to understand, situate and govern power is central to how the institutions within society evolve and the roles they seek – and choose – to play. It is here that the personal is political, and the political is personal.

As we examine the issue of power in philanthropy, we should be mindful that too often the ways in which power plays out are often directly rooted in the broader power inequalities within society. Yet in philanthropy the question of power is often relegated, even ignored. This is to our peril: without acknowledging, examining and confronting the power question, we risk being untrue to ourselves and, in the process, undermining our efforts at achieving a more just society.

The politics of power

During a recent conversation on philanthropy and power at the Working Group for Social Justice and Peace, a question was asked: is there a common discourse in the Global North and the Global South around power? Perhaps the real question is whether there is a discourse at all? The international aid system and the way in which its resources have been used as tools to determine agendas has been much discussed (one need only look at the many critiques of the IMF and the World Bank), and international foundations have supported voices to advance this discourse. Surprisingly, those international foundations often fail to recognize that they are themselves a part of that same aid system. As a result, the discourse is seen to apply to 'others' out there –

bilateral/multilateral aid agencies, global financial institutions, international NGOs, etc. The foundations do not look at themselves and consider whether they too are complicit in perpetuating this imbalance.

A second question is: should there be different discourses? While there are increasing concerns about external funding reproducing the colonial structure of the economy; about social and political agendas for Africa being set outside Africa; and about philanthropic funding as a tool for establishing the legitimacy of external frameworks, power imbalances are not just the domain of international aid. There is also a power dynamic within local philanthropy. In Africa, a variety of formal philanthropic institutions exist. Some emerged with local money, some rely almost entirely on international funding and some are a mix; each has to negotiate and manage the power associated with the funds they have. There are increasing concerns about African elites' interests setting agendas that are not in the interests of all; about the use of philanthropy to offset exploitative business practices; and about philanthropy deliberately ignoring the web of social, political and economic structures through which it exists. So, while where the resources come from matters at one level – African resources provide legitimacy, a better seat at the table, increased say in decisions, and leverage to assert local agendas – geography alone is not a predictor of how power will play out. Neither is size. The question of how power is exerted should be as much a concern for a Congolese or Namibian community foundation as it is for an international foundation based in the US or Europe.

The third question that needs to be asked is: what should a discourse on philanthropy and power be mindful of? While power can be experienced and exerted in various ways by different types of institution, and while strategies to negotiate and manage power may differ, the core issues around local agency and how agendas are developed needs to lie at the centre of the discourse on power. But in doing so, several challenges present themselves.

Challenging the dominant narrative

At one level, the narrative of philanthropy in Africa has long been dominated by a 'Global North' perspective, and this has shaped not just how our formal philanthropic institutions operate but the very nature of what is acknowledged as 'philanthropy'. At another level, even within Africa, many philanthropic institutions have emerged from segments of society that are elite and urban or from the private sector; or have been created by international actors with a particular approach. Together, these have developed a narrative of philanthropy – from rich to poor, through formal institutions, based on money and individual (high net worth) giving at scale. This is often far from what philanthropy in Africa is actually like – where giving emerges across socioeconomic classes; through individual and communal channels (formal or informal); often not involving money and through simple and complex communal arrangements that, cumulatively, occur at significant scale.

As we look at power and philanthropy in Africa, we first need to change the dominant narrative to one that gives due place to the informal giving that is most characteristic of African philanthropy. This narrative should also take account of the fundamental role that this 'unrecognized' giving plays within African society and seek to challenge the notion of Africans as the 'undeserving' poor – undeserving of aid and power. We do not imply here that these African systems may not themselves include relations of power; as we seek to build knowledge and develop our narratives, we must also constantly be questioning the power dynamics inherent within them.

Dissociating power from identity

Who the money comes from is often just as important a determinant of power as where it comes from. In a context where power is intricately bound to notions of identity, or configurations of identities – class, race, gender, age, education, background, experience and geography among others – the ways in which power relations play out are very much influenced by the identity(ies) of the parties on both sides of the power equation. For instance, a challenge to the philanthropic directions of an African male, who was educated at a prestigious foreign university and holds significant weight within his traditional cultural system, becomes a challenge not just to his philanthropic leanings but to the identities that have informed these leanings.

Or look at any of several African governments and compare the ways in which they engage with local foundations that support civil society efforts to increase state transparency and accountability with the ways in which they engage with a foundation led by an ex-president from the Global North such as Bill Clinton, talking about the same thing. Or how much easier it is for someone like Bill Gates or Aliko Dangote to convene African leaders than it would be for the African Grantmakers Network. In Africa, unless and until power is dissociated from identity, a critical examination of power in philanthropy and development will be extremely difficult.

Letting go of control

History has taught us that development agendas in Africa can rarely be called Africans' own unless those agendas have been self-financed. History has also taught us that, irrespective of where the support comes from, funding is rarely just funding. It is often accompanied by strings – from prods to highlight a particular direction to parameters or restrictions on whom and what to fund (or not), to explicit instructions on what kind of agenda is appropriate. Many philanthropic institutions bring a distinct level of expertise, experience and insight, but the ways in which these things determine the parameters within which local agendas are set is problematic. While there are certainly examples of foundations that engage in ways that place local agency at the forefront of decision-making, too often local contexts, expertise and insight are 'considered' in ways that don't extend to fundamentally informing programmatic priorities. Those who receive funds (whether community organization or African public charity) find themselves constantly having to compromise between the ideal of local ownership of agendas and the leveraging power that external funders exert. More often than not what we end up with are limitations on agency for change and dilution of local agendas at the tables of power. It is too early to tell if the story will be different with local sources of money, especially with high net worth individuals.

The power of process

Power is not just about explicit/overt control. Any discussion of philanthropy and power must acknowledge the implications of our processes on power dynamics. For African philanthropic institutions, several questions need to be looked at:

Does philanthropy speak truth to power?

To what extent are African philanthropic agencies willing and able to challenge the dominant consensus and ways of working? Is a community foundation able to challenge a well-resourced international foundation (from which they receive funds) when there is a clash between the priorities of the international funder and the agenda of the beneficiary groups it supports? Is an African foundation, working at national level, able to drive the issues they believe require priority or are these things subject to a constant process of mediation and negotiation with international partners or funders?

On the other hand, African foundations must bear some responsibility for allowing this power imbalance to continue. Does our ongoing acceptance of the terms of engagement, and our failure to publicly discuss this issue, not make us as much a party to this dynamic as those who hold the power? Reflections from Sarah Mukasa of the African Women's Development Fund sum up this dilemma very well:

> This thing always brings it back down to me and to us as African philanthropic institutions. What are we to do with the messiness in front of us? What choices are we making? In what way/s are these choices challenging, mirroring or enabling these power inequalities to continue (both in what we say and do)? It has to begin with us. And the questions we need to ask ourselves of our thought and conduct are very difficult ones.

How accountable are local philanthropic actors for how money is made?

With private and corporate philanthropy rapidly increasing, philanthropic agencies need to be accountable for how money is made just as much as for how it is spent. If a resource-based corporation has made its profits from land where people have been dispossessed of their land rights and then engages in philanthropic activity, serious questions need to be asked. Are we to consider that our role as philanthropic agencies justifies our overlooking practices that have produced poverty and injustice? We certainly want to advocate for an increase in organized private philanthropy in Africa, but not at all costs – we need to be mindful of where the line is and set standards for accountability and transparency.

Do the ways in which African philanthropic actors operate entrench elite consensus?

At a social justice philanthropy convening in Johannesburg [in 2012], the point was raised that many African philanthropic organizations are in danger of mimicking the processes and procedures of the Global North. Specifically, the question came out of a discussion about our preference for funding large NGOs with good track records, which perpetuates inequalities within our civil societies, reduces the voices of social movements and community-based organizations, and takes no account of voices that do not fit in with the norm. We were asked to think seriously about whether and how our processes perpetuate forms of exclusiveness.

For too long power imbalances in philanthropy have dictated and dominated development agendas in Africa. The question for us now is whether we are ready to examine what roles philanthropic actors play, whether these roles are relevant and appropriate to the realities of African societies, and whether we are willing to change them.

As Yao Graham of Third World Network remarked at the Power Panel at the AGN Assembly in 2012: 'If you don't have clarity of your own agency, you become someone else's project'.

This is really the gist of the relationship between power and philanthropy in Africa.

Section 5

PHILANTHROPIC PRACTICES AND INSTITUTIONS

Editors' introduction

Overview

Everything this Reader has explored so far about philanthropy – from the definitions and debates, to the history and cultural variations, to the motivations and complex relationships – must ultimately be enacted through everyday practices and actual institutions. The real work of philanthropy takes place through real organizations and activities, all of which have their own history, structure, and norms.

These philanthropic practices and institutions are not mundane or simplistic, as some might think. There are often quite thorny questions raised when we take a close look, questions that connect back to many of the complex issues covered in previous sections:

- What are the origins of our accepted philanthropic practices? How are new institutions created and new philanthropic approaches innovated? What are the most telling or notable variations across time and place?
- What makes one sort of practice or institution more or less legitimate or effective than others? What justifies their widespread use and the roles they play in society? Should certain kinds of institutions have privileged status and get special treatment?
- What are the ethical hazards of different practices and institutions, especially as they change or adapt over time? How do certain philanthropic practices and institutions perpetuate and/or challenge the status quo?

These questions go beyond the mere "how to" issues that one would expect to confront when talking about practices and institutions. While these practical matters of organisational management or technical skills are very important to the success of any philanthropic endeavour, this Reader is not focused on those administrative concerns. Rather, the readings in this section explore broad questions about the roles and core practices of institutionalised philanthropy, about what place they have in society, and about the implications of, and disagreements over, these roles. The readings here also focus on fundamental and rapid changes in philanthropic practices and institutions.

The readings start with the often misunderstood, complementary practices of asking for philanthropic support and of making grants to give support. Both of these practices involve a combination of art and science, and raise questions of ethics and values, pride, power and trust. The section then considers in depth two major types of institutions for philanthropic giving – the foundation and the corporation – both of which have been the subject of strong critique as well as thoughtful analysis. The section ends by examining recent creative – yet also controversial – innovations in practices and institutions that are blurring boundaries between sectors that previously seemed clearly distinct.

The practice of asking, the practice of granting

The practice of fundraising and the practice of grantmaking are both often misjudged and mischaracterised, usually in ways that see them as more crass and unsubtle than they really are. The readings here depict asking and granting as positive, complex, ethical practices that are necessary to the health of philanthropy. All three readings argue that these practices are "values-based," as fundraising guru Henry A. Rosso puts it. Both fundraising and grantmaking are essential to the mission of the institutions being served by the practitioners, and should be judged by how well they advance that mission.

The extracts from Rosso and the famous American educator Booker T. Washington address the common perception that asking for funds is a necessary yet unfortunate profession, and both of them insist instead that fundraising is actually a noble and essential profession, something to be proud of rather than apologise for. Rosso frames fundraising as providing the opportunity for contributors to support missions they believe in and to fulfil their moral duty. Washington is more blunt in making the same point, saying it is wrong to think of fundraising as "begging." Instead, fundraising involves giving donors the "honour" of an opportunity to give. Both authors also prioritise ethical discernment by fundraisers, as befits the moral purpose and stature of their profession.

Whereas too little pride is a common danger for fundraisers (and those who misjudge them), grantmakers have the opposite problem. Joel J. Orosz reviews what he calls the "Seven Deadly Sins" of philanthropy, urging professional foundation professionals to be careful as they "walk the line between arrogance on the one hand and cynicism on the other." Like fundraising, grantmaking carries ethical temptations as well as moral value for society, and we necessarily place a great deal of trust in practitioners working in both roles.

Foundations: roles and critiques

Building from the Orosz excerpt, the next section of readings cover a primary institution used for much elite giving: the philanthropic foundation. Foundations play significant social roles, although their specific form and function varies – like other expressions of philanthropic impulse – across cultural, historical, and national contexts. In many societies foundations enjoy a privileged status as valued institutions. But this does not mean they are uncontroversial. In fact, they are subject to many of the same sorts of criticisms levelled against elite philanthropists that were covered in Section 3 of this Reader.

Joel L. Fleishman gives a useful summary of the often taken-for-granted contributions of foundations in a democratic society such as the US, and how they adapt their role to the social problem or context. Helmut K. Anheier and Diana Leat provide a similar summary for foundations across Europe and elsewhere, agreeing with Fleishman that foundations make distinctive contributions in a democracy, as a source of creativity and innovation outside the constraints of market forces and the political and electoral context. Foundations can take risks and "think the unthinkable."

Anheier and Leat also note many of the common critiques of foundation behaviour and processes, raising some issues that are then forcefully taken up in the next reading from Joan Roelofs. Levelling some of the sharpest criticisms of foundations in this field, Roelofs adopts a Marxist/Gramscian perspective to accuse foundations of perpetuating the hegemonic powers-that-be. Roelofs disagrees with the view of foundations as outsiders taking risks and thinking the unthinkable, seeing them instead as the epitome of power elite insiders.

The final reading from Filiz Bikmen on foundations (*vakifs*) in Turkey is not only a reminder that philanthropic foundations exist well beyond the European and American contexts, but provides a case study of how their role and status has changed in one society over time.

Should corporations give?

While foundations exist for the primary purpose of philanthropic giving, corporations exist for the primary purpose of creating wealth and profit. Still, corporations routinely give to charity in a number of different ways and, like other individual and institutional donors, do so for a variety of reasons. It shouldn't be surprising, then, that whether corporations *should* give, and how effective they are when they do so, are issues that have long been debated, as the selections here illustrate.

Milton Friedman's classic 1970 essay denounces what was then a fairly new and limited idea of "corporate social responsibility" (CSR) as a dangerous practice of businesses giving away "someone else's money" – namely, the stockholders'. Better, he argues, to focus on using the genius of the market to make profits and then let the owners use their dividends to be philanthropists on their own if they so wish.

Friedman's view seems quaint now, as CSR and corporate philanthropy have become widespread and highly legitimised. Thomas W. Dunfee offers some explanations for this, showing how corporate philanthropy can be motivated by business reasons as much as social ones, and how social norms now create the expectation that companies will give, even if we cannot definitively determine whether being philanthropic serves profitability. Finally in this subsection, Felipe Aguero presents a case study of the practice of corporate giving in one region, Latin America, over recent decades. He too points to the power of expectations on businesses to demonstrate social responsibility, especially in a region where increasingly powerful companies must try to stave off "the threat of social discontent" caused by inequality and other economic and social troubles.

New methods and blurring boundaries

Previous sections of this Reader have shown the many ways that philanthropy changes over time, displaying innovation in both form and practice. However, there is strong evidence that the pace of change has quickened considerably in the recent past. This recent change is seen most pointedly in the emergence of new methods and vehicles for giving, and new organisational forms. Many recent innovations have sought creative new ways of generating revenue and returns, producing financial and social value together, and in doing so these new methods and institutions deliberately blur the boundaries between sectors, especially between traditional "non-profit" and "for-profit" practices and entities.

Antony Bugg-Levine and Jed Emerson call this constant churn of new innovations "the mighty wave," and Lester M. Salamon calls it a "significant revolution" on the "frontiers of philanthropy." The Mark R. Kramer reading shows how these major changes are in part borne from dissatisfaction with the ineffectiveness of "traditional philanthropy."

Many of the new innovations relate to the use and deployment of money in new ways – such as providing seed money to create social enterprises, making socially responsible impact investments and distributing microloans using online means – but others, in what Salamon calls "a bewildering array of new instruments and institutions," go beyond funding mechanisms. Kramer, for instance, focuses on new kinds of "catalytic" donors who first focus on results, create campaigns with advocacy and lobbying, and use all available assets. Salamon's extensive lists include many new entrepreneurial entities that go "beyond grants," "beyond foundations" and "beyond cash." Similarly, though usually on a much smaller scale, Angela M. Eikenberry shows how giving circles are an increasingly popular approach to giving that are transformative (for both donors and recipients) for reasons beyond the mere change in funding structure.

In a sense, the readings in this section show how far we have come from Friedman's scepticism about blurring the boundaries between the marketplace and philanthropy. Today, there is a deep-seated social expectation that capital and markets should serve the public good. All types of investments are now to be considered for how they create multiple types of value – not just financial value but social and environmental value as well, what Bugg-Levine and Emerson call "blended" value. And technological mechanisms are being developed to better facilitate global giving, as Lucy Bernholz, Edward Skloot, and Barry Varela show in their review of the new online marketplaces for giving.

Weiyan Zhou and her colleagues reveal that these innovations are now spreading in China, which many people in this field consider the vast new frontier of philanthropy and social investment. What is happening there could have a tremendous effect on what happens globally in the next several decades – just as what happens in the Chinese economy already profoundly affects the global economy.

Many of the authors in this section are careful to point out that this type of innovation – and even some of these specific "new" mechanisms – has been going on for a while, a point made in many readings in other sections as well. More telling, though, is the fact that these authors also note we do not have a clear idea of where all these developments are leading. Perhaps all we can say for sure is that philanthropic practices and institutions will continue to evolve, and so the everyday reality of how philanthropy will operate in the future is uncertain.

Discussion questions

- How can fundraisers and grantmakers address the inevitable power imbalance between them? And how can wider society appreciate the work of both those who ask and those who make grants as ethically valid and important to achieve philanthropic missions?
- How do the challenges facing grantmakers and fundraisers compare to the challenges facing individual donors and recipients that were reviewed in the previous section? For example, how do these challenges relate to the issues of donor control and the temptation to "chase the money" discussed in Section 4?
- How do the critiques of foundations mirror the critiques of elite donors in Section 3? What is convincing about these critiques and what is not?
- What justifies corporate giving if we can't be sure that it increases profitability? Why has the expectation that business should be socially responsible become so widespread in the past couple of decades?

- What are the advantages and possible dangers of blurring the boundaries between philanthropy and the marketplace, between non-profit and for-profit? How can we take advantage of the benefits these new market-oriented changes can bring, while minimising the ethical or other hazards?
- Why do you think that the pace of change and innovation in philanthropy has accelerated so much in recent years? What will the field look like in 10 or 20 years?

5.1 The practice of asking, the practice of granting

A philosophy of fundraising

Henry A. Rosso, 1991

Fundraising is the servant of philanthropy and has been so since the seventeenth century, when Puritans brought the concept to the new continent. The early experience of fundraising was simple in form, obviously devoid of the multifaceted practices that characterize its nature in the contemporary United States. These practices now make fundraising more diversified and more complex than ever before.

The American spirit of giving is known and respected in other nations. American fundraising methods are equally known and admired abroad, as foreign citizens who have attended classes taught by The Fund Raising School will attest. Ironically, the practice of resource development that is so much a part of the culture, necessity, and tradition of not-for-profit organizations in the United States is not sufficiently understood, often misrepresented, and too often viewed with suspicion and apprehension by a broad section of our own population, particularly by regulatory bodies. Few still argue with the observation that fundraising has never been considered the most popular practice in this country.

Dean Schooler of Boulder, Colorado, a scholar and student of fundraising, takes the teleological view of a vitalist philosophy that phenomena not only are guided by mechanical forces but also move toward certain goals of self-realization. Indeed, fundraising is never an end in itself; it is purposive. It draws both its meaning and essence from the ends that are served: caring, helping, healing, nurturing, guiding, uplifting, teaching, creating, preventing, advancing a cause, preserving values, and so forth. Fundraising is values-based; values must guide the process. Fundraising should never be undertaken simply to raise funds; it must serve the large cause.

Organizations and their reasons for existing

Organizations of the independent sector come into existence for the purpose of responding to some facet of human or societal needs. The need or opportunity for service provides the organization with a reason for being, as well as a right to design and execute programs or strategies that respond to the need. This becomes the cause that is central to concern of the organization. The cause provides justification for more intervention, and this proved justification for fundraising.

The organization may claim a right to raise money by asking for the tax-deductible gift. It must earn the privilege to ask for gift support by its management's responsiveness to needs, by the worthiness of its programs, and by the stewardship of its governing board. An organization may assume the right to ask. The prospective donor is under no obligation to give. The prospect reserves the right to a "yes" or a "no" response to any request. Either response is valid and must be respected.

Each organization that uses the privilege of soliciting for gifts should be prepared to respond to many questions, perhaps unasked and yet implicit in the prospect's mind. These may be characterized as such: "Why do you exist?" "What is distinctive about you?" "Why do you feel that you merit this support?" "What is it that you want to accomplish and how do you intend to go about doing it?" and "How will you hold yourself accountable?"

The response to "Who are you and why do you exist?" is couched in the words of the organization's mission statement. This statement expresses more than justification for existence and more than just a definition of goals and objectives. It defines the value system that will guide program strategies. The mission is the magnet that will attract and hold the interests of trustees, volunteers, staff, and contributors.

The answer to "What is distinctive about us?" is apparent in the array of goals, objectives, and programs that have been devised to address the needs of the value system as well as to serve as symbols of fidelity to it.

"What is it that you want to accomplish and how do you intend to go about doing it?" is closely linked to "Why do you merit this support?" People give to people with causes. To be worthy of support, the organization must show that it has not only a vision of what it wishes to accomplish but also a clear plan for making the change it wishes to effect feasible and achievable.

"How do we hold ourselves accountable?" is the primary question. It is a continuing call for allegiance to the mission. It acknowledges the sacredness of the trust that is inherent in the relationship with both the constituency and the larger community. The organization is the steward of the resources entrusted to its care.

It is axiomatic that change is a constant. Shifting forces within the environment quicken the pace of change, thus posing a new constant. Not-for-profit organizations must always be prepared to function in the center of whirling pressure.

Organizations cannot afford to be oblivious to the environment that surrounds and engulfs them. Forces within the environment – such as demographics, technology, economics, political and cultural values, and changing social patters – affect daily business performance, whether this performance pertains to governance, program administration, fiscal responsibility, or fundraising.

To govern or not to govern

Governance is an exercise in authority and control. Trustees, directors, or regents – the interchangeable nomenclature that identifies the actors in governance – are the primary stewards of the spirit of philanthropy. As stewards, they are the legendary "keepers of the hall." They hold the not-for-profit organization in trust to ensure that it will continue to function according to the dictates of its mission.

The trustees must bear the responsibility to define and interpret the mission and ensure that the organization will remain faithful to its mission. Board members should accept the charge that trusteeship concerns itself with the proper deployment of resources and with the accompanying action, the securing of resources. Deploying resources is difficult if the required resources are not secured through effective fundraising practices. It stands to reason that trustees as advocates of and stewards to the mission must attend to the task of pressing the resources development program on to success.

Institutionalizing fundraising

Fundraising projects the values of the total organization into the community whenever it seeks gift support. All aspects of governance – administration, program, and resources development – are part of the whole. As such, these elements must be part of the representation when gifts are sought. Fundraising cannot function apart from the organization; apart from the organization's mission, goals, objective, and programs; or apart from a willingness to be held accountable for all of the organization's actions.

Fundraising is and must always be the lengthened shadow of the not-for-profit entity, reflecting the organization's dignity, its pride of accomplishment, and its commitment to service. Fundraising by itself and apart from the institution has no substance in the eyes and heart of the potential contributor.

Gift making as voluntary exchange

Gift making is based on a voluntary exchange. Gifts secured through coercion, through any means other than persuasion, are not gifts freely given. They do not have the meaning of philanthropy. Rarely will gifts obtained under pressure or through any form of intimidation be repeated. These gifts lose their meaning.

In the process of giving, the contributor offers a value to the not-for-profit organization. This gift is made without any expectation of a material return, apart from the tax deductibility authorized by government. The reasons for making a gift are manifold.

In accepting the gift, it is incumbent upon the organization to return a value to the donor in a form other than material value. Such a value may be social recognition, the satisfaction of supporting a worthy cause, a feeling of importance, a feeling of making a difference in resolving a problem, a sense of belonging, or a sense of "ownership" in a program dedicated to serving the public good.

Trustees, administrators, or fundraising practitioners often misconstrue the true meaning of this exchange relationship, and they violate the acknowledgement process by offering a return of substantive value. This alters the exchange, reduces the meaning of philanthropy, and diminished the gift in its commitment to the mission. The transaction is one of a material exchange, a self-centered quid pro quo with none of the spirit of philanthropy in the exchange.

Substituting pride for apology

Giving is a privilege, not a nuisance or a burden. Stewardship nourishes the belief that people draw a creative energy, a sense of self-worth, and a capacity to function productively from sources beyond themselves. This is a deep personal belief or a religious conviction. Thoughtful philanthropists see themselves as responsible stewards of life's gifts to them. What they have they hold in trust, in their belief, and they accept the responsibility to share their treasures effectively through their philanthropy. Giving is an expression of thankfulness for the blessings that they have received during their lifetime.

The person seeking the gift should never demean the asking by clothing it in apology. Solicitation gives the prospective donor the opportunity to respond with a "yes" or a "no." The solicitation should be so executed as to demonstrate to the prospective contributor that there can be a joy to giving, whether the gift measures up to the amount asked for or not. Fundraising professionals must teach this joy by asking properly and in a manner that puts the potential contributor at ease.

The first task of the solicitor is to help the potential contributor understand the organization's case, especially its statement of mission. When a person commits to contribute to a cause and does so because of an acceptance of and a belief in the mission, then that person becomes a stakeholder in the organization and the cause and work for which it stands. This emphasizes that philanthropy is moral action, and the contributor is an integral part of that action.

Fundraising as a servant to philanthropy

Philanthropy is voluntary action for the public good through voluntary action, voluntary association, and voluntary giving. Fundraising has been servant to philanthropy across the millennia. Through the procession of the centuries, the thesis has been established that people want and have a need to give. People want to give to causes that serve the entire gamut of human and societal needs. They will give when they can be assured that these causes can demonstrate their worthiness and accountability in using the gift funds that they receive.

Ethical fundraising is the prod, the enabler, the activator to gift making. It must also be the conscience to the process. Fundraising is at its best when it strives to match the needs of the not-for-profit organization with the contributor's need and desire to give. The practice of gift seeking is justified when it exalts the contributor, not the gift seeker. It is justified when it is used as a responsible invitation, guiding contributors to make the kind of gift that will meet their own special needs and add greater meaning to their lives.

I am not a beggar

Booker T. Washington, 1907

During the last fifteen years I have been compelled to spend a large proportion of my time away from the school [the Tuskegee Institute in Alabama, of which he was President], in an effort to secure money to provide for the growing needs of the institution. In my efforts to get funds I have had some experiences that may be of interest to my readers. Time and time again I have been asked, by people who are trying to secure money for philanthropic purposes, what rule or rules I followed to secure the interest and help of people who were able to contribute money to worthy objects.

As far as the science of what is called begging can be reduced to rules, I would say that I have had but two rules. First, always to do my whole duty regarding making our work known to individuals and organizations; and, second, not to worry about the results. This second rule has been the hardest for me to live up to. When bills are on the eve of falling due, with not a dollar in hand with which to meet them, it is pretty difficult to learn not to worry, although I think I am learning more and more each year that all worry simply consumes, and to no purpose, just so much physical and mental strength that might otherwise be given to effective work. After considerable experience in coming into contact with wealthy and noted men, I have observed that those who have accomplished the greatest results are those who "keep under the body;" are those who never grow excited or lose self-control, but are always calm, self-possessed, patient, and polite.

[. . .]

In order to be successful in any kind of undertaking, I think the main thing is for one to grow to the point where he completely forgets himself; that is, to lose himself in a great cause. In proportion as one loses himself in this way, in the same degree does he get the highest happiness out of his work.

My experience in getting money for Tuskegee has taught me to have no patience with those people who are always condemning the rich because they are rich, and because they do not give more to objects of charity. In the first place, those who are guilty of such sweeping criticisms do not know how many people would be made poor, and how much suffering would result, if wealthy people were to part all at once with any large proportion of their wealth in a way to disorganize and cripple great business enterprises. Then very few persons have any idea of the large number of applications for help that rich people are constantly being flooded with. I know wealthy people who receive as many as twenty calls a day for help. More than once, when I have gone into the offices of rich men, I have found half a dozen persons waiting to see them, and all come for the same purpose, that of securing money. And all these calls in person, to say nothing of the applications received through the mails. Very few people have any idea of the amount of money given away by persons who never permit their names to be known, I have often heard persons condemned for not giving away money, who, to my own knowledge, were giving away thousands of dollars every year so quietly that the world knew nothing about it.

[. . .]

Although it has been my privilege to be the medium through which a good many hundred thousand dollars have been received for the work at Tuskegee, I have always avoided what the world calls "begging." I often tell people that I have never "begged" any money, and that I am not a "beggar." My experience and observation have convinced me that persistent asking outright for money from the rich does not, as a rule, secure help. I have usually proceeded on the principle that persons who possess sense enough to earn money have sense enough to know how to give it away, and that the mere making known of the facts regarding Tuskegee, and especially the facts regarding the work of the graduates, has been more effective than outright begging. I think that the presentation of facts, on a high, dignified plane, is all the begging that most rich people care for.

While the work of going from door to door and from office to office is hard, disagreeable, and costly in bodily strength, yet it has some compensations. Such work gives one a rare opportunity to study human nature. It also has its compensations in giving one an opportunity to meet some of the best people in the world – to be more correct, I think I should say the best people in the world. When one takes a broad survey of the country, he will find that the most useful and influential people in it are those who take the deepest interest in institutions that exist for the purpose of making the world better.

At one time, when I was in Boston, I called at the door of a rather wealthy lady, and was admitted to the vestibule and sent up my card. While I was waiting for an answer, her husband came in, and asked me in the most abrupt manner what I wanted. When I tried to explain the object of my call, he became still more ungentlemanly in his words and manner, and finally grew so excited that I left the house without waiting for a reply from the lady. A few blocks from that house I called to see a gentleman who received me in the most cordial manner. He wrote me his check for a generous sum, and then, before I had had an opportunity to thank him, said: "I am so grateful to you, Mr. Washington, for giving me the opportunity to help a good cause. It is a privilege to have a share in it. We in Boston are constantly indebted to you for doing our work." My experience in securing money convinces me that the first type of man is growing more rare all the time, and that the latter type is increasing; that is, that, more and more, rich people are coming to regard men and women who apply to them for help for worthy objects, not as beggars, but as agents for doing their work.

In the city of Boston I have rarely called upon an individual for funds that I have not been thanked for calling, usually before I could get an opportunity to thank the donor for the money. In that city the donors seem to feel, in a large degree, that an honor is being conferred upon them in their being permitted to give. [. . .] I repeat my belief that the world is growing in the direction of giving. I repeat that the main rule by which I have been guided in collecting money is to do my full duty in regard to giving people who have money an opportunity to help.

Humane grantmaking

Joel J. Orosz, 2000

[T]he quality of any foundation's work, and the amount of positive change that it can effect in the world, is directly dependent on the capabilities of its employees. And of all these employees, no position matters more than that of the program officer. Everything that the foundation knows of its grantees – and everything that the grantees know of the foundation – ultimately filters through this individual. Program officers are truly at the vital center of the entire enterprise.

Because all roads in philanthropy lead to (and through) program officers, it matters greatly what kind of people they are, how well they can resist the peculiar temptations of philanthropy, how they treat applicants and grantees, and what kind of qualities they need to excel at their position.

[. . .]

It must be acknowledged at the outset that the sheer number of foundations and the bewildering variety of their interests render it all but impossible to come up with a universal set of best practices that will fit all program officers, in all settings, at all times. There are, nonetheless, a certain number of generic challenges and a certain level of general skills and aptitudes that characterize efficient, ethical, and humane ways to conduct grantmaking.

[. . .]

The temptations of philanthropy

In his study of the Ford Foundation, author Dwight Macdonald puckishly defined a foundation as "a large body of money completely surrounded by people who want some." To change the metaphor, a foundation, to most people, is the pot of gold at the rainbow's end, and program officers are its guardian leprechauns. This means, of course, that everyone wants to catch – or at least, catch the attention of – grantmakers. The competition to capture the interest of program officers is intense, which ensures that their paths will always be strewn with numerous snares and temptations. If you are taking on the role of program officer, your first test is to avoid the blandishments of seven temptations: philanthropy's version of the Seven Deadly Sins. Surrendering to any one of these can utterly destroy your effectiveness as a grantmaker.

Believing the flattery

Clearly some grantseekers feel that flattery will get them everywhere – or, at any rate, somewhere. Grantmakers actually receive letters with opening lines that read like this one: "What a delightful, sincere, knowledgeable individual you are!" A little flattery does wonders for anyone's self-esteem, but a steady diet of it distorts the perspective and raises the danger that the recipient may actually begin to believe it uncritically. To be a successful program officer, you must learn to discount a large proportion of the praise that you will receive from those outside the foundation. You need to equip yourself with an internal gyroscope to allow for self-assessment of performance. After all, those who want a grant or who have gotten a grant have a vested interest in praising the grantmaker. Even those whose grant requests have been declined have a vested interest (the hope of securing a grant in the future) in avoiding overt criticism of the program officer. As a result, all feedback you receive is highly likely to be skewed unrealistically to the favorable side, thus making the internal gyroscope an indispensable tool.

Surrendering to the whims of arrogance

The unending flattery leads directly to this second temptation. Few grantseekers are so bold – or so foolhardy – as to disagree with you to your face. A prolonged drought of constructive criticism, coupled with the ongoing cloudburst of flattery, leads almost inevitably (unless you strenuously resist) to a growing sense of entitlement and infallibility – in short, arrogance. Pifer framed the problem perfectly: "These are the individuals – and we all know some – who go around exuding an air of self-importance and apparent infallibility, who have fallen into the habit of pontificating rather than listening, who have become name droppers, who surround themselves with an aura of wealth, power, and prestige, and who are patronizing toward grantseekers and are largely insensitive to their feelings and inconsiderate of their needs. These people would be shocked if they were charged with such faults because they quite genuinely believe that simply being part of a profession as worthy as philanthropy automatically makes them worthy people too."

It is difficult, indeed, to resist this overblown sense of self-worth when so many people, day after day, line up to proclaim your worthiness. People toiling in more feedback-rich environments (an umpire perhaps, or a public school teacher) experience no shortage of those willing to be critical, whether constructively or otherwise. In contrast, you will only rarely find anyone so bold. One solution to this problem comes from the David and Lucile Packard Foundation, which in 1996 and again in 1998 mailed anonymous surveys to their grantees and those whose grant requests they had turned down. The cloak of anonymity served to protect the respondent while providing the foundation with valuable unfiltered feedback on its performance. As a result of this approach, the foundation received constructive criticism – including specific ideas for improvement – that they could have received in no other way. Such anonymous responses are a powerful corrective to the flattery and fear that prevents honest feedback from occurring naturally.

It is worth noting, however, that there is another, cheaper method of receiving candid criticism. It is also a somewhat older approach, having been in operation as long ago as AD 43. In that year, the Roman emperor Claudius returned from his successful campaign in what is now Great Britain. The Roman Senate voted him the exceptional right to make a triumphal entry into Rome at the head of his legions. Mindful of the dangers of arrogance, however, the Senate prescribed that the slave who stood behind the emperor, holding the laurel wreath above his head, repeatedly whisper the words

"Remember, you are not a god." You should have at least one friend who is empowered specifically to provide you with such timely and unminced words.

[. . .]

Surrendering to cynicism

The third temptation of grantmaking is really an overreaction to the first two. It is entirely possible for you to overdiscount the flattery and to overestimate the amount of criticism you might receive if only people dared to offer it. A program officer can become tempted to consider every compliment, no matter how sincerely meant or well intended, as immediately suspect. "They only love me for the money I might get for them" becomes the mantra of this poor soul. After a while, it may occur to the suspicious grantmaker that the only reason that she or he is treated with respect is because of employment with the foundation. The program officer therefore slides into a cynical Catch-22. To stay at the foundation is to be inundated with praise that is insincere and unmerited, but to leave the foundation would mean risking being treated as a nonentity.

To avoid this situation, again you must be able to assess your self-worth. If you are able to walk the line between arrogance on the one hand and cynicism on the other, you must have a self-generated sense of just how many of the compliments are truly earned.

Regarding the foundation's money as your own

Grantseekers report this as a widely indulged peccadillo among program officers, complaining that their requests for grants are sometimes treated as if they were pleas for personal loans. This attitude toward grantseekers is fundamentally unkind, but more than that, it is dead wrong. The corpus of the foundation, of course, is not your property. Nor is it any longer the property of the donor or donors of the corpus. It is not, strictly speaking, even the property of the foundation that employs you. US foundations exist as a result of a social contract: the US government has agreed to forego taxes on the donor's capital in exchange for the donor's irrevocably dedicating that capital to projects that will advance the common good. Thus the corpus ultimately belongs not to any single entity but to the public. Ironically, the money belongs just as much to those who are seeking it as to those who are dispensing it.

The fifth and sixth temptations of grantmaking are mirror images of each other, and were identified in a jocular vein some years ago by a California community foundation executive named Jack Shakely.

Doubting the worthiness of all applicants

The fifth temptation, says Mr. Shakely, is to believe that no applicant is worthy of funding. As a program officer, you are essentially in the business of making decisions about who gets money and who does not, and for every applicant who gets money there is a long line of those who do not. Your critical faculties must be sharp, you must make hard decisions, and people (unfortunately, many very good people) must be disappointed. Every program officer must have a strongly analytical streak and must be decisive in making the call as to which proposals are funded and which are rejected. If taken to excess, however, a purely analytical approach will miss many of the most creative and daring ideas. Compassion, imagination, and a generous spirit must also come into play. As Shakely notes, you can reach a point at which you find fault with everything. Overanalyzing proposals, if taken to its logical conclusion, results in the foundation being unable to fund anything. Grantmaking requires you to have a good head, but that is not enough; you also need to have a good heart.

Finding value in all applicants

If all head and no heart is a problem, so too is its mirror image, all heart and no head. Bighearted grantmakers see worthiness in every proposal and try to nurture them all to funding. Such an approach cannot work, for foundations get more proposals than they can possibly fund, and some are much more worthy of funding than others. As a program officer, you simply must make hard decisions and disappoint good people. Bighearted grantmakers frequently respond to this hard truth by dithering – that is, they defer making decisions and neither decline nor fund proposals. Typically, the proposal does not fit the foundation's guidelines, but the submitting organization is so admirable or the people leading it are so likable that the program officer cannot bear to say no, so the proposal goes into limbo. The grantmaker might hope that a change in foundation priorities or a need to pay out more funds due to endowment growth (to take but two rationalizations) will allow him or her eventually to slip the proposal through. What almost always happens instead is an endless, inconclusive wait for the grantseeker, and frustration for all involved. It seems safe to say that neither the pure head approach nor the pure heart approach works in philanthropy; these are two temptations that must be strenuously resisted.

Taking the easy way out

The life of the average program officer is nothing if not hectic. Grantseekers continually clamor for meetings, both face-to-face and by telephone. Projects must be visited, both prior to and after funding. Colleagues within the organization require attention, as do colleagues working for other foundations or potential funding partners. And there is always a mountain of material to read: proposals, annual report narratives, reports from evaluators, and background material needed to keep current in fields of the foundation's interests. Add to this imposing workload the knowledge that most grantmakers are driven by a desire to serve good causes, and it all totals overload. "None of what I do is rocket science," commented one program officer, "but the sheer volume of it all is overwhelming." The typical program officer works very hard. It is commonplace for grantmakers to take home work at night, put in hours on weekends, even to toil on holidays and while on vacation. Against this background of sheer busyness, there is sometimes an overwhelming temptation to cut corners. Phone messages are easy to ignore, general correspondence can be tossed in the circular file, long proposals can be skimmed or not read at all. Grantseekers are unanimous in complaining that too many program officers are unresponsive, not even giving the simple courtesy of a civil reply to a polite inquiry.

Such behavior on the part of grantmakers, no matter how busy they might be, is simply inexcusable. It is, for starters, unprofessional. It is also a train wreck in the making. Sooner or later one of these ignored applicants will turn out to be a key player in a critical field, or a friend or relative of a foundation trustee, or, worse, a prominent constituent of a member of the House Ways and Means Committee. Any ephemeral savings in time or spurious increase in efficiency realized by ignoring grantseekers will be more than counterbalanced by the damage that discourtesy and unprofessional behavior inevitably cause.

This discourtesy, it should be noted, too often crosses the line into rudeness. Grantseekers have horror stories to tell of repeated phone calls that are never returned, urgent letters that are pointedly ignored, contemptuous and dismissive behavior during meetings, and broken promises of follow-through. Regrettably, this boorish behavior is probably the most common failing among grantmakers. Again, there can be no possible justification for such performance on the part of program officers, for though grantmakers must deliver bad news regularly, there is no reason why they must deliver it badly.

[. . .]

A grantseeker's bill of rights

A straightforward way to systematize this kind of "right behavior" for program officers is to draw up a bill of rights for grantseekers. [. . .] My choice of offering ten rights is a deliberate one. Not only is this pleasing historically, but my aim is to present a concise statement of the most important things that all program officers should honor in their dealings with applicants:

1. The right to receive a clear statement of the foundation's funding interests.
2. The right to have all communications answered.
3. The right to an explanation of, and timeline for, the foundation's proposal review process.
4. The right to a prompt acknowledgment of receipt of a proposal.
5. The right to have all proposals read in full and seriously considered.
6. The right to a timely and unambiguous funding decision.
7. The right to receive an explanation of the reasoning behind funding decisions.
8. The right to have all requirements for the grant relationship clearly spelled out, in writing (including the right to have any components of the grant required by the foundation paid for by the foundation).
9. The right to have all reports completely read and carefully considered.
10. The right to be informed if continued funding is a possibility.

5.2 Foundations: roles and critiques

What foundations do

Joel L. Fleishman, 2007

Consider these basic, familiar aspects of contemporary life. What do they all have in common?

- The first 911 emergency telephone system was set up in Alabama in 1968. By the 1970s, the simple, uniform system had spread throughout the United States. Since then, millions of Americans faced with an emergency have rushed to phone 911, and thousands of lives have been saved as a result. Have you ever wondered how this national emergency response system came into being?
- Most Americans have heard about India's newly dynamic, rapidly growing economy. But do you know the story of how India, plagued for centuries by famines, became not only self-sufficient in food production but also a food-exporting nation – the essential platform on which the subcontinent's newfound prosperity is being built?
- Millions of people depend on PBS's *NewsHour with Jim Lehrer* for their daily supply of serious news. Millions more habitually tune in to National Public Radio to stay in touch with the world throughout the day. When you watch or listen, have you ever asked yourself how the institution of public broadcasting in the United States came to be?
- Every year, billions of dollars' worth of financial assistance is provided to college students through the Pell Grant program. Millions of students and their families take this aid for granted. Do any think to inquire about the origin of a government program that has enriched so many lives?
- In three hundred run-down inner-city neighborhoods and impoverished small towns, local community-development corporations (CDCs) are working to create jobs, build housing, and incubate small businesses. Countless Americans have benefited from their efforts. Where did the notion of the CDC come from?

In each case, the explanation is the same – the central force promoting the creation of these valuable social institutions was a *foundation*.

There are thousands of foundations actively working for the betterment of society here in the United States and around the world. And behind each foundation stands a wealthy individual or family that chose to declare "enough is enough," and then gave away a significant portion of their wealth for the benefit of the wider community rather than hoard it, invest it, or spend even more of it on personal pleasures. Why did they do so? As we will see, for many different reasons. But perhaps the motivation of the founders of major foundations – from Carnegie and Rockefeller to Gates and Buffett – was poignantly stated most recently by Joseph Hirschhorn, the wealthy art collector for whom the Hirschhorn Collection on the Mall in Washington was named: "I tried eating more meals a day and got sick. There are only so many suits you can wear or houses you can live in. So I collected art [and then gave it away]."

It's a remarkable phenomenon, a testament to human generosity and creativity, and one whose story has never been adequately told [. . .] Foundations, after all, are among our most powerful, least accountable, and significantly tax-benefited institutions, so it is all the more unacceptable that they are also among our least understood institutions.

[. . .]

[F]oundations, along with the organizations that they support, are the great secret of the dynamism of America's civic sector. The civic sector is not just about social change in the narrow sense but rather about all kinds of organizations that are created, supported, and staffed by Americans acting independently of government. Just as private investors and venture capitalists spark the creation of new products and services in the for-profit sector, foundations provide the capital that powers innovation and diverse experimentation in the civic sector.

Foundations enable the creation of countless civic-sector organizations – groups dealing with human rights, civil liberties, social policy experimentation, public advocacy, environmental protection, knowledge generation, human capital building, and service delivery, among other causes – and assist them in building national, regional, and local constituencies that move into the forefront of continuing social change. Those organizations, together with the foundations that support them, play an influential role in the constant reinvention of American society, including the redistribution of power and wealth.

Three roles that foundations play

At the most basic level, what foundations do is very simple. The leaders of a foundation – usually a staff of professionals guided by a board of trustees – provide funds from the foundation's income or endowment to support not-for-profit organizations, charities, or other programs and organizations in accordance with the mission designated by the founder. But within this broad framework, many variations are possible. One way to analyze the work of foundations is by describing three different roles that foundations can choose to play. Of course, the lines dividing these roles are often blurred. But this three-part breakdown is a useful jumping-off point for a deeper exploration of what foundations do and how they do it.

The first role is that of *Driver*. When a particular social, economic, or cultural goal can be visualized clearly and a practical strategy can be developed to attain it, a foundation may choose to play the role of Driver. In this case, the foundation itself maps out and directs the change effort, making grants to organizations that will simply carry out the strategy devised by the foundation.

The second role is that of *Partner*. Here, the foundation shares the power to shape a strategy and makes crucial decisions together with other partner organizations, making grants to support those organizations as well as others that simply implement the strategy.

The third role is that of *Catalyst*. When tackling a problem for which a strategy is inconceivable, inappropriate, or premature, a foundation may make grants to organizations that generally deal with the problem, without specifying or expecting particular outcomes. Here, the foundation acts as a kind of "Johnny Appleseed," broadcasting resources in many directions, knowing that most of the grants are unlikely to produce lasting change, but hoping that a few at least will take root and grow.

These roles do not have crisp, clean boundaries, however. The differences among them depend on the character, specificity, and ripeness of the problem in which the foundations are interested, and the nature of those institutions whose behavior they are seeking to change.

Let's take a closer look at these roles and consider some examples of each.

The foundation as Driver

All of the examples listed at the start of this chapter illustrate what foundations can accomplish when they act as Drivers, pursuing specific objectives according to a strategy they develop and whose implementation they guide.

The so-called Green Revolution, which was launched in 1945 and came to full fruition during the 1950s, 1960s, and 1970s, was driven by the work of the Rockefeller Foundation. The goal was to develop new varieties of wheat, corn, and rice adapted to particular climates that would significantly increase crop yields and thereby help to alleviate the lack of adequate food, which was costing the lives of millions of people in the developing nations of Asia, Africa, and Latin America. The research agenda was formulated by Rockefeller Foundation staff scientists, and the research itself was carried out by scientists working full-time on the foundation's payroll in laboratories in Mexico. Rockefeller Foundation control was key to maintaining a focused pursuit of the objective of increased grain yields and to implementing the strategy as rapidly as possible.

As a result of the Green Revolution, the world increase in per capita production of agricultural commodities outstripped population growth in every year after 1950. So successful was the Mexican program, led by Rockefeller scientist Dr. Norman Borlaug, that Mexico, which had formerly imported half its wheat, attained self-sufficiency by 1956 and was exporting half a million tons of wheat by 1964. The program was expanded to India and Pakistan, where it is credited with saving over one *billion* people from starvation.

[. . .]

When the national 911 emergency-response system was created, the Robert Wood Johnson Foundation took the Driver role. It catalyzed and financed 911 organizations across the United States, brought together emergency responders who hadn't previously cooperated, and created a national confederation that could easily work with the US government on the details of implementation.

The Public Broadcasting System and Pell Grants were both driven by blue-ribbon commissions envisioned, organized, financed, and run by the Carnegie Corporation of New York.

Finally, community-development corporations were similarly driven by the Ford Foundation, which was later joined by many other foundations.

When a foundation can define and limit a problem, and believes that it can map a strategy for solving the problem, then the Driver role may be appropriate, especially when no other institution can play that role as well or as faithfully as the foundation. If you're familiar with the workings of venture capital, you might think of the Driver role as similar to that of the general partner, who invests a large – often the largest – share of the money required to start a new venture, occupies one or more seats on the venture's board, and plays a decisive role in hiring the CEO and making other critical decisions.

[. . .]

The foundation as Partner

The second role, that of Partner, can be just as strategic as that of Driver, but is both less hands-on and less controlling of the initiative. Typically, the Partner foundation shares control and accountability with the grant-receiving organization.

As examples, consider the academic field-building activities of the Rockefeller Foundation in molecular biology, the Ford Foundation and the Carnegie Corporation of New York in foreign area studies, the Alfred P. Sloan Foundation in computational neurobiology, John M. Olin Foundation in law and economics, and the Hewlett Foundation in dispute resolution. In each case, the foundation had a specific goal to achieve and a strategy that involved making grants to universities to create centers, programs, or departments to conduct research, offer new courses, and finance student fellowships and postdoctoral study. In so doing, the foundations acted as Partners with the universities. By contrast, in the example of the Green Revolution, the Rockefeller Foundation placed researchers on its own payroll and created a new freestanding organization to conduct research in its chosen field.

The role of Partner is likely to be appropriate whenever a foundation has a strategic objective that can be accomplished by working with an existing, usually nonprofit, organization that shares with the foundation both the goal and the strategy for attaining it. The role of Partner is generally more cost-effective for the foundation than that of Driver, demanding less commitment of time and energy by the foundation's staff. The trade-off, of course, is a corresponding loss of control by the foundation. If things go wrong in the implementation of the strategy, the Partner foundation cannot set things right as quickly and easily as if it were the Driver.

And sometimes things do go wrong – occasionally very wrong. The most common problem is a poor choice of leadership by the nonprofit responsible for implementation or by the foundation itself. Other times, the foundation and the implementation organization are at odds about the goal, the strategy, or both. And still other times, the foundation's own practices may be faulty or its interference in implementation unwarranted. For all these reasons, some foundations are nervous about the risks involved in the Partner role and prefer to be Drivers whenever possible.

Nevertheless, most foundations choose to operate as Partners, and not just as a way of saving energy, time, and money. Most foundation initiatives are about promoting change, and the best way to achieve that goal is usually to engage and involve the organizations whose behaviors are to be changed. Thus, when a foundation wants to change academia by giving new vitality and prominence to a field of study that is currently neglected (as in the examples cited above), the fastest way to promote such change is by partnering with existing universities, which can then serve as role models for the rest of the academic universe.

[. . .]

The foundation as Catalyst

The Driver role is difficult for foundations to assume. It is time – and labor – intensive, and committing one's foundation to the achievement of a specific objective is risky and anxiety-producing. It requires a high degree of resolve to commit the organization to a particular strategic focus and much deeper knowledge of the field of focus than the other roles. And, of course, when a foundation commits to a particular strategy and fails to achieve the goals it sets, the public failure is psychologically and organizationally painful.

For all these reasons, it's easy, even tempting, for foundations to deliver most of their resources through projects at the other end of the spectrum – lower-commitment grants in which the foundation restricts itself to the role of Catalyst, scattering resources like Johnny Appleseed in hopes that some of the initiatives supported will bear fruit.

There are also good reasons to emphasize the Catalyst role in dealing with particular types of social problems. Some problems are simply not ripe enough to lend themselves to a clear-cut strategic solution. They may be too big, too complex, or too unwieldy; they may be relatively new and little-understood; or they may require intervention by government agencies or the for-profit sector. In such cases, rather than undertake a high-risk strategic effort that is likely to fail, a foundation is wise to take a Catalyst approach, donating to a number of initiatives in the spirit of experimentation.

The Catalyst role may seem less impressive than the grandly strategic roles of Driver or Partner. The Catalyst is unlikely ever to receive a Nobel Prize for its efforts. Yet the role of Catalyst is important for foundations to fill. The fact is that, at any given time, relatively few significant problems are ripe for solution. Moreover, very few foundations have the resources to mount a strategy of sufficient scale to solve any really large problems in the first place. Thus, the ground is always in need of preparation so that ripeness can be hastened. Organizations need to be established and supported to research new solutions, to raise awareness, and to educate the public. For this reason, most foundations do most of their grantmaking in the hands-off role of Catalyst, scattering seeds for the future by supporting the existing efforts of grant-receiving organizations.

[. . .]

The limits of foundation power

The examples I've mentioned so far indicate the remarkable scope and influence that foundations can have when they tackle major social problems well and with intelligence. But there are clear limits to what foundations are capable of doing. When a social problem is *not* discrete and well-bounded, when it permeates large segments of society, or when it is created in part by dug-in interest groups, a foundation can usually do little to solve the problem beyond ameliorating some of its symptoms and suggesting through research or pilot programs some directions in which ultimate solutions may be found.

The creative value of foundations in a democracy

Helmut K. Anheier and Diana Leat, 2006

Foundation renaissance

After decades of stagnation and then decline, philanthropic foundations are enjoying a renaissance. Countries as different as the United States, the UK, Australia, Japan, Italy, Germany, Sweden, Turkey and Brazil are displaying renewed interest in creating foundations. In 2004, the *Economist* reported 'an explosion' in new private foundations in the United States. According to the Foundation Center, foundation numbers are up from about 22,000 in the early 1980s to 65,000 today. In Europe there has also been growth. In Germany, for example, formation of philanthropic foundations has risen from around 200 per annum in the 1980s to between 800 and 900 per annum today. The inter-generational transfer of wealth looks set to increase the number of philanthropic foundations in Germany yet further from the present count of 12,000. The UK has about 9,000 foundations, which is about the same number as Switzerland, whereas the Netherlands has about 1,000, and Italy 3,000. In these countries, too, further growth is expected.

This significant and prolonged growth notwithstanding, the 'golden age' of philanthropy is usually seen as being the early 20th century when the 'big foundations' were established by Rowntree, Nuffield, Rockefeller, Ford, Carnegie and others. We suggest that the early 21st century, with foundations enjoying unprecedented global growth and increasing policy importance amid heightened expectations, could become a new golden age. For policy makers, and others, the hope is that greater philanthropy will capture greater private wealth for the public good, take some of the pressure off government spending, and both reflect and enhance the renewal of civil society.

But despite the hopes attached to philanthropic foundations there are important questions about the capacity of foundations to make a real, sustainable difference in the 21st century. In many countries foundations have been around for centuries, and have poured huge sums of money into a variety of problems that remain obstinately entrenched, with poverty and social exclusion as perhaps the most obvious examples. Are foundations essentially 19th-century institutions, dispensing charity to relatively small numbers of grantees, or funding to scientists sequestered in ivory towers? More fundamentally, do foundations, spending money as and where they choose with very little accountability, have a place in modern democracies without greater calls for openness and transparency?

As one leading commentator on foundations, Nielsen, remarked in *The Big Foundations*, 'foundations, like giraffes, could not possibly exist, but they do'. As quasi-aristocratic institutions, they flourish on the privileges of a formally egalitarian society; they represent the fruits of capitalistic economic activity; and they are organized for the pursuit of public objectives, which is seemingly contrary to the notion of selfish economic interest that originally created their wealth. Seen from this viewpoint, foundations are not only rare, they are also unlikely institutions, 'strange creatures in the great jungle of American democracy', to paraphrase Nielsen.

The case against foundations

In most countries, renewed interest in philanthropy in general, including foundations, has gone hand in hand with greater scrutiny of the freedoms and privileges enjoyed by both public and private foundations. The media have stepped up their interest in foundations, and in the United States in particular have found sufficient salacious stories to whet their appetites for more. It may be merely a matter of time before journalists in other countries develop similar interests.

Foundations, especially in the United States, are under attack from across the political spectrum – from various House and Senate committees, government agencies, advocates for the nonprofit sector, and from within their own ranks. The debates over pay-out and estate duties and taxes, as well as actual and proposed restrictions on foundations' freedom to give grants where they see fit, have all served to bring foundations into the limelight. At the same time, from within their own ranks, foundations are suffering the effects of abuse and mismanagement by a minority, as well as criticisms that they have become 'flabby' and 'complacent'.

The charges against foundations in the United States are varied. Issues of contention include insider relationships between foundations and outside vendors, corporate abuses including use of charitable gifts as bribes to overlook financial improprieties (as in the Enron case), conflicts of interest with grantees, issues around donor-advised funds, trustee self-dealing, salaries and severance packages, trustee compensation, and so on.

In 2004 and 2005, the US Senate Finance Committee responded with a series of recommendations, including a requirement that nonprofit organizations file detailed information every five years showing that they continue to operate for tax-exempt purposes, tougher conflict-of-interest standards, a requirement for detailed descriptions of performance goals and measures for meeting them, controls on donor-advised funds, and tougher controls on administrative costs and pay-out.

Foundations in other countries, such as the UK and Australia, are facing similar and growing demands for greater oversight and accountability, even though the particular issues may be different. The European Union, too, is taking a more pronounced interest in foundations, and some philanthropic leaders in Europe are calling for the establishment of a new legal instrument, the European Foundation, to overcome the complexities and inefficiencies of national laws and the weaknesses of oversight regimes in many member states.

[. . .]

Reframing the question

[. . .]

Rather than responding to a debate the terms of which have been set by others, foundations urgently need to redefine those terms and vigorously defend, define and illustrate their unique strengths and the roles that they, and only they, can play in strengthening and defending democracy. In this way they can turn a low-key crisis into an opportunity.

To make this happen, foundations need to move the debate away from concerns with processes to the more fundamental question of what value they add in society. They need to illustrate their unique roles with success stories, and consider ways in which these success stories can be replicated. What is more, foundations must do more in promoting these messages to policy makers, the media, the nonprofit sector and the public.

[. . .]

The unique value of foundations in a democracy

Foundations' value does not lie in their assets or expenditure per se. Their unique value lies in what they uniquely can do. Endowed foundations need to stop playing to their weaknesses and start playing to their strengths. Lack of both resources (relative to the costs of provision) and democratic mandate are foundations' key weaknesses, but they are also among their key potential strengths. The key is that foundation resources are 'free' relative to both governments and markets. Foundations enjoy the luxury of freedom from market and political constraints and constituencies. Many also enjoy the luxury of perpetuity.

Foundations have sufficient resources and 'space' to allow them to think, to be truly innovative, to take risks, to fail, and to take the longer-term view. Furthermore, in an important sense, foundations exist in a world of their own. They do not fully belong to any one sector but have, or could have, a foot in all. They are not, yet, dominated by any one professional group and thus have the freedom and space to think and work across conventional wisdoms, and disciplinary, organizational and sectoral boundaries.

These characteristics of endowed foundations give them the potential to make a contribution to society way beyond that which their limited resources might suggest. Furthermore, building on these characteristics enables foundations to build a robust role that harnesses their 'privateness' for the public good. Susan Berresford, president of the Ford Foundation, has called for a revisiting of the implications of the 'public' definition of foundations, calling attention to the intersection of philanthropy, democracy and freedom. We argue that the characteristics of foundations outlined above should be recognized as a cause for celebration rather than apology, providing one of the keys to unlocking the 'private/public' conundrum.

At a time when many commentators see democracy in the United States and elsewhere as under threat from a combination of the demands of global capitalism and overly powerful political parties, we argue along with other experts that foundations have never been more important. The role of the wider nonprofit sector, dependent for resources on contracting, corporate fundraising and popular sympathies moulded by the media, is constrained in what it can offer.

Foundations have to acknowledge that they have neither the resources nor the democratic mandate to fill all the gaps, provide everything the state does not provide, and support unpopular causes in the long term. What is more, foundations should no longer use resource limitations as an excuse to turn down grant-seekers, but to make it very clear that they are not in the business of stepping in for what governments, or market firms might be better at.

Endowed foundations are uniquely placed to bring genuinely creative, innovative ideas to the intransigent problems of our age. Free of market and political constraints, they are uniquely able, if they choose, to think the unthinkable, ignoring disciplinary and professional boundaries. They can take risks, consider approaches others say can't possibly work – and they can fail with no terminal consequences. Equally important, foundations can take a longer-term view. Foundations are free to be imaginative and creative, working across sectoral, organizational, professional and disciplinary boundaries, without the stifling constraints of short-term, ill-conceived performance measurement criteria. They can change the way in which we think about things, our priorities and our ways of creating a truly civil society characterized by respect and dignity for all. As Carson has noted, foundations need to spend more time and money on 'projects that have the promise of changing how an issue is viewed or handled'. We refer to this as 'creative grant-making'.

[. . .]

Opening up debate

We are supporters of foundations and philanthropy, and we defend the right of independent private action for common benefit, and would like to see such actions encouraged by public policy. We believe that foundations ultimately add to the problem-solving capacity of modern societies in dealing with the challenges they face, be it in the field of education, health, culture, or policy development, among others. The freedom that foundations have from both ballot box and shareholder expectations affords them great latitude in pursuing private objectives and agendas while serving a public purpose. Some foundations take full advantage of this freedom; others are not achieving their full potential and the great promise they hold for modern societies.

[. . .]

Creative philanthropy

A key element of our argument for a renewal of philanthropy so far has been that much of what foundations do could be done, and perhaps done equally well, by other nonprofit organizations, and even public agencies and businesses. We also suggest that other foundation-like forms such as donor-advised funds and community foundations could take on roles more conventional foundations play. Foundations should therefore concentrate on doing those things only they have the potential to do better than other institutions.

Foundations have, in an important sense, had it right all along. The only justification for independence from government and market accountability (as distinct from transparency) is their potential to be a source of innovation – and, we would add, creativity – that is unconstrained by short-term market forces and political–electoral considerations, and that in the aggregate contributes to greater pluralism. In so doing, creative philanthropy provides a space for alternative thinking, voices and practices. In encouraging constructive conversations about new approaches to old and new issues, creative foundations increase the problem-solving capacity of society and reinvigorate civic engagement and democracy.

Foundations and hegemony

Joan Roelofs, 2003

> A part of the bourgeoisie is desirous of redressing social grievances, in order to secure the continued existence of bourgeois society. To this section belong the economists, philanthropists, humanitarians, improvers of the condition of the working class, organizers of charity, members of societies for the prevention of cruelty to animals, temperance fanatics, hole-and-corner reformers of every imaginable kind.
>
> (Marx and Engels, *The Communist Manifesto*)

Antonio Gramsci's theory of hegemony suggests a conceptual framework useful for understanding foundations. Gramsci, an Italian socialist imprisoned by the Fascists, argued that any political system, such as democratic capitalism, is maintained in two ways. The more obvious is the political realm, or "the state," which controls through force and laws. It is complemented by subtle but overarching system maintenance performed by "civil society," or the private realm, which produces consent without the resort to force.

> These two levels correspond on the one hand to the function of "hegemony" which the dominant group exercises throughout society and on the other hand to that of "direct domination" or command exercised through the State and "juridical" government. The functions in question are precisely organisational and connective.
>
> The intellectuals are the dominant group's "deputies" exercising the subaltern functions of social hegemony and political government.

Gramsci's category of "intellectual" is a broad one; he maintained that all men [sic] were intellectuals, although they do not all perform that function in society. Those who did included artists and scholars, the clergy, teachers, journalists, political party and other activists, engineers, administrators, doctors, lawyers, social workers, and professional reformers. Gramsci did not discuss foundations; there were few in the Italy of his day, although there were corporate grants for ameliorative projects. The Catholic Church was the dominant structure in the Italian nongovernmental world.

To elaborate on Gramsci, in the modern foundation we find the domain of intellectuals par excellence. Furthermore, a central group of liberal foundations exerts "hegemonic" power over civil society, including all of these intellectuals and their institutions, and it has a large role in shaping governmental policies. Hegemony now operates on a global scale, facilitating the globalization of both political and civil society.

Gramsci meant by "the dominant group" what is generally called "the ruling class," or the owners of major productive resources. Intellectuals act on their behalf, whether or not they are members of "ruling class" families. System maintenance, according to Robert Michels, requires attractive positions for ruling class scions not needed to direct industry. Political systems are most secure when all educated, artistic, and ambitious people can find interesting, well-rewarded work; the defection of intellectuals is the chief destabilizing factor.

Foundations provide an institutional basis for the hegemonic function. They appear distant from their corporate origins and support, so they may claim a neutral image. Unlike universities, they are not hobbled by disciplinary traditions or professional qualifications, so they can include anyone and can fund all kinds of projects.

Incorporation of the restless and cheeky is one function of our vast "third" or nonprofit sector. Michels thought that government employment would do the trick, but nongovernment employment is even better as a stabilizer [. . .] Marx and Engels probably never imagined that whether or not reformers fixed anything, capitalism would be solidified by their operations. Nonprofits are a reliable source of employment that does not build up the unsettling pile of surplus manufactured goods.

Hegemonic institutions elicit consent by the production and dissemination of ideology that appears to be merely common sense. Deviations from the central myths are considered "extremism," "paranoia," "utopianism," "self-defeating dogmatism," and the like. Dissent is thereby neutralized, often ridiculed, but dissenters are welcomed and may be transformed. Raymond Williams observed that hegemonic control is so invincible because it is a dynamic process, creatively incorporating emergent trends.

Intellectuals are attracted to these institutions because they offer prestige, power, perks, and/or social mobility; access to resources needed for their own creations or the "good work" they are doing; and legitimation. Technological changes have upped the ante for doing most anything, whether artistic, scholarly, or activist; consequently, control of resources becomes even more influential.

We also may understand foundations using the power elite theory of C. Wright Mills, later developed and empirically supported by G. William Domhoff and others. Domhoff argues that the corporate community dominates the federal government, local governments, and all significant policy-making institutions.

> The corporate rich and the growth entrepreneurs supplement their small numbers by developing and directing a wide variety of nonprofit organizations, the most important of which are a set of tax-free charitable foundations, think tanks, and policy-discussion groups. These specialized nonprofit groups constitute a *policy-formation network* at the national level.

[C]orporate-created institutions not only dominate but also tend to supplant governmental ones, local to international. Today there is no replay of the heated debate in our early Republic, when all corporations, including "voluntary associations," often were regarded as a threat to democracy.

Domhoff identifies the power elite as the leadership group in society. However, it is not coextensive with the "corporate rich."

> The concept of a power elite makes clear that not all members of the upper class are involved in governance; some of them simply enjoy the lifestyle that their great wealth affords them. At the same time, the focus on a leadership group allows for the fact that not all those in the power elite are members of the upper class; many

> of them are high-level employees in profit and nonprofit organizations controlled by the corporate rich [. . .] The power elite, in other words, is based in both ownership and in organizational positions.

My studies also have been guided and inspired by educational theorist Robert Arnove's anthology, *Philanthropy and Cultural Imperialism*, and its contributors. Arnove maintains that:

> [. . .] [F]oundations like Carnegie, Rockefeller, and Ford have a corrosive influence on a democratic society; they represent relatively unregulated and unaccountable concentrations of power and wealth which buy talent, promote causes, and, in effect, establish an agenda of what merits society's attention. They serve as "cooling out" agencies, delaying and preventing more radical, structural change.

[. . .]

Historians Barry Karl and Stanley Katz acknowledge and document the vast power of the foundations, both in providing essential services to the polity, such as planning, and in training elites for efficient and enlightened leadership.

> The creation of the modern foundation and its legitimation as a national system of social reform – a privately supported system operating in lieu of a governmental system – carried the United States through a crucial period of its development: the first third of the twentieth century.

They generally approve of these interventions and do not probe the contradictions to both "free enterprise" and democratic theory implied by the need for extra-constitutional planners.

Resource mobilization theory has illuminated the fate of social change movements – why they live, grow, die, or are transformed. Resources are crucial for all forms of political action, far beyond the campaign and lobbying funding emphasized in "money in politics" studies. Sociologist J. Craig Jenkins, who takes particular notice of foundations, states:

> The foundations have been political "gatekeepers," funding the movement initiatives that were successfully translated into public policy and institutional reforms. In the process, they have also selected the new organizations that became permanent features of the political landscape.

This applies as well to foundation funding of political parties, governmental factions, and overthrow movements. Although illegal in the United States, such grants are considered quite proper when foreigners are recipients.

Foundations in Turkey

Filiz Bikmen, 2008

There is a common saying about the extent to which foundations (*vakif*, in Turkish) in the Ottoman Era affected people's lives – it was possible for a person to be born in a *vakif* hospital, study in a *vakif* school, work in a *vakif* institution, and be buried in a *vakif* graveyard. Given that more than 35,000 foundations were functioning during this period, it is quite likely the saying held true for many.

The history of Ottoman foundations is full of richness in both assets and activities and considered a very important part of Turkish (not just Islamic) culture and tradition. Although foundations have continued to play some role in society, they are still more commonly known through their rich legacy.

Foundations reached their peak in the 18th century, ranging from Anatolia to the present-day Balkans and Thrace, and reaching into Syria and Egypt. With significant assets in the form of land and, later, cash, foundations constructed caravansaries, schools, hospitals and roads, serving many of the same functions of basic service provision performed by today's modern welfare state. Yet the role of foundations was significantly curtailed, starting in the late Ottoman period, and this continued throughout the beginning of the new Turkish Republic – from the mid-to-late 19th century to the early 20th century.

The foundation sector was weakened greatly by both external forces and internal politics, yet the philanthropic impulse of Turkish people remained. While fewer incentives and strict state controls made foundations less appealing for many, this did not prevent a small but powerful segment of society from continuing this tradition, and allocating private wealth for public good – and today, reaching beyond that to supporting positive social change. Currently there are more than 3,000 privately established foundations in Turkey.

The view of Turkey as a 'paradox of tradition and modernity' or a 'bridge between east and west' can also be applied to the foundation sector. Today, many foundations – characterized as 'traditional' – in Turkey bear a striking resemblance to their ancestors of the Ottoman period. Their most common characteristic is the practice of building institutions such as schools, hospitals and museums. There is also a 'modern' generation of foundations that have gone beyond building institutions to undertaking policy analysis, advocacy and innovative programs aimed at social change, taking an active role in creating a democratic and civil society. In this sense, foundations are beginning to search within and across borders for new ways to serve – perhaps even redefine – the public good, in a society undergoing a remarkable political, economic, social and cultural transformation.

A great deal of this momentum for change is owed to the EU accession process, yet the effects of changes in the greater global context are also felt within Turkey's borders.

Some call this momentum a 'silent revolution', indeed its effects may not be seen or heard immediately. Yet these changes are slowly carving out a more prominent role for modern foundations, parallel to Turkey's political and economic development.

[. . .]

A rich past

What is commonly known in the West as a 'foundation' is in its most basic form very similar to the institution known as *waqf* in Arabic (or *vakif*, in Turkish). At their very core, *vakifs* and foundations share the following main characteristics:

- There is an endowment of private wealth for a specified activity of public benefit.
- Objectives, purpose and detailed directives on how revenue from the endowment is to be managed and allocated are stated in a founding document.

Philanthropic endowments have a history considerably older than Islam, and are likely to have been influenced by earlier civilizations including ancient Mesopotamia, Greece, Rome and pre-Islamic Arabs. It is still unresolved to what extent Islamic *waqfs* were influenced by these traditions; however, it is likely that Muslims adopted this practice from earlier civilizations. Some scholars suggest that medieval Europe may have learned of these institutions through the *vakif* system. Some go as far as to suggest that it was not Roman or Germanic law but Islamic *waqfs* that greatly influenced the development of the trust law of England and throughout the Christian Mediterranean.

Despite the lack of agreement on the various factors that may have influenced its emergence, the institution of *vakif* become known after the death of the Prophet Mohammed and its legal structure was firmly established during the second half of the second century. According to the Foundations Directorate of Turkey, the earliest documentation of a *vakif* in Anatolia dates back to 1048. Yet this was probably just one of many, as there were an estimated 2,773 foundations active in year 986.

The role of *vakifs* in Ottoman society

Vakifs are often referred to in an Islamic context, leading many to think that they are actually part of the religious text and practice. They were established within the framework of Islamic law, which was in practice during the period when *vakifs* emerged. However, what fascinates scholars about the emergence of the *vakif* as an institutional form is that it is not referred to specifically in the Koran, but it was – and continues to be – widely used as a vehicle through which pious Muslims could realize, in perpetuity, their religious obligations. Such obligations include charitable deeds, which are described in great detail in the Holy Book. While many foundations during this period did adopt religious observation as a central objective, their role was much broader in serving public benefit. And, as described in this chapter, this would change significantly in the era of the modern Turkish Republic where foundations now play a very limited role in promoting religious practice.

Although foundations were active for many centuries, it was during the Ottoman Era that these institutions reached their peak in terms of numbers, acquisition of assets, services to the public and institutional development. It was, in fact, a vibrant sector. In the absence of government or centralized regulation – which came at a later point

– common procedures and frameworks were developed that practitioners today would consider self-regulatory.

One of the most important reasons for this exponential growth was the major role foundations played in delivering basic services to society. The responsibility of the Ottoman state to its people was solely to provide justice, safety, freedom of religion and the possibility of individual self-development. As such, there was no budget or system for the provision of all other basic services. In the absence of this, foundations became the sole providers of basic services, from municipal services (the water system in Istanbul was entirely developed by foundations) to education, health, culture and religion.

Foundations also developed sophisticated tools for economic generation, offering services similar to microfinance and modern banks, at times providing major injections of capital into the economy. Funds endowed were lent to borrowers without the borrowing rate charge and gains with interest were put back into the foundation, with revenues spent on social and pious purposes.

The rise and fall of the *vakif*

There are many gaps in figures and statistics, mainly due to the lack of centralized registries for many centuries. Yet scholars estimate more than 35,000 foundations were established and operational throughout the Ottoman Era. During the 16th century, there were approximately 2,860 foundations in Istanbul alone and 485 in Aleppo. Foundations were established not only by elite segments of society, but also by middle-income individuals and families. Even more fascinating is that women established almost 40 per cent of these foundations. Although no statistics are available, this number is likely far smaller today.

Given the vast scope and sophistication of foundation services, their financial assets constituted a significant portion of the Ottoman State budget. Foundations had two major forms of 'corpus' or endowed assets: cash (movable) or property (immovable). By the 16th century, most foundations were cash foundations, giving them greater liquidity. It is estimated that foundation assets comprised approximately 12 per cent of the state budget in the 16th century, slightly higher at 18 per cent in the 17th century, and peaking at 27 per cent in the 18th century.

Until the early part of the 19th century, foundations enjoyed a relatively *laissez-faire* relationship with the state and were granted full autonomy. However, this was to change dramatically in the 19th century due to internal politics and economic challenges, as well as external pressures from guarantors in Europe on the Ottoman state following the Crimean War, which mandated the weakening of the *vakif* system. As a result, the revenue base of foundations was cut almost in half and a majority of their assets were centralized through many state operations.

Yet their wealth was of such great proportions that, regardless of these conditions, foundation revenues continued to be a vital source for funding of basic public services in the first ten years of the establishment of the Republic in 1923.

The turn of the 20th century brought a new paradigm of state administration, and with it a school of thought influenced greatly by the French, which at one point discouraged the emergence of intermediary actors such as foundations serving public needs and services to citizens. The ethos of the Turkish Republic reflected this position, and it was not until after the new Civil Code of 1926 that a new legal framework for foundations was created.

A portrait of the present

Even today, the revenues and assets of Ottoman foundations are of massive proportions and continue to play a significant role in modern Turkish society. There are currently more than 65,000 movable and immovable assets of Ottoman foundations (commonly referred to as *eski vakif* or simply "old foundations"), which are managed directly by the Foundations Directorate, the central regulatory authority.

Most are property and land; the buildings, including mosques, *medreses* (Islamic theological elementary schools), libraries, bridges and schools, are considered historical artefacts. The Foundations Directorate ensures they are preserved according to cultural heritage regulations and, if possible, used as public spaces and/or museums. Their revenues continue to provide charitable support to the poor and needy in the form of food, assistance and scholarships. Valuable properties are now being rented and sold for real estate development projects, and revenues being re-invested in foundation endowments to serve their original charitable purposes. In this way, 'old' foundations are revalued within the system of Turkey's vibrant market economy.

The 4,449 foundations established since the new Civil Code in 1926 are referred to as 'Civil Code' or 'new' foundations; these are also regulated by the Foundations Directorate. Though governed by a new set of laws, the *vakif* has retained its main institutional characteristics as inherited from the Ottoman period – an endowment, a specific purpose and a founding document outlining management details. Yet, as times have changed, so has the way in which foundations realize their charitable purposes.

5.3 Should corporations give?

The social responsibility of business is to increase its profits

Milton Friedman, 1970

When I hear businessmen speak eloquently about the "social responsibilities of business in a free-enterprise system," I am reminded of the wonderful line about the Frenchman who discovered at the age of 70 that he had been speaking prose all his life. The businessmen believe that they are defending free enterprise when they declaim that business is not concerned "merely" with profit but also with promoting desirable "social" ends; that business has a "social conscience" and takes seriously its responsibilities for providing employment, eliminating discrimination, avoiding pollution and whatever else may be the catchwords of the contemporary crop of reformers. In fact they are – or would be if they or anyone else took them seriously – preaching pure and unadulterated socialism. Businessmen who talk this way are unwitting puppets of the intellectual forces that have been undermining the basis of a free society these past decades.

The discussions of the "social responsibilities of business" are notable for their analytical looseness and lack of rigor. What does it mean to say that "business" has responsibilities? Only people can have responsibilities. A corporation is an artificial person and in this sense may have artificial responsibilities, but "business" as a whole cannot be said to have responsibilities, even in this vague sense. The first step toward clarity in examining the doctrine of the social responsibility of business is to ask precisely what it implies for whom.

Presumably, the individuals who are to be responsible are businessmen, which means individual proprietors or corporate executives. Most of the discussion of social responsibility is directed at corporations, so in what follows I shall mostly neglect the individual proprietors and speak of corporate executives.

In a free-enterprise, private-property system, a corporate executive is an employee of the owners of the business. He has direct responsibility to his employers. That responsibility is to conduct the business in accordance with their desires, which generally will be to make as much money as possible while conforming to the basic rules of the society, both those embodied in law and those embodied in ethical custom. Of course, in some cases his employers may have a different objective. A group of persons might establish a corporation for an eleemosynary purpose – for example, a hospital or a school. The manager of such a corporation will not have money profit as his objective but the rendering of certain services.

In either case, the key point is that, in his capacity as a corporate executive, the manager is the agent of the individuals who own the corporation or establish the eleemosynary institution, and his primary responsibility is to them.

Needless to say, this does not mean that it is easy to judge how well he is performing his task. But at least the criterion of performance is straightforward, and the persons among whom a voluntary contractual arrangement exists are clearly defined.

Of course, the corporate executive is also a person in his own right. As a person, he may have many other responsibilities that he recognizes or assumes voluntarily – to his family, his conscience, his feelings of charity, his church, his clubs, his city, his country. He may feel impelled by these responsibilities to devote part of his income to causes he regards as worthy, to refuse to work for particular corporations, even to leave his job, for example, to join his country's armed forces. If we wish, we may refer to some of these responsibilities as "social responsibilities." But in these respects he is acting as a principal, not an agent; he is spending his own money or time or energy, not the money of his employers or the time or energy he has contracted to devote to their purposes. If these are "social responsibilities," they are the social responsibilities of individuals, not of business.

What does it mean to say that the corporate executive has a "social responsibility" in his capacity as businessman? If this statement is not pure rhetoric, it must mean that he is to act in some way that is not in the interest of his employers. For example, that he is to refrain from increasing the price of the product in order to contribute to the social objective of preventing inflation, even though a price increase would be in the best interests of the corporation. Or that he is to make expenditures on reducing pollution beyond the amount that is in the best interests of the corporation or that is required by law in order to contribute to the social objective of improving the environment. Or that, at the expense of corporate profits, he is to hire "hardcore" unemployed instead of better qualified available workmen to contribute to the social objective of reducing poverty.

In each of these cases, the corporate executive would be spending someone else's money for a general social interest. Insofar as his actions in accord with his "social responsibility" reduce returns to stockholders, he is spending their money. Insofar as his actions raise the price to customers, he is spending the customers' money. Insofar as his actions lower the wages of some employees, he is spending their money.

The stockholders or the customers or the employees could separately spend their own money on the particular action if they wished to do so. The executive is exercising a distinct "social responsibility," rather than serving as an agent of the stockholders or the customers or the employees, only if he spends the money in a different way than they would have spent it.

But if he does this, he is in effect imposing taxes, on the one hand, and deciding how the tax proceeds shall be spent, on the other.

This process raises political questions on two levels: principle and consequences. On the level of political principle, the imposition of taxes and the expenditure of tax proceeds are governmental functions. We have established elaborate constitutional, parliamentary and judicial provisions to control these functions, to assure that taxes are imposed so far as possible in accordance with the preferences and desires of the public – after all, "taxation without representation" was one of the battle cries of the American Revolution. We have a system of checks and balances to separate the legislative function of imposing taxes and enacting expenditures from the executive function of collecting taxes and administering expenditure programs and from the judicial function of mediating disputes and interpreting the law.

Here the businessman – self-selected or appointed directly or indirectly by stockholders – is to be simultaneously legislator, executive, and jurist. He is to decide whom to tax by how much and for what purpose, and he is to spend the proceeds – all this guided only by general exhortations from on high to restrain inflation, improve the environment, fight poverty and so on and on.

The whole justification for permitting the corporate executive to be selected by the stockholders is that the executive is an agent serving the interests of his principal. This justification disappears when the corporate executive imposes taxes and spends the proceeds for "social" purposes. He becomes in effect a public employee, a civil servant, even though he remains in name an employee of a private enterprise. On grounds of political principle, it is intolerable that such civil servants – insofar as their actions in the name of social responsibility are real and not just window-dressing – should be selected as they are now. If they are to be civil servants, then they must be elected through a political process. If they are to impose taxes and make expenditures to foster "social" objectives, then political machinery must be set up to make the assessment of taxes and to determine through a political process the objectives to be served.

This is the basic reason why the doctrine of "social responsibility" involves the acceptance of the socialist view that political mechanisms, not market mechanisms, are the appropriate way to determine the allocation of scarce resources to alternative uses.

On the grounds of consequences, can the corporate executive in fact discharge his alleged "social responsibilities?" On the other hand, suppose he could get away with spending the stockholders' or customers' or employees' money. How is he to know how to spend it? He is told that he must contribute to fighting inflation. How is he to know what action of his will contribute to that end? He is presumably an expert in running his company – in producing a product or selling it or financing it. But nothing about his selection makes him an expert on inflation. Will his holding down the price of his product reduce inflationary pressure? Or, by leaving more spending power in the hands of his customers, simply divert it elsewhere? Or, by forcing him to produce less because of the lower price, will it simply contribute to shortages? Even if he could answer these questions, how much cost is he justified in imposing on his stockholders, customers and employees for this social purpose? What is his appropriate share and what is the appropriate share of others?

And, whether he wants to or not, can he get away with spending his stockholders', customers' or employees' money? Will not the stockholders fire him? (Either the present ones or those who take over when his actions in the name of social responsibility have reduced the corporation's profits and the price of its stock.) His customers and his employees can desert him for other producers and employers less scrupulous in exercising their social responsibilities.

[. . .]

The difficulty of exercising "social responsibility" illustrates, of course, the great virtue of private competitive enterprise – it forces people to be responsible for their own actions and makes it difficult for them to "exploit" other people for either selfish or unselfish purposes. They can do good – but only at their own expense.

Many a reader who has followed the argument this far may be tempted to remonstrate that it is all well and good to speak of Government's having the responsibility to impose taxes and determine expenditures for such "social" purposes as controlling pollution or training the hardcore unemployed, but that the problems are too urgent to wait on the slow course of political processes, that the exercise of social responsibility by businessmen is a quicker and surer way to solve pressing current problems.

Aside from the question of fact – I share Adam Smith's skepticism about the benefits that can be expected from "those who affected to trade for the public good" – this argument must be rejected on grounds of principle. What it amounts to is an assertion that those who favor the taxes and expenditures in question have failed to persuade a majority of their fellow citizens to be of like mind and that they are seeking to attain by undemocratic procedures what they cannot attain by democratic procedures. In a free society, it is hard for "evil" people to do "evil," especially since one man's good is another's evil.

I have, for simplicity, concentrated on the special case of the corporate executive [. . .] But precisely the same argument applies to the newer phenomenon of calling upon stockholders to require corporations to exercise social responsibility (the recent G.M crusade for example). In most of these cases, what is in effect involved is some stockholders trying to get other stockholders (or customers or employees) to contribute against their will to "social" causes favored by the activists. Insofar as they succeed, they are again imposing taxes and spending the proceeds.

The situation of the individual proprietor is somewhat different. If he acts to reduce the returns of his enterprise in order to exercise his "social responsibility," he is spending his own money, not someone else's. If he wishes to spend his money on such purposes, that is his right, and I cannot see that there is any objection to his doing so. In the process, he, too, may impose costs on employees and customers. However, because he is far less likely than a large corporation or union to have monopolistic power, any such side effects will tend to be minor.

Of course, in practice the doctrine of social responsibility is frequently a cloak for actions that are justified on other grounds rather than a reason for those actions.

To illustrate, it may well be in the long run interest of a corporation that is a major employer in a small community to devote resources to providing amenities to that community or to improving its government. That may make it easier to attract desirable employees, it may reduce the wage bill or lessen losses from pilferage and sabotage or have other worthwhile effects. Or it may be that, given the laws about the deductibility of corporate charitable contributions, the stockholders can contribute more to charities they favor by having the corporation make the gift than by doing it themselves, since they can in that way contribute an amount that would otherwise have been paid as corporate taxes.

In each of these – and many similar – cases, there is a strong temptation to rationalize these actions as an exercise of "social responsibility." In the present climate of opinion, with its wide spread aversion to "capitalism," "profits," the "soulless corporation" and so on, this is one way for a corporation to generate goodwill as a by-product of expenditures that are entirely justified in its own self-interest.

It would be inconsistent of me to call on corporate executives to refrain from this hypocritical window-dressing because it harms the foundations of a free society. That would be to call on them to exercise a "social responsibility!" If our institutions, and the attitudes of the public make it in their self-interest to cloak their actions in this way, I cannot summon much indignation to denounce them. At the same time, I can express admiration for those individual proprietors or owners of closely held corporations or stockholders of more broadly held corporations who disdain such tactics as approaching fraud.

Whether blameworthy or not, the use of the cloak of social responsibility, and the nonsense spoken in its name by influential and prestigious businessmen, does clearly harm the foundations of a free society. I have been impressed time and again by the schizophrenic character of many businessmen. They are capable of being extremely farsighted and clearheaded in matters that are internal to their businesses. They are incredibly shortsighted and muddleheaded in matters that are outside their businesses but affect the possible survival of business in general. This shortsightedness is strikingly exemplified in the calls from many businessmen for wage and price guidelines or controls or income policies. There is nothing that could do more in a brief period to destroy a market system and replace it by a centrally controlled system than effective governmental control of prices and wages.

The shortsightedness is also exemplified in speeches by businessmen on social responsibility. This may gain them kudos in the short run. But it helps to strengthen the already too prevalent view that the pursuit of profits is wicked and immoral and must be curbed and controlled by external forces. Once this view is adopted, the external forces that curb the market will not be the social consciences, however highly developed, of the pontificating executives; it will be the iron fist of Government bureaucrats. Here, as with price and wage controls, businessmen seem to me to reveal a suicidal impulse.

The political principle that underlies the market mechanism is unanimity. In an ideal free market resting on private property, no individual can coerce any other, all cooperation is voluntary, all parties to such cooperation benefit or they need not participate. There are no values, no "social" responsibilities in any sense other than the shared values and responsibilities of individuals. Society is a collection of individuals and of the various groups they voluntarily form.

The political principle that underlies the political mechanism is conformity. The individual must serve a more general social interest – whether that be determined by a church or a dictator or a majority. The individual may have a vote and say in what is to be done, but if he is overruled, he must conform. It is appropriate for some to require others to contribute to a general social purpose whether they wish to or not.

Unfortunately, unanimity is not always feasible. There are some respects in which conformity appears unavoidable, so I do not see how one can avoid the use of the political mechanism altogether.

But the doctrine of "social responsibility" taken seriously would extend the scope of the political mechanism to every human activity. It does not differ in philosophy from the most explicitly collectivist doctrine. It differs only by professing to believe that collectivist ends can be attained without collectivist means. That is why, in my book *Capitalism and Freedom*, I have called it a "fundamentally subversive doctrine" in a free society, and have said that in such a society, "there is one and only one social responsibility of business – to use its resources and engage in activities designed to increase its profits so long as it stays within the rules of the game, which is to say, engages in open and free competition without deception or fraud."

The legitimacy of corporate philanthropy

Thomas W. Dunfee, 2011

Corporate philanthropy involves a transfer of money, goods, or services by a public for-profit organization based upon a significant social motive. In the United States, the level of corporate philanthropy appears to have averaged a little more than 1 percent of net profits for many decades. It typically accounts for about 5 percent of total charity in the United States. In 2005, the total amount given was around $14 billion. About a quarter of corporate tax returns reflect deductions for charitable contributions.

Although the amounts are nontrivial and the potential for improving the social good is high, the practice of corporate philanthropy remains distressingly opaque and shrouded in controversy. Critics on the right charge that corporations are not proper agents for distributing charity, a function that should be left to individual shareholders who are free to disperse dividends and capital gains as they prefer. Critics on the left are skeptical of corporate motives, believing that business strategies and financial engineering goals dominate any desire to improve the social good. This has led some to question whether the term *strategic philanthropy* is a classic oxymoron. Aggregate data are imprecise, because many firms either do not report their data to independent organizations or only selectively disclose donations. More than a third of the top 150 firms in the Fortune 500 fail to disclose information about their giving to the *Chronicle of Philanthropy* whereas 60 percent of the S&P [Standard & Poor] 500 failed to provide data to *Business Week* when the respected publication initiated an annual report on philanthropy, and even in the most recent report the percentage responding stays well less than 50 percent. A visit to the website of virtually any major corporation will quickly make clear how difficult it is to obtain a comprehensive picture of a particular firm's philanthropic activity.

Definitions concerning what falls within the domain of corporate philanthropy are uncertain in practice and, perhaps surprisingly, also in the academic literature. The inability to define with precision what corporate philanthropy includes creates measurement problems that make comparisons difficult. Should, for example, noncash distributions such as the donation of drugs by pharmaceutical companies be counted and, if so, how should the distributions be valued? Should they be valued at cost or at a marked-up price? Similar issues arise in the treatment of employee volunteer programs. How should employee time be valued? Does it make a difference whether the employee is given credit by the firm for a workday? The answers to these types of valuation questions can have a major impact on reports of the level of corporate giving and in studies seeking to compare activity across firms or industries.

The use of corporate foundations has an impact on assessments of philanthropy. Some corporations set up separate foundations funded directly by distributions from the firm. This allows the business entity to time and control the tax efficiency of its donations (it may give more in a highly profitable year) while the foundation employs a professional staff to distribute resources in a manner attuned to donor need. WalMart has the largest corporate foundation. Corporate foundations accounted for about $4 billion in 2005, which represented about 11 percent of all foundation giving.

[. . .]

A working definition of corporate philanthropy

Corporate philanthropy is a special category or form of philanthropy. The defining characteristic, of course, is that the philanthropic act is carried out by a business corporation, ordinarily understood to be a for-profit organization. The act itself involves a net transfer intended to create value for a donee. In contrast to ordinary market exchanges, a philanthropic act involves a desire to provide a social good. A much-debated issue is the prominence to be given to the altruistic, social benefit component of the donor's motivation.

Multiple motives underlie corporate giving programs. Even a single project may involve a variety of seemingly contradictory motives. For example, a firm may engage in philanthropy (1) to improve the general reputation of the company, (2) to induce customers to buy their products or services, (3) to smooth earnings, (4) to reduce taxes, (5) to improve their competitive position in the industry, (6) to motivate or attract employees, (7) to access important social networks, (8) to forestall regulation, (9) to insulate against negative public reaction to bad acts, and (10) to achieve a particular social goal. The Committee Encouraging Corporate Philanthropy provides annual reports of the results of surveys of slightly more than 100 large corporations. In their 2006 report, they described the results of a survey of motivations for giving. The allocation of a typical company was found to be 54 percent charitable, 35 percent strategic, and 11 percent commercial. In a recent McKinsey Global Survey of chief executive officers (CEOs) and high-level executives, nearly 90 percent indicated that their firms seek business benefits from their philanthropy programs.

Philanthropy may be a component of a business strategy. Social cause marketing involves creating an alignment between values of the company and those of customers. The assumption is that customers will try and then be loyal to the company's products and services because of the perceived commonality of values. Iconic academic consultant Michael Porter now advocates strategic philanthropy as a means by which firms can develop a competitive edge: "If systematically pursued in a way that maximizes the value created, context-focused philanthropy can offer companies a new set of competitive tools that well justifies the investment of resources. At the same time, it can unlock a vastly more powerful way to make the world a better place." Evidence indicates that firms are indeed becoming more strategic in their approach to philanthropy.

Philanthropy may be a component of financial engineering. Properly timed and framed, philanthropy may minimize tax liability or assist with earnings management. Deductions may be increased or reduced in a given year to smooth earnings. Deductions may be increased when a firm faces higher than usual taxes.

Agency problems may be associated with philanthropy. Corporate donations may be designed to fulfill the desire of the CEO or other top managers to be named to the boards of artistic or educational institutions. Membership on such boards brings prestige and social connections. Bartkus, Morris, and Seifert describe the claim that when Ross Johnson wanted to take RJR Nabisco private, he attempted to influence several key members of the board of directors by making large company donations to Duke University in their names.

Suppose that a company were to make a large anonymous donation to the Red Cross. There is no public notice involving the donation. Assume further that the company does not even let its own staff or employees know. Instead, only a senior corporate official has knowledge of the gift. The company appears to receive no benefit, while at the same time there is a major social benefit. This would seem to be a case of pure social philanthropy. Presumably, there are very few cases like this in which a company has a purely altruistic motivation.

At the other extreme would be a company that decides the best way to introduce a new product (for example, a new shampoo) is by promising that it will make a small donation to the Red Cross for every bottle purchased. The action is taken at a time in which there has been a disaster that has created a significant blood shortage. Public support for the Red Cross as an institution is high. The shampoo donation program is designed by the marketing department on their budget, and the success and continuation of the project will be determined solely on the basis of the sales of the new product. In this case the "philanthropy" is purely a business strategy in which any social motivation is purely instrumental.

Most cases of corporate philanthropy fall in between these two extremes. Social purposes and business strategies are liberally intermixed.

[. . .]

The ersatz issue: questioning the legitimacy of corporate philanthropy

Corporate philanthropy is ingrained in US culture and is widely practiced and praised. At least a quarter of all firms engage in the practice with a bias toward greater involvement by larger firms. The Friedmanite claim that, in general, corporations should not engage in philanthropy has had little real world impact. One can imagine the chorus of concern and criticism that would greet an announcement from the Fortune 500 that they were going to adopt Friedman's ideas and stop all giving and social initiatives immediately. The protesting choir would be quite diverse. The ensemble of protesting choral sections would include university presidents, directors of museums and ballets, leaders of human services organizations, heads of major nongovernmental organizations (NGOs), politicians, heads of hospitals and medical research clinics, leaders of professional business associations, and even some investor-based groups.

Why has the Friedman view failed to have much impact? One explanation might be that philanthropy is so good for business that shareholders support it because they understand that it enhances long-term profitability. This win-win idea is an ever more popular idea as consultants push the concept of strategic philanthropy. Despite the general claims and arguments advanced in support of the win-win view. Hard evidence of a relationship between philanthropy and profits is hard to come by. Seifert Morris and Bartkus state that "there is little research evidence that giving has a positive effect on firm financial performance," noting that "the path coefficient between company size and relative corporate philanthropy was not significant in any model we tested." Fisman, Heal, and Nair model corporate philanthropy and use economic databases to conclude that profits and philanthropy appear to be positively related only in industries with high advertising intensity and high levels of competition.

Corporate philanthropy programs justified significantly on the basis of their contribution to the financial bottom line would have a hard time satisfying the rigorous standards typically followed when firms evaluate ordinary business investments. When firms make business investments, they are unlikely to rely on vague statements or projections about improved reputation or morale. Instead, they insist on the best available direct evidence concerning probable contributions to the bottom line or to a successful competitive strategy. They require hard data demonstrating that the business goals are being realized. A comparable approach doesn't appear to be possible for most types of corporate philanthropy. Meaningful "hard" numbers for the impact of philanthropic programs cannot be identified. End points cannot be specified with precision. Results are amorphous. So although advocates of corporate philanthropy may claim that there are business benefits, they cannot demonstrate the actual benefits in the same serious manner expected for a business investment.

If the business case is marginal at best, then why does the practice persist? One answer, supported by institutional theory in management and consistent with social contract-based approaches to business ethics, is that corporate philanthropy, at least in some markets and nations, is supported by influential business norms. Pro-philanthropic norms are often reflected in peer pressure influencing individual executives and organizational management. Professional organizations such as the Business Roundtable support the practice. Chief executive officers interact socially in venues such as boards associated with educational and arts organizations in which corporate philanthropy is recognized and applauded. Galaskiewicz studied the Twin Cities of Minneapolis and St. Paul, famous for the 5 percent club that supports generous giving among major local firms, and concluded that socialites were critically important influencers of firm behavior. Philanthropic actions provoke responses from competitors. Merck's much-praised development and distribution of a drug designed to combat the ravages of the affliction called river blindness was followed by other major pharmaceutical companies developing similar programs.

The business norm supporting philanthropy is clearly supported by key stakeholders and by broader society. Tax laws allow a deduction for charitable giving. The policy of granting a tax exemption can be seen as a direct subsidy of the practice because tax revenues decrease in response. In the United States, a National Corporate Philanthropy Day was initially promulgated jointly by the US Secretary of Commerce, the governor of New York, and the mayor of New York City. The broad social norm found in many countries and cultures supports voluntary action by a corporation in support of a social good. Not only is such action seen as a way by which business legitimates itself. John Manzoni, a senior executive at British Petroleum, puts it as follows: "Part of the bargain, the social contract which allows companies to be as large as they are, is that they become engaged in the challenges the world faces, rather than dismissing them as someone else's problem."

Today, when many argue that corporate philanthropy is fundamental to a company's license to operate, and the websites of more than 80 percent of the Fortune 500 explicitly describe social endeavors, the time has come to declare the Friedmanite criticism officially moribund. However, even as its legitimacy is now unquestioned, serious issues remain concerning the effectiveness of corporate philanthropy in contributing to the social good.

Corporate social responsibility in Latin America

Felipe Aguero, 2005

Philanthropy is nothing new for business leaders in Latin America. Even in the previous context of a statist sociopolitical matrix, in which all socially oriented expenditure was viewed as an exclusive state responsibility, business leaders promoted donations and foundations, created universities and technical schools and developed social assistance initiatives toward the poorest groups, often alongside church programs. What is new, however, is the discourse of corporate social responsibility, and the flurry of initiatives undertaken under that concept, including the creation of organizations by business leaders with the specific purpose of advancing it.

Corporate social responsibility (CSR) is often presented as distinct from the idea of philanthropy, which is presumed to follow altruistic motivations, with little or no expectation of a direct benefit for the firm, using resources that come from profits and involving only individuals or, at the most, the board of directors. Philanthropy is exerted in fields not necessarily associated to the activity of a particular business or firm. In contrast, CSR, in its ideal version, seeks benefits for the firm that may include image and reputation, improvements in productivity, and sustained earnings while simultaneously pursuing community improvement. It relies primarily on the firm's general budget, equipment and human resources, and not necessarily profits and, still ideally, on the participation of officers and workers at all levels of the firm, and sometimes of shareholders. In this way CSR brings in a more strategic perspective involving planning, targets, impact, and evaluation.

In the language of international meetings and of major foundations involved in the promotion of philanthropy the terms are either used indistinctly or CSR is viewed as one subset of philanthropic activity. In Latin America, the prevalent use of one or another concept to capture both sets of activities varies according to national context and experiences. However, it is the more demanding concept of corporate social responsibility that pervaded the recent discourse on business' social orientation.

The recent adoption of this concept among significant sectors of the business elite might have appeared unlikely in the context of market reforms, increased international competition, and sluggish growth. Milton Friedman's dictum that there is no social responsibility for corporate officials "other than to make as much money for their shareholders as possible," or its updated formulation in *The Economist* – "The proper business of business is business. No apologies required" – could have sufficed as legitimacy buffers to resist or at least postpone the admission of an active social role for business. Yet, and despite the actual gap between discourse and reality, the dissemination of the idea of corporate social responsibility (CSR) has taken off and expanded vigorously across the region.

Beginning in the late 1990s organizations created by business to promote this concept began to sprout throughout the region. The vigorous Instituto Ethos in Brazil was created in 1998, followed by Acción Empresarial in Chile in 1999 and Fundemas in El Salvador in 2000. "Older" organizations, such as the Mexican Center for Philanthropy (Cemefi), created in 1988, or Peru 2021, founded in 1994, began engaging in the promotion of CSR at about the time of the founding of their younger partners in the region. Similar organizations emerged in countries such as Argentina, Colombia, and Panama.

What accounts for the emergence of all this activity in a short period of time and in a context that could not be seen as the most propitious? Perhaps the answer must be sought in the heightened visibility of the private sector in a context provided by a relatively weaker state, the social impact of sluggish and uneven growth, and the inegalitarian consequences of economic reform. Viewed in this way, CSR provides a defensive buffer against the threat of social discontent. At the same time, economic internationalization, accompanied by features of globalization such as the development of transnational networks and movements, has demanded ethical behavior and social responsibility on the part of firms, particularly if these firms export to developed markets or are based in advanced countries. These networks facilitate the circulation of ideas and their reflection in international norms, influencing the expansion of CSR promotion to Latin America.

[. . .]

The origins of CSR in Latin America: a preliminary framework

Three interrelated factors can be posited as the basis for the emergence of CSR in these countries: a) social mobilization or pressures from below; b) changing views among business leaders; and c) developments in management theory and practice. These are presented here in the manner of hypotheses that require further research, especially in terms of the different ways in which they combine in each of the countries of concern.

The factors have operated in the new context of an invigorated business sector after the termination of state-led inward-oriented development; strategies that prevailed in Latin America until two or three decades ago and the promotion of market oriented reforms. The contrast with the situation of business a few decades back is stark. Dependent on the dynamics of the public sector and public policy, business was subdued by controls and regulations ranging from price controls to tariffs through exchange rates, quotas, and wages. Today, although with variation across countries, a much weightier private sector often is the one that sets the tone for the public sector. The change in the balance of power, raising the visibility of business and its leaders, presents new issues of legitimacy and accountability.

Within this context the role of social pressure, business leaders' views, and management concepts in the promotion of CSR in Latin America may be addressed.

Social pressure

Interest in programs that portray business as concerned with social problems must be viewed, in the first place, as a response to social pressure. In fact, some scholars have made it part of the definition of CSR. David Vogel, for instance, views CSR as "those business policies that are primarily undertaken in response to changes in political or societal pressures, norms or expectations." In Latin America, social pressure appears in the context of economic reforms that have had dramatic social effects jointly with enhanced opportunities for political expression of previously suppressed social and political actors. Argentina, Brazil, and Chile saw the end of military rule at different points in the 1980s, and social and political actors that had been severely repressed under those regimes found new opportunities for organization and expression. Except in Chile, neoliberal reforms were pursued only after democratic rule had been attained. Also in Mexico liberalization and eventual democratization of the political regime went along with economic reforms, also opening up avenues for civil society organization and opposition. In all of these cases, high levels of unemployment combined with high rates of poverty and levels of inequality, and often with a dramatic expansion of urban crime and violence, laid bare the shortcomings of a weakened public sector as well as the responsibilities of an ascendant private sector. Business organizations for CSR emerged at about the time in which these pressures were being felt.

At the level of individual firms, business executives became more aware of public scrutiny of the behavior of firms and of a better educated and demanding consumer. Firms increased their resort to consulting in communications and public relations and their attention to public opinion surveys that focus on the public's perception of the behavior of firms and consequence on consumer loyalty. Many businesses also became sensitive to empowered social and civil organizations at the local and national level, and felt urged to propose solutions to social problems in areas adjacent to their particular area of activity and to anticipate crises through the establishment of links to the community. Social pressure from below operates objectively, as an increase in popular mobilization and organization, but most often operates subjectively, as business' anticipated response to a perception of crisis or social pressure, and as awareness of the magnitude and complexity of social problems.

Changing views among business leaders

The initiative of enlightened individuals in the business community and the development of new ideas among significant sectors of this community have helped conceive strategies for business that address its social responsibility in the face of large and complex social problems. In many ways, in some elite sectors, this development may best be captured as a transition from a segmented and particularistically oriented mindset and behavior, to one decidedly more assertive and national-universalistic in orientation. This movement can be presented in Mancur Olson's terms as the passing from a narrower strategy of redistribution to a broader strategy of collective gain; from the pursuit of particularistic gain in a zero-sum game, to the pursuit of gain by collective improvement. Put differently, a stronger and wealthier business sector is freer to think beyond its corporate boundaries and to consider taking on responsibilities that were previously the exclusive domain of the public. Beyond defensive corporate claims, business may now aspire to assume a national leadership role in shaping debates over modes of social organization and coordination, taking on directly the role of disseminating a private, market-based ethos throughout society.

A parallel development has been the strengthening of the role of economists in public policy and political leadership, and, more generally, of a cadre of intellectuals with diverse disciplinary foundations. Business relations with this cadre – its "organic intellectuals" – have helped it advance a view about the connection between an improved social context (stable political relations, an educated work force, expanded consumption opportunities) and business performance. These intellectuals have aided in challenging business to move beyond its corporate frontiers into collective-universalistic pursuits. Along these lines appears the recent development of the notion of social entrepreneurship, supported by business school programs in major US and European universities, a trend which is beginning to develop in Latin America.

Changing views among business leaders are also often the result of religious inspiration. This is the case with Uniapac (International Christian Union of Business Executives), "an ecumenical movement of business executives who take inspiration from the Christian social thinking and ethical principles of Christianity concerning their economic and social responsibilities toward enterprise and society, in order to accomplish their tasks and professional duties." This organization, with members in Latin America, stands for liberalism, globalization, and subsidiarity, and maintains close relations with other organizations similar in its Christian inspiration, including the International Christian Democracy. However, this older Christian organization, dating back to the 1930s, appears to be less influential in the current tide of CSR than are recent strands of more conservative Catholic organizations, such as the Legionarios de Cristo, influential in Mexico and Chile. In most cases, however, CSR promotion is secular in orientation and has often been aided by orientations generated from within early immigrants' associations.

Management theories and practice

A third factor in the emergence of CSR comes from developments in management theory and practice that stress new roles for the corporation and new tasks for effective long-term management that emphasize links with the community. In this view the corporation is a part of society, and responsiveness to the community must be built into the daily practices of the firm and into its management and strategic design. This ultimately makes business sense as is reflected in the ability to attract better quality employees and in its beneficial impact in "human resource management, culture building, and business generation."

In the ideal type presented by these new concepts CSR emerges as business that integrates a concern for ethics, people, the community and the environment both in the daily operations of the firm and in its strategic planning and decision-making process. It ideally engages all or most of its human resources, and includes an internal dimension focused on labor relations, personnel, working standards, and management practices, and an external dimension focused on respect for the environment, a commitment to aiding the community's economic and social development, and the conduct of responsible trade and marketing practices.

[. . .]

The short recent history of the emergence of CSR in Latin America also appears related to crisis: the enduring signs of poverty and inequality in the 1980s and 1990s, in the context of a less able state and a vastly more powerful private sector. Business perceives political and societal pressures, and reacts alongside a network of civil society organizations, think tanks, research centers, and multilateral agencies that circulate, multiply, and legitimize ideas about social responsibility. Across the different countries, the factors listed above combine in different and particular ways, confronting their own specific landmarks of crisis. History, politics, and culture are important factors in establishing these differences.

5.4 New methods and blurring boundaries

Catalytic philanthropy

Mark R. Kramer, 2009

Thomas Siebel does philanthropy differently from other donors. As the founder of the software company Siebel Systems Inc., he is one of a handful of philanthropists who have the resources to devote substantial time and money to charity. His approach and the results he has achieved, however, dramatically distinguish him from most of his peers.

In 2005, while spending time on his Montana ranch, Siebel became concerned about the rampant local use of methamphetamine, or "meth." Meth is a highly addictive and physically destructive drug, and it is a particularly acute problem in rural America. In 2005, Montana had the fifth worst level of meth abuse among all US states. Half of its inmates were imprisoned for meth-related crimes. The direct cost to the state was estimated at nearly $300 million per year, and the cost in human lives and suffering was far greater.

Rather than writing a check to a local nonprofit, Siebel took the time to find out why people become addicted to meth. After learning that first-time users were typically teenagers who were unaware of meth's risks, Siebel created the Meth Project to change teenage perceptions about the drug. He brought together experts and hired a major San Francisco advertising agency to develop a hard-hitting campaign that would reach 80 percent of Montana teens with at least three ads every week.

The ads were world-class: With production budgets of $500,000 to $1 million each, they were directed by leading Hollywood figures such as Alejandro González Iñárritu, director of the Academy Award-nominated film *Babel*. The ad campaign has won 43 awards in national and international advertising competitions.

The ads were gut-wrenching: Tested in focus groups to capture a teenager's attention, they were far more brutal than anything the community had seen on television before. The 30-second spots begin with an ordinary teen whom kids can relate to, and end by showing the badly scarred and disfigured ravages that come from using meth. Teens are shown attacking and robbing their own families, prostituting themselves, or dying from an overdose. In one ad, a boy describes how his mother has always been there for him, while the screen shows him stealing her purse, hitting her, and kicking her away as she screams and desperately tries to grab his leg while he runs out the door.

And the ads were pervasive: Because Montana is a small media market, Siebel's $2 million annual advertising budget generated more than 45,000 television ads, 35,000 radio ads, and 1,000 billboards in the first two years. The Meth Project became the largest purchaser of advertising in the state. The results have been stunning. Between 2005 and 2007, meth use in Montana dropped 45 percent among teens and 72 percent among adults, while meth-related crimes fell 62 percent. The percentage of teenagers who were aware of meth's dangers increased from 25 percent to 93 percent, and teenagers have even begun to dissuade their friends from trying meth. Montana's ranking among US states in meth abuse fell from fifth to 39th.

Siebel has continued the campaign, using teen focus groups to develop new advertising campaigns every nine to 12 months. He has convinced other funders to support the campaign and encouraged schools and community organizations to sponsor anti-meth events. Siebel has also personally lobbied Congress to combat the meth problem. Six other states have adopted the Meth Project's program.

Siebel's success in fighting meth abuse stands in stark contrast to the modest and often indiscernible results that most philanthropists have achieved, whether individually or collectively. Between 1980 and 2005, US annual charitable giving in constant dollars grew by 255 percent and the number of nonprofits more than doubled to 1.3 million. Today, per capita giving in the United States is three times greater than any other country in the world. Yet, during this same 25-year time period, the United States dropped from second to 12th among the 30 countries that are members of the Organisation for Economic Co-Operation and Development (OECD) in basic measures of health, education, and economic opportunity.

To be sure, philanthropy cannot be blamed for the persistence of childhood poverty and failed schools that result from much larger political and economic forces. Without philanthropy, conditions would likely be even worse. Yet whatever benefits philanthropy may provide, it is not delivering the kind of social impact Siebel achieved. If philanthropy is to become an effective way of solving pressing social problems, donors must take a new approach.

Siebel is one of the exemplars of this new approach, but there are others. These exceptional donors – whether foundations, corporations, or individuals – do not write the largest checks, but they do act differently from other donors. They have expanded the toolkit of strategic philanthropy beyond even the most recent thinking of venture philanthropists and social entrepreneurs, creating a new approach to bringing about social change that I call "catalytic philanthropy." Before turning to a discussion of the practices that distinguish this new form of philanthropy, it is important to understand why the conventional approach so rarely produces measurable impact.

Limitations of traditional philanthropy

For most donors, philanthropy is about deciding which nonprofits to support and how much money to give them. These donors effectively delegate to nonprofits all responsibility for devising and implementing solutions to social problems. Despite the sincere dedication and best efforts of those who work in the nonprofit sector, there is little reason to assume that they have the ability to solve society's large-scale problems.

The overwhelming majority of the 1.3 million US nonprofits are extremely small: 90 percent of their annual budgets are under $500,000 and only 1 percent have budgets greater than $10 million. Each nonprofit is capable of helping hundreds or even thousands of people in need, and many of them do so in creative and highly effective ways. Despite their often-heroic efforts, these nonprofits face severe limitations.

Each nonprofit functions alone, pursuing the strategies that it deems best, lacking the infrastructure to learn from one another's best practices, the clout to influence government, or the scale to achieve national impact. A majority of the very largest nonprofits that might have the resources to effect national change are hospitals, universities, and cultural organizations that focus primarily on their own institutional sustainability. Collaboration throughout the sector is almost impossible, as each nonprofit competes for funding by trying to persuade donors that its approach is better than that of any other organization addressing the same issue. Very few systematically track their own impact.

However generous the donors or hardworking the nonprofit staff, there is no assurance – nor even any likelihood – that supporting the underfunded, non-collaborative, and unaccountable approaches of the countless small nonprofits struggling to tackle an issue will actually lead to workable solutions for large-scale social problems. The contributions of conventional donors and the good work of effective nonprofits may temporarily improve matters at a particular place and time, but they are unlikely to create the lasting reform that society so urgently requires.

Four practices of catalytic philanthropy

What is needed is a new approach to philanthropy, one that catalyzes the kind of social change exemplified by Siebel's Meth Project. Over the past decade, the consulting firm that I cofounded, FSG Social Impact Advisors, has studied many examples of this new approach to social change. We have distilled what makes catalytic philanthropists so effective into four distinct practices: They have the ambition to change the world and the courage to accept responsibility for achieving the results they seek; they engage others in a compelling campaign, empowering stakeholders and creating the conditions for collaboration and innovation; they use all of the tools that are available to create change, including unconventional ones from outside the nonprofit sector; and they create actionable knowledge to improve their own effectiveness and to influence the behavior of others.

Each of these practices stands in distinct contrast to the practices that most donors, foundations, and corporations follow today. [. . .] To understand why these four practices are important, each will be considered in turn.

1. Take responsibility for achieving results

Two years ago, the Bill & Melinda Gates Foundation asked FSG to explore why some donors are more effective than others. We interviewed several dozen wealthy donors of different ages and backgrounds, all of whom had been identified by their peers as highly effective, and we found a surprisingly common theme. When these donors first began giving away money, they followed conventional philanthropic practice, responding to those who asked them for funds with little awareness of what impact they actually achieved. They gave large sums to many different organizations and were viewed as prominent philanthropists in their communities, but had not yet distinguished themselves as highly effective donors.

After some time, these donors became involved in an issue of great personal significance: A donor's child was diagnosed with a rare disease; a wilderness preserve a donor hiked in as a child was about to be sold to a developer; or a donor went on a trip to a developing country and was exposed firsthand to a level of poverty and disease that she had never imagined. The urgency of the cause and the intensity of their commitment compelled each of these donors to take an active role in solving the problem.

These newly energized donors became deeply knowledgeable about the issue and actively recruited collaborators, sometimes even creating a new nonprofit to further the cause. The donors stopped thinking about which organizations to support, and started to think about how to solve a specific problem, using every skill, connection, and resource they possessed. The donors formulated clear and practical goals that enabled them to identify the steps needed to succeed. Above all, the donors took responsibility for finding solutions to the problem instead of waiting for the nonprofit sector to approach them with a proposal. Like Siebel's campaign against meth abuse, the difference in impact was remarkable.

[. . .]

Our research suggests that if donors want to solve a problem, they must decide to do so themselves. This doesn't mean that they need to create their own nonprofit or that they should ignore the efforts of others. It does mean that funders have a powerful role to play that goes beyond merely supporting existing nonprofits. Private donors, foundations, and corporations have the clout, connections, and capacity to make things happen in a way that most nonprofits do not. By becoming directly involved and taking personal responsibility for their results, these donors can leverage their personal and professional relationships, initiate public-private partnerships, import projects that have proved successful elsewhere, create new business models, influence government, draw public attention to an issue, coordinate the activities of different nonprofits, and attract fellow funders from around the globe. All of these powerful means for social change are left behind when donors confine themselves to simply writing checks.

Catalytic philanthropists, however, must be as cautious as they are bold. Considerable havoc has been wrought, and billions of dollars wasted, by donors whose success in business or other fields has convinced them that they can single-handedly solve a social problem that no one else has solved before. Philanthropists cannot catalyze change by acting alone or imposing a solution, convinced that they have the answer before they begin. Instead, they must listen to and work with others, enabling stakeholders to develop their own solutions.

2. Mobilize a campaign for change

In "Leading Boldly," an article that Ron Heifetz, John Kania, and I wrote for the winter 2004 issue of the *Stanford Social Innovation Review*, we suggested that many of the problems foundations tackle are adaptive in nature: The people with the problem have to become engaged in solving it for themselves. Teenagers, for example, need to dissuade other teenagers from using meth. In other cases, effective solutions may already be known but cannot be externally imposed on the existing system. It is well known, for example, that better qualified teachers produce better educated students, but the systemic changes needed to act on that simple solution are mind-bogglingly complex. The obstacle isn't that no one knows any answers, but rather that the uncoordinated actions, narrow constraints, and conflicting incentives of different stakeholders and different sectors of society perpetuate the status quo.

Catalytic philanthropy cuts through these divisions by stimulating cross-sector collaborations and mobilizing stakeholders to create shared solutions. Building alliances that create the conditions for a solution to emerge and take hold is a very different pursuit from the usual grantmaking process of trying to direct funds to the one organization that offers the most appealing approach. Systemic reform requires a relentless and unending campaign that galvanizes the attention of the many stakeholders involved and unifies their efforts around the pursuit of a common goal.

[. . .]

Mobilizing and coordinating stakeholders is messier and slower than funding a compelling grant request from a single organization. Systemic change depends on a sustained campaign to increase the capacity and coordination of an entire field, together with greater public awareness and, often, stronger government policies. Catalytic philanthropists have the wherewithal to heighten awareness, raise expectations, and coordinate the many disparate efforts of other funders, nonprofits, corporations, and governments.

3. Use all available tools

The prominence of the US nonprofit sector and the tax deductibility of donations have lulled people into thinking that IRS-sanctioned philanthropy is the only way to solve social problems. Donors have the freedom, however, to complement traditional grantmaking with a wide array of other tools from outside the nonprofit sector, including many that can influence social, economic, and political forces in ways that traditional charitable giving cannot.

Siebel employed an unconventional tool by hiring world-class advertising talent and purchasing prime-time advertising for his anti-meth campaign, rather than accepting the less effective tools of donated public service announcements. Other catalytic philanthropists have used a variety of unconventional tools for social change, including corporate resources, investment capital, advocacy, litigation, and even lobbying [. . .]

[. . .]

4. Create actionable knowledge

Most donors rely on their grant applicants and recipients to provide them with information about the social problems the nonprofit is tackling, focusing their inquiries narrowly on the program to be funded without researching the issue more broadly. Catalytic philanthropists, by contrast, gather knowledge about the problem they are tackling and use this knowledge to inform their own actions and motivate the actions of others. Making knowledge actionable requires more than just gathering and reporting data. The information must also carry emotional appeal to capture people's attention and practical recommendations that can inspire them to action.

The revolution on the frontiers of philanthropy

Lester M. Salamon, 2014

On September 28, 2011, *Microfinance Africa*, a newsletter serving the microfinance industry on the African continent, reported news of an important, if unusual, development designed to help East Africa cope with the region's food shortage and resulting skyrocketing food prices. An unexpected consortium had come together to channel $25 million to a series of small and medium-sized East African agricultural enterprises whose businesses could help link the region's small-holder farmers to improved production and marketing opportunities. Although the US Agency for International Development was a party to this consortium, this was not your normal top-down, government-funded development project. Rather, USAID had teamed up with three foundations (the UK-based Gatsby Charitable Foundation, and the US-based Rockefeller and Gates Foundations), a major US investment firm (J.P. Morgan Social Finance), and Pearl Capital Partners, a private, Kampala-based investment company dedicated to channeling private equity to small-holder agricultural enterprises in Africa.

What may be most unusual about this deal in the current climate of development assistance, philanthropy, and finance, however, is that it is no longer unusual at all. Rather, it is an example of what students of the field have begun referring to as "yin-yang" deals, deals that bring together, as in Chinese thoughts, seemingly contrary forces that turn out to be uniquely capable of producing new life forms when taking advantage of their interdependencies. In the present arrangement, USAID managed to stimulate the investment of $25 million into building a robust agribusiness sector in East Africa with only $1.5 million of its own money, and all of that in the form of technical assistance to small and medium-sized businesses funded out of President Obama's flagship Feed the Future initiative. The investment fund itself was assembled by combining a USAID guarantee of an $8 million loan from J.P. Morgan's Social Finance Unit that was further leveraged by $17 million in equity investments made by the three foundations, which functioned in this deal as "philanthropic banks" rather than traditional grant-making charities.

Sizable yin-yang deals of this sort are slowly becoming the new normal in efforts to combat the enormous social, economic, and environmental problems that confront our world at the present time. And none too soon. With the resources of both governments and traditional philanthropy barely growing or in decline, yet the problems of poverty, ill-health, and environmental degradation ballooning daily, it is increasingly clear that new models for financing and promoting social and environmental objectives have become urgently needed.

Fortunately, a significant revolution appears to be underway on the frontiers of philanthropy that is providing at least a partial, though still embryonic, response to this dilemma. The heart of this revolution is a massive explosion in the tools of philanthropy and social investment, in the instruments and institutions being deployed to mobilize private resources in support of social and environmental objectives. Where earlier such support was limited to charitable grants and gifts made available directly by individuals or through charitable foundations and corporate giving programs, now a bewildering array of new instruments and institutions has surfaced – loans, loan guarantees, private equity, barter arrangements, social stock exchanges, bonds, secondary markets, investment funds, and many more. Indeed, the world of philanthropy seems to be experiencing a Big Bang similar in kind, if not in exact form, to the one thought to have produced the planets and stars of our solar system.

Even a quick glance at the emerging landscape on the frontiers of contemporary philanthropy around the world yields a rich harvest of unfamiliar names and terms: Bovespa in Brazil; Social Capital Partners in Canada; Impact Investment Exchange in Singapore; Acumen Fund, Root Capital, and New Profit in the US; Bridges Ventures, Big Society Capital and NESTA in the UK; Blue Orchard in Switzerland; Aavishkaar International in India; Willow Tree Impact Investors in Dubai; Calvert Foundation; the Schwab Charitable Fund; the Community Reinvestment Fund; community development finance institutions; TechSoup Global; conversion foundation; and many more.

At the core of this enormous proliferation of entities lie four important processes of change. In particular, contemporary philanthropy is moving:

- *Beyond grants*: deploying a variety of new financial tools for promoting social purposes – loans, loan guarantees, equity-type investments, securitization, fixed-income instruments, and, most recently, social-impact bonds.
- *Beyond foundations*: creating a host of new actors as the institutional structures through which social-purpose finance is proceeding – capital aggregators, secondary markets, social stock exchanges, social enterprise brokers, internet portals, to name just a few.
- *Beyond bequests*: forming charitable or social-purpose capital pools not simply through the gifts of wealthy individuals, but also from the privatization of formerly public or quasi-public assets or the establishment of specialized social-purpose investment funds.
- *Beyond cash*: utilizing new barter arrangements and internet capabilities to facilitate the giving not just of money, but of a variety of in-kind forms of assistance, whether it be volunteer time or computer hardware and software.

Behind these movements is a common imperative, usefully summarized in a single word: *leverage*. Leverage is the mechanism that allows limited energy to be translated into greater power. It is what allowed Archimedes to claim that, given a lever and a place to stand, he could "move the whole world." In the philanthropic context it means finding a way to go beyond the limited flow of charitable resources generated by the earnings of foundation assets or the annual contributions of individuals to catalyze for social and environmental purposes some portion of the far more enormous investment assets resident in banks, pensions funds, insurance companies, mutual funds, and the accounts of high net worth individuals.

The upshot is the emergence of a "new frontier" of philanthropy and social investing that differs from twentieth-century philanthropy in at least four ways. It is:

- *More diverse*, involving a wider variety of institutions, instruments, and sources of support.
- *More entrepreneurial*, moving beyond "grant-making," the giving resources, to capture the possibilities for greater leverage that comes from adopting an investment orientation, focusing more heavily on measurable results, and generating a blend of economic, as well as social, returns.
- *More global*, engaging problems on an international scale and applying models developed in cross-national settings.
- *More collaborative*, interacting explicitly not only with the broader civil society sector, but also with new social ventures serving the "bottom of the pyramid," as well as with a broad array of private financial institutions and government agencies.

The result, as outlined in Table 5.1, is a new paradigm emerging on the frontiers of philanthropy and social investing. Where traditional philanthropy relied chiefly on individuals, foundations, and corporate philanthropy programs, the new frontiers of philanthropy engage a broad assortment of private financial institutions, including banks, pension funds, insurance companies, investment advisors, specialized investment funds, and foundations that function as philanthropic banks. Whereas traditional philanthropy concentrated mostly on operating revenue, the new frontiers concentrate far more heavily on investment capital, which funds long-term development. Whereas traditional philanthropy channels its assistance almost exclusively to nonprofit organizations, the new frontiers support as well a wide assortment of social enterprises, cooperatives, and other hybrid organizations. Whereas traditional philanthropy brings a charity perspective to its works, focusing exclusively, or at least chiefly, on social return, actors on the new frontier of philanthropy bring an investment orientation, focusing on social and financial return and seeking to build self-sustaining systems that bring permanent solutions. Whereas traditional philanthropy mobilizes a relatively small share of its own resources, the new frontiers of philanthropy leverage the deeper reservoirs of resources resident in the private capital markets. And whereas traditional philanthropy has historically tended to be satisfied with *output* measures, the new frontiers put greater emphasis on reliable *outcome* metrics.

Table 5.1 The *new frontiers of philanthropy* paradigm

Philanthropy = "The provision of private resources for social or environmental purposes"	
Traditional philanthropy	*New frontiers of philanthropy*
Foundations, individuals	Individuals and institutional investors
Operating income	Investment capital
Grants	Diverse financial instruments/capital tranches
Nonprofits	Nonprofits + social ventures
Social return	Social + financial return
Limited leverage	Expanded leverage
Output focus	Outcome focus/metrics

To be sure, these differences are hardly universal. What is more, the changes are far from fully developed. But neither are they trivial. Indeed, as reflected in Figure 5.1, a complex social-purpose finance ecosystem is emerging to channel funds from banks, pension funds, insurance companies, foundations, high net worth individuals, and others through a variety of social-impact investment organizations, support institutions, and new types of grantmakers, to an increasingly diverse set of nonprofits, social ventures, social cooperatives, and related organizations to achieve poverty alleviation, environmental improvement, improved health and environment, strengthened civil society organizations, and improved life chances.

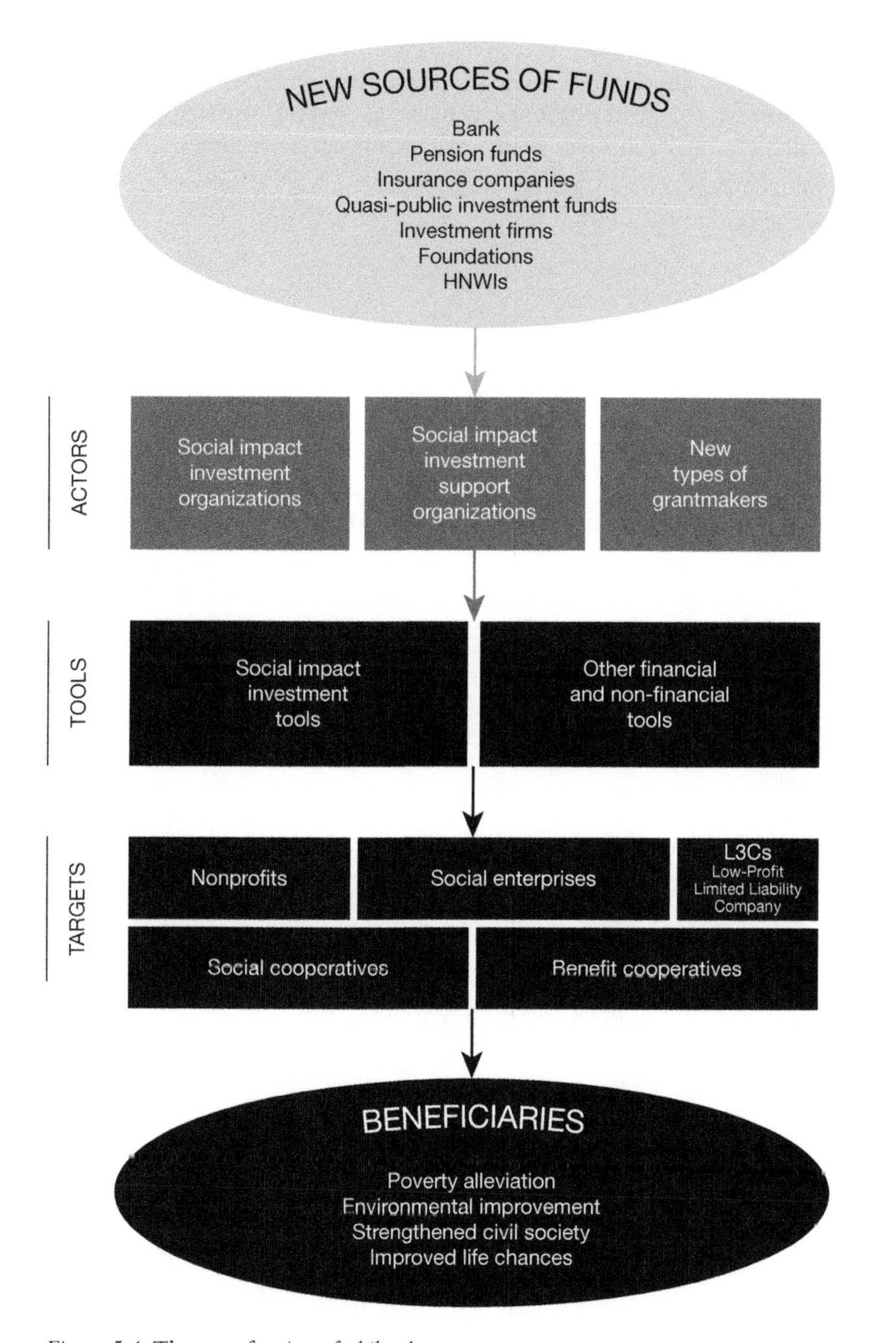

Figure 5.1 The *new frontiers of philanthropy* ecosystem

[. . .]

While the changes under way are inspiring and by no means trivial, however, they remain scattered and largely uncharted in any systematic fashion. Individual practitioners typically have a handle on one or another of the relevant innovations, but the full scope of the changes has yet to be visualized, let alone pulled together and examined in a systematic way. Even the terminology used to depict these developments is in flux. Established terms such as "program-related investments" (PRIs), "mission investing," "market-rate investments," all of which tended to apply narrowly to foundations, have recently been superseded by the term "impact investing," which itself covers only a portion of the emerging field and involves its own significant ambiguities.

Impact investing and blended value

Antony Bugg-Levine and Jed Emerson, 2011

A mighty wave

- An investor in Hong Kong wants to secure her children's economic future. But she also wants to use her wealth to address the social and environmental challenges she cares about and thereby leave a deeper legacy. She becomes convinced that simply giving her money away cannot be the only way she can make a difference. So she redirects her assets into investments that preserve her wealth and also directly tackle problems of poverty and environmental degradation.
- A group of friends volunteering for a nonprofit organization look for ways to help reduce poverty in rural Mexico. They stumble onto the idea of lending small amounts of money to poor people who cannot access loans from banks. But they struggle to secure donations and instead take on loans. When their success exhausts their available charitable capital, they convert to a for-profit enterprise and eventually hold an initial public offering on the Mexican stock market that raises more than $300 million. Suddenly they find themselves in the middle of a global media storm, lionized as saviors and vilified as greedy capitalists.
- A senior investment banker in New York decides to shift career tracks to contribute to the fight against global poverty. But instead of leaving Wall Street to do it, she sets up a unit in one of the world's leading finance firms to provide banking services to enterprises around the world that tackle the issue of poverty. Within a week of the announcement of the unit's creation, nearly a thousand employees of the investment bank contact her to offer to collaborate in this work.

It's easy to miss these pioneers in the crowded and complex worlds of investment and traditional philanthropy. After all, a lot has been going on in both worlds recently. And maybe these individuals are just eccentrics we can easily ignore. Perhaps they are just barely visible and unimportant ripples atop the roiling waves we seem to find ourselves in so often these days.

We believe they are something more. These ripples are related and part of a shifting tide. These three people are pioneers in the rapidly evolving global industry of impact investing [. . .] Each of them is discovering a new realm of possibility. They are maximizing the total value of their investments and organizations, creating a high-octane blend of economic performance and sustained environmental and social impact. And their discoveries are upending long-held and jealously guarded beliefs that profit-making and charitable activities must be kept separate in isolated silos of thinking and practice.

These are the early signs of a long-forming undercurrent that is poised to reshape how society deploys its resources and solves its problems. As Robert Kennedy famously noted, even tiny ripples can become a powerful current that sweeps aside the established order when they are multiplied and brought together. Powerful in its simplicity, the idea of impact investing for blended value – investment strategies that generate financial return while intentionally improving social and environmental conditions – is disrupting a world organized around the competing principle that for-profit investments should seek only to pursue financial return, while people who care about social problems should give away their money or wait for the government to step in. But one person's disruption is another's opportunity. Impact investing pioneers are jumping into these fast-flowing waters, creating new enterprises, ideas, and approaches to match the aspirations of investors and entrepreneurs eager to harness the full power of capital.

[. . .]

The grand global swell of impact investing is growing as the dynamics that precipitated the movement gather force. We cannot predict what will happen when this water crests. But we will all be well served to develop the insights and strategies that can ready us for the changes it will bring.

Impact investing for blended value: a definition

Impact investing recognizes that investments can pursue financial returns while also intentionally addressing social and environmental challenges. Despite, or perhaps because of, this simplicity, it can seem threatening to some people. Many mainstream investors reject the idea that they should pay attention to the social impact of their investing, insisting instead that these considerations be left to governments and charities. And for their part, most traditional philanthropists reject the idea that they should use their investments to advance their mission or that businesses generating profits have a right to stand alongside philanthropy and civil society in the noble work of promoting equality and justice.

But impact investing is not a modern aberration. The idea that our investment decisions can have an impact on the wider world beyond financial return did not begin when Jed first described "blended value" in 2000 or when Antony was part of the group that coined the phrase "impact investing" seven years later. In many ways, it reconnects with a centuries-old tradition that held the owners of wealth responsible for the welfare of their broader community. It is a story that goes back at least to the Quakers in seventeenth-century England who sought to align their investment and purchase decisions with their values. It is linked as well with the Shaker congregations in the 1800s that launched businesses in alignment with social values and to fund religious communities. It traces its arc through the environmental movement of the 1970s, the anti-apartheid divestment campaigns of the 1980s, and the modern fair trade consumer and socially responsible investing movements. In one form or another, aspects of impact investing have been playing themselves out on the global stage for centuries. What we see before us today is simply its latest iteration, linking economics with social and environmental aspects of the human experience.

What is new is that impact investors are profoundly optimistic about the role business can play in advancing the common good and the leverage that social enterprises can achieve by applying financial tools. We see business practices as a powerful force that can be harnessed for good rather than a necessary evil that must be curtailed.

This optimism is not ideological: we are not capitalist triumphalists, eager to spread the gospel of free market greatness to the far corners of the world. Moreover, we are not ignorant of the limits of market-based strategies for social change. But we have observed what is going on in diverse corners of an increasingly connected planet. And we cannot help but marvel at how many people in both rich and poor countries enjoy a better life because of successful profit-seeking investment.

We also know that new challenges require new approaches. Every one of us is confronting the shared reality that regardless of who is in political office or what the latest social trend is, our social and environmental challenges are too vast and our financial resources too limited for our current approaches to work. We can no longer afford to waste capital and talent by organizing ourselves around the separate poles of financial return and social good, which forces us to play the middle against itself. Instead blended value offers a new way to integrate our activity around the recognition that we do not seek appropriate wealth or social justice; rather, we seek both.

We are neither purely economic creatures nor social beings. By extension, all of our organizations have elements of financial, social, and environmental performance embedded within them, regardless of whether they are for profit or nonprofit. The sooner we recognize that and organize our public persona and institutions around this basic, seemingly self-evident truth, the sooner we will be able to move beyond the bifurcated approaches to both investing and social change that have dominated our world over past centuries. They have locked us into supposed solutions that have failed to consistently move our communities into a sustainable, just, and personally powerful future.

[. . .]

What an impact investment is

Defining exactly what is (and what is not) an impact investment has become increasingly important as the term has taken off. And, unfortunately, many people approaching this task are still locked in old language and mind-sets. They are used to orienting themselves around financial return and therefore define impact investments as below-market-rate investments that trade off financial return for social impact. Although these investments certainly form part of the impact-investing universe, the heart of the movement is the reorientation around blended value as the organizing principle of our work: using capital to maximize total, combined value with multiple aspects of performance.

For now, the industry is coalescing around a definition that focuses on intention and the attention an investor pays to blended value returns: impact investors intend to create positive impact alongside various levels of financial return, both managing and measuring the blended value they create.

What does this mean in practice?

All investments are capable of generating positive social impact, but some are closer to the action than others. Public equity investors can generate impact, for example, through a shareholder advocacy campaign, and investors pursuing this approach have had meaningful impact on some corporate practices. Indeed, virtually all the impact investors we know place a portion of their portfolio in impact-oriented public equity funds. In this way, impact investing is a strategy across all asset classes. But the shortest line we can draw between our investment choices and their social impact is to place capital directly into companies and projects and make loans and private equity investments as the vehicles to do so. Therefore, the impact investing movement tends to focus on venture investing, private equity and direct lending because of the unmatched power of these investments to generate social impact.

Of course, not all venture or private equity investments are impact investments, even when they seem to focus on high-potential sectors or geographies. Simply putting capital to work in a poor country does not qualify an investor as an impact investor. Funds and firms earning a seat at the impact investment table focus on strategies that intentionally seek to uplift rather than exploit poor customers and treat impact reporting as a central business management practice – not an afterthought for external reporting and marketing. Similarly, a clean energy investment that inadvertently destroys critical habitat could destroy rather than create value. These distinctions matter to impact investors who are developing strategies to allocate capital where it can generate the most integrated, blended value.

What blended value is

If impact investing is what we do, blended value is what we produce. Value is what gets created when investors invest and organizations act to pursue their mission. All organizations, for-profit and nonprofit alike, create value that consists of economic, social, and environmental components. All investors, whether market rate, charitable, or some mix of the two, generate all three forms of value. But somehow this fundamental truth has been lost to a world that sees value as being only economic (created by for-profit companies) or social (created by nonprofit organizations or government). And most business managers, as well as investors, miss out on the opportunity to capture their total value potential by not managing for blended value on an intentional strategic basis.

The concept of blended value reintegrates our understanding of value as a nondivisible combination of these three elements. Blended value is its own distinct force to be understood, measured, and sought. It is not just something we can achieve by adding up its component parts because it is more than the sum of the parts of a triple-bottom-line analysis. At the same time, blended value does not mean one loses the distinct taste and flavors of the component ingredients of value creation. It is not a blurring of these components, and the components do not lose their unique attributes and characteristics. It is not a weaving together of separate parts, but rather a recombining of core elements that, through their natural integration, transform into a new, stronger, and more nuanced organizational and capital structure. Blended value is the recognition that capital, community, and commerce can create more than their sum and is less a math exercise of zero-sum pluses and minuses than a physics equation of an expanding universe of investments in organizations, people, and planet.

The coming disruption

Impact investing has gained its foothold following an historic period of upheaval in the capital markets. In fact, the financial crisis of 2008 precipitated the largest impact investments of all time. Just like pioneering impact investors, governments around the world recognized the need and opportunity to go beyond donations in their scramble to protect jobs and social stability by shoring up private companies. They invested tens of billions in loans, equity investments, and guarantees, the basic tools of the impact investors that we describe extensively in this book. And the forces that set off the first ripples of the impact investing movement continue to grow:

- With gathering intensity, wealthy investors and philanthropists have become impatient with old approaches in the face of intractable and increasingly visible environmental damage and poverty.
- A new generation of business and socially savvy entrepreneurs is launching ventures across an array of geographies and sectors that creatively structure investment capital to tackle society's challenges and pursue new market opportunities.
- Cash-strapped governments are redefining their relationships with private business as demographic realities force a re-examination of fundamental components of the social contract.
- The rise of online social networking platforms creates the potential for thousands of investors to talk, share, and engage with each other as they identify, vet, and place investments in social entrepreneurs the world over.

These forces are finding their outlet in impact investing for blended value. Implementing this simple concept is not easy. Although impact investors see the opportunities in an integrated approach, our systems have not yet caught up. Frustration abounds as the old only grudgingly gives way to the new.

The current of impact investing is washing along the shores of a bifurcated world still organized to separate profit making from social and environmental problem solving. For now, this bifurcated world channels the energy of impact investors into the hidden pools and underground rivers on the margins of mainstream investment and philanthropic activity. But water has a powerful ability to reshape the world it flows through. The gathering weight of impact investment activity is wearing away the bedrock of seemingly immovable institutions and investment practices.

[. . .]

The power of capital

We have seen the true power of capital:

- It is the green of heavy banana bunches on the slopes of Mt. Kenya in the dry season, watered with irrigation equipment funded by a microloan.
- It is the anticipation on the face of the woman on Chicago's South Side who tapped a local community development fund to launch her bakery.
- It is the professional pride of a foundation program officer whose investment in an educational services company in New York has helped provide teachers with the tools they need to raise students' performance to heights that grants alone never could.
- It is the satisfaction of a family in India that has just moved out of a slum into a new brick home purchased from an equity-backed, low-income-housing developer.
- It is the light shining through the window of a home in rural Nicaragua that is powered by a micro-hydropower plant built with investment from a renewable energy fund.

- It is the investment banker in London signing the closing documents for a new fund that will channel client capital into businesses that provide affordable, essential services to poor people.

These are the realities we can create when we remove our blinders and realize the potential for blended value all around us. There are some dear paths and promising trails but no one way to go or right way to execute the strategy.

Social enterprises and impact investing in China

Weiyan Zhou et al., 2013

Social enterprises, a calling of our times

In the past few years, an increasing number of commercial entrepreneurs are no longer satisfied with pure economic returns. Instead, they hope to make a significant social impact by using commercial means to address social issues. At the other end of the spectrum, an increasing number of nonprofit organizations are trying to decrease their dependence on traditional donations and achieve financial sustainability. The first wave of Chinese social enterprises has arisen from the confluence of these forces. Simply put, social enterprises use commercial methods to achieve social goals. But why does our society need social enterprises?

First, market imperfections exist. The market mechanism inherently contains many limitations, and there are many issues that the market cannot solve. Each player in the market pursues profit, often overlooking social needs in order to maximize returns. A new approach is needed to address these social issues.

Second, government alone cannot solve all problems confronting society. Government resources are limited and direct income from taxation can only be directed towards a finite number of projects. In addition, operational inefficiencies exist within the government, and it is unrealistic to expect the government to resolve all social issues.

Third, it is unrealistic to expect NGOs to solve societal issues. NGOs are by and large charity organizations. Charity organizations require a continuous flow of donations for their operations. Therefore, their impact is limited and dependent on the continuous inflow of funding. Such an organization cannot solve many problems that society faces at present.

If government, NGOs, and businesses cannot solve these problems, then we need a new form of solution. Social enterprises are born in this environment. Social entrepreneurs have begun to appear en masse, social impact investors are eager to participate, academia is heavily interested, local governments have begun experimenting with social enterprise incubators, and the media is calling for a spirit of social entrepreneurship. After years of preparation, a group of outstanding social entrepreneurs and social impact investors are emerging.

Yet, the definition of "social enterprise" in China remains nebulous. "Social enterprises" operate in many different areas using many different operational models. A social enterprise may be a nonprofit organization employing a business's operational management model. Or it could be a financially profitable organization transitioning into the nonprofit area. It could also involve joint investments by several nonprofit organizations in order to achieve social objectives created by a for-profit company. The definition of "social enterprise" in China is still being heatedly debated.

[. . .]

Chinese social enterprise development stage, distinguishing characteristics, and operational scope

[. . .]

In recent years, social enterprise member organizations, incubators, and conferences continue to appear. As a result of advocacy by the media, capacity-building by foundations, and incubation by businesses and various sources of capital, the field of Chinese social enterprise has begun to develop. Social enterprises have a short development history in China. At present, there is no uniform definition and concept for social enterprise. If we borrow from the international standard of social enterprises, as of now, there are only a handful of strictly defined social enterprises of real scale in China. According to our interview with social enterprises, their distinguishing characteristics are the following:

- A significant portion of social enterprises transitioned from NGOs. Possible reasons include: first, NGOs share social enterprises' strong sense of social mission; second, NGOs have motivation to transition due to funding constraints; third, many of the British Council's training participants came from the NGO community. NGO-turned-social enterprises typically work in their traditional sectors of poverty alleviation and support for disadvantaged groups. These are similar to the sectors they had been in as NGOs. The successful transition of an NGO depends largely on leadership capacity. The largest challenge to NGO-turned-social enterprises is the lack of operational business experience, talent, and infrastructure. There is also a large difference between the NGO and business culture, resulting in failure for a significant number of the NGOs attempting transformation.
- Some social enterprises at inception did not classify themselves as "social enterprises," but the organization's mission statement clearly showed such a value orientation. One example is Global Leadership Adventures (GLA). Their founders did not know the concept of social entrepreneurship. The business model of GLA is through organizing youth training camps to participate in volunteer projects in poor countries with the goal of cultivating young people's compassion and sense of social responsibility. However, this is an organization with the potential to be a social enterprise. For this type of organization, the founders typically have a certain amount of business operational experience, but are not overly restricted by rules and possess innovative thinking.
- Unclear profit distribution model. An important metric for the current international definition of social enterprise is the distribution of profits. As far as China is concerned, if social enterprises are registered as a civil non-enterprise unit, according to Chinese law, civil non-enterprise units cannot pay dividends. For example, the Beijing Fuping Development Institute is founded by a number of shareholders and operates according to market rules. They have two subsidiary microfinance companies with an annual profit of 3 million RMB, and Fuping Corporation has an annual profit of 300,000 RMB. However, profits are re-invested into the development of the organization and, since its establishment in 2002, Fuping has not paid any dividends.

[. . .]

- Most social enterprises interviewed are relatively small, and few have annual turnover of more than 1 million RMB. This is mainly because social enterprises are still in their infancy – most are no more than three years old – and have limited funding and experience, and a profit model that still needs to be affirmed. Many NGO-turned-social enterprises must maintain financial sustainability through diverse revenue streams such as donations, government procurement, and sales revenue.

[. . .]

China social impact investment development

Rapid growth of social impact investment institutions

In recent years, with the appearance of different types of impact investors, there is a rapid growth in the establishment of specialized social venture capital funds. At the same time, an increasing number of social impact venture capital case studies have been written, proving the practical feasibility of such funds.

[. . .]

China's earliest social impact investors came from philanthropy, typically from traditional private foundations. Narada Foundation serves as an example. The mission of Narada Foundation is the promotion of social innovation and the development of a civil society. It specifies in its mission statement that it will: "prioritize the public interest. Public interest takes precedence over any direct or potential interest of companies or individuals." Most foundations resemble Narada in their prioritization of public interest. For them, business profits only serve as capital to support the sustainable development of the foundations' public interest projects. These types of foundations do not conform to the "triple standard," as they do not prioritize social and economic goals equally. YouChange Foundation (China Social Entrepreneur Foundation) was founded on the combined support of many business entrepreneurs, and YouChange's council members include the Chairman of Hong Kong Sino Group Huang Zhixiang, the Chairman of Taikang Life Insurance Chen Dongsheng, among others. Following the trend of foundations supporting social entrepreneurship, YouChange, very early on, began directing financial support, know-how and other social resources towards eligible social enterprises, non-profit organizations, and research institutions. YouChange uses long-term sustainable social value as the primary measure of return on investment. As such, the concept of YouChange is very close to the standard definition of "impact investment." Another of YouChange's innovations is its establishment of its own asset management company. It hopes to invest the foundation's reserve funds in order to ensure the safety of the fund under management and to maximize the value-added benefit. This method of investing and expanding the funds of high net worth individuals into public welfare projects using standard capital market operations may in the future become a widely adopted method of investing business profits. The "patient capital," under this type of management, can better focus on producing social benefits, allowing a certain leeway for producing economic returns.

As increasing domestic attention turns to public welfare and charity, overseas foundations have also begun participating in the China market, leveraging their relatively mature social impact investment techniques. The SOW Asia Foundation uses humanity as its key value guideline for investment decisions. SOW Asia focuses on education, environment, and poverty alleviation. In 2009, SOW Asia invested in the Shanghai-based environmental technology company GIGAbase. In addition to supporting

GIGAbase with a five-year interest-free loan, SOW Asia also used its networks to help the GIGAbase (a WOFE, wholly owned foreign enterprise) to overcome its legal and technological issues.

Since 2010, there has been continuous establishment of private equity and venture capital funds focused on social enterprise. Chinese impact investing, thus, is no longer pure philanthropy but has also begun exhibiting characteristics of commercial investment. In 2012, the China team of the World Resources Institute founded the China Impact Fund. It is China's first impact fund that specializes in financing and accelerating small and medium-sized enterprises (SMEs) providing environmentally friendly products and services as well as start-up companies with an environmental value proposition for the country's Base of Pyramid (BoP) population, primarily those in sustainable land use, clean energy and water access. In March of the same year, Xinhu Group, Amity Foundation, and Yu Venture Philanthropy co-founded Xinhu-Yu Venture Philanthropy Fund. Xinhu-Yu's founding capital is 10 million RMB, managed by Yu Venture Philanthropy. Through start-up capital and operational management support, the Xinhu-YU VP Fund aims to help China's high-potential social enterprises achieve social impact and scale up their operations.

Giving circles are changing philanthropy

Angela M. Eikenberry, 2006

There has been revived attention to community in recent years especially at the local level in the United States. Embedded within this larger societal focus, several claim a new era has begun in American philanthropy. This "new philanthropy" is unique in that it is more engaged, guided by individual donors with an emphasis on collaboration; hands-on, unconventional modes of giving and volunteering; and a focus on small organizations and grassroots, entrepreneurial problem solving. Leading the shift in philanthropy are what some have called "new and emerging donors." Dissatisfied with the mainstream approach to philanthropy, these donors have sought out a more engaged philanthropy. As noted by one of these donors, "the traditional approach of writing a check to a charitable organization or serving on a board did not seem very fulfilling. There was a desire to be more engaged in the process of giving back."

A funding mechanism to emerge within this environment is the "giving circle." A *giving circle* has been described as a cross between a book club and an investment group and entails individuals "pooling their resources in support of organizations of mutual interest." More than this, as discussed in more detail below, giving circles include social, educational, and engagement components that seem to connect participants to community, perhaps to a greater degree than other forms of philanthropy.

[. . .]

Giving circles are changing philanthropy

Data indicate that giving circles generally attract younger (younger than age 40 years) and female participants, thereby bringing "new money" to the (organized) philanthropic table. However, for those who have already been philanthropically active, participation serves to increase members' level of giving and extend their giving to organizations with which they were not previously familiar. In addition, through participation, members are more thoughtful, focused, and strategic in their giving inside and outside of the giving circle. Because they begin to see their giving in the context of issues and needs in the community, in which they want to have some impact, their donations are more targeted. For this reason, members say they have started giving fewer, but larger gifts. This is especially the case for small group and formal organization members.

There are also new relationships being formed between giving circle members and nonprofit professionals in the community. This takes place inside the giving circle as several nonprofit professionals are participating in giving circles as members. Beyond this, however, are the new links being made between giving circle members and nonprofit staff who head organizations funded by the giving circle. The interactions take place when nonprofit professionals meet with giving circle members at a site visit, through guest speaking or presentations at meetings, at receptions or events, through informal meetings over lunch, or when a giving circle member volunteers with a nonprofit organization. Some members also work directly with nonprofit professionals as they create proposals to submit to the giving circle for funding. Through these encounters, giving circle members become networked into the nonprofit and philanthropic sector to a degree perhaps only open to major donors previously. This has served to expand the understanding giving circle members have regarding the needs of nonprofit organizations and the issues and problems they are trying to address.

[. . .]

Giving circles are something different

What makes giving circles unique? This question can be answered by looking at their key characteristics and why people say they have joined a giving circle. First, giving circles appear to share varying degrees of six major characteristics. They tend to:

1. Pool funds – This is often but not always in equal amounts from each member, ranging from $25 in loose networks to $5,000 or more in small and formal groups. Several giving circles also raise money from outside their membership.
2. Give away resources – This includes giving money, in-kind gifts, and in some cases members' time and talents to mostly small, local nonprofit organizations or to individuals in need or doing good works. Funding tends to go to fewer organizations for (relatively) larger amounts, and there seems to be a split in funding either capacity building and day-to-day operations or programs and projects. Several of those interviewed noted the difficulty their giving circle had in finding appropriate fundees to match funding objectives.
3. Educate members about philanthropy and issues in the community – Education takes place informally through the running of the giving circle and giving away of money – that is, learning about the grantmaking process, going on site visits, and so on – and formally through educational sessions such as workshops, seminars, and presentations by guest speakers.
4. Provide a social dimension – This social aspect varies in importance depending on the type of giving circle. For some, it is a primary focus – as in many women's and young leader giving circles – whereas for others it is very much peripheral to the task of giving and volunteering. By default, when a group of people come together to do anything, there is social interaction; however, some groups are very intentional about providing networking and other social opportunities for members.
5. Engage members in volunteering – Nearly all giving circles are run by volunteers, though some have staff or receive administrative support from elsewhere. A few giving circles also encourage or require direct volunteer engagement with nonprofit agencies. This volunteering tends to be at a professional or administrative level.
6. Maintain their independence – Giving circles are typically not tied to any one charity, though some (as donor-advised funds) do rely on community foundations to be fiscal agents and provide administrative support. However, it is the donors, rather than philanthropic professionals, who decide to what charities or individuals funds should be distributed. This is a new way of thinking about philanthropy that gets beyond particularistic, institutional fundraising.

[. . .]

If one were to look at each of these key characteristics independently, they certainly do not seem like unique or new contributions to philanthropy (one can see similarities in Women's Clubs of the Progressive Era and Kiwanis or Rotary, for example); however, the environment in which they have emerged and in which they operate – a philanthropic sector that is increasingly modernized and where voluntary associations are losing numbers rapidly – and the combination of all six aspects are new for today's philanthropy. What is also unique is the underlying, express purpose for creating giving circles: to give away money for community betterment. Earlier institutions such as Women's Clubs and Rotaries often did not start or sustain such a focus; the philanthropic aspect either emerged later or was secondary to the main intent of the group.

One could argue that this is old wine in new bottles (or even new wine in old bottles); however, for those participating in the giving circle, this is a new and exciting way to be more engaged in their giving. Overall, compared with other philanthropic mechanisms, those interviewed see giving circles as "something different." Compared to individual check writing or giving individually through donor-advised funds, it is a more engaged, personal process.

Technology and the future of philanthropy

Lucy Bernholz, Edward Skloot and Barry Varela, 2010

Introduction

A decade ago, the landscape of philanthropy was relatively simple. There were foundations – private, community, and corporate – that awarded grants to nonprofits. Some of the larger staffed foundations also offered "technical assistance" to their grantees and undertook other activities such as convening meetings, engaging in advocacy, and financing litigation. Community foundations administered unrestricted, restricted, and donor-advised funds. Individuals gave money to nonprofits as well, mainly through personal checks or cash (while living) and bequests (upon death).

Ten years ago, givers both institutional and individual gathered information about nonprofits mainly through word-of-mouth. There was no easy way for foundation executives, let alone average citizens, to compare the financial health or budget-allocation practices of different organizations. Today, ratings services like Charity Navigator and Charity Guide assemble, analyze, and make available data on tens of thousands of organizations.

Ten years ago, commercial investment firms were small players on the philanthropic landscape. Today, companies like Charles Schwab and Fidelity Investments offer wide ranges of products for donors, including advised funds, foundation management services, and socially responsible investment vehicles.

Ten years ago, socially responsible investment was a niche concern mainly of universities, labor unions, and a few pension funds. Today, socially responsible investment accounts for more than 10 percent of professionally managed investment funds and is expected to total $3 trillion by next year.

Ten years ago, individual citizens were unable to contribute directly in response to a natural disaster like the 2001 Gujarat, India, earthquake. The best they could do was send money to a large international nonprofit like the American Red Cross. Today, a worldwide community of "crisis mappers," using satellite imagery and on-the-ground information reported via cell phone, helps coordinate responses to complex humanitarian emergencies.

Ten years ago, microfinance was entirely top-down – from large institutional lenders to small borrowers. Today, anyone can lend $25 to entrepreneurs located anywhere on the globe.

Information networks – the Internet primarily, and increasingly SMS (text-messaging) and 3G (smart-phone) cell phone technologies – are overturning core practices of philanthropic foundations and individuals. Enormous databases and powerful new visualization tools can be accessed instantly by anyone, at any time. A decade of experimentation in online giving, social enterprise, and collaboration has brought us to a place from which innovation around enterprise forms, governance, and finance will only accelerate.

The legal scholar Yochai Benkler has observed that the "networked information economy" that emerged over the past two decades is rooted in a "communications environment built on cheap processors with high computational capabilities, interconnected in a pervasive network" (i.e., the Internet) and is "centered on information (financial services, accounting, software, science) and cultural (films, music) production." The shift from a centralized, top-down, often impenetrable information economy to a networked information economy has allowed "nonmarket, nonproprietary motivations and organizational forms [to become] more important to the information production system." It has also enabled "the rise of effective, large-scale cooperative efforts – peer production of information, knowledge, and culture."

As we scan the landscape of philanthropy, we'll see these themes – the importance of *nonmarket, nonproprietary motivations and organizational forms* and the emergence of *effective, large-scale cooperative efforts* – lurking constantly just below the surface.

The widespread availability of broadband Internet access and the near ubiquity of SMS and 3G cell phone networks give everyone the tools of both production and consumption. They expand individuals' sense of empowerment and lead to profound changes in expectations and norms. What information matters to funders and nonprofits? Who has it? Who owns it? How do we share it? How do we collaborate around common issues? How quickly can individuals and groups act when information is accessible 24/7?

In 1911, Andrew Carnegie created a general-purpose philanthropic entity – the foundation in its modern form. Two years later, John D. Rockefeller established the Rockefeller Foundation. Both men found that, to provide money and know-how in support of the social good, they needed to create centralized, vertically integrated institutions modeled on the big businesses (steel, oil) from which their fortunes derived. This institutional structure has remained the predominant model for organized philanthropy for almost a century. Today, peer-supported, data-informed, passion-activated, and technology-enabled networks represent a new structural form in philanthropy, and the institutions that support them will need to be as flexible, scalable, and portable as the networks they serve.

On the cusp of the first modern foundation's centennial, we may be looking at the dawn of a new form of organizing, giving, and governing that is better informed, more aware of complex systems, more collaborative, more personal, more nimble, and ultimately, perhaps, more effective.

Philanthropy's long tails

The *long tail* is a marketing strategy that connects products that have relatively small customer bases to those customers. Large companies such as Amazon and Netflix service the long tail by stocking not only very popular titles like the latest Dan Brown novel or Jim Carrey movie – products that may have millions of customers – but also thousands of things like poetry collections and documentaries: products that may have only a few hundred customers each. Cumulatively, the long tail of books sold by Amazon – ten copies of a scholarly study here, twenty copies of a memoir there – exceeds the sales of bestsellers.

In the same way that Amazon allows the 200 individuals in the world who are interested in reading about some esoteric topic find the 10 books written on that topic, online philanthropy marketplaces allow individuals to find, evaluate, and invest in or fund the small enterprise or project that is of interest to them. And conversely, online marketplaces allow the small enterprise to find the few individuals willing to invest in or fund it. The long tail of philanthropy describes this dispersion of resources contributed for social good: millions of people, each providing small amounts of money to tens of thousands of enterprises.

Figure 5.2, "The long tail of giving," shows how the funder market is organized. (Figures drawn from the Foundation Center's *Foundation Directory Online*.) In 2008, the 400 largest foundation givers ranged from the Gates Foundation, which gave $2.8 billion, to the Greater St. Louis Community Foundation, which gave $14.4 million; cumulatively, the 400 gave $22.2 billion. The 60 largest individual donors ranged from the late Leona Helmsley, who left $5.2 billion to create a charitable foundation, to Oscar Tang, who gave $25 million to Phillips Andover Academy; cumulatively, the 60 gave $10.6 billion. Together, the 400 foundations and 60 individuals gave about $32.8 billion to charitable causes in 2008 – a small portion of the $307.7 billion given by all donors.

Online information exchanges focus on the long tail that makes up the right-hand side of Figure 5.2: the millions of smaller donors who, cumulatively, account for about eight times as many dollars as do the very biggest institutional and individual givers. It is the similarity between marketing on the long tail (poetry chapbooks v. best-sellers) and giving on the long tail (you and I, each with $200, v. the Gates Foundation) that is crucial to understanding one feature of the new philanthropic landscape.

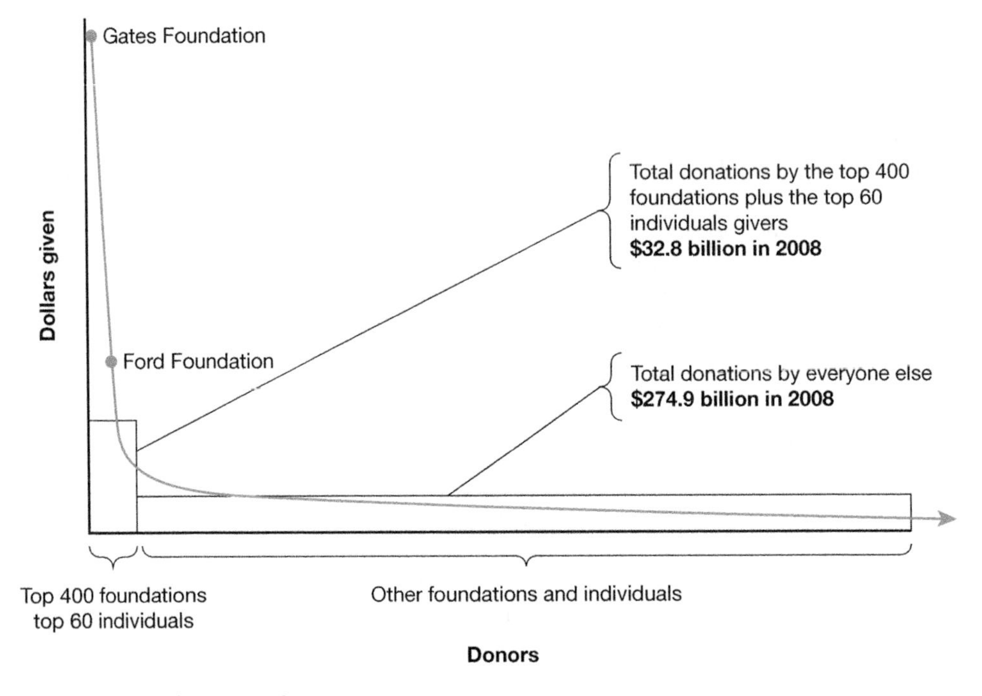

Figure 5.2 The long tail of giving

Figure 5.3 shows how the nonprofit market is organized. (Figures come from the National Center for Charitable Statistics and are based on the approximately 355,000 non-foundation nonprofits that filed tax returns in 2008.) As with the funder market, which is populated on the left-hand side by big foundations and high-net-worth individuals, large organizations such as the United Way, the Salvation Army, and major universities and medical centers make up the left-hand side of the recipient market. In contrast to the giving market, in which the big foundations and high-net-worth individuals do not outweigh the millions of small donors, the large nonprofits in the recipient market take in the lion's share of donations. In 2008, the approximately 40 percent of nonprofits with assets greater than $250,000 received almost 95 percent of donations. The over 200,000 nonprofits with assets less than $250,000 received only about 5 percent of donations. There is a long tail of receiving, but it's a starved tail.

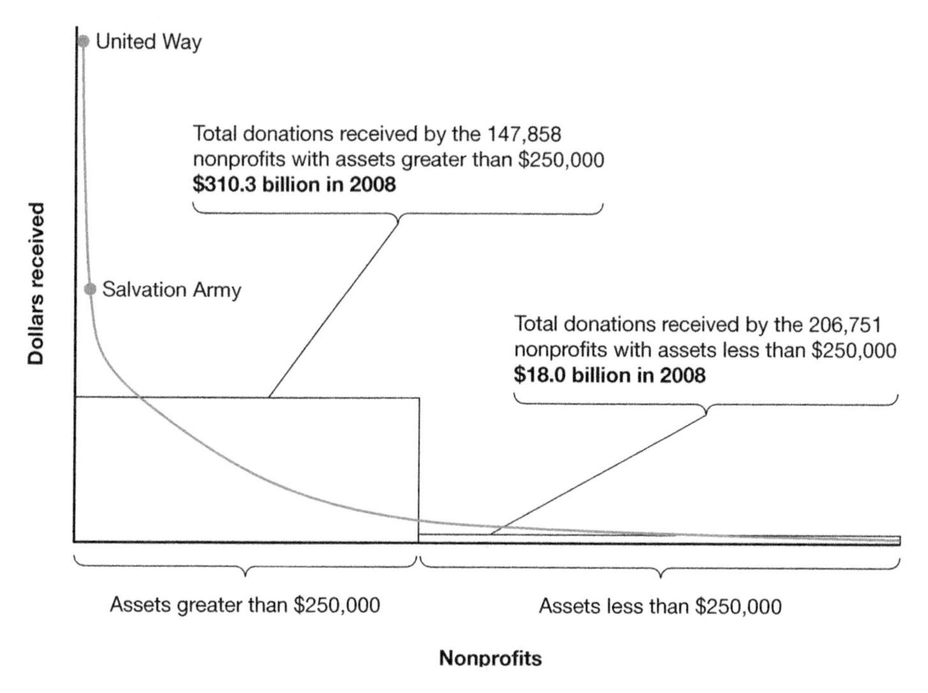

Figure 5.3 The long tail of receiving

Transactional philanthropy sites facilitate direct giving and lending by individuals to enterprises *without regard to geographical location*. The novelty of this arrangement can't be overstated. Ten years ago, the average American's philanthropic activity was limited to volunteering or donating to a local nonprofit (often a church or church-run operation like a soup kitchen), participating in a United Way fund drive, volunteering at the local chapter of one of the large civil-society organizations (Rotary, Habitat for Humanity, Boy Scouts of America), or writing a check to a prominent national or international nonprofit (American Cancer Society, World Wildlife Fund, Amnesty International). Today, individuals can lend money to small business owners in Tanzania, learn about the leanest, closest-to-the-ground nonprofits in Haiti, or buy art supplies for a fourth-grade teacher in a rural school half a continent away. While it's true that, in the case of the Haitian earthquake for example, most Americans donated to the American Red Cross rather than seeking out indigenous Haitian nonprofits, the trend is clear: With each passing year, more people learn about alternative candidates for their charitable dollars, in fuller and more revealing detail. In 2008, online giving surpassed $15 billion dollars (more than 5 percent of total giving), and in 2009, while foundation giving fell by a record 8.4 percent, online giving rose by 5 percent.

While we typically focus on online giving and lending marketplaces for their financial transactional value, they have as a byproduct also created two large new information repositories that are invaluable resources for both donors and doers. The first repository contains information about entrepreneurs, organizations, and causes around the world or around the corner. Every project featured on one of these sites is its own data point about needs and opportunities. The second repository contains data about giving patterns.

The networked information economy is now beginning to influence the left-hand side of the funder market as well. The professionals who run foundations, donor-advised funds, trusts, and other philanthropic institutions increasingly rely on electronic grant application and management systems, online reporting forms, and so on. Foundations are beginning to experiment with sharing with peer organizations these systems and the data they produce, creating collaborative databases that can be remixed, re-sorted, and reconfigured.

Different uses of data are at the core of the behavioral and expectation changes fostered by information networks. Our individual use of search engines is proof enough of this. For many of us, the ability to find instantaneously what we are looking for whether it's a restaurant, a news item, or the balance in our retirement accounts – has changed how we behave. We're now so used to immediate access to data from almost anywhere that we're more likely to take note of it when we can't find it than when we can. Think of the last time your browser was slow, your connection to Google lost, or you were out of cell phone range. The degree to which we're comfortable with and depend on information networks indicates the degree to which we will demand more from them. A brief example: It's no longer enough to be in an unfamiliar city and be able to find an Indian restaurant within five blocks; we also expect to be able to find user-generated reviews of it.

We see this same rise in expectations around online philanthropy. We now have sites such as Social Actions or All for Good that pull together and make available multiple donation or volunteer opportunities in a given locale or on a certain issue. We can barter for or donate goods simply by posting on FreeCycle or Craigslist. Smartphone applications such as The Extraordinaries and Catalista let us donate mental labor wherever we are and whenever we like.

The next frontier is the blending of donations with investments. Online giving markets that manage charitable donations are merging with investor-level exchanges that manage social investments. In some cases, such as the Denmark-based site My C4, the user determines on a case-by-case basis whether she is making a gift, a loan, or a profit-seeking investment. Other sites, such as Kickstarter, which supports artistic and cultural projects, acknowledge that the funds they drive to projects can be classified as investments, gifts, loans, or any combination of the above – leaving the decision to the funder and recipient and broadening the options of both.

On the soon-to-launch NeXii, individual registered users will be able to manage portfolios of grants and investments, track them against financial and social indices, and compare their own performances against those of other investors. NeXii is designed to be useful to individual investors, commercial investors with social goals, and endowment managers seeking to track all of their grants and social investments in one place.

Sites like NeXii are built on software developed for financial markets and data derived from the social sector. It remains to be seen whether these sites will become popular enough to significantly reduce the amount of money that now goes into donor-advised funds administered by commercial banks and community foundations – and if so, whether those institutions will find a way to adapt to, or even adopt, online social-investment platforms.

While we cannot predict which of today's online marketplaces will be leading in transactions processed a decade from now, it's clear that the aggregated data from those transactions will themselves be a key source of information for and about the sector. They will then become the starting point for the next round of innovation.

Section 6

DEBATES ABOUT MAKING PHILANTHROPY BETTER

Editors' introduction

Overview

Many writers and donors say that philanthropy is much harder than it looks. Seneca and Maimonides said this long ago, and the same conversation continues feverishly in contemporary debates about philanthropy. This sixth and final section is focused on the question of doing philanthropy well: what that might look like, how we can recognise it, whether contemporary philanthropists are 'better' than their predecessors, and what 'better' actually means in practice.

The history of philanthropy is a history of reinvention, with repeated attempts to improve philanthropy – to make it more strategic, more effective, more impactful – by creating 'new' approaches to giving. Over the years, as the readings in this section show, these purportedly new approaches have been labelled in many ways: 'scientific philanthropy', 'strategic philanthropy', 'philanthrocapitalism' and most recently 'effective altruism'. In most cases, these new approaches involve applying business or scientific principles and methods to philanthropy in some way. These approaches embrace the sort of blurring of boundaries in institutions and practices covered in the previous section of the Reader.

Of course, there has also been repeated pushback against these new approaches. Some critics claim they overemphasise the 'head' and forget the 'heart' that is essential for meaningful philanthropy. Other common dissents are rooted in resistance to the suggestion that *any* type of giving should be designated superior to any other. Some note that as voluntariness and donor autonomy are defining principles of philanthropy, all giving should be celebrated and promoted as long as it is legally allowable. Others suggest that being 'cause-neutral' is not only morally and legally the correct stance, but will also generate greater quantities of giving, because a more permissive environment reduces the barriers to entry facing donors, whose philanthropic enthusiasm might be deterred by a fear of 'getting it wrong'. This section includes readings from both sides of the recent versions of this long-standing debate.

Consider, for example, the recent emergence of 'effective altruism', which sounds superficially uncontroversial because it combines two terms generally viewed as positive ('effective' and 'altruism'). Yet as with so many ideas related to philanthropy, this concept is contested. The contemporary philosopher, Peter Singer, who has done the most to popularise and promote it, defines 'effective altruism' as 'a philosophy and social movement which applies evidence and reason to working out the most effective ways to improve the world'. Effective altruists believe that every life has equal value, and the goal of philanthropy should be, simply, to save as many lives as possible. Given the vast difference in the number of lives that can be saved using the same amount of money in different places, we should differentiate between better and worse ways of allocating philanthropic resources using technocratic methods and metrics. Such analytical approaches are intended to ensure donors remain focused on measureable and maximum impact, and avoid falling into the trap of giving to what makes them feel good, rather than what achieves the most good. It is important here to recall from the Gates and Singer readings in Section 3 that this ethic of 'every life has equal value' – and this corresponding interest in measuring impact – is the guiding belief of the largest philanthropic foundation ever to have existed: the Bill and Melinda Gates Foundation.

Yet as readings in earlier sections have shown, the simultaneous pursuit of personal and public goals is a defining feature of philanthropy, and this raises a vexing problem for effective altruism – one raised often by its critics. Most donors are not cause-neutral; they become invested in specific issues because those issues have affected them personally in some way. Most donors also prioritise helping those closest to them, including those who share the same community or interests.

It would be wrong to overstate either the degree of consensus or the extent of disagreement in this particular example of the recurring debates over how to make philanthropy better. One point on which both sides agree is that it is impossible to help everyone – even the world's richest donors must focus their efforts on a restricted set of issues. And as Singer notes, effective altruists have different opinions on what counts as 'the most good' and those who reject the language of 'effective altruism' usually remain keen to ensure their money is well spent.

From this example, we can see how there is often a space in the middle for compromise approaches between the opposing sides in these debates. For instance, some current proponents of strategic philanthropy advocate for agnosticism on the choice of cause, combined with heavy emphasis on how funds are spent within the chosen area. The Paul M. Connolly reading in this section proposes a similar combination of the 'technocratic' and 'humanistic' approaches.

The impulse that drives both proponents and critics of new approaches is ultimately to make philanthropy work well, and achieve, in Singer's words, 'a world with less suffering and more happiness in it'. This takes us full circle to the reading from Payton and Moody that began Section 1, which argued that philanthropy is a response to the human condition in which 'things often go wrong' and 'things could always be better'.

The 14 readings in this section address this question of making philanthropy better from many different angles, and are divided into four subsections.

On philanthropic decision-making

It is something of a cliché to note that it is easier to earn money than to give it away wisely, but much evidence shows that it is nonetheless true. The two extracts in this first subsection illustrate the nature of the problem of philanthropic decision-making from the past and present.

John D. Rockefeller (1839–1937) is one of the best-known and biggest US philanthropists. In this extract, written well into his philanthropic career but five years before he endowed the Rockefeller Foundation, he sets out underlying principles to achieve what he calls 'scientific giving', including 'enquiry' to ensure the expenditure is effective and leverage to ensure the 'largest and surest returns'. Despite sounding like an early effective altruist, Rockefeller disputes the notion that some causes are more important than others, saying that if his committee were asked what is the most fundamental cause area, 'they would not attempt to answer, that the question is purely an academic one, that all these go hand in hand'.

Over 100 years later, Charles Bronfman and Jeffrey Solomon echo Rockefeller's starting point, concurring that philanthropy is hard to do well because there is no single, universally agreed-on measure of success. Arguing that time and effort are needed to work out how 'best' to invest philanthropic monies, Bronfman and Solomon warn that the difficulty in philanthropic decision-making lies in there being no wrong answers, only a 'galaxy' of ideas that can never be fully considered.

How do we know if philanthropy does any good?

The difficulties of measuring the impact and value of philanthropic giving are long-standing. The subjectivity involved in making philanthropic decisions is compounded by the lack of widespread agreement on how to assess philanthropic success.

The extracts in this section explore the notion of 'outcome-oriented philanthropy', which involves clearly defined goals and evidence-based strategies, and the pros and cons of conducting empirical research to discover which interventions work and which do not. Social experiments can take many forms, and use both qualitative and quantitative methods. Randomised controlled trials are considered the gold standard for assessing the impact of specific interventions, but involve half the sample receiving no – or a placebo – treatment, which may be considered morally questionable in some situations, such as where lives are at stake. However, without such evidence, some argue, we are fighting poverty or other social problems the way medieval doctors fought illness.

Paul Brest notes that the phrase 'outcome-oriented philanthropy' ought to be tautologous, but that in practice few donors follow its principles. He identifies two broad approaches taken by those who are results-focused: 1) supporting charitable organisations to achieve outcomes, using a variety of strategies including providing risk capital, and impact investing; and 2) designing and implementing 'problem-solving philanthropy' directly. While acknowledging the challenges and criticisms of these methods, Brest argues that the current 'underperformance' of philanthropy can only be tackled by the spread of outcome-oriented approaches.

Michael Hobbes reviews the role that newfound enthusiasm for evidence is playing in international development work, arguing that the hunger for data-driven big ideas is leading to miniscule impact or even negative unintended consequences. Instead of unrealistic expectations of 'game-changing' interventions, he argues that funders should be prepared to pay for overheads and settle for 'baby steps and trial-and-error and tweaks' – even if they do not attract celebrity support or make the headlines.

Meanwhile, Dan Pallotta tackles the issue of charities hitting the headlines for the wrong reason: when they are accused of profligate spending on salaries and overheads. His argument that it is 'unethical' to choose crowd-pleasing processes, like lowering pay for charity leaders or minimising spending on fundraising, if they lead to suboptimal ends, is intended to 'change our whole approach to changing the world . . . [so that] things can really begin to change'.

New – or not so new – ways of improving philanthropy

The claim that philanthropy has recently been 'reinvented', and now differs substantially from the philanthropy of past decades and centuries, is examined in this subsection. Matthew Bishop and Michael Green believe the application of private sector principles in the nonprofit sector is key to a shift towards a bigger, better and 'world changing' philanthropy, and coin the term 'philanthrocapitalism' to describe what they see as a 'new movement'. Michael Edwards then takes issue with the 'seductive' suggestion that philanthrocapitalists can – or should – be encouraged to 'save the world', noting the 'flaw' in relying on business methods because these can also be a cause of social problems. Further, he emphasises the undemocratic consequences of allowing rich donors to determine society's priorities, echoing the critiques of elite donors covered in Section 3 of this Reader.

Charles Handy concurs with Bishop and Green that something distinctively new is afoot, and describes the kind of people who are 'new philanthropists': 'hands-on, pioneering and entrepreneurial . . . in the prime of life, with goals still to achieve, passions to satisfy, and the energy that is needed to start something new'. Beth Breeze draws on historical evidence to suggest there is more evidence of continuity than change, with most differences being in degree rather than in kind, and argues that any 'new philanthropy' is due to a process of adaptation to changing circumstances rather than a paradigmatic shift.

The final extract in this subsection, by Olga Alexeeva, is concerned with the inconsistent application of principles in donors' private lives and in their philanthropy, much as Edwards highlights the role of entrepreneurs in both creating and solving social problems. Further, Alexeeva notes that the potential for any 'new philanthropy' to be a powerful instrument of change will not be realised as long as it is viewed – like a 'Gucci bag' – as the fashionable, rather than the right, thing to do.

Is 'being effective' the only worthwhile yardstick?

The extracts in this subsection set out the parameters of the 'effective altruism' debate that was discussed above. The readings include both those who argue for 'effectiveness' as the primary metric to judge philanthropic success, and those who question this, noting the essential subjectivity of philanthropy that involves choosing between right and right.

We begin with Singer, the foremost proponent of 'effective altruism', who charts its emergence as a response to donors wishing to give more and to give more effectively. He describes the key people and ideas involved in advancing the movement and addresses key questions such as: what counts as 'doing the most good', and can supporting the arts be considered an effective use of philanthropic money?

The preference for metrics is apparent in the next extract. Eric Friedman argues that philanthropy is 'broken' because globally effective charities can save a life for between $200 and $2,000, yet most US donors prefer to fund domestically, where the median life-saving intervention costs about $2.2 million. He illustrates this point with an emotive comparison of the philanthropically funded health care available to two sick children – one in the US and one in Angola; despite the latter being vastly cheaper, funding was not available and the child died. Friedman's solution is to encourage donors to move away from 'expressive giving' to causes with which they have a personal connection, and move towards 'instrumental giving' to causes that create the most positive social change.

The extract from William Schambra sees no merit in the ideas of 'effective altruism', viewing it as a threat to civil society and to democratic self-government and calling it 'a radical utilitarian approach to giving that might best be described as "strategic philanthropy on steroids"'. Dismissing the 'metric madness' of its adherents, he argues that lives-saved-per-dollar calculations will always favor spending philanthropic money in poor countries, making it indistinguishable from long-distance altruism. Yet Schambra claims there is more to philanthropy than maximising utility as it has other moral purposes and an important role in strengthening all neighbourhoods and communities.

The final two readings offer two versions of a compromise position that seeks to take advantage of the benefits of giving a little more with the head while retaining the value of giving from the heart. Connolly describes how what he terms the 'technocratic' and 'humanistic' approaches to giving are not necessarily opposed, and that compromise can be reached by reframing the debate to 'creatively unite both the art and science of philanthropy'.

Similarly, Thomas J. Tierney and Joel L. Fleishman suggest that donors 'give smart' by complementing heartfelt generosity with a rigorous approach to practising philanthropy. Noting a triumverate of 'terrible truths' ('All philanthropy is personal. Results can confound. Excellence is self-imposed'.), they identify traps that can befall even the most capable and experienced philanthropists who must operate in a 'Galapagos Island-like world, where there are no natural predators': being 'fuzzy-headed'; 'flying solo' rather than in partnership; 'underestimating and underinvesting;' and contributing to the nonprofit starvation cycle by resisting funding overheads.

Taking steps to avoid such traps, and realising that the aspirations of almost every philanthropist far exceed their resources, should enable donors to be confident that they have accomplished as much with their philanthropy as they possibly could have – whether they describe themselves as a traditional philanthropist, a new philanthropist, an effective altruist, or something else altogether.

Discussion questions

- Why do so many people suggest that giving money away is harder than earning it? What do these readings tell us, specifically, might be so difficult about giving?
- Is the desire to be effective, strategic, and impactful in one's giving something that is more common among contemporary donors? Is this approach unique to Western donors and Western countries? Looking back at the previous sections of the Reader, come up with some examples of donors from other times and other places that exemplify this strong focus on making philanthropy better.
- What do critics of the 'effective altruism movement' mean by the phrase 'metrics madness'? How can measurement, and being outcome-oriented in your giving, cause unintended problems?
- Is some giving really better than other giving, or should all philanthropy be equally valued? In what way does this question change when we talk about the methods of giving versus the causes of giving? Can we rank methods from better to worse but not causes?
- How can donors strike the right balance between giving with their head and giving with their heart? Describe some specific techniques for doing this that you find in these readings.

6.1 On philanthropic decision-making

The difficult art of giving

John D. Rockefeller, 1908

The very rich are just like all the rest of us; and if they get pleasure from the possession of money, it comes from their ability to do things which give satisfaction to someone besides themselves.

The mere expenditure of money for things, so I am told by those who profess to know, soon palls upon one. The novelty of being able to purchase anything one wants soon passes, because what people most seek cannot be bought with money. These rich men we read about in the newspapers cannot get personal returns beyond a well-defined limit for their expenditure. They cannot gratify the pleasures of the palate beyond very moderate bounds, since they cannot purchase a good digestion; they cannot lavish very much money on fine raiment for themselves or their families without suffering from public ridicule; and in their homes they cannot go much beyond the comforts of the less wealthy without involving them in more pain than pleasure. As I study wealthy men, I can see but one way in which they can secure a real equivalent for money spent, and that is to cultivate a taste for giving where the money may produce an effect which will be a lasting gratification.

[. . .]

The best philanthropy

The best philanthropy, the help that does the most good and the least harm, the help that nourishes civilization at its very root, that most widely disseminates health, righteousness, and happiness, is not what is usually called charity. It is, in my judgment, the investment of effort or time or money, carefully considered with relation to the power of employing people at a remunerative wage, to expand and develop the resources at hand, and to give opportunity for progress and healthful labor where it did not exist before. No mere money-giving is comparable to this in its lasting and beneficial results.

If, as I am accustomed to think, this statement is a correct one, how vast indeed is the philanthropic field! It may be urged that the daily vocation of life is one thing, and the work of philanthropy quite another. I have no sympathy with this notion. The man who plans to do all his giving on Sunday is a poor prop for the institutions of the country.

[. . .]

The generosity of service

Probably the most generous people in the world are the very poor, who assume each other's burdens in the crises which come so often to the hard pressed. The mother in the tenement falls ill and the neighbor in the next room assumes her burdens. The father loses his work, and neighbors supply food to his children from their own scanty store. How often one hears of cases where the orphans are taken over and brought up by the poor friend whose benefaction means great additional hardship! This sort of genuine service makes the most princely gift from superabundance look insignificant indeed. The Jews have had for centuries a precept that one-tenth of a man's possessions must be devoted to good works, but even this measure of giving is but a rough yardstick to go by. To give a tenth of one's income is well nigh an impossibility to some, while to others it means a miserable pittance. If the spirit is there, the matter of proportion is soon lost sight of. It is only the spirit of giving that counts, and the very poor give without any self-consciousness. But I fear that I am dealing with generalities again.

The education of children in my early days may have been straight-laced, yet I have always been thankful that the custom was quite general to teach young people to give systematically of money that they themselves had earned. It is a good thing to lead children to realize early the importance of their obligations to others but, I confess, it is increasingly difficult; for what were luxuries then have become commonplaces now. It should be a greater pleasure and satisfaction to give money for a good cause than to earn it, and I have always indulged the hope that during my life I should be able to help establish efficiency in giving so that wealth may be of greater use to the present and future generations.

Perhaps just here lies the difference between the gifts of money and service. The poor meet promptly the misfortunes which confront the home circle and household of the neighbor. The giver of money, if his contribution is to be valuable, must add service in the way of study, and he must help to attack and improve underlying conditions. Not being so pressed by the racking necessities, it is he that should be better able to attack the subject from a more scientific standpoint; but the final analysis is the same: his money is a feeble offering without the study behind it which will make its expenditure effective. Great hospitals conducted by noble and unselfish men and women are doing wonderful work; but no less important are the achievements in research that reveal hitherto unknown facts about diseases and provide the remedies by which many of them can be relieved or even stamped out.

To help the sick and distressed appeals to the kindhearted always, but to help the investigator who is striving successfully to attack the causes which bring about sickness and distress does not so strongly attract the giver of money. The first appeals to the sentiments overpoweringly, but the second has the head to deal with. Yet I am sure we are making wonderful advances in this field of scientific giving. All over the world the need of dealing with the questions of philanthropy with something beyond the impulses of emotion is evident, and everywhere help is being given to those heroic men and women who are devoting themselves to the practical and essentially scientific tasks. It is a good and inspiring thing to recall occasionally the heroism, for example, of the men who risked and sacrificed their lives to discover the facts about yellow fever, a sacrifice for which untold generations will bless them; and this same spirit has animated the professions of medicine and surgery.

The fundamental thing in all help

If the people can be educated to help themselves, we strike at the root of many of the evils of the world. This is the fundamental thing and it is worth saying even if it has been said so often that its truth is lost sight of in its constant repetition.

The only thing which is of lasting benefit to a man is that which he does for himself. Money which comes to him without effort on his part is so seldom a benefit and often a curse. That is the principal objection to speculation – it is not because more lose than gain, though that is true – but it is because those who gain are apt to receive more injury from their success than they would have received from failure. And so with regard to money or other things which are given by one person to another. It is only in the exceptional case that the receiver is really benefited. But, if we can help people to help themselves, then there is a permanent blessing conferred.

[. . .]

We must always remember that there is not enough money for the work of human uplift and that there never can be. How vitally important it is, therefore, that the expenditure should go as far as possible and be used with the greatest intelligence!

I have been frank to say that I believe in the spirit of combination and cooperation when properly and fairly conducted in the world of commercial affairs, on the principle that it helps to reduce waste; and waste is a dissipation of power. I sincerely hope and thoroughly believe that this same principle will eventually prevail in the art of giving as it does in business. It is not merely the tendency of the times developed by more exacting conditions in industry, but it should make its most effective appeal to the hearts of the people who are striving to do the most good to the largest number.

Some underlying principles

At the risk of making this chapter very dull, and I am told that this is a fault which inexperienced authors should avoid at all hazards, I may perhaps be pardoned if I set down here some of the fundamental principles which have been at the bottom of all my own plans. I have undertaken no work of any importance for many years which, in a general way, has not followed out these broad lines, and I believe no really constructive effort can be made in philanthropic work without such a well-defined and consecutive purpose.

My own conversion to the feeling that an organized plan was an absolute necessity came about in this way.

About the year 1890, I was still following the haphazard fashion of giving here and there as appeals presented themselves. I investigated as I could, and worked myself almost to a nervous break-down in groping my way, without sufficient guide or chart, through this ever-widening field of philanthropic endeavor. There was then forced upon me the necessity to organize and plan this department of our daily tasks on as distinct lines of progress as we did our business affairs; and I will try to describe the underlying principles we arrived at, and have since followed out, and hope still greatly to extend.

It may be beyond the pale of good taste to speak at all of such a personal subject – I am not unmindful of this – but I can make these observations with at least a little better grace because so much of the hard work and hard thinking are done by my family and associates, who devote their lives to it.

Every right-minded man has a philosophy of life, whether he knows it or not. Hidden away in his mind are certain governing principles, whether he formulates them in words or not, which govern his life. Surely his ideal ought to be to contribute all that he can, however little it may be, whether of money or service, to human progress.

Certainly one's ideal should be to use one's means, both in one's investments and in benefactions, for the advancement of civilization. But the question as to what civilization is and what are the great laws which govern its advance have been seriously studied. Our investments not less than gifts have been directed to such ends as we have thought would tend to produce these results. If you to go into our office, and ask our committee on benevolence or our committee on investment in what they consider civilization to consist, they say that they have found in their study that the most convenient analysis of the elements which go to make up civilization runs about as follows:

1st. Progress in the means of subsistence, that is to say, progress in abundance and variety of food-supply, clothing, shelter, sanitation, public health, commerce, manufacture, the growth of the public wealth, etc.
2nd. Progress in government and law, that is to say, in the enactment of laws securing justice and equity to every man, consistent with the largest individual liberty, and the due and orderly enforcement of the same upon all.
3rd. Progress in literature and language.
4th. Progress in science and philosophy.
5th. Progress in art and refinement.
6th. Progress in morality and religion.

If you were to ask them, as indeed they are very often asked, which of these they regard as fundamental, they would reply that they would not attempt to answer, that the question is purely an academic one, that all these go hand in hand, but that historically the first of them – namely, progress in means of subsistence – had generally preceded progress in government, in literature, in knowledge, in refinement, and in religion. Though not itself of the highest importance, it is the foundation upon which the whole superstructure of civilization is built, and without which it could not exist.

Accordingly, we have sought, so far as we could, to make investments in such a way as will tend to multiply, to cheapen, and to diffuse as universally as possible the comforts of life. We claim no credit for preferring these lines of investment. We make no sacrifices. These are the lines of largest and surest return.

[. . .]

Quite as interesting as any phase of the work have been the new lines entered upon by our committee. We have not been satisfied with giving to causes which have appealed to us. We have felt that the mere fact that this or the other cause makes its appeal is no reason why we should give to it any more than to a thousand other causes, perhaps more worthy, which do not happen to have come under our eye. The mere fact of a personal appeal creates no claim which did not exist before, and no preference over other causes more worthy which may not have made their appeal. So this little committee of ours has not been content to let the benevolences drift into the channels of mere convenience – to give to the institutions which have sought aid and to neglect others. This department has studied the field of human progress, and sought to contribute to each of those elements which we believe tend most to promote it. Where it has not found organizations ready to its hand for such purpose, the members of the committee have sought to create them. We are still working on new, and, I hope, expanding lines, which make large demands on one's intelligence and study.

To give is to choose

Charles Bronfman and Jeffrey Solomon, 2010

Philanthropy is hard to do well. It is far more difficult to design and run a nonprofit than it is to manage a for-profit company of equivalent size. Why? Because in the nonprofit world, there is no single, universally agreed-on measure of success. Now we believe in measures, and work very hard to create them, and we use them to evaluate our own endeavors. But it is not obvious what those measures are, for there is no built-in bottom line of profit and loss of return on investment. Without such measures, nonprofits too often are flying blind, relying on guesswork as to where they are and where they are headed. And those guesses can be way off.

Plus, nonprofits are being buffeted about by enormous changes in the world of philanthropy, not the least of them stemming from the baby boomers' new approach to giving. Their parents largely believed in funding umbrella institutions like the United Way and Catholic Charities, which decided for them how the funds were to be spent. This was that generation's idea of saluting society for the benefits it had received. The baby boomers, by contrast, believe in making a difference personally. They want to choose for themselves the recipients of their donation and monitor the effects. Their parents usually called their giving "charity." The boomers prefer to call theirs "philanthropy."

There is a plethora of nonprofits in the United States, over 1.7 million in all, and they are often staffed by untrained volunteers who can be difficult to manage without financial inducements. The talent pool for paid management staff is shallow. Who do you know who made it his life's ambition to run a nonprofit? Not too many people, most likely. Compared to for-profit equivalents, the salaries are paltry, the status not much better, and precious few university programs offer these professionals any serious instruction. And the objectives are daunting: curing Alzheimer's disease, feeding the poor in Africa, developing new models for elementary school education.

Now into this jumble comes you, the neophyte donor, eager to make a difference with your money. Most likely, you have no direct experience with nonprofits beyond having been a consumer of some nonprofit service in a hospital or school, or done some volunteer work, or perhaps served on a board. Typically you have given the topic a fraction of the attention that you have lavished on your career, family, social life, hobbies, or investments. And yet you expect to engage in serious philanthropy before the week is out.

If it were that easy, those of us who have made philanthropy our life's work would have written novels, or composed symphonies, or engaged in many other extracurricular activities in our copious free time. Truth is, philanthropy makes serious demands not only on your pocketbook but also on your intellect, feelings, attention, and time.

Nothing of value comes for free. If you are willing to give fully of yourself, you will receive satisfactions that are hard to come by on the for-profit side: the thrill of seeing your idea sent forth into the world to improve countless other people's lives. It's the joy of connection, of enlarging yourself. Yes, there truly is a joy to giving.

Philanthropy as we practice it shares one of the major principles of the for-profit world, and that is accountability. In some respects, old school charity was quick and easy in that it freed donors from significant social obligation. Donors could give a few hundred dollars to the United Way or place a few bills in the plate at church without having any particular idea where that money was going, who decided, why, and what good, if any, came of it. The institutions were unassailable repositories of probity and good sense. They knew better than anyone else how to fix any ills that beset society.

It's unclear how many people ever believed that, but few believe it now. Most people, quite rightly, believe that they are entitled to follow their money and see what it does, and if it's nothing, to look elsewhere for a nonprofit investment. Nowadays a donor can rightly expect that the nonprofit will make the most of his gift by leveraging it to the hilt. And he should feel free to ask tough questions when it fails to. This new business-mindedness is the norm. Nonprofits should be run just as crisply as for-profits. Meetings should start on time and end on time too. They should not be social gatherings that drag on endlessly for no purpose. A nonprofit isn't church either. It should not fall for a charismatic leader who gives the operation a charged-up, religious feeling – and loses sight of what it is actually created to do.

[. . .]

In philanthropy, there are no wrong answers. It is hard sometimes for donors to appreciate that fact; it is so different from everything else they are used to. In other realms, there are plenty of wrong answers – wrong because a suggestion violates company policy, wrong because we already tried that and it was a disaster, wrong because it's just plain stupid and everybody says so. Not so when it comes to philanthropic objectives. You might want to fund an antigravity machine or a museum of dust mites. There may be more constructive uses for your money, and these objectives may sound crazy, but there is nothing wrong with them. In philanthropy, the choices are not between right and wrong, but between right and right. This makes it all the harder to choose. If an option is wrong, it can be eliminated instantly. If it is right, you have to think some more, and then some more after that.

[. . .]

Would-be philanthropists peer out at this vast world of need and see mostly a blur of smudgy colors. But in time, and with some effort, certain parts of this world will start to clarify and exert a certain unmistakable pull. Our techniques can hasten this process, but they are not guaranteed to yield The Thing – that subject of consuming passion – promptly, and they almost certainly won't deliver it in the few minutes that it has taken you to read this chapter. No, these are lengthy practices, as the Buddhists say, but if you keep your mind open, that moment of clarity will come. And when it does, you'll be amazed. You'll wonder how you could have ever failed to see it. The answer is, you were looking in the wrong place. It was never out there, not really; it was inside you the whole time, buried down deep where the truest things lie.

[. . .]

The decision about where to invest your philanthropic money is not likely to be made in one swoop. A tentative notion might lead to vigorous enthusiasm followed by anxious reconsideration and scornful rejection. From its ashes, another idea might spring up to suffer the same fate or emerge as The Thing. It's a process of exploration and retrenchment and then exploration again. All the stars in the galaxy of nonprofit ideas are never under full consideration. But the donor shouldn't limit herself to just one or two either. It is a big world out there, and donors might be astonished to discover the satisfaction of connecting to some distant corner of it.

6.2 How do we know if philanthropy does any good?

A decade of outcome-oriented philanthropy

Paul Brest, 2012

Outcome-oriented philanthropy is at least a century old, but the past 10 or so years have seen an upsurge in both its intensity and its extent. It has been the subject of many articles, talks, and conferences, and has given rise to new organizations dedicated to facilitating its practice. An increasing, albeit still small, number of foundations seem to have adopted an outcome orientation.

"Outcome-oriented" is synonymous with "result-oriented," "strategic," and "effective." It refers to philanthropy where donors seek to achieve clearly defined goals; where they and their grantees pursue evidence-based strategies for achieving those goals; and where both parties monitor progress toward outcomes and assess their success in achieving them in order to make appropriate course corrections.

This approach can take different forms. A classic example from many decades ago was the Rockefeller and Ford Foundations' funding of research and development to improve agricultural production in developing countries – what became known as the Green Revolution. More recent examples include the John D. and Catherine T. MacArthur Foundation's efforts to build the field of digital media and learning, and Acumen Fund's and Omidyar Network's "impact investments" to benefit the world's poorest people.

The common theme of these approaches, the idea that philanthropy should seek results, may seem so obvious as to make the modifier "outcome-oriented" superfluous. But despite the increasing belief that the work of the sector should rest on goal-oriented, evidence-based strategies, very few donors actually follow these principles.

I caught the start of the wave of outcome-oriented philanthropy when I joined the William and Flora Hewlett Foundation as president in 2000, and it's been a great ride. As I prepare to leave the foundation, I'd like to reflect on the currents that have brought outcome-oriented philanthropy this far, and the shoals and reefs that lie ahead.

[. . .]

Approaches to outcome-oriented philanthropy

The last decade has seen the emergence of an infrastructure to support outcome-oriented philanthropy, including new organizations, services, consultants, evaluators, donor education programs, online forums and advocates who have written important texts, as well as critics who argue against the practice, or at least its inclination toward measurable outcomes.

But the important question is the extent to which it has taken root in practice. Outcome-oriented philanthropy has two major focal points: *supporting organizations* and *problem-solving philanthropy*. Examples of *supporting organizations* range from grants to after-school programs for under-served children and gifts to universities to create, teach, and disseminate knowledge, to investments in for-profit entities distributing malaria bed nets. There are three different strategies for supporting organizations: *philanthropic buying, providing risk and growth capital,* and *impact investing.*

Outcome-oriented philanthropic buyers look for the best service in their areas of interest for the lowest cost, and make gifts and grants to help pay the operating costs of nonprofits providing those services. Philanthropic investors provide risk capital to social entrepreneurs and nascent organizations, or growth capital to enable relatively mature organizations to expand the scope, efficiency, and quality of their work. Impact investors seek the double or triple bottom line objectives of achieving social or environmental impact as well as financial returns. Their investments may buy services or provide risk or growth capital with the aims of, say, improving the lives of the poor through microfinance or reducing energy consumption by investing in clean tech startups, while earning financial returns.

The second major type of outcome-oriented philanthropy is *problem-solving philanthropy.* Whereas philanthropists often buy services and support organizations in order to solve problems, problem-solving philanthropists put the problem rather than the organization at the center, and actively engage with their grantees in designing and implementing strategies. Here philanthropists act as architects, general contractors, or engineers, and their work often verges on the operational. As a practical matter, only a foundation staffed with experts in a field can undertake this work. During the past decade, foundations played increasingly active and visible problem-solving roles by building fields, brokering collaborative arrangements, and supporting systems change and advocacy.

Supporting organizations

Philanthropic buying – Of the three strategies for supporting organizations, philanthropic buying accounts for the vast majority of contributions, and it is also the area where outcome-oriented philanthropy has shown the least gains. The "Money for Good" research published by Hope Consulting in 2010 found that although 21 percent of US donors inquire into performance, only 3 percent actually use the information to determine which organizations to support. This may be partly explained by the challenges of obtaining adequate information about nonprofits' performance. Despite the existence of third-party ratings groups, there is nothing approaching the comprehensiveness of, say, *Consumer Reports.* As a result, philanthropic buyers must often do their own due diligence, which requires knowledge of the substantive area and detailed information about a particular organization's goals, strategies, and actual outcomes. Staffed foundations are relatively well equipped to acquire this information. Other foundations and high net worth individuals must rely on consulting firms or else follow the lead of staffed foundations in which they have confidence – a practice that has not yet gained much adherence.

Apart from these difficulties, many philanthropic buyers subvert their contributions by earmarking donations for particular projects rather than providing unrestricted general operating support. Even outcome-oriented buyers impose these restrictions, often in the misguided beliefs that general operating support grants cannot be evaluated and that donors can have more impact by designating funds for programs.

Providing risk and growth capital – Well before the current decade, philanthropists supported social entrepreneurs' early-stage ventures through organizations such as Ashoka and Echoing Green. Although the interest in social entrepreneurship has grown, the sector is still lacking in patient capital to build, sustain, and grow promising nonprofit organizations – for example, funding to pay for new computer systems or train staff members, as well as funding to allow successful enterprises to operate at a larger scale.

[. . .]

One particular area of need is funding to allow successful enterprises to operate at a larger scale. The Edna McConnell Clark Foundation (EMCF) does this by helping build the capacity of promising youth services organizations, and by aggregating capital toward this end.

Philanthropic investors must perform the same tasks as philanthropic buyers – and then some. They must assess organizations' capacities, needs, and potential for growth and sustainability; understand how to replicate successful model programs; and provide capacity-building support, directly or through consultants, in areas including strategic planning, management, evaluation, governance, fundraising, and communications. As with philanthropic buying, these activities call for experienced foundation staff members. Individual donors and unstaffed foundations have the option of investing in a fund managed by organizations that have those capabilities.

Impact investing – The idea that markets can be important vehicles for creating social impact was recognized in the US by the Internal Revenue Service as early as 1969 in its favorable treatment of program-related investments – typically investments that have a lower market-adjusted return than ordinary investments. This paved the way for impact investing some 30 years later. Impact investors invest capital or make loans to business or nonprofit entities with the goal of achieving social, environmental, and financial returns. In addition to affirmative investment strategies, an increasing number of foundations engage in "socially responsible investing" by voting proxies on issues of social concern or using negative screens to avoid investing in companies that they believe cause social harm.

[. . .]

In addition to needing the skills of philanthropic buyers and investors, impact investors need the financial acumen to identify and analyze investment opportunities that promote the foundation's goals at whatever financial return and risk level fit their social and financial parameters. This requires marrying the knowledge of a foundation's program officers with the skills of its investment staff. Program-related investments typically require legal expertise as well. Donors who lack the staff to perform these activities in-house can turn to the increasing number of consultants in this area.

[. . .]

As with all philanthropic giving, the main challenge of impact investing is to assess the social impact of one's investment decisions. The issue is most apparent for impact investing that seeks to achieve market rate returns at market risk levels: If clean tech is just as attractive to investors just out to make a buck, will a mission-related investment in clean tech make even a slight additional difference in improving the environment? (Similar questions can be asked about negative screens for investing in publicly traded stocks.) As tools are developed to measure the "blended value" of impact investing, they may ultimately benefit all outcome-oriented philanthropy.

Problem-solving philanthropy

Problem-solving philanthropy focuses on solving social, environmental, or other problems rather than supporting individual nonprofits as such. This approach is essential when a field lacks strong organizations whose missions and activities are closely aligned with a funder's goals – which may happen if the funder's goals are novel or not mainstream, or if the field is new or is not well developed. But even in a fairly mature field, organizations are often disconnected and competitive with one another at the expense of transparency and collaboration, and lack the capacity or will to act in coordination to solve multifaceted problems. In short, the whole sometimes is less than the sum of its parts.

In these situations, the problem-solving philanthropist plays a coordinating role, drawing on the resources of various organizations and linking them with each other and with experts, policymakers, and practitioners. Problem-solving philanthropists use all available philanthropic tools, including investing and buying, to achieve particular goals. With expertise in the field, they often possess a perspective that no single organization does. Like philanthropic buyers and investors, problem-solving philanthropists often help grantees improve their organizational effectiveness, but they typically go beyond this role to be partners in strategic planning and implementation.

Here are several vignettes of different types of problem-solving philanthropy from the Hewlett Foundation's work as well as one in which we were not involved.

Building fields – For decades, international donors' support for primary and secondary education in developing countries focused on expanding access to schools without attention to learning outcomes. In 2001, the Hewlett Foundation began to try to improve outcomes in reading, math, and problem-solving skills. Because few existing organizations were closely aligned with this goal, the foundation had to draw on diverse entities to put together a strategy. For example, the foundation made grants to the Center for Universal Education for research on quality education in developing countries. It made grants to the Aga Khan Foundation to develop a more effective approach to teaching reading and math, and then to implement the approach in Kenya and Uganda. And it engaged the African Population and Health Research Center to assess whether these approaches actually worked. Over time, the foundation hopes to foster the development of in-country organizations to which it and others can make general operating support grants. But for now, the work continues to require considerable engagement by foundation staff.

Brokering – Hewlett Foundation staff played a major role in assisting with the transfer of the *Stanford Social Innovation Review* from the Stanford Graduate School of Business (whose priorities no longer included the journal) to Stanford University's Center on Philanthropy and Civil Society, and gaining financial support for the enterprise. The foundation also facilitated the acquisition of Philanthropedia by GuideStar and the formation of a strategic alliance among Independent Sector, the Wise Giving Alliance, and GuideStar to create Charting Impact, a framework for organizations to describe their goals, strategies, and outcome measures.

Collaboration and linking organizations – The Hewlett, Moore, Packard, Tosa, and Wilburforce foundations and the Rockefeller Brothers Fund collaborated to protect about 21 million acres of largely undeveloped coastal land in the Great Bear Rainforest in British Columbia, Canada. The foundations' staffs brought together conservation grantees with the provincial and Canadian governments, First Nations tribes, and the timber industry – interests that had fought one another for years. The foundations saw an opportunity to facilitate negotiations among these parties to protect the forest, deliver economic development opportunities to coastal First Nations, and put the timber industry on a path toward sustainability. In the process, the foundations created the

Rainforest Solutions Project to put together an environmental deal among nonprofits and supported similar partnerships among the First Nations people and private sector companies.

Policy advocacy – The Hewlett Foundation's Environment Program has made grants to a variety of organizations to advance climate change and air quality policies in California. Traditional environmental groups like the Natural Resources Defense Council and the Environmental Defense Fund have provided critical advocacy and analytical capacity to help develop California's climate change policies, which ultimately can have a large effect on private investments as well as public resources. On the local and regional level, public health, environmental justice, and community groups like the Fresno-Madera Medical Society, the Coalition for Clean Air, Communities for a Better Environment, and the East Yard Communities for Environmental Justice have achieved significant improvements in air quality.

Collective impact – Foundations have sometimes played a role in multi-stakeholder collaborative efforts. For example, "Strive" is a project in which foundations, nonprofit organizations, corporations, school district leaders, and universities have collaborated to address the problem of low student achievement in Cincinnati, and created an intermediary organization to coordinate their efforts.

In addition to calling for all the skills involved in supporting organizations, problem-solving philanthropy requires understanding the dynamics of complex social and political systems; developing sound strategies that take both benefits and risks of failure into account; helping develop strategies, and monitoring and evaluation plans; and linking nonprofit organizations, funders, experts, and policymakers. It also calls for the resilience to abide both great uncertainties and great failures.

Criticisms of outcome-oriented philanthropy

Outcome-oriented philanthropy – particularly the problem-solving approach – has been subject to various criticisms. Some critics embrace the practice and seek to improve it, and others challenge the very concept. I'll begin by mentioning an argument between the two main outcome-oriented schools. Some proponents of problem-solving philanthropy imply that (merely) supporting organizations is not an impactful use of philanthropic dollars. Indeed, the frequent characterization of problem-solving philanthropy as "strategic" might be taken to imply that supporting organizations is *un*strategic. On the other side, some commentators accord general operating support an almost religious status, and denigrate problem-solving philanthropy as inherently top down and inimical to the autonomy and vitality of nonprofits. My view is that both approaches have great potential, but that their true value depends on their actual outcomes.

These internecine squabbles aside, internal critics of outcome-oriented philanthropy voice the concerns that it can be incompetently executed, and that funders may exercise inappropriate control over grantees, thereby impinging on their autonomy and stifling innovation. For example, in their 2011 article in *The Foundation Review*, "Beyond the Veneer of Strategic Philanthropy," Patricia Patrizi and Elizabeth Thompson note that, after engaging in a lengthy strategic planning process, some foundations put their plans in a drawer and do not engage in the ongoing monitoring and evaluation that would inform necessary corrections. They also observe that foundations often don't consider in advance the tasks that their staffs must perform to design and implement a strategy, and that staff members may lack the requisite skills.

Some of Patrizi and Thompson's points resonate with the Hewlett Foundation's experience over the past decade. Early on, we mouthed the concepts of outcome-oriented philanthropy and asked grantees to do likewise, without fully understanding how the concepts played out in practice. Though we always treated strategic plans as living documents, it is only in the last several years that we have engaged in the systematic monitoring and evaluation necessary to see if strategies are working, and correct them when they're not. We have also learned through painful experiences about the challenges of implementing even well-thought-out strategies. The Hewlett Foundation's support for strengthening grantees' capacities has grown year by year. And our understanding of the tasks performed by program officers, the skills needed, and the implications for hiring, support, and training has also grown tremendously.

Patrizi and Thompson note that some foundations treat grantees merely as agents for implementing strategies designed in-house, rather than as partners in their design, leading to weak strategies, limited buy-in by grantees, and poor feedback. In "Letting Go," an article in the spring 2011 issue of the *Stanford Social Innovation Review*, Kristi Kimball and Malka Kopell levy the similar criticism that foundations are prone to the "not invented here" syndrome in adopting strategies and their underlying theories of change.

The critics' basic concern is legitimate. Workable theories of change cannot be developed by foundation staff alone, but only through extensive and ongoing consultations with grantees, practitioners, experts, policymakers, and others. But in their zeal to prevent the not-invented-here error, Kimball and Kopell adopt the mirror-image error of demanding that "it must be invented there," where "there" is a grantee. This fundamentally mistakes the way knowledge develops. It is seldom possible to trace the origins of ideas to one or another institution. As ideas are tested, refined, mixed with others, or discarded, they don't belong to any particular organization but instead enter the public domain.

Kimball and Kopell also complain that a given foundation typically funds interventions based on only one or two theories of change, rather than supporting a diverse group of promising ideas. But although supporting a number of ideas may sound good in theory, most foundations lack the financial and human resources to pursue more than a couple at any time.

In contrast to the preceding critics who want to improve outcome-oriented philanthropy, others question its core tenets. These include both conservatives like William Schambra and liberals like Bruce Sievers and Bill Somerville, whose positions sometimes converge and sometimes diverge. The critics share a radical skepticism about social science as well as the belief that an emphasis on metrics leads philanthropists to focus on measurable results at the expense of outcomes that are truly important. The conservative critics, following the political theorist Edmund Burke, argue that efforts at broad-scale social change are fraught with uncertainty and unanticipated bad consequences. They would have philanthropy support local community organizations without demanding particular outcomes. The liberals share this emphasis on local communities, but they also extol philanthropy's big bets on social movements, whether involving the environment or civil rights – again, without the constraints of specific outcomes and metrics.

Of course, there is good reason for caution in acting on social science findings. But the implication that we can never make good bets on social interventions is demonstrably false; it isn't the way we live our own lives when we make decisions, say, about what kind of education to provide our children. For all of the complexities of evaluating social interventions and assessing whether they can be generalized to different settings, we sometimes know "what works" and what doesn't. Indeed, the past decade saw the emergence of organizations that attempt to answer these questions at a granular level.

The concern that an obsession with metrics may limit a philanthropist's ambition or scope is legitimate. My own view is that one should first choose goals and then make a serious effort to define measurable targets or reasonable proxies for them. Our experience at the Hewlett Foundation is that this usually takes us pretty far, but that sometimes we must make do with qualitative indicators of progress that fall far short of ultimate outcomes. Statistical analysis can provide a reasonable picture of the success of a de-worming program in Africa. But broad-scale social movements require long time horizons and patience with setbacks and periods of stasis.

Sievers argues that philanthropy should focus primarily on empowering civil society. Doubtless, this is a valuable goal, but so too are curing cancer and reducing poverty. Certainly the engagement of citizens is often an important means of achieving philanthropic goals as well as an end in itself. But not always. The proposition that philanthropy must devote itself to particular goals has surfaced in every decade. Rather than choose among the myriad possible candidates, I would prefer to continue the rich tradition of diverse ends and means that has characterized American philanthropy.

The coming decade

The decade ends with healthy debates on these issues in journals and blogs that did not exist at its inception, and with many of the institutions and practices mentioned above flourishing. It also ends with considerable interest in the use of social media to improve impact, and in crowdsourcing, design thinking, and other approaches to developing innovative ideas – though, unfortunately, less enthusiasm for scaling successful strategies.

Some of the most interesting innovations have involved nonprofit financing, including "pay-for-performance" schemes, in which funders pay grantee organizations only if they achieve agreed-upon outcome targets. There has been some experimentation with social impact bonds, which combine pay-for-performance with financial markets to scale up successful strategies. For example, in 2010, the United Kingdom offered £5 million of bonds to fund interventions by organizations with proven records of reducing recidivism among prisoners. The bondholders, who take greater than market risks, are repaid only if the organizations achieve certain milestones.

For all of the improved practices and new ideas of the past decade, philanthropy remains an underperformer in achieving social outcomes. One cause of this may be that philanthropists are essentially unaccountable. Businesses have shareholders, politicians have constituents, and nonprofits have funders. In contrast, philanthropists are spending their own money subject to only minimal constraints on their judgment. Of course, foundations have boards, but the boards are often themselves the primary decision-makers and, in any event, are not externally accountable. In theory, the media can play a watchdog role. But even if they had the data and capacity necessary to monitor outcomes, their audiences tend to be more interested in personal anecdotes, especially tales of malfeasance.

Despite these shortcomings, I cannot think of a system of external accountability with bite that would not threaten the valuable diversity of American philanthropy – especially its ability to experiment and take risks. A more promising approach would center on self-imposed philanthropic transparency, which could provide donors with feedback that would inform their practices as well as improve sector-wide knowledge.

[. . .]

It is not surprising that donors who are unconcerned with improving their own practices are not interested in improving the practice of philanthropy more broadly. Perhaps because supporting the field seems self-indulgent, or because its benefits are indirect, abstract, and long term, some of the promising new organizations are underfunded.

Despite these problems, outcome-oriented philanthropy continues to have momentum. If there's still more talk than action, talk often precedes action. With many new large foundations likely to come into being during the coming decade, there is a great opportunity to increase the sector's impact. But for outcome-oriented philanthropy to take root will ultimately require a change in the mindset of high net worth donors about what it means to be a good philanthropist.

The problem with big ideas

Michael Hobbes, 2014

It seemed like such a good idea at the time: A merry-go-round hooked up to a water pump. In rural sub-Saharan Africa, where children are plentiful but clean water is scarce, the PlayPump harnessed one to provide the other. Every time the kids spun around on the big colorful wheel, water filled an elevated tank a few yards away, providing fresh, clean water anyone in the village could use all day.

PlayPump International, the NGO that came up with the idea and developed the technology, seemed to have thought of everything. To pay for maintenance, the elevated water tanks sold advertising, becoming billboards for companies seeking access to rural markets. If the ads didn't sell, they would feature HIV/AIDS-prevention campaigns. The whole package cost just $7,000 to install in each village and could provide water for up to 2,500 people.

The donations gushed in. In 2006, the US government and two major foundations pledged $16.4 million in a public ceremony emceed by Bill Clinton and Laura Bush. The technology was touted by the World Bank and made a cameo in America's 2007 Water for the Poor Act. Jay-Z personally pledged $400,000. PlayPump set the goal of installing 4,000 pumps in Africa by 2010. "That would mean clean drinking water for some ten million people," a "Frontline" reporter announced.

By 2007, less than two years after the grants came in, it was already clear these aspirations weren't going to be met. A UNICEF report found pumps abandoned, broken, unmaintained. Of the more than 1,500 pumps that had been installed with the initial burst of grant money in Zambia, one-quarter already needed repair. *The Guardian* said the pumps were "reliant on child labour."

In 2010, "Frontline" returned to the schools where they had filmed children laughing on the merry-go-rounds, splashing each other with water. They discovered pumps rusting, billboards unsold, women stooping to turn the wheel in pairs. Many of the villages hadn't even been asked if they wanted a PlayPump, they just got one, sometimes replacing the hand pumps they already had. In one community, adults were paying children to operate the pump.

Let's not pretend to be surprised by any of this. The PlayPump story is a sort of Mad Libs version of a narrative we're all familiar with by now: Exciting new development idea, huge impact in one location, influx of donor dollars, quick expansion, failure.

I came across the PlayPump story in Ken Stern's *With Charity For All*, but I could have plucked one from any of the dozen or so "development doesn't work" best-sellers to come out in the last ten years. In *The Idealist* – a kind of "where are they now?" for the ideas laid out in Jeffrey Sachs's *The End of Poverty* – Nina Munk discovers African villages made squalid by the hopes and checkbooks of Western do-gooders.

Esther Duflo and Abhijit Banerjee's *Poor Economics* finds dozens of "common sense" development projects – food aid, crop insurance, microfinance – either don't help poor people or may even make them poorer.

[. . .]

I am conflicted about this moment. I have worked at international development NGOs almost my entire career. I've been frustrated by the same inefficiencies and assumptions of my sector that are now getting picked apart in public. Like the authors, donors, and governments attacking international development, I'm sometimes disillusioned with what my job requires me to do, what it requires that I demand of others.

Over the last year, I read every book, essay, and roman à clef about my field I could find. I came out convinced that the problems with international development are real, they are fundamental, and I might, in fact, be one of them. But I also found that it's too easy to blame the PlayPumps of the world. Donors, governments, the public, the media, aid recipients themselves – they all contribute to the dysfunction. Maybe the problem isn't that international development doesn't work. It's that it can't.

Evidence-based interventions and RCTs

In the late 1990s, Michael Kremer, then an economics professor at MIT [Massachusetts Institute of Technology], was in Kenya working on an NGO project that distributed textbooks to schools in poor rural districts. Around that time, the ratio of children to textbooks in Kenya was 17 to 1. The intervention seemed obvious: Poor villages need textbooks, rich donors have the money to buy them. All we have to do is link them up.

But in the early stages of the project, Kremer convinced the researchers to do it differently. He wanted to know whether giving kids textbooks actually made them better students. So instead of handing out books and making a simple before-and-after comparison, he designed the project like a pharmaceutical trial. He split the schools into groups, gave some of them the "treatment" (i.e. textbooks) and the others nothing. Then he tested everyone, not just the kids who got the books but also the kids who didn't, to see if his intervention had any effect.

It didn't. The trial took four years, but it was conclusive: Some of the kids improved academically over that time and some got worse, but the treatment group wasn't any better off than the control.

Then Kremer tried something else. Maybe the kids weren't struggling in school because of what was going on in the classroom, but because of what was going on outside of it.

So again, Kremer split the schools into groups and spent three years testing and measuring them. This time, the treatment was an actual treatment – medication to eradicate stomach worms. Worm infections affect up to 600 million children around the world, sapping their nutrition and causing, among other things, anemia, stomachaches, and stunting.

Once more, the results were conclusive: The deworming pills made the kids noticeably better off. Absence rates fell by 25 percent, the kids got taller, even their friends and families got healthier. By interrupting the chain of infection, the treatments had reduced worm infections in entire villages. Even more striking, when they tested the same kids nearly a decade later, they had more education and earned higher salaries. The female participants were less likely to be employed in domestic services. And compared with

Kremer's first trial, deworming was a bargain. Textbooks cost $2 to $3 each. Deworming pills were as little as 49 cents. When Kremer calculated the kids' bump in lifetime wages compared with the cost of treatment, it was a 60-to-1 ratio.

This is perfect TED talk stuff: Conventional wisdom called into question, rigorous science triumphing over dogma. As word of Kremer's study spread, he became part of a growing movement within international development to subject its assumptions to randomized controlled trials.

Dozens of books and articles have tracked the rise of the randomistas, as they've come to be called. The most prominent of these, and the most fun to read, is *Poor Economics*, sort of the *Principia Mathematica* of "obvious" development interventions tested and found wanting.

[. . .]

Armed with his rigorously gathered results, Kremer founded an NGO, Deworm the World. He launched it at the 2007 World Economic Forum and committed to deworming ten million children. He was feted by the Clinton Global Initiative; GlaxoSmithKline, and Johnson & Johnson pledged $600 million worth of deworming treatments a year, enough for every infected primary school student in Africa. The World Health Organization issued a statement of support. Kenya asked him to help create a national program to deworm 3.6 million children. Two states in India initiated similar programs, aiming to treat millions more. The organization now claims to have helped 40 million children in 27 countries.

But wait a minute. Just because something works for 30,000 students in Kenya doesn't mean it will work for millions of them across Africa or India. Deworm the World's website talks a lot about its "evidence-based" approach. (It has now been folded into an NGO called Evidence Action.) Yet the primary evidence that deworming improves education outcomes is from Kremer's single Kenya case and a post-hoc analysis of deworming initiatives in the American South in 1910. In 2012, the organization said that it had treated 17 million children in India, but didn't report whether their attendance, school performance, or graduation rates improved.

I keep thinking I'm missing something really obvious, that I'm looking at the wrong part of their website. So I call up Evidence Action and ask: Are you guys really not testing how deworming affects education anymore?

"We don't measure the effects on school attendance and school performance," says Alix Zwane, Evidence Action's executive director. At the scale they're going for in India, entire states at a time, splitting into control and treatment groups simply wouldn't be feasible.

Kremer tells me that enough trials have been done to warrant the upscaling. "There's more evidence for this than the vast majority of things that governments spend money on." Every time you want to build a new road, you can't stop to ask, Will this one really help people get from place to place?

"Meanwhile," he says, "there's a cohort of children that, if you don't implement the policy now, will go through years of schooling without treatment."

It's an interesting question – when do you have enough evidence to stop testing each new application of a development idea? – and I get that you can't run a four-year trial every time you roll out, say, the measles vaccine to a new country. But like many other aid projects under pressure to scale up too fast and too far, deworming kids to improve their education outcomes isn't the slam-dunk its supporters make it out to be.

[. . .]

Then there's the comparison to textbooks. Kenya, it turns out, is a uniquely terrible place to hand out textbooks to kids and expect better academic performance. When Kremer reported that textbooks had no overall effect, he also noted that they did actually improve test scores for the kids who were already at the top of the class. The main problem, it seems, was that the textbooks were in English, the second or third language for most of the kids. Of the third-graders given textbooks, only 15 percent could even read them.

In the 1980s and early '90s, a series of meta-analyses found that textbooks were actually effective at improving school performance in places where the language issues weren't as complex. In his own paper reporting the Kenya results, Kremer noted that, in Nicaragua and the Philippines, giving kids textbooks did improve their test scores.

But the point of all this is not to talk shit on Kremer – who has bettered the world more with his career than I ever have with mine – or to dismantle his deworming charity, or to advocate that we should all go back to giving out free textbooks. What I want to talk shit on is the paradigm of the Big Idea – that once we identify the correct one, we can simply unfurl it on the entire developing world like a picnic blanket.

There are villages where deworming will be the most meaningful education project possible. There are others where free textbooks will. In other places, it will be new school buildings, more teachers, lower fees, better transport, tutors, uniforms. There's probably a village out there where a PlayPump would beat all these approaches combined. The point is, we don't know what works, where, or why. The only way to find out is to test these models – not just before their initial success but afterward, and constantly.

I can see why it's appealing to think that, once you find a successful formula for development, you can just scale it up like a Model T. Host governments want programs that get more effective as they get bigger. Individual donors, you and me, we want to feel like we're backing a plucky little start-up that is going to save the world. No international institution wants to say in their annual report: "There's this great NGO that increased attendance in a Kenyan school district. We're giving them a modest sum to do the same thing in one other district in one other country."

The repeated "success, scale, fail" experience of the last 20 years of development practice suggests something super boring: Development projects thrive or tank according to the specific dynamics of the place in which they're applied. It's not that you test something in one place, then scale it up to 50. It's that you test it in one place, then test it in another, then another. No one will ever be invited to explain that in a TED talk.

[. . .]

Unintended consequences

Dertu isn't a place very many people go on purpose. Located in northeastern Kenya, close to the Somali border, and next door to a sprawling refugee camp, in 2004 it was little more than a rest stop, a place for the local pastoralists to refresh their animals and catch up on local news. Its chief attraction was fresh water from a UNICEF-drilled borehole in the clay. Of the few thousand people living there permanently, more than 80 percent relied on food aid. Ninety percent were illiterate.

This is the "before" picture of Dertu that Jeffrey Sachs found when he initiated his Millennium Villages Project there in 2006. Sachs, a professor at Columbia University, became a Bono-approved development celebrity with his book *The End of Poverty*, a screed against the rich world's complacency in letting easily solvable problems – malaria, literacy, clean water – damn an entire continent to misery.

Sachs's book tour culminated in the establishment of the Millennium Villages Project, an ambitious plan to jump-start development with a huge influx of cash, in-kind support, and infrastructure to some of the poorest settlements in the world. Sachs's premise was that millions of people, dozens of countries, had fallen into the "poverty trap:" Living in substandard housing leads to problems concentrating at school. Which leads to not graduating. Which leads to working in low-skilled jobs. Which leads to living in substandard housing. And on and on.

The only solution, Sachs argued, was to dramatically boost people to a level where they could start to develop themselves.

This is, it turns out, an incredibly persuasive idea, and in the two years after the book came out, Sachs raised $120 million (including $50 million from George Soros's personal checkbook) and identified 14 villages throughout sub-Saharan Africa to test his theory.

As described in Nina Munk's book, *The Idealist: Jeffrey Sachs and the Quest to End Poverty*, things looked promising in Dertu at first. Sachs convinced GE and Ericsson to donate medical equipment and cell phones. He hired local managers who knew the culture and language to ensure his project was responding to Dertu's needs. His teams built housing, schools, roads, health clinics. They set up a livestock market to attract farmers from all over the region.

But soon, the momentum faltered. Without electricity to run it or specialists to maintain it, the advanced medical equipment gathered dust – in Kenya, that means literally. The managers of the project, so knowledgeable about the local culture and mores, eventually succumbed to them, doling out benefits on the basis of tribal favoritism and tit-for-tat back-scratching. The borehole broke down and water had to be shipped in by truck.

The core of the problem, as Munk describes it, was that Dertu became a sort of company town, with the Millennium Villages Project providing the only reliable source of employment, benefits, and public services. Thousands of new residents came from the nearby refugee camp and other parts of Kenya, seeking jobs or handouts. Where Dertu was once a stopover for nomads, the influx of donor money, the improved infrastructure, the free housing and education and health care, had given people a reason to stay. Sachs's funding couldn't keep up. And eventually, it ran out.

In an interview about her book for EconTalk, Munk describes what Dertu looked like the last time she saw it, in 2011:

> They were now really living in a kind of squalor that I hadn't seen on my first visit. Their huts were jammed together; they were patched with those horrible polyurethane bags that one sees all over Africa . . . There were streams of slop that were going down between these tightly packed huts. And the latrines had overflowed or were clogged. And no one was able to agree on whose job it was to maintain them. And there were ditches piled high with garbage. And it was just – it made my heart just sink.

This is the paradox: When you improve something, you change it in ways you couldn't have expected. You can find examples of this in every corner of development practice. A project in Kenya that gave kids free uniforms, textbooks, and classroom materials increased enrollment by 50 percent, swamping the teachers and reducing the quality of education for everyone. Communities in India cut off their own water supply so they could be classified as "slums" and be eligible for slum-upgrading funding. I've worked in places where as soon as a company sets up a health clinic or an education program, the local government disappears – why should they spend money on primary schools when a rich company is ready to take on the responsibility?

There's nothing avaricious about this. If anything, it demonstrates the entrepreneurial spirit we're constantly telling the poor they need to demonstrate.

My favorite example of unintended consequences comes, weirdly enough, from the United States. In a speech to a criminology conference, Nancy G. Guerra, the director of the Institute for Global Studies at the University of Delaware, described a project where she held workshops with inner-city Latina teenagers, trying to prevent them from joining gangs. The program worked in that none of the girls committed any violence within six months of the workshops. But by the end of that time, they were all, each and every one, pregnant.

"That behavior was serving a need for them," she says in her speech. "It made them feel powerful, it made them feel important, it gave them a sense of identity . . . When that ended, [they] needed another kind of meaning in their lives."

The fancy academic term for this is "complex adaptive systems." We all understand that every ecosystem, each forest floor or coral reef, is the result of millions of interactions between its constituent parts, a balance of all the aggregated adaptations of plants and animals to their climate and each other. Adding a non-native species, or removing one that has always been there, changes these relationships in ways that are too intertwined and complicated to predict.

According to Ben Ramalingam's book called *Aid on the Edge of Chaos*, international development is just such an invasive species. Why Dertu doesn't have a vaccination clinic, why Kenyan school kids can't read, it's a combination of culture, politics, history, laws, infrastructure, individuals – all of a society's component parts, their harmony and their discord, working as one organism. Introducing something foreign into that system – millions in donor cash, dozens of trained personnel and equipment, UN Land Rovers – causes it to adapt in ways you can't predict.

[. . .]

Conclusions

So international development sucks, right? I've just spent thousands of words telling you all the ways the incentives of donors, recipients, and NGOs contradict each other. Why not just scrap it altogether?

Because I don't think that's the conclusion these examples suggest. I think they suggest something much less dramatic: It's not that development is broken, it's that our expectations of it are.

First, let's de-room this elephant: Development has happened. The last 50 years have seen about the biggest explosion of prosperity in human history. China, India, Taiwan, South Korea, Turkey, Mexico – these aren't the only countries where you'd rather be born now than 50 years ago. Even the poorest countries in the world – Burundi, Somalia, Zimbabwe – are doing way better on stuff like vaccinations and literacy than they did earlier in our own lifetimes.

You sometimes hear this Cambrian proliferation of well-being as an argument against development aid, like: "See? China got better all by itself." But the rise of formerly destitute countries into the sweaters-and-smartphones bracket is less a refutation of the impact of development aid than a reality-check of its scale. In 2013, development aid from all the rich countries combined was $134.8 billion, or about $112 per year for each of the world's 1.2 billion people living on less than $1.25 per day. Did we really expect an extra hundred bucks a year to pull anyone, much less a billion of them, out of poverty?

Development, no matter how it happens, is a slow process. It wasn't until about 30 years after Mao's death that China's per capita GDP reached lower-middle-income status. The country's growth is arguably the fastest of any country's since we, as a species, started gathering economic statistics. Even in the most cartoonishly successful scenario imaginable, countries like the Central African Republic (per capita GDP: $700, adjusted for purchasing power), Burundi ($600), and the Democratic Republic of Congo ($400) will take decades just to reach the point where China is now.

The ability of international development projects to speed up this process is limited. Remember how I said the deworming project had a 60-to-1 ratio between the price of the pills and the increase in wages for the kids who got them? The increase was $30. Not $30 per year. The kids earned $30 more over their lifetimes as a result of the deworming treatment. You find this a lot in the development literature: Even the most wildly successful projects decrease maternal mortality by a few percent here, add an extra year or two of life expectancy there.

This isn't a criticism of the projects themselves. This is how social policy works, in baby steps and trial-and-error and tweaks, not in game changers. Leave the leaps and bounds to computing power. If a 49-cent deworming treatment really does produce a $30 increase in wages for some of the poorest people on Earth, we are assholes for not spending it.

And this is where I landed after a year of absorbing dozens of books and articles and speeches about international development: The arguments against it are myriad, and mostly logistical and technical. The argument for it is singular, moral, and, to me anyway, utterly convincing: We have so much, they have so little.

If we really want to fix development, we need to stop chasing after ideas the way we go on fad diets. Successful programs should be allowed to expand by degrees, not digits (direct cash payments, which have shown impressive results in Kenya and Uganda, are a great candidate for the kind of deliberate expansion I'm talking about). NGOs need to be free to invest in the kinds of systems and processes we're always telling developing countries to put in place. And rich countries need to spend less time debating how to divide up the tiny sliver of our GDP we spend on development and more time figuring out how to leverage our vast economic and political power to let it happen on its own.

[. . .]

PlayPump International, the charity I started with, doesn't exist anymore. The pumps, however, are still being installed by Roundabout Water Solutions, an NGO that markets them as a "niche solution" that should only be installed at primary schools in poor rural areas. Four years ago, the same evaluations that so harshly criticized the rapid expansion of the project also acknowledged that, in some villages, under the right circumstances, they were fabulously helpful.

In 2010, "Frontline" interviewed the director of PlayPump about its failures, and he said, "It might have been a bit ambitious, but hey, you gotta dream big. Everyone's always said it's such a great idea."

And it was. But maybe when the next great idea comes along, we should all dream a little smaller.

What if everything we've been taught about charity is dead wrong?

Dan Pallotta, 2013

How would you react if you knew someone was getting wealthy in charity? How would you feel if you saw your favorite charity run a $3 million ad on the Superbowl using charitable donations to fund it? What would you think if a charity lost a million dollars on a brand new fundraising idea that flopped? Lastly, what if you learned that a charity had just paid an investor a 100 percent return on a loan?

These are the kinds of scenarios that make our blood boil with rage and the kinds of practices that give charities a bad name, right?

But what if we're wrong about all of it? What if the things that send us into a rage are actually the things it would take to end humanity's most vexing and extreme forms of suffering? And what if you are only being given half of the story?

These are the issues that have consumed me for the last fifteen years and that were the subject of my closing talk at the 2013 TED conference.

Ask yourself how you would feel if you were given the whole story.

Suppose that the person getting wealthy in charity was worth it. Imagine, for example, that the Boys & Girls Clubs hires a leader that triples revenues in 8 years from half a billion annually to $1.5 billion annually. This allows the clubs to *double* the number of kids served. She gets a total compensation package of about $1 million annually. This is not a fairy tale. It really happened. And the Boys & Girls Clubs were criticized for it. Is $1 million not a cheap price to pay for $1 *billion* in new revenues and double the kids served? Would we rather they hire a leader for a more modest $150,000 who is incapable of increasing revenues and serving more kids? Save $850,000 in salary expense and lose a billion dollars a year in revenue?

And what if the $3 million Super Bowl ad brings in $6 million in new revenues in just the first showing, and another $6 million in gifts over time from new donors who repeat their gifts? The charity would have turned each original donor's dollar into four dollars.

What if the $1 million lost on a charity fundraiser that flopped taught the charity something they never knew that allowed them to create a new fundraiser that raised many millions, in the way, say, a cancer researcher's big failure points them to their next big breakthrough? That would mean the donors that funded the "loss" were actually funding an investment in learning that reaped millions.

And as for the investor getting a 100 percent return on a loan, what if the loan was to finance a brand new, risky fundraising event idea – a new triathlon for the cause, for example. The charity needs a million to cover the upfront costs to launch it. But it's risky. It could fail. There's no data on it. It's never been done before. No bank will touch it. So an investor comes along and says I will put up the million, but I want

$2 million back if it succeeds, to compensate me for the potential risk of the loss of my money. The charity agrees. The event is a huge success, netting $10 million in the first year. The investor gets $2 million, leaving $8 million for the cause – a figure that would have been zero without the investor. Because the concept is now proven, banks are willing to finance the event in future years at much lower interest. The event nets $8 million a year for ten years – $80 million total, all for the tiny cost of $1 million paid to the original investor.

None of these are fantasy. I've seen versions of these examples manifest in the real world, many times.

When you hear the whole story, suddenly it seems unconscionable *not* to do the things we've all been taught it would be unconscionable to do.

Could it be that everything we've been taught about charity, and about giving, and about change is backwards? That when we show people only the means, without revealing the ends, we mislead them? Is it possible that in the name of an ethic we are actually prolonging the suffering of millions of adults and children the world over? Do we really think it is of some comfort to a mother who has just lost her little boy to bird flu that at least no one made a profit in the failed effort to save her son?

We allow the for-profit sector to feast on the tools of capitalism, while we deny those tools to the nonprofit sector, and all in the name of charity, no less. Real charity, as in grace, could not be undermined with more reverence paid to the notion of something noble. It is perhaps the greatest injustice ever perpetrated against all those citizens of humanity most desperately in need of our aid. But it is an injustice about which we have been largely unconscious. If we take responsibility for the thinking that has been handed down to us, revisit it, and revise it, we could change our whole approach to changing the world. And then things could really begin to change.

It is a staggering question – what if everything we've been taught about charity is dead wrong?

6.3 New – or not so new – ways of improving philanthropy

How the rich can save the world

Matthew Bishop and Michael Green, 2008

Shortly before lunchtime of June 26, 2006, the then second-richest man in the world stepped onto a stage in the New York Public Library to be greeted by a standing ovation from several hundred of the wealthiest and most powerful people in the city. After saying a few words, Warren Buffett, whose record of brilliant investment decisions had earned him the nickname "Sage of Omaha," reached into his jacket pocket, took out a pen, and with a flourish began to sign five letters, each one promising a part of his fortune. "The first three letters are easy to sign. I just sign Dad," he joked, before handing a billion-dollar letter starting "Dear Suze" to his only daughter. The next letter he gave to his elder son; the third, to his second son; the fourth to a representative of his late wife, Susan, who had died two years earlier.

So far, these letters had promised to give away a combined $6 billion or so. Finally, he held only the fifth letter, alone worth an estimated $31 billion. He signed it and handed it to the wife of the only man on the planet who was then richer than himself, Bill Gates, the cofounder of Microsoft, the world's biggest software firm. Then the two tycoons smiled and shook hands as the crowd cheered wildly.

Not one of these gifts was for the personal benefit of those accepting the letters. Buffett had long made it clear that his children should expect to receive far smaller sums for themselves in his will. Rather, each gift was for the charitable foundation that the grateful recipient had established. At a combined total estimated at $37 billion, Buffett's philanthropic donation was the largest ever. It beat even the $31 billion that Gates had by then given to the foundation that bears his name and that of his wife (although Gates had already said that most of his remaining fortune – estimated at over $50 billion – would go the same beneficent way). By 2009, the Bill & Melinda Gates Foundation plans to give away over $3 billion of that endowment every year, unprecedented in the history of philanthropy.

Buffett and Gates are leading a revival and reinvention of an old tradition that has the potential to solve many of the biggest problems facing humanity today. Making the announcement in the New York Public Library was a deliberate nod to that tradition. The striking marble beaux arts building had been paid for more than a century before by a previous generation of great American philanthropists. But modern philanthropy was invented several centuries before that, in Europe, at the same time as the emergence of what we now call capitalism. The Buffetts and Gateses of this first golden age of philanthropy were the merchants of Tudor England and Renaissance Europe, who helped the poor in growing trading cities like London, Florence, and Bruges. Next, in the eighteenth century, philanthropy was embraced by the inventors of the joint stock company and the original hedge-fund-like speculators such as Thomas Guy, who sold at the top of the South Sea Bubble and used his profits to found Guy's Hospital in London. This was also the age of the enlightened financiers who backed crusading activists such as William Willberforce, destroyer of the slave trade. In the nineteenth century, philanthropy became a way of life for Britain's newly wealthy Victorians, as reflected in the novels of Charles Dickens.

But the fortunes that Buffett and Gates are giving away dwarf those of the leading philanthropists of golden ages past, even those of Andrew Carnegie and John D. Rockefeller a century ago. Nor are Buffett and Gates, the leading examples of a fast-growing army of new philanthropists, merely doing the same old thing. The new philanthropists believe they are improving philanthropy, equipping it to tackle the new set of problems facing today's changing world; and to be blunt, it needs improvement – much philanthropy over the centuries has been ineffective. They think they can do a better job than their predecessors. The past couple of decades have been a golden age for capitalism, and today's new philanthropists are trying to apply the secrets behind that money-making success to their giving. That is why we call them philanthrocapitalists.

Today's philanthrocapitalists see a world full of big problems that they, and perhaps only they, can and must put right. Surely, they say, we can save the lives of millions of children who die each year in poor countries from poverty or diseases that have been eradicated in the rich world. And back home in the United Sates or Europe, it is we who must find ways to make our education systems work for every child, instead of failing so many students. And if these children are to have a decent life when they grow older, we must find a solution to climate change and the underlying causes of terrorism. And so on.

As evidence of the seriousness of his philanthropy, Bill Gates had made a big announcement of his own a few days before Buffett handed out his letters. At the end of June 2008, he would leave his day job at Microsoft, which he had cofounded in 1975, and start working full time at his foundation – a significant career change for a man aged only fifty-two, still at the peak of his powers, and proof that when it comes to philanthropy, he means business.

Sitting in his huge office in Microsoft's Seattle headquarters in September 2007, Bill Gates rocks back and forth in his chair as he gets excited about what he is saying. "You know, if you picked the five most interesting and important things that have happened in my time frame, I think that these two would be in the top five, if not at the top," he says, now tapping his pen to the rhythm. "The personal computer, which I got a chance to participate in, has had this amazing, almost unbelievably great impact on billions of lives, so I'm very proud to be involved in that." But now he is looking to have at least as great an impact on at least as many lives through his philanthropy as he takes on some of the world's deadliest diseases. "Now I get to put more into what is sort of a new frontier – more like Microsoft at age three than at age thirty-three."

In business, the philanthrocapitalists are used to achieving success on a grand scale, to thinking big and going for it. If that approach works in making money, they reason, why wouldn't it work when it comes to giving the stuff away?

In the United States, Gates wants to transform the entire government-funded public school system. Already, his money is starting to make a difference, and Gates believes this is just the beginning. In New York City, for example, Gates has provided money to start dozens of small schools, such as the Bronx Lab. One of four new schools sharing the former campus of the Evander Childs High School in one of New York's poorest areas, which was closed due to persistently low levels of educational achievement, the Bronx Lab opened its doors in 2004. After three years, a remarkable 90 percent of its first class of students was on track to graduate in 2008, compared with a typical graduation rate of under 31 percent at Evander Childs. Gates thinks this sort of success can be repeated through the education system, in New York and nationwide.

But what gets Gates rocking and tapping even more excitedly are the things his philanthropy could achieve outside America by ending disease and reducing poverty. More than one million people die from malaria every year, most of them children in poor countries. That is the equivalent of losing every student in the New York public school system in one year. "We're sort of crazy enough to say, 'Let's eliminate malaria,'" says Gates. And it is not just malaria that is on his hit list. His foundation also wants to dramatically reduce deaths from other diseases that annually kill millions of people in the developing world, such as acute diarrhoea, pneumonia, tuberculosis, and HIV/AIDS. And it is funding research into fourteen "grand challenges in global health," ranging from creating new vaccines to finding economically efficient ways to measure public health.

Gates is also giving hundreds of millions of dollars a year to accelerate economic development in poor countries. In 2006, he announced a partnership with one of the foundations created during an earlier gold age of philanthropy, the Rockefeller Foundation, to increase the productivity (and thus, income) of poor farmers in Africa. The Alliance for a Green Revolution in Africa aims to build on what many people believe is philanthropy's greatest ever success: the first "green revolution." Over many years the Rockefeller Foundation, guided by Normal Borlaug, funded research into how to increase crop yields in poor countries, which is reckoned to have saved over one billion lives since the 1940s. But most of those lives were in Asia, not Africa. As global food prices soar increasingly beyond the reach of the poor, Gates believes something just as dramatic can now be done about that.

None of this will be easy. Buffett admits that his gift amounts to only "one dollar each per year for the poorest half of the world population" and describes philanthropy as a "tougher game" than business. Gates concedes that, "given the scale of the problems of global development, education, we will only be a small part of the solution." But there is no doubting their determination. Nor is it just the two richest men on the planet who are thinking such world-changing thoughts. The massive commitment of Gates and Buffett to philanthropy is the most dramatic evidence so far of a movement – philanthrocapitalism – that is growing hand in hand with the rise in the number of very rich people on the planet. Since the early 1980s, the world has enjoyed a remarkable period of prosperity that, whilst spread quite broadly, has benefited the people at the top of the pyramid considerably more than the rest of the population. According to *Forbes* magazine, in 2008 the world had a record 1,125 billionaires, up from a mere 140 in 1986, as well as thousands of multimillionaires.

Buffett and Gates were relatively slow to join the movement. In 1997, Ted Turner, the founder of the CNN cable news channel, made headlines by giving $1 billion to support the United Nations and criticizing his fellow tycoons for being tightfisted. He called specifically on Gates and Buffett – and other people "awash with money" – to "give the money away that you have no idea what you're going to do with."

It remains to be seen how many of today's newly wealthy will become serious philanthrocapitalists, but the omens seem good – not least because Buffett, Gates, and others are challenging the rest of the rich to join their movement. "There is a great question of all the wealth that has been created in this era," says Gates. As he throws down the philanthropic gauntlet to his fellow tycoons, he is optimistic. "This is a momentum thing: the more people that are involved, the more it draws other people in." "But what proportion of the new rich will ultimately start to give back? I think it'll be a high percentage," says Gates, "more like seventy percent than fifteen percent."

The annual Capgemini/Merrill Lunch World Wealth Report noted a 20 percent surge in giving by the rich in North America in 2006. This trend is not confined to America. "Led by the ranks of the ultra-wealthy, [high-net-worth individuals] are increasing the financial resources, time and thought they donate to philanthropic causes," concluded the report, which found that those wealthy individuals who engaged in philanthropy typically gave away around 7 percent of their wealth, far more than did the average citizen. "Veteran fundraisers say the outlook for giving is the most upbeat in a generation," reported the house journal of the American giving business, the *Chronicle of Philanthropy*, in 2006.

This impressive picture is reinforced by various rankings of philanthropists. Since 1997, online magazine *Slate* has been publishing its Slate 60 ranking of the largest philanthropic donations of the year. This was inspired by Turner's complaint that the rich are always measured in terms of what they own rather than what they give. ("I think that the culture towards philanthropy has changed," says Turner. "Why? Because we drew attention to it. We should have lists of givers, which is why I came up with the Slate 60. That is why rich people own sports teams – wealthy people like to get their name in the paper.") Since it began, the minimum gift needed to get on the list has tripled to $30 million.

A similar picture emerges from the fast-growing number of charitable foundations in America and abroad. New bequests, combined with strong investment returns on the endowments of older foundations, drove a doubling in real terms of American foundation giving from $13.8 billion in 1996 to $31.6 billion in 2006.

As they apply their business methods to philanthropy, philanthrocapitalists are developing a new (if familiar-sounding) language to describe their businesslike approach. Their philanthropy is "strategic," "market-conscious," "impact-oriented," "knowledge-based," often "high-engagement," and always driven by the goal of maximizing the "leverage" of the donor's money. Seeing themselves as social investors, not traditional donors, some of them engage in "venture philanthropy." As entrepreneurial "philanthropreneurs," they love to back social entrepreneurs who offer innovative solutions to society's problems. (Inevitably, some charity traditionalists dismiss all this as empty jargon.)

As well as seeking better ways to work with charitable nonprofit, non-governmental organizations (NGOs), philanthrocapitalists are increasingly trying to find ways of harnessing the profit motive to achieve social good. This is controversial, to say the least: isn't philanthropy supposed to be about giving away money, not making more of it? But as the philanthrocapitalists see it, if they can use their donations to create a profitable solution to a social problem, it will attract far more capital, far faster, and thus achieve a far bigger impact, far sooner, than would a solution based entirely on giving money away. Thus, their money can lever, in a good cause, some of the trillions of dollars in the for-profit business world.

At the same time as individual philanthropists are embracing the profit motive, a growing number of big for-profit businesses are catching the philanthrocapitalism bug and getting into giving – or at least trying to do good. Gates sees this as potentially the start of a "system innovation" in how business operates, which he calls "creative capitalism."

This is very different from traditional corporate philanthropy, which has often been ineffective: giving away small sums of money typically to generate positive publicity rather than change the world. Nor is it like old-fashioned corporate social responsibility, which is too often nothing more than a cynical exercise in public relations. Indeed, the ineffectiveness of both these traditional approaches is one reason why many people view with skepticism the notion that large companies can be a force for good.

To prove the skeptics wrong, some of the world's biggest firms are now making advancing the good of society an integral part of their business strategy. Wal-Mart, for instance, is championing environmentalism, seeing it as a profit opportunity because it will both cut costs (of packaging, for example) and allow the retailer to sell new products (long-lasting low-energy light bulbs). Oil giant Shell is redeeming its reputation by helping to develop small businesses in Africa on the basis that job creation is the only sustainable strategy for ending poverty.

Arguably the most innovative firm of all is Google. When the Internet search and advertising company first sold shares to the public in 2004, it promised to give 1 percent of its shares, 1 percent of its profits, and 1 percent of its employees' time to Google.org, which the firm's thirtysomething founders, Sergey Brin and Larry Page, hope will one day "eclipse Google itself in overall world impact by ambitiously applying innovation and significant resources to the largest of the world's problems." Given the impact achieved already by Google.com, that would be something to behold.

The test of these fine words will be whether rich philanthropists and companies can walk the walk as well as they talk the talk. The road to hell is paved with good intentions. And the problems they are addressing are highly complex. Will they have the humility to listen to others who have been grappling with these problems for far longer? Will they be willing to learn from their mistakes? Will they stick at it when the going gets tough, as it surely will?

A few miles from the proliferating skyscrapers of Bangalore, the centre of India's booming high-tech business-process outsourcing industry, is a camp of metal huts housing the families of labourers who have come from far-off villages to work on the city's many construction sites. A bright yellow bus stops in the dirt square, and immediately it is surrounded by about thirty children, aged four to ten. Once on board, they sit – three per screen – by computers where specially developed software teaches them language and mathematical skills. The children are clearly comfortable with the computers, absorbed in their learning.

The bus is provided by the Azmin Premji Foundation, which is head-quartered next to the modern campus of the Indian tech firm Wipro. The company's boss, who established the eponymous foundation in 2001, was the sixtieth-richest person on earth in 2008, according to *Forbes*, with an estimated fortune of $12.7 billion. "A more educated child is very critical for democracy," Premji says, worrying that India's population is growing dangerously fast. "If a girl is educated up to level five or six, she is aware of the need for a smaller family. A little basic education improves knowledge of primary health care."

Just as globalization has been one of the driving forces of the current golden age of capitalism, so the idea that the wealthy winners should engage seriously in philanthropy has gone global. Even ten years ago it was easy to regard large-scale philanthropy as a US exception to the global consensus that the state, not private giving, offers the best solutions to society's biggest problems. Today philanthropy is booming everywhere there is entrepreneurial wealth creation. In 2007, the then third-richest man in the world announced he would give away $10 billion through his foundation. He was not from the United States, but from Mexico: telecommunications boss Carlos Slim Helu.

Shakira's hips don't lie – and Bill Clinton can't keep his eyes off them. Nor, to be fair, can most of the audience, a strange mix of students, social activists, and billionaires, in the legendary Apollo Theater in Harlem. This particular evening, in September 2007, the Colombian pop star is singing her latest hit, "Hips Don't Lie," at a debate-cum-party, screened live on MTV, at the end of the annual meeting of the Clinton Global Initiative (CGI). Since the former president, now as much a celebrity as a politician, first held this annual giving fest in 2005, it has become a must-attend event for philanthrocapitalists eager for recognition at what the Economist has christened "the Philanthropy Oscars."

At least since the Live Aid concert in 1985, celebrities and philanthropy have become ever more entwined. Now, movie and rock star "celanthropists" are serious partners with the superrich. Rock star and activist Bono and Bill Gates – who, with Melinda Gates, were named *Time* magazine's "People of the Year" in 2005 – have "had a common cause" ever since their first meeting in New York in 2002, says Gates: "He's been great." Some celebrities are even superrich philanthropists in their own right. Oprah Winfrey, for example, the billionaire television host and producer, has paid for a school in Africa and also works in partnership with the Gates Foundation.

This makes some people uneasy. What does a rock star really know about the poor in Africa? Yet just as celebrities are now an integral part of capitalism, due to their ability to touch and influence the mass market, so too they are becoming a key ingredient of philanthrocapitalism, particularly on issues in which mobilizing public opinion is crucial.

When rich people get involved in what are essentially political issues, it is easy for everyone else to fear the worst. Today's democratic freedoms have been hard-won; voters do not want to trade their rights for plutocracy. "For traditional-minded Americans, George Soros is public enemy number one," thunders TV pundit Bill O'Reilly in *Culture Warrior*, his 2006 bestseller. "We ignore him at our peril." A financier who has given away billions to promote democracy around the world, Soros has provoked conservatives like O'Reilly by backing liberal causes in America. Yet, even for those who would support Soros' goals, his philanthropy can raise troubling questions, such as why should the rich determine society's priorities?

Many people are also suspicious of how the rich made their money, and mistrust them accordingly. Gates and Soros have been accused of exploitation, whether through monopoly or financial market manipulation. Questions about the source of wealth can seem even more pertinent when the philanthropist is, say, a Russian oligarch who stands accused of stealing assets from the public.

If philanthrocapitalists are to be a legitimate part of the solution to the world's problems, a new "social contract" is needed to spell out what it means to be a good billionaire, in terms of how much is given and in what way, how much tax is paid, whether the money has been made in a legitimate way, and what the rich can expect from everyone else in return. Soros, for one, believes the public should hold philanthropists to account. "I always tell people who question my motives that they are right to do so. When I claim to be disinterested, the burden of proof is on me." He says that it is "very important to have transparency as the basis on which a judgment can be made." The onus in the social contract should be on the rich to be transparent and accountable. If not, they run the risk of being forced to do so by government regulation.

Given the difficulties presented by the rise of philanthrocapitalism, wouldn't it be better to simply tax the rich more heavily and let governments solve the world's problems? For much of history, it has been possible to see the state and philanthropy as alternatives. The previous golden ages of philanthropy each ended with the state significantly increasing its role in areas where philanthropists had tried to find solutions, such as educating the poor. In some cases, the state stepped in with alternative approaches; in others, the state took successful philanthropic ideas to a much larger scale.

But it is the state that has been retreating over the past thirty years. Today, it looks unlikely that big government will return. A government's ability to raise taxes is constrained, not least by the need to generate economic growth, which means attracting investment and wealthy residents who are increasingly globally mobile. In rich countries, aging populations are likely to only intensify the pressures on the state. In poorer countries, governments are struggling to meet the challenges of accelerating economic development and of public health, not least diseases such as malaria and HIV/AIDS. At the same time, genuinely new global challenges have emerged, from climate change to international nonstate terrorism, that existing multilateral governance organizations, such as the United Nations, struggle to address. In these circumstances, no wonder governments, of both right and left, seem increasingly keen for wealthy individuals to give them a helping hand. Even so, if the rich do not take on this responsibility, they risk provoking the public into a political backlash against the economic system that allowed them to become so wealthy.

In short, a new division of labor is needed between governments, businesses, charitable NGOs, and philanthropists. Philanthrocapitalists can play a key role in this – certainly a far greater role that their relatively limited financial resources might suggest. (Even the billions that Gates is giving away pale in comparison to most government budgets.) This is not to underplay the importance of the changes taking place within governments, businesses, or NGOs, nor the role that every individual citizen can play. Bono may be right to claim that "as great as some of the philanthropists in your book are, the real change comes through social movements." Yet when he wanted to start DATA, a professional organization to drive forward a social movement to reduce the debt burden and increase aid and trade to help some of the poorest people on the planet, it was to philanthropists such as Gates and Soros that he turned for money and advice. Nor is Bono's experience particularly unusual. Over the centuries, behind many a great social movement there has been a wealthy philanthropist.

Philanthrocapitalists are "hyperagents" who have the capacity to do some essential things far better than anyone else. They do not face elections every few years, like politicians, or suffer the tyranny of shareholder demands for ever-increasing quarterly profits, like CEOs of most public companies. Nor do they have to devote vast amounts of time and resources to raising money, like most heads of NGOs. That frees them to think long-term, to go against conventional wisdom, to take up ideas too risky for government, to deploy substantial resources quickly when the situation demands it – above all, to try something new. The big question is, will they be able to achieve their potential?

The emperor's new clothes

Michael Edwards, 2008

A new movement is afoot that promises to save the world by revolutionizing philanthropy, making non-profit organizations operate like business, and creating new markets for goods and services that benefit society. Nicknamed "philanthrocapitalism" for short, its supporters believe that business principles can be successfully combined with the search for social transformation.

There is no doubt that this is an import phenomenon. Very large sums of money have been generated for philanthropy, particularly the finance and IT industries. But despite its great potential, this movement is flawed in both its proposed means and its promised ends. It sees business methods as the answer to social problems, but offers little rigorous evidence or analysis to support this claim, and ignores strong evidence pointing in the opposite direction. Business will continue to be an inescapable part of the solution to global problems, and some methods drawn from business certainly have much to offer. But business will also be a cause of social problems, and as Jim Collins, author of *Good to Great*, concluded in a recent pamphlet, "we must reject the idea – well intentioned, but dead wrong – that the primary path to greatness in the social sectors is to become more like a business."

Philantrocapitalism's other promise is to achieve far reaching transformation by resolving entrenched social problems. Yet its lack of understanding of how change occurs make it unlikely that this promise will be achieved. There is a huge gulf between the hype surrounding this new philanthropy and its likely impact. Some of the newer philanthropists have come to recognize this – and have shown humility and a readiness to learn about the complexities of social change. But too many remain captivated by the hype.

Philanthrocapitalism has seized on an important part of the puzzle of how to square democracy with the market, but is in danger of passing itself off as the whole solution, downgrading the costs and trade-offs of extending business and market principles into social transformation. I argue that:

- The hype surrounding philanthrocapitalism runs far ahead of its ability to deliver real results. It's time for more humility.
- The increasing concentration of wealth and power among philanthrocapitalists is unhealthy for democracy. It's time for more accountability.
- The use of business thinking can damage civil society, which is the crucible of democratic politics and social transformation. It's time to differentiate the two and re-assert the independence of global citizen action.
- Philanthrocapitalism is a symptom of a disordered and profoundly unequal world. It hasn't yet demonstrated that it provides the cure.

The stakes are very high. Fifty-five trillion dollars in philanthropic resources are expected to be created in the United States alone in the next forty years. It matters whether these vast resources are used to pursue social transformation or just to address the symptoms of global problems. And for philanthrocapitalists themselves, it matters that they are seen to be serious about engaging with this question. If they aren't, they may find themselves on the receiving end of the same kind of backlash that greeted previous concentrations of private wealth and power. It is time for a different kind of conversation, less dominated by hype, more critical, and more open to evidence and dissenting voices. The result could indeed be a world transformed.

Across the universe, meanwhile, a very different form of philanthropy is taking place. Nick-named "philanthrocapitalism" by journalist Matthew Bishop, its followers believe that business thinking and market methods will save the world – and make some of us a fortune along the way. Bobby Shriver, Bono's less famous partner in the Red brand of products, hopes that sales will help "buy a house in the Hamptons" while simultaneously swelling the coffers of the Global Fund for TB, malaria and AIDS. It is a win-win situation – gain without pain – and the price of entry to the world's "most elite club," as *Business Week* describes the "Global Philanthropists' Circle" that is sponsored by Synergos in New York. If only we can make foundations and non-profits operate like businesses and expand the reach of markets, great things will be within our reach, much greater than all the traditional activities of civil society combined.

From Bill Clinton to Bill Gates, the rich and famous are lining up to boost the claims of this new paradigm. According to journalist Jonathan Rauch, ex-President Clinton wants to "repurpose business methods and business culture to solve the world's problems . . . and he hopes to reinvent philanthropy while he's at it."

"The profit motive could be the best tool for solving the world's problems, more effective than any government or private philanthropy," says Oracle founder Larry Ellison.

"Wealthy philanthropists have the potential to do more than the Group of Eight leading nations to lift Africa out of poverty," says "rock star" economist Jeffrey Sachs.

"If you put a gun to my head and asked which one has done more good for the world, the Ford Foundation or Exxon," says Buffet and Berkshire Vice Chairman Charles Munger, "I'd have no hesitation in saying Exxon."

"The most pressing environmental issues of our time will be . . . solved when desperate governments and non-governmental organizations (NGOs) finally surrender their ideologies and tap the private sector for help."

"This," says Jeff Skoll, who created eBay, "is our time."

Some even believe that terms like "business" and "civil society" are redundant: "We are beginning to understand that the old categories of commerce, capitalism, and philanthropy do not serve the new generation of either social problems or market opportunities. We are at the end of definitions." "I have difficulty not thinking of any non-profit as a business," says Buss Schmidt, chief executive officer of the non-profit (or is it business?) Guidestar. What lies behind the rise of this phenomenon?

The philanthrocapitalists are drinking from a heady and seductive cocktail, one part "irrational exuberance" that is characteristic of market thinking, two parts believing that success in business equips them to make a similar impact on social change, a dash or two of the excitement that accompanies any new solution, and an extra degree of fizz from the oxygen of publicity that has been created by the Gates-Buffet marriage and the initiatives of ex-President Clinton.

There is justifiable excitement about the possibilities for progress in global health, agriculture and access to micro-credit among the poor that have been stimulated by huge investments from the Gates Foundation, the Clinton Global Initiative and others. New loans, seeds and vaccines are certainly important, but there is no vaccine against the racism that denies land to "dalits" (or so-called "untouchables") in India, no technology that can deliver the public health infrastructure required to combat HIV, and no market that can re-order the dysfunctional relationships between different religions and other social groups that underpin violence and insecurity.

Philanthrocapitalism should certainly help to extend access to useful goods and services, and it has a positive role to play in strengthening important areas of civil society capacity, but social transformation requires a great deal more than these two things. Despite their admirable energy and enthusiasm and genuine intent, the philanthrocapitalists risk misfiring when it comes to much more complex and deep-rooted problems of injustice. Before analyzing the evidence for and against that proposition, what exactly does philanthrocapitalism mean?

[. . .]

Continuing the conversation

Philanthrocapitalism offers one way of increasing the social value of the market, but there are other routes that could offer equal or better results in changing the way the economic surplus is produced, distributed and used: the traditional route that uses external pressure, taxation and regulation; the philanthrocapitalist route that changes internal incentives and gives a little more back through foundations and corporate social responsibility; and more radical innovations in ownership and production that change the basis on which markets currently work. We don't know which of these routes carries the greatest long-term potential, though all of them rely on civil society as a vehicle for innovation, accountability, influence and modified consumption, and especially for getting us from reformist to transformational solutions. I suspect that civil society will be able to play those roles more effectively from a position of diversity and strength. "It's the difference that makes the difference" remember, so working together but independently may be a better way forward than dissolving our differences in some soggy middle ground. In the real world, there is no gain without pain, no seamless weaving of competition and cooperation, service and self-interest, inequality and fairness. If something seems too good to be true, it probably is.

"What could possibly be more beneficial for the entire world than a continued expansion of philanthropy?" asks Joel Fleishman in his book that lionizes the venture capital foundations. Well, over the last century, far more has been achieved by governments committed to equality and justice, and social movements strong enough to force change through, and the same might well be true in the future. No great social cause was mobilized through the market in the twentieth century. The civil rights movement, the women's movement, the environmental movement, the New Deal, and the Great Society – all were pushed ahead by civil society and anchored in the power of government as a force for the public good. Business and markets play a vital role in taking these advances forward, but they are followers, not leaders, "instruments in the orchestra" but not "conductors."

"We literally go down the chart of the greatest inequities and give where we can affect the greatest change," says Melinda Gates of the Gates Foundation, except that some of the greatest inequities are caused by the nature of our economic system and the inability of politics to change it. Global poverty, inequality and violence can certainly be addressed, but doing so requires the empowerment of those closest to the problems and the transformation of the systems, structures, values and relationships that prevent most of the world's population from participating equally in the fruits of global progress. The long-term gains from changes like these will be much greater than those that flow from improvements in the delivery of better goods and services. After all, only the most visionary of the philanthrocapitalists have much incentive to transform a system from which they have benefited hugely.

[. . .]

Organizing a better conversation

The first thing we need to do is to pause, take a very deep breath, and create space for a different kind of conversation. Philanthrocapitalism is seductive for many different reasons – the allure of a new magic bullet, set against the reality of plodding along, step by step, in the swamps of social change; the glitz and glamour of gaining entry to a new global elite; and the promise of maintaining a system that made you rich and powerful while simultaneously pursuing the public good. We all want our place in history as the ones who saved the world, but this is surely immature. Will "social enterprise end up intoxicated by virtue, breathing its own exhaust," as a report from Sustainability concluded? At least Bill Clinton's enthusiasm is tempered by some boundaries: "What I long to do," he says, "is to see this [approach] integrated into every philanthropic activity from now on, *where it is appropriate*," and "where it's appropriate" may be a small but not unimportant part of the pictures as a whole. I think it is time to launch a "slow food movement" for the philanthrocapitalists, in order to help them savor the complexities of what's involved. It's not that our old ideas about social transformation were perfect; it's that our new ideas are imperfect too, and almost certainly won't turn out as planned. There is no place for triumphalism in this conversation.

What we do need is a good, old-fashioned, full-throated public debate, to sort out the claims of both philanthrocapitalists and their critics, and to inform the huge expansion of philanthropy that is projected over the next forty years. So here's the $55 trillion-dollar question: Will we use these vast resources to pursue social transformation, or just fritter them away in spending on the symptoms? The stakes are very high, so why not organize a series of dialogues between philanthrocapitalists and their critics, on the condition that they shed the mock civility that turns honest conversation into Jell-O. There isn't much point in staying in the comfort zone, forever apart in different camps, like the World Economic Forum and the World Social Forum that take place in splendid isolation each and every year. Deep-rooted differences about capitalism and social change are unlikely to go away, so let's have more honesty and dissent before consensus, so that it might actually be meaningful when it arrives.

Philanthrocapitalism is the product of a particular era of industrial change that has brought about temporary monopolies in the systems required to operate the knowledge economy, often controlled by individuals who are able to accumulate spectacular amounts of wealth. That same era has produced great inequalities and social dislocations, and past experience suggests that such wealth will be politically unsustainable unless much of it is given away, just as in earlier decades when Ford, Rockefeller and Carnegie found themselves in much the same position.

Effective philanthropists do learn from their experience and the conversations they have with others. Melinda Gates, for example, describes this process well: "Why do something about vaccines but nothing about clean water? Why work on tuberculosis but not on agricultural productivity? Why deliver mosquito nets but not financial services?" Of course, there is another set of questions waiting to be answered at a much deeper level – why work on agricultural productivity but not on rights to land? Why work on financial services but not on changing the economic system? But these are challenges that face all foundations and they are best addressed together, since all of us have much to learn from others. Rather than assuming that business can fix philanthropy, why not put all the questions on the table and allow all sides to have their assumptions tested? Who knows, this kind of conversation might lead us far beyond the limitations of the current debate and closer to that ultimate prize of an economic system that can sustain material progress with far few social, personal and environmental costs.

The New Philanthropists

Charles Handy, 2006

The inevitable first questions are: who are these New Philanthropists, why are they new, and what is it that they have done that deserves celebration?

They are individuals, still in the prime of life, who have been successful in their chosen careers, made money, sometimes a lot of it, either in business or in their profession. Having made enough for their own needs they now want to use their money, their skills and their abilities to get things done to create something transparently useful in society. They talk of making a difference, of giving something back, but they aren't satisfied by writing cheques to worthy causes, valuable though such charity can be. These people want to be in the driving seat, because that's where they belong and, being by nature entrepreneurs of one sort or another, they like to fill gaps and to meet needs neglected by others. There is a feeling now in Britain that there are niches that the government can't or isn't filling; that if you have talent, energy and money you should move into these gaps and show the way. 'The chance to do this,' one interviewee said, 'makes the whole business of making money worthwhile.'

We need new words. Some shudder at the very word 'philanthropy,' feeling it still carries overtones of Victorian *noblesse oblige*, of paternalistic and interfering do-gooding.

'Please don't call me a philanthropist, I am just trying to be useful,' one of them said. Others, such as Tom Hunter, like to describe themselves as venture philanthropists. They are true 'social entrepreneurs', but unlike most such people, they don't have to spend their time trying to raise the funds for their initial investments. They can write themselves a cheque without having to ask anyone else.

Philanthropy has almost become the new status symbol. To have your own foundation or a wing of a building named after you can be an outward and respectable mark of success. We should not sneer. If status is measured by how much one gives to others, society is the richer. But our new philanthropists are not driven by a desire for status. They required a lot of persuading to be featured in this book, lest they be thought to be parading their wealth or their good works. The best philanthropy, we were constantly told, was anonymous. The New Philanthropists featured here do what they do because they care and because they know how to make things happen. That is what their success is built on.

They are 'new' philanthropists because they don't fit the old mould of grant-giving foundations, responding to requests and applications. They are hands-on, pioneering and entrepreneurial, their resources dedicated to their own causes. They are new because they are still in the prime of life, with goals still to achieve, passions to satisfy, and the energy that is needed to start something new. Not for them any idea of what one termed 'post-mortem philanthropy' – they want to use their money while they are around to see the results. They are new because, since the end of the Victorian age, Britain has not until recently, with rare exceptions such as the Sainsbury family, had an entrepreneurial class capable of growing a business that would in time generate substantial wealth. The salaried clan of the large organizations and the public sector that have been the mainstay of British life for most of the past century never accumulated enough wealth to be able to make sizeable endowments, however charitably inclined they might have been. Only lately have the salaries and bonuses of some professionals been sufficiently big to create large disposable surpluses.

The example of these New Philanthropists is important. Not only does their entrepreneurial flair enrich the whole area of social enterprise but, by using the money that they made by their business acumen to improve the lot of others, they provide a social justification for the free enterprise system that is has often lacked. People should be judged, many of them feel, not only by how they made their money, but, as importantly, how they spend it. These individuals spend it well, on purposes and causes beyond themselves, and they enjoy doing so. As Dr Frederick Mulder, an art dealer and the founder of The Funding Network, has said, 'using my profits to fund what I believe in is immensely satisfying.'

Not everyone likes the New Philanthropists, however, or what they do. Some accuse them of jumping into situations without doing enough research or of not understanding the longer-term implications of their initiatives. They can cross swords with established charities that have been working in the same areas for longer and resent the intrusions of the newcomers. In their efforts to get things moving the New Philanthropists can ruffle bureaucratic feathers, short-circuit procedures by going over the heads of local officials, or draw unwelcome publicity to faults in the system. As Geoff Mulgan, the director of the Young Foundation, has pointed out, profound social change does not come from a few inspiring projects or individuals. It generally needs a host of interlocking shifts in attitudes, social movements and markets, as well as involvement by government. But the change has to start somewhere and those whom we interviewed would claim that they are well aware of the pitfalls and do their best to work with others in the field as well as with the relevant authorities. If their initiatives are to have a lasting effect, they realize, they must eventually be integrated into the bigger system. Leverage is all, they say.

How new is the "new philanthropy"?

Beth Breeze, 2011

The idea of new philanthropy implies a paradigmatic change in the charitable giving of rich people. A review of both academic and non-academic literature indicates that this alleged paradigm shift has three different manifestations. Firstly, it is used to refer to new types of donors: New philanthropists are said to be younger, richer, more likely to be self-made and living a cosmopolitan lifestyle. They are, "in the prime of life, with goals still to achieve, passions to satisfy, and the energy that is needed to start something new." The youthfulness of new philanthropists is often cited as a defining feature: "Many of the new breed of philanthropists have made their money in the City or computing. Some are still in their thirties." The emergence of new sources of wealth from industries such as information technology and the financial sector, notably hedge funds, have also been cited as factors behind the creation of new multi-millionaires who are able to make significant philanthropic commitments at a younger age. As a media report on the 'new philanthropists' claims, "most of them are self made [. . .] they are hedge funders, bankers, corporate raiders, venture capitalists, dot-com millionaires, fashion tycoons or global magnates".

Secondly, the term "new philanthropy" refers to support for new types of causes. Prominent new philanthropists are said to support emerging issues such as global health problems, notably HIV/AIDS, and the environmental crisis, especially climate change.

[. . .]

Thirdly, new philanthropists are said to conduct their giving in new ways by setting up their own foundations and projects instead of funding existing charities. They are alleged to be distinctive in terms of being catalysts, rather than just responding to requests for money to support established charities. They are said to use their power to leverage money from other funders (especially the government) and claim to pay far greater attention to how their money is spent, by demanding targets, performance indicators and measurable outcomes. It is this aspect of new philanthropy that lies behind the synonymous label of "Philanthrocapitalism" which refers to the application of businesslike skills to the charity sector. New philanthropists are also said to be distinctive in their preference for intensive personal engagement with the causes that they fund.

[. . .]

[. . .] Despite finding some support for all three aspects of "new philanthropy" (i.e. that it involves new types of donors, new causes and new methods of giving), a review of the historical literature, and of wider claims about changes in behaviour that are characterized as "new," indicates there is insufficient evidence to suggest that these variables are wholly new, particularly widespread or a result of changes that are specific to philanthropic behaviour.

[. . .]

The first suggestion, that new philanthropists are distinctively younger, entrepreneurial and "first-generation" rich, was found to be historically typical rather than exceptional. The historical roll call of donors includes many self-made entrepreneurs who began giving before retirement, notably Andrew Carnegie and John D. Rockefeller. In the UK, Thomas Guy, Isaac Wolfson and Joseph Rowntree all fit this description. Indeed one of the standard historical explanations of Victorian philanthropy is that it offered an opportunity for "new money" to buy the status required to be integrated into the elite. Other types of "new donor" emerged as a result of changes in the sources and distribution of wealth. Rubinstein's studies of the patterns of wealth-creation in nineteenth- and twentieth-century Britain demonstrate a long-standing experience of constantly emerging means of becoming rich such that, "men of every type and of high and low degree could amass a fortune." In her 1934 book called *The New Philanthropy* (a title which demonstrates the currency of this phrase long before the present era), Elizabeth Macadam suggests that "new philanthropists" emerged after the Great War when "the class accustomed to generous giving gave place to a different class – the 'new rich', not bred in the same tradition." Having surveyed the philanthropic terrain in the first third of the twentieth century, Macadam concluded it was no longer "the prerogative of the 'older families' or the 'upper class'".

Macadam's account of the ways in which the profile of the rich has altered over time offers an explanation for possible changes in the profile of philanthropists: as a sub-set of those possessing wealth, philanthropists reflect the characteristics of the group from which they are drawn. Within the ranks of the UK's richest people there has been a shift over recent decades from a majority that inherited their wealth to a majority that are self-made. If a distinctive feature of the new philanthropists is that they are likely to be self-made entrepreneurs, this could be due to the changing composition of the rich rather than the changing nature of philanthropists. The types of people who are drawn to philanthropy can also be seen to change over time. Shapely's study of charity and power in Victorian Manchester, for example, found that being associated with philanthropy became a crucial, if unwritten, criterion for parliamentary candidates in that era.

The second suggestion is that new philanthropists support "new causes," such as global health and the environment. Yet similar shifts in the focus of philanthropic attention have occurred throughout history as the most urgent social problems changed over time. AIDS and climate change are prevailing concerns at the start of the twenty-first century just as, for example, it was popular to help poor maids to marry in the fifteenth century; to pay ransoms for people captured by pirates in the sixteenth century; and to make contributions to rebuild London after the Great Fire in the seventeenth century. Clearly the social problems facing sixteenth century philanthropists, such as the loss of poor relief contributions made by the monasteries following their dissolution and the consequences of epidemic disease, were not the same as those faced by donors living during the Industrial Revolution which "posed problems for philanthropists different in degree and kind from those they had faced in the past."

Given that philanthropy can be seen as part of a mixed economy of welfare, the role it plays in any given period will depend to a large extent on the kinds of needs that the private or public sectors are failing to address. It will also be shaped by the wider cultural context and prevailing social norms that affect every aspect of public life. In the seventeenth century, for example, factory schools which set children to work in a factory by day and taught them by night, were considered an appropriate response to the challenge of educating poor children who needed to contribute to the family budget. Factory schools would be viewed as unacceptable child labour today but received enthusiastic support from prominent contemporary philanthropists. As different social problems emerge in different ages, it is to be expected that the philanthropic individuals of the time will offer what seems to them to be new and appropriate solutions. As Macadam observed:

> The worthy citizen of the eighteenth century relieved his conscience by a gift to an orphanage; the benevolent lady of the nineteenth century distributed soup and blankets. Her daughter 'taught the orphan boy to read and the orphan girl to sew'; her grand-daughter went 'slumming'. The twentieth-century lady is on the committee of the village institute; her daughter is a guide captain and her son helps at an unemployment centre.

Any perceived "newness" in terms of causes is therefore more a consequence of external forces, notably changes in social need, social norms and provision by other sectors, than the result of internal decisions made by individuals to seek out and support new types of recipients.

[. . .]

The third suggestion is that new philanthropy involves new approaches to giving. New philanthropists are said to emphasize their "hands on" engagement with the causes they support, for example by sitting on charity boards and interacting with staff and beneficiaries. But again, a review of the historical literature shows that giving time, skills and energy as well as money is not a new approach. In Victorian England, for example, Himmelfarb notes:

> The dispensers of charity [. . .] were expected to give generously of their time and resources and to have a sustained personal involvement in their work. This was not 'checkbook philanthropy' satisfied merely by the contribution of money.

The rise of "scientific philanthropy" in the late eighteenth century provides further evidence that new approaches have arisen throughout the history of philanthropic activity.

Another facet of the newness claimed for contemporary philanthropic approaches is the implementation of businesslike models in the charity world, such as providing venture capital and using key performance indicators to monitor the impact and progress of donations. Yet the transfer of techniques from the business world into charities has a long history. For example, accounts of seventeenth-century philanthropy note the emergence of "associational philanthropy," based on the private sector model of joint-stock principles, which was frequently used to fund schools and hospitals. The introduction of associational philanthropy was as revolutionary in its day as the introduction of "venture philanthropy" (a method commonly associated with new philanthropists) is today, and exemplifies how "old" philanthropists "pioneered a range of new forms in which aid could be delivered". Another idea developed by philanthropists in previous centuries (yet often assumed to be a modern innovation) was the use of loans to provide funding to hospitals in need of cash injections. Loans were often necessary due to the proclivity of founders for providing the capital but not the running costs of such institutions. This was clearly a major difficulty before the introduction of the UK's state-funded National Health Service.

The concept of "Five Per Cent philanthropy," pioneered in the second half of the nineteenth century by advocates of the social housing movement, offers a further example of the historic transfer of business approaches into the philanthropic world. This concept combined commercial and philanthropic responsibilities by offering investment opportunities in house-building companies that built dwellings for the labouring and artisan class. Tenants paid an affordable rent and investors' returns were capped at a maximum rate of five percent, with any surplus re-invested in efforts to tackle the shortage of decent housing. Five percent philanthropy demonstrated the long-standing compatibility of altruism with business acumen as investors sought to make a profit (albeit restricted) whilst doing good. This model also demonstrates a pre-existing concern with something often assumed to be a contemporary philanthropic obsession: that of sustainability. The policy of "philanthropy and five percent" was implemented as a concerted attempt to ensure the self-perpetuation of the social housing movement, "so that future generations might gain some benefit." Pursuing sustainability through revenue-generating schemes is revealed as yet another *leitmotiv* of the "new philanthropy" that does not withstand scrutiny.

[. . .]

In addition to the idea that strategies such as pursuing sustainability are unique to the modern philanthropic era, it is also suggested that the approaches taken by new philanthropists are more innovative, bolder and "cutting edge" than their predecessors. For example, Handy claims that "they like to fill gaps and to meet needs neglected by others". Yet some "old philanthropists" tackled the difficult issues of their times with groundbreaking initiatives. A prime example is London's Lock Hospital, which opened in 1747 to treat people with venereal diseases, described as: "a courageous attempt on the part of mid-18th-century philanthropists to grapple with one of the more noisome evils of their time." Also in the health field, philanthropists were early supporters of contentious issues such as birth control, as well as backers of pioneering work in the new field of maternal health.

Finally, an archetypal feature of new philanthropy is said to be a desire for impact or "value for money" which involves calculating the precise consequences achieved by philanthropic donations. For example, it is suggested that effective philanthropy involves, "being confident that your gift will make a difference, and being assured that your donation is an efficient use of your money". Yet there is no basis for the suggestion that all old philanthropists indulged in careless benevolence without concern for outcomes, and again the historical evidence reveals that concerns about ineffective philanthropic acts are not new. An example of a careful approach to philanthropic spending can be found as far back as 1758 when one of the life-governors of the Founding Hospital, Jonas Hanway, resigned after calculating that it cost £60 to raise a foundling in the institution, which was more than twice the £25 needed to raise a child within their own family. Similarly, late-19th-century proponents of the Five Percent movement deployed research to demonstrate the effectiveness of their approach, publishing a report showing that mortality rates fell by two-thirds as a result of better housing, and that infant mortality in "model houses" was just a fifth of that found in the metropolis generally. A concern with measuring need and demonstrating the effectiveness of philanthropic interventions is therefore clearly not the sole preserve of new philanthropists.

This review of historical precedents for the allegedly defining characteristics of new philanthropy indicates that previous generations of givers demonstrated similar properties, and therefore might equally have been perceived to be as "new" and "groundbreaking" in their time as those who live and give at the start of the twenty-first century. It appears that "newness" is a feature of every successive era, rather than the preserve of any specific generation.

[. . .]

Philanthropy has undergone continual processes of change and has appeared "new" at many points in its history. The role of the philanthropist is continually being reinvented to reflect contemporary needs, dominant values, available wealth, technological developments and the broader socio-political context. Philanthropy is now, as it always has been, a product of its time.

The Gucci bag of new philanthropy

Olga Alexeeva, 2009

I once attended an evening party organized by a wealthy family in a South American country, devoted to philanthropy. Guests, similarly ultra-wealthy families, gathered to talk about their giving, share experiences and possibly form alliances. I was invited as an outside expert with a knowledge of philanthropic trends in other places.

As I listened to the other guests talking, I began to realize that if giving is seen as just an accessory to a wealthy lifestyle rather than an act that implies a complete moral worldview, such giving, new or old, will make no great changes in the world. That perhaps it is time to embrace the idea of 'private social responsibility'.

I heard one impeccably dressed lady share with a friend her frustration over peasants in the northern part of the country who did not want to move from their land despite 'generous' offers from the company she owned. Her friend nodded sympathetically and replied with a similar story of poor workers demanding some right or other.

My glass of wine was forgotten, so shocked was I by such apparent contempt and disregard for people lower on the social ladder than these two ladies. Growing up in the Soviet Union, for all its faults, created in me a strong sense that all people are equal, regardless of their wealth or lack of it. Even more than this, I was shocked by the contrast between the real feelings of these ladies and their philanthropic aspirations.

Development of giving in BRIC [Brazil, Russia, India & China] economies

Organized philanthropy, for many years associated mostly with the Western world, is today a growing phenomenon in the East and South. Individual giving in Russia more than tripled in 2008 alone despite the economic crisis. In China, where five years ago less than 3 per cent of the population gave to charity, in 2009, after a powerful impulse provided by the Sichuan earthquake, over 84 per cent of Chinese consider giving an important part of their lives. In Brazil, the first endowed private foundations were created in the past ten years, and India has also seen a surge of non-religious giving, especially by the new middle classes.

I can only welcome these developments. For many years, I have been a staunch advocate of Eastern and Southern giving and have urged the Western philanthropic sector to see the potentially important new partners they can have in the East and South. But while I applaud new giving, that discussion at the party in South America keeps coming back to me. I still cannot shake off the feeling of acute disconnect between the scorn and negligence that were their everyday attitudes towards the poor and the patronizing care that characterized their philanthropy. Talking to a number of people in Asia and Africa confirmed to me that these are widespread attitudes. It clearly demonstrated that we need to address the issue of private as opposed to corporate social responsibility.

Towards a philanthropic ethics

Philanthropic ethics, along with the whole topic of philanthropy, was for many years an area dominated by US or UK donors. Even in the US, widely recognized as a flagship philanthropy development space, ethics in giving started to be widely discussed only relatively recently, and I am sure that same disparity between lifestyles and philanthropic practices still exists among donors even there. However, in relation to 'new' donors from the East and South, philanthropic ethics have never been properly discussed.

It is a common notion, especially in less sophisticated philanthropic environments, that the term philanthropic ethics applies only to the technicalities of giving, such as the grantmaking rules of foundations or areas of endowment investment (avoid tobacco, etc.). I would argue that this term should be understood much more widely and should encompass the private life of philanthropists, especially the wealthy; their relationships with employees, including domestic servants; businesses they own (and those they influence), and even sometimes their conversations.

Just as in the corporate world the term corporate social responsibility now applies to the whole range of company activities, not just their community support budgets, we should start to demand from those actively and publicly involved in giving, or private social investment, adhesion to certain moral and ethical standards. We should insist that they extend the principles and objectives they employ in their giving – alleviation of poverty and social exclusion, environmental protection, access to education and health care – to those whom they employ or come across in their daily lives. Philanthropic missions and ideas should stem from acknowledged values and inform those values, but they should also be informed by them.

Donors practising what they preach

Unfortunately, especially among donors from the East and South, it is normal practice to strike your servants in the morning or evict farmers from your land with laughable compensation, and then in the afternoon sign cheques to charities helping the poor. It is absolutely acceptable to build a chemical plant in the delta of a life-saving river and the next day make an inspirational speech about global warming at an international conference.

A passage in the Bible adjures you not to let your right hand know what your left hand is doing. This phrase, at least in the Eastern Orthodox Christian tradition, is often used to support and encourage quiet philanthropy, generous anonymous giving. But it has a different twist in many parts of the world, where the right hand of donors deprives the poor and destroys the environment, while their generous left hand creates foundations and engages in venture philanthropy.

An organic tradition of giving

Another issue that is closely connected with the ethics of giving is the power of tradition. Philanthropy is not a Western phenomenon, as Barbara Ibrahim rightly points out; it is an ancient tradition in many parts of Asia and the Middle East. But if we ask ourselves whether philanthropy has changed there since then, the answer in many cases would be 'no'.

Philanthropic tradition, preserved and nurtured, is an important motive for people to give; it is a benchmark against which many newcomers in philanthropy check their performance. But what if philanthropic tradition is set in the stone of centuries and only supports the status quo, and tradition is simply a justification for not changing anything, and not challenging current practices and approaches? In that case, I think such traditions need to be revisited. Like anything else, tradition should evolve with time and reflect the changes in the economic, political and social life of countries. Just as the quantity of giving does not equal the quality of it, the longevity of philanthropic tradition does not prove that it has made lasting change in those societies.

Questions of how to preserve the long-term cultural capital and the frameworks of non-western societies, while achieving equality and social justice and decreasing social exclusion stretch far beyond philanthropy. But philanthropy is, and is becoming even more so, a powerful instrument to find solutions to this complex riddle. Philanthropy, by definition free of political games and fears, and able to experiment, can and should seek this balance between tradition and modernity. It should nurture models and ideas that respect the past but provide an equal and just future for everyone. For years these questions haunted western donors working in the East and South. But today, as the financial resources and the influence of western philanthropists diminish, these are questions we should ask donors in India and China, in Brazil and in the Gulf.

'Fashion' philanthropy

Finally, questions related to ethics and the direction of philanthropic development in the East and South are also key issues for philanthropy development organizations and for major fundraising charities who work with new donors in these areas. Too often, donor support organizations and fundraising charities content themselves with the fact that such-and-such a rich family has finally started giving at all. They do not put in front of them hard questions about the quality or ethics of their giving.

I admit I am guilty of this myself. For many years, I was just happy that we pushed wealthy Russians to open their pockets. How effective that giving was and what change it made in Russian society seemed much less important. As a result, we now have to struggle with two trends in the otherwise exponentially growing Russian philanthropy: the culture of 'wants', when donors fund something that appeals to them without thinking about whether it is actually needed and what beneficiaries think about it; and the culture of 'direct help' when masses of Russian middle-class donors reject the non-profit sector and prefer to give directly to individuals in need.

In a number of other countries, the tendency of donor support organizations to follow their clients instead of leading them has resulted in the appearance of what I call 'fashion' philanthropy, where new words such as social investment or new models of giving such as venture philanthropy are adopted but neither donors nor support organizations actually ask: is it working? Do we need this or that nice-looking new giving framework, or do we copy it just because it is fashionable, a new philanthropic Gucci bag?

Whatever we call philanthropy in Brazil or India, Russia or China, the Middle East or Africa – social investment, creative giving, philanthrocapitalism – these will just be words without changes in attitudes, without respect for and acknowledgement of people, without debate on private social responsibility and philanthropic ethics. We can bask in the sunshine of growing giving, but this sunshine will eventually dim if we don't create a culture where donors start thinking not only how they want to give but also what is truly needed and what beneficiaries of their generosity think about it.

If we want to ensure that, in the coming years, philanthropy in all corners of the world truly enhances social justice, I think it is time to start exploring the notion of private social responsibility.

6.4 Is 'being effective' the only worthwhile yardstick?

What is effective altruism?

Peter Singer, 2015

I met Matt Wage in 2009 when he took my Practical Ethics class at Princeton University. In the readings relating to global poverty and what we ought to be doing about it, he found an estimate of how much it costs to save the life of one of the millions of children who die each year from diseases that we can prevent or cure. This led Matt to calculate how many lives he could save, over his lifetime, assuming that he earned an average income and donated 10 percent of it to a highly effective organization, for example, one providing families with bed nets to prevent malaria, a major killer of children. He discovered that he could, with that level of donation, save about one hundred lives. He thought to himself, "Suppose you see a burning building, and you run through the flames and kick a door open, and let one hundred people out. That would be the greatest moment in your life. And I could do as much good as that!"

Two years later Matt graduated. His senior thesis received the Philosophy Department's prize for the best thesis of the year. He was accepted by the University of Oxford for postgraduate study. Many students who major in philosophy dream of an opportunity like that – I know I did – but by then Matt had done a lot of thinking about and discussing with others what career would do the most good. This led him to a very different choice: he took a job on Wall Street, working for an arbitrage trading firm. On a higher income, he would be able to give much more, both as a percentage and in dollars, than 10 percent of a professor's income. One year after graduating, Matt was donating a six-figure sum – roughly half his annual earnings – to highly effective charities. He was on the way to saving hundreds of lives, not over his entire career but within the first year or two of his working life and every year thereafter.

Matt is an effective altruist. His choice of career is one of several possible ways of being an effective altruist. Effective altruists do things like the following.

- Living modestly and donating a large part of their income – often much more than the traditional tenth, or tithe – to the most effective charities.
- Researching and discussing with others which charities are the most effective or drawing on research done by other independent evaluators.
- Choosing the career in which they can earn most, not in order to be able to live affluently but so that they can do more good.
- Talking to others, in person or online, about giving, so that the idea of effective altruism will spread.
- Giving part of their body – blood, bone marrow, or even a kidney – to a stranger.

[. . .]

What unites all these acts under the banner of effective altruism? The definition now becoming standard is "a philosophy and social movement which applies evidence and reason to working out the most effective ways to improve the world." That definition says nothing about motives or about any sacrifice or cost to the effective altruist. Given that the movement has altruism as part of its name, these omissions may seem odd. Altruism is contrasted with egoism, which is concern only for oneself, but we should not think of effective altruism as requiring self-sacrifice, in the sense of something necessarily contrary to one's own interests. If doing the most you can for others means that you are also flourishing, then that is the best possible outcome for everyone. Many effective altruists deny that what they are doing is a sacrifice. Nevertheless they are altruists because their overriding concern is to do the most good they can. The fact that they find fulfillment and personal happiness in doing that does not detract from their altruism.

Psychologists who study giving behavior have noticed that some people give substantial amounts to one or two charities, while others give small amounts to many charities. Those who donate to one or two charities seek evidence about what the charity is doing and whether it is really having a positive impact. If the evidence indicates that the charity is really helping others, they make a substantial donation. Those who give small amounts to many charities are not so interested in whether what they are doing helps others – psychologists call them warm glow givers. Knowing that they are giving makes them feel good, regardless of the impact of their donation. In many cases the donation is so small – $10 or less – that if they stopped to think, they would realize that the cost of processing the donation is likely to exceed any benefit it brings to the charity.

In 2013, as the Christmas giving season approached, twenty thousand people gathered in San Francisco to watch a five-year-old boy dressed as Batkid ride around the city in a Batmobile with an actor dressed as Batman by his side. The pair rescued a damsel in distress and captured the Riddler, for which they received the keys of "Gotham City" from the mayor – not an actor, he really was the mayor of San Francisco – for their role in fighting crime. The boy, Miles Scott, had been through three years of chemotherapy for leukaemia, and when asked for his greatest wish, he replied, "To be Batkid." The Make-A-Wish Foundation had made his wish come true.

Does that give you a warm glow? It gives me one, even though I know there is another side to this feel-good story. Make-A-Wish would not say how much it cost to fulfill Miles' wish, but it did say that the average cost of making a child's wish come true is $7,500. Effective altruists would, like anyone else, feel emotionally drawn toward making the wishes of sick children come true, but they would also know that $7,500 could, by protecting families from malaria, save the lives of at least three children and maybe many more. Saving a child's life has to be better than fulfilling a child's wish to be Batkid. If Miles' parents had been offered that choice – Batkid for a day or a complete cure for their son's leukemia – they surely would have chosen the cure. When more than one child's life can be saved, the choice is even clearer. Why then do so many people give to Make-A-Wish, when they could do more good by donating to the Against Malaria Foundation, which is a highly effective provider of bed nets to families in malaria-prone regions? The answer lies in part in the emotional pull of knowing that you are helping *this* child, one whose face you can see on television, rather than the unknown and unknowable children who would have died from malaria if your donation had not provided the nets under which they sleep. It also lies in part in the fact that Make-A-Wish appeals to Americans, and Miles is an American child.

Effective altruists will feel the pull of helping an identifiable child from their own nation, region, or ethnic group but will then ask themselves if that is the best thing to do. They know that saving a life is better than making a wish come true and that saving three lives is better than saving one. So they don't give to whatever cause tugs most strongly at their heartstrings. They give to the cause that will do the most good, given the abilities, time, and money they have available.

Doing the most good is a vague idea that raises many questions. Here are a few of the more obvious ones, and some preliminary answers:

What counts as "the most good?"
Effective altruists will not all give the same answer to this question, but they do share some values. They would all agree that a world with less suffering and more happiness in it is, other things being equal, better than one with more suffering and less happiness. Most would say that a world in which people live longer is, other things being equal, better than one in which people live shorter lives. These values explain why helping people in extreme poverty is a popular cause among effective altruists, because a given sum of money does much more to reduce suffering and save lives if we use it to assist people living in extreme poverty in developing countries than it would do if we gave it to most other charitable causes.

Does everyone's suffering count equally?
Effective altruists do not discount suffering because it occurs far away or in another country or afflicts people of a different race or religion. They agree that the suffering of animals counts too and generally agree that we should not give less consideration to suffering just because the victim is not a member of our species. They may differ, however, on how to weigh the type of suffering animals can experience against the type of suffering humans can experience.

Does "the most good you can do" mean that it is wrong to give priority to one's own children? Surely it can't be wrong to put the interests of members of the family and close friends ahead of the interests of strangers?
Effective altruists can accept that one's own children are a special responsibility, ahead of the children of strangers. There are various possible grounds for this. Most parents love their children, and it would be unrealistic to require parents to be impartial between their own children and other children. Nor would we want to discourage such bias because children thrive in close, loving families, and it is not possible to love people without having greater concern for their well-being than one has for others. In any case, while doing the most good is an important part of the life of every effective altruist, effective altruists are real people, not saints, and they don't seek to maximize the good in every single thing they do, 24/7. As we shall see, typical effective altruists leave themselves time and resources to relax and do what they want. For most of us, being close to our children and other family members or friends is central to how we want to spend our time. Nonetheless, effective altruists recognize that there are limitations to how much they should do for their children, given the greater needs of others. Effective altruists do not think their children need all the latest toys or lavish birthday parties, and they reject the widespread assumption that parents should, on their death, leave virtually everything they own to their children rather than give a substantial part of their wealth to those who can benefit much more from it.

What about other values, like justice, freedom, equality and knowledge?
Most effective altruists think that other values are good because they are essential for the building of communities in which people can live better lives, lives free of oppression, and have greater self-respect and freedom to do what they want, as well as experience less suffering and premature death. No doubt some effective altruists hold that these values are also good for their own sake, independently of these consequences, but others do not.

Can promoting the arts be part of "the most good you can do?"
In a world that had overcome extreme poverty and other major problems that face us now, promoting the arts would be a worthy goal. In the world in which we live, however, donating to opera houses and museums isn't likely to be doing the most good you can.

How many effective altruists could there be? Can everyone practice effective altruism?
It's possible for everyone who has some spare time or money to practice effective altruism. Unfortunately, most people – even professional philanthropy advisors – don't believe in thinking too much about the choice of causes to support. So it isn't likely everyone will become an effective altruist anytime soon. The more interesting question is whether effective altruists can become numerous enough to influence the giving culture of affluent nations. There are some promising signs that that may be starting to happen.

What if one's act reduces suffering, but to do so one must lie or harm an innocent person?
In general, effective altruists recognize that breaking moral rules against killing or seriously harming an innocent person will almost always have worse consequences than following these rules. Even thoroughgoing utilitarians, who judge actions to be right or wrong entirely on the basis of their consequences, are wary of speculative reasoning that suggests we should violate basic human rights today for the sake of some distant future good. They know that under Lenin, Stalin, Mao, and Pol Pot, a vision of a utopian future society was used to justify unspeakable atrocities, and even today some terrorists justify their crimes by imagining they will bring about a better future. No effective altruist wants to repeat those tragedies.

Suppose I set up a factory in a developing country, paying wages that are better than local workers would otherwise earn and enough to lift them out of extreme poverty. Does that make me an effective altruist, even if I make a profit from the factory?
What are you going to do with your profits? If you decide to manufacture in the developing country in order to make it possible for people to escape extreme poverty, you will reinvest a substantial part of your profits in ways that help more people escape extreme poverty. Then you are an effective altruist. If, on the other hand, you use your profits to live as luxuriously as you can, the fact that you have benefited some of the poor is not sufficient to make you an effective altruist. There are all kinds of intermediate positions between these two extremes. Reinvesting some of your profits to help more people earn a decent income, while retaining enough to live at a much better level than your employees, puts you somewhere on the spectrum of effective altruism – you are living at least a minimally decent ethical life, even if not a perfect one.

What about giving to your college or university? You teach at Princeton University, and this book is based on lectures you gave at Yale University, thanks to the generous gift of a Yale alumnus. Do you deny that giving to such institutions counts as effect altruism?
I count myself fortunate to be teaching at one of the finest educational institutions in the world. This gives me the opportunity to teach very bright, hardworking students like Matt Wage, who are likely to have a disproportionately large influence on the world. For the same reason, I was pleased to accept the invitation to give the Castle Lectures at Yale. But Princeton has an endowment, at the time of writing, of $21 billion, and Yale's is $23.9 billion. At the moment there are enough alumni donating to these universities to ensure that they will continue to be outstanding educational institutions, and the money you donate to one of them could probably do more good elsewhere. If effective altruism ever becomes so popular that these educational institutions are no longer able to do important research at a high level, it will be time to consider whether donating to them might once again be an effective form of altruism.

A movement emerges

Effective altruism is an offspring with many parents. I can claim to be one of them because in 1972, when I was a junior lecturer at University College, Oxford, I wrote an article called "Famine, Affluence and Mortality" in which I argued that, given the great suffering that occurs during famines and similar disasters, we ought to give large proportions of our income to disaster relief funds. How much? There is no logical stopping place, I suggested, until we reach the point of marginal utility – that is, the point at which by giving more, one would cause oneself and one's family to lose as much as the recipients of one's aid would gain. Over the next forty plus years, the essay has been widely reprinted and used by professors around the world to challenge their students' beliefs that they are living ethically.

Here's the rub: even though I argued that this is what we ought to do, I did not do it myself. When I wrote the article, my wife and I were giving away about 10 percent of our modest income (she was working as a high school teacher, earning a little more than I was). That percentage increased over the years. We are now giving away about one-third of what we earn and aiming to get to half, but that still isn't anywhere near the point of marginal utility. One of the things that made it psychologically difficult to increase our giving was that for many years we were giving away a bigger slice of our income than anyone we knew. No one, not even the mega rich, seemed to be giving a higher proportion.

Then in 2004, the *New Yorker* published a profile of Zell Kravinsky. Kravinsky had given almost his entire $45 million real estate fortune to charity. He did put some money into trust funds for his wife and children, but the children were attending public schools, and he and his family were living on about $60,000 a year. He still did not think he had done enough to help others, so he arranged with a nearby hospital to donate a kidney to a stranger. The article linked my then 32 year old essay to Kravinsky's way of living and quoted him as saying, "It seems to me crystal clear that I should be giving all my money away and donating all of my time and energy."

By this time I was teaching at Princeton, not far from where Kravinsky lived, so I invited him to speak to one of my classes, something he has done regularly ever since. Kravinsky is a brilliant man: he has one doctorate in education and another on the poetry of John Milton. He taught at the University of Pennsylvania before turning from academic life to real estate investment, so he is at home in the university environment. Despite his interest in poetry, he puts his altruism in mathematical terms. Quoting scientific studies that show the risk of dying as result of making a kidney donation to be only 1 in 4,000, he says that not making the donation would have meant he valued his life at 4,000 times that of a stranger, a valuation he finds totally unjustified. He even told Ian Parker, the author of the *New Yorker* profile, that the reason many people don't understand his desire to donate a kidney is that "they don't understand math."

Around the time I was reading about Kravinsky I became aware of the work of Abhijit Banerjee and Esther Duflo, professors of economics at MIT [Massachusetts Institute of Technology], who founded the Poverty Action Lab to carry out "social experiments" – by which they meant empirical research to discover which interventions against poverty work and which do not. Without such evidence, Duflo points out, we are fighting poverty the way medieval doctors fought illness by applying leeches. Banerjee and Duflo pioneered the application of randomized controlled trials, the golden standard of the pharmaceutical industry, to specific aid projects. By 2010 researchers associated with the Poverty Action Lab – now known as the Abdul Latif Jameel Poverty Action Lab, or J-PAL – had carried out 240 experiments in 40 countries. Dean Karlan, once a student of Banerjee and Duflo and now himself a professor of economics at Yale, started Innovations for Poverty Action, a nonprofit organization to bridge the gap between academic research and the practical side of development. Innovations for Poverty Action has grown to have a staff of nine hundred and a budget of $25 million, and the idea of randomized trials is clearly catching on.

In 2006 Holden Karnofsky and Elie Hassenfeld were in their midtwenties, working for a hedge fund in Connecticut, and earning far more than they had any desire to spend. Together with some of their colleagues, they talked about giving significant amounts to charity – but to which charity? (The Poverty Action Lab and Innovations for Poverty Action evaluate specific interventions, such as distributing bed nets to protect people against malaria, but not the charitable organizations themselves, most of which have several programs.) Karnofsky, Hassenfeld and their colleagues were used to analyzing large amounts of data in order to find sound investments. They contacted several charities and asked them what a donation would accomplish. They got lots of glossy brochures with pictures of smiling children but no data that told them what the charities were achieving and at what cost. Calling the charities and explaining what they wanted to know got them no further. One charity told them that the information they were seeking was confidential. Karnofsky and Hassenfeld sensed a vacuum that needed to be filled. With financial support from their colleagues, they set up GiveWell, an organization that has taken the evaluation of charities to a new level. They soon found they could not run it part-time and so left the hedge fund, a move that cut their income by more than half. Their assumption is that if enough people follow the recommendations on GiveWell's website, the charities will realize that it is in their interest to be transparent and to demonstrate their effectiveness. GiveWell estimates that in 2013 more than $17 million went to its top-ranked charities as a result of those rankings. Although that is not enough to have a major impact on the charitable field as a whole, the figure has risen sharply each year since GiveWell was launched. GiveWell's existence has been critical to the development of the effective altruism movement. Now, when skeptics ask, "How do I know that my donation will really help people in need?" there is a good reply: If you give to one of GiveWell's top-rated charities, you can be confident that your donation will do good and be highly cost-effective.

Around the time Karnofsky and Hassenfeld were setting up GiveWell, Toby Ord was studying philosophy at the University of Oxford. As an undergraduate, Ord, an Australian, had initially studied computer science and mathematics at the University of Melbourne, but he often got into arguments about ethical and political issues. When he expressed his views about poverty, his friends would retort, "If you believe that, why don't you just give most of your money to people starving in Africa?" His friends thought that this conclusion was absurd, but Toby asked himself, "If my money could help others much more than it helps me, then why not?"

Ord's growing interest in ethics led him to do a second undergraduate degree in philosophy. He did so well that he got a scholarship to Oxford, where he wrote a doctoral thesis on how we should decide what to do. He remained interested in practical ethics, and read my article "Famine, Affluence and Mortality." He began to think seriously about what he could do for people in extreme poverty. At the time he was living quite comfortably on his graduate student scholarship, which paid him £14,000 a year, a sum that put him, he noticed, in the richest 4 percent of the world's people, even after adjusting for how much further money goes in developing countries. When he graduated he would be earning more. He decided to calculate how much he would be able to give away over his lifetime, after meeting his own needs, assuming he earned a standard academic salary. His earnings, he estimated, might come to £1.5 million, or US$2.5 million (in 2005 dollars), and of this, he thought he could donate two-thirds, that is, £1 million, or US$1.7 million. Then he asked himself what that sum could achieve if it were donated to the most effective charities. He estimated that, while maintaining an attractive quality of life, he could donate enough to cure eight thousand people of blindness or to save around fifty thousand years of healthy life. In other words, his donations would achieve the equivalent of saving the lives of one thousand children, each of whom would live another fifty years in good health, or enabling five thousand people to live an extra ten healthy years. Such benefits so dramatically outweighed the small sacrifice Ord imagined he would be making that he committed himself to living on £20,000 per annum (adjusted for inflation and equivalent to US$34,000) and giving away the rest. His wife, Bernadette Young, a physician, pledged to give away everything above £25,000 (US $42,600). Ord subsequently lowered his own allowance to £18,000 (US$30,600), as he found that £20,000 was more than he needed to live comfortably and even take a holiday in France or Italy.

Ord wanted to share his knowledge of how easy it is to make a huge positive difference to the world. In 2009 he and Will MacAskill, another Oxford philosophy graduate student, founded Giving What We Can, an international society dedicated to eliminating poverty in the developing world. Members pledge to give at least 10 percent of their income to wherever they think it will do the most to relieve suffering in the developing world. At the time of writing, 644 people have taken the pledge, and Giving What We Can estimates that if the donors all do what they have pledged to do, $309 million will go to the most effective charities.

In addition to helping Ord launch Giving What We Can, MacAskill had an idea for another organization. Students and other young people get plenty of career advice, but none of it is directed toward the question an effective altruist would ask: What career will enable me to do the most good over my lifetime? In 2011 MacAskill and five friends founded 80,000 Hours, so named because that is roughly the number of hours people spend working in their careers. 80,000 Hours does research on which careers do the most good, offers free career coaching, and is building a global community of people seeking to change the world for the better.

The term *effective altruism* was born when Giving What We Can and 80,000 Hours decided to apply for charitable status under a common umbrella organization. The umbrella organization needed a name. After tossing around some names, including High Impact Alliance and Evidence-Based Charity Association, the group took a vote, and Centre for Effective Altruism was the clear winner. Effective altruism soon caught on and become the term for the entire movement.

Philanthropy is broken – here's how to fix it

Eric Friedman, 2013

A few years ago, the following story was highlighted on St. Jude Children's Research Hospital's website as an inspiring testament to the hospital's work:

> Sabrina developed bruises on her arms and legs that didn't go away, even after a few weeks. Then one night, during bath time, Sabrina's mom, Vicky, was startled to see a rash across her little girl's chest. When she noticed that her usually sunny daughter was becoming more and more lethargic, mother's intuition kicked in. This was something serious, Vicky felt. The next day, she took Sabrina to the pediatrician.
>
> At the doctor's office, Sabrina underwent an ultrasound and blood work. When Sabrina's doctor referred the family to the local St. Jude Children's Research Hospital affiliate, Vicky felt her dread rising. At the affiliate, Sabrina underwent more tests. The results were devastating: Sabrina suffered from t-cell acute lymphoblastic leukemia.
>
> The next day, Sabrina and Vicky arrived at St. Jude, where Sabrina quickly started chemotherapy on a two-and-a-half-year treatment plan . . .
>
> "Something like this puts life in perspective," Vicky said. "We thank St. Jude every day for saving Sabrina." Sabrina is able to do her weekly chemotherapy at the local St. Jude affiliate. She takes oral chemotherapy each day, and returns to Memphis once a month for intense chemotherapy. Happily, she is responding well to treatment.
>
> Vicky and her husband are grateful for the donors who support St. Jude . . . "Never receiving a bill from St. Jude . . . that is a true blessing," said Vicky.

Sabrina is lucky to be alive, thanks to St. Jude and the donors who help maintain its high standards of care.

[. . .]

Halfway around the world, in Malanje, Angola, Domingos Antonic struggled with a different illness. He was sick with malaria for several days before being brought to the Malanje Provincial Hospital, already underweight for an eight month old. Domingos suffered from acute anemia and had difficulty breathing. He needed oxygen, but the hospital did not have an oxygen tank. His veins were so small that the staff was unsuccessful at giving him the transfusion he needed; a surgeon could have cut to find a vein, but there was no surgeon available. A $10 mosquito net probably would have prevented his illness, but the hospital received only 300,000 of the 1.2 million needed to cover everyone in the area.

Domingos died.

Two innocent children got sick. One received the best treatment in the world. Another barely received any treatment. One lived; one died.

In a perfect world, neither would have died. But that's not the world we live in. We live in a world with limited resources, and bad things happen that more resources could prevent. That fact drives many philanthropists to donate their wealth to make the world a better place, and for most of them, giving feels good.

But there's a dark side to giving that is rarely discussed in the world of philanthropy. For every person a donor helps, countless others are not helped. It isn't the donor's fault – it's impossible to help everyone – but it is reality. Donors who chose St. Jude over Malanje Provincial implicitly chose Sabrina over Domingos. Just as every donor to St. Jude deserves credit for saving Sabrina's life, they also made a decision that influenced the ultimate outcome for Domingos. They certainly didn't kill Domingos, but the choices that helped save Sabrina's life also influenced Domingos's death. Many find this way of thinking offensive – and it is – but it is also reality. It makes giving seem less fun. Some donors might respond by splitting their gift among many different organizations to help both children, but spreading resources around doesn't effectively tackle the broader issue: scarce resources prevent them from helping everyone in need. Choices must be made.

[. . .]

When the stakes are so high, doesn't Domingos deserve more consideration? Shouldn't donors think about their options more carefully? Maybe you believe that it is more important to save Sabrina's life than Domingos's because you're American and "charity begins at home." But the decision isn't as simple as Sabrina versus Domingos: one child here versus one there. Considering the $1.8 million daily operating costs of St. Jude, it is fair to ask: Would a donation to Malanje Provincial Hospital have saved more lives? If there ever has been a question whose answer affected life-and-death situations, this is it. Even without perfectly reliable "cost-per-life-saved" measures from each institution, we can still make comparisons. This is not about criticizing one institution and taking money away from it to promote another, but about trying to do the most good with limited resources to balance the needs of the world's Sabrinas and Domingoses.

[. . .]

Failings of philanthropy

Answering the question of Sabrina versus Domingos is no easy task, and it is worthwhile to start by stepping back and considering why people give.

[. . .]

Too many donors give to charities that affect them emotionally rather than to charities where their money will do the most good. They excuse themselves from effective giving under the rubric of "giving back."

[. . .]

One way of thinking about this issue is to classify giving as being either expressive or instrumental. The purpose of an expressive gift is to express the donor's feelings. Examples include:

- Donating in memory of someone who recently passed away.
- Giving to the donor's alma mater as a gesture of gratitude, to repay the support given, or to help someone in similar circumstances to the donor.

- Giving to a medical cause or facility because its particular area of focus is something that has personally touched the donor's life.
- Donating within a particular geographic region because the donor has lived there and wants to help those near home.

Although most expressive donors hope their gifts help others, it is important to realize that their focus in selecting the gift's recipient is largely based on expressing personal emotions rather than having an impact.

Instrumental gifts, on the other hand, are designed to create positive social change. Instrumental gifts are much less likely to be specifically directed at meeting the emotional needs of the donor. They are also much more likely to meet the needs of the recipients.

To give in a way that is fully instrumental, the donor must be focused on impact in making decisions about which philanthropic goals to pursue as well as how to pursue those goals. For example, consider a donor who focuses on increasing the public's appreciation of sousaphone music. The donor extensively researches the many different ways to accomplish this goal and funds the program he believes will be most effective at accomplishing his goal. This donor could be considered very instrumental in one aspect of his giving because of his research into the most effective ways to increase the public's awareness of sousaphone music. However, he probably was not instrumental in choosing to focus on promoting sousaphone music; more likely, he chose this area because of a personal passion he wanted to express.

Many experts in philanthropy do not make a distinction between instrumental and expressive choices in terms of the donors' goals, only in how the donors pursue those goals. As an example, Philanthropedia, an organization that provides information to help guide donors, tells donors on its "Guide to Better Giving" webpage, "Wondering where to begin? Think about what you care about most. Our motto is: Pick a cause with your heart and then an organization with your mind." They appear to believe that if a donor who cares about sousaphone music picks the best organization to increase its public appreciation, the gift would be extremely instrumental. But this logic is drawing a bright line where none should exist. The key difference between philanthropy and spending money on oneself is that philanthropy helps others, so all decisions about philanthropy should be considered in terms of how instrumental they are at helping others. In that respect, the importance to the world of having slightly greater public appreciation of sousaphone music should be a factor in considering how instrumental this donor is, just as the donor's effectiveness in pursuing this goal is.

Most giving tends to be a combination of expressive and instrumental. Even the most expressive donor would be unlikely to make a gift without believing it would do some good. And even the most instrumental donor is unlikely to write a large check without feeling some passion for the cause. However, there is a spectrum, and some philanthropy is closer to the expressive side while some is closer to instrumental.

[. . .]

There is no requirement for donors to do thorough research or give thoughtful consideration on whether there are other areas that should be of higher priority. It's their money, so donors are in control. In a free society, this is okay – people can do whatever they want with their money, and certainly doing something good for others is better than being completely selfish, even if that "something good" isn't attempting to do the most good for others. Some donors may not care, though they probably won't admit it. It's their money and they're in control, so they certainly don't have to care. But one of the major reasons philanthropy is failing is because of the imbalance in focus on what will make donors feel good to the detriment of what will do the most good – it is hard to characterize philanthropy as "successful" if donations are not directed primarily to help others as much as possible.

This is not the only failure of philanthropy, as many donors do care about the effectiveness of their donation. Another major reason for philanthropy's failure to get close to its potential is the lack of critical analysis regarding how donors can make the most impact. There is very little willingness to explicitly acknowledge that some good causes are better than others. This results in a severe lack of constructive criticism for donors. It is socially taboo to do anything other than enthusiastically praise donors or those working for good causes, with rare exceptions in the case of politically motivated charities and outright corruption. It's time for philanthropy to be reinvented.

[. . .]

Philanthropy reinvented

There is a perverse system in philanthropy: the charities that survive are the ones that satisfy the donors, not necessarily the ones that are effective at their core mission. That is, and will always be, the case. Some people have told me that there's no point in trying to reinvent philanthropy – donors won't change their behavior. The reasons they've cited include the following:

- Donors and nonprofits are already doing a good job maximizing impact; there's no need for anything to be reinvented.
- The moral implications are too burdensome, appearing to require an almost superhuman level of self-control and sacrifice.
- People are too emotional; philanthropy will never be as heartless as seemingly required by the do-bester approach.
- It is too time-consuming and difficult to be a do-bester; this book doesn't present a simple step-by-step process for deciding where to give.

I don't expect there's much chance to completely reverse the practices of philanthropy that donors have been applying for decades, but I am not as cynical as the naysayers about making incremental progress. Let's consider these points one by one.

1. Donors and nonprofits are already doing a good job maximizing impact; there's no need for anything to be reinvented

How impactful can the most effective nonprofits be relative to the typical ones? As an example, there have been several studies analyzing the cost to save a life in various places and with different interventions. Although the world's most effective charities can save a life for between $200 and $2,000, the median life-saving intervention in America costs about $2.2 million.

The ultra-cheap ways to save lives are funding things like mosquito nets to prevent malaria, measles immunizations, and clean water – things that typically don't get funded by donors who choose their area of giving emotionally. Most people from developed countries don't relate to these causes because we don't often know people who have died of malaria, measles, or unsanitary water. The difference between the impact of do-gooders and do-besters can be several orders of magnitude.

This is not to imply that do-besters must focus on saving lives, but simply to illustrate the relative cost-effectiveness of different causes. Comparing these to education, the environment, human rights, hunger, and other interventions is an extremely important part of the process – and one that will also yield large differences between typical charities and the most effective ones.

2. The moral implications are too burdensome, requiring an almost superhuman level of self-control and sacrifice

Though there are certainly moral undertones to many of the issues discussed in this book, there should not be a moral imperative for philanthropists to attempt to become absolute do-besters. Nor should there be a moral imperative for people to donate every dime of their disposable income. While it is okay for people to spend their money on things other than necessities, those with more money than they need should help others. There is a lot of gray area in assessing the level of such obligations and the appropriate balance between spending on oneself and helping others.

Philanthropy is one way people can fulfill their obligations to help others. Those with a do-bester approach are purely focused on maximizing the benefits of others, while those with a do-gooder approach are typically trying to balance helping others with connecting to their individual emotional passions. Giving in a way that reduces the impact to others in order for the donor to get those emotional benefits is a combination of helping others and consumption.

Ironically, a do-bester donor can actually donate less than a do-gooder donor and fulfill the same obligation to help others, because the do-bester's donations are doing more to help others. Do-gooders need to donate much more to have a comparable impact. In my experience, however, donors passionate about a do-bester philosophy tend not to use this as an excuse to donate less, but rather a reason why they choose to donate more. Regardless, the moral implications of a do-bester approach are not necessarily more burdensome than that of other approaches.

3. People are too emotional; philanthropy will never be as heartless as seemingly required by the do-bester approach

The do-bester approach may not be for every donor, but a donor doesn't have to be emotionless to subscribe to it. Most donors are not masochists. They enjoy giving money away, deriving pleasure from helping others. This is why people feel good about themselves when giving. Do-besters are no different, other than being more aware of whether and how much they are helping. A do-bester who knowingly chose to give to an "average" cause instead of a "top" cause would not get as good of a feeling. Some might actually get a bad feeling from "wasting" money. Do-besters may simply be more knowledgeable and aware versions of do-gooders. A reinvented world of philanthropy should not be about all head and no heart, but about doing a better job of focusing on what many people's hearts want to do: help others. It is not cold and calculating, but warm and smart. And ironically, it may lead to even greater emotional benefits from giving because do-besters will have more conviction in the impact of their giving.

4. It is too time-consuming and difficult to be a do-bester; this book doesn't present a simple step-by-step process for deciding where to give

This may be the most damming of the four criticisms, claiming that the approach this book recommends is not implementable for most donors. The reality is that it is a lot easier to donate to an average charity than it is to evaluate which charity is likely to have the greatest impact. A simple how-to manual with a step-by-step process wouldn't accurately portray the complexity of the decisions donors face. There is no single best approach, philosophy, cause, or charity. In short, a simple solution would be disingenuous. However, presenting only complex, difficult solutions is not practical. Some donors simply don't have the time or interest to dedicate to their giving. They just want their giving to be extremely impactful. For them, a simple, practical solution is needed. The solution: Get someone else to do the hard work.

Warren Buffett did it by giving his money to the Gates Foundation. The choices Bill Gates made about how to set up his foundation, who to hire, which causes to focus on, and which organizations to support represent a composite of all of his beliefs. Gates and Buffett are both thoughtful individuals. They must have agreed on many aspects of philanthropy in order for Buffett to give his life savings to the Gates Foundation, but it is unlikely that they agree on everything. While Buffett has some influence as a board member and was able to give direction about how his donation is used, ultimately he delegated so much responsibility to Gates that he almost assuredly is incorporating aspects of Gates's beliefs that he doesn't share. That is the sacrifice that Buffett made in taking the simple solution. He wanted to spend his time running Berkshire Hathaway rather than thinking about every issue in philanthropy (and due to the sheer amount of his giving, he has more issues to consider than most of us), so he adopted Gates's belief set as his own. One of the biggest problems with the simple solution is that donors can't always pick and choose the specific, shared views of whoever they get to "do the work" for them.

In Buffett's case, Gates wasn't the only option he had to get others to make decisions for him. Surely there were plenty of other foundations that would have taken his money. But he chose the one that he thought would do the best job. Similarly, GiveWell [a US-based charity ratings organization] built itself around helping donors make these decisions. And many foundations publish lists of their grantees in hopes of encouraging others to give to them. So donors who want to be do-besters can limit their time commitments by making only one decision: who to piggyback.

[. . .]

Almost everything in philanthropy originates with donors, because they decide which organizations and projects to fund. A large group of active donors with a do-bester philosophy, even if it is far from a majority, could substantially change the philanthropic sector. My vision for reinventing philanthropy involves three major improvements over how it is practiced today.

First, there should be a general acceptance of the do-bester philosophy as legitimate. Unfortunately, that is not the case today. The dominant view of today's "best practice" in philanthropy is that donors should let their personal interests and passions dictate major decisions such as how they select causes and geographies. This view is treated as a given axiom in almost every other book on philanthropy that has been published recently. Almost all of the major consulting firms for philanthropists advocate a similar perspective as the standard for how donors should think. This implicitly rejects a more issue-agnostic, utilitarian goal of trying to provide the greatest help to the greatest number of people. Though the do-bester approach is often considered void of passion or too unfocused to be implemented, neither is true. This philosophy should be accepted as a legitimate way of approaching philanthropy, at least on par with the traditional approach.

Second, there should be better information on the impact of various charitable alternatives, and nonprofits should compete for donors based on their potential for impact. More donors would demand that nonprofits demonstrate that their programs work and are cost effective, and that proof would be documented transparently on their websites. Further, more charity evaluators would exist and focus on greater impact. The watchdog organizations like Charity Navigator, CharityWatch, and the Better Business Bureau would continue their trend of focusing less on the financial aspects of the organizations they rate, and increasing their emphasis on impact. There would also be more rigorous comparisons of different causes. Further, there should be a stronger role for charity evaluators, like GiveWell, that include more subjectivity in their evaluations. Unlike the charity rating agencies, the evaluators would emphasize deep evaluations of a small number of organizations to try to identify the best ones. More of these charity evaluators would be formed, each with its own process and philosophy, so donors could have more options to consider. These organizations would even have a certain amount of competition with each other for the attention of donors. Having this support system in place would make it easier to be a do-bester.

Third, with greater acceptance of the do-bester philosophy and greater resources for those types of donors, more philanthropic funds would go to the top organizations and most cost-effective solutions. Because there is a significant amount of subjectivity in determining these organizations and causes, there would be a range of causes and organizations funded by this emerging breed of donor. But those most often viewed as having the greatest potential and likelihood of succeeding would be well funded. Further, more of the gifts would be unrestricted, as the organizations will have earned the trust of donors to make the best decisions about how to use their funding.

[. . .]

It is easy to find flaws in other people's giving processes, and hard to find processes without flaws. That is one reason why so many within mainstream philanthropy emphasize that philanthropy is about what donors are emotionally drawn to. Since there is no single "correct" answer, they say that donors can do whatever they want and imply that their actions are equally good. This is an easy solution to a difficult problem, but its validity is questionable.

If I were the parent of a child with cancer, I'd almost certainly want my child to have access to medical care as good as what is offered at St. Jude – hopefully they wouldn't penalize my child because of this book – and I'd want no expense spared for my child. I would want the best resources to be dedicated to my child, even if that might prevent those resources from going to others. But as a donor, I may prefer to give to Malanje Provincial Hospital over St. Jude if I think Malanje Provincial can make better use of my donation to help other people's children. This is not hypocritical. My motivation and decision criteria can (and should) be very different in the role of a relatively neutral donor than someone with a vested personal interest. This is often forgotten, though it is a central difference between philanthropy and consumption.

Putting together all the pieces of the do-besters puzzle is difficult – in fact, it is impossible. It is only a dream, a vision that donors can try to make progress toward, but will never truly achieve. Reinventing philanthropy is not about taking the emotion out of giving or finding an objective answer to solving the world's problems, Rather, it is about channeling the emotions and intellect of donors into a framework for better solutions. And donors who genuinely understand and embrace this approach will not only do better, they'll also feel better.

The emerging threat of effective altruism

William Schambra, 2014

We face the challenge of a new movement called "effective altruism" – a radical utilitarian approach to giving that might best be described as "strategic philanthropy on steroids."

[. . .]

We will be hearing more and more over the coming years about "effective altruism," a cause inspired by Princeton professor Peter Singer's strict utilitarianism; developed in books by Eric Friedman and William MacAskill; put into action by groups like charity evaluator GiveWell and the Robin Hood Foundation; and explored and promoted by websites like Effective Altruism Blog, 80,000 Hours, and Giving What We Can.

The upshot of this new movement is that metrics should determine not only which among similar groups pursuing a given cause deserves support. Rather, *metrics should be the basis for choosing which cause to support in the first place*. Paul Christiano calls it "cause prioritization." Giving should seek to save or improve the most lives per dollar, no matter what a program does or where it's located.

In his much-viewed TED talk "The How and Why of Effective Altruism," Singer notes that the $40,000 spent providing "one guide dog for one blind American" could instead "cure between 400 and 2,000 people of blindness" in a developing country. He concludes, "I think it's clear what's the better thing to do."

In *Reinventing Philanthropy*, Friedman similarly juxtaposes art museums in a wealthy city against illness in the developing world: "I think the relative merits of supporting art museums versus saving people dying of diseases that are easily preventable or curable are pretty clear. Both are 'good' causes, but one is likely to do a lot more good than the other."

Effective altruism vs. strategic philanthropy, left and right

Although this might sound like just another manifestation of strategic philanthropy's metric-mindedness, it's critical to understand that it is in fact a profound radicalization of it. Effective altruists make strategic philanthropists look like sloppy sentimentalists. Strategic philanthropists like Paul Brest seek only to apply metrics to the selection of groups once a cause has been selected. But, altruist critics note, this foolishly leaves the choice of the cause itself willy-nilly to the all-too-often idiosyncratic, short-sighted, selfish impulses of the donor.

Here, effective altruism constructs a powerful critique of strategic philanthropy. Why should one seek such rigor in the technical details of giving, but be unwilling or unable to make any judgments about its larger purposes or ends?

Does it really make sense for an advisor to say to a donor: "We have no authoritative advice to give you about the cause you should pursue, so just pick any one that strikes your fancy. But once you do that, we're here to help you calculate down to the third decimal how effectively your grantees reach that arbitrary goal?"

Measurement, which is omnipotent in the realm of philanthropic means, seems to be impotent in the realm of ends. But, effective altruists sensibly argue, the choice of ends surely influences the overall impact of charitable spending far more decisively than merely fine-tuning the means.

In defense of strategic philanthropy's agnosticism about the ends of philanthropy, however, it must be said that it is at least consistent with the principle of moral relativism, which is at the heart of so much of progressivism today. Who can say which purpose is better than another, when all such decisions, liberals argue, are just matters of personal opinion?

Although the progressive philanthropy watchdog group National Center for Responsive Philanthropy (NCRP) takes a strong moral stand for anti-poverty giving, the more consistently relativist liberal position would be: "Who are you to judge if I prefer art museums to fighting poverty?"

Curiously, many conservative philanthropists today seem to end up in the same place, embracing strategic philanthropy's combination of objective means with subjective ends. They have no problem with metrics, of course, since the demand for measurable outcomes resonates with the business backgrounds many of them bring to giving. But in recent years, conservatism has had less and less to say about the appropriate purposes of philanthropy. In their desire to safeguard the private legal status of foundations against public intrusion, conservative lobbyist and leaders have shied away from making judgments about good and bad giving, lest such self-criticism invite unwelcome congressional attention. Conservative philanthropic publications have become almost as mindlessly upbeat and vacuous as those of the Council on Foundations, endlessly celebrating and promoting giving itself in all its forms – as if it didn't matter what the giving were for.

NCRP's powerful moral demand for more spending against poverty is considered a particular threat to conservative philanthropy. After throwing up a few half-hearted skirmish lines (museums benefit the poor too!), conservatives quickly fall back on their main rhetorical fortress: the concept of "donor intent." Before its walls, moral demands utterly lose their power. For here they come up against the only standard that truly counts: The donor is always right.

Donor intent is of course legally unassailable. But it's also philosophically debilitating. It's a quick, cheap way to cut off any substantive debate about the proper ends of philanthropy, because in the final analysis only the donor's opinion counts.

Oddly, then, the normless drift of liberalism's moral relativism – typically a prime target for conservatism – is faithfully echoed in conservative philanthropy's almost-Nietzschean devotion to the groundless but resolute Will of the Donor.

The problem of localism for effective altruism

However antagonistic effective altruism is to strategic philanthropy in its liberal or conservative form, philanthrolocalism [defined by Jeremy Beer as "a philosophy of giving that prioritizes the use of resources to help one's own place, including one's neighbors, community members, churches, businesses, cultural institutions, civic associations, and ecology"] had best brace itself, for it must soon find itself in the bull's eye. In effective altruism's view, the tendency to focus charity within one's own backyard is nothing less than a profound failure of moral imagination. But unlike institutional conservative philanthropy, philanthrolocalism dares fight back on the field of morality itself, without retiring behind the walls of donor intent.

Singer observes that the thousands of annual deaths from preventable illness tend to occur in communities where donors are unlikely to live. But "does it really matter that they're far away? I don't think it does make a morally relevant difference. The fact that they're not right in front of us, the fact that they're of a different nationality or race, none of that seems morally relevant to me."

Friedman similarly complains that "90 percent of all foundations in the United States are restricted by their donors to specific geographic regions, usually to the city, county, or state in which donors live." Yet, "a donor is unlikely to live in the region where a donation will have the most impact." He continues:

> Are the homeless shelters and food pantries near you the best ways to reduce hunger and poverty? For most donors, the answer to these questions is "no." . . . Donors shouldn't fool themselves into thinking that it is easy to focus on their favored region without also reducing the impact of their donations.

Note that in its willingness to attack local-mindedness outright, effective altruism is far more corrosive to local giving than strategic philanthropy has ever been. True, once one starts down the metrics road, it isn't long before the local grassroots groups so critical for teaching self-governance begin to seem bumbling, amateurish, and deficient. Soon measurable outcomes demand the displacement of such haphazard, decentralized efforts with centralized, data-driven, professional service programs. In this light, strategic philanthropy's tension with philanthrolocalism is just the latest skirmish in the century-old war between root-causes philanthropy and "band-aid" charity.

Still, if a donor insists that his giving, albeit now technically more proficient, must be confined to a given locale, strategic philanthropy cannot object. It must remain resolutely agnostic about such choices.

[. . .]

Unlike strategic philanthropy, effective altruism finds *any* qualification of the purely utilitarian calculus of maximum human benefit to be morally unacceptable. So it must take particular umbrage at the notoriously widespread limitations "arbitrarily" imposed by localism. Effective altruism cannot hope to spread among the public until it has loosened the constraints imposed by local allegiances.

Mainstream liberal and conservative philanthropy cannot be counted on as allies in the coming showdown. They are obliged by principle simply to shrug their shoulders and concede that whatever the donor wants, the donor gets, whether it's localism or universalism.

But philanthrolocalism must do better than this. It claims to affirm a specific, well-defined moral purpose for philanthropy. It must present a substantive argument on behalf of giving that aims to strengthen one's own neighborhood or community, rather than to maximize utility wherever it is to be found.

[. . .]

Community-embeddedness versus detached godliness: not a bad summary of the coming conflict between philanthrolocalism and effective philanthropy. Given philanthrolocalism's view of human nature, moral sentiments can only be cultivated within the small, immediate communities that surround us and that press neighborly obligations upon us. Local communities are built upon and cultivate a mutual dependence among and compassionate attentiveness to those in our midst.

It may not be morally significant to Singer whether or not a person in need is "right in front of us." But it *is* significant to Tocqueville, who warned us that we can no longer count on grand, detached, noble moral sentiments to sustain benevolence in our democratic future. In this fragmented, individualistic age, only an immediate, face-to-face encounter with others – those "right in front of us" – would stir us out of our introspective, selfish concerns to pay attention to others' needs.

Democratic self-governance as well as moral development depends on localism: The gritty, unpleasant, contentious world of local politics and civic association is a magnificent school of citizenship. It teaches us that others have views very different from ours, with seemingly obscure and illogical origins, perhaps expressed and pursued clumsily, and even obnoxiously. But we must learn to accommodate those views, not as an abstract humanitarian exercise, but rather as the only way to pave a road, secure a variance, or lay some drainage tiles. Tocqueville points out that what originates in this limited calculus of self-interest becomes over time a solid, reflexive civic habit. But the cultivation of this humble democratic virtue demands immediate involvement in local community.

Clearly, the global aspirations of effective altruism are unlikely to be satisfied by localism's petty disputes and small satisfications. Localism is messy, complex, fragmented, parochial, and sustained by the concrete, unremarked fulfillment of the small daily obligations that bespeak neighborliness. Down this path there are no million-view TED talks, no seats on a glittering panel at Davos alongside Bill Gates and Bono.

The detached god of effective altruism is so much more appealing. Freed from entanglement in the messy reality of any particular community (where one's manifest benevolence is so frequently misconstrued as self-righteous meddling), the effective altruist can scan the globe for the best lives-saved-per-dollar bargain. This is almost by definition not in our own backyard but probably in Africa. "In general, where human welfare is concerned, we will achieve more if we help those in extreme poverty in developing countries, as our dollars go much further there," argues Singer.

As it turns out, such charitable activity at considerable remove is highly congenial to the altruistic but very busy young intellectual: to determine the good accomplished, the giver has only to glance at the reams of promising data generated by distant, professional service providers summing up faraway programs. There is no need ever to encounter face-to-face the unintended consequences generated by those interventions.

[. . .]

The unpromising terrain ahead for philanthrolocalism

One final note of caution: In the coming showdown between effective philanthropy and philanthrolocalism – the detached god and embedded particularity – it should be clear that the institutional lay of the land within the field of philanthropy clearly favors the former.

This was true from the moment early on when philanthropy proudly broke free of mere charity's concerns with meeting immediate local needs and set out resolutely to solve problems once and for all by getting to their root causes. Since then, everything about philanthropy has pushed it away from localism toward globalism; away from particularity toward universalism; away from the concrete toward the abstract.

The very language of philanthropy today – with its collaborating and synergizing, its convenings and learnings and collective impacts, its thought leadership and social entrepreneurialism – betrays a profession that prides itself on detachment and abstraction, on models, theories, strategies, and formulas. Philanthropic argot even hesitates to be precise about the issues it aims to address: it funds "around" an issue, or "in that space." Our large foundations today are almost completely untethered from the workaday world of their grantees, who finally must sit down face-to-face with a particular person and help him or her deal with an all-too-concrete and immediate problem.

As hostile as the institutional realities of philanthropy may be for philanthrolocalism, it still has one critical asset: the established habits of the individual donors who constitute the vast majority of charitable giving in the United States. While their durable good sense has managed to resist the relentless propaganda of strategic philanthropy, it now faces a much more formidable challenge from effective altruism. A critical task before us is to translate the sound opinion and practice of everyday Americans into a coherent doctrine of philanthrolocalism.

We must be able to respond when our philanthropic elites deride localist sentiments as intellectually deficient and morally bankrupt. That means building a compelling moral claim on behalf of the centrality of localism for the preservation of American democracy and the kind of human being it requires. It means refusing to tone itself down in the face of donor intent, or yielding to the relentless calculus of utilitarianism.

Balancing the head and heart in philanthropy

Paul M. Connolly, 2011

Over the past 15 years, a technocratic approach to philanthropy has become more common and brought numerous benefits to the field. While the term "technocratic" may carry negative connotations, it embodies elements that are positive: It typically involves experts applying business principles to help foundations define their goals clearly, devise focused strategies, measure results rigorously, and engage with grantees to increase impact. While modern features are now part of the mix, this way of thinking is not new. In the early 20th century, funders like the Rockefeller Foundation followed a "scientific philanthropy" course that similarly employed objective business and social science disciplines to address the root causes, rather than just the symptoms, of systemic problems.

Part of the current emphasis on the technocratic stems from economic and societal forces that shape the philanthropic landscape. In 2008, there were approximately 75,000 foundations in the United States, almost double the number of just a decade earlier. Yet the $46 billion in grants those foundations made during that year represented only a small portion of nonprofit revenues – meaning that it is even more essential to create a "bigger bang for the buck." Especially in light of the recent recession, philanthropies are striving to find ways to create a wider ripple effect and amplify their impact. Greater scrutiny by regulators, the media, and the public has also contributed to a laudable desire to be more accountable and better demonstrate results.

As with any high-profile idea, the technocratic approach can get blurred or even distorted – and it is worth pausing to define the term. The field tends to use "strategic philanthropy" to refer to what this article is calling "technocratic." That phrase, however, does not appear in these pages because it may imply that other foundations do not act strategically, a position not shared by the author. For the sake of simplicity, however, this article does at times refer to technocratic practices – such as focusing on clear goals and plans with built-in accountability – as the work of "strategy" or "being more strategic."

Demystifying the sometimes elitist terminology attached to the technocratic approach reveals an underlying common sense. Strategy can simply be defined as a decision-making framework, based on a foundation's external context and internal capacity, for selecting goals and activities to accomplish results. Performance measurement – also part of the technocratic landscape – is a way to assess progress and make course corrections. Devising a program strategy requires articulating purpose and values, developing a clear understanding of the larger environment, creating well-defined and integrated aims and plans, and then evaluating programs and using what is learned to modify them.

Straightforward as these ideas might sound, the evolving emphasis on technocratic practices – along with the vastly differing degrees to which foundations have embraced them – has led to confusion and a rift in the field. The technocratic paradigm has become a source not just of misunderstanding, but even of rancorous debate. It is now discussed in opposition to the humanistic, positing a false choice that obscures the most effective option of all: a blending of the two approaches. One does not have to listen hard to hear how heatedly divided the field has become about which form of philanthropy is best. While vigorous dialogue can help test assumptions and identify effective practices, the arguments have become narrow-minded and detrimental. By focusing on two extreme points on the spectrum, this debate gives the impression that these possibilities are mutually exclusive when they need not be.

A counterproductive "either-or" debate and the need for nuance

Prominent authors such as Matthew Bishop (*Philanthrocapitalism: How the Rich Will Save the World*) and Michael Edwards (*Small Change: Why Business Won't Save the World*) have been at the forefront of this dispute. So have Paul Brest, president of the Hewlett Foundation and co-author of *Money Well Spent: A Strategic Plan for Smart Philanthropy*, and Bill Somerville, who is executive director of Philanthropic Ventures Foundation and wrote *Grassroots Philanthropy: Notes of a Maverick Grantmaker.* Other thought leaders in the field – while not using the terms "technocratic" or "humanistic" per se – give conflicting advice that sends readers in different directions and reveals the current schism. In *The Foundation*, for example, Joel Fleishman suggests that foundations methodically frame problems, employ evidence-based decision-making, conduct due diligence to fund competent nonprofits, and hire intelligent staff to carry out strategies to increase their impact. By contrast, in *How to Change the World*, David Boorstein argues that local initiatives should drive change and recommends a more bottom-up approach that supports the work of empathetic, innovative, and values-driven social entrepreneurs.

Some technocrats go so far as to arrogantly accuse other funders of following a scattershot and arbitrary "spray and pray" approach that is based on "magical thinking" and leads to scandalous squandering of money with few results. On the other hand, some with a bias against technocratic practices complain about a "philanthro-industrial complex" and patronizingly dismiss due diligence, theory of change, and social return on investment as the empty jargon of soulless business experts. They charge that performance measurement is just a "fetish" or an "obsessive measurement disorder" that creates excessive data that suffocate nonprofits and undermines social impact.

[. . .]

If the black-and-white dichotomies are indeed false, then what would it look like to include gray shades, rather than simple labels of "unstrategic" and "strategic," or "old" and "new?" Figure 6.1 shows a framework for thinking about these different options along a continuum. At one end is a "humanistic" approach and at the other a more "technocratic" one. As the figure illustrates, these two major models have different assumptions about values, grantmaking styles, relationships with grantees, and evaluation. Foundations in the humanistic school tend to be driven by values and passions, exhibit a responsive and flexible grantmaking style, have hands-off relationships with grantees, and employ qualitative evaluation primarily for learning. Funders in the technocratic

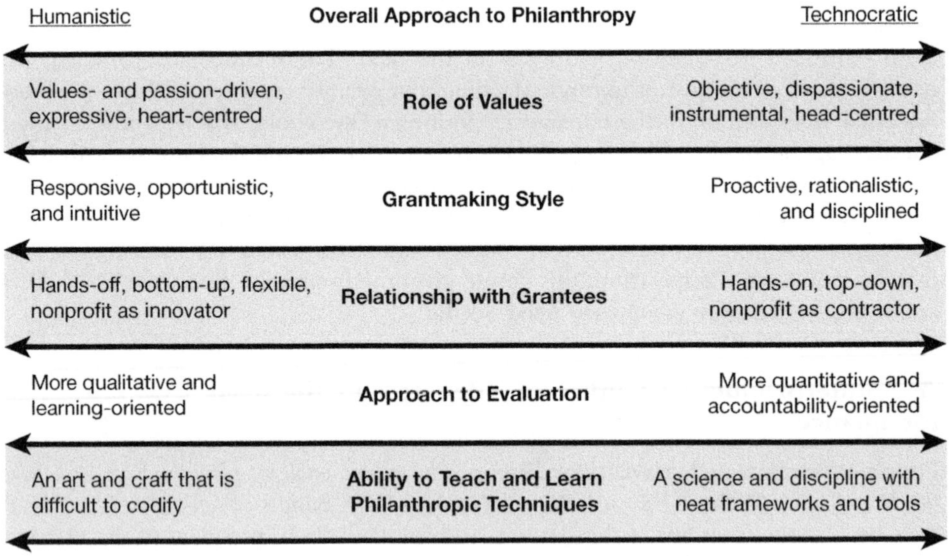

Humanistic	Overall Approach to Philanthropy	Technocratic
Values- and passion-driven, expressive, heart-centred	**Role of Values**	Objective, dispassionate, instrumental, head-centred
Responsive, opportunistic, and intuitive	**Grantmaking Style**	Proactive, rationalistic, and disciplined
Hands-off, bottom-up, flexible, nonprofit as innovator	**Relationship with Grantees**	Hands-on, top-down, nonprofit as contractor
More qualitative and learning-oriented	**Approach to Evaluation**	More quantitative and accountability-oriented
An art and craft that is difficult to codify	**Ability to Teach and Learn Philanthropic Techniques**	A science and discipline with neat frameworks and tools

Figure 6.1 Finding the humanistic-technocratic balance in philanthropy

camp embrace objective and rational analysis, use a proactive grantmaking style, forge hands-on relationships with nonprofits, and rely heavily on metrics-oriented evaluation for accountability to monitor and prove returns. Despite the sometimes black-and-white debate about the technocratic versus humanistic approach, most funders acknowledge that they do not fall at one end of the range but somewhere in the middle. They may also be at different points at different times for a wide variety of reasons.

Muddying the landscape further is the fact that neither of these two schools is directly aligned with any one political ideology. It is true that progressive funders who support social justice tend to be more humanistic, while conservative, market-conscious funders who advocate social enterprise are apt to be more technocratic. Yet some conservative philanthropic leaders espouse a populist philosophy calling for nonprofits and ordinary citizens – rather than professional elites – to address our most pressing social problems. And more liberal philanthropic leaders believe that rational strategies and performance assessment can be beneficial. Moreover, many wealthy donors schizophrenically check their business acumen at the door when they get involved with philanthropy. And some of the most innovative, free-market crowd-sourcing techniques are being utilized for highly responsive and grassroots social problem-solving.

Neither the humanistic nor technocratic model has cornered the market on taking risks or on being innovative – or even strategic or effective. As stated earlier, this article is not suggesting that humanistic funders don't think or act strategically – they often do. But they tend not to embrace the technocratic practices described in these pages. Often the most effective course is to accept the tensions between the two approaches – in other words, to creatively unite both the art and science of philanthropy. A similar rationale lies behind the ever-more-popular call to utilize both right- and left-brain thinking. The point is not to ignore differences, but to use appreciative inquiry, weigh trade-offs, and try to balance frictions given the particular complicated circumstances.

As the philanthropy field matures, it needs a hybrid model that incorporates the best of the humanistic and the technocratic. These seemingly contrary forces are in fact interconnected in a dynamic yin-and-yang-style system. When joyful and passionate conviction converges with judicious and dispassionate analysis, a powerful creative energy emerges. Another way to think of this melding of different mindsets is that they employ multiple intelligences, encompassing logical, emotional, and creative abilities. The way forward requires holding these differing perspectives in balance and productive tension. Sometimes an oxymoron, in its capacity to mix up ideas and make us think in unpracticed ways, holds hidden value. What would it mean to ponder such ideas as humble ambition, rigorous values, passionate discipline, rational exuberance, soulful strategy, planned opportunism, proactive responsiveness, flexible engagement, strategic intuition, irrational insight, immeasurable outcomes, and poignant data? The answer is "soft" and "hard" practices at the same time, which will ultimately lead to heightened effectiveness.

[. . .]

Advancing the philanthropy field by building bridges, not walls

There is no doubt that the social and environmental problems we face are enormous and multifaceted. It only follows that no one approach will successfully tackle them. Philanthropy is marked by a history of innovation, guided by people who are not just capable of understanding complexity, but welcome it to foster greater creativity and impact. The dynamic energy between the technocratic and the humanistic comprises rich territory that has not been fully mined. Both approaches are needed, and together unlock new potential. A more integrated philosophy also makes it more likely that philanthropy will move beyond its traditional boundaries in other ways, such as forging new collaborations with government and business.

Joshua L. Liebman, a rabbi who sought to reconcile religion and psychiatry, said that "maturity is achieved when a person accepts life as full of tension." Similarly, fields progress when tension arises as new paradigms emerge and clash with previous ones, and leaders combine the best elements of both. During the 20th century, for example, the business world benefited from "scientific management" methods involving analysis of operations, while later mixing in more humanizing approaches such as organizational development and values-based leadership. Likewise, more recently, the psychology field, after decades of fierce infighting between behavioral/cognitive and psychodynamic schools, now mostly supports multimodal treatments that are tailored to the person and the problem.

It is time for courageous and bold leaders in philanthropy to step above the fray, sound a wake-up call, and reframe the debate. They need to encourage others to appreciate the tensions between the technocratic and humanistic modes, acknowledge the trade-offs, and respect and learn from each other. The thought-provoking questions in Figure 6.2 can help start a fieldwide discussion to move people from an "either/or" to a "both/and" perspective. Leaders should call for more research that compares the efficacy of the models and identifies practices for synthesizing them, ensuring that they are applicable to smaller foundations, too.

They should also encourage educators to teach an eclectic and integrated range of philosophies and techniques. Seemingly paradoxical concepts – such as values-driven business planning, strategic intuition, and deliberate improvisation – should be promoted.

Questions for More Humanistic Funders	Questions for More Technocratic Funders
How can we incorporate and gain from more dispassionate analysis in our philanthropy work, without losing too much of the joy and heartfulness?	How can we do a better job clarifying and expressing the values and passions that guide our philanthropic work?
When would it be valuable for us to offer more direction to grantees and less flexibility and lenience?	In what cases might it be beneficial for us to be less directive and more nimble, opportunistic, and patient with grantees?
Could we profit from more research on needs and best practices to avoid duplicating effort and reinventing the wheel?	How can we get a broader array of constituents (beyond outside "experts") to weigh in on what they see as the needs and how to address them?
Can we do a better job articulating what specifically we are trying to achieve and explaining the interconnections among the inputs, strategies, and outcomes?	Is our theory of change really feasible? Might there be opportunities for us to improvise more and make more "leaps of faith," based on intuition?
Are there times when we delegate too much to a grantee so that our own knowledge is not tapped sufficiently and the nonprofit accountable enough for its performance?	Are there times when our engaged relationships with grantees end up being too meddlesome, putting them in a servile role, creating too many hoops to jump through, suppressing their innovation, and overlooking their full organizational capacity? How and when could we give grantees more leeway?
How can we build in more rigorous performance measurement into our evaluation so that we document evidence of success and inform our future funding decisions?	How can we share evaluation findings with a broad array of stakeholders – including nonprofit grantees and maybe even beneficiaries – and refine program strategy based on reflection and learning about what worked, why and under what conditions?
What is the best way for us to learn more about and become more at ease with the disciplines, tools, and frameworks associated with strategy and performance measurement? What might nonprofits be able to learn from business?	How can we learn more about the softer, "art and craft" side of philanthropy, including practicing and grooming bold leadership, making sound judgments, encouraging innovation, and building trusting relationships and collaborations? What might business be able to learn from nonprofits?

Figure 6.2 What can we learn from each other?

Since the tools and frameworks associated with technocratic disciplines are usually easier to codify, effort should be put into documenting, teaching, and providing mentoring for more humanistic approaches.

The Rev. Martin Luther King Jr. observed that "power without love is reckless and abusive, and love without power is sentimental and anemic." To advance as a field, philanthropy must tap its own ability to think through paradox to cultivate a deeper wisdom. At its most effective, philanthropy will require combining objectivity with passion, discipline with agility, proactivity with responsiveness, and top-down with bottom-up. This broader perspective depends on making a shift that is not just more nuanced and sophisticated but potentially game-changing. Funders devote their lives to breaking down walls to find solutions to the problems of communities and society. It is time to break down the walls that have come up closer to home.

From aspirations to impact

Thomas J. Tierney and Joel L. Fleishman, 2011

> I'm giving away money – some would say lots of money. And yet it pales in comparison to the needs I see all around me: urban slums and rural poverty, children in failing schools and children without access to any schooling whatsoever, deforestation and unclean water, crippling diseases of many kinds. The needs are immense, at home and abroad. My aspirations are so much greater than my resources that at times it feels as though I'm trying to hold back the tide. I want my giving to do the most it can . . . but how?

We have heard these sentiments from every corner of the philanthropic universe, across America and around the world. They are echoed by experienced donors giving away hundreds of millions a year and rookies with newly established donor-advised funds; by families engaged in private foundations, as well as by their independent trustees and advisors; by all manner of foundation decision-makers, from chief executives to program officers. The speakers' roles and circumstances vary widely, but they share the aspiration to get the most from their philanthropy – and a nagging concern that they could indeed accomplish more.

The concern is warranted. Every donor wants his or her money to make a difference, and nobody wants to see hard-earned wealth (their own or a benefactor's) go to waste. Yet philanthropy's natural state is underperformance. The generosity that causes people to use their wealth on others' behalf is a wonderful expression of humanity at its best, and it can bring enormous joy into a donor's life. But generosity alone is rarely sufficient if you aspire to leave a legacy of exceptional results. Outstanding philanthropy is distinguished by what it achieves as well as by the act of charity itself. It requires you to complement your heartfelt generosity with a disciplined consideration of what you hope to accomplish: the results that will define success, what it will take to achieve them, and how those results will get better over time.

This rigorous approach to how you practice philanthropy is what we mean when we say, "Give smart." It may sound unexceptional. In practice, it is much less straightforward – and far more valuable – than it may first appear.

Philanthropy's "terrible truths"

Giving money away is easy. If you can sign your name at the bottom of a check, or approve the slate of grants at a family foundation board meeting, or accept proposals from aspiring grantees, you can give money away. Giving it away smartly, so that it not only gets results but also gets more and better results over time, is hard. In addition to the sheer difficulty of the issues many philanthropists choose to tackle, you also have to reckon with some "terrible truths" that are rooted in the realities of how the social sector works: All philanthropy is personal. Results can confound. Excellence is self-imposed.

All philanthropy is personal. In the United States alone, there are more than one million nonprofit organizations engaged in every sort of activity, from promoting the arts to organizing zoological expeditions. This diverse and dynamic landscape is the product of the freedom enjoyed by individuals and foundations to support whatever causes they care most about. This same freedom also explains why, quite understandably, not all philanthropic giving is motivated purely or even primarily by the desire to achieve results.

All philanthropy is personal and, as donors, we make gifts for many different reasons: responsibilities to our communities or colleagues ("doing my share"), personal relationships ("can't say no"), giving back, returning a favor, fulfilling our volunteer commitments ("we need 100 percent participation from the board"). Such gifts may be relatively small, given our circumstances, or they may be substantial, as evidenced by the large number of six-, seven-, and even eight-figure gifts given to educational, medical, and cultural institutions each year. Either way, the motivation behind the gift is primarily personal. Results matter, of course, but results are not the driving force.

When institutions replace individuals as the source of funds, philanthropy's personal taproots do not disappear, even if they are seldom discussed publicly. In family-run foundations, trustees naturally feel a certain sense of ownership of the institution's assets, and their interests and worldviews are likely to influence the focus and nature of its grants. Professionally staffed foundations typically have well-defined institutional priorities and processes, yet their program managers often have considerable discretionary latitude in proposing grants, as do the executive directors who ultimately decide what will go before the board. Since many of these individuals are recruited on the basis of their expertise and experience, institutional confidence in their judgment is not at all surprising. But neither should it be surprising that many day-to-day decisions bear their personal stamp.

Results can confound. In the complex world of giving money away, tangible philanthropy – funding the construction of a new marine biology laboratory for instance, or buying up conservation land – is about as straightforward as it gets. As donors, we can take pride in our contributions without worrying that we may not have gotten quite what we paid for. In contrast, the results of other philanthropic initiatives – funding an after-school tutoring program, sponsoring research on global warming, supporting a local neighborhood's revitalization – can be defiantly difficult to pin down. We bet that such gifts and grants will "make a difference." But unlike a construction site, we cannot easily see the work in progress, nor can we be certain that whatever results we do see are directly attributable to our efforts.

In addition, feedback on the results of our philanthropic efforts can be ambiguous, even suspect. When you are in the business of giving away money, people have a tendency to tell you what they think you want to hear. Surrounded by smiling faces and awash in reassuring rhetoric, it's natural for even the most objective and disciplined donors to think they are really achieving outstanding results. Personal incentives are surreptitiously aligned: givers want to feel good about their contributions; current and potential recipients of those funds need to be liked if they hope to secure future funding. Without hard facts to help, even the most well-intentioned individuals can easily be overwhelmed.

Excellence is self-imposed. This is the last and most terrible truth of all: philanthropy has no built-in systemic forces to motivate continuous improvement. The absence of external accountability is what gives philanthropy its freedom to experiment, take risks, and pursue long-term initiatives on society's behalf. At the same time, it also means that if you do not demand excellence of yourself no one else will require it of you.

Unlike business leaders, philanthropists have no market dynamics with which to contend. There are no competitors fighting to take market share away from them, no customers who will take their money elsewhere if they fail to deliver, no shareholders poised to dump their stock. Nor do they need to answer to the public, as politicians ultimately must. Quite the contrary: grant making is often accomplished through foundations established in perpetuity, insulated (and isolated) from any external pressure other than being required to abide by regulatory and tax laws.

In this Galapagos Island-like world, where there are no natural predators, philanthropy is inclined to persist, but not to excel. Therefore, whether you are a donor, a trustee, or a foundation officer, if you want to narrow the gap between your aspirations and the results your giving achieves, you must be willing to set your own standard of excellence and hold yourself accountable for meeting it.

This is no small challenge. Self-imposed accountability is not a natural act. It requires extraordinary determination and discipline to pursue outstanding results year after year, when nothing in the surrounding environment requires you to do so. It is especially unnatural when you are tackling complicated issues, where there are no proven strategies and results are difficult to assess. Helping to change the life of a child born into poverty or forestall the effects of global warming is fundamentally harder than making the proverbial widget.

[. . .]

History lessons

Giving smart is not a recent phenomenon. After selling the Carnegie Steel Company to J.P. Morgan in 1901, Andrew Carnegie (aged sixty-six) devoted the remainder of his life to philanthropy. His results ultimately included establishing some twenty-five hundred public libraries, launching the Carnegie Institute of Technology (now Carnegie Mellon University), and building Carnegie Hall in New York City. In 2006, 105 years after Carnegie "reported" himself, Bill Gates (aged fifty-one) left Microsoft to devote his extraordinary energies to advancing the mission of the Bill & Melinda Gates Foundation. One of its earliest philanthropic initiatives was to install computers in libraries across America. Since then, the foundation has expanded into a wide range of initiatives, from eradicating polio to transforming public education in the United States.

If these two extraordinary philanthropists could compare notes over dinner (we'll assume that Melinda is away on foundation business), they would quickly discover how much they had in common: a relentless ambition to deliver exceptional results through their giving; a deep belief in enabling others to help themselves by leveling the playing field; the willingness to use their brain power, relationships, and influence as well as their money to improve society; the ability to leverage their efforts with other people's money and government support. Rigorous, disciplined, and deeply strategic, the industrial baron and the software tycoon would be highly compatible.

If Gates were to mention "strategic philanthropy," "social entrepreneurs," or "scaling what works" in the course of the conversation, Carnegie might not recognize the phrases, but he would immediately understand the concepts: the need to think hard about your giving, bet on talented people, and pay careful attention to results. A voracious reader, Gates would likewise grasp the continuities, recognizing that language changes faster than principles and that what pass as contemporary insights often fail to appreciate, or fully build upon, relevant lessons from the past.

In fact, when it comes to basic principles, the philanthropy of the industrial era and the philanthropy of the era of nanotechnology are remarkably similar. What is new and constantly evolving is the context within which philanthropists work and the means available to them for getting results. Were Carnegie to spend a few days with the Gateses and their foundation staff, there's no question he would be amazed by the changes from his day to theirs.

Technology is an obvious case in point: the advent of the Internet has enabled all manner of new social-sector business models and tools, from online giving marketplaces like Donors Choose and Kiva, to better methods for measuring and evaluating results. The compounding effect of knowledge is another powerful force: never before has there been so much wealth – or such a wealth of relevant and accessible ideas and information. Changing talent flows that are bringing more people of all ages into careers of public service; new laws and hybrid business-nonprofit models; creative financial structures; blurring boundaries between the sectors: all these and more are creating new opportunities for philanthropists eager to help drive positive change.

Equally important, just as the work that philanthropy does is becoming more global, so are its benefactors. In the years ahead, philanthropists already in the field will increasingly be joined by legions of wealthy contemporaries in India, China, Brazil, and other countries around the globe. Like their predecessors, they will be working in a relentlessly dynamic context, relying upon technologies, tools, and techniques yet to be discovered. And they, too, will be learning some enduring lessons – about the fundamental relationship between thoughtful, considered decision-making and philanthropy that gets results; and about the need to avoid the traps that can cause even the most well-intentioned philanthropists to go astray.

Traps for the unwary

Getting better – steadily better – requires better decisions on every front, from fundamental strategic decisions (like how to define success) to key operational decisions (like whom to hire for a senior staff role). Decisions, after all, are how we allocate resources, and as a donor, your resources – not just your money but also your time and influence – are ultimately the only lever you have to effect change.

The challenge for philanthropists is that many, if not most, of these decisions are often clouded by ambiguity and uncertainty, because the objective data and feedback that could make them more straightforward don't exist, or because they aren't easily available. As a result, more often than not, you're apt to find yourself relying largely if not entirely on your own judgment to make important calls. And that, in turn, means keeping a watchful eye out for some insidious traps that lie in wait at every turn, undermining good intentions and impeding results, even among astonishingly capable and experienced philanthropists.

The first of these traps is fuzzy headedness, which occurs when donors allow their emotions and wishful thinking to override logic and thoughtful analysis. Replying to the question "What are you trying to accomplish?" with a response as undefined (and therefore unattainable) as "curing cancer," or "ending poverty," or "stopping global warming" is a common symptom. So is relying on a miracle to get your giving to its desired result: assuming that a $10 million gift can transform an urban school district with an $800 million budget, for example. Another common symptom is falling in love with a charismatic nonprofit leader's plan without examining it through the lens of rational analysis. One consequence of fuzzy headedness is "feel-good" philanthropy, where happy sentiments abound, but the odds of success are small.

The second trap that donors often fall into is flying solo. One of philanthropy's great ironies is that very little can be accomplished by individuals acting on their own, even when those individuals are extraordinarily wealthy. The grander your ambitions, the more certain it is that success will require working with and through a broad range of other players, including the nonprofit or nongovernmental organization (NGO) grantees you support; other donors who are passionate about the same issue or issues; government agencies at home or abroad; or members of the public whose views you will have to influence in order to effect change. The list of potential candidates is long and varied. Yet far too many donors and foundation leaders fall prey to trying to go it alone, arrogantly assuming that they have all the answers and can achieve success unilaterally!

The third trap is underestimating and underinvesting. It is astonishing how often donors fall into it, given how much philanthropic wealth is created in the high-pressure crucible of business, where mastering the intricacies of finance is essential to survival. The old saying "Everything takes longer and costs more than you expect" holds as true when you are trying to repair the world as it does when you are engaged in home repairs. Yet, as donors, we chronically underestimate what it will actually cost to deliver results and underinvest in the capacity required to make those results a reality.

The consequences of falling into this trap are predictable. The organizations we depend on receive less than they need to perform successfully, and so the next time around we give them even less (or nothing), because they didn't perform as we expected in the first instance.

The corollary to this shortfall, and the fourth trap for the unwary, is nonprofit neglect. It manifests itself chiefly in philanthropy's widespread resistance to providing general operating support, which grantees can use to develop their organizational capacity. No one likes wasting money, and funding for "overhead" can feel like a waste. But is such money always wasted? Suppose we all decided to fly on the airline that reported the lowest maintenance costs? Or went to the hospitals with the oldest, most depreciated equipment? In many circumstances, consumers gladly pay for more overhead if it delivers value to them.

Nonprofits, too, have good overhead and bad overhead. Paying excessive rent or entertaining lavishly is obviously a waste of money. But what about hiring a chief operating officer who can take on crucial management responsibilities for which the executive director has no time, or a chief financial officer who can develop a long-term funding model to sustain the organization's programs? Are those bad investments? Definitely not, and yet we consistently fall into the trap of believing that nonprofits can deliver A-level results with a malnourished team.

"Prudent" boards of directors make this mistake all the time. They'll have an executive director who is doing a fabulous job of raising money and growing the organization, but is also burning out. And the board will resist funding a chief operating officer, even though it would help the organization sustain its results and ultimately do more, because the position would cost $120,000 a year. Colleagues of ours rightly call the consequences of this trap the "nonprofit starvation cycle."

The starvation cycle is the most egregious manifestation of nonprofit neglect. For the most part, donors' results depend on the performance of the nonprofits they support. Great giving is not accomplished in a vacuum. Yet philanthropists routinely impose an excessive "cost of capital" on their grantees, which erodes the value of their contributions as surely and as imperceptibly as water flowing through a corroded pipe seeps away.

What does this hidden cost of capital look like? It comes in many forms: the philanthropist who thinks he knows how to run an after-school program better than the folks who have been doing just that for twenty-five years and insists on imposing his strategic ideas; the grant maker who annually requires her grantees to fill out fifty-page reports about how the grant was used and what results were achieved, but never acknowledges the reports – and probably never reads them in their entirety. The costs of such behavior in disrupted strategies and unproductive working relationships are real, though rarely tabulated. And because of the enormous power imbalance between those with money and those who need to raise it, they can remain invisible and persist for years on end.

Finally, in a world without competition but overflowing with appreciation and praise, grant makers quite naturally fall into the trap of satisfactory underperformance: accepting things as they are without really pushing toward what might be possible. Results are calibrated as "good enough," or perhaps even outstanding, but the motivation to excel, to improve future results by even 10 percent is lacking.

[. . .]

Acknowledging the existence of these traps, and recognizing that they will never really go away, however experienced and wise we become, offers some help in avoiding them.

[. . .]

There is, however, a smarter way to go about choosing your path. That is to engage in a process of rigorous inquiry around six separate but related questions:

- What are my values and beliefs?
- What is "success" and how can it be achieved?
- What am I accountable for?
- What will it take to get the job done?
- How do I work with grantees?
- Am I getting better?

Taken together, these questions create an approach for donors and grant makers who want to give smart. Wrestling with them will require you to develop strategic clarity, about what you hope to accomplish and what you believe will have to happen for your hopes to be realized, before you leap into action and start making decisions. It will require you to identify a set of results for which you'll hold yourself accountable, so that you can develop real feedback loops for learning and continuing improvement. Last but not least, it will bring you face to face with the harsh realities of what it takes to make change happen when you work with and through nonprofit partners, as well as help you understand how you can be most productive in bettering their performance, and therefore your own.

[. . .]

We recognize that not every question will be equally relevant for every reader, and that their relative importance is likely to change over time, as your circumstances and the arc of your philanthropy evolve. So whether they merit several hours of consideration – or several days, months, or even years – will depend on the specifics of your circumstances as well as on the sum of money involved, the difficulty of the issue (or issues) you're choosing to focus on, and the extent of your ambitions.

Whatever those specifics may be, however, choosing to ignore these questions will reduce the probability of achieving results. Philanthropy almost always involves a fair degree of trial and error. By prioritizing thought as well as action – thinking through the relevant questions with appropriate rigor and discipline – you will reduce the frequency of your errors and make your trials more valuable. The good news is that even a modest amount of thought can help you avoid philanthropy's insidious traps and start you on a path toward better performance. The rewards of doing so will multiply over time, as communities are better served and society's thorniest issues are more effectively addressed.

There will be rewards for you personally, as well. Your legacy may help to establish standards of excellence, inspiring others to use their philanthropic resources more effectively in pursuit of their own ambitious aspirations. Your success at giving will provide an enhanced sense of meaning and fulfillment in your life. And when you close your eyes at night, you will do so confident that you have accomplished as much with your philanthropy as you possibly could have.

Sources and copyright information

Adam, T. (2004) Introduction, in T. Adam (ed.), *Philanthropy, Patronage and Civil Society: Experiences from Germany, Great Britain and North America*, Bloomington, IN: Indiana University Press. Copyright © 2004 Indiana University Press. Reprinted with permission.

Addams, J. (1899) *Democracy and Social Ethics*, New York: The Macmillan Company. In public domain.

Aguero, F. (2005) The promotion of corporate social responsibility in Latin America, in C. Sanborn and F. Portocarrero (eds), *Philanthropy and Social Change in Latin America*, Cambridge, MA: Harvard University Press. Copyright © 2005 Harvard University David Rockefeller Center for Latin American Studies. Reprinted with permission.

Alexeeva, O. (2009) The Gucci bag of new philanthropy, *Alliance Magazine*, 14(4). Copyright © 2009 Alliance Publishing Trust. Reprinted with permission.

Andreoni, J. (2006) Philanthropy, in S. Kolm and J. M. Ythier (eds), *Handbook of the Economics of Giving, Altruism and Reciprocity*, Amsterdam, The Netherlands: Elsevier. Copyright © 2006 Elsevier B. V. Reprinted with permission.

Anheier, H. and Leat, D. (2006) *Creative Philanthropy: Towards a New Philanthropy for the Twenty-First Century*, New York: Routledge. Copyright © 2006 Routledge. Reprinted with permission.

Aristotle ([350 BC] 2008) Selection from *Nicomachean Ethics* (trans. L. R. Kass), in A. A. Kass (ed.), *Giving Well, Doing Good: Readings for Thoughtful Philanthropists*, Bloomingon, IN: Indiana University Press. In public domain.

Bekkers, R. and Wiepking, P. (2011) Adapted by the authors from: A literature review of empirical studies of philanthropy: the eight mechanisms that drive charitable giving, *Nonprofit and Voluntary Sector Quarterly*, 40(5): 924–973. Copyright © 2011 Sage Publications. Reprinted with permission.

Bernholz, L., Skloot, E. and Varela, B. (2010) *Disrupting Philanthropy: Technology and the Future of the Social Sector*, Durham, NC: Duke University: Center for Strategic Philanthropy and Civil Society. Copyright © 2010 Duke University. Reprinted with permission.

Bikmen, F. (2008) The rich history of philanthropy in Turkey: a paradox of tradition and modernity, in N. MacDonald and L. T. de Borms (eds), *Philanthropy in Europe: A Rich Past, a Promising Future*, London: Alliance Publishing Trust. Copyright © 2008 Alliance Publishing Trust. Reprinted with permission.

Bishop, M. and Green, M. (2008) *Philanthrocapitalism*, New York: Bloomsbury Press. Copyright © 2008 Bloomsbury Press. Reprinted with permission.

Breeze, B. (2006) *UK Philanthropy's Greatest Achievements*, London: Institute for Philanthropy. Copyright © 2006 Institute for Philanthropy. Reprinted with permission.

Breeze, B. (2011) Is there a 'new philanthropy'?, in C. Rochester, G. Campell Gosling, A. Penn and M. Zimmeck (eds), *Understanding the Roots of Voluntary Action: Historical Perspectives on Current Social Policy*, Brighton: Sussex Academic Press. Copyright © 2011 Sussex Academic Press. Reprinted with permission.

Brest, P. (2012) A decade of outcome-oriented philanthropy, *Stanford Social Innovation Review*, Spring. Copyright © 2012 *Stanford Social Innovation Review*. Reprinted with permission.

Bronfman, C. and Solomon, J. (2010) *The Art of Giving: Where the Soul Meets a Business Plan*, San Francisco, CA: Jossey-Bass. Copyright © 2010 Jossey-Bass. Reprinted with permission.

Bryson, J., McGuinness, M. and Ford, R. G. (2002) Chasing a 'loose and baggy monster': almshouses and the geography of charity, *Journal of Royal Geographic Society*, 34(1): 48–58. Copyright © 2002 Royal Geographic Society. Reprinted with permission.

Bugg-Levine, A. and Emerson, J. (2011) *Impact Investing: Transforming How We Make Money While Making a Difference*, San Francisco, CA: Jossey-Bass. Copyright © 2011 Jossey-Bass. Reprinted with permission.

Burlingame, D. F. (1993) Altruism and philanthropy: definitional issues, *Essays on Philanthropy: No. 10*, Indianapolis, IN: Indiana University Center on Philanthropy. Copyright © 1993 Dwight Burlingame. Reprinted with permission.

Carnegie, A. (1889) Wealth, *North American Review*, 148(391): 653–65. In public domain.

Connolly, P. M. (2011) The best of the humanistic and technocratic: why the most effective work in philanthropy requires a balance, *The Foundation Review*, 3(1 & 2): 120–36. Copyright © 2011 *The Foundation Review*. Reprinted with permission.

Cunningham, H. (2016) The multi-layered history of Western philanthropy, in T. Jung, S. Phillips and J. Harrow (eds), *The Routledge Companion to Philanthropy*, London: Routledge. Copyright © 2016 Routledge. Reprinted with permission.

Dalai Lama (1999) The Ethics of Compassion, in *Ethics for the New Millennium*, New York: Riverhead Books. Copyright © 1999 by His Holiness the Dalai Lama. Used by permission of Riverhead, an imprint of Penguin Publishing Group, a division of Penguin Random House LLC.

Daly, S. (2012) Philanthropy as an essentially contested concept, *Voluntas*, 23(3): 535–57. Copyright © 2012 Springer. Reprinted with permission of Springer Science+Business Media.

Davis, S. (1996) Philanthropy as a virtue in late antiquity and the middle ages, in J. B. Schneewind (ed.), *Giving: Western Ideas of Philanthropy*, Bloomington, IN: Indiana University Press. Copyright © 1996 Indiana University Press. Reprinted with permission.

Dees, J. G. (2007) Taking social entrepreneurship seriously, *Society*, 44(3): 24–31. Copyright © 2007 Springer. Reprinted with permission.

Dunfee, T. W. (2011) The unfulfilled promise of corporate philanthropy, in P. Illingworth, T. Pogge and L. Wenar (eds), *Giving Well: The Ethics of Philanthropy*, Oxford: Oxford University Press. Copyright © 2011 Oxford University Press. Reprinted with permission.

Edwards, M. (2008) *Just Another Emperor? The Myths and Realities of Philanthrocapitalism*, New York: Demos. Copyright © 2008 Michael Edwards, Demos, & Young Foundation. Reprinted with permission.

Eikenberry, A. (2006) Giving circles: growing grassroots philanthropy, *Nonprofit and Voluntary Sector Quarterly*, 35(3): 517–32. Copyright © 2006 Sage Publications. Reprinted with permission.

Fleishman, J. (2007) *The Foundation: A Great American Secret*, New York: Public Affairs Books. Copyright © 2007 Public Affairs Books. Reprinted with permission.

Fowler, A. and Wilkinson-Maposa, S. (2013) Horizontal philanthropy among the poor in southern Africa: grounded perspectives in social capital and civic association, in T. A. Aina and B. Moyo (eds), *Giving to Help: Helping to Give: The Context and Politics of African Philanthropy*, Senegal: Amalion Publishing. Copyright © 2013 Amalion Publishing. Reprinted with permission.

Friedman, E. (2013) *Reinventing Philanthropy: A Framework for More Effective Giving*, Washington, DC: Potomac Books. Copyright © 2013 by Eric Friedman. Reprinted by permission of the University of Nebraska Press.

Friedman, M. (1970) The social responsibility of business is to increase its profits, *The New York Times*. Copyright © 1970 *The New York Times*. Reprinted with permission.

Frumkin, P. (2006) *Strategic Giving. The Art and Science of Philanthropy*, Chicago, IL: University of Chicago Press. Copyright © 2006 University of Chicago Press. Reprinted with permission.

Gates, B. (2007) Remarks of Bill Gates, Harvard commencement, *Harvard Gazette*, 7 June. Copyright © 2007 Harvard Gazette. Reprinted with permission.

Handlin Smith, J. (1998) Reflections on Chinese philanthropy based on the case of famine relief in Shan-yin County, Shao-hsing, 1640–1642, in S. Katz, W. Ilchman and E. Queen II (eds), *Philanthropy in the World's Traditions*, Bloomington, IN: Indiana University Press. Copyright © 1998 Indiana University Press. Reprinted with permission by The Random House Group Limited.

Handy, C. (2006) *The New Philanthropists: The New Generosity*, London: William Heinemann. Copyright © 2006 William Heinemann. Reprinted with permission by The Random House Group Limited.

Himmelfarb, G. (1995) *The De-Moralization of Society: From Victorian Virtues to Modern Values*, New York: Random House. Copyright © 1995 by Gertrude Himmelfarb. Used by permission of Alfred A. Knopf, an imprint of the Knopf Doubleday Publishing Group, a division of Penguin Random House LLC. All rights reserved.

Hobbes, M. (2014) Stop trying to save the world, *New Republic*, 17 November. Copyright © 1999 Riverhead Books. Reprinted with permission.

Ignatieff, M. (1984) *The Needs of Strangers*, New York: Penguin Books. Copyright © 1984 by Michael Ignatieff. Used by permission of Viking Books, an imprint of Penguin Publishing Group, a division of Penguin Random House LLC.

Ilchman, W. F., Katz, S. N. and Queen II, E. L. (1998) Introduction, in W. F. Ilchman, S. N. Katz and E. L. Queen II (eds), *Philanthropy in the World's Traditions*, Bloomington, IN: Indiana University Press. Copyright © 1998 Indiana University Press. Reprinted with permission.

Kramer, M. (2009) Catalytic philanthropy, *Stanford Social Innovation Review*, Fall. Copyright © 2009 *Stanford Social Innovation Review*. Reprinted with permission.

Lacey, J. J. (2011) Gates, Buffett, and misguided philanthropy, *The National Review*, 11 May. Copyright © 2011 National Review Online. Reprinted with permission.

LaMarche, G. (2014) Democracy and the donor class, *Democracy Journal*, 34(Fall): 48–59. Copyright © 2014 *Democracy Journal*. Reprinted with permission.

McCarthy, K. D. (2001) Introduction, in K. D. McCarthy (ed.), *Women, Philanthropy, and Civil Society*, Bloomington, IN: Indiana University Press. Copyright © 2001 Indiana University Press. Reprinted with permission.

Mahomed, H. and Moyo, B. (2013) Whose agenda? Power and philanthropy in Africa, *Alliance Magazine*, 18: 39–41. Copyright © 2013 Alliance Publishing Trust. Reprinted with permission.

Maimonides, M. ([1170–1180] 2002) Eight levels of giving, from *Hilchot Matanot Ani'im ('Laws Concerning Gifts to the Poor'), Mishneh Torah* (trans. J. Mandelbaum), in A. A. Kass (ed.), *The Perfect Gift: The Philanthropic Imagination in Poetry and Prose*, Bloomington, IN: Indiana University Press. In public domain.

Martin, M. W. (1994) *Virtuous Giving: Philanthropy, Voluntary Service and Caring*, Bloomington, IN: Indiana University Press. Copyright © 1994 Indiana University Press. Reprinted with permission.

Moody, M. (2011) A Hippocratic oath for philanthropists, in R. F. Donelson and C. L. Hoyt (eds), *For the Greater Good of All: Perspectives on Individualism, Society and Leadership*, New York: Palgrave Macmillan. Copyright © 2011 Palgrave Macmillan. Reprinted with permission.

O'Brien, A. (2014) *Philanthropy and Settler Colonialism*, New York: Palgrave Macmillan. Copyright © 2014 Palgrave Macmillan. Reprinted with permission.

Odendahl, T. (1990) *Charity Begins at Home: Generosity and Self-interest Among the Philanthropic Elite*, New York: Basic Books. Copyright © 1990 Basic Books. Reprinted with permission by Basic Books, a member of the Perseus Book Group.

Okasha, S. (2013) Biological altruism, *Stanford Encyclopedia of Philosophy*, available at http://plato.stanford.edu/entries/altruism-biological. Copyright © 2013 Stanford Encyclopedia of Philosophy & Samir Okasha. Reprinted with permission.

Olasky, M. (1996) *Renewing American Compassion*, Washington, DC: Regnrey. Copyright © 1997 Simon & Schuster. Reprinted with permission.

Orosz, J. J. (2000) *The Insider's Guide to Grantmaking*, San Francisco, CA: Jossey-Bass. Copyright © 2000 Jossey-Bass. Reprinted with permission.

Ostrander, S. and Schervish, P. G. (1990) Giving and getting: philanthropy as a social relation, in J. V. Til (ed.), *Critical Issues in American Philanthropy*, San Francisco, CA: Jossey-Bass. Copyright © 1990 Jossey-Bass. Reprinted with permission.

Ostrower, F. (1995) *Why the Wealthy Give*, Princeton, NJ: Princeton University Press. Copyright © 1995 Princeton University Press. Reprinted with permission.

Pallotta, D. (2013) Why I think nonprofits should act more like businesses, *Huffington Post*, 20 November. Copyright © 2013 Huffington Post. Reprinted with permission.

Payton, R. L. and Moody, M. P. (2008) *Understanding Philanthropy: Its Meaning and Mission*, Bloomington, IN: Indiana University Press. Copyright © 2008 Robert L. Payton and Michael P. Moody. Reprinted with permission of Indiana University Press.

Philanthropy New York (2008) *Key Contributions to Society. Online Resource*, New York: Philanthropy New York. Copyright © 2008 Philanthropy New York. Reprinted with permission.

Pinchuk, V. (2013) My giving pledge. Copyright © 2013 Pinchuk-Eastone Group. Reprinted with permission.

Prochaska, F. K. (1990) Philanthropy, in F. M. L. Thompson (ed.), *The Cambridge Social History of Britain 1750–1950*, Cambridge: Cambridge University Press. Copyright © 1990 Cambridge University Press. Reprinted with permission.

Reich, R. (2011) Toward a political theory of philanthropy, in P. Illingworth, T. Pogge and L. Wenar (eds), *Giving Well: The Ethics of Philanthropy*, Oxford: Oxford University Press. Copyright © 2011 Oxford University Press. Reprinted with permission by Oxford University Press, USA.

Robbins, K. (2006) The nonprofit sector in historical perspective: traditions of philanthropy in the West, in W. W. Powell and R. Steinburg (eds), *The Nonprofit Sector: A Research Handbook*, New Haven, CT: Yale University Press. Copyright © 2006 Yale University Press. Reprinted with permission.

Rockefeller, J. D. (1908). Some random reminiscences of men and events, *The World's Work*, October. In public domain.

Roelofs, J. (2003) *Foundations and Public Policy: The Mask of Pluralism*, New York: State University of New York Press. Copyright © 2003 State University of New York Press. Reprinted with permission. All rights reserved.

Ross, E. (1996) Human communion or a free lunch: school dinners in Victorian and Edwardian London, in J. B. Schneewind (ed.), *Giving: Western Ideas of Philanthropy*, Bloomington, IN: Indiana University Press. Copyright © 1996 Indiana University Press. Reprinted with permission.

Rosso, H. A. ([1991] 2010) A philosophy of fundraising, in E. R. Tempel, T. L. Seiler and E. E. Aldrich (eds), *Achieving Excellence in Fundraising* (3rd edn), San Francisco, CA: Jossey-Bass. Copyright © 2010 Jossey-Bass. Reprinted with permission.

Salamon, J. (2003) *Rambam's Ladder: A Meditation on Generosity and Why it is Necessary to Give*, New York: Workman Publishing. Copyright © 2003 by Julie Salamon. Used by permission of Workman Publishing Co., Inc., New York. All rights reserved.

Salamon, L. (2014) *Leverage for Good: An Introduction to the New Frontiers of Philanthropy and Social Investment*, New York: Oxford University Press. Copyright © 2014 Oxford University Press. Reprinted with permission by Oxford University Press, USA.

Sanborn, C. A. (2005) Philanthropy in Latin America: historical traditions and current trends, in C. Sanborn and F. Portocarrero (eds), *Philanthropy and Social Change in Latin America*, Cambridge, MA: Harvard University Press. Copyright © 2005 Harvard University David Rockefeller Center for Latin American Studies. Reprinted with permission.

Schambra, W. (2014) The coming showdown between philanthrocapitalism and effective philanthropy, *Philanthropy Daily*, 22 May. Copyright © 2014 Capital Research Center. Reprinted with permission.

Schervish, P. (2007) Why the wealthy give: factors which mobilize philanthropy among high net-worth individuals, in A. Sargeant and W. Wymer Jr. (eds), *The Routledge Companion to Nonprofit Marketing*, London: Routledge. Copyright © 2007 Routledge. Reprinted with permission.

Schmid, H. and Rudich-Cohn, A. (2012) Elite philanthropy in Israel: characteristics, motives, and patterns of contribution. *Society*, 49: 175–81. Copyright © 2012 Springer. Reprinted with permission.

Seneca ([AD 63] 1887) *De Beneficiis* Book 1 (trans. A. Stewart). In public domain.

Silber, I. (2012) The angry gift: a neglected facet of philanthropy, *Current Sociology*, 60(3). Copyright © 2012 Sage Publications. Reprinted with permission.

Singer, P. (2006) What should a billionaire give – and what should you? *The New York Times Magazine*. Copyright © 2006 The New York Times. Reprinted with permission.

Singer, P. (2015) *The Most Good You Can Do: How Effective Altruism is Changing Ideas about Living Ethically*, New Haven, CT: Yale University Press. Copyright © 2015 Yale University Press. Reprinted with permission.

Smith, C. and Davidson, H. (2014) *The Paradox of Generosity: Giving We Receive, Grasping We Lose*, New York: Oxford University Press. Copyright © 2014 Oxford University Press. Reprinted with permission.

Smith, D. H. (2005) Introduction: doing good, in D. H. Smith (ed.), *Good Intentions: Moral Obstacles and Opportunities*, Bloomington, IN: Indiana University Press. Copyright © 2005 Indiana University Press. Reprinted with permission.

Smith, J. A. (2006) In search of an ethic of giving, in W. Damon and S. Verducci (eds), *Taking Philanthropy Seriously: Beyond Noble Intentions to Responsible Giving*, Bloomington, IN: Indiana University Press. Copyright © 2006 Indiana University Press. Reprinted with permission.

Soskis, B. (2014) The importance of criticizing philanthropy, *The Atlantic*, 12 May. Copyright © 2014 *The Atlantic*. Reprinted with permission.

Sulek, M. (2010a) On the modern meaning of philanthropy, *Nonprofit and Voluntary Sector Quarterly*, 39(2): 193–212. Copyright © 2010 Sage Publications. Reprinted with permission.

Sulek, M. (2010b) On the classical meaning of *philanthrôpía*, *Nonprofit and Voluntary Sector Quarterly*, 39(3): 385–408. Copyright © 2010 Sage Publications. Reprinted with permission.

Sundar, P. (2013) Philanthropy in the building of modern India, in M. Cantegreil, D. Chanana and R. Kattumuri (eds), *Revealing Indian Philanthropy*, London: Alliance Publishing Trust. Copyright © 2013 UBS AG. Reprinted with permission.

Tierney, T. J. and Fleishman, J. L. (2011) *Give Smart: Philanthropy That Gets Results*, New York: Public Affairs Books. Copyright © 2011 Public Affairs Books. Reprinted with permission.

Tocqueville, A. de (1840 [1899]) How the Americans combat individualism by the principle of self-interest rightly understood, *Democracy in America*, Vol. 2 (trans. Henry Reeves). In public domain.

Toynbee, P. (2009) Thank goodness the poor don't rely on philanthropy, *The Guardian*, 9 January. Copyright © 2009 *The Guardian*. Reprinted with permission.

Van Leeuwen, M. H. D. (2012) Giving in early modern history: philanthropy in Amsterdam in the golden age, *Continuity and Change*, 27 (Special Issue 02): 301–342. Copyright © 2012 Cambridge Journals. Reprinted with permission.

Venkatesh, S. A. (2002) Race and philanthropy: an introduction, *Souls: A Critical Journal of Black Politics, Culture, and Society*, 4(1): 32–4. Copyright © 2002 Routledge. Reprinted with permission.

Washington, B. T. (1907) *Up from Slavery: An Autobiography*, New York: Doubleday, Page. In public domain.

Wesley, J. (1760) The use of money, Sermon 50. In public domain.

Wright, K. (2002) Generosity versus altruism: philanthropy and charity in the US and the UK, *Civil Society Working Paper*, 17, London: The Centre for Civil Society. Copyright © 2002 Springer. Reprinted with permission.

Wuthnow, R. (1991) *Acts of Compassion*, Princeton, NJ: Princeton University Press. Copyright © 1991 Princeton University Press. Reprinted with permission.

Zhang, X. (2014) The rise of the Chinese philanthropist, *New York Times*. Copyright © 2014 *The New York Times*. Reprinted with permission.

Zhou, W. A. *et al.* (2013) *China Social Enterprise and Impact Investment Report*, Shanghai University of Finance & Economics Social Enterprise Research Center, Peking University Center for Civil Society Studies, 21st Century Social Innovation Research Center, & University of Pennsylvania School of Social Policy & Practice. Copyright © 2013 UBS Wealth Management. Reprinted with permission.

Zunz, O. (2011) *Philanthropy in America: A History*, Princeton, NJ: Princeton University Press. Copyright © 2011 Princeton University Press. Reprinted with permission.

Index

Abdul Latif Jameel Poverty Action Lab (J-PAL) 472
Abrams 166
Acción Empresarial 365
accountability 52, 172, 310, 311, 324, 326, 342–343, 345, 416, 450, 490, 495
Acumen Fund 421
Adam, Thomas 90, 119–120
Addams, Jane 247, 276–278
Addison, Joseph 32
Africa 304–307, 308–312, 376, 443, 445; *see also* individual countries
African Population and Health Research Center 424
African Women's Development Fund 311
Aga Khan Foundation 424
Agarwal, P D 143
agenda-based strategy 288, 289
Aguero, Felipe 317, 364–368
AIDS epidemic 20
Alexeeva, Olga 406, 460–463
Allen, Paul 186–187
Alliance for a Green Revolution in Africa 443
Alliance for Progress 146
almshouses 164–166
altruism: biological 63–66; economics and 45; effective 403–404, 406–407, 467–474, 483–487; as mechanism for giving 69; philanthropy vs. 75–77; reciprocal 65
American Cancer Society 25
American individualism 54–55, 56
Amsterdam 299–303
Amsterdam Catholic Charity 301
Andreoni, James 5, 45–49
Andrews, William 51
Anheier, Helmut K. 316, 342–345
Antonic, Domingos 475–476
Appiah, Kwame Anthony 188
Aquinas, Thomas 132, 197
Arendt 89
Argentina 145, 366
Aristotle 97, 199–200, 246, 253–254, 264–265
Arjomand, Said 153
Arnold, John 223, 225, 226
Arnold Foundation 225
Arnove, Robert 348
Art Gallery of Toronto 119–120
Ashoka 422
Australia 39–41, 162, 343
autonomy 269
awareness of need 67–68
Azmin Premji Foundation 445

Bacon, Sir Francis 32, 100
Bajaj, Jamnalal 142
banality of benevolence 89
Banerjee, Abhijit 430, 472
Bangladesh 238
Baptist Missionary Society 103
Barkan, Joanne 225
Barker-Benfield, G. J. 100
Bartkus 361, 362
Beckhert, Sven 120
Beer, Jeremy 484–485
Bekkers, René 5, 67–71
Benedict 132
Benetech 238
Benkler, Yochai 395
Bentham, Jeremy 58
Bernholz, Lucy 318, 394–399
Berresford, Susan 344
Beveridge, William 126, 164
Beveridge Report 19
biblical tradition 58, 103
Bijtebier, Neeltje 299

Bikmen, Filiz 317, 349–352
biological altruism 63–66
Birla, G D 142
Bishop, Matthew 406, 449, 489
Bishop, Michael 441–447
Bittker, Boris 51
Boas, Franz 115
Bono 446, 447, 449
Boorstein, David 489
Booth, Charles 136
Borlaug, Norman 339, 443
Boston Public Library 119
Bowery Residents' Committee (BRC) 291, 294–295
Brants, Christoffel van 300
Brazil 145, 147, 148, 162, 163, 365, 366, 377
Breeze, Beth 4, 17–22, 406, 455–459
Brest, Paul 405, 421–428, 483, 489
Brin, Sergey 445
Bronfman, Charles 405, 415–417
Bryson, John R. 92, 164–166
Buffett, Warren: children of 187–188; in China 210; encouragement from 171; pledges from 183–184, 224, 441–442, 443, 480; religion and 185
Bugg-Levine, Antony 317, 318, 381–386
Burke, Edmund 426
Burlingame, Dwight F. 6, 75–77
Burundi 435
Büsch, Johann Georg 99–100
Bush, Laura 429
business 229–230
business, social responsibility of 355–359; *see also* corporations
Butler, Josephine 102
Byers, Brook 242

Calhoun, Craig 271
Cameron, David 233
Canada 119, 377, 424–425
cancer, cervical 24–25
Carnegie, Andrews: Buffett compared to 184; critiques of 235; establishment of foundation by 342, 395; Gates and 495–496; Gospel of Wealth and 171, 201–204; public libraries and 12, 19, 23, 102; religion and 185; as self-made entrepreneur 456; self-reliance and 34; Sesame Street and 26; Tata and 141
Carnegie Corporation 23, 24, 26, 235, 339, 340
Carnegie Foundation 104
Carnegie UK Trust 19
Carson 345
Carter, Dr. Nathaniel 24
Casey, Jack 53–54, 55–57
catalytic philanthropy 371–375
Catholic Church 145, 147, 162, 346
Catholic Relief Services 117, 147
celanthropists 446
Center for Universal Education 424
Central African Republic 435
Centre for Effective Altruism 474
Cham, Elizabeth 39
Chan, Ronnie 210
Charitable Uses Act 98
Charity Organisation Society 134, 135, 282, 283
Chettiar, Rajah Sir Annamalai 141
Children's Television Workshop 26
Chile 147, 365, 366, 367
China 121–124, 170, 208–210, 318, 387–390, 435, 460
China Impact Fund 390
choice 413–414, 415–417
choice utility 48
Christian Social Union 135
Christiano, Paul 483
Cicero 264
civic anger 171, 213–214
Clarkson, Thomas 19
Claudius 330–331
Clinton, Bill 429, 446, 449, 451
Clinton Global Initiative (CGI) 446, 450
Coffin, William Sloane 261
Collins, Jim 448
Collins, John 112
Colombia 148
colonialism 39–41, 160
Comfort, John Fiske 119
Comic Relief 20
Committee Encouraging Corporate Philanthropy 361
Commonwealth Fund 25
community-development corporations (CDCs) 337
compassion 53–59, 180–182, 232
compassion fatigue 231
Comte, Auguste 75
Connolly, Paul M. 404, 407, 488–492
Constantelos, Demetrios 131
consumption philanthropy 197–198, 288

corporate philanthropy 360–363
corporate social responsibility (CSR) 317, 355–359, 364–368
Corporation for Public Broadcasting (CPB) 26
corporations 317, 355–368; *see also* business
Costigan, Edward P. 235
costs and benefits 68–69
Crisp, Roger 97
Cromhuysen, Abraham and Johanna Maria 302
crowding out effect 46, 47, 69
cultural explanations 53–59
Cunningham, Hugh 90, 97–104

Dalai Lama 170, 180–182
Daly, Siobhan 5, 37–38
Darwin, Charles 63
Davidson, Hilary 5, 60–62
Davis, G. Scott 91, 131–132
Dawkins 64
Dean, William 75
Dees, J. Gregory 173, 238–242
Dekker, Jeroen 101
Democratic Republic of Congo 435
Deutz, Agneta 300
Deworm the World 431
diabetes 24
Diebolt, Evelyne 162
diversity 11
Doerr, John 242
Domhoff, G. William 347
donor-oriented strategies 287
donor-recipient relationship 245–249, 253–257, 264–265, 281–295, 299–312
Dorr, Dr. John V. N. 25
Dorr Foundation 25–26
Douglas, Mary 264
Drayton, Bill 238
Dubai 377
Duflo, Esther 430, 472
Dunfee, Thomas W. 317, 360–363
Dwight, Henry E. 119
Dyer, George 100
dynamic capitalism 241

Echoing Green 422
economics 45–49, 68–69, 100–101, 229–230
Edison, Thomas 25
Edna McConnell Clark Foundation (EMCF) 423
education 18, 19, 208–210, 219, 225, 430–432, 442–443
Edwards, Michael 406, 448–452, 489
effective altruism 403–404, 406–407, 467–474, 483–487
Effective Altruism Blog 483
efficacy 70–71
Egypt 162, 163
80,000 Hours 473–474, 483
Eikenberry, Angela M. 318, 391–393
El Salvador 365
elite donors: calling and 183–188; civic anger and 213–214; critiques of 170–171, 217–226; motivations for 169–170, 195–200; statements from 201–212
Ellison, Larry 449
emergency medical response system 26–27, 337, 339
Emerson, Jed 317, 318, 381–386
Engels, Friedrich 346, 347
England: history of philanthropy and 100; *see also* United Kingdom
enlightened self-interest 45, 126
ethics, philanthropic 460–463
European Foundation 343
European Union 343
Evidence Action 431

Fabian Society 135
Fairchild 301
Fairchilds, Cissie 98
famine relief 20, 21
financial security, as motivation 198–199
Fisman 362
five percent philanthropy 458
Fleishman, Joel L. 316, 337–341, 407, 450, 489, 493–499
Ford, Henry, II 117
Ford, Robert J. 92, 164–166, 342
Ford Foundation 26, 117, 147, 236, 329, 339, 340, 344, 421
Foundation Center 342
foundations: critiques of 223–226, 316–317, 346–348; role of 316, 337–341; in Turkey 349–352; value of 342–345
Fowler, Alan 248, 304–307
France 100, 101, 160, 162, 163
Francis 132
Franklin, Ben 242
Friedman, Eric 406–407, 483, 485

Friedman, Milton 317, 318, 355–359, 362, 364, 475–482
Fruchterman, Jim 238
Frumkin, Peter 6, 38, 81–85
FSG Social Impact Advisors 373
Fundemas 365
fundraising 316, 323–326, 327–328
Fuping Development Institute 388

Galaskiewicz 363
Gallie 37
Galston, William 127
Gandhi 142
Garrett, Laurie 236
Gates, Bill: Bono and 446; Buffett's pledge to 441–442; Carnegie and 495–496; in China 210; donation from 184; foundation work and 442–445, 480; as high-profile 39; moral biography and 171; percent of wealth donated by 186, 187; religion and 185; statement from 205–207, 404; value of human life and 183
Gates, Frederick 34, 104
Gates, Melinda 39, 171, 183, 184, 446, 450–451, 452
Gates Foundation 52, 183, 185, 210, 224, 235–236, 373, 376, 404, 441, 446, 450–451, 480, 495
Gatsby Charitable Foundation 376
gender 92, 159–163, 351
generosity, well-being and 60–62
geography 92, 164–166, 185, 484–486
Germany 119, 120, 159, 342
gift relationships 247, 261–265
GIGAbase 390
GiveWell 472, 480, 481, 483
giving circles 391–393
Giving What We Can 473–474, 483
Global Alliance for Vaccines and Immunizations (GAVI) 184
Global Leadership Adventures (GLA) 388
Global North perspective 248, 309
Global South, study of philanthropy in 37
Goddard, Robert H. 24
Goenkas 143
Goodpaster 275
Google 445
Gospel of Wealth 171
government 231–232, 238–241
government grants 10
Graham, Yao 312
Grameen Bank 238, 242
Gramsci, Antonio 346
Grand Tour 119
grantmaking 316, 329–333
grants, gifts versus 263–265
gratitude, as motivation 198
Grayling, Chris 233
Greece, ancient 106, 131
Green, Michael 406, 441–447
Green Revolution 339, 340, 421
Greg, W. R. 112
Grill, Anthony and Elizabeth 300
Grim, John A. 153
Gross 38
Guerra, Nancy G. 434
Guggenheim, Harry 24
Guggenheim Foundation 24
Guidestar 424, 449
Guy, Thomas 441–442, 456

Habib, Adam 308
Hagenauer, Frederick 40
Hale, Victoria 238
Hamburg 99–100, 101
Hamilton 64
Hamilton, Alexander 33
Handy, Charles 406, 453–454, 458
Hanway, Jonas 134, 458
Harkness Foundation 104
harm 247, 269–276
Hassenfeld, Elie 472
Hatch 166
Heal 362
health services 20
Heavenly Interest 302–303
hegemony, theory of 346–348
Heifetz, Ron 374
Helmsley, Leona 271
Helu, Carlos Slim 446
Herman 286
Hewlett Foundation 340, 421, 424–425, 426, 427, 489
highway shoulder lines 25–26
Hill, Matthew Davenport 101
Hill, Octavia 20
Hillquit, Morris 235
Himmelfarb, Gertrude 91, 133–136, 241, 457
Hippocrates 247
Hippocratic oath 247, 269, 270–271
Hirschhorn, Joseph 337–338
Hobbes, Michael 405, 429–436

Hobbes. Thomas 184–185
Hochman 46
Hodgkins Fund of the Smithsonian Institution 24
Holmes, John Haynes 235
Hoover, President 117
Hope Consulting 422
horizontal philanthropy 304–307
hospices 20
Howard, John 100, 101, 134
human condition 14
Human Genome Project 21
human nature 14, 15
human problematic 14–16
humanistic approach 488–492
Hume, David 58
Hunter, Sir Tom 233, 453
Hurlburt, Heather 224
Hyde, Lewis 261
hyperagency 170–171, 172, 195, 200, 447

Ibrahim, Barbara 461–462
identification 197–198
Ignatieff, Michael 37, 170, 171, 189–192
Ilchman, Warren F. 92, 151–155
impact investing 381–386, 387–390, 421, 422, 423
India 139–143, 163, 337, 339, 377, 431, 434, 445, 450
individual philanthropy 10
industrialization 140–141
innovation 17
Institute for One World Health 238
institutional efflorescence 89
Instituto Ethos 365
insulin 24
Inter-American Foundation 147
international cooperation 147
Ireland 162
Israel 137–138, 170, 213–214
Italy 98

J N Tata Endowment Scheme 141
Jay-Z 429
Jeejeebhoy, Jamsetji (J J) 141
Jenkins, J. Craig 348
Johnson, Ross 361–362
Johnson, Samuel 32
Johnson Foundation 27, 339
J.P. Morgan Social Finance 376
Jubilee Debt campaign 20
Juergensmeyer, Mark 154

Kahneman 48
Kandil, Amani 162
Kania, John 374
Kanorias 143
Kant, Immanuel 185, 269
Karl, Barry 348
Karlan, Dean 472
Karnofsky, Holden 472
Katz, Stanley N. 92, 151–155, 348
Kauffman Foundation 239
Kennedy, Robert 382
Kenya 424, 430–434
Kimball, Kristi 426
King, Martin Luther, Jr. 492
Kirkpatrick, David 184
Knetsch 48
Knight 166
Kolm 46
Kopell, Malka 426
Korea 162, 163
Kozlowski, Gregory C. 154
Kramer, Mark R. 317–318, 371–375
Kravinsky, Zell 187, 471–472
Kremer, Michael 430–432

Lacey, Jim 173, 229–230
Lalbhai, Kasturbhai 142
LaMarche, Gara 173, 235–237
Landim, Leilah 162
Lange, Cornelis de 299
Laslett, Peter 98
Latin America 144–148, 161, 317, 364–368; *see also* individual countries
League of Pity 113
Leat, Diana 316, 342–345
leisure opportunities 18, 19
Lettsom, J. C. 101
Levi-Strauss 282
Liberation Theology 161
Liebman, Joshua L. 491
Lindbergh, Charles 24
Lindenmeyr, Adele 154
Litan, Robert 239
Live 8 20
Live Aid 20
Lloyd, Theresa 195
Loch, Charles 164
London Missionary Society 103
London Society for the Improvement of Prison Discipline 101
long tail 395–399
Low, Sampson 164

Luddy, Maria 162
Lutheran Charity 302

Ma, Jack 210
Macadam, Elizabeth 103, 456, 457
MacArthur Fellowship 238
MacAskill, Will 473, 483
Macdonald, Dwight 329
Macquarie 40
Madaliar, Pachaiyappa 141
Mahomed, Halima 248, 308–312
Maimonides, Moses 246, 247, 257, 292, 294, 403
Make Poverty History 20, 21
Make-A-Wish 468
Malinowski, Bronislaw 115
Manzoni, John 363
Martin, Mike W. 75, 247, 269
Martineau, Harriet 197
Marx, Karl 200, 346, 347
Mauss, Marcel 115–116, 247, 261
Mavor, James 119
McCarthy, Kathleen D. 92, 102, 159–163
McGuinness, Mark 92, 164–166
McMahon, Darrin M. 154
Medecins Sans Frontieres (Doctors Without Borders) 240
mediated-engagement strategies 287, 289
Mekeren, Johanna van (nee Bontekoning) 300
Merck 363
Meth Project 371–372
Metropolitan Museum of Art 119–120
Mexican Center for Philanthropy 365
Mexico 145, 339, 366, 367
Michels, Robert 347
Mill, John Stuart 58
Millennium Villages Project 432–433
Mills, C. Wright 347
Misereor 147
modeling effect 71
Modi, Gujarmal 143
Montaigne 79
Moody, Michael 4, 9–16, 247, 270–275, 404
Moore Foundation 424
moral biography 171, 196, 199–200
More, Hannah 134
Morleys, Charles 282
Morris 361, 362
Moyo, Bhekinkosi 248, 308–312
Mukasa, Sarah 311
Mulder, Frederick 454
Mulgan, Geoff 454
Munger, Charles 449
Munk, Nina 429, 433
Murphy, Liam 188
Murugappa Group 142
Muukkonen 37

N M Wadia Foundation 141
Naidu, Kuppuswamy 142
Nair 362
Narada Foundation 389
National Benevolent Institution 113
National Center for Responsive Philanthropy (NCRP) 484
National Corporate Philanthropy Day 363
National Education Association 26
National Educational Television system 26
National Public Radio 26
National Safety Act 26–27
National Trust 20
natural selection 63–65
needs and obligations 189–192
needs-based strategy 287, 289, 290
Netherlands 68, 342
'new philanthropists' 453–459
New Schools Venture Fund 242
NeXii 398–399
Nicaragua 432
Nielsen 342–343
911 26, 337, 339
North, Douglas 240
Norway 162
Nuffield 342

obligations, needs and 189–192
O'Brien, Anne 5, 39–41
O'Connor, Alice 157
Odendahl, Teresa 172, 220–222
Okasha, Samir 5, 63–66
Olasky, Martin 173, 231–232, 241
Olin Foundation 340
Olson, Mancur 366
Omidyar Network 421
opportunity-based strategy 287, 289
Ord, Tony 473
O'Reilly, Bill 446
Orosz, Joel J. 316, 329–333
Ostrander, Susan A. 76, 77, 248, 284–290
Ostrower, Francie 38, 172, 217–219
outcome-oriented philanthropy 405, 421–428

Oxford Committee for Famine Relief (Oxfam) 20, 21, 273–274

Packard Foundation 330, 424
Page, Larry 445
Pakistan 339
Palatre, Gabriel 122
Palestine 162
Pallotta, Dan 405, 437–438
Pan American Health Organization 25
Pan Shiyi 208
Pap smear 24–25
Papanicolaou, Dr. George N. 25
Patrizi, Patricia 425–426
Payton, Robert 4, 9–16, 34, 37, 75, 152, 270, 404
Pearl Capital Partners 376
Pell Grants 337, 339
Penslar, Derek J. 154
personal-engagement strategies 286, 289–290
Peru 365
Pew, Howard 117
Phelps, Edmund 241
Philadelphia Society for Alleviating the Miseries of Public Prisons 101
philanthrocapitalists 442–447, 448–452, 455
philanthrolocalism 484–487
Philanthropedia 424, 477
Philanthropic Society 100
Philanthropic Ventures Foundation 489
philanthropy: conceptualisation of 37–38, 125–126; context for 14; definitions of 9, 13–14, 31–36; diversity of 11–12; moral dimension of 14; motives for 197–200; new frontiers of 376–380; new physics of 196–197; scope of 12–13; summary of 9–11
Philanthropy Australia 39
Philanthropy New York 4, 23–27
philanthropy of community (PoC) 304–307
philia 199–200
Philippines 432
Pifer 330
Pinchuk, Victor 171, 211–212
PlayPump International 429, 435–436
Pogge, Thomas 186
polio vaccine 25
political theories 50–52
Poor Laws 19, 39, 41, 98
Population Council 117
Porter, Michael 361
Porterfield, Amanda 154
poverty 231–232
Poverty Action Lab 472
Powell, John 157
power, resources and 308–312
prestige 217–219
prisons 154
private donations 10
private values 82–83, 84–85
probation service 18
problem-solving philanthropy 421, 422, 423–425
Prochaska, Frank 89, 90, 111–114
psychological benefits 69–70
public broadcasting 26
Public Broadcasting Service (PBS) 26, 337, 339
public goods 46–47
public libraries 12, 19, 23, 102, 119
public needs 81–82, 84–85

Queen, Edward L., II 92, 151–155

race relations 92, 156–158, 237
Ram, Lala Shri 142
Ramalingam, Ben 434
Rauch, Jonathan 449
Rauhes Haus 101
Readymoney, Kavasji Jehangir 140
recipients of philanthropy 12; *see also* donor-recipient relationship
Reformed Charity 302
Reich, Rob 5, 50–52
religion: calling and 170, 177–179; charity in Amsterdam and 299–303; corporate philanthropy and 367; role of 91–92, 102–103, 117, 121–122, 131, 135, 145, 153, 160–161, 162–163; Turkish foundations and 350–351
reputation 69
Research in African-American Studies conference 156–157
resource mobilization theory 348
Richard, Timothy 121
Rijp, Gerard van de 300
risk-taking 17
RJR Nabisco 361–362
Robbins, Kevin 90, 105–107
Roberts, Russell 46
Robin Hood Foundation 483
Rockefeller, John D.: Buffett compared to 184; critiques of 169, 223, 235;

establishment of foundation by 342, 395; on scientific giving 404–405; as self-made entrepreneur 456; statement from 411–414
Rockefeller, John D., III 117
Rockefeller Brothers Fund 424
Rockefeller Foundation 23–24, 104, 223, 224, 235, 236, 339, 340, 376, 395, 421, 443, 488
rocket science 24
Rodgers 46
Rodgers, Daniel 120
Roelofs, Joan 316–317, 346–348
Rome 116, 131, 330–331
Rosenwald, Julius 230
Ross, Ellen 248, 281–283
Rosso, Henry A. 316, 323–326
Rotary Foundation 25
Roundabout Water Solutions 435–436
Rowntree, Joseph 19, 342, 456
Rowntree, Seebohm 19, 342
Roychand, Premchand 140–141
Rubinstein 456
Rudich-Cohn, Avishag 91, 137–138
Rush, Benjamin 101
Rusk, Dean 236
Russell Sage Foundation 104, 235
Russia 154, 460, 462

Sachs, Jeffrey 230, 429, 432–433, 449
Salamon, Julie 248, 291–295
Salamon, Lester M. 33–34, 317–318, 376–380
Salk, Dr. Jonas 25
Salvation Army 135
Sanborn, Cynthia A. 91, 144–148
Sansum, Dr. William 24
Say, J. B. 239
Say's law 48
Scaife Foundation 25
Schambra, William 407, 426, 483–487
Schervish, Paul G. 34–35, 37–38, 76, 77, 170–171, 172, 195–200, 248, 284–290
Schmid, Hillel 91, 137–138
Schmidt, Buss 449
Schmitt, Mark 224
Schooler, Dean 323
Schramm, Carl 239
Schumpeter, Joseph 239
scientific charity 241
scientific philanthropy 457, 488
Scott, Miles 468
Seifert 361, 362
self-interest: American philanthropy and 116–117; rightly understood 77, 78–80, 116–117, 197
Seneca 246, 255–256, 264, 403
Sesame Street 26
Shakely, Jack 331–332
Shakira 446
Shankarshet, Jagannath 140
Shapely 456
Sharp, Granville 19
Shell 445
Shri Ram Charitable Trust 142
Shriver, Bobby 449
Siebel, Thomas 371–372, 375
Sievers, Bruce 426, 427
Silber, Ilana 171, 213–214
Singapore 377
Singer, Peter: on Buffett's pledge 224; effective altruism and 403, 406, 467–474, 483; statement from 183–188; on value of human lives 170, 171, 404, 486
Singhania, Kamalapat and Lakshmipat 142–143
Sir Dorabji Tata Trust 141
Sirota 225
Skloot, Edward 238, 318, 394–399
Skoll, Jeff 449
slave trade, abolition of 18, 19, 135
Sloan Foundation 340
Smith, Adam 115, 116, 357
Smith, Arthur 121–122
Smith, Christian 5, 60–62
Smith, David H. 247, 261–262
Smith, Iain Duncan 233
Smith, James Allen 247, 263–265
Smith, Joanna Handlin 90, 121–124
Sober, Elliott 66
social change, campaigns for 20–22
Social Democratic Federation 135
social entrepreneurship 238–242
social services 18
Société Philanthropique de Bruxelles 98
Société Philanthropique de Paris 100
Societies of Public Benefit (*Sociedades de Beneficiencia Publica*) 146
Society for the Abolition of the Slave Trade 19
SOHO China Scholarships 209–210
solicitation 48, 68
Solomon, Jeffrey 405, 415–417

Somerville, Bill 426, 489
Soros, George 446–447
Soskis, Benjamin 172, 223–226
SOW Asia Foundation 389–390
speed 17
Spencer, Harriet 203
Srivastava 37
St. Jude's Children's Research Hospital 475, 476
Stern, Ken 429
Stonewall 21
Stowe, William W. 119
Su Shi 124
Sulek, Marty 5, 31–36, 38
Sulston, Sir John 21
Sundar, Pushpa 89, 91, 139–143
supporting organisations 421–423
Swain, Shurlee 162
Switzerland 342, 377

Taine, Hippolyte 134
Talhami, Ghada Hashem 162
Tata, Sir Dorabji 141
Tata, Sir Jamsetji 141
tax incentives/exemptions 10, 50–52, 195, 236, 363
Taylor, J. Bayard 119
technocratic approach 488–492
technology 394–399
Teles, Steve 224
Tensini, Octavio Francisco 299
Thatcher, Margaret 133
Theiler, Dr. Max 24
'third sector' 12
Third World Network 312
Thomas, Robert 240
Thomas, St. 132
Thompson, Elizabeth 425–426
Ticknor, George 119
Tierney, Thomas J. 407, 493–499
Tocqueville, Alexis de: on duality in philanthropy 6; on local philanthropy 486; on philanthropy 33; on self-interest 77, 78–80, 116–117, 197
Toppler, Francis 200
Tosa Foundation 424
Toynbee, Polly 173, 233–234
Trajan 131
Trivers 65
Tsai, Joe 210
Turkey 317, 349–352
Turner, Ted 443, 444
Twells, Alison 102
tzedakah 257

Uganda 424
Ukraine 170, 211–212
Uniapac (International Christian Union of Business Executives) 367
UNICEF 25
United Kingdom: accountability and 343; almshouses in 164–166; children's meals and 282–283; generosity versus altruism in 125–128; greatest achievements in 17–22; growth of foundations in 342; history of philanthropy and 100; influence of on United States 119; innovative philanthropy in 377; philanthropic tradition in 111–114; social impact bonds in 427
United States: charges against foundations in 343; donor-recipient relationship in 291–295; drug use in 371–372; European influence on 119–120; generosity versus altruism in 125–128; giving circles in 391–393; history of philanthropy and 101–102, 103, 115–118; innovative philanthropy in 377; religion and 162; separation of church and state in 161; solicitation and 68; tax incentives in 50–52; Tocqueville on 78–80; volunteerism in 53–59
Uruguay 145
US Agency for International Development (USAID) 376
utilitarianism 58

vakifs 349–352
value creation 83–85
values 70
Van Leeuwen, Marco H. D. 248, 299–303
Van Til, Jon 34, 37, 77
Varela, Barry 318, 394–399
Venkatesh, Sudhir Alladi 92, 156–158
venture philanthropists 457
Veyne, Paul 131–132
Vives, Juan Luis 98, 99
Vogel, David 366
voluntarism 53–59, 161, 233–234
voluntary association 13

Wadia, N. M. 84–85, 91
Wage, Matt 467
Walker, Sir Edmund 119

Walmart 361, 445
Walsh, Frank P. 235
'warm glow' 45, 46–49, 70, 468
Warr 46
Washington, Booker T. 316, 327–328
Water for the Poor Act 429
Webb, Beatrice 134–135
Weber, Max 133
Webster, Noah 32–33
Weiyan Zhou 318, 387–390
welfare state 231, 234
well-being 60–62, 69–70
Wellcome, Sir Henry 21
Wellcome Trust 20, 21
Wesley, John 133, 170, 177–179
West Birmingham Relief Fund 112
West Street Chapel Benevolent Society 112
Wichern, Johann Hinrich 101
Wiepking, Pamala 5, 67–71
Wilberforce, William 19, 442
Wilburforce Foundation 424
Wilkinson-Maposa, Susan 248, 304–307
Williams, Raymond 347
Williams, Ronald 294
wills 299
Winfrey, Oprah 446
Winthrop, John 58
Wipro 445
Witherspoon, John 58
Wolfson, Isaac 456
Wolpert, Julian 126
women 159–163, 351
working-class philanthropy 111–112
World Council of Churches 147
World Health Organization 25
World Relief 147
World Resources Institute 390
World Vision 147
Wright, Karen 90, 125–128
Wuthnow, Robert 5, 53–59

Xin Zhang 171, 208–210
Xinhu-Yu Venture Philanthropy 390

Yardley Great Trust 164–165
yellow fever vaccine 23–24
YouChange Foundation 389
Young, Bernadette 473
Young, Robert 100
Young Foundation 454
Yunus, Muhammad 238, 241, 242

Zambia 429
Zunz, Olivier 90, 115–118
Zwane, Alix 431